THE LAST FOLK HERO

ALSO BY JEFF PEARLMAN

The Bad Guys Won

Love Me, Hate Me

Boys Will Be Boys

The Rocket That Fell to Earth

Sweetness

Showtime

Gunslinger

Football for a Buck

Three-Ring Circus

THE LAST
FOLK HERO

THE LIFE AND MYTH
OF
BO JACKSON

JEFF PEARLMAN

MARINER BOOKS

New York   Boston

HarperCollins books may be purchased for educational, business, or sales promotional use. For information, please email the Special Markets Department at SPsales@harpercollins.com.

FIRST EDITION

Designed by Jen Overstreet

Library of Congress Cataloging-in-Publication Data has been applied for.

ISBN 978-0-358-43767-3

22 23 24 25 26 LBC 10 9 8 7 6

To Joan Pearlman, my mother and hero.

When I was a kid, Mom worked as a probation officer.
Every man in her office carried a gun.

She was tough enough not to.

CONTENTS

Paul Bunyan, (you have heard of Paul?)
He was the king pin of 'em all,
The greatest logger in the land;
He had a punch in either hand
And licked more men and drove more miles
And got more drunk in more new styles
Than any other peavey prince
Before, or then, or ever since.

"The Round River Drive"
by Douglas Malloch and James MacGillivray
April 25, 1914

INTRODUCTION

The other day I was walking through the airport in Atlanta, working my way past security and toward the gate, when a TSA agent pulled me aside and asked, pointedly, "What's in your suitcase?"

My L.L.Bean roller had just cruised through the X-ray machine, and now Carlton required an explanation as to the large rectangular blemish appearing on the screen before him.

"Oh," I said. "That."

"Yeah," he replied. "That."

"It's a brick," I said.

Carlton's face suggested disbelief.

"A what?" he snapped.

"A brick," I said. "Like—you know. A brick."

Carlton didn't like bricks.

"Sir," he said, "you can't travel with a brick in your carry-on."

"Really?" I replied.

"Really," he said. "There's really no good reason for bringing a brick on a plane."

That's when I stopped him and explained I had the best reason in world history for bringing a brick on a plane.

"OK," Carlton said. "Tell me."

I cleared my throat.

"Do you know who Bo Jackson is?" I asked.

He looked at me as one stares down a moron.

"Right," I said. "Well, I'm writing a biography of Bo Jackson. A definitive biography. I've been working on it for well over a year. And yesterday I was at his childhood home in Bessemer, Alabama. Middle of nowhere. And he lived on this abandoned street, on this now-abandoned lot. And his childhood home is totally gone. Not there. But I was standing in the spot where he grew up, and beneath the leaves and the sticks and a whole lot of garbage were a few bricks from the house's foundation. So I took one, because it's Bo Jackson's house, and I'm obsessed with Bo Jackson's life. So why wouldn't I take a brick home with me?"

Charged by two trenta cold brews, I kept going. And going. And going. About Auburn and Kansas City; about Los Angeles and Chicago and Anaheim. About scaling an outfield wall and breaking a bat atop his head and running over a mohawked, steroid-stuffed Seahawks linebacker. About boar hunting and hip replacements and a long-ago television show called *Ben Casey.*

A few days earlier I'd attended services at the all-Black, side-of-the-road Mount Zion Baptist Church (which Bo attended as a boy), and the spirit of Pastor Dwight Miller's sermon had moved me.

Praise Bo!

At long last I stopped, and Carlton called over a supervisor. "Hey, Melissa," he said. "This gentleman is writing Bo Jackson's biography. And he's trying to fly home with a brick from the guy's childhood house."

Melissa picked up the brick. Smoothed it over with her hands. I smiled and nodded.

"A brick?" she said.

"Yeah," Carlton replied.

Pause.

"Hmm," she said. "We don't get many bricks in suitcases. But Bo Jackson—that's a pretty big deal."

Melissa smiled.

"Go on through," she said. "Fly with Bo Jackson's brick."

JEFF PEARLMAN
AUGUST 15, 2021

PROLOGUE

On the night of September 15, 1991, the sixty-five members of the Chicago White Sox traveling party knew they were about to die.

This is neither exaggeration nor hyperbole.

No.

This is an airplane that seemed all but destined to crash.

Earlier that day, the White Sox wrapped a four-game series at the California Angels with a 9–2 victory. The players and coaches immediately retreated to the visitors' clubhouse at Anaheim Stadium, where they showered, changed and bolted to nearby Ontario International Airport. They then walked toward the jetway and climbed up the steps onto the team's chartered Boeing 737-300, operated by America West Airlines.

As the pilots prepared for the three-and-a-half-hour flight to the Windy City, the players, coaches, and executives found their familiar spots. Carlton Fisk, the gruff veteran catcher, plopped down in the back row alongside Matt Merullo, his young understudy. Ozzie Guillen, the loquacious shortstop, found a seat a few rows up from Dan Pasqua, the slugger and regular midflight poker afficionado. Lance Johnson and Warren Newson, a couple of young outfielders, sat side by side.

For the first two and a half hours of travel, all was calm. The flight attendants offered drinks and food. Playing cards were dealt among teammates. Frank Thomas, the burly first baseman, listened to music on his Walkman. Robin Ventura, the young third baseman, started to—

BOOM!

Everyone remembers the sound—a loud, unsettling explosive reverberation that caused the aircraft's 126 seats to shake. Then Craig Grebeck, the utility infielder, pulled up the shade on his window, looked out toward the engine and spotted the flames. "A huge flash," he recalled. "Gobbling everything up."

Grebeck turned toward Tim Raines, the speedy outfielder. "Rock," he said, "the fucking engine's on fire."

"What?" Raines said, before craning his neck to gaze outside. "Oh, shit!" Raines screamed. "Ohhhhh, shiiiiiiit!"

Pasqua dashed toward the window, saw the inferno, rushed back to his seat and buckled it as tight as possible. Donn Pall, a relief pitcher, pressed-pressed-pressed-pressed-pressed the flight attendant call button until someone arrived. "Look out the window!" Pall screamed.

"Holy shit!" the flight attendant said, then yanked down the blind.

Thomas—the 6-foot-5, 240-pound mountain of a man—collected every pillow he could find and cocooned himself in a preposterous nest of cotton and fleece. Scott Radinsky, relief pitcher, screamed (*Almost Famous*–like), "We're going down boys! We're . . . allllll. . . . gonnnnnna . . . diiiiiiiiiiiiiiiiie." Barry Foote and Dave LaRoche, coaches and long-ago Yankee teammates, sat in silence and listened as a player two rows back called a friend to tell him the whereabouts of a hidden bank account. Others used the seat-back phones to reach out to family members.

"Mom, I love you . . ."

"Dad, I love you . . ."

"Honey, I love you . . ."

The plane banked hard left, the flames crawling up the metal, lighting up the craft's innards in a terrifying orange-red glow. Screams. Tears. Religious medallions rubbed between index fingers and thumbs.

And then—*it happened.*

The cockpit door swung open, and out stepped Bo Jackson.

Three decades later, many of the White Sox players can still see it. The world's greatest athlete—the two-sport phenom; the Bo Knows embodiment; the man who loved picking the brains of the pilots—marching down the aisle, aware of the danger but shrugging it off, urging his teammates to buckle up. It was John Wayne. It was Clint Eastwood. It was Harrison Ford. It was . . .

"Don't worry, everyone!" Jackson commanded in his deep baritone. "The crew knows exactly what it's doing. We'll be fine."

Jackson strutted from man to man before taking a seat. When the pilots somehow touched down at Des Moines International Airport, placing the jet between dozens of emergency vehicles, the members of the White Sox burst out in applause. Joey Cora, a young second baseman, turned his head to look at Bo Jackson.

"That," he thought, "is a hero."

There is a second version to this story—one also verified by multiple members of the Chicago White Sox.

The engine is on fire.

The passengers are terrified.

No one is moving.

Prayers are being said aloud.

The plane banks hard to the left.

And then . . .

"I can tell you *exactly* what happened," said Merullo, the reserve catcher. He was twenty-six at the time, a struggling-to-stick once-upon-a-heyday prospect out of Winchester, Massachusetts. Merullo was sitting on the Boeing 737 alongside Fisk, bracing for impact and taking notes with his eyes.

"Bo had been limping that year, because his hip was hurt," Merullo recalled. "But with the plane on fire, he gets out of his seat near us and he sprints—and I mean *sprints*—to the cockpit like Mighty Mouse coming to save the day. Bo Jackson literally opens the cockpit door and enters. I know he was a pilot, so I'm guessing he helped land the plane or something. There wasn't anything he couldn't do."

Fisk, approaching his forty-fourth birthday and in his twenty-second Major League season, was one of the few unfazed. According to Merullo, the veteran surveyed the scene, grabbed a Budweiser from a nearby cooler, cracked it open and gazed slyly toward Jackson.

"Go get 'em, Bo," Fisk said. "*Gooooo* get 'em.'"

Both stories are true.

I wouldn't write that about a similar circumstance involving Michael Jordan or Carl Lewis, Mike Tyson or Ja Morant. I wouldn't write that about Renaldo Nehemiah, Michael Phelps, Randy Moss, Brett Favre or Wayne Gretzky.

But, in this case, both stories are true.

Bo Jackson ran from the cockpit and ran toward the cockpit. He flew the plane, served as his own copilot and delivered Coca-Cola products to every passenger. He climbed out onto the wing and extinguished the fire while simultaneously writing a poem about the perils of Laura Branigan rock operas.

This is what it means to be mythological; to exist in a world that is both factual and fantastical; to do things so unprecedented, so spectacular, that one must wonder if they were ever actually done at all.

It was Joe Posnanski, the journalist and occasional Bo chronicler, who referred to Jackson as "the last folk hero"—and the more I thought about it, the more I came to embrace Joe's take. Nowadays, everything that happens in the world can be found seconds later on YouTube and Twitter. Kevin Durant dunks—it's right there. Ronald Acuña, Jr., blasts a 450-foot home run—also right there. There is no longer such a thing as "You won't believe this," because there's nothing *not* to believe. It exists in front of us. And, in many ways, that's wonderful. Sports have never been more accessible, and in dark times (say, like, during a worldwide pandemic) being able to observe the splendor of a 130-mph Serena Williams serve can balm the soul.

And yet . . .

Sports without mythology is David Blaine without levitation. Did Babe Ruth really point into the distance before homering at Wrigley Field in Game 3 of the 1932 World Series? Did Earl Manigault really grab a quarter off the top of a backboard before dunking a basketball? We don't know. But the beauty is in the mystery. It's in the debate; in the descriptive adjectives; in having a cousin whose uncle's brother's sister's nephew's wife's maid of honor (from her second wedding, not her third) was at the game, and swears to God it happened.

Bo Jackson is, as Posnanski says, the last folk hero, because he's the last legendary athlete to do these impossible-to-conceive feats without the benefit (or curse) of a thousand camera angles. Dating back to his boyhood in Bessemer, Alabama, and through his years at Auburn University, then as a Memphis Chick, a Kansas City Royal, a Chicago White Sox, a California Angel, a Los Angeles Raider, there are fables that may well be more than fables. Bo, age seven, side-arming a rock yards. Bo, high school senior, blocking two oncoming linebackers 40 yards down the field. Bo, at Auburn, soaring over a Volkswagen; standing waist-deep in a pool and leaping—flat-footed—onto the cement lip. Bo throwing a football straight into the air and hitting the New Orleans Superdome scoreboard—140 feet above his head. Even one of his all-time-great highlights—the 1989 throw from the left-field corner to gun down Seattle's Harold Reynolds at home—is an incomplete video experience. Watch the clip, and you never actually see Bo release the baseball.

So did he?

It's the reason, nearly thirty years since his final moment as a professional athlete, Bo Jackson continues to feel relevant and important. He was far from charismatic or charming. He hated signing autographs, and told plenty of people (friends and foes alike) to back off, to keep their distance, to read the scowl. But Jackson rendered sour personality moot. There have been other two-sport athletes of some note. D. J. Dozier played for the Min-

nesota Vikings and New York Mets. Brian Jordan was both a fantastic Atlanta Falcons safety and Atlanta Braves outfielder. On and on. They came,
they vanished. What Jackson accomplished (and, via campfire stories, still
does) was forcing oneself to ask, "Did I just see that? Did that *actually* happen?" You would rub your eyes, look again. Rub once more, look again. The
mythology is a paradox—by not quite believing what you witnessed, you
remember what you witnessed. It's permanence via dumbfoundedness, and
it makes a man whose time in the sun was disappointingly brief far more
interesting/discussed than statistically superior contemporaries like, say,
Andre Dawson or Eric Dickerson.

Those men—Hall of Famers in their respective sports—were beholden
to gravity.

When the Boeing 737 pulled up to the gate in Des Moines, it was one o'clock
in the morning.

The sixty-five members of the White Sox traveling party entered an
empty terminal. There was little chatter. Ballplayers exist off of banter, but
this wasn't the time. Minutes earlier, the aircraft was on fire.

Now they were being told another America West plane would arrive
shortly. In the meantime, they were to have a seat and collect themselves.
"Like it was *that* easy," recalled Pasqua.

A stone's throw from the gate was a kiosk—one that, when opened, peddled pretzels, hot dogs and beer. Positioned toward the side of the business
was an industrial-size keg, protected with a large stainless-steel Master
Lock. A half dozen or so White Sox found themselves staring longingly at
the object, noting aloud that they could *really* use a drink.

Bo Jackson stepped forward. "I got this," he said—then wrapped his
right hand around the lock, squeezed tightly and (*pop!*) cracked it open.
"He broke the fucking lock," said Radinsky. "Just . . . broke it."

With that, Jackson lifted the keg high into the air and poured beers for
his gleeful teammates. "Like a bartender," said Merullo, "when we needed
one most."

How, exactly, did the Chicago White Sox drink, when there were no
cups?

No one remembers.

It's the stuff of folk heroes.

CHAPTER 1

"THE LITTLE ROCK CHUCKER"

The house no longer exists.

Of course, it no longer exists.

For its existence would be proof, and folk heroes don't leave behind much proof. Because folk heroes aren't tangible. Their actions, their movements, their existences—it all comes and passes like a wink.

And yet . . .

If you look hard enough, and place your eyes close to the ground, there are traces. Beneath the brown leaves, beneath the twigs, to the right of the rusted mop handle, a few inches away from the shards of shattered beer bottles—you will find a reddish-orange brick. Then, to its left, another reddish-orange brick. Two more over there. Another three or four over there.

Some of the bricks are whole. Most are worn and crumbled, time's white flag to the relentlessness of hot Alabama summers.

But the bricks are, in fact, here and they are verification that once upon a time a house stood on the vacant lot that is 612 Butler Avenue in the Raimund neighborhood of Bessemer, Alabama.

The place where Bo Jackson was born.

It is, admittedly, difficult to imagine. The Butler Avenue before you is not the Butler Avenue of long ago. It is a dead-end dirt road, with a string of abandoned homes pocked by shattered windows, peeled-off paint, caved-in roofs. The lawns are overtaken by weeds and wildflowers. Garbage is everywhere. A yellowed mattress. A smattering of playing cards. A thirtyish man named Symphoney Adams lives in a gray home near the dead end, and he points toward a patch of scorched earth beside his driveway. "I burn my trash," he said nonchalantly. "Cheaper than having it collected."

The cliché biography trope would offer, "Squint and you can still see Bo Jackson." But try as one might, you can't. What one beholds are the bloody remains of a once-thriving iron ore, coal and limestone mining industry that began to abandon Birmingham and its nearby suburbs (like Bessemer, which is fifteen miles to the city's south) in the early 1970s. "Pretty much everyone who lived here worked in the mines," said Carolyn Williams, one of the few remaining Butler Avenue residents from back in the day. She is seventy-five, African American, with short hair, embedded dimples and three stray cats on a front porch. Her home is the one she was born in, and as others bolted she stuck. Now she wonders why. With a crime rate of 118 per 1,000 residents, Bessemer—long known as "The Marvel City"—is one of the most dangerous places in America. "It's a far cry from what it was," she said. Then, a pause. A sigh. "But I'm telling you, this was once a place to be. Believe it or not, it *really* was . . ."

And the words are uttered with such conviction that, perhaps, some vague vision of Butler Avenue is recoverable. It's the early 1960s. The mines are still mostly open. The houses on Butler Avenue are well-maintained and fully occupied. The Scotts live over there—they're bootleggers. The Johnsons are down thataway—they sell ice cream out of the freezer. The Evans family. The Leonard family. The Williamses. And here, at 612 Butler Avenue, resides Florence Mae Jackson. She is a single Black woman who was reared by her parents, George and Margaret Jackson, in a little blue home on an adjacent street. Those who know her well call her "Bebe." But those who don't know her well keep a measured distance. Florence is a not a "Bebe." She is hardened. Takes no shit and doesn't suffer phonies. There is a stereotype of the Southern Black woman who refers to you as "Sugar" and insists you sit on down and try a slice of her out-of-the-oven rhubarb pie. That's *not* Florence Jackson.

Back in 1949, when she was eighteen, Florence married a local World War II veteran named Johnnie Jackson, Sr. He jumped ship after a handful of years, leaving her with multiple kids and a house (the green one at 612 Butler) the size of a sneaker.

The home was built in the mid-1930s, constructed primarily of plywood and reddish-orange brick on a plot that measures roughly three quarters of an acre. Inside, there were three rooms: a miniature kitchen (which doubled as a bedroom), a miniature living room (which doubled as a bedroom) and a miniature bedroom. There was no running water. If one needed to defecate he had to open the rickety front door and walk ten feet to a green rectangular outhouse with a tar paper roof and concrete floor.

Florence worked jobs one wouldn't choose to work—cleaning houses, cleaning rooms at the local Holiday Inn and Ramada Inn. She never held a driver's license, so the older children took her where she needed to go.

By the early 1960s, Florence was mother to seven—several with Johnnie Jackson, Sr., another bunch with A. D. Adams, a steel mill worker from Leflore, Mississippi, who moved to Bessemer in the late 1950s. Adams was a burly man with short-chopped hair, a pronounced mustache and forearms that doubled as anvils. His nickname was "Big Track." A. D. had a warm laugh; the kind that began in the belly and shot up. He worked hard, spending four decades employed by the Woodward Iron/Coppers Coke Plant. He wasn't one to bemoan his lot in life. "Everyone liked A. D.," recalled Stephanie Wilson, his niece. "He would give you the shirt off his back without a second's pause."

There was one small issue: A. D. Adams lived in a house four miles away on 26th Street North—*with his wife, Louise.*

The two married on October 26, 1961, in a small church ceremony in Montgomery. So, when thirteen months later (on November 30, 1962, to be exact) Florence was taken to the nearby Black hospital, Bessemer General, to give birth to A. D.'s child, the father was nowhere to be found.

He wasn't there to hold Florence Jackson's hand.

He wasn't there to embrace a new life.

He wasn't there to swaddle his baby boy.

His absence was expected.

It would come to sculpt the life of the child.

After the requisite one-day recovery, Florence Mae Jackson and her newborn returned to the house at Butler Avenue. This was familiar turf—along with her seven other children (Jennifer, twins Jerry and Sherry, Louella, Janet, Anthony and Ronald), Florence had miscarried two sets of twins, as well as two individual babies. She had been through the drill. So when it came to naming the latest baby, Florence didn't seek out deep meaning via biblical influences or family history.

Nope, she simply turned to the twelve-inch black-and-white Zenith positioned in the living room where the television show *Ben Casey* aired on Channel 6 every Monday night at nine o'clock.

The star of Florence's favorite program was an actor named Vince Edwards, who portrayed a rugged neurosurgeon with, in the words of Newhouse News Service's Richard Freedman, "virile intensity."

Florence looked at the television.

Florence looked at her nearby baby.

Vincent Edward Jackson it would be.

Florence recalled her eighth child as being something of a nightmare.

He cried a lot. He ate a lot. When he didn't get his way, he threw objects. He stomped until Florence picked him up.

Before long, there were three more children—a year-younger sister, Millicent (whose father was also A. D.), then two boys, Clarence and Anthony, with a different man. And while Butler Avenue was a long way from the skippy-dippy-doo Mayberry portrayed on *The Andy Griffith Show*, it was a fairly safe environment for Florence and her offspring. Neighbors watched out for other neighbors. Your friend's mother was your (unofficial) auntie. The homes all used the same skeleton key—so if someone required a cup of sugar, she was welcome to go a house over, unlock the door and take it.

On the day of Vincent Edward Jackson's birth, George Wallace, the state's governor-elect, found himself addressing the Alabama Farm Equipment Association's convention in nearby Montgomery. The headline atop the next day's *Birmingham News* piece was WALLACE ONCE MORE SAYS HE WILL DISOBEY INTEGRATION STATUTES.

Save one story on the newspaper's second page (headline: NEGROES LACK BOND, STAY BEHIND BARS), the entire *Birmingham News* reads as a celebration of the region's whiteness. Despite the city's 39.6 percent Black population, there were no images of nonwhite faces. There were no odes to Black accomplishments. The day's weddings were white weddings. The day's deaths were white deaths.

So while, yes, Raimund felt safe, much of that was because it was a small, cocooned region of Bessemer—Black residents, Black businesses, Black schools, little day-to-day interactions with white hostilities. Until 1963, when the state of Alabama finally complied with the 1954 decision in *Brown v. Board of Education of Topeka*, there were two Raimund Elementary Schools in Bessemer—one deliberately painted white (for the white students), one deliberately painted brown (for the Black students). "I lived in the white area. Bo lived in the Black area," recalled Lynn Payne, a white Bessemer native who graduated from high school in 1967. "We weren't raised to hate Blacks. You just knew to keep a certain divide."

Not that little Vincent Edward Jackson thought much about such matters. When you're young, and you're one of eight . . . nine . . . ten children in a three-room house, and your father doesn't exist in your sphere, and your stomach is hollow, the last thing on your mind is the civil rights movement. Years later, Jackson had vivid memories of resentfully watching *The Brady Bunch*, wondering why Mike and Carol's kids always seemed so happy. "Nobody [in my house] had a bed all for himself," he recalled of his childhood. "We had two beds in the bedroom, and usually we'd sleep two to a bed, one at the top and one at the bottom. The rest of us would sleep on the floor. Get a blanket and sleep on the floor. In the winter we had a coal stove for the bedroom and a gas heater for the living room, and most of the time I tried to sleep right in front of the heater. Sometimes I'd wake up with burn marks on my butt where I bumped against the heater during the night."

Florence worked long hours, so her children spent much time with neighboring relatives. Her sister Beatrice was employed as a janitor at a nearby school, often bringing her nieces and nephews leftover scraps from the cafeteria. And Florence's parents, George and Margaret, lived within walking distance and helped raise the grandchildren. With A. D. Adams not around, Vincent's idea of manhood was molded by George.

He was sixty-three when Vincent was born, a former semipro catcher who barnstormed the region with an array of Black teams. Most people called him "Snag"—an ode to the unusually large hands that allowed him to snag baseballs minus a glove. Some of Vincent's earliest memories involve sitting on the porch of his grandparents' house and observing his grandfather. "He would wake up early in the morning, get his old coon dog and they'd go up in the mountain, come back around nine or ten o'clock, he'd have one or two possum," Jackson recalled. "When he came home and he'd empty out the croker sack and have two, three rabbits, two, three coons. I'd sit there and watch him skin 'em, wash 'em out, hang 'em in the smokehouse."

A treat for little Vincent was an oatmeal cookie made with cheese. Or a foil-wrapped sweet potato. Most meals involved wild game—"rabbit, squirrels," he recalled. "You name it, we've eaten it." If a Jackson found a turtle in the road, he brought it home, scooped out the innards, dumped the goop into boiling water and drank turtle soup. "There were times we didn't have anything but grits," he said. "It always puzzled me. 'How in the hell can we live in this house and not have food to eat?'" Every item of clothing was handed down. The local bootlegger, Pap Scott, was always in need of plastic bags, so the Jackson kids scavenged Bessemer and passed them to Scott for three cents apiece.

On December 21, 1968, less than a month after his grandson's sixth birthday, George died. It was Vincent's first experience with death—the idea that someone can exist, then cease to exist. "We buried him either the day before or the day after Christmas," Jackson recalled. "For about five or six Christmases after that, it rained. Christmas was always sad."

This is a moment in time when something changes. Young Vincent was supposed to imitate George—a steadfast and decent man who believed in family, hard work and Sunday mornings at the Mount Zion Baptist Church. He trudged forward—left boot on, right boot on. In an ideal world, Vincent Edward would wind up just like him.

Now George Jackson was gone.

Florence did not dream on behalf of her children. She did not stress over their futures. Certainly never thought of college, or careers in business or law. Her lone goal was to have them survive in one piece, to navigate childhood and emerge unscathed and available to work in one of the nearby mines. This was no easy task.

The Jackson kids were rough, wild and physical. Were one to walk past 612 Butler Avenue on certain nights, he'd see the children on the porch, decked out in soiled clothing, armed with shotguns and bricks. "Waiting," Vincent recalled, "for mom to come home." They trusted few outside of family. A person's word meant little. Promises were viewed skeptically. That type of outlook generally exists for a reason, and with the Jacksons it wasn't hard to interpret. The children were fatherless and broke.

For Vincent, there was an added component: He stuttered.

When he wanted a slice of bread, it was "C-c-c-c-c-c-an I-I-I-I-I ha-ha-have s-s-s-s-s-some buh-buh-buh-buh-buhread." If he wanted to go outside, it was "I-I-I-I-I'm g-g-g-g-going out-out-out-outside." The stutter was almost certainly genetic. His father, A. D. Adams, gave Vincent nothing but a speech impediment that would damn his son until his adulthood.

In poor, rural, Black Bessemer, there was no such thing as a speech therapist. Certainly, the Raimund School District didn't provide one. So when Vincent enrolled at now-integrated Raimund Elementary for first grade in 1969, his stutter presented a problem. "I was probably one of the smartest kids," he recalled, "but my stuttering was so bad I couldn't keep up with the normal kids. I was the first in my class to actually write my name instead of print, and I could read better than any of the kids in class. I was slowed down because of my stuttering."

Five decades ago, "stutterer" was often seen as a crass synonym for "stupid." So Vincent, at the urging of Florence, was forced to re-enroll in first grade and take Mrs. McDonnell's class again. It was humiliating— having a November birthday, he was already nearly a year older than many of his classmates. The school was minuscule. A single coal heater. Thin walls. There were four rooms and a cafeteria for the roughly seventy-five kindergarten through grade 5 students. A husband and wife janitor (Robert Harris) and cafeteria worker (Annie Harris) kept things running. Every Friday a man pulling a cart filled with sugarcane stopped outside the main entrance and sold nickel stalks. One teacher, Mr. Hopson, kept a stick wrapped in duct tape by his desk, and used it to whip misbehaving students. Another, Mrs. Smith, preferred an old-school wood paddle. "I was caught eating peanuts in class," recalled Michael Cox, Jackson's classmate. "Mrs. Smith gave me one hundred licks—ten per day for ten days. Your parents didn't care. It was fair game." Inside Raimund, everyone knew everyone, so everyone knew the grumpy first grader who st-st-st-stuttered all his words. As a result, the Vincent Jackson walking the halls of Raimund Elementary as a second-time first grader was a quiet terror. "When I started to read and I got stuck on a word," he said, "the kids started laughing and it made me mad."

How mad?

"If you laughed at me when I stuttered in class," he added, "I was going to beat the shit out of you when we got out of school. I did that religiously from the first through the sixth grades."

Vincent looked for reasons to start fights. One day, he wore his sister's hand-me-down sneakers to school, and someone laughed. Vincent beat him up. A couple of times, lacking shoes, he arrived in dirty, torn socks. People laughed. He beat them up. One day, Vincent stuttered over the word "h-h-h-home" while reading aloud to the class, and someone laughed. Vincent beat him up.

It was while languishing at Raimund that Vincent first discovered a wholesome way to generate income: steal the lunches of classmates, then force them to buy back the food. If they refused, he punched them. Sometimes even if they *did* buy the food back, he punched them. "He'd line us up and say, 'I want this from your plate, this from your plate,'" said Bobby Clayton, Jr., a classmate. "He challenged you one time, and after that you learned to give him what he wanted." The class photo from that year tells the story—a scowling Vincent Edward Jackson in a ratty, hand-me-down pink shirt, doing his all to conceal a missing front tooth.

Away from school, Vincent's life could sound—beneath a certain lens—somewhat idyllic. Butler Avenue was backed by acres of wooded terrain, and he and his friends and cousins (Bessemer was home to dozens of Jackson kin) spent hours climbing, sprinting, leaping, riding. "We would get up in a tree and jump into the honeysuckle bushes to break our fall," Jackson recalled warmly. There was a nearby fishing hole with water the color of blood from the reddish clay bottom, and on hot days the children sought out frogs and tadpoles and, on occasion, snakes. They held lengthy crab apple battles. Mr. Simon, a few streets over, paid the boys a dime for every robin they could kill with a BB gun ("He ate them birds," said Greg Johnson, a child of Bessemer). Vincent's closest running buddies were three cousins—Michael, Lodge and Jason Jackson—who lived around the corner.

On Friday nights his aunt Bea (referred to as "Sister" by most everyone) threw parties for the neighborhood—fish sandwiches, greens, cobblers. "People wouldn't even go home to change," he recalled. "They'd stop by on the way home from work. They wanted to get drunk." Vincent served as caddie, shuffling back and forth to the refrigerator, bringing the men their Falstaffs, making sandwiches, occasionally slipping his hand into a drunkard's pocket and picking out a ten-spot. "That's when you could buy two-for-a-penny cookies," he said. "Twelve-ounce sodas for twelve cents. A bag of potato chips cost a dime." There can be a Rockwellian feel to it all; a simpler time with simpler needs.

But that's largely illusion. A. D. Adams lived across town with his own family (he and his wife, Louise, wound up having their own fleet of children, and in his 2010 obituary he was unironically remembered as someone who was "loved and adored by many who called him Daddy"), and Vincent lashed out. Once, because a friend issued a dare, he stood along the side of a road and launched a rock at the front window of a passing car. The glass splintered into hundreds of pieces and the vehicle swerved off the street. Vincent bolted into the woods. "I was best known in the community for throwing rocks," he said. "I hit somebody every day with a rock."

Another time, he and his brother Jerry engaged in a heated backyard rock-throwing contest. Jerry ducked behind a doghouse, and when he raised his head Vincent hurled a rock that nailed him flush above the eyes. "We didn't have rock fights anymore," Jackson said. He was anointed with a new nickname: "The Little Rock Chucker."

Before discovering sports, his true gift was stealing bicycles, then stripping them down. "I'd throw it in a fire," he said, "burn the paint off, spray-paint it another color, ride it down the street past the house I stole it from. Nobody would know."

In the Jackson household, violence begat violence. Because food was hard to come by, Florence made clear the few items in the refrigerator were to be cherished. When she bought, say, three or four bananas, they were not to be gratuitously touched. Her line was "Don't bother [fill in the blank]"—as in, "Don't bother these bananas, because I'll be making a pie on Saturday." And if a child *did* bother the bananas, brutality ensued. If Florence punished her children, it wasn't with a stern lecture. No, she hit them with a switch, or a pipe, or a shower rod. Or multiples of the above.

When Vincent was six or seven, he took to crawling into the kitchen, rummaging through his mother's purse and grabbing the loose change. Sometimes it'd only be a quarter. Different days, fifty cents. On a memorable Saturday morning, Vincent was caught in the act.

"Don't you move!" Florence barked. "You keep your hands right there!"

She went back to sleep for another hour and a half, then woke, tied her son to the bedpost, grabbed the nearest extension cord and—his words—"wore my ass out." Jackson walked away from the beating with a back resembling a bloodied tic-tac-toe board. Which was nearly as bad as the time she whipped him with an extension cord in one hand, a .38 pistol in the other. "You run or you try to take the extension cord from me," she said, "and I'm gonna bust you in the ass with this pistol."

Vincent did not run.

Most Sunday mornings, Florence dragged her children to the neighboring Mount Zion Baptist Church, where she sang in the choir as her offspring sat on the wood benches and squirmed as the deacon spoke of God and Satan, heaven and hell. He was a bombastic orator, and his warnings—*"In Revelation 12:9 we learn that Satan is a dangerous enemy. He is a serpent who can bite us when we least expect it. He is a destroyer . . ."*—were meant to terrify the two dozen or so children in attendance.

It didn't work.

When Vincent Jackson was seven, he and the other neighborhood children enjoyed playing house.

Now, that might read a bit strange. Vincent was the kid stealing bikes and punching noses and throwing rocks at passing cars. House seems genteel.

Here's how he explains it: "We would use the outhouse to play house in. There was a shelf and a toilet. We would get old cans out of the garbage and put them high on the shelf and pretend they were groceries and we would put the toilet seat down and it was a table. If somebody in the neighborhood got a new refrigerator or a new stove, we would get the box and it would be our bedroom and we'd make holes in it for windows . . ."

It sounds lovely. In the darkness of poverty and a fatherless world, young Vincent and his pals sought out domestic bliss and tranquility and . . .

Or, not.

". . . We'd go inside [the house] and get a blanket and we'd do the nasty. We'd do the grown folks."

In 1979, a study conducted by the Johns Hopkins School of Public

Health found that the average age of first sexual intercourse among teenagers was 16.2 years.

Vincent Jackson insists he was seven.

"I never told anybody," Jackson recalled. "Back there in the country, kids did that because we would see the grown-ups do it." It began, innocently, with a game called "Hump"—the boys counted to one hundred as the girls hid in the woods. When a boy found you, he could hump against you—"clothes against clothes," Jackson said. "There's somebody always looking to see where the pretty girls are gonna hide. I always peeked."

For the most part, Florence had no idea what her eighth child was up to. Yes, she was aware he could be stubborn and obstinate. But the era was one of distanced relationships between a child's behaviors and a parent's involvement. There weren't a thousand after-school clubs to join. Your kid came home, had a snack, hopped on his bike and vanished until dusk. He would be fine.

One Sunday morning, when Vincent was eight or nine, he and some friends walked through the woods to a local dairy farm. The property belonged to a white man. The kids ran down to a lake on the property, dove into the cool water and were confronted by the owner. "If I ever catch you swimming in that lake," he said, "I'm gonna whip your ass!"

A few weeks later, the boys returned. First, they picked bushels of blackberries off the man's bushes. Then they removed all their clothing and dove back into the forbidden waters. A man who worked the land was riding horseback when he spotted the trespassers. He galloped forward, fired his rifle into the air, hopped off the horse and threw all the clothing down a drain.

The nude boys dashed from the lake, through a barbed-wire fence ("Which wasn't easy without anything on," Jackson said) and roughly five hundred yards into the woods. The walk home, Jackson recalled, was anything but normal. "We had to pass one house where the old lady sat on the porch," he said.

One of Jackson's cousins hushed his comrades. "Don't say nothing," he whispered, "and they'll think we're from Florida."

Later in his life, as he came into contact with people from different parts of America, Jackson was often asked what it was like to grow up Black in the Deep South. The presumption was that there would surely be stories of KKK marches and burning crosses.

The presumption was wrong.

Jackson never actually heard racial epithets directed toward him until he was midway through elementary school. One day, while walking home after the final bell, he was headed toward the woods when a blue Mustang approached. Filled with white kids, it sped in his direction.

Jackson bolted into the woods, and the whites followed. "Come here, n-----!" one screamed. "We're gonna kick your ass!" As the boys moved in, Jackson stopped atop a hill and slung rocks. The taunts continued—"We're gonna getcha! We're gonna getcha!"

"That," Jackson later said, "was the first time that I really experienced prejudice."

This, of course, was not *really* true. Vincent Jackson was born at Bessemer General because Birmingham's better hospitals didn't take Black patients. He lived in the Raimund section because that's where Blacks were relegated. The house he called home had little resale value. His mom worked as a housekeeper because those were the jobs available to uneducated Black women. His mom was an uneducated Black woman because society did not grant her the luxury of dreams or expectations. The church he attended— Mount Zion Baptist—was all Black, and had the Jacksons tried entering the nearby Second Baptist Church, an army of aspiring Moseses would have risen to stop them. "I went there as a girl," recalled Gigi Smart, who is white. "Our deacon said he would *never* go to church with Blacks." The teachers Vincent learned from at Raimund Elementary were almost all white. The white classmates he had at Raimund were, for the most part, not allowed to have Black children over and certainly not allowed to go to a Black friend's house. Rex Parker, a white student one year ahead of Jackson at Raimund Elementary, considered his best childhood pal to be Langston Leonard, a Black classmate from the Butler Avenue neck of Bessemer. When the two were in third grade, Langston was diagnosed with leukemia. Rex's parents would not allow him to pay a visit. After Langston died, a crestfallen Rex was forbidden to attend the funeral. "My dad was a racist, and he wouldn't let me go," said Parker. "Someone told me Langston asked about me during his last days. That still eats at me. I let him down. Any why? Because he was Black and I was white? What a waste . . ."

Prejudice was all around Vincent Jackson.

He just didn't realize it yet.

So when—and how—did Vincent Edward Jackson become "Bo"?

Well, to certain residents of Bessemer, never. As a young boy, he was handed the various young boy type of nicknames many of us are assigned.

He was "Boo," "Nap," "Nappy Head." Some referred to him as "Vinson," an absentminded shortening of Vincent. A good number of people who attended school with him still (in 2022) think of him as "Vincent," and spit out "Bo" as one would a mouthful of sour milk.

Back in the late 1980s, Jackson told a *Sporting News* reporter: "My older brother and cousin said I was tough like a wild boar. After a while they just cut it short and called me 'Bo.'" He has mainly stuck by the story— and perhaps it's true.

But maybe there's a different reason.

On May 31, 1972, when Vincent was nine, going on ten, Florence wed Joseph Bond, a miner who was twenty-five years her senior. The union was as much of convenience as affection—Bond lived on a parallel street, had saved his money and was financially well off for the area, which was something Florence had never known. "He was an old man," one family friend said. "What do *you* think the gossip was?"

Shortly after the marriage the couple—along with Florence's children— relocated to a new house a half mile away at the top of Merritt Street in the Erie Heights neighborhood. It was, in the eyes of nine-year-old Vincent, a literal mansion. Three levels! Back *and* front yards! Twelve rooms! Two bathrooms—both indoors! This was huge. Plus, when Bond died less than a year after the wedding, the house was all Florence's.

The relocation also placed Vincent significantly closer to 408 Republic Avenue, where a man named Willie Norville Harris resided. Harris was one of the guys everyone in Black Bessemer knew. He was (simultaneously) the owner of Harris Sanitation, an employee at Dickie Clay (maker of fine bricks) and the assistant pastor at the Good Samaritan True Holiness Church.

The Harris property was home to cows, goats, horses, chickens, pigs. Norville (no one called him "Willie") and his wife, Elizabeth, were parents to eight children, all of whom woke early every morning to feed the beasts. "We worked like dogs," recalled Tony Harris, the sixth of the eight offspring. "My dad was very strict. *Very* strict. He definitely would break out the switch if we didn't listen. Those animals were our dinner, but they were also sold to other people for their dinners. I hated every moment of the work. But we had no choice."

The Jackson family knew the Harris family, but only casually. What Vincent Jackson *did* know was that Norville Harris owned a bunch of really enormous hogs.

Not that this was unusual. Some of the best days of Vincent's childhood involved his uncle Jesse (Florence's brother), who lived close by and raised his own slew of hogs. Come fall Saturday mornings, Vincent and some of his brothers would walk through the woods and over to their uncle's house, then watch as he'd place feed in the trough. "The hogs would come out," Jackson recalled, "and he'd pick one that he was gonna slaughter and he'd take his little .22 rifle and hit him right between the eyes and drop him right there."

Jesse would order the boys to drag the carcass toward a cast-iron pot overflowing with boiling water, dump it on the animal and scrape off the hair. Then, Jackson recalled, "we'd hang him up and you'd just gut him— and when you'd do that, you get the saws out and just cut him up. [Then] they would take the head up to the house, wash it, clean it out, cook it, and make 'country souse.'"

Last, Vincent and his brothers scooped up the pig intestines and (*splat*) threw them (*splat*) at one another (*splat*).

It's hard to measure the impact of exposure to such violence at the age of ten . . . eleven . . . twelve. But the experiences hardened Vincent to animal cruelty. Which is probably why, at age thirteen in the summer of 1976, he and twenty or so friends and cousins walked over to the Harris property, checked to make certain no one was looking, found a bunch of sticks—and beat the living shit out of Norville's hogs.

For.

Three.

Straight.

Days.

Twenty-two years after William Golding wrote *Lord of the Flies*, the Jackson-led posse surrounded one boar hog after another and unleashed a merciless bevy of blows to the head and body. "We wouldn't beat on people," recalled Wayne Leonard, who was part of Bo's crew. "But animals? One summer some neighborhood kids caught a stray dog, poured gasoline on it, lit a match and watched it run. Animals were fair game." Hence, there was no empathy toward the hogs. When one died, the kids moved on to the next one.

Except that the biggest of the boar hogs refused to give in. He was approximately five hundred pounds, and absorbed his daily pounding, crumbled to the ground, then rose to live for yet another attack. On the third day, Jackson recalled, "We finally got him down. We were all gathered around him, beating him with the sticks." Then, a sound from behind— "Hey! Get out of here!" A shotgun blast, and the boys dropped their sticks and ran.

Jackson scaled the fence and sprinted toward a ditch that he remembered being about twenty yards wide. "I hit that ditch full speed and leaped over and as I looked down there were all those dead pigs," he recalled. Jackson headed for the woods where he ran left, right, right, left, right before returning home and locking himself inside his room. He changed his clothes, wiped the mud from his shoes.

Knock, knock, knock.

It was William Lumpkin, the local barbershop owner who for years cut Vincent Jackson's hair. If Lumpkin wasn't trimming fades, he was assisting Harris with his farm.

When Florence answered the door, Lumpkin explained to her what had transpired. "I do your boy's hair every month," he said, "and he was one of the boys who killed the hogs."

Florence was livid. Her son was trouble. Always trouble. Beating kids up. Throwing rocks through windows. Stealing lunch money. "Look," she said, "if Mr. Harris wants to send his ass to reform school, then send him. Because I'm tired of him."

Reform school?

Lumpkin demanded that Vincent name the other boys who helped kill the animals. This was a youngster who feared no pain, feared no suspension, feared no labor. But . . . reform school? One of his brothers had attended reform school for several years, and returned with stories of other boys trying to rape him.

Reform school?

"I ratted on everybody," Vincent said. "They all got grounded for the summer. They couldn't be pissed at me, because nobody could beat me up."

The story quickly turned to local lore, and from local lore to local legend.

Vincent Edward Jackson had killed a bunch of hogs—*boar hogs.*

Boar hog, when enunciated, sounds just as it reads. But when uttered quickly, with a hardy Alabama twang, it's more like *bo hog.*

Bo, for short.

CHAPTER 2

A BLACK BRUCE JENNER

There are three moments that could have changed everything.

Three moments, where instead of Bo Jackson becoming a mythological sports icon, Vincent Edward Jackson becomes another fatherless poor Black inmate in a state (Alabama) not lacking the model.

The first moment: He is twelve, and it is summer. There's a recreation center not far from the family home where local kids are provided free meals and inexpensive snacks. In the center of it all is a battered ping-pong table.

Two kids are playing, and Jackson has next. He reaches for a paddle, only his cousin reaches for the paddle, too. She tugs hard, digging her fingernails beneath his skin. The paddle is now in her hand. Bo shoves her, then fires off a weak hook. She punches him in the face.

Vincent storms off to the adjacent baseball field and returns moments later with an aluminum bat. His first swing is wild and off the mark. He falls, and a bunch of kids laugh aloud. He swings again, misses again. More laughter—the kind he hears while stuttering in class.

There is a third swing. It is the hardest so far, and it lands just below her rib cage, in the kidney. She falls to the concrete floor and lets out a guttural moan. Bo is unmoved. He is standing over her, preparing to take another shot. He raises the bat, begins to chop downward, and . . . out of nowhere, his sister Sherry (who works at the rec center) grabs Bo and pulls him away.

"Vincent," she screams, "you could kill her!"

He drops the bat and walks away, leaving his victim writhing in pain.

The second moment: He is still twelve, back at the rec center waiting to shoot pool. An older kid arrives and shoves Bo. "Get lost," he says. "It's my turn."

Bo is overmatched in size and strength. So he says, "You be here when I get back," then leaves, walks home and returns with his mother's shotgun.

The culprit is gone. But Bo knows where he lives, and tracks him through the woods. "I saw him," he said, "and I threw the gun up, fixin' to shoot. If he hadn't stepped behind the tree, I would have blew him away."

When he arrives home, one of his sisters locks the front door. For three hours, Bo sits in the backyard, watching birds fly toward a pecan tree on the neighbor's property. He fires at one—*BOOM!*—and "nothing fell down but feathers and a beak," he recalled.

Florence hears the sound, drags Bo in by his ear, and beats him with an extension cord.

The third moment: He is a seventh grader at McAdory Junior High. There is a kid he doesn't like—some chubby boy named Danny Terrell. One afternoon, while standing in the hallway, Bo pounces, leaping toward Danny with the intent to hurt.

It does not work out.

Terrell is bigger and stronger than his assailant. A pair of punches to the nose throw Bo back against a locker and knocks him out. Both students are suspended, and that should be that.

But, no. The Terrells and the Jacksons live in the same neighborhood, and a school bus leaves Danny off on Merritt Avenue, right in front of Bo's home. In the aftermath of the fight, nursing a black-and-blue nose, Bo rushes inside and grabs the .22 rifle belonging to one of his brothers.

He loads the clip, finds a good spot, sets his sight on Danny Terrell, prepares to fire.

Against all odds, a thought enters his mind: *If I shoot Danny Terrell, I'm either going to jail or I'm going to reform school. And if I go to reform school, I'll be up all night trying to keep people from raping me.*

So, instead of shooting Danny Terrell, Jackson fires at a tree. "He turned and looked, dropped his books and hauled his ass home," Jackson recalled. "I could have filled him so full of lead they would have had to pick him up with a magnet. But something tapped me on the shoulder and said, 'Hey, this isn't a good thing.' So I shot the tree."

The Terrell family left town shortly thereafter.

So, yes, the Bo Jackson you know could have been the Vincent Edward Jackson you never knew. The line is thin. But something saved him.

Jackson found sports.

He was, from the start, uniquely athletic. Carolyn Williams, a next-door neighbor, recalled little Vincent, no older than seven or eight and "just a big-headed ol' boy," picking up a rock and launching it down Butler Avenue. In her mind's eye, the rock soars through the air, from one end of the street to the other—which would be well over two hundred yards. "I don't know exactly how far," she said. "But it *went*."

Back in Bessemer, there weren't a ton of sports opportunities for young children. But the town's landscape provided its own training grounds. Vincent Jackson wasn't running 40s in singlets, but he was sprinting up, over, under and through the woods in tattered jeans and hand-me-down Keds. He wasn't lifting weights or tossing javelins, but the 12,471 rocks that left his hand traveled at high velocities. His boxing workouts involved beating up kids. His endurance training was Florence's extension-cord whippings. His shiftiness came in avoiding crab apples.

In the summer of 1973, ten-year-old Vincent took his first major leap into organized athletics, signing up to play Bessemer Little League. He was assigned to a team coached by Florence's cousin-in-law, and lasted a month. It wasn't fair—squads were delegated by grades, and Vincent (November birthday, held back a year) was dominant. "I was too physical for the boys I was playing with," he said.

Promoted to Pony League, he joined the Raimund Pirates and found himself surrounded by older kids with more developed skills. Any records documenting the league have long vanished. But fleeting memories abound. Vincent Jackson blocking the plate like a brick wall. Vincent Jackson gunning down a runner at second, then pointing an imaginary gun his way. Curtis Wilson, a future high school classmate, was an outfielder for the rival Jonesboro Astros. In a game at Bessemer's diamond, Wilson stole home plate and ran over Jackson for the winning run. "He didn't budge," Wilson remembered. "But he dropped the ball."

After the field was cleared and high fives were exchanged, a dirt-covered Jackson ran up behind Wilson.

"Curt," he said, "we'll meet again."

There was one forbidden sport: football.

Which, if you think about it, is sort of strange. Florence Bond would beat her kids, whip her kids, threaten her kids with a gun, lock her kids out of the house, strap her kids to a bedpost.

But football was too violent.

"She did not want me to play—period," Jackson recalled. "I guess she . . . um . . . seen it on TV. She saw the pros play on TV. How hard they're hit."

Raimund Elementary ran through sixth grade, and after that, in the fall of 1976, Jackson began attending the seventh-through-ninth McAdory

Junior High, which was located alongside the high school four miles from his home in neighboring McCalla.

Steered away from football (recalled Bobby Clayton, a classmate: "Most of Bo's friends would stay after school for junior high football practice, but Bo just took the bus home; it was sorta sad") and not yet ready for high school track, Vincent followed the path of his older brother Anthony, who spent two years playing baseball at nearby Lawson State Community College. The sport was Vincent's first athletic passion, and he devoted many a day to starring for the Raimund Pirates and, later, the Ben All-Stars of the local industrial league. The games were played on tattered fields, in front of sparse crowds. He *loved* it. As a younger child, he had enjoyed stickball in his yard—"my aunt would bring old mops and brooms for us," Jackson recalled. Now, with the Ben All-Stars, he was holding a real aluminum bat, wrapping his left hand in a genuine leather glove, squaring off against bigger, stronger, better players. "Usually kids weren't playing in those games," said Curtis Wilson. "But Bo was just too talented not to have in uniform." One of his teammates, a pitcher named Reggie Patterson, wound up spending four Big League seasons with the White Sox and Cubs. He was four years Bo's senior.

When he began the ninth grade, Jackson defied his mother and tried out for a football team. He made the junior varsity roster. "My mother was the motivator," said Earl Jackson, Vincent's brother. "Because of her doubting him so much."

At the time, McAdory's do-it-all superstar athlete was junior halfback Larry Mason. He was one year older but two grades ahead of Jackson. Mason stood 5-foot-11 and was built like a chimney. He ran over people and around people, and the scouts flocked to McCalla to watch the kid play (Mason later spent several years in the NFL and USFL). Jackson, by comparison, languished in the shadows. "At the beginning Vincent was just sort of average," said Lester Haney, a JV teammate. "You have to remember, he'd never played football before. So it wasn't like, 'Look, everyone, it's Bo Jackson!' Not at all. We were all raw kids."

"He was a good JV running back," recalled Michael Weeks, another teammate. "But was there a reason to think, 'Holy cow! This guy is special'? Nah."

Jackson's first taste of scholastic athletic glory came in the spring of his ninth-grade year, when he joined the McAdory High track team. He had always enjoyed running, but this was about more than competition. At age sixteen, he was starting (albeit slowly) to look around and see his life was heading in a bad direction. Far too many of the kids from his neighborhood were turning toward drugs and violence. Gradually, familiar faces disappeared, victims to temptation. Plus he was tired of getting in trouble, of staring down a mother with an extension cord and reason to believe her son was worthy of a beatdown.

"I finally realized that all the crap I had been doing when I was younger could get me sent to jail," he said. "Something just clicked where I wasn't that bad a person."

One day, during the early spring of 1979, Vincent was walking off the McAdory baseball diamond when he happened upon Dickey Atchison, the varsity track coach, mentoring a high jumper. The boy was working his way up toward clearing six feet, but it was going slowly. He would clear five feet four inches. Then five feet five. Then stumble. Then stumble again. Then . . .

Jackson, wearing pants, took three elongated steps and cleared five feet six with room to spare.

Whoa.

"Hey kid," Atchison asked, "wanna do varsity track?"

What the coach could not have realized was that Jackson had been inadvertently training for this moment since his family moved to the house on Merritt Avenue. It was surrounded by a five-and-a-half-foot-high gated fence, which the Jackson children were forbidden to cross sans permission. "My mom would tell me not to leave the house, and her bedroom was around by the back gate and she could see anybody coming," Jackson recalled. "The two front gates were locked, so I'd walk up to the gate, and I would stand flat-footed and just jump over the fence. She'd say, 'One of these days that damn fence is gonna catch you in the seat of your pants and cut your ass up and I ain't gonna take you to the doctor.'"

Jackson never failed to clear the fence. He was an elite high jumper, waiting to be discovered.

Over his first sixteen years, Jackson had been denied any male role models of substance. His grandfather had died long ago. His father, A. D. Adams, was MIA. Elementary school teachers found him frustrating (if not a bit scary), and middle school teachers struggled to get past the severe stutter that caused him to languish in the rear of classrooms and speak only if called upon.

Atchison, however, saw a spark. A McAdory High guidance counselor, he was employed by the school district to, more than anything, help students who needed a boost. Jackson—dirt-poor, lacking confidence (Atchison had other students who stuttered, and knew of the crippling impact), missing one of his two front teeth and in desperate need of structure and affection—fit the bill. Up until ninth-grade track, Jackson tended to thrust his anger and frustration upon classmates—"I had this mean streak in me," he said, "where if somebody would say something to me I'd just beat the shit out of them." Atchison, however, changed the focus. Vincent could unleash his fury differently. More productively. "I'd [now] take that meanness out on running the hurdles or just high jumping," he recalled

McAdory High had neither track nor much track equipment. The teams practiced on the football field, or outside the stadium, or sometimes in the hallways. Howard Beckner, the school's band director, was once sitting in his office after school when he heard a nearby *BAM! BAM! BAM!* He opened his door to a visual shock. "Here's Vincent Jackson, leaping over hurdles in the hallway, jumping so high his head was hitting the ceiling," Beckner said. "They were trying to teach him to jump lower. It wasn't working."

In the spring of 1979, the McAdory boys track team was small, yet spectacular. Larry Mason, the star running back, won the 220 at the Class 3A Alabama High School Athletic Association championships, then placed third in the 100. Timmy Reese, who would go on to run track at Troy State, came in second in both. A look through the old newspaper agate shows one impressive performer after another.

Now, look closely.

Right there—in the May 6, 1979, *Selma Times-Journal*, buried at the bottom of page 15B. You might need your reading glasses. It's the results of the 3A state championships, and the first time the name "Vincent Jackson" ever appears in print . . .

BROAD JUMP: Phillip Hunt, UMS, (22'2¼") Mark Tate, Buckhorn (2nd) Vincent Jackson, McAdory (3rd)

There is no statistical recording of how far Jackson jumped. There is no quote raving about a ninth grader placing third in an event he first tried only a few weeks earlier. The writer of the accompanying piece, Tommy Hicks, has no memory of seeing Jackson perform that day.

Two weeks later Jackson competed in the 3A state decathlon championships—a ten-event do-it-all sports buffet he knew not existed. Atchison did his best to educate the youngster on the finer points of the various contests. How to slide over a high jump bar backward. How to clear hurdles without killing yourself. How to spring up into a leap. How to pole vault witho— actually, scratch that. The pole vault was no man's land. McAdory owned zero poles. Jackson borrowed one belonging to John Carroll High and somehow cleared ten feet six inches. Which was farcical. "Remember, we had no facilities," said Johnny Benavidez, who coached the girls team. "We practiced everything on the football field. We'd create a four hundred. We'd make hurdles out of the horses you cut wood on. It was all sort of organic."

How raw was Vincent "Bo" Jackson? The first time he picked up a discus at the state meet was the first time he ever picked up a discus. He threw it as one would a Frisbee—wrist back, step, chuck . . .

Plop. It went nowhere.

Sidney Reed, Opelika High's decathlete, approached. "Listen," Reed said, "when you get ready to throw it, have it slide out of your hand instead of trying to actually throw it. And you don't need to spin so much . . ."

Jackson lined up for his second attempt, stepped back and let loose.

"That fucker," Jackson recalled, "took high off."

Two weeks earlier, Joseph Grant of Charles Henderson High had won the 3A state discus championship with a toss of 146 feet 7 inches. Jackson's throw went *20 feet* farther.

Done in by inexperience, Jackson wound up tenth in the overall decathlon. He was the only ninth grader to compete, and to those in attendance his accomplishments screamed I AM COMING!

Alas, the decathlon went uncovered by all media.

The world would have to wait.

In the fall of 1979, Jackson was a tenth grader, approaching his seventeenth birthday and the occupant of an adult body. He had reached six feet in height, with 195 pounds of well-packaged muscle running up and down his frame. In a grade where boys were spindly and gawky, with voices that cracked and quivered, he was mostly man. Yes, the stutter was as bad as ever, and prevented him from speaking up in class, but he otherwise rolled with the radiant confidence of an athlete in control of his athleticism.

Now a decade removed from the end of segregation, the region's social dynamics were . . . intriguing. In 1976, when McAdory began busing in more students of color (its first Black student, Jasper Minnifield, arrived in 1969), a dozen or so white parents tried to strike up a boycott. It didn't take. "There was some turmoil," recalled Renee Morris, a white classmate of Jackson. "Some people acting the fool. But that faded."

Bessemer fed three public schools, and the vast majority of the town's

Black students were zoned to attend either Jackson S. Abrams High or Jess Lanier High, both routinely dismissed as "city schools" in the ugly jargon of prideful racism. Abrams's student body was almost entirely Black, while Lanier's was roughly 85 percent Black, and most of its white students were too poor to afford tuition at one of the area's white-flight Christian academies.

Of the 156 students in Jackson's class at McAdory High, 39 were Black. With rare exception, the races lived in separate neighborhoods, grew up experiencing different childhoods. Blacks had their churches, whites had their churches. Blacks had their hangouts, whites had their hangouts. There were unspoken-yet-entrenched rules. A white classmate could drive a Black classmate home. A white classmate could not invite the Black classmate inside his/her home. "My daddy would say, 'You might have to go to school with them, but you better not bring one here,'" said Michael Cox, a white classmate. "He didn't care if I made an F. But a Black friend over? No way. Years later my wife and I tried adopting a Black child. My dad disowned me for two years." White classmates and Black classmates could not date. Ever. Under *any* circumstances. "It was a huge taboo," said Greer Outlaw, a white student. "No mixed-race couples allowed. I blame the parents more than the kids. It's what we were told." There would never be a mixed-race homecoming king and queen. There would never be more than two Black cheerleaders on the twelve-person squad. "We went to a cheerleading camp one year in Oxford, Mississippi," said Rhonda McMillian, a white cheerleader. "Two of my teammates were Black girls, and a lot of the other families refused to drive them. It's sickening. My mama wasn't like that. She said, 'Hey, girls, load up!' But she was rare."

Ten of McAdory's forty-seven teachers were Black, and there was an unspoken dividing line among faculty. These were people who grew up in a segregated world; the descendants of slave owners and the enslaved.

"Generally, white students ran with white students and students of color ran with students of color," said Teresa Browning Lee, a white 1985 McAdory grad. "You'd be friendly with someone Black in your class. That wasn't unusual. But it wasn't often a very deep friendship."

If there had been any racial animosity aimed toward Jackson, he has never devoted much time toward recapping it. Once, a classmate named Ricky Pennington accused him (wrongly) of stealing his watch. Born with an enormous noggin, Pennington's nickname was "Head." The two met up after school behind the locker room—white student v. Black student—and Jackson pummeled the boy. Head's head was a bloodied cacciatore. "There were probably fifteen of us watching," said Carl Smith, a white classmate.

"We were all white. We all cheered for Bo. Ricky thought he was tough shit. He had it coming."

Although Jackson's ninth-grade track-and-field success was impressive, few at McAdory knew much about it. There was one sport that mattered at the school, and it was varsity football. In 1978, the team went a disappointing 5-5 in the first season under head coach Jim Berryman. The Yellow Jackets returned most of the roster for 1979, including Leroy Mason, Larry's younger brother and a high-powered ball carrier.

Vincent Jackson, increasingly known as either "Bo Hog" or "Boar Hog" to classmates, was (by comparison) just a guy. Berryman heard good things about his performance as a JV player, but hardly *amazing* things. The kid was physically gifted but raw; quick and tough but often out of position and bewildered. He would alternate breathtaking plays and boneheaded plays.

Entering 1979 there was plenty of uncertainty—was Jackson a running back? A defensive lineman? A linebacker? No one was entirely sure. He barely saw the field in McAdory's season opener, a 14–12 nail-biter over Pell City, and did little a week later when the Jackets stormed out to a 28–0 third-quarter lead at Midfield High. By the fourth, Berryman had removed most of his starters. The staff was beginning to pack up equipment. The coaches were starting to think about the following week's game against Fairfield High. On a fourth and long, Midfield sent out Butch Hudspeath to punt. McAdory placed (*eh, why not?*) Jackson on the field to return it. Hudspeath took the snap, stepped forward and launched a spiral high into the air and toward the awaiting arms of little-known number 40.

Jackson tucked the ball beneath his right arm, dashed toward the middle of the field, juked a tackler, juked another tackler, spun wildly. And . . . he . . . was . . . gone. "I mean, gone, gone, gone," said Johnny Benavidez, an assistant coach. "He just broke away from everyone, and before you knew it he was in the end zone. All the coaches were standing there, sort of in awe. I turned to someone and said, 'Damn, he's pretty good.'"

The next afternoon's *Birmingham News* wrote of "Timothy Reese" returning a punt 89 yards, but the error mattered little. In that single play, Jackson showed an explosiveness the coaches either had not seen or somehow ignored. "It was an eye-opener," said Benavidez. "We decided we needed to find ways to get this kid the football."

The Yellow Jackets' third game of the season was a home clash against Fairfield High. The night before, a handful of McAdory's white players caught a movie at the nearby Fairpark Drive-In Theater. "Bo will say this didn't happen," Glenn Todd, his teammate, said years later. "But we know it did. I assure you, it's legit." According to Todd, as the boys readied for the film, Jackson was spotted in a nearby car with a white female classmate. This was an enormous no-no in early-1980s Alabama. Before the next evening's game, the five offensive linemen—all white—hatched a plan. "Not only did we take the play off," Todd said, "we let Fairfield know he was getting the ball."

According to Todd, as soon as the ball was snapped he and his fellow linemen froze and Jackson was blasted. The running back, he recalled, returned to the huddle and said, "What the hell was that for?"

One of McAdory's players stared Jackson down. "Leave the white girls alone," he said.

Jackson, Todd said, nodded and the game resumed. McAdory won, 7–6.

"Back then, the preachers told us that lions don't mate with leopards," Todd said. "They said if God intended us to mix he wouldn't make the different skin tones. I'm not proud of it, but at the time I agreed. We all did.

"And Bo paid the price for that."*

Jackson kept at it. He continued to practice, continued to dress for games. If the coaches lined him up at defensive end, that was fine. If he took four or five handoffs, also fine. Deep down, he realized the sport kept him out of trouble. He also was beginning to realize that he was gifted.

One week later, McAdory played Abrams High in downtown Bessemer at Snitz Snider Stadium. The Blue Devils were 2-2 and coming off a recent 34–0 loss to Wenonah High. They averaged 7 points per outing, and—in Todd's words—"really sucked." The game was scoreless at halftime. Berryman entered the locker room, looked at his players and barked three words: "Start playing football!"

McAdory was set to receive the second half kickoff, and as Jackson jogged back toward the 15-yard line, he yelled toward his teammates, "If they kick it to me, I'm scoring!"

They kicked it to him.

Jackson plucked the ball off the mud at the 13-yard line and stashed it beneath his right elbow. He sliced left across the field, eluded two tacklers and bolted down the sideline for the touchdown. McAdory won, 9–0. "He saved our asses," Todd said. "Seriously, he saved us."

---

* A similar circumstance occurred Jackson's senior year, when—after school—he and a football teammate changed from sweatpants to shorts in an empty hallway. A white girl saw from afar and complained to the principal. "I had to paddle both of them," said Randy Haught, a teacher. "It was ridiculous, and I felt terrible. They did nothing wrong—the shorts were under their sweatpants. But racism was real."

From a physical standpoint, there was no comparing Jackson with Mason, Keith Mack and Vinson Rivers, the Jackets' three primary ball carriers. They were wonderful teenage prep players with far more experience than their teammate. Jackson, though, *was a man*. Despite rarely lifting weights, his chest was carved and his arms miniature bazookas. His stomach was a rock. "The kid was a physical freak," said Berryman. "Off the charts." Once, in the school's dilapidated weight room, Jackson told everyone he could squat 975 pounds. Had he ever done so? No. Had he ever come close to doing so? No. Hell, the all-time high school record is 1,025 pounds. "Ten of us surrounded him to get the weight off him if he failed," said Todd. "The coaches told him he was crazy. He exploded and lifted it like a pro. We were blown away."

During the 1979 season, Berryman bought the team its own Nautilus machine, a steel-and-chains contraption primarily used for squats. It was the coach's attempt at making his players a bit stronger, and Jackson was one of the first to give it a go. "He jumped on the thing and—RIP!—first time, tore up the gears," said Berryman. "When the repairman came to fix it, he looked at me like, 'What sort of creature did this?'"

"We had another machine that was homemade," said Ricky Dunn, McAdory's noseguard. "You got on a platform, got underneath it and you'd push up these bars that were connected with chains to a car tire. There were settings that controlled the tension on the tire. Most of us were happy to hit twenty-five, thirty. Well, Bo, once he got going, that needle would stick at forty and never come back. It was phenomenal—just the power and quickness. No one else was close."

McAdory's 1979 season remains one of the best in school history. The team finished its regular season by winning all ten of its games before losing at Gardendale in the first round of the 3A state playoffs. But for all his potential and the handful of sparkly moments, Jackson did fairly little. Two newspapers ran recaps of every Yellow Jackets outcome, and of the dozens of players credited with tackles, sacks, touchdown runs, booming punts, bursts of glory—Vincent Jackson is referenced only three times.

"You knew he was an athlete," said Tim German, a member of McAdory's special teams unit. "I'm not sure it was clear yet that he was an elite football player."

The life of a high school underclassman involves a good amount of slinking. You are in the shadows of the cool kids, the smart kids, the older kids. Even if you dwell in their solar system, you are but a distant planet, orbiting from afar. Seniors are the stars. Freshmen and sophomores are space debris.

Such was life for Vincent Jackson, tenth grader.

Classmates remember him, but not vividly. He wore ragged outfits. Stuttered. He dated a girl in his grade named Marilyn Strother who—like Jackson—was quiet and reserved (and whose hair featured eye-catching gray streaks). "A lot of us figured they'd get married one day," said Alesia Carter, a cheerleader and Jackson family friend. "They dated the whole time they were at McAdory." In Mrs. Anchors's biology class, Jackson's lab partner was a girl named Laura Felton, who called him "Vinson" and liked that he took the lead when it came to dissecting frogs. Susan Powers worked in the principal's office, and can still picture Vincent seeing her and saying hello. "He was a sweet kid," Parsons said. "Warm smile." Tina Pate sat behind Jackson in tenth-grade math, and described him as "agitating—but in a good way. When he was bored he would turn around and say something funny."

Put simply, Vincent Jackson was an ordinary student.

Until Gail Pilkinton showed up.

She was a cub scribe for the *Birmingham News*—just twenty-three years old in 1980 and new to the newspaper world. When the *News* hired her a year earlier, it was to serve as a metro reporter. One memorable day, an editor approached her desk and said, "We'd like to put a woman in the sports department."

"Wonderful," she replied. "Who do you have in mind?"

Pause.

"Oh, me."

Yikes.

"There were one hundred sports reporters in the state of Alabama, and ninety-nine were men," Pilkinton recalled. "They hated me. I had to cover games, I had to go in locker rooms. I had coaches slam the door in my face and say, 'I'll wait for the real reporter to come.'"

In the spring of 1980, Pilkinton was told to profile a local kid from Bessemer who was making some noise on the track circuit. His name was Vinny. Or Vincent. Something like that. So she reached out to the coaches at McAdory High, but received no response. "It was common back then," she said. "Coaches shielded their athletes from the media."

Pilkinton's strength was her pertinacity. She learned early on that the gateway to a young athlete—and, in particular, a young, Southern Black athlete—was via the mother. Pilkinton was told Florence Bond did her grocery shopping at Mr. Looney's store down on Easter Valley Road, then scouted her out. "I told her that the coaches weren't helpful," Pilkinton said, "but I'd love to write something nice about her son."

"Honey," Florence said, "come home with me. Vincent will be back in thirty minutes."

The two retreated to the house at Merritt Avenue, and when her son walked through the front door, Florence introduced Pilkinton. The shy stutterer beamed. "You're here," he asked, "to talk to me?"

Indeed.

Over the next hour, Jackson provided the reporter with a backyard track-and-field exhibition unlike anything she had ever witnessed. "So which event in track do you like best?" she asked.

"Long jump and high jump," Jackson replied. "Wanna see?"

The boy sprinted and leapt and soared across the yard. At one point he grabbed a stick, took some steps backward, charged forward, stuck the stick in the grass and vaulted onto a wood platform. "I thought he was about to kill himself," Pilkinton said. "But he really lit up. He was a kid who clearly didn't grow up in the best circumstances, and sports seemed to give him something extra."

On April 16, 1980, readers of the *Birmingham News* sports section were greeted with the headline MCADORY HIGH'S VINCENT JACKSON IS ALL-AROUND ATHLETE, BUT IN TRACK NO ONE BELIEVES HE'S JUST A SOPH. The accompanying photo showed Jackson, in street clothes, leaping through the air. The caption informed readers that Jackson "calls himself a Black Bruce Jenner."

> Vincent Jackson began his track career by using a stick to jump over the fence in the backyard of his Raimund home and by seeing how far he could jump off the porch.
>
> Even today, the 17-year-old sophomore at McAdory High School doesn't have any fancy equipment. He practices his hurdles over folding chairs and does his other events on the football field which has to double as a track.
>
> But it just doesn't seem to matter to Jackson because he manages to beat just about everybody anyway.

In an era when local newspaper pieces mattered, this piece *really* mattered. McAdory wasn't a big enough school to warrant regular profiles, and here was sophomore Vincent Jackson, blossoming sports phenomenon.

Everyone at McAdory read it. Everyone talked about it. Classmates asked Jackson to sign their copies.

Most important, the hype was warranted. The football season had been ordinary, but what followed was an electric rainbow of physicality. On February 8, Jackson and his McAdory track-and-field teammates traveled to Montgomery's Garrett Coliseum, home of the state indoor championships. Not only did Jackson win the long jump, he shattered the Alabama 3A record with a leap of 21-8½. Then, after the indoor season concluded, he shifted over to baseball and outdoor track and field, usually practicing both sports on the same day. It was unheard of at McAdory. When the school day ended, Jackson would scoot to the locker room, change into shorts and a T-shirt, participate in track for two hours, then sprint over to the diamond for an hour of baseball work. "By the time I get home," he said, "I just shower, eat dinner and go to bed."

In a track meet at Homewood, Jackson placed second in the high jump, then won four other events, breaking records in three of them. This was mere days after he threw a no-hitter for the baseball team (he was batting .400 at the time). "I don't think there's a limit," Dickey Atchison, his coach, said at the time. "He's a natural."

On May 3, Jackson led McAdory to the state 3A boys track-and-field title, capturing the 120 high hurdles, placing second in the triple and long jumps and third in the 300 intermediate hurdles. Two weeks later, at the same venue, he finished second in the state decathlon championships behind Tom Powers of Berry High, who would go on to star as a decathlete at Auburn University. "Bo had it won going into the last event," recalled Curt Linder, Auburn High's star decathlete. "But he couldn't score any points in the mile. He couldn't beat the maximum time, and that killed his chances. Still, it took everything Tom had to beat him." The coaches in attendance couldn't believe what they were witnessing—an unparalleled blending of size, speed, power and hustle. Vincent Jackson didn't win in total points, but he dominated when it came to showmanship and dropped jaws.

"This kid," Atchison told a reporter, "is something special."

CHAPTER 3

EMERGENCE

The big man with the bald head would show up on occasion.

On *rare* occasion.

A. D. Adams was, after all, Vincent Jackson's father. And even if that meant having almost nothing to do with the child, or the two other kids he ultimately sired with Florence Jackson, he would still pop by from time to time. Come to Florence's house with a small present. Arrive randomly at a sporting event, watching from a shadowy corner. A quarter of football. A few innings of baseball. Then (*poof*) leave. Without a word. "I vividly remember walking out to the field one day and this man standing by the gate," recalled Renee Morris, a cheerleader and friend of Jackson's. "I wondered who it was. And then it dawned on me—'Oh, that's Vincent's dad. That's his father.'"

What was Adams's motivation? More than a decade after his passing, it's difficult to say. Guilt? The voice in your head that whispers, "Do the right thing"? Perhaps it was raising children in his own home with his own wife. Attending church most Sunday mornings, praying to God and knowing, deep down, this wasn't a righteous way to be.

Or maybe, just maybe, it was more than that.

Maybe it was the increasing realization that this Vincent Edward Jackson . . . this Boar Hog . . . had talent. That his son was destined to be something special.

Whatever the case, A. D.'s limited presence brought his offspring no joy. He didn't merely view his father as a missing piece. No, he resented him and, on occasion, *loathed* him. Vincent's mother worked all the time—starting the day on a seven- or eight-hour shift with the cleaning crew at Bessemer's Carraway Methodist Hospital, then heading over to the nearby Ramada Inn and straightening rooms. She would come home exhausted—eat something, flop into bed, then wake up at five a.m. and start all over again. What Florence Bond lacked in overt warmth, she made up for with hard work, steeliness, determination. Her kids would be taken care of, and she sure as hell didn't need a deadbeat to *not* pay the bills. "People think a man is important," she once said. "They're OK in their place."

"I saw my daddy once a month, twice a month," Jackson said. "He'd come down and stay for an hour or so. I'd see him. That was daddy. I never had what my friends called 'a father' that was there every day, helping them fix their bikes or giving them spankings when they needed it, taking them to the park, taking them on camping trips. To me, that was a father back then and I envied all my friends that had both parents home with them."

With no male role model in the house, and with his mother always working, Vincent turned to the next best thing: his football and track coach.

This was no stretch for Dickey Atchison. He was a short man—"built close to the ground," Jackson once said with a laugh—with a pronounced drawl and a pit bull's snarl when needed. Some at the school were in it for the extra paycheck, and some loved sports. But Atchison—white, financially secure, husband and father of three—viewed himself as a guardian for his athletes; as both a teacher and a role model. Most days after practices ended, one would see Atchison with a car filled with boys (usually all Black), dropping them off house by house. Sure, he had a home life to cater to. He and his wife, Jody, had been sweethearts at Banks High School in Birmingham who married at twenty-two and devoted themselves to working in education (Jody brought women's sports programs to Homewood Middle School via Title IX in the 1970s). But Atchison considered *this* to be his calling. Young athletes weren't just young athletes. They were young people, oftentimes shit on by society based upon race and economics. "I love him to death," Jackson said. "He taught me so much."

Heading into his junior year of high school, Jackson was changing. Now almost eighteen, he was built like a Greek statue. Jackson stood six feet, and weighed roughly 195 pounds. His arms were cut. His chest was cut. His neck was iron. He hated lifting weights, but when he did the results were astonishing. He'd wait for the heaviest amount to be hoisted by a teammate, throw on ten, twenty, thirty additional pounds, smirk and raise the bar without so much as a grunt. "That good enough for you?" he'd say—then walk off.

Following his second year coaching the McAdory football team, Jim Berryman left to take over as the offensive line coach at Troy State. His replacement—to Jackson's delight—was Atchison. Players were thrilled. "I used to come to school really early because I was the yearbook editor," recalled Lori Ledbetter, a McAdory student. "I'd arrive at six a.m., and I'd look out and Coach Atchison would be there, midway through mowing the school lawn. That told you something about the man."

Entering the 1980 football season, Atchison salivated at all the weapons. He was a first-year head coach gifted with a trio of junior ball carriers who would all wind up playing collegiately. The neon name of the bunch was Leroy Mason, whose brother Larry was now the featured back at Southern Miss. Leroy stood about 5-foot-9, and ran with a straight-ahead ferocity. "A lot of people thought of Leroy as you would Earl Campbell," said Bobby Clayton, a halfback and defensive back. "Just ran you over and stepped on your body." The second name was Edwin (Keith) Mack, whose shiftiness evoked comparisons to Baltimore's Joe Washington. "Couldn't touch him," said Clayton. "Too quick."

The third was Jackson. Only, as the August 29 kickoff against Jones Valley High approached, few outside of McAdory knew this to be true. In most minds, Vincent Jackson was a track kid who dabbled in baseball and returned some kicks. Leroy Mason rambled for nearly 1,200 yards as a sophomore. Edwin Mack rambled for nearly 600 yards as a sophomore. Those were the go-to guys for the Yellow Jackets. Jackson was merely the fullback for a fantastic squad.

The Jones Valley Brownies, by contrast, were not a good football team. They'd completed the 1979 season with a 3-7 record that featured a seven-game losing streak during which they were outscored 157–13. Their head coach, John Galloway, was a strategy-light guidance counselor. Their roster was undersized and pocked by non-athletes. They had one good player, a halfback named Sanford Benjamin.

The Yellow Jackets expected to dominate.

The Brownies expected to be dominated.

No expectations went unfulfilled.

Football nights at McAdory Stadium were marquee events, filled with black-and-yellow shirts and signs and pom-poms. Admittedly, the facility was an ode to 1980s dumpiness—dilapidated wood bleachers with certain steps that creaked and groaned; an outdated press box that slept three comfortably; a field with unsightly patches of browns and oranges. But in a neck of the woods where, for most teenagers, weekend excitement involved hanging out in the Burger King parking lot, Yellow Jackets football mattered.*

Starting alongside Mack and Mason in the triple option backfield,

---

* Really, the Burger King parking lot on 9th Avenue. A police officer named Billy Jack would check in from time to time to make sure the high schoolers were behaving themselves.

Jackson was an initial afterthought for the Brownies. A concern, but far from a major one. Everyone knew that to beat the Jackets, you needed to shut down their two halfbacks. But then Jackson ran wild—first plowing through the defense for a one-yard score, later taking the pitch from quarterback Scott Davis, bursting around the right side and scooting through the secondary for a 33-yard touchdown. He was simply too big and too powerful for a defense whose average player stood 5-foot-10 and weighed 165 pounds. It was an unfair fight. The final score, 28–6, could have been 50–0.

"Very quickly, people went from having no idea who Vincent Jackson was to hearing about him every week," said Herb Winches, the sports anchor at Channel 6 in Birmingham. "I saw him early that junior year and I thought, 'Holy cow, this might be the best high school athlete I've ever seen.'"

Atchison didn't consider Jackson to be strictly a fullback. He was a fullback who also started on the defensive side as a linebacker/defensive end hybrid. Who also returned kickoffs. Who also returned punts. Who also handled kickoff and field goal duties. He went from a sophomore fringe player to the utility knife of a coach who understood the unique talent before him. Yes, Mack and Mason were excellent. But Jackson was proving to exist on a different level. He dwarfed them, both in physicality and pure football ability.

Before long, teammates saw that talent, too. He was a human rubber band. Jackson would goof around inside the McAdory gymnasium, standing beneath a hoop, leaping flat-footed and grabbing it with both palms. He would run toward goalposts, football in hand, and dunk over the bars. Surrounding the football field was a fence, approximately five feet high and undefeated in scarring students dumb enough to attempt a leap. "Bo Hog would go over that thing all the time—flat-footed," said Frank Hopkins, a classmate. "No running start. No exaggerated arms. Just standing there, bends his knees a bit, up and over. Like Superman."

Jackson was not a hard practice player, but when he *did* practice hard, you noticed. There are stories of Jackson running over teammates, running through teammates, leaving teammates in a temporary coma. Rex Parker, who had a very brief tenure as the team's fourth quarterback, recalled an afternoon when Jackson charged him from the defensive end. "He hit me," Parker said, "and my ancestry shook. I couldn't have told you which way was up. I couldn't have told you my name. He basically drilled me into the ground. The next day I returned to playing in the band."

One month after the Jones Valley mashing, members of the 3-1 Mc-

Adory High football team boarded their two yellow school buses and headed forty miles north to Dora, home of Horace Roberts Field and the Dora Bulldogs.

A farming community of just two thousand residents, Dora was best known as the birthplace of Ivy Andrews, long-ago New York Yankees pitcher . . . and a whole lot of nothing. "We had a Hardee's," said Wayne Sanford, the team's starting center.

And?

"That's about it," he said. "A Hardee's."

Because Dora was a geographical armpit, the stadium's small press box was nearly empty. There was no local radio broadcast; no throngs of reporters. The single media representative was Charles Lloyd, a staff writer for the *Birmingham News*.

What unfolded over the ensuing sixty minutes was something those involved in the game have not forgotten. "It was," said Clayton, "the Bo Jackson football coming-out party."

Wrote Lloyd in the next day's paper:

McAdory crushed Dora 36–6 in a prep football game Friday night.

Vincent Jackson scored four touchdowns, kicked three extra points and even added a field goal.

Jackson's nine-yard run on the first play of the second quarter capped a 59-yard drive. Jackson converted.

Eric Benison recovered a fumble at the Dora nine in the second period, and three plays later Jackson bounced over from the five. He added the PAT.

After a punt of minus one yard, McAdory, now 4-1, scored on the game's only pass, a 25-yarder from Scott Davis to Jackson. Jackson added the point with six minutes to play in the first half.

The winners drove 51 yards to open the second half, Jackson going in from the five. He missed the conversion.

Edwin Mack's 45-yard run was a big play as McAdory drove 69 yards to score in the third. Jackson went over from the five and kicked the point.

Jackson added a 27-yard field goal in the fourth.

Jackson scored *30* points.

He also spent the final minutes of the game in shorts and a T-shirt. "It was such a blowout he didn't dress for the fourth quarter," recalled Clayton. "Think about that."

One thing worth noting about the 1980 McAdory Yellow Jackets: There were, for the first time, pictures.

Pictures in the *Birmingham News*.

Pictures in the *Birmingham Post-Herald*.

Pictures upon pictures.

Over the previous half decade, McAdory games were rarely covered by local outlets. Birmingham was a big city with more than a dozen high schools. The Yellow Jacket results were mere dial-ins—meaning, after the sixty minutes wrapped, a host school employee would call the area newspapers and explain what happened. Someone working in the newspaper office then jotted down the information and turned it into a paragraph and a box score.

That, however, was changing, and the reason isn't hard to decipher. "I think people were starting to understand the potential greatness of this guy they had at McAdory," said Rubin Grant, a preps reporter for the *Post-Herald*. "Word was getting around and we needed to write about it."

The week after the Dora win, the *Birmingham News* sent reporter Race Seale *and* photographer Steve Barnette to McAdory to cover the Yellow Jackets' home clash with Fairfield. With 90 seconds left and the Tigers up, 13–12, the Yellow Jackets received the kickoff. "We're pumped because we're about to win," recalled Mark Trammell, a Fairfield linebacker. "They were the better team, but we had them. Finally. Well, Bo gets the kick deep and he just bursts down the field until he's finally tackled at the fifty. I was like, *'Who is that kid?'*"

Moments later, with 21 seconds remaining, Jackson booted a 25-yard field goal for the 15–13 victory. Wrote Seale: "Vincent Jackson provided a dramatic ending to a dramatic game . . .".

Jackson's name recognition was growing. On October 24, against visiting Brookwood, he ran for touchdowns of 37 and 45 yards, finishing the night with 118 yards on nine carries. He passed to Jimmy Craig on a two-point conversion. He kicked a point after. He twice sacked the quarterback. He stole the manhood of an opposing defensive back named Harold Hannah. "I was 5-foot-5 and 142 pounds, and our starter got hurt so I was put in," recalled Hannah. "They teach you to tackle by putting your forehead in the opponent's chest. Well, Bo is coming toward me, and I smoked him with everything I had. He ran completely over me, and I ended up between his legs and both his ankles are between my arms. I locked on to him, and his knees were in my forehead and my helmet was bouncing-bouncing-bouncing on the ground. Somehow he tripped over me and fell. My coaches praised me for saving a touchdown. They should have praised me for not dying."

In the following morning's *Tuscaloosa News*, Mike Bolton led his game recap with: "McAdory's Bo Jackson did everything you can do in Brookwood except mine a ton of coal."

When the season ended, Jackson's numbers leapt from the page: More than 800 rushing yards, 19 touchdowns. "Vincent probably would have had better stats . . . but we had two other backs we ran just as much," Atchison said. "No doubt if I had put him in the 'I' as the tailback, he would have had 1,500 yards rushing."

In the aftermath of his personal decimation of Brookwood, the first recruiting letter arrived. It was sent via the University of Indiana, and signed by the head coach, Lee Corso. The vague wording was nothing to get overly excited about, but Jackson was blown away by the nifty letterhead, by the praise for his game. Really, that a school located some five hundred miles to the north knew of his existence. The note was accompanied by a small red-and-white Hoosiers pen that Jackson proudly showed around school, then placed in a trophy case back home. Within weeks, a pile of mail accumulated on the kitchen counter—pitches from UCLA and Nebraska, from Kansas and Kansas State, from Oklahoma and Nebraska and Tennessee. Most came with a pen or pencil or pin or patch. Something that suggested, *"Hey, we want you, kid. And this made-in-China, 20-cent token is the proof."*

"He's going to be an outstanding college prospect in football," said Atchison. "A lot of colleges have already expressed an interest in him."

When people look back and marvel over Vincent Jackson's high school accomplishments, they talk football, they talk baseball, they talk track and field.

They never talk wrestling.

Yet in the winter of 1980–81, after the gridiron season concluded, McAdory High's wrestling coach asked Jackson to come out for the team.

Admittedly, Joe Powers had few expectations. Jackson tried wrestling for a second or two in junior high, and hated everything about it. "He went out, picked up the guy, slammed him, and the slam was illegal so he was disillusioned," said Powers. "He lost the match, said, 'This sucks,' and it was over."

The sport incorporated too much touching. Jackson was OK with lifting an opponent off the ground and pummeling him, à la Andre the Giant. But the whole sweat-swapping, armpit-eating, two-become-oneness was not to his liking.

Powers, though, offered a sweet deal. His varsity team was loaded with three future state champions. But McAdory had nobody listed as a heavyweight. "And here's the thing," said Frank Bunn, a member of the wrestling squad. "Most of the other schools didn't have heavyweights either. So Coach basically told Bo he'd be our heavyweight, he'd show up to the meets, the other team wouldn't have anyone to wrestle against him, he'd get the wins via forfeit without doing a thing and he'd wind up with another varsity letter."

And that's how it went week after week after week. Jackson was an undefeated heavyweight wrestler; one of the few in 3A competition.

"So one week we go to an event, and the other team has a heavyweight," Bunn said. "The kid was about three hundred pounds. Just enormous."

Powers sat down with Jackson to explain the necessary steps toward winning.

"I ain't wrestling that guy," Jackson said.

"But I need you out there," Powers replied.

"Not doing it."

With that, Vincent Jackson's undefeated wrestling run came to an end. With a forfeit.

On a late summer day in 1980, a man named Terry Brasseale found himself inside the McAdory High principal's office, hoping to catch a break.

A former outfielder at the University of Montevallo, Brasseale was twenty-six years old and interviewing for the Yellow Jackets' open head baseball coaching position. He'd spent the four previous years in Dora, Alabama, at Corner High, but wanted to move closer to home to care for his father, who had recently suffered a heart attack.

So he sat across from Nelle Salamone, the McAdory principal, talking about various subjects, when he gazed out the nearby window and spotted a mountain carrying a shovel. The entity was Black, with muscles rippling from muscles.

"Whoa," Brasseale said. "Who is that guy?"

He assumed it was a janitor. Or a maintenance man. Perhaps a coach.

"That's Vincent Jackson," Salamone said. "He's about to be a junior. If we offer you this position, you'll be coaching him."

Dang.

A couple of days later, Brasseale was hired. Baseball practices began in the middle of January 1981. At Corner High, he had coached a team of "all white, all slow kids." McAdory was the opposite—a rainbow coalition of skills, backgrounds, experiences. There were speedsters, sluggers, power pitchers and junkball specialists. "But Bo," Brasseale recalled. "I mean, I watched Bo throw, hit, move and I thought, 'My God . . .'"

That first week, Brasseale reached out to a scout and begged him to attend a McAdory practice and check out this Vincent Jackson kid. So that's what Kenny Gonzales, in his second year with the Kansas City Royals, did. He and Brasseale went back a ways—Gonzales had been an assistant coach at Montevallo when Brasseale played third and outfield for the Falcons. He trusted his former player, even though the call about Jackson was probably the five hundredth Gonzales had taken in his time as a scout. There was always another "next" somebody. The next Hank Aaron. The next Nolan Ryan. "Coach," Brasseale said, "I'm telling you—on my word—that something about this kid is special."

Gonzales's scouting territory was the South. Specifically Alabama, Mississippi and Louisiana. On his next journey to the Yellowhammer State, he drove to McAdory, a school he had never before visited. "OK," he said to Brasseale, "where's this phenomenon?"

He was directed toward Jackson.

"Whoa," he said.

By now, Jackson was 6-foot-1 and 200 pounds. He had a 19-inch neck, a 32-inch waist. Gonzales plopped down in a seat alongside the field and spent the next hour and a half watching an unrivaled combination of speed, power and coordination. Brasseale had his young star jump around the diamond—a little shortstop here, a little outfield there. Jackson pitched, and Gonzales clocked him in the low 90s. He hit, and his balls traveled toward Hydra, Pluto's fifth moon. Gonzales wasn't watching a baseball player—he was beholding a freak of human physicality.

When the practice ended, Brasseale asked his old coach for an impression.

"Terry," he said, "I've never seen anyone like that in my life."

A few hours later, after leaving the field and returning to his hotel room in Birmingham, Gonzales called Art Stewart, Kansas City's director of scouting and a man who had witnessed everything there was to see over thirty-six years working in baseball. "Art," Gonzales said, "I saw this player down here and I don't know if he's a boy or a man."

Pause.

"And he's a high school *junior*."

It was far too early for Gonzales to make any real advances. But over the months that followed he checked in on Jackson. Watch a McAdory game. Attend a practice. Never say a word to the player himself. Just observe and admire and breathe a deep sigh of relief when no other scouts showed up. The smartest move—no, the *savviest* move—is Gonzales would always stay at the Ramada Inn where Florence Bond worked as a housekeeper. "He found out when she took her coffee break, and he planned his day around it," Stewart recalled. "He would sit with her, eat with her, take her for coffee and talk."

Jackson batted .432 as the Yellow Jackets' starting shortstop (and occasional center fielder), with 7 home runs and a 5-1 mark as a pitcher. He averaged 12 strikeouts per start, and never allowed more than two runs. "Someone from McAdory would call in the game stats," said Rubin Grant, a *Birmingham Post-Herald* scribe, "and whenever Bo pitched it seems like he'd have 14 or 15 strikeouts and hit a couple of home runs." Gail Pilkinton, the *News*'s preps writer, found herself habitually nominating Jackson for the newspaper's weekly Metro West Region athlete of the week award. Editors ignored her pleas until the junior's dominance was too much. On April 14, 1981, after striking out five batters against Dora High en route to a 1–0 three-hitter, then rapping three hits in a 14–4 drubbing of Vincent High, readers opened the paper to see JACKSON WINS WEST SPORTS AWARD. "He just has raw ability," Brasseale told Pilkinton, "and, to tell you the truth, the best thing for me, as a coach, to do is to just leave him alone."

Yet to watch Jackson on the mound was to watch someone who didn't belong on the mound. Jackson hated pitching. Found it boring and detached. He told Brasseale the position didn't interest him, but the coach was unmoved. The idea (Vincent on the mound) was born of a moment from Brasseale's early days at McAdory, when during practice Jackson—standing flat-footed in center field—launched a baseball over the backstop behind home plate. "When the coach saw me do that he said, 'Can you pitch?' Jackson recalled. "I said I did it when I was little but I don't like it."

Jackson's windup resembled that of Luis Tiant, the then–Pittsburgh Pirates right-hander whose corkscrew-exaggerated leg kick combo made him the stuff of baseball folklore. Unlike Tiant, Jackson was never quite certain where the ball might travel. He threw a fastball with a mind of its own, a sinker (that didn't sink) and a slider (that didn't slide). "You never dug in against him," said Darel McKinney, Jess Lanier High's second baseman. "He'd throw ninety miles an hour down the middle for a strike, then the next pitch went a foot over the umpire's head." Against Pinson Valley, Jackson tossed a one-hitter without breaking a sweat. "He was a beast," recalled Dwight Harper, Pinson Valley's ace pitcher. "A lot of us were excellent baseball players, but he had this raw talent we all lacked. His fastball was scary—but it was all he had. But in high school that's enough. If you can scare opposing hitters, you'll win."

Were Jackson merely devoting his spring to dominating suburban Birmingham prep diamonds, it'd be impressive. But baseball was his second best seasonal sport. That one hitter against Pinson Valley came two days after Jackson's five first-place finishes in the regional track sectionals. At the Class 2A-3A Jefferson County Track Meet, Jackson captured the MVP trophy by winning three events, placing second in two more and single-handedly giving McAdory the title. A few weeks later, in the state outdoor track-and-field championships, Jackson won the long jump, the 120-yard high hurdles, the 330-yard intermediate hurdles and the triple jump. "He's the best athlete I've ever been around," said Atchison, who failed to mention Jackson's triple jump leap of 48 feet, 7¼ inches smashed the state record by more than 3 inches. Just for kicks, Jackson ran a leg on McAdory's second-place 440 relay.

On May 14, 1981, Alabama's best high school decathletes gathered at Vestavia High for the two-day state championship meet. Because the event featured a limited number of participants, there were no classifications. It was everyone against everyone in ten events: On day one, the 100, the shot put, the discus, the long jump and quarter mile. On day two, the hurdles, the triple jump, the pole vault, the discus and the 1,500. "I never did figure out the proper way to throw the discus, but I did get it around 150 feet," Jackson recalled. "And even without practicing the pole vault I managed to clear 12 feet, which was probably a state record for a Black kid."

Jackson captured five of nine events, and was so far ahead that he was able to skip out on the 1,500. The bulk of the competition featured a gaggle of spindly Alabama teenage athletes staring, mouths agape, at a Terminator-like machine that could not be stopped by modern devices. A mouse cannot beat up a bear. None of these kids had a shot against Bo. "There's an explanation, and it's simple," said Curt Linder, the Auburn High decathlete. "Bo Jackson was better than us. That's it, that's all, no debate. We were good athletes. He was the best athlete in the state. Period."

More than four decades later, Jackson's 8,340 total points have yet to be eclipsed.

The secret was still a national secret.

Sure, a Kansas City Royals scout was monitoring Vincent Jackson and his mother. And, sure, the college letters were arriving. And sure, the Birmingham newspapers now kept semiregular tabs on the kid out of McAdory.

Really, though, the secret was still a national secret. In the summer of 1981, the high school athlete garnering the most national attention was a seven-foot center out of the Cambridge Rindge and Latin School in Massachusetts named Patrick Ewing. A distant runner-up was Marcus Dupree, a running back from tiny Philadelphia, Mississippi.

Few outside of Alabama had heard of Vincent Jackson.

That's why, in early July, Rubin Grant of the *Birmingham Post-Herald* sent a letter to the New York offices of *Sports Illustrated*. At the time, the magazine (boasting a circulation of 2.4 million) was the most important and respected voice in American sports journalism. So Grant nominated Jackson for the weekly "Faces in the Crowd" section, where six unknown athletes were pictured and hailed (in a paragraph or two) for their regional achievements. Past Faces inductees included a little-known Ohio golfer named Jack Nicklaus, a little-known San Diego basketball player named Bill Walton, a little-known St. Louis tennis champion named Arthur Ashe. "I just thought he deserved it," Grant said. "There was nothing he couldn't do."

On July 20, 1981, the cover of the new *Sports Illustrated* featured Vince Ferragamo, quarterback for the Canadian Football League's Montreal Alouettes. The magazine also included a profile of boxer James "Quick" Tillis, an ode to runner Sebastian Coe, an exploration of a champion yacht. And there, on the bottom of page 69, alongside a swimmer from Danville, California, named David Bottom and a fencing coach out of Waban, Massachusetts, named Lisel Judge, rests the photograph (taken by Grant) of Vincent Jackson of Bessemer, Alabama.

Vincent, who recently completed his junior year at McAdory High, won four events at the state AAA track meet, including the triple jump with a state-record of 48' 7¼". He also won the state decathlon title and hit .432 for the baseball team.

Less than a week after the magazine hit newsstands, *Sports Illustrated* sent Grant the silver bowl it presented to anyone who scored a Faces in the Crowd spot. The writer brought it to McAdory High and awarded it to Jackson, who smiled for the newspaper's photographer while caressing the prize in his hands.

"It's a real nice feeling," he said. "It's something I never thought I'd be able to do, getting in the magazine." He looked toward the bowl. "That's something," Jackson said. "It'll sit on my trophy case for a long time."

He shook Grant's hand, walked out of the building, and never gave the bowl much thought again.

CHAPTER 4

DON'T MESS WITH BO JACKSON

They began coming to Bessemer en masse in the summer of 1981.

One scout.

Two scouts.

Three scouts.

Ten scouts.

The men (and they were *always* men) were not particularly difficult to recognize. White. Sunburned necks. Khaki pants. Some offshoot of a wrinkled Hawaiian shirt. Sandals or dusty sneakers. A cap. A pack of Camels, Marlboros or Viceroys. The ages varied—late twenties to early seventies—but the rooster strut of a once-upon-a-time jock was unmistakable.

Oh, and a notepad and pen.

They *always* carried a notepad and pen.

In the wake of the *Sports Illustrated* mention, and with the *holy-shit-is-that-for-real?* cobbling together of otherworldly football stats plus otherworldly baseball stats plus otherworldly track-and-field stats, Vincent Edward Jackson sat on the doorstep of a haughty status most prep athletes never touch: He was a burgeoning phenom.

So the scouts—Major League Baseball *and* college football—came to Bessemer, to catch whatever glimpse was available.

They would not leave disappointed.

Whereas the younger Vincent once devoted his June and July days to stealing bicycles and assassinating boar hogs, he was now all in on summer baseball. That meant multiple leagues, multiple teams and dozens of opportunities for scouts to drool over the 6-foot-1, 205-pound sculpture. What the men witnessed in the flesh somehow exceeded expectations. First, there was the body. No matter the fit of the uniform or the name across the chest, Jackson's bulging muscles turned baggy into elastic. You could literally see the rocklike curvatures of his arms and legs. Calves like melons. Quads like toasters. A head-to-toe fluidity. "That boy before us," recalled Joe Mason, a Mets scout, "was no child."

Then there were the moments. The flashes of Willie Mays and Carl Yastrzemski, of Josh Gibson and Babe Ruth. Leaping over fences. Uncorking throws that had no business traveling such distances. The kid was raw steak on the block, but bursting with potential. In one game, at the rec field in Bessemer, Jackson crushed a home run that dented a fire truck parked a block beyond the outfield fence. In another contest, at Roosevelt Park in Bessemer, Jackson hit a shot that cleared the center-field fence and disappeared into two enormous oak trees. "The ball was still climbing when it vanished," said Steve Dabbs, who played that night. "Everyone just froze. We all stood and watched it go far away."

One afternoon, also at Roosevelt, Jackson was playing shortstop for a McAdory squad when Barry Brand, the speedy leadoff hitter for a Jess Lanier team, roped a liner that got past the third baseman and headed into the outfield. Jackson dove, stretched out his body, somehow corralled the ball with his glove, positioned himself on his knees and unleashed a bullet that beat the runner by two steps. "It was a dart," said Darel McKinney, a Jess Lanier player. "Just unreal. But not the most amazing play of the day."

That came a few innings later, when Jackson laced a line drive into center field that somehow levitated over the fence. "I swear to God, the ball never rose more than ten feet off the ground," said McKinney. "It flew right past my head. Not *above* my head—past it." An overmatched umpire fell for the optical illusion and Jackson was ordered to stop at second with a ground-rule double. When the inning concluded, McKinney grabbed the Jess Lanier center fielder to ask whether it had cleared the fence.

"Man, of course it did," he said. "But I wouldn't say nothing."

This is what the scouts were watching, and while their notepads filled with superlatives, their attempted conversations with Jackson began and ended with "Hello." This was partly attributable to the stutter, which remained a barrier in day-to-day communication. This was also partly attributable to Jackson's general reluctance to trust.

He was, even at eighteen, the little boy whose daddy lived crosstown, but couldn't muster the energy to visit. Jackson wore the deliberately detached veneer of a stone wall. Yet he wasn't blind. Even at these meaningless summer games, many of his teammates could turn and see a father in the stands, or leaning along the fence. Maybe a dad was berating the umpire. Maybe a dad was sitting in a chair outside the third base line, drinking his third Piels. Jackson didn't have that.

As a result, depth was not something Jackson surrendered. He didn't do small talk. He wasn't letting a stranger in on his plans. Did he want to go to college or jump straight to pro ball? He wasn't entirely sure. And besides, how was that anybody's business? "Bo was a nice guy if you knew him," said Jay Sherron, a high school teammate. "But if you didn't, he wasn't giving out hugs."

For the most part, scouts came and went. *Hi. Bye. Here's my card.* One man, however, was able to eke his way into the Vincent Jackson stratosphere. He was a scout. Well, *sort* of a scout. "Invested observer" might be a better way of putting it. To Jackson, Frelon Abbott was just a local guy who came off as friendly and charged up about sports. Back two decades earlier, Abbott had been a basketball standout at McAdory High—ol' number 13 for a Yellow Jackets team referred to as "one of the most talented in the country" by the *Birmingham News*. He remained in the area, earning a degree from the University of Montevallo, then operating a business that sent women into offices to clean at night. One of his employees happened to be (if you believe in coincidences) Florence Bond, Jackson's mother. He signed her checks.

From time to time, Abbott paid Vincent to mow his lawn. It was appreciated pocket change. A ten-spot here, a twenty-spot there. On other occasions, he slipped him some dough. Take-your-girlfriend-out-to-dinner clams. "He would come around, talk to me," Jackson said. "He would loan me a little money, not big money." Like hundreds of others in his shoes, Jackson never thought much about the stranger's kindness. Abbott was an around-the-way fella being nice. Someone acting as a protective quasi-uncle.

This is how it often worked in the Deep South—poor, naive Black high schoolers the uncomfortable objects of affection. Before the major universities began to desegregate in the late 1960s, these kids were all but invisible to the Southern white world. A Black halfback with 4.4 speed was as useful as a tree stump. Then integration kicked in. The Division I college recruiters were white men who not only came up via segregation, but embraced it. There was a raw ugliness to the whole setup, and while Black parents often knew to view these interlopers with suspicion and skepticism (*"Oh, you're interested in my son now . . ."*) their children did not. "Young Black guys are gullible to that type of thing," Jackson said years later, "because ninety-five percent of us grew up poor, with nothing. Somebody comes to you and says, 'Look, here's five hundred dollars, here's a thousand dollars to hold you over for a month. And when you need more, just give me a call . . .'"

Abbott wasn't necessarily handing Vincent Jackson five hundred or a thousand bucks. But he was slipping him money and ingratiating himself to the young man with the large future.

He also was (cough, cough) a booster for Auburn University.

It was weird, though not entirely uncommon in the sports-mad state of Alabama, where one was either "Roll Tide!" (Alabama) or "War Eagle!" (Auburn). Here was Abbott, husband, father of two, seemingly sane and a reasonable adult—living and dying with the exploits of Auburn football, and doing his all to help the program gain as many qualified adolescents as possible. That, technically, was (and still is) the task of a booster. He isn't paid by the university. He's certainly not an employee of the university. He's someone who loves the school and speaks to potential prospects on its behalf, with the payoff being free tickets, a nod from the head coach, the special feeling of being in the loop and the opportunity to brag to friends, "Hey, I'm the one who got [fill in the name] to come to Auburn."

"I can't speak for everyone, but I viewed being a booster as a chance to talk to people about the greatness of Auburn and showing them all the things Auburn offered," said Caleb Pipes, an Auburn grad who served as a booster throughout the 1980s. "You go to their games, you congratulate them when they play well, you hope they ultimately want to become part of the Auburn family."

Abbott was in regular contact with the Auburn football coaching staff, and his enthusiasm for Jackson's talent and college readiness was unbridled. "Frelon was big into Bo Jackson way before other people knew who he was," said one of Abbot's longtime friends. "I think he saw it as his job to make sure that if Bo went to college out of high school, he would wind up going to the *right* college."

The first time Auburn's coaches saw Jackson in person wasn't actually at a football game, but in the state decathlon championships. Bobby Wallace, the Tigers' defensive backs coach, attended the meet, then returned to campus raving about a "world-class athlete" sitting beneath their noses. Pat Dye, Auburn's head coach, digested the information, but failed to lay eyes on Jackson until the spring of 1981, when he was sent some grainy film of McAdory's game against Leeds High School. He was told to keep an eye on number 40 in the Yellow Jackets uniform. "This kid Jackson is out front, leading a play, and [he] blocks three people at one time," recalled Dye. "He just runs through 'em, stacks 'em up like cord wood. I'm not sure he ever hits the ground, just runs through the three of 'em.

"Like dominoes. I never saw anything like it."

By the time late summer rolled around and the sticky hundred-degree Alabama days turned into sticky ninety-five-degree Alabama days, most of the baseball scouts had vanished into the bushes. It was the coming of football season, which meant—at McAdory High's field—the coming of Vincent Jackson season.

Only, he was no longer Vincent Jackson. Or Boar Hog Jackson. Or Bo Hog Jackson. Nope. Somewhere around this time, when asked for autographs by locals, he started to sign—nonchalantly—*Bo Jackson*. Mythology has it that "Bo" was easier off the stutterer's tongue than "Vincent" and simpler to say than "I." Yet mythology, in this area, is incorrect. "Bo" was a thing because Bo Jackson liked it. The sound. The feel. It was an athlete's name—much more so than Vincent Edward. So while classmates continued to refer to him as "Vincent" and "Vince" and "Boar Hog," to those who knew no better he was, officially, *Bo*.

Bo Jackson.

College recruiters flocked to McAdory practices to witness the specimen, as did media members, and they were rarely disappointed. One day, a reporter and cameraman from Birmingham's Channel 13, WVTM, drove out to McCalla to film a segment on Jackson. Jeff Meadows, a sophomore defensive back, saw the cameras and, despite an inverted chest and kindling arms, decided now was the time to be seen. The first time Jackson took a handoff, Meadows charged forward. What the boy lacked in physicality, he made up for with heart and determination and drive and . . .

WHOP!

Knees rising, quads pumping, arms churning, Jackson charged into Meadows like brick into butter. He ran through—then over—the defensive back, and as Meadows's body crumpled toward the turf, he could taste the blood squirting from his chin and onto his lips. "He busted me open something good," Meadows said. "I wanted to be on TV. Thank God I *wasn't* on TV."

When practice ended, Meadows was taken to the local hospital for ten stitches. Some forty years later, the scar on his chin continues to spin a wise yarn.

"Don't," he said, "try tackling a bull on your own."

One hundred and forty-five miles away, in the two-traffic-light town of Philadelphia, Mississippi, much of the nation was abuzz over a senior running back named Marcus Dupree who was 6-foot-3, 229 pounds and the closest thing anyone had seen to a refrigerator cross-pollinated with a roadrunner.

As a sophomore at Philadelphia High, Dupree had rushed for 1,850 yards and scored 28 touchdowns, and his head coach was receiving more than a hundred phone calls per day from colleges. Lucious Selmon, the University of Oklahoma's defensive line coach, spent six weeks living in Philadelphia's Motor Inn with the single task of convincing Dupree to become a Sooner. When the running back committed to the University of Texas, Oklahoma sent Billy Sims, Detroit Lions star/former Sooner Heisman winner, to Philadelphia to beg Dupree to change his mind. Which he did.

It was the most highly anticipated recruiting battle in college football history, and spoke to the powers of perception. Running out of the I, carrying the football thirty to forty times per game, Dupree provided a weekly highlight reel of stompings and sprints, of stiff arms and high knee kicks.

By comparison, the newly minted "Bo" Jackson had been a part of Dickie Atchison's wishbone, where he played fullback and shared carries with Keith Mack and Leroy Mason. His size was off the charts, as was his speed (he was timed in high school running a 4.3 40—faster than Dupree's 4.4). But the samples were sparse. There wasn't much tape on Jackson, and available footage oftentimes featured him throwing a block, or tackling a ball carrier, or kicking an extra point. Also, there was the matter of Jackson's overall attitude and demeanor. In Philadelphia, recruiters found Dupree to be shy yet respectful and endearing in that awkward-high-school-kid sort of way. Jackson was also shy, but zero percent endearing. He barely spoke, his handshake was a dead fish. He didn't look adults in the eyes. His stutter made conversations uncomfortable and, on occasion, impossible. He could be intimidating and brooding and hard to read. Not all that long ago he was wearing his sister's hand-me-down sneakers to school, and now he was being courted by the biggest universities in the land. It was abnormal. "People thought he was rude," said Johnny Benavidez, a McAdory assistant coach. "But that's not fair. He'd rather hold in his feelings than talk about things. He wasn't standoffish, he was embarrassed."

If recruiters pressed the McAdory football coaches, they'd hear the stories. Having grown up without a ton of discipline (outside of his mother's gun, belt and switch collection), Jackson did not adjust to schedules and orders and regimentation. As a boy, he had been a leaf in the wind, blowing there, gusting here. That did not mix with organized sports. Jackson hated practice. He quit teams on more than one occasion, only to be corralled back by a fellow player or staff member. He dreaded time in the weight room, and extra running was, well, there would be no extra running. Bo Jackson refused. "Bo just didn't like to work out," said Steve Mann, McAdory's quarterback. "We'd go into the weight room and if a coach was looking he'd get under the bar like he was preparing to lift. As soon as the coach looked away he'd take his hands off the weights and say, 'Man, that was tough.'"

"He rarely went full speed in practice," said Bobby Clayton, the halfback/ defensive back position. "If he didn't have to put in extra work, he wouldn't."

His grades were . . . fine. Ish. Some D's. Mostly C's. Not the most inquisitive kid in school, but certainly intelligent. Once, in his economics class, Jackson and a handful of peers were caught using a textbook during an exam. Larry Baker, the teacher, berated his student. "Bo," he said loudly, "you do realize I can change the course of your future, yes?"

In Grayce Parsons's English class, Jackson taped test answers to the back of Tony Minnifield, the boy who sat in the desk in front of him. While walking the room, Parsons—a white-haired taskmaster whom one classmate called "mean as the meanest snake"—spotted the piece of paper and ripped it from Minnifield's shirt. "Bo," she said, "I'm going to think of a really good punishment for this."

Knowing of Jackson's stutter, she ordered him to stand before the class and recite the Elizabeth Barrett Browning sonnet "How Do I Love Thee?"

"Every time you stutter," Parson said, "you need to start over again."

Recalled Lori Ledbetter, a classmate: "It was one of the cruelest things I've ever seen one person do to another person. But Bo handled it well. I don't remember him stuttering once."

Word of Jackson's work habits and demeanor turned off certain schools (a handful of recruiters checked in, visited, then never returned). The other obstacle—perhaps the biggest obstacle—was geography. In his nineteen years, Jackson had left the state of Alabama one time. It happened his junior year of high school, when he accompanied his girlfriend Marilyn on a three-hour church group bus trip for a day at Atlanta's Six Flags amusement park. He was a mama's boy, and the opportunity to play football by the Pacific Ocean for USC or near the Rocky Mountains as a Colorado Buffalo failed to intrigue him. Tennessee and Nebraska invited him to make visits—all expenses covered. No and no. Houston came hard. No. So did Mississippi State. No. "Every coach in the South tried to recruit the kid," said Frank Burns, Rutgers's football coach. All efforts proved futile. He had to be near his mother. "I wasn't going to leave her alone," Jackson said years later. "She needed me, and I needed her."

As recruiters came and went, Frelon Abbott stayed. He was always there, like a fern in the corner of the room. At practices. Around the school. Lingering. Lurking. Not necessarily in a bad way. Or a good way. Merely there for Bo Jackson. To offer a ride, to offer some scratch. A word of encouragement. If Oklahoma could send an assistant coach to live in Philadelphia, Mississippi, and stalk out Marcus Dupree, was it all that wrong for an Auburn booster to do his small part?

"You'd see the Abbott man regularly," recalled Renee Morris, a McAdory cheerleader and Jackson pal. "It was strange, because you knew all the parents, and here was this guy, with sort of a used-car-salesman look, at all the games, kind of touting himself as a scout. To be honest, I always thought he was kind of a shyster."

The other Auburn representative to plant his flag in Bessemer was Wallace, the Tigers' defensive backs coach. When it came to recruiting, Dye's approach to the state of Alabama was simple: divide and conquer. Following every Thursday-afternoon practice during the season, the program's twelve assistant coaches boarded one of two airplanes (a Beechcraft King Air and a Piper PA-31 Navajo) and were dropped off at various spots across the state. "So the plane would fly to Birmingham, leave me there, then fly to, say, north Alabama and drop another coach off," said Wallace. "I'd watch high school games on Thursday, stick around Friday, watch more games Friday night. Then the plane would pick us up and take us to wherever we were playing next. We had to do that, because there were so many rural areas without major airports."

Scores of players filled Wallace's radar. But there was only one Bo Jackson. To watch him practice, Wallace recalled, was to watch a tiger dash through an open field. He was sleek and powerful and beautifully controlled. "I had people ask me why I wasn't going after that kid in Philadelphia, Mississippi, named Dupree," Wallace said. "Well, I was recruiting an even better athlete in Bessemer. The difference was everyone knew of Marcus. Not everyone knew about Bo."

The McAdory football season opened on the road against Jones Valley on a Friday night in late August, and Fair Park Stadium was filled with spectators and a gaggle of recruiters anxious to finally witness Bo Jackson in a legitimate game. Yet what they saw was underwhelming. The Yellow Jackets won, 20–14, and the star was Mack, who flashed around left end for a 60-yard touchdown scamper. When the next morning's *Birmingham News* left the presses, Jackson's name was mentioned just twice in the recap. Wrote J. W. Ward: "Vincent Jackson kicked the extra point" and "Jackson's PAT attempt was good."

It was hardly Marcus Dupree–esque material.

One week later, at Midfield's Winfred E. Jackson Stadium, the Yellow

Jackets put up yet another sluggish showing, losing 12–11 in a sloppy game on a sloppier field. Jackson performed admirably, catching a 37-yard touchdown pass, picking up the fumbled snap on the extra point and running in for two points, then later booting a 20-yard field goal. But where were the explosives? Where was the dynamic physical specimen folks had raved about?

Entering the season, the two best prep running backs in Alabama were said to be Jackson and a kid out of Enterprise named Alan Evans. But in actuality, the best running back in Alabama *was* Evans, whose team (Enterprise High) won a state championship his sophomore year and was a state semifinalist when he was a junior. Evans was 6-foot-2, 195 pounds and reminded nostalgists of legendary Bears halfback Gale Sayers for his ability to shed tackles and make defenders miss. Recruiting-wise, Evans was closer to Dupree status than Jackson—the University of Pittsburgh had Tony Dorsett call, Auburn had James Brooks call, USC had Marcus Allen call and Georgia had Herschel Walker call. Paul "Bear" Bryant, the legendary Alabama coach, paid a visit to Enterprise, as did Georgia's Vince Dooley. "They used to just call at night," Evans complained at the time. "But now they call in the morning, too."

If Evans and Jackson began the season as 1 and 1A among Alabama high school running back prospects, the early results widened the gap. As Jackson was slow to get going, Evans broke one long run after another, shifting, sliding, dashing, winding his way to a series of 100-yard games. When, on October 8, 1981, the *Montgomery Advertiser* ran a story headlined EVERYONE AFTER EVANS, it was no exaggeration. *Everyone* was after Evans.

But, truth be told, Bo Jackson didn't *want* to have everyone after him. "Here I am, probably not knowing what a college campus looked like, and I got all these damn coaches fighting over me and wanting to visit with me and talk," he recalled. "After a while it got boring. Coaches calling your house any time of night, early in the morning. We just took the telephone off the hook."

Jackson soon found a line that worked perfectly: "Look," he told distant-land recruiters, "I'm not leaving the state, and there's nothing you can say to me to leave the state."

Which was exactly what representatives of Auburn University and the University of Alabama wanted to hear.

About to begin his first year coaching the Tigers after one season at Wyoming, Pat Dye was in desperate need of athletes. While SEC rivals boasted fast, quick, powerful game-changers like Herschel Walker (Georgia) and Willie Gault (Tennessee), Auburn's teams were plodding and poorly conditioned. The Tigers went 5-6 in 1980 under the since-discarded Doug Barfield, and it easily could have been 3-8. They were an empty vessel.

If Bo Jackson wasn't the best student, and wasn't the hardest worker, and didn't put up Marcus Dupree–level statistics, Pat Dye was willing to overlook such things. So, for that matter, was Bryant, who could live with a top prospect not signing with the Crimson Tide, but sure as hell could not live with said prospect choosing Auburn.

Now sixty-eight years old and in his twenty-fourth year heading the program, Bryant was losing heat off his fastball. His decision-making skills had deteriorated. His relationships with players barely existed. He'd forget names, forget formations, doze off at random times. He drank *a lot*. It was still a dream of most Alabama kids to one day play for the Bear, but it was no longer *The* Dream. Jeff Parks, a highly regarded senior tight end from Gardendale High, had recently declined Alabama's scholarship offer to attend Auburn—and while that was shocking, it was also sort of understandable. Tim Jessie, a fantastic halfback from Opp, Alabama, took a recruiting visit to Tuscaloosa around the same time as Parks, and was turned off from the moment he arrived. "I sat next to Bear Bryant at a meal," Jessie recalled, "and when he turned to me his breath reeked of alcohol. My father's an alcoholic, and I hated that smell. There was no way I was going to play for Coach Bryant." Gerald Williams, a standout defensive lineman from Valley, Alabama, knew he would be signing with the Tide—then visited and was informed he'd be third string. "I mean, OK," Williams recalled. "I guess I'll go to Auburn." Which he did.

The Tide staff seemed to do everything within its power to turn off Jackson. First, Bryant never took the time to visit Bessemer, or catch a McAdory game. "He called on the phone," Jackson said. "That's how it was." Second, when Jackson visited campus, there was no red carpet. He bummed a ride to Tuscaloosa in the silver Pontiac Firebird driven by Alex Dudchock, a defensive lineman for Birmingham's Minor High who was also being recruited. Once there, Jackson was treated as one would any potential student. A tour of campus. A free lunch. He attended practice, but Bryant refused to speak with him on the ground. Instead, Jackson had to climb to the top of the coaching tower, from where Bryant—binoculars in hand—overlooked the field as a general overlooks his soldiers. "Bo," Bryant said, "we'd love to have you down here as part of our team. We think you could help us in a lot of ways—whether it be defense or offense."

Those last three words—*defense or offense*—dangled. In the lead-up to the visit, Jackson had been primarily recruited by Ken Donahue, Alabama's defensive coordinator. Donahue was a well-regarded football lifer who had played at the University of Tennessee in the 1940s, but to young Black kids coming up in the MTV '80s, he was a fossilized tyrannosaurus. In discussions with Jackson, Donahue ran off the Tide's fleet of running backs and insisted he would have to wait his turn. It was the least effective recruiting pitch in modern history: *Come here and one day you may well possibly perhaps if you're lucky play.* "The first time I met [Donahue] we sat and talked in front of my washer and dryer in my laundry room," Jackson said. "He said, 'Bo, we'd love to have you in Tuscaloosa. But personally, I don't think you'll have a chance to play until the end of your sophomore or beginning of your junior season.' I just looked at him with a look on my face like, 'You gotta be out of your damn mind.'"

Knowing the other university Jackson was considering, Donahue added a zinger: "Auburn," he told the running back, "will never beat us."

Damn.

"Auburn was my second choice," Jackson said. "I was going to Alabama before that day."

Negotiations with Auburn were far more positive. First, there was Abbott, the enthusiastic booster who attended every McAdory game, who slipped Jackson wads of dough, who (Auburn) brought up (Auburn) the (Auburn) university (Auburn) in every (Auburn) possible conversation (Auburn) he and Jackson (Auburn) had. "Frelon kept Auburn up to date on everything Bo was doing," said one of Abbott's close associates. "His job was to keep it all positive for Auburn, and run interference when it came to other schools."

Second, there was Wallace, the coach who regularly showed his face and insisted to his colleagues this Jackson kid was on a different level. "Bobby gave me some tape of Bo and I said, 'Maybe we should have him come here as a linebacker,'" said Jack Crowe, Auburn's offensive coordinator. "He said, 'Shut up, Jack! That's the reason he doesn't wanna go to Alabama.' So, wisely, I shut up."

Third, there was Dye, who decided he was all in on adding Jackson to his roster. One day, after returning home from a sporting event, Jackson entered the front door of the house on Merritt Avenue and saw his mother, Florence, sitting at the kitchen table with Dye and Wallace. The three were drinking coffee, eating small tea cakes, chatting up a storm. "My dad's strength was just being comfortable with people of all walks of life," said Pat

Dye, Jr. "He wouldn't just visit a recruit's house and eat the food. He'd walk right in and right up to the stove and start stirring the collard greens. He was great—just great—with mothers, because he was sincere." Dye waved when Bo arrived, then continued gabbing with Florence as the boy walked downstairs to place his soiled laundry in the washing machine. "I was a very, very quiet person," Jackson later explained. "Coach thought I didn't like them because I never talked, just came in and said hi and bye."

After a few moments, Dye excused himself and walked down the steps to the basement. "Bo," he said, "I just came down to ask if you're considering coming to Auburn."

Jackson, softly, said, "Yes, sir. I am."

"All right," Dye replied. "That's what I wanted to know."

There was no talk of being redshirted. There was no talk of playing defense. "There were some universities that flat-out said, 'Look, if you come here we'll take care of you. Transportation, you won't have to worry about that, we'll take care of your mom,'" Jackson recalled. "They would say absolutely anything to get you to their school. But whenever I talked to Coach Dye, there was nothing like that."

Dye, according to Jackson, gave the most refreshing sales pitch he had heard from a coach. Namely—if you pick Auburn, and you work hard, and you perform, you'll play. "He always said, 'I'm gonna treat you just like I treat the other kids,'" Jackson said. "'Once you get out there and you screw up, you're gonna get burned. I'm not gonna give you anything. You've gotta earn it. Earn the respect, the loyalty, the honesty.'"

On the third weekend of September 1981, Florence, Bo, and his sister Janice took an official visit 120 miles west to Auburn. Instead of having to drive, they were flown via private jet. It was Bo's first time on an airplane. The three were served steak and shrimp inside the cafeteria at Sewell Hall, the athletic dormitory. They were offered a private tour of the campus, and on the morning of September 19, before Auburn's game against Wake Forest, the trio met with Dye, who was living inside a Sewell Hall apartment while his house was being built. This was heady stuff for Jackson—instead of game-planning for the Demon Deacons, Dye was talking *with him*.

"We need you in our program," Dye said. "You can be our Herschel Walker."

Walker, Georgia's star halfback, was college football's brightest light. Six days earlier he had run for 167 yards in the Bulldogs' win over Cal. There was only one Herschel Walker.

Jackson told Dye he might want to also play college baseball. "Fine."

Could he dabble in track and field, too? "Fine."

"Vincent," Dye finally said, "how would you like to come here?"

Jackson's mind was made up.

"I'd like that," he said.

Dye looked over Jackson and his mother and knew their word was as strong as oak. Jackson looked over Dye and knew this was a man he could play for. Although the official college signing day was February 18, 1981, the five months in between brought little worry to Auburn's coach. He trusted Bo from day one.

"I think I asked Bo one other time if he was coming to Auburn," Dye said, "and then I never asked him again."

Maybe it was the comfort of knowing college awaited.

Maybe it was the peace of mind.

Whatever the case, once Bo Jackson agreed to attend Auburn University on a full athletic scholarship, he was able to kick back, relax and focus on the remainder of the McAdory High football season.

It was a sight to behold.

After splitting their first two games, the Yellow Jackets headed to Oxford High. It was pouring rain at Lamar Field, and the surface was mud and goop. Still, roughly five thousand spectators packed in to watch the visiting supernova.

One of Oxford's better players was a junior defensive tackle named Rick Burgess.* He never forgot the day. "I played against Bo the year before and I didn't recall him as particularly outstanding," said Burgess. "But now he's a senior, and I'm standing there in warm-ups and I see him and I think, 'Man, that's a pretty stout running back.' Well, it turns out he's also their kicker. And he walks back to kick the opening kickoff, and just—*BOOM!* He kicks it, and nobody moves. Nobody. The ball flew out of the end zone. I'd never seen that happen. Not one time."

Oxford's star was a defensive end named Thomas Jackson, who was regionally known for decapitating opposing ball carriers. Thomas was fast, strong and built like a grand piano—"he killed many people who came his way," said Burgess. Midway through the first quarter, Bo Jackson took the handoff from quarterback Steve Mann, cut to his right, then shifted in the

---

* Rick went on to regional notoriety as the host of the *Rick & Bubba* radio show on stations spanning the South.

other direction. Thomas Jackson was waiting, and went shoulder-first into the ball carrier. "He hit Bo as hard as you can hit a man," Burgess said. "And Thomas bounced off Bo's shoulder like he ran into a car."

As Thomas Jackson slumped to the ground, Bo Jackson sprinted 20 yards into the end zone. When he finally rose, Thomas looked at Burgess, who had helped him up. "Listen, man," he said. "We've gotta gang tackle that guy."

McAdory won, 15–7.

As the season progressed, Jackson—still splitting carries with Mack and Mason, still starting at defensive end/linebacker and kicking—put on an all-world football clinic. In a 28–14 triumph over undefeated Abrams High he ran for an 11-yard touchdown, then caught a short pass from Mann and danced through the opposition for a 79-yard score. A week later, after a 48–20 takedown of Dora High, Jackson's picture was featured on the front sports page of the *News*, a reward for his 20-yard scoring scamper through the heart of the Bulldogs defense.

"His talent was just at a higher level," said Mann, the quarterback. "There were a lot of guys who could play football. But Bo was on a different planet."

If there was a singular moment that exemplified Bo Jackson's rise, it came in the lead-up to the October 16 game at Jess Lanier, the downtown Bessemer school whose players had little love for the Yellow Jackets. Unlike McAdory, what with its relatively new building, Jess Lanier was a dump— old school, dilapidated materials, an outdated, overgrown stadium that smelled of mold and rust. There was a belief among many that Jackson should have actually been a Jess Lanier student; that somehow the white influencers of McAdory stole him from his rightfully zoned school (this was untrue). The resentment was palpable.

Three days before the October 16 kickoff, a letter arrived at McAdory High, with ATTENTION VINCENT JACKSON scribbled on the envelope. Inside, a warning—SCORE A TOUCHDOWN THIS FRIDAY, YOU DIE. The note was attributed to BAQ, the youth street gang whose initials stood for Beat Yo' Ass Quick. The members of BAQ were no joke—one year earlier, a McAdory game against Brookwood was played with police officers surrounding the field after BAQ members threatened to shoot spectators. The writer D. Winston Brown referred to them as "the terror of Birmingham" in his essay "Ghost Children." One of its leaders, eighteen-year-old Kenneth Blaylock, had recently been sentenced to thirty-five years in prison for forcing a mother and two children into a closet at gunpoint (all for two dollars, a bike and a radio). "BAQ was right before people around here started referring to themselves as Bloods and Crips," said Frank Easterling, a former lieutenant in the Bessemer Police Department. "At that point they were sort of mysterious. We knew they existed, but not much about their movements or whereabouts."

"When you dig deep into Bessemer, it's not a pretty scene," said Mike Hill, a former Fox Sports host and city native. "In a lot of ways it's like being from South Central or Houston's Fifth Ward. A gang threatening an athlete should be surprising. But it's not."

Word of the note made its way throughout the Yellow Jackets locker room. Jackson was presented with the option to skip. He already had his college scholarship in hand. Why play a seemingly meaningless high school game?

"That wasn't Bo," said Mann. "No way he sits out."

Snitz Snider Stadium's wooden bleachers were filled to capacity. The Bessemer Police Department sent extra enforcements to walk the sidelines, cruise the stands. On the opening drive, McAdory marched down the field—87 yards on 16 plays. On first and goal from the Jess Lanier seven, Jackson took a pitch from Mann, cut toward his right and sliced into the end zone. Upon reaching pay dirt, he flipped the ball to the nearest official, high-fived some teammates, lined up for the extra point and booted it through the uprights.

Beat Yo' Ass Quick? Whatever . . .

A couple of series later, the Tigers kicked off to McAdory's 21-yard line, where Jackson caught the ball, cradled it beneath his right forearm—and exploded. Past one defender. Past three defenders. Past all eleven defenders. Down the sideline and into the end zone once again. "I'll never forget how to spell his last name," said Steve Dabbs, a Lanier tackle, "because I was chasing him down the field, looking at the back of his jersey."

All told, Jackson scored two touchdowns, kicked two extra points and caught a pass for a two-point conversion. Jess Lanier won, 22–21, but the message was delivered.

Don't mess with Bo Jackson.

CHAPTER 5

THE EPITOME OF SUPERMAN

The 1981 McAdory High football season doesn't go down as particularly remarkable.

The team finished 8-2, and Bo Jackson was its lone representative on the *Birmingham News*'s All-Metro squad. He ran for 1,173 yards and 17 touchdowns—excellent but hardly historic numbers. By comparison, America's number 1 recruit—Philadelphia (Mississippi) High's Marcus Dupree—compiled 2,955 rushing yards and 36 touchdowns.

When, that December, the *Alabama Journal* ranked the state's top 20 high school prospects, Jackson was fifth, two slots behind Alan Evans, the Enterprise High all-everything tailback, and one below David Johnson, a lineman from Butler High.

In other words, while Jackson was a big deal, he wasn't the biggest of deals.

Until 1982.

In Alabama, indoor track and field is largely invisible. Newspapers cover the sport by rarely covering it at all. Nobody cares.

But in McCalla, at McAdory, Bo Jackson—referred to as a "one-man track wrecking crew" by the scribe Phillip Marshall—made it impossible *not* to care. On the last weekend of January, Jackson competed in Auburn High's annual indoor meet. He and his teammates were known for their hideous mustard-colored sweatsuits, as well as for showing up late. ("Our coaches drove the bus," Jackson recalled. "*Slowly.*") They were also known for dominating. At Auburn, Jackson won three events. He ran a 6.2 in the 60-yard dash, soared 21-9 in the long jump (wearing tennis shoes, not spikes!) and took the 60-hurdles in 7.6 seconds against athletes whose schools had both tracks and training equipment. That's what blew rivals away—while back home they were leaping over hurdles, Jackson was leaping over desk chairs. "We didn't have any mats to land on," Jackson said, "so we just bought these big nets and sewed these nets together, and go down to the stores and get all the foam that they didn't want. We'd stuff it in these big nets and those were the cushions for us to land on."

On February 15, 1982, the *Birmingham News* ran a lengthy piece beneath the headline MCADORY'S VINCENT JACKSON SETS THREE STATE MARKS AT TRACK MEET. Later that month the *Montgomery Advertiser* published a story, "BO" SHOULD WEAR AN "S" ON HIS CHEST. What both articles told, without having to exaggerate, was the saga of a young man with never-before-seen athleticism. Or, put differently: Even though he barely practiced for track events, Jackson traveled to Garrett Coliseum in Montgomery for the state indoor championships and put on a show for the ages. Beforehand, he told peers his goal was to smash four state records. He disappointed, and only broke three—the 60-yard high hurdles (7.29), the high jump (6 feet 8 inches) and the long jump (22 feet 6½ inches). Wrote Phillip Marshall in the *Advertiser*: "When you are 6-foot-1, weigh 215 pounds, leap like a kangaroo and run like the wind, you draw attention."

For most high school athletes, the football–indoor track double-double would have been the cherry atop four years of prep sports participation. The varsity letters. The jacket. Walking through the halls with the jocular strut. Jackson was, truly, the region's most discussed and admired star, and at McAdory he was royalty. "There was Bo," said Mann, "and there were the rest of us."

What came next would dwarf it all.

There is a story about young Bo Jackson you won't believe.

It's one of those fables that sounds exaggerated. A wide receiver floating through air. A pitcher throwing literal smoke. On and on. Sports and bullshit are bedfellows.

And yet, unless witnesses are all lying, and participants are all lying, and coaches are all lying . . . perhaps this holds up.

The game was a county baseball tournament semifinal matchup between Fairfield High and McAdory. It took place at Bessemer's Roosevelt Park, on a mid-May evening so hot a billowing steam rose from the dirt. Here, at yet another dilapidated Alabama facility, the bleachers were rotting wood and the unmowed grass brushed ankles. Mosquitoes gathered by the thousands around the halogen lights, their collective hum supplying a familiar chorus to the three hundred or so attendees.

The score? No one remembers the score. But it was a late inning, and up to the plate stepped Bo Jackson.

"That was never something we wanted to see," said Wayne Byram, Fairfield's head coach. "Never, ever."

McAdory baseball wasn't a program people generally noticed. Yet Jackson's presence changed that. He was an Auburn-bound local celebrity, batting in the .470s, approaching what would become a national prep record of 20 home runs (in just 25 games). The scouts showing up were all affiliated with Major League teams, and a consensus was building that this was home to one of the greatest physical specimens of all time. Paul Bunyan in the flesh.

Julian Mock, a Cincinnati Reds scout, filed a report to the organization that included these words on a Post-it: "He's the only guy I've ever seen who can hit it 400 feet, run and catch it before it comes down and throw it back to where it came from." Kenny Gonzales, the Royals scout and the first in his position to identify the talent, filled out a sheet labeled FREE AGENT REPORT. Wrote Gonzales: "Has present ML bat speed. Show ML power on occ. Has good composure in gut check situations for high school player. Has strength and can run. Can steal many bases."

Ellis Dungan was the Toronto Blue Jays southeastern scouting supervisor. He'd observed crappy prospects and stellar prospects; kids who reminded him of Joey Tama and kids who reminded him of Dave Parker. What he saw in Bessemer was different. "He was the best pure natural talent I ever saw," Dungan recalled. "Not just high school. Anywhere."

And now Jackson was standing alongside the Roosevelt Park home plate, digging his cleats into the moist dirt, his aluminum Easton waving above his cocked right elbow. In a game against Fairfield earlier in the season, Jackson homered three times on three pitches—"balls that went distances I'd never even seen adults reach," said Keith McKeller, a Fairfield football star who witnessed the matchup.

The first pitch was a fastball, and Jackson swung low and loopy, popping the ball to left field, where Fairfield's Eddie Scott stood a few feet in from the fence. It was all very ordinary-looking—save the baseball was rising. And rising. And rising. And rising. And rising. No one could remember seeing a ball rise this high, this quickly. Scott, who would go on to play for Samford University, tried tracking the ball with the expectation of catching it. "It's literally in orbit," Scott recalled. "I'm looking up, and I've got nothing. Nothing at all. And I've got my hands up, sorta like, 'Where is this thing?' And Bo—he sensed it."

Somewhere between home and first base, Jackson realized Scott was lost. Terry Brasseale, the McAdory coach, screamed, "Run!"—and Jackson proceeded to bolt down the line and turn toward second. "He starts kicking up rooster tails," said Steve Mann, a McAdory pitcher. "The dirt was flying off the back of his shoes." He was booking at full Bo Jackson speed—a blur of white and yellow and black. "Holy cow, it was unlike anything we'd ever seen," said Don Holmes, a spectator. "No human can move that fast without rockets."

"That ball reached the solar system," said Barry Dunn, also watching from the stands. "The ball got lost in the lights because it . . . actually . . . approached . . . the lights."

By the time the baseball *finally* fell to Earth between Scott and Tigers shortstop David Cooper, Jackson was rounding third base—right past the hold sign from Brasseale. "The ball hit the ground so hard it popped up high off the grass," said Keith Langston, a McAdory pitcher. "On the bench, we just sat there with our mouths wide open." There was no throw home. Safe without debate.

When the inning ended, Brasseale grinned toward Jackson. "Hey," he said, "you ran through my stop sign."

"Coach," Jackson said, "there wasn't no stopping me."

"Now, think about it," said Scott. "My instinct when I picked up the ball was to throw to third—and he was already past the base. By a lot. He ran from home to first, first to second, second to third and halfway to home *as the baseball was in flight*. It was the most amazing thing I've ever seen."

> HOLMES: "It was the most amazing thing I've ever seen."
> DUNN: "It was the most amazing thing I've seen."
> MANN: "Of all the stuff, it was the most amazing I've ever seen."
> BYRAM: "That was the most amazing thing I've ever seen."

In that game, Jackson had three more hits, including a home run. He wound up batting .493 for the season, with seven triples and twelve doubles. He had one twelve-for-twelve stretch that included six home runs and four doubles. Against Thompson High, he blasted a shot that—later measured by Brasseale—traveled 501 feet. It was his second bomb to exceed 500 feet. In another game, he hit a routine one-hopper back to the pitcher. "Kid catches it and takes a little crow hop and throws to first," recalled Brasseale, "and Bo beats it by half a step."

Over three high school baseball seasons, Jackson stole ninety bases in ninety-one attempts. Re-read that. *Ninety for ninety-one.* "How is it even possible?" said Sam Doss. "I'll never know."

A Jess Lanier High junior in 1982, Doss was the only catcher to ever throw Jackson out. "We had a guy named Gary Gilmore pitching this one afternoon," Doss said. "It was at Roosevelt Park. Bo was on first. I told Gary, 'Just don't throw it in the dirt. Whatever you do.'"

Though only 5-foot-7, Doss was a self-described "big ol' country boy" who exasperated his mother by wearing out new jeans within two or three weeks. "My legs were that thick, that strong," he said. "I was made to be physical."

Now Jackson took off—head down, arms pumping—and Gilmore threw a high fastball on the outside portion of the plate. Doss popped up, whipped the ball from his right hand and uncorked a perfect dart to second. "I got him!" Doss said. "I really caught Bo Jackson stealing! The only one ever!"

His next at-bat, Jackson launched a moon shot that traveled, by Doss's estimation, 450 feet. After crossing the plate, the slugger glanced at the catcher and winked. It was all ludicrousness, and even opponents learned to laugh at the Herculean feats of Bo Jackson.

One person who did not laugh was Frelon Abbott, the McAdory regular/ Auburn booster who surely found himself alarmed by the attention Jackson was drawing. Although the sporting universe now knew the Yellow Jackets star was committed to Auburn, that detail mattered little to Major League scouts. Long was the list of high school stars who planned on attending X University, then changed course when the potential dough piled up. "Frelon was the shield between Bo and anywhere other than Auburn," recalled a longtime Abbott associate. "There was very little Bo did that Frelon didn't know about. He filtered Bo's activities and tried to keep him from dealing with anyone but Auburn."

"There's somebody from Auburn at just about all our games," Brasseale said at the time. "[Auburn] is afraid that he's going to be talked into playing baseball."

Inside the Jackson household, Florence Bond, Bo's mother and a doggedly steadfast advocate for her son becoming the first Jackson to attend a four-year university, began screening calls in her own uniquely aggressive way.

FLORENCE BOND: "HELLO."
BASEBALL EXECUTIVE: "Hello, Mrs. Bond, I'm calling from the Milwau—"
FLORENCE BOND: *Click.*

When scouts knocked on the front door of his home, Jackson either pretended he wasn't home or hid out at a neighbor's house. "He'd wait with us until the scouts and recruiters left," said Alesia Carter, a classmate and family friend. "He'd call his mom and say, 'Are they gone?' He didn't want to be tempted. He wanted to be the first in his family to go to college." According to Randy Haught, a McAdory social studies teacher, one day a red Cadillac Eldorado convertible pulled into the school parking lot. The man behind the wheel identified himself as a representative of the Philadelphia Phillies, and when he popped the trunk there was a briefcase, laying open, with hundreds of stacked bills on display. "He told me he wanted to talk to Bo about the Phillies," Haught recalled. "I told him Bo was going to Auburn, and he said—and I'll never forget this—'A Black kid in the South, when he sees this car and knows it can be his, and when he sees the money, he'll sign.'"

Jackson, Haught remembered, came down, shook the man's hand, said, "I'm going to Auburn," and left.

"The guy drove off," Haught said, "dejected."

Dick Egan, working for the Major League Scouting Bureau, traveled to Bessemer specifically to see Jackson play a doubleheader against Ensley High. Before the first game Egan introduced himself to Brasseale, who was raking down the infield. "The kids will be coming out to take BP in a minute," Brasseale said. "Vincent will be there."

When Jackson arrived, Egan's eyes popped—"Oh, my," he recalled. "An athlete's athlete." As soon as the prospect took his swings, Egan approached.

"Hey, Bo," he said, "I'm Dick Egan with the Major League Scouting Bureau . . ."

Jackson turned his back and walked away.

Moments later, Egan tried a different approach. "Bo," he said, "I just wanted to know what offense y'all ran in football."

"Wishbone," Jackson said—then walked away again.

Oy.

"I'd been warned Auburn had people guarding him, and told him to have nothing to do with scouts," Egan said. "Clearly, he listened."

Egan stayed for the games. In the first, Jackson batted left-handed—just because, on occasion, he liked to bat left-handed. For the hell of it. "He lays down this bunt," Egan said, "and I clock him in 4.1 seconds to first. Holy shit! Four. Point. One." In the second game, Jackson hit a ball that, forty years later, Egan still pictured. "It went over everything," he said. "Fences. Trees. Everything." That, however, wasn't the moment that caused the scout to remove his glasses, rub them on his shirt and make sure what he saw was, well, what he saw. Here's how Egan tells it:

He was playing shortstop. There was a kid on third for the other team, and the batter popped up a shallow ball down the left-field line. Bo went over there, about five feet from foul territory. The ball is coming down and somebody is yelling, "Tag! Tag!" The kid on third is going to tag. Bo gets under the pop-up, decides he can no longer wait and jumps up to meet the ball coming toward him. And this part is etched in stone in my mind. The ball clanged off Bo's glove and bounced away. And he bent over to pick it up, let it go from a hunched-over position and threw the runner out by ten feet. It was an absolute fucking laser. This guy was the epitome of Superman.

Frustrated by Jackson's lack of engagement, and put off by Auburn's blockade, scouts did everything within their power to gauge the phenom, to understand his makeup and potential, to observe and plot and plan. The kid would certainly be drafted. Of this, there was no doubt. But how high? By what team? And would he actually consider escaping the clutches of Frelon Abbott and Auburn football, jumping straight to pro ball and skipping college? So many questions, so few answers.

Which meant, in the spirit of scouting ingenuity, representatives of Major League Baseball's twenty-six franchises found themselves sitting in the stands of not only McAdory baseball games, but central Alabama track-and-field meets.

It was not always by choice. As much as Jackson enjoyed baseball, he loved running, and missed seven games in order to compete in track. On occasion, he'd participate in both on the same day. "First time I saw Bo he was walking across the baseball field in his track uniform, track spikes on his feet, baseball spikes hanging around his neck," said Marty Maier, a St. Louis Cardinals scout. "Then he changed into a baseball uniform and hit a ball that's still traveling." On multiple occasions, scouts would arrive at McAdory's diamond only to be told, "Bo's not here. He's running in [fill in the Birmingham suburb]." It happened to Harry Minor, the New York Mets birddog who, fifteen years earlier, signed Tom Seaver. It happened to Bob Zuk, beating the bushes for the Atlanta Braves.

Jackson was 75 percent of McAdory's track-and-field scoring. He was the fastest, strongest, most explosive and most daring. His favorite event was the high jump, because it combined power and velocity with a moment's terror. "I would go out and raise the bar and raise the bar and raise the bar until it beat me—which was seven feet," he said. "I cleared seven feet once. It was in practice in high school. The [regional] record was 6-foot-6, and I would wait until everybody else went, then I'd raise the bar to 6-foot-6, jump that and clear that."

McAdory's meets turned into the Bo Jackson Show. Over the course of the season he set state records in the 100-yard dash (9.59 seconds), the 60-yard high hurdles (7.29 seconds), the triple jump (48 feet 7¼ inches), the high jump (6 feet 9 inches) and the long jump (23 feet 1 inch). The events also provided scouts with a chance to see Bo Jackson in the (near-literal) flesh. In a baseball uniform, he appeared enormous. In McAdory's running singlet, he was a jacked-up puma.

The track-and-field magnificence of Bo Jackson was on full and final display on the weekend of May 22 and 23, when the layers of his athletic genius merged. Two weeks earlier, Jackson had traveled to Selma for the state high school track-and-field championships, where he captured the long jump on Friday night, then (after landing clumsily in the triple jump) came back to win the 100 and 120 hurdles on a severely sprained ankle. It rained throughout the weekend, and opponents were shocked/confused/impressed by the visage of a man following Jackson around with an umbrella. "We're all getting wet, and he's dry," said Jay French, an Auburn High senior distance runner. "It was an older white guy, almost serving as his personal butler. None of us had that."

Now, ankle caked in medical tape, Jackson was off to Vestavia Hills High School to defend his state decathlon championship.

In normal circumstances, a wounded favorite inspires optimism. *Maybe I can beat him.* Not here. "You knew you had no shot," said Don Murphy, an Auburn High decathlete. "None." The majority of Jackson's rivals came from Auburn High, located in the shadow of his soon-to-be-collegiate home. Unlike McAdory, the school had its own track and first-rate practice equipment. Their coaches specialized in the sports they taught, and knew whereof they spoke.

Over the course of the two-day championship, Jackson never bothered to remove his sweatpants. Not during the five Saturday events—the 100, shot put, discus ("He had no clue how to throw that thing," said Auburn High's Bud Nesmith, "and then on his first throw he beats everyone by a lot."), long jump and quarter mile. Not during Sunday's four other events—hurdles, triple jump, pole vault and discus. They were thick and tight—and he kept them on the entire time. "Which," said Murphy, "is just incredible. And, if you're an opponent, really intimidating."

Jackson's ankle injury caused him to borrow a page from Bruce Jenner, the legendary American decathlete who, while once injured in a meet, was forced to high jump off the opposite foot. The technique was referred to as "goofy-footing"—and, said Curt Lindner, Auburn High's standout decathlete, "you never wanted to have to goofy-foot." But a severely hobbled Jackson had no choice. "And this is what makes Bo Jackson Bo Jackson," said Linder. "In the high jump he jumped off his right foot, and not only that but he came to the bar from the wrong side and was still able to clear six feet. You can't possibly understand how hard that is. To twist the body the opposite way that it wants to turn. It's just not done."

The pole vault was even more staggering. McAdory High owned absolutely nothing to help Jackson prepare for the event. So he never practiced until it was time to compete, and upon arriving at Vestavia Hills Jackson had to hope another school would loan him a pole.

Nesmeth of Auburn High was both the state champion in the event and a decathlete. His school allowed Jackson to borrow its pole—which, technically, was built for far smaller humans. At 6-foot-1 and 215 pounds, Jackson was seven inches taller and 90 pounds heavier than Nesmeth. "It was sorta scary watching him," said Nesmeth. "He didn't know how to bend the pole and his body weight was a lot. He and I were practicing together, and I showed him what I knew. It was basically five minutes of tutoring, then go get 'em . . ."

Jackson didn't win the decathlon pole vault, but he cruised over the 9-foot entry height and wound up topping out at an impressive 12 feet 6 inches—"remarkable for that big of a kid," said Atchison, his coach.

Of the decathlon's ten events, Jackson won seven en route to edging out Auburn High's Linder, 8,30 points to 8,205 points, for the title. It was, however, a significantly wider margin than numbers suggest. Throughout the decathlon, Jackson obsessed over two thoughts:

1. I need to win.
2. I need to be ahead by so much that I don't have to do the final event—the 1,500.

In the following day's *Birmingham News*, writer Rick Lowry explained that Jackson's "leg problems kept him from competing in the mile run." This was not true. He simply led Linder by more than 1,000 points—the maximum one could score in a single event. The 1,500 would do without him.

So how did he feel about capturing back-to-back state decathlon titles?

"Tired," Jackson said. "I'm going home and getting some rest."

But here's the crazy thing.

The crazy

Crazy

Crazy

Crazy

Crazy

Thing.

He didn't go home and get some rest. Because the day after the decathlon wrapped, McAdory's baseball team headed to Birmingham's Rickwood Field to face Pinson Valley High in a doubleheader for the Class 3A Jefferson County championship.

In Alabama, a trip to Rickwood was akin to a trip to Yankee Stadium. When it first opened in 1910 as home to the city's lone professional baseball team, the Coal Barons, Rickwood was America's finest minor league ballpark—a semi-replica of Pittsburgh's fabulous Forbes Field. Through the years, Rickwood served as the base of the Negro League's Black Barons, and had luminaries like Babe Ruth and Rogers Hornsby play within its confines. By the 1980s, it was run-down, but still home to the Birmingham Barons, the Detroit Tigers Double A affiliate.

It was also the host to central Alabama's annual prep baseball tournaments.

The setup was uncomplicated: Should Pinson Valley, the lower seed, sweep both games, it would be the Class 3A title holder. Should McAdory win one of the two, it would be the champion.

"It was definitely an uphill battle," said Barry Dunn, Pinson Valley's second baseman. "But we all thought we'd do it."

The opening game was a matchup of aces—Pinson Valley's Joe Chambers against McAdory's Dale Burnett—and the stands were loaded with both bystanders and Major League scouts itching to get a last look at He-Man. Florence Bond, Bo's mother, sat in a seat a few rows behind home plate, wedged between two hulking security guards sent by Auburn to ward off scouts.

The Indians jumped out to an early lead, and by the fifth inning Chambers was cruising along. He had faced Jackson dozens of times, and knew precisely how to pitch him. "He couldn't hit the curveball," Chambers said.

"I mean, not to save his life. He'd screw himself in the ground just trying." As Jackson approached the plate for his third (and final) at-bat of the game, he pointed his bat at Chambers and stuttered, "I-i-i-i-i d-d-d-are you to throw m-m-m-e a-a-a-a f-f-f-f-fastball."

Chambers laughed, then yelled, "You dare me?"

"Y-y-y-eah," Jackson said. "I-I-I-I d-d-d-are y-y-you."

"OK," Chambers said. "I'll give you what you want."

Russell Justice, Pinson Valley's catcher, put down two fingers for the curveball. Chambers shook him off.

Justice did it again. Chambers shook him off.

And again. Chambers shook him off.

Finally, Justice flashed a single finger. *Fastball.*

Chambers let fly an absolute dandy—lower part of the plate, an inch inside, tough for a guy with long arms to hit with force. But Jackson swung and connected, and as the baseball headed toward Chambers's skull, the pitcher wisely ducked. "Bo nearly took my head off," he recalled. The ball reached center field, and Jackson—speed personified—motored in to second base for a double. It was the reason so many scouts were here, and Chambers always remembered the sound of clicking stopwatches. "For anyone else, that's a single," Chambers said. "It was one of the greatest single displays of athleticism I'd ever seen."

Actually, that would come moments later. The 6-3 Pinson Valley victory forced a second game, and with Burnett already used, Brasseale told Jackson he would be starting. This was noteworthy because: (a) Jackson hated pitching; (b) Jackson had spent the past two days winning the state decathlon; (c) Jackson's left ankle was wrapped in tape; and (d) Jackson had pitched a grand total of zero innings in 1982.

"We didn't know much about Bo as a guy on the mound," said Dwight Harper, the Indians first baseman. "Just that he threw hard, but didn't have much beyond a fastball."

This was fair—Jackson *didn't* have much beyond a fastball. But, damn. *The fastball.* Jackson had a high release point, and when the baseball left his palm it rocketed toward the plate and cut in—hard—on right-handed batters. "He was about ninety-one, ninety-two all game," said Barry Dunn, the Indian left fielder. "It was as hard as you'd see at that level." One after another, Jackson chopped down the Pinson Valley hitters, and by the end of the eighth inning he had allowed but seven hits while fanning fourteen in McAdory's 6-3 win. All of the Indians' runs were unearned. "But, honestly, his pitching wasn't what sold me," said Dunn. "There was a moment when he was on third, and all we could think about was Bo stealing home. Don't let him steal home. Don't let him steal home." Eric Hays, the Pinson Valley pitcher, nervously eyed Jackson. He'd throw to third baseman Scott Hodge, stop, throw to third again, stop, throw to thi— "he balks, and Bo walks home with a run," said Dunn. "I've never seen another kid change the dynamics of a baseball game like Bo Jackson did that night. Baseball doesn't bend, but the field was at the mercy of his talent."

After striking out the final Pinson Valley batter, Jackson quickly hugged his teammates and walked back to the dugout. Rubin Grant of the *Birmingham Post-Herald* asked for a comment, but the kid was overcome by exhaustion. "I don't think I can," he said before plopping down on the bench and leaning his head against the wall.

Sitting in the Rickwood Field stands was Tim Wilken, Toronto Blue Jays area scout. He was late to the Bo Jackson frenzy—Pat Gillick, the team's general manager, heard all the buzz and ordered Wilken to fly to Alabama for the season's last two games. "I don't care what you do," he told Wilken, "but you get inside that family's home."

"How do you expect me to do that?" Wilken replied.

"I don't care," said Gillick. "Just make it happen."

Later in the day, the Blue Jays sent Leroy Stanton, a longtime Major League outfielder now serving as a minor league hitting coach, to join Wilken in Bessemer. When the doubleheader ended, Wilken and Stanton drove to the Jackson household. Wilken remained in the car and Stanton— an African American man who grew up poor in South Carolina—knocked on the front door. Watching from afar, Wilken was shocked when Florence Bond ushered Stanton inside.

A few minutes later, Stanton returned to the vehicle. "Tim," he said, "come on in."

The three chatted, then Wilken worked up his nerve and said, "Mrs. Bond, I would really like to speak to your son."

"I'll tell you what," she replied. "Call here at nine o'clock Monday morning, I'll have Vincent Edward talk to you."

As promised, come Monday morning at nine o'clock Wilken was on the phone with Jackson. The teen was soft-spoken, with a stutter that elongated sentences from seconds to minutes. The conversation was exasperating.

WILKEN: "Vincent, we'd like to work you out before the draft."
JACKSON: "I-I-I-I h-h-have t-t-to check with m-m-my m-m-mom."
WILKEN: "Well . . ."

JACKSON: "And I-I-I-I h-h-h-have to c-c-c-check with m-m-my c-c-coach."

WILKEN: "Would there be a time that might work?"

JACKSON: "I-I-I-'m v-v-v-ver-y-yy b-b-b-usy."

WILKEN: "Bo, it was a pleasure speaking with you. I hope you do well in the upcoming draft."

Click.

"He was the best prospect I scouted," Wilken said. "But I told Pat we shouldn't take him. He wasn't interested."

On June 7, 1982, the New York Yankees used their second-round pick in the amateur draft to select Vincent "Bo" Jackson, shortstop out of McAdory High School. Gus Poulos, a Yankee scout who had watched Jackson on dozens of occasions, celebrated the selection by raving, "He's the youngster with the best overall ability, raw-talent wise, in my 21 years of scouting."

"To tell you the truth, we were surprised he lasted as long as he did," added Bill Livesey, New York's director of player development. "He's the kind of young man the Yankees like to deal with."

Because of his commitment to Auburn, Jackson fell to fiftieth overall in a draft that included future neon names like Shawon Dunston (first overall to the Cubs), Dwight Gooden (fifth, Mets) and David Wells (thirtieth, Blue Jays). Had he been willing to commit to baseball, and only baseball, there is little doubt Jackson would have been selected number 1.

Dunston was a tremendous talent who projected to a Garry Templeton–type player.

Jackson projected to Mickey Mantle.

On the day of the draft, the Yankees called the Jackson household to offer congratulations, and no one answered. On the day after the draft, the Yankees called the Jackson household again, and no one answered. They reached out to Brasseale, asking that he intervene on the organization's behalf. "They can't understand why he won't talk," the coach said. "I'm sure they'll try to show him the glamour side, like playing in Yankee Stadium. But Bo's not a glamour guy."

A few days later, Brasseale was teaching when he received another call from the Yankees. The team wanted to fly him and Jackson to New York for a game against the Red Sox at Yankee Stadium. "Let me talk to Bo and get back to you," he said.

At the conclusion of that afternoon's practice, Brasseale shared the news with his superstar.

"No," Jackson said.

"No?" replied the coach.

"I don't want to go to New York," Jackson said.

"But it's Yankees–Red Sox!" said Brasseale.

He could have been speaking Choctaw. Jackson never watched televised sports. He couldn't have named more than a player or two on either team. He had no clue Yankees–Red Sox was a thing.

"I called the Yankees to tell them thanks, but we were passing," Brasseale said, "and they were dumbfounded."

Steve Renfroe, an assistant baseball coach at Auburn, was once a Yankees prospect. The organization called and asked, "Do you have any idea where Vincent Jackson might be?"

"I told them the truth," recalled Renfroe. "I had no knowledge."

Finally, on Wednesday evening—two days after Jackson was picked—Poulos flew from New York to Birmingham, rented a car and drove to Bessemer, where he knocked on the front door of the family home and hoped to offer a six-figure signing bonus that couldn't be refused.

No one answered.

When Don Kausler, Jr., of the *Birmingham News* caught wind of what was (and wasn't) transpiring, he tracked down Poulos and found a man at his wit's end. "This confuses me a little," he said. "Suppose two years from now something happens to Bo (like an injury). Don't you think he'll be wishing then, 'If only I had listened to the Yankees'? All I want to tell Bo is that we've got some outstanding instruction at all levels of our farm system to offer him."

Poulos was never granted a one-on-one with the family, and he departed Alabama depressed, bewildered and lost. Plenty of prospects had turned down professional baseball for other opportunities. But this was a first for Poulos: The kid wouldn't even meet with him.

"There wasn't a snowball's chance I was ready for the Big Apple," Jackson said later. "They talked to my coach, but that was it."

What Poulos didn't realize is Auburn's representatives had been tipping the scales for months. The Yankees scouted Jackson hard throughout the spring, and—through whispered sneers—Auburn made certain their future running back knew the organization was rotten. That the owner, George Steinbrenner, was a crook. The front office was inept. New York City was a big scary place that would eat a bumpkin like Jackson for lunch.

"[The Yankees] put out lies about me," Jackson said years later. "When they found out I had signed to Auburn they put out lies like, well, the reason

Bo Jackson is at Auburn is because Auburn made his mother the proud owner of a chain of seventeen stores, a supermarket, his mom now drives a new Cadillac. They put all that out. They said I was driving a brand-new forty-thousand-dollar sports car."

The lies, in fact, were created by Auburn University, not the New York Yankees.

And they worked.

Bo Jackson was heading to college.

CHAPTER 6

VILLAGE ON THE PLAIN

Bo Jackson arrived on the campus of Auburn University in the summer of 1982, a mere ten days after graduating from McAdory High. Jackson was a backwoods kid with little understanding of what college life would entail, and when the coaching staff told him to come early for a summer job, a couple of classes (history and geography) and daily workouts, he did as instructed.

Although he twice visited during the recruiting process, the early culture shock had to be dizzying. In Bessemer, Jackson lived in a small house in an all-Black neighborhood with mostly Black friends. The campus of Auburn University, on the other hand, was a sprawling 1,875 acres, lined with classic brick buildings and carpeted by lush green landscapes. The nearby town was a quaint ode to the homogeneous college setting. Best known for its agricultural program, Auburn University was safe and comfortable and lily-white.*

"For a lot of us Black players, it was a change from the norm," said Lionel James, an African American running back. "I remember taking an English class, and I was the only Black student, and the teacher asked me, directly, 'So, how do you feel about Martin Luther King?' I looked around and said, 'I think you need to ask some of these other people, because my answer probably won't fit your narrative.' It was that type of thing."

When Jackson first entered Sewell Hall, the university's official athletic dormitory, he carried a duffle bag stuffed with clothing and a thirteen-inch color television purchased as a farewell gift by (of all people) A. D. Adams, his 99-percent-unavailable nonfather father. Jackson was cursed with a pronounced shyness and a stutter that remained unforgiving ("God, it was *so* bad," said Pat Arrington, a teammate), and making new friends

---

* In the fall of 1982, Auburn University was 2 percent Black—with a faculty that was .6 percent Black.

was never something that came easily. Many of Jackson's early Auburn meals were eaten in solitude. Many of his conversations were with himself. "I was scared," Jackson recalled. "First time living away from home. Afraid I wouldn't fit in."

"When I was growing up my mom always told me to look a person in the eyes if he's talking to you," said James. "But Bo didn't look anybody in the eyes."

His assigned roommate for apartment 221 was Jeff Lott, a freshman offensive guard from Gainesville, Georgia. Jackson and Lott had never before met, but within days the running back knew this union could not last. Lott was 6-foot-3 and 266 pounds, and specialized in eating, disco dancing, and Rich Little impersonations. He also smelled, and liked leaving garbage everywhere. "He was a big, nasty guy," Jackson said. "I would come in and he would have his sweaty clothes right on the door. I got tired of him and I said, 'Look, you've got to get your ass out of here . . .'"

Jackson's debut task at Auburn wasn't running the lines of a football field, but painting the lines of a parking lot. He was told to head out every morning to the nearby Auburn Mall, where he was presented with a barrel of yellow paint and instructed to lay down parking space markings. "We painted all the little parking lines and the arrows and the stops," Jackson recalled. "The hottest summer of my life." The pay was minimum wage ($3.35 per hour), and the joy was equally minimal. Pat Dye, the school's second-year head football coach, liked seeing what his new charges were made of; liked noting whether they handled the tasks without gripe, or moaned and whined their way through labor. It was the first of many tests Dye issued his legions, and it revealed plenty. Jackson was miserable, but he never complained. "It was about a hundred and twenty degrees in that parking lot," he later recalled with a laugh.

There was a perk. During breaks, Jackson liked to head inside the shopping center, where he met a young woman working at one of the stores. No longer dating Marilyn Strother, his high school squeeze, Jackson was free to pursue as he pleased, and he later boasted of the summer romance resulting in twenty-seven sexual escapades in a single week. "I would get out of practice, run over to her place, get laid once or twice, come back," he said. "I'm telling you, those were the good ol' days."

Freshman practices officially commenced on Tuesday, August 17, and Jackson didn't know what to expect. One season earlier, Auburn finished 5-6, and its leading rusher had been James, an undersized sophomore halfback who ran for a paltry 561 yards and one touchdown. With a gaping hole at the position, and an emphasis on employing the run-first wishbone offense, Dye and his staff had emphasized the recruiting of ball carriers. Eight running backs were a part of the newest class, including Tommie Agee (the Montgomery Advertiser's 1-A Player of the Year and a kid who averaged 8.2 yards per carry as a senior for Maplesville High), Collis Campbell (a 6-foot-1, 210-pound bowling ball from Coffee High who gained 873 yards on 142 carries as a senior), Tim Jessie (a three-time 1,000-yard rusher from Opp High), and Danny Robinson (the *Atlanta Constitution*'s Metro Player of the Year for Fulton High).

The crème de la crème was Alan Evans. If Marcus Dupree, the manchild out of Philadelphia, Mississippi, had been America's number 1 high school halfback, the runner-up was Evans, a two-time Alabama All-State selection. Inside Auburn's football offices, Evans was considered the answer to many of the program's prayers. Four years earlier, when Doug Barfield was still head coach, the Tigers boasted a backfield featuring three future NFL stars—James Brooks, Joe Cribbs, William Andrews. The school's fans expected their Tigers to run over the competition, and now here was Evans. "Coming in, all we heard about was Alan," said Jessie. "I grew up thirty miles from him, and he was something. He ran a 4.3 40, he was really smooth, he was in newspapers all the time. But there was a problem, and it didn't take people long to see it."

Namely, Alan Evans wasn't particularly tough. In high school, running out of the wishbone, he never blocked and rarely took a hard direct blow. To watch a prep Evans run was to watch a man glide, slip, slide, shift, twirl. Evans was beautiful and balletic and borderline artistic—Baryshnikov on grass—but soft as cottage cheese. "Getting hit in high school isn't getting hit in college," said Alex Dudchock, an Auburn defensive tackle. "He started getting hit *hard*."

At Auburn, Evans was exposed. Or, if not exposed, overshadowed. "The first three practices, Alan owned the field," said David King, an Auburn defensive back. "And then we knew his moves, and that was it. Wasn't much to him."

When asked by the Associated Press about his new freshmen runners, Dye raved that they were "the best-looking group I've been around." But "best-looking group" was code for *best freshman running back I've ever seen*. And he wasn't thinking of Alan Evans.

From the start, Jackson did things ordinary freshmen didn't. They were surprising little moments, suggesting an inner confidence cloaked by shyness. (Said Yann Cowart, an offensive lineman: "He literally said nothing for a while. *Nothing.*") First, Jackson demanded a new roommate, and the irksome Lott was kicked to the curb and replaced by the affable Agee. Second, he was adamant about wanting uniform number 40, which he'd worn at McAdory. Yet to Jackson's chagrin, the number already belonged to Greg Tutt, a senior cornerback from Rome, Georgia, who only donned number 40 because—as an incoming freshman in 1980—his desired number 4 jersey was worn by Skip Johnston, a punter. "Bo asked me for 40," said Tutt. "But, I mean, come on. I was a senior, he was a freshman. Had number 4 been available, sure. But I wasn't giving a freshman my number." As a compromise, Jackson took number 41, then quickly traded down for number 34, the era's halfback digits de jour. At the time, the greatest runner in college football was Georgia's Herschel Walker—number 34. The NFL's two best ball carriers—Chicago's Walter Payton and Houston's Earl Campbell—both wore 34. It fit.

Third, during early drills Jackson demanded Bud Casey, the running backs coach, stop having him line up at fullback. Jackson, all of nineteen years old, didn't *ask*. He entered Casey's office and *insisted.* "Look," he said, "I didn't come here to get down on all fours and be a damn blocking back. I came here to be a running back."

Casey was forty-two years old. Over fourteen years he had coached at Northeast Oklahoma State, the University of Tampa, Georgia Tech, Texas Tech and now Auburn. Never before had a first-year player exhibited such audacity.

Casey dug it.

"OK, Bo," he said. "We'll move you to halfback."

Like the other incoming backs, Jackson was aware of the buzz surrounding Evans. "He was a blue chipper and I wasn't," Jackson said. "He was cream of the crop. He was going to beat me out." Then Dye had every player—new and returnee—line up and run the 40. One running back after another took a turn, and the 4.6 and 4.5 clockings were as expected. When it was Jackson's time, he lined up, waited for the whistle, fired into his first step, and ran a *what-did-we-just-see?* 4.2. It was not merely the fastest on the team, but the fastest ever recorded at Auburn. "Alan Evans," said Forrest Benson, an Auburn linebacker, "didn't turn out to be worth a crap. Bo Jackson was the truth."

Of the ninety-nine players on Auburn's roster leading up to the 1982 season, *maybe* 5 percent had ever heard of Jackson. Because college teams are so enormous, it can take players weeks, if not months, to recognize and know one another. Freshmen, in particular, blend in like beige carpeting.

Jackson, however, glowed. When he stretched, his nose touched his knee-caps. His thighs, recalled a quarterback named Ken Hobby, "were these black steel pipes." When he ran, the punter Fred Murphy noted, "he sounded like a train passing you by at full speed." Every member of the roster was an athlete. But Jackson walked like an athlete, ran like an athlete, ate like an athlete, slept like an athlete. It oozed off of him.

Recalled Chuck Clanton, a junior cornerback: "When I saw him the first time I was like, 'Jesus Christ, what the fuck is that?' When he walked, his thighs naturally rubbed together. There was no fat. None. He had Earl Campbell thighs. But he was faster than Earl Campbell. If he had three per-cent body fat, that'd be a lot. He was all muscle. Like a tank from the future."

Todd Rubley, a junior tight end, remembered sitting in the weight room with a handful of veterans when Jackson stopped, placed 350 pounds on a bar and laid across the bench. "Doesn't say a word," said Rubley. "Just—one, two, three, four, five. Then he puts the bar back and walks out."

"I think," Rubley said to the group, "that guy can help us win."

Randy Campbell was the Tigers new starting quarterback. In his two years with the team, he had seen a lot. On one of Jackson's first days, Camp-bell headed over to the training bubble with a gaggle of running backs to work on the intricacies of the wishbone offense. Because of Jackson's size (he now weighed 220 pounds), he was still positioned in the fullback slot behind Campbell and to the right. With Casey, the running backs coach, standing off to the side, Campbell took a snap and turned to hand off to Jackson. "I take one step with my right foot and I put the ball out suppos-edly right into his stomach," Campbell recalled. "But the point of the ball kind of stuck into the side of his ribs. Our timing was off just a bit."

They ran the play again, and the same thing happened.

They ran the play again, and the same thing happened.

Finally, an exasperated Campbell looked toward Casey and said, "Coach, you need to get him lined up in the right place. He's lined up too close to me."

The play was run again, and again the football wound up in Jackson's ribs.

"And that's when it hit me," said Campbell. "It was like, '*Ohhhhhh*, shit! This guy's so fast I can't spin and get the ball to him in time. That's not his problem. That's *my* problem."

In the late summer days of 1982, the biggest problem for Auburn's football players wasn't Bo Jackson's speed, or Alan Evans's mediocrity. It wasn't an upcoming schedule that included four nationally ranked opponents, or the eternally high expectations of a fanbase starved of success.

No, it was Pat Dye.

Or, to be precise, Pat Dye's madness.

On the recruiting trail, the Tigers' head coach was everything you'd want in a dinner guest. Dye was gregarious, polite, even funny. He'd help Mama clear the dishes, help Pops fix a blown tire. He was well versed in 1,001 different subjects, and could easily drop back-to-back Rutherford B. Hayes and Kool & the Gang references without batting an eye.

So when freshmen arrived on campus, they largely expected to find *that* Pat Dye waiting for them.

They did not.

Before Dye was hired by Auburn on January 2, 1981, the program had been headed for five years by Doug Barfield, an unflinchingly decent man ("one of the finest people I have ever known," said David Housel, Auburn's media relations director at the time) who knew his X's and O's but treated football practices and conditioning drills like a sunny day at Camp Kiwi. As a result, despite an abundance of talent, Barfield's teams compiled a 29-25-1 record. They were outworked.

He resigned under pressure toward the end of the 1980 calendar year, and while he blamed boosters and limited university support for his demise (indeed, he inherited a team that had been under NCAA investigation for recruiting violations), a culprit could be found in the mirror.

"A coach needs to hold people accountable," said Jeff Jackson, a defensive end. "Coach Barfield really didn't. It was sort of a free-for-all."

With Barfield gone, the board of trustees turned its attention toward Vince Dooley, the fantastic University of Georgia head coach and a 1954 Auburn grad. He was flown in for multiple interviews, and offered financial incentives few men could refuse.

Dooley—embedded in Georgia—refused.

The next choice was Dye, best known as . . . well . . . um . . . nothing. In 1980, Dye coached the Wyoming Cowboys of the Western Athletic Conference to a 6-5 record, and before that he spent six years as the head coach at East Carolina, where his Pirates were always good against programs that were rarely good. In many ways, Dye's most important qualification was that he had served as a nine-year assistant coach under Bear Bryant at the University of Alabama—a school that would be Auburn's archrival had the Crimson Tide thought of the Tigers as anything more than a gnat on an elephant.

Dye was forty-one when he accepted the Auburn position, and the re-action from the community was a one-handed clap.

Pat Dye? Yawn.

Auburn's returning players felt similarly. Vince Dooley was legend, and the idea of playing for such a man was thrilling. But Dye felt like sloppy sec-onds, and no one knew what to expect when they reported to a Sewell Hall lounge for the coach's first team meeting.

It was scheduled to begin at 7 p.m., and as players waddled in at 6:57 ... 6:58 ... 6:59 ... they were greeted by the visage of Pat Dye's psychotic scowl.

"He wouldn't let anyone enter who came late," said Campbell, the quarterback. "He told them to get the hell out if they couldn't be there on time. In my time at Auburn, nobody had ever done that."

"He said, 'Gentlemen, you're not welcome at this meeting,'" recalled Ar-rington. "But I'll see you at six tomorrow morning at the stadium. You'll be running for me.'"

At one point, as Dye—whose speeches cooooulllllllld droooooone onnnnnn foooooooor hooooouuuurrrs—rambled about expectations, a player sitting near the front fell asleep, his light snores filling the room. A couple of Tigers snickered, until Dye approached and slammed his fist on the table. "You!" he said to the suddenly stirred napper. "Get the hell out of the room! And do not come back!"

He shuffled off.

"Listen," Dye said. "I've won a championship at every level. In high school. In college. In the pros. Either as a coach or a player. And I can prom-ise you we'll win one here at Auburn. I was at Alabama for nine years, and starting today we no longer fear Alabama. You understand?"

The players nodded.

"Look around," he said. "Half of you won't be here next year. That's a promise. And for those who want to do this, you will go through hell. Start-ing now."

Dye—referred to as a "benevolent tyrant of the old school" by *Inside Sports*'s Hank Nuwer—walked the walk. He was raised on a farm in Bly-the, Georgia, and woke up daily before dawn to complete the tasks, then hitched a ride on a milk truck to school so he could make it on time. He rarely wore shoes, and boasted feet with soles so tough that his father, Wayne Dye, used to have his boy entertain guests by cracking Brazil nuts with his toes. Later, after graduating from Georgia, he served in the United States Army, and won a Timmy Award as the outstanding football player in the armed services. Hard work? Going the extra five miles? Fighting through sore muscles, raw hands, battered psyches? Those were Pat Dye calling cards.

"He ran a lot of Coach Barfield's guys off," said Rubley. "A ton of the returning starters quit. These were guys whose asses had been kissed for far too long. Who didn't work hard. But it was a new world."

In the lead-up to the start of a season, many Division I coaches implemented two-a-day practices. Dye implemented three-a-day practices. "You went from five thirty until seven in the morning, ate breakfast, took a break," said Arrington. "Then you practiced from ten to eleven thirty. You ate lunch and you came back and you practiced from three until six. You did that shit for two weeks in summer camp. No limitations. We would weigh ourselves at the morning practice, then weigh ourselves again at day's end. I'd lose ten, twelve pounds. In one day."

"Maybe we'd get two hours off, total," said Joel Gregg, a fullback. "You'd find somewhere soft and sleep. Then right back at it."

Water was allowed—rarely. The higher the temperature, the better. The brighter the sun, the better. The more stifling the humidity, the better. "To this day," said Arrington, "the smell of cut grass makes me want to vomit." One didn't bench-press until he felt tired. One bench-pressed—said Mike Cowart, a running back—"until a coach told you you were tired." For every penalty committed during practices, all players had to run a hundred-yard sprint. If you violated a team rule, you were punished with stadium steps—a task even worse than it sounds. "A cinder block in each hand, and you have to walk to the top of the stadium, then walk down," said James, the halfback. "If you're late by ten minutes, you do ten stadium steps. If you're late by an hour, you're doing sixty. Coach Dye brought the prison camp mentality to Auburn University."

"We started Coach Dye's first spring with about a hundred and seventy-five players," said Chris Woods, a wide receiver, "and ended it with sixty-five." The biggest loss was that of Sam Dejarnette, a halfback out of Selma who wanted nothing to do with Dye's hell; he left for the University of Southern Mississippi and rushed for 1,545 yards in 1982. "He was gifted," said James. "But he was like, 'Screw this. I don't need this shit.'"

By the time the 1981 season wrapped, a slimmed-down, toughed-up Auburn Tigers squad finished . . . 5-6, the same as it had under Barfield in 1980. But those paying attention recognized the change. Dye's squad—often overmatched thanks to a string of subpar recruiting classes—played hard and fought through the fourth quarter. The *Auburn Plainsman*, the school's weekly student newspaper, celebrated Dye's first season with a glowing piece headlined THE WINNING DYE ERA. The Tigers, sports editor Stuart Blackwell noted, "have begun to turn around to SEC and national prominence."

The Pat Dye who returned for his second season in 1982 was one convinced that he now had the horses to compete. Which meant—"we were in for hell," said Tim Jessie, the running back. "The hell of a coach set on driving his players to the brink."

On August 24, 1982, readers of the *Atlanta Constitution* sports section opened to a piece headlined AUBURN SHOWS OPTIMISM BY THE DAWN'S EARLY LIGHT.

Wrote Ed Hinton . . .

Auburn's returning football players were on the practice fields at dawn Monday for the first of three workouts on their opening day of preseason practice.

Coach Pat Dye roused his players at 5:45 a.m., fed them orange juice and worked them an hour on the kicking game before breakfast. The Tigers then worked two hours in mid-morning and two hours in late afternoon, all in shorts and T-shirts.

Three-a-day drills, beginning with the 6:20 a.m. kicking game practice, are scheduled to continue through Wednesday.

"It was so awful I remember one day standing on the field and praying," said Steve Wallace, an offensive lineman. "I said, 'God, if you allow me to blow out both of my arches right now and stop practicing football, I would very much appreciate it.'"

Like Bryant, his mentor, Dye observed much of practice via the top of a coaching tower positioned between two fields. He was God, judging from up above. How would these young men respond to the pre-dawn alarm clock? How quickly would they dress? Were they groggy or wide awake? Did they have a pep in their step?

In late August, the Tigers held an intrasquad scrimmage inside Jordan Hare Stadium. Though closed to paid spectators, enough people were present to witness a moment that would be forever spoken of in hushed tones. On an ordinarily designed run play meant to gain a few yards, Jackson took a handoff from Randy Campbell, burst toward the line, leaned outside and headed straight for Donnie Humphrey.

In the 1982 Auburn football media guide, Humphrey's listed hobbies were "work[ing] with children and watch[ing] soap operas on television."

Omitted were the 6-foot-2, 275-pound defensive tackle's additional dual passions of eating rusty nails and kicking opposing players in the testicles. The team's lone preseason All-American was an ornery bull who forced offensive coordinators to game plan toward the opposite side of the field.

In the lead-up to the scrimmage, Humphrey had approached Jackson in the locker room and said, "Boy, wait until we put our pads on you tomorrow. Just wait until you see what we're gonna do to your freshman ass . . ."

"He was talking all sorts of trash," said Barry Garber, a freshman tight end. "Bo listened and smiled."

Now Jackson and Humphrey were about to collide. Two men, both future NFL players, barreling straight toward one another. Humphrey lowered his head, reached out with his arms, lunged at Jackson's midsection . . . and got stampeded. *Hard.*

The noise. Decades removed, players still remembered the noise. Like a hammer slamming into a piece of wood. Jackson charged into Humphrey, then through Humphrey, then *over* Humphrey, and glided toward the end zone otherwise untouched. The offensive players whooped and hollered. The defensive players whooped and hollered, too. "Donnie was the meanest motherfucker on the team," Jackson said. "I figured if I could run over him I could run over motherfucking anybody."

Afterward, in the locker room, a straight-faced Humphrey approached, extended a hand and smiled.

"Damn, Bo," he said. "You are the real fucking deal."

The freshman from Bessemer, according to Wallace, averaged about 10 yards per carry during those early weeks. "It was so obvious he was special," Wallace said. Evans was left in the dust and reduced to playing Sunday junior varsity games. (After one more season at Auburn, he transferred to UT-Chattanooga.)

"During workouts a few scouts came one day to clock some seniors in the forty," said Murphy, the punter. "They're all standing at the finish line, and Bo jumps in. Just . . . because. Well, he runs a 4.2 and sounded like a Mack truck coming through. Destroyed all the other guys. Everyone there was like, 'Did that just happen?'" Another time, Randy Campbell asked Jackson how far he could throw a football. "He stood on the twenty, stepped and skipped to the twenty-five and launched it past the end line of the opposite end zone," said Campbell. "That's about ninety yards—*in the air!* I was the starting quarterback. I couldn't touch that." In one scrimmage, Jackson caught a short screen pass, broke eight different tackles and ran for an 80-yard score. "And that," said Kyle Collins, an H-back, "was probably the hundredth most amazing thing I witnessed." The first, for many, had to be the time he jumped over a parked Volkswagen. On a dare. For shits and giggles. "There was no one like him," said Woods. "Anywhere, ever."

On August 28, 1982, an Associated Press piece headlined AUBURN'S JACKSON MAY BE NEW PHENOM hit the wires. It served as the nation's first real introduction to Vincent "Bo" Jackson, and opened thusly . . .

> Vincent "Bo" Jackson was everything Bear Bryant wanted in a running back.
> Size. Speed. Remarkable athletic ability. A physique that is presumably able to leap tall buildings in a single bound.
> He is, in short, a leading candidate for the freshman who will be most often compared to Herschel Walker this year. And everybody, from Alabama to Southern Cal, was after him.

> Pat Dye hated it.

The head coach was OK with rising expectation, but Jackson felt like a secret weapon that could be surreptitiously detonated. The less bluster, the better. "Pat was very uptight about Bo," said Marvin West, the *Knoxville News Sentinel* writer. "He thought he could shelter him and keep all of us from knowing."

For the first time in years, Auburn football had legitimate expectations of competing in the loaded Southeastern Conference. The Tigers returned all but seven starters, including the entire defensive backfield. But, in the eyes of the gridiron media, the difference maker was Jackson. In advance of the September 11 opener against Wake Forest, a surprising number of journalists found themselves in Auburn, trying to separate hype from reality. MEET AUBURN'S NO. 34—screamed a headline in the *Atlanta Constitution.* BO JACKSON MAY BE SPARK FOR AUBURN OFFENSE—raved the *Anniston Star.* Dye tried extinguishing the hype, with little success. "We're glad we have a player the fans feel excited about," he said. "If Bo Jackson rushes for two hundred yards against Wake Forest, I wouldn't get too excited. We all know Bo can run fast and jump high. We know all the wonderful things he can do. We're just waiting for him to prove them on the grass during a game."

Kickoff was at six o'clock, and a crowd of 59,350 fans entered Jordan-Hare Stadium. As the Bo Jackson buzz intensified, Dye kept pressing the mute button. First by insisting the kid had much to learn. Second by insisting the kid might not play a ton. Third by starting a backfield of James, halfback Willie Howell and fullback Ron O'Neal. Behind the scenes, however, Dye recognized the weapon at his disposal. "Ignore everything I say to the press," he whispered to Jackson. "Expect to play a lot."

Dye insisted his men arrive at the stadium four hours early. Football was a game of highs and lows, and he wanted the Tigers in the right emotional place to play with what he often referred to as a "controlled fury." So as Dye strolled from locker to locker in the lead-up to the opener, he found some players pacing, some players bobbing their heads to music, some players chatting, some players chanting, some players gazing over scouting reports.

And Bo Jackson sleeping.

Yes, sleeping. In two folding chairs in front of a locker, shoulder pads set aside, feet propped up, the sound of gentle snoring emerging from his nostrils. None of the Tigers coaches had seen anything like it. "Maybe," Dye recalled thinking, "that's a sign he is nervous." Was this Bo Jackson preparing, or Bo Jackson not taking the afternoon particularly serious? Could he arise from a deep slumber and perform? Would he sleepwalk through the Deacons?

"Snoozing before a football game?" said James. "*That* was weird."

To attend an Auburn home game is to have one's senses exposed to five hundred competing sights, smells and sounds. The "War Eagle!" battle cry is screamed once every 1.3 seconds. The fight song, also titled "War Eagle!," is played incessantly. One cannot hear himself think. Or talk. Tigers players are gladiators entering the round. "The fans are as loyal as any in the country," said James. "As long as you're playing well."

When Jackson first jogged onto the field to start Auburn's second possession, it was as if a crown prince was entering his kingdom. Everything about the nineteen-year-old felt regal. The upright way he walked on the tip of his toes. The perfectly horizontal shoulder pads. Local fans had heard enough about the newbie to develop expectations, and the literal sight of Jackson somehow exceeded them.

Then—he carried the ball.

In his 1990 autobiography, *Bo Knows Bo*, Jackson recalled a disastrous first-ever run, when he took the ball from Randy Campbell and slammed into the line for no gain. This is not what happened. Or even close to what happened. Jack Crowe, the offensive coordinator, wanted to break the freshman in easily, so he told Campbell to call a straight, up-the-middle handoff to Jackson. Standing in the huddle alongside his new teammate, James said loudly, "When we get you the ball, haul ass!" Seconds later, Campbell took the snap from center Bishop Reeves, turned, placed the ball in the freshman's chest and

ZOOM!

At first blush, the play appears relatively conventional. But watch again. Jackson bursts up the middle, past Reeves's (large) posterior and into the Wake Forest defensive line, where he causes a pair of oncoming tacklers to miss with barely perceptible jukes that combine one hundred twitches into one. The run, all of 11 yards, doesn't make the list of Jackson's ten thousand greatest sports moments. But from the sideline, Crowe was thunderstruck. "This guy," he yelled to Dye, "is different level!"

Jackson scored from the Wake Forest one-yard line when he bowled over two defensive backs for a touchdown. Later in the fourth quarter, with the Tigers up 21–10, Campbell rolled right, with the option to either keep the ball or pitch it. He kept it, kept it, kept it, kept it—then, a quick backward flip. Jackson reached up with both hands, ripped the ball from the air and exploded down the right sideline, rolling 44 yards untouched. The noise was deafening, and teammates swarmed their new superstar.

The 28–10 win was special, and afterward Dye did his best to spread the love. Campbell, he said, ran the offense like a conductor. James was the type of veteran any competitive team needed. The defense made the life of Gary Schofield, Wake's savvy quarterback, miserable. But the storyline was obvious. Jackson ran for 123 yards and two touchdowns on 10 carries.

"[Jack Crowe and I] were walking off the field after the game," Dye recalled. "I said to Jack, 'I don't want to tell you how to do your business over there, but you might want to think about making that guy your featured back.'"

Football stardom at Auburn University is a magical thing.

You are the king of the land.

You are easily recognized.

You sign autographs. You pose for photos. You have a harem of women to choose from.

"It is," said Campbell, the quarterback, "pretty darn sweet."

In the aftermath of his debut, Jackson was promoted to the starting lineup, and the next two weeks he soared in home wins over Southern Miss (Jackson ran for 99 yards and a touchdown) and Tennessee (17 carries, 110 yards, one touchdown). He was an instant phenomenon, and area sporting goods stores rushed to stock as many number 34 jerseys and "Go Bo" bumper stickers as possible. A month earlier, Jackson could walk on campus unbothered and unrecognized. Those days were over.

So, again, football stardom at Auburn is a magical thing. Yet there is also something inherently off-putting. When Jackson arrived, he and the vast majority of football and basketball players were assigned to Sewell Hall, a twenty-year-old brick building with three stories located on the corner of Samford and Donahue. Named after a deceased booster named Roy B. Sewell, the dormitory housed 144 athletes, and provided a private dining hall run by Anne Graves, the head dietician. "Sewell was the most fantastic place on campus," said David Jordan, a junior offensive lineman. "We all had this bond of being athletes, we all ate together. You'd have guys blasting music, guys talking trash. It felt like a community within a community."

There is much truth to this. Sewell was home to the biggest on-campus celebrities—Charles Barkley and Chuck Person, basketball stars with bright NBA futures. Lionel James and, now, Jackson. There were regular pizza deliveries, and balcony water balloon launches, and . . .

It was an isolation chamber.

A solid 95 percent of Jackson's engagements involved fellow athletes. He would walk to classes, then sit in classes, then leave classes. Peers pointed and waved and, on occasion, complimented the latest win. But otherwise, he was not an Auburn student, so much as an Auburn celebrity athlete who happened to partake in the bare minimum of campus life. And while this wasn't entirely by sinister design, the whole jocks-in-a-bubble arrangement served a purpose in the socially restrained universe that was (and remains) Auburn University—where 2 percent of the student body was Black. Namely, white parents who sent their precious daughters to college to (a) land an education and (b) land a husband wouldn't have to worry about Annabelle Blanche, recent high school magnolia queen, fucking/dating/marrying someone Black. "There was a good amount of, 'Why are all these n----s in here,'" said David King, a defensive back. "Then, 'Oh, no, that's David King. He's on the football team.' Like knowing that made my presence acceptable."

As Jackson was emerging as the king of Auburn football, the redbrick Kappa Alpha fraternity house was one of the centerpieces of student life. Born in 1865 with Robert E. Lee as its "spiritual founder," KA was best known for its enormous confederate flag that waved in the wind and its annual Old South Parade—a procession from the frat house down College Street and back where (according to fraternity literature), "we turn back the hands of time to the period when the South flourished." The event was held every April, the month of Confederate Memorial Day.

The vast majority of Auburn's student body seemed to love the Old South Parade. The all-white KA brothers dressed in confederate Civil War uniforms while riding horses. Their (all-white) girlfriends, meanwhile, transformed into Southern belles by breaking out antebellum dresses with matching parasols. It was a return to the good ol' plantation days, capped off (and this is not a misprint) by the dozen or so local Black children the brothers of Kappa Alpha hired to (again—not a misprint) dress as slaves. Once a Black student named Nedra Dodds led a petition drive to end the Old South celebration. She approached James Everett Martin, a former KA brother and now the university president, seeking support.

Martin's response: "What's the big deal?"

In the October 14, 1982, edition of the *Auburn Plainsman*, a columnist named Sean Bowlin wrote of his experience attending a fraternity party after transferring from the University of Montana.

> The brothers were nice guys—they treated me with the hospitality that the South is renowned for. I really felt at ease.
>
> That is, until the subject of race came up.
>
> "What? Y'all had n-----s in your frat out there?" one of my hosts inquired.
>
> I replied affirmatively.
>
> The guy shook his head. "I can't believe that, man. If we ever did anything like that here, we'd be the laughingstock of the campus."

In its one-hundred-twenty-three-year history, Auburn had never had a Black student pledge a (non-Black) fraternity. Or a Black student win homecoming king or queen. Or a Black student serve as editor of the student newspaper or student yearbook. When, in 1954, the Supreme Court overruled the separate-but-equal doctrine with its *Brown v. Board of Education* decision, Ralph B. Draughon, the acting president, spoke out against the decision for fear that it would spark "demagogues." The university didn't accept a Black applicant for ten more years, until Harold Franklin transferred in from Alabama State. "They made it clear I wasn't wanted," recalled Franklin. "I lived on campus, and they gave me a whole wing of a dormitory to myself. They emptied the entire wing and allowed me no neighbors. A few whites shook my hand. Most ignored me. And some would call me on the phone, call me a n----r and hang up. That was my Auburn experience."

During Jackson's freshman year, George Wallace, the former (and future) governor and renowned segregationist, came to campus and spoke before a fawning crowd. When, in 1985, a federal judge ruled that Auburn was the most racially segregated of Alabama's state universities, the news was greeted with a nod and a shrug. Wrote Judge U. W. Clemon: "The evidence tends to support the widespread perception of Blacks in Alabama that, except for the presence of Black athletes and the changes mandated by federal laws and regulations, Auburn's racial attitudes have changed little since the '50s."

To be a white student at Auburn was to love every second of the experience. The university, one and all (white alum) insist, is less school, more family.

To be a Black (non-athlete) Auburn student in the 1980s was to face loneliness, skepticism, strange looks, and stranger questions. Talk to most white alum from the era, and they'll rave about their favorite local restaurants and bars. For the majority of Black students at Auburn, weekends out involved a nineteen-mile drive southwest to Tuskegee, home to famed HBCU Tuskegee Institute. "If you were a Black Auburn student, you understood where you were welcome and where you weren't welcome near campus," said Dorcas Washington, an African American 1988 Auburn grad. "It wasn't stated, but you knew." In 1985 the *Detroit Free Press* ran a piece headlined BLACK STUDENTS AT AUBURN FIGHT FEELINGS OF ISOLATION, which included a quote from one Black student, Mary McGowan Robinson, that spoke for nearly all: "When I first came here, I could walk on campus and not see another Black the entire day. I remember sitting outside my dorm waiting for a Black person to pass. That's how badly I wanted somebody to talk to. I just sat there and waited."

Because they lived in their own building, with their own chef and their own dining hall and their own dorm monitors (home-away-from-home parents Rusty and Sally Dean), Auburn's minority football players were usually lulled into a sense of blissful unawareness. Dodds, who dated King, a Black defensive back, repeatedly explained to her boyfriend, "You have no real idea what it's like to be Black here."

"Sure I do," King would reply. "I'm Black. I see stuff, too."

"No," Dodds said. "You don't."

And he didn't. Not really. He and his fellow gladiators were campus royalty, to be feted and admired. For example, Auburn's football players were welcome to show up at Kappa Alpha events, because they were Auburn football players. But at the university there was a rule, rarely discussed yet understood, that Auburn's Black football players knew to take seriously: They were not to date white girls.

To be more precise: They were *not to be seen* dating white girls.

Shortly before Dye was hired, a fringe Black player was dismissed from the team after impregnating two white students. "That was the end of him," said one teammate, who requested anonymity. "There were things you could not do." Although Dye was fairly progressive in his views of race, certain lines were not to be crossed. Before he dated Dodds, for example, King—a sophomore from Fairhope, Alabama—was in a relationship with a white coed. "And I was fairly vocal about it," he said. "Meaning I'd go out dancing with her, I brought her to meetings, to team parties. And I think Coach Dye would have been more OK with it were we not being seen. It was made very clear it was not a thing to be doing as a representative of Auburn football."

James, the standout halfback, loved much about his Auburn experience, and thought warmly of the university until his death in 2022. But there were nights, he admitted, when he would lie awake in his Sewell Hall bed and find himself horrified by the hypocrisy. "I'm bleeding for y'all," he said. "I'm giving everything I have for y'all. But God forbid I date one of your women. God forbid I date a white girl on this campus. Before one game against Florida I broke all of my fingers, but played through it. I did that for Auburn. *For Auburn.* But what was I to these people? Was I part of the family? Or was I a n----r who carried a football?"

King and James were two of many African American players to have sexual relations with white girls. Jackson—who received an endless number of "lust letters" (his words) from female fans—was another. In the aftermath of a lengthy high school courtship, the freshman rarely turned down the opportunity to fool around. "I've had some of my best games right after I got laid," he said. "When I was in college that was a ritual. To get laid Friday night before a game. Or to get up early Saturday morning, run across campus and get laid, then be back at the dorm before anybody wakes up."

If the coaches knew (and, according to several Auburn players, they did know), eyes were diverted elsewhere. Yes, sexual relations between people of different races were strongly discouraged. But exceptions could be made for generational halfbacks with 4.2 speed.

"So," said King, "Bo got away with it."

With increased production, Jackson pretty much got away with everything. Seven games into the season, Auburn sat at 6-1 and Jackson was a darling of the SEC. "Failure to get Jackson the ball," wrote Mike Babcock of the *Lincoln* (Nebraska) *Star*, "is like trying to win the Kentucky Derby with a mule." His 520 rushing yard through seven games ranked second in the conference (first among all freshmen—despite missing 1½ games because of a bruised thigh), and the comparisons to Herschel Walker, Georgia's splendid junior halfback, were appropriate. Wrote Mark Stevenson, assistant sports editor of Auburn's student newspaper, the *Plainsman*:

> Both are big, strong and outrageously fast. Both were high school All-Americans and both run track. Both run through arm tackles as if they weren't there, and both can accelerate like a scared Maserati. And both wear number 34. Does Jackson mind the inevitable comparisons with Walker? "No. They go in one ear and out the other," he says, carefully measuring each word. "I am myself."

The major difference was approach. Walker was tireless. His nightly fitness regimens had gained mythological status (depending on who you asked, Walker either did five hundred, five thousand, or fifty thousand crunches before bed), as had his restrictive eating habits. Georgia's star was *only* about achieving greatness. Jackson, on the other hand, was privately picking up the reputation as a half-assed practice player who coasted on ability and avoided the weight room at all costs. Back at McAdory, the football and baseball coaching staffs occasionally struggled to have Jackson give 100 percent effort. Even 60 percent effort. They assumed college life would awaken the kid to the importance of hard work.

Over the final week of October, the Tigers prepared for a trip to Gainesville to take on the University of Florida in what was deemed one of the marquee SEC matchups of the season. "This is not football," sports editor Darryal Ray wrote in the *Alabama Journal*. "This is war." With a 4-2 record, the Gators were a strong test. Their defense, in particular, was led by two of America's elite linebackers, Fernando Jackson and future Chicago Bears star Wilber Marshall. "There were six or seven guys on our unit who were NFL caliber," said Tony Lilly, Florida's free safety. "We'd been hearing about this freshman, and when you're an upperclassman all you want to do is shut that kid down. So our focus in practice, really, was killing Bo Jackson."

Jackson was no longer a secret weapon. If anything, he was a flashing bolt of lightning. But he didn't act like it. His work habits stunk. His moderate interest in the playbook was irritating. Nothing was crisp or precise. The Florida contest meant everything to Dye and Co., but seemingly little to

Jackson. Perhaps that's why, during a practice leading up to the game, Bud Casey greeted Jackson's listlessness by grabbing him by the face mask and screaming—for all to hear—"Bo, wake the fuck up!"

Everything stopped.

Casey was an ornery lawn gnome. He spoke with a thick Alabama drawl and was raised to believe college players (especially Black college players) existed to take a coach's abuse. He had two catchphrases—"Fast backs and Cadillacs!" and "Blood on the saddle!"—that were repeated ad nauseam. A few years earlier, he tried motivating the halfback Sam Dejarnette by head-butting his helmet. A huge gash opened up above Casey's eyes, but he refused to wipe away the blood.

"Lord, Coach Casey was nonstop," said Forrest Benson, a linebacker. "Bo got so sick and tired of him."

Jackson could take some yelling. The grabbing of the face mask was a step too far. He wildly shook his head back and forth, dislodging Casey's hand.

"Coach," he said. "Don't you ever do that again."

Casey chuckled awkwardly.

"No," Jackson said. "I mean it. Don't ever grab me."

This had never happened before to Bud Casey. It had been a mere thirteen years since James Owens, a running back out of Alabama's Fairfield High, became the program's first Black player, and while the barrier had been broken, real cultural changes dragged at a snail's pace. Black players were expected to know their place. Black players were expected to speak when spoken to. Black players were expected to understand that this gift could be taken away at any moment. Plenty of white Tiger players comfortably dropped the N-word in conversation, and it was incumbent upon Black players to turn the other cheek. Skim through the early to mid-1980s Auburn media guides, and a high percentage of white players are described as "hardworking" and "tough," a high percentage of Black players are "gifted" and "athletic." Auburn's thirteen-man coaching staff included but two African Americans, and one of the job requirements was reporting back to Dye on the attitudes of Black players. "Spy on us," said Chuck Clanton, a defensive back. "Keep us in check."

And now here was Bo Jackson, a freshman, threatening an assistant coach?

Pat Dye did nothing. By now he had enough of a feel for his freshman star to know he marched to a different beat. If Jackson didn't practice quite as hard as the others, that would have to be OK. And if he napped during an occasional talk—also OK. And if he told Bud Casey to back off—was anyone really being hurt?

The kickoff in Gainesville was scheduled for 1:30, and despite a pulsating sun and temperatures that hit the eighties, a record 73,532 Gator loyalists filed into Florida Field to observe what they hoped would be the crushing of freshman hype. Over the next sixty minutes, Jackson and James endured a steady stream of trash talk from Florida's defenders, while being held to a combined 57 yards on 16 carries. Jackson even fumbled an exchange with Randy Campbell—a first for both men. "Wherever Jackson went," Mike Marshall wrote in the *Plainsman*, "four or five Gators were sure to be." But despite the Tigers being outgained by more than 200 yards, they led until the final second of play, when a walk-on kicker named Jim Gainey booted a 42-yard field goal to give the home team a shocking 19–17 triumph.

Afterward, the Auburn locker room was silent. Elliott Laudermann, representative of the Sugar Bowl, had been on hand to watch Auburn in person—the idea being that a Bo Jackson appearance could boost bowl buzz. Now, with two losses, that was out of the question.

"There were games when Bo didn't show up," said Jack Crowe, the offensive coordinator. "Either he wasn't into it, or he wasn't motivated. When that happened, we were in trouble.

"We needed Bo all in to win."

CHAPTER 7

BUS STATION

He was, by most appearances, happy.

That's the thing about being a rapid rise college football star with a shy demeanor, a crippling stutter and a skin color that doesn't align with an isolated bubble's majority.

Happiness can be more perception than reality.

So, to observe Bo Jackson as an Auburn freshman was to observe someone who seemed to be living atop the world. Inside Sewell Hall, he and his roommate, fullback Tommie Agee, got along splendidly, and they split a suite with two other agreeable teammates—halfback Lionel James and defensive end Jeff Jackson. "There was a little hallway that connected the rooms," said James, "and we all shared a bathroom. We only had one shower, so you were always waiting for someone to finish. But other than that, it was good living." The athletes-only dining hall was paradise of steak, shrimp and lobster. "SEC football players," Melissa Harris, an Auburn student, wrote in the school paper, "eat better than your typical OPEC head of state." The travel to road games was, for a kid who'd never before flown on a commercial airplane, exciting and glamorous.

And yet, decades before college programs knew to focus on the mental health of its students, the star freshman was struggling with loneliness, homesickness and depression. He missed his mother, missed his siblings, missed the familiarity and ease of McAdory High. His discomfort could be seen in the morning-to-night habitual bending and chewing of a soda straw. It was his (sort of gross) security blanket. In college, everything moved so swiftly. There was always somewhere to go, something to do. An interview with yet another nameless reporter. A request to speak with a disabled kid. Boosters to chat up. Alum to bore him with stories of yesteryear. The practices and workouts, meanwhile, were interminable. What was the point? Whether he lifted weights or not, he was the baddest cat on the field. Pat Dye was a taskmaster. Bud Casey, the running backs coach, was an asshole. The offensive coordinator, a first-year import from Wyoming named Jack Crowe, could not have been less imaginative or inventive. "He was the worst fucking offensive coordinator ever, and we all knew it," said Vince Thompson, a student assistant sports information director. "All the things Bo could do, and Crowe didn't see it."

The week after the Florida loss, Auburn rebounded with a resounding 30–7 homecoming destruction of Rutgers, during which Jackson ran wild for 114 yards on 15 carries. Within twenty-four hours, however, focus shifted to Herschel Walker and the number 1 Georgia Bulldogs, who would travel to Auburn the following Saturday. The worst part—the part that Jackson wanted no part of—was the inevitable machine-gun firing line of questions. And questions. And questions. And questions.

He was the unofficial second coming of Walker, and reporters needed to know about it. Walker was 6-foot-1, 222 pounds. Jackson was 6-foot-1, 224 pounds. Both wore number 34, both came from small towns (Walker hailed from Wrightsville, Georgia) with a long string of siblings (Walker was one of seven), both had patched-jeans upbringings, both reinvigorated downtrodden home-state college football programs. Both were soft-spoken and a little awkward. "Bo could be another Herschel Walker," Dooley said in the days before the game. "There's no doubt in my mind I would not like to see him run the ball thirty-five times like Herschel does."

Lord, Bo Jackson hated the attention. He played football because he wanted to sprint and leap and pummel the opposition. Not to talk to a reporter from a newspaper he'd never heard of for an article he'd never read. By the time that Saturday's game arrived, he was exhausted. Georgia took a surprisingly close 19–14 decision, and while Walker soared with 177 yards on 31 carries, it was James (111 yards and a touchdown on eight attempts) who kept the Tigers close. Jackson's 58 rushing yards meant little. He was, on this rare occasion, invisible.

One regular season game remained.

But to reduce Auburn-Alabama to mere "regular game" status is to refer to Marilyn Monroe as *just* a movie star; to refer to the Beatles as a *mere* rock 'n' roll band.

Long considered one of the two or three most revered rivalries in college football, the Iron Bowl dates back to either (according to Alabama) 1892 or (according to Auburn) 1893. There's an exasperatingly dull saga about the Hows and Whys of the matchup's origins, but the story of Alabama v. Auburn isn't a history tale, so much as a Hatfields v. McCoys sociological study.

In the book *The Uncivil War: A Look at the Rivalry That Divides Families, Friends, and an Entire State!*, author Scott Brown breaks it down thusly . . .

In general, Alabama people think of Auburn followers as low-class rednecks lucky to have the Crimson Tide on their schedule. Auburn, in turn, views Bama as a bunch of spoiled smoke blowers living off Daddy's money. Obviously, neither perception is true, but a deep socially based resentment between the two camps has existed since the beginning.

"I'd rather beat Alabama on a technicality and listen to them bitch for a year than blow them out," said Forrest Benson, an Auburn linebacker. "I hate them." Entering the 1982 meeting, Alabama had won twenty-eight of the forty-six all-time Iron Bowls, including the last nine in a row. And while Auburn was coached by the impressive Pat Dye, the Crimson Tide program was headed by the greatest of all legends, Bear Bryant.

Moment of silence, please.

In 1981, at age sixty-eight, Bryant became college football's all-time winningest coach, surpassing Amos Alonzo Stagg with his 315th triumph against (of all the schools) Auburn. He was the icon of icons—houndstooth hat and jacket, ironworker's jaw, a look that could melt ice sculptures. But he was also losing it. Bryant was often intoxicated. He fell asleep during events. Whereas once he was America's greatest recruiter, he was now often outworked and outhustled. Not merely by the Southern Cals of the landscape. By Auburn. Even though the 1982 season was yet to reach its conclusion, Alabama was pilloried for its inability to add Bo Jackson, the type of in-state star who should have automatically signed with the Tide.

In the days before Alabama and Auburn would meet at Birmingham's Legion Field (the standard neutral site), there was much to discuss and much to debate. In the midst of a two-game losing streak, the Tide had sunk from perceived national championship contender (Alabama was once ranked in the Top 5 in every poll) to a ship spiraling out of control. After a loss to LSU in Birmingham, Don Kauser, Jr., of the *Birmingham News* did the unthinkable and called for Bryant's retirement. Over the following days a slew of death threats streamed into the newspaper's office. In his defense, Kauser was correct. Interviewed by the *Atlanta Constitution* a few weeks later, Bryant admitted, glumly, "I can't coach them anymore."

Auburn, on the other hand, was earning praise for nearly toppling

Georgia. The Tigers were a program on the rise, and media near and far wanted to hear about all the excitement.

Bo Jackson had no interest.

None.

As a kid from Alabama who had been marginally recruited by the Crimson Tide, this game was supposed to stir his soul. In the minds of local reporters, it *had* to stir his soul. But Jackson was never a rah-rah type. He didn't clap when his team won, didn't sob when his team lost. The term "grudge match" wasn't a concept. "He was just a young guy who liked to play football," said Chris Woods, an Auburn wide receiver. "All the extra stuff meant nothing to Bo."

And now, with the pressure mounting and the season feeling interminable and the requests pouring in, he aspired to disappear.

So, in the lead-up to Alabama, that's what he did.

It was a weeknight, and when no one was paying attention Jackson slipped into Woods's dormitory room, grabbed the keys to his car and drove the ten miles to the Greyhound bus station in Opelika. "He left me an apologetic note," Woods recalled, "and told me where the car would be parked."

Jackson paid the eight dollars for a one-way ticket to the Fourth Avenue North station in Bessemer. And then he sat. And sat. And sat. And sat. One hour passed. Two hours passed. Three hours passed. "Every time a bus would leave," Jackson said, "I'd say to myself, 'I'll catch the next one.'" When Woods saw the note on his desk, he reached out to a handful of teammates. "There was a little ice cream place, Sani-Freeze, near the station," recalled Joel Gregg, a freshman fullback. "Tommie Agee and I went over there, got some ice cream, then walked in to talk to Bo. I swear, all he had was a damn paper bag with some of his stuff in it."

If Gregg and Agee weren't overly alarmed, it's because this wasn't Jackson's first threat of departure. Earlier in the season, after a particularly rough practice, he had entered Dye's office to say, bluntly, "I quit."

"What?" Dye said.

"I'm done," Jackson replied. "I'm not having fun."

The head coach asked Lionel James to speak with the youngster. "I told Bo the truth," James recalled. "That this won't get easier. That football is hard work. But that he'll regret it for his entire life."

Now Jackson again prepared to leave it all behind. Gregg and Agee departed the station, uncertain how this would end. Buses came, buses went, Jackson remained. "I sat for about seven hours," he said. "Then after a while the guy that was cleaning up said, 'Look, you're either gonna have to get on a bus, or you're gonna have to leave."

Jackson dropped a dime in a pay phone and dialed the home number of Bobby Wallace, Auburn's defensive backs coach and the man who had recruited him. It was about one thirty in the morning—three and a half hours past curfew. A groggy Wallace answered, shocked to hear the gentle voice of a lost superstar.

"Coach," Jackson said, "I'm at the bus station and I'm thinking of leaving."

By the time Wallace arrived it was after two o'clock. He and Jackson sat outside, on a wood bench beneath a lamp, and chatted for an hour and a half. Of all the Auburn staffers, Wallace was the one who best understood Jackson wasn't a player moved by threats or a sucker for overblown oratory.

"Let me ask you a question," Wallace said. "Have you thought about what your life would be if you leave college?"

The halfback had not.

Wallace explained to Jackson that the world was filled with bypassed opportunities. That for every star athlete living the dream, there were a hundred who gave up because they were too scared, or too overwhelmed, or too lazy.

"I sat there," Jackson recalled. "At that point, everybody at home thinks the world of me. And my mom's proud of me, my brothers and sisters are proud of me. What the hell would they think if I just up and quit? When I literally got the world in my hand, what would they think if I just quit? I'd just go home and hang around the neighborhood doing nothing. And the more I thought about that, the more I realized I didn't want that to happen to me. [I thought about] some guys I grew up with hanging around the neighborhood. I just said that is not what I wanted."

The next day, Jackson found himself back at practice, holding a pair of cinder blocks and completing stadium steps.

He had no complaint.

The Auburn-Alabama kickoff was scheduled for 11:35 a.m. on November 27.

For both teams, the nerves were real and the lead-up unusually rocky. Citing a lack of a "winning attitude," Bryant dismissed three of his players from the roster, including halfback Ken Simon, a former captain. "They just aren't helping the team and I think it best for them to spend all their time studying," Bryant explained.

On the Auburn side, Jackson's near-departure was only part of the drama. Three Tigers—fullback Ron O'Neal and defensive backs Johnny Cheeks and Greg Tutt—were caught smoking marijuana in their hotel room the night before the game. Dye was furious, and walked up to Cheeks during a team meal and said, "Hey, Johnny, you're feeling really good, huh? I bet you're feeling really good." After initially deciding to send all three home, Dye changed his mind and benched the trio for much of the first half.

In his defense, Dye had much on his mind. That week the coach relocated practices from outdoors to the enclosed bubble, where he and Crowe surreptitiously switched from the familiar wishbone offense to the I—two backs lined up directly behind quarterback. It was not unlike a lifelong right-handed boxer going southpaw for a title shot. In this case, Dye believed a senile Bryant would be unable to adjust to a different look. Wrote Will Collier, "Dye intended to walk into Legion Field loaded for Bear."

And now, at long last, the Iron Bowl was here.

An hour or so before kickoff, players jogged out for warm-ups beneath a leaden gray sky and the slight chance of rain. The temperatures hovered in the low sixties. Legion Field held 78,170 seats, and with its proximity to the University of Alabama (the Crimson Tide had 54 miles to travel, the Tigers 112), the vast majority would be filled with fans wearing crimson and white. Every spot in the press box was filled. The Goodyear Blimp hung in the sky. This wasn't merely a football game. "Everything else in the state stops that day," Christopher J. Walsh once wrote, "and those who relocate there are asked to declare an allegiance almost immediately."

The general consensus was that 'Bama, recently ranked as high as seventeenth nationally, had enough firepower to vanquish unranked Auburn for a tenth straight year. Keith Jackson, however, wasn't so certain. The veteran broadcaster would be calling the game on ABC, and beforehand he told Jim Fyffe, the Tigers play-by-play announcer, that he thought the Tide would be upset. "Auburn," Jackson said, "is simply hungrier."

Alabama felt old and outdated, Bing Crosby in a Twisted Sister era. Whereas Bryant was once an elite motivator, he now shuffled along as an old man, chain-smoking cigarettes and downing whiskey out of his players' view. "He'd be gone from practices for a couple of days," said Tommy Wilcox, a defensive back. "We'd hear rumors that he fell in the shower or something like that. Then he'd return like nothing had happened." One week earlier, Bryant's team lost to Southern Mississippi and the coach appeared zombie-like.

In the moments before Auburn-Alabama, Bryant and Dye met on the field for a chat. "Coach," Bryant said, "this may well be my last season walking the sideline."

It wasn't a well-hidden secret.

"If you're really getting out," Dye told his former boss, "I'll let you have this one last win."

"Well," Bryant said, "that'd sure be appreciated."

An enormous chunk of Dye's pitch to recruits involved Alabama, and how the bigger, more successful, more famous program didn't want them. "Coach Dye came to my house and said to me, 'How would you like to go change the history of the state of Alabama?'" recalled Steve Wallace, an offensive lineman from Atlanta. "'How would you like to change the culture?' That's a pretty powerful sales pitch."

"There was a stretch of time when we practiced five times per day," said Tim Jessie, the halfback. "It sounds crazy, right? But Coach Dye knew Alabama was practicing four times a day. So we had to do better."

Auburn held a 14–13 halftime advantage, and Alabama's biggest first-half accomplishment was keeping Jackson in check. The Tigers had gained a paltry 99 yards in total offense. Alabama gained 284. "It was one of the hardest-hitting games I ever played in," said Paul Tripoli, a Tide defensive back. "We brought everything out."

Alabama opened the second half with a lengthy drive capped by Paul Ott Carruth's 8-yard touchdown run and a 19–14 lead. On the Auburn sideline, Dye was turning testy. This was not the plan. In Jackson and James, he had two of the best college runners on the planet. But Jackson was often a sleepy starter—unmoved by pep talks or pep bands; a tad unengaged until a series of jolts served as wake-up calls. "He was sometimes frustrating to coach, because his head would be elsewhere," said Casey. "And you'd be like, 'Bo, there's a game to be played! A really important game!' And suddenly, he'd come to life."

The exact moment occurred with nine minutes and six seconds remaining in the fourth quarter and Alabama up 22–14. It was second down and three, and the Tigers had the ball at their own 34. The I-formation plan had been a dud, and Auburn was back to its familiar wishbone—Randy Campbell lined up under center, Greg Pratt up front at fullback, James to the rear left, Jackson by his side. The Tide was playing a four-man front, with an extra lineman, Emanuel King, cheating up over the tight end.

Campbell handled the snap and flipped the ball to Jackson, who was sliding left behind James. Cornerback Mike O'Toole charged forward and

James sprung toward his knees. Jackson burst through the hole between left guard and tackle, past Steve Booker, a lunging linebacker, and into the secondary. With no one in sight, Jackson rocketed down the field (yelped Keith Jackson from the booth: "Bo Jackson! He! Breaks! It! Big!")—a terrifying white-and-blue tanklike blur. Jackson was a vision. Faster than any wide receiver. Stronger than any lineman. Perfect form. Perfect control. Finally, at the 13, he was crunched out of bounds by cornerback Jeremiah Castille.

Four plays later, Al Del Greco booted a 23-yard field goal, and with 9:06 remaining the Tigers trailed, 22–17.

"Auburn," Keith Jackson said, "is still in the hunt."

Randy Campbell was not a gifted Division I quarterback.

This might sound strange, considering that when he came out of Morgan County High in 1978, Campbell was Alabama's top-ranked prep signal caller. But back in the day, being highly regarded at the position was mostly about one's ability to not screw up. "Nowadays, if you're number one in the state you've been throwing thirty to forty times a game and you expect to be in the lineup as a college freshman," Campbell said in 2020. "But back then my goal was to start one year for Auburn. Just one."

Campbell entered the 1982 season having played only 13 varsity snaps. One season earlier he tore his quadricep. The year before that he injured his knee. His arm was below average. His strength was below average. Spirals were rare. His legs were pipe cleaners. Wrote Darryal Ray in the *Montgomery Observer*: "He is not fancy or flashy or even a very good passer, but Randy Campbell seldom makes mistakes." In the Auburn media guide, Campbell is described as "A Can't-Run-Can't-Throw-All-He-Does-Is-Beat-You Quarterback"—and clichéd-white-guy-descriptives aside, it was accurate. "Randy didn't have a lick of talent," said Ken Hobby, an Auburn quarterback in 1981–82. "I could do much more than he could, physically. But he had an enormous heart."

Entering the Alabama game, Campbell had yet to exceed 18 passing attempts in a single contest. His main job was game manager. But in the heart of the Iron Bowl, he was the center of attention. The Tide failed to score on its next drive, and with 7:06 left in the game the Tigers' offense took over at its own 33. Using a mix of throws, handoffs and pitches, he methodically marched Auburn into Alabama territory. "One thing about Randy," said James, "is you'd never see him sweat." On a third and 14 from the Alabama 45, the quarterback dropped back and hummed a tight spiral to wide receiver Mike Edwards, who corralled the ball along the sideline just beyond the 31. First down. "This is a great throw by Campbell!" raved Frank Broyles, Keith Jackson's broadcast partner. "Watch him rifle this ball!"

It was everything Campbell had dreamed of. Biggest game of the year, leading a charge.

But in high-level sports, talent (or lack thereof) tends to reveal itself. Two plays later, Campbell faked a handoff and lofted a helium balloon over the middle toward a streaking Chris Woods, the Tigers' best wide receiver. In the 17 hours it took for the pass to arrive, Castille slid inside of the wideout, extended his hands and snatched the ball from midair. The All-American returned it 18 yards, charged onto the Alabama sideline, threw his arms toward the sky and was absorbed by a sea of crimson-and-white teammates.

The game was over.

But, wait.

As Castille was basking in the glow of a lifetime of paid bar tabs in the greater Tuscaloosa area, Billy Teas, the back judge, tossed his yellow flag and called pass interference. It was a brutal miscarriage of football justice—Castille and Woods were both going for the ball.*

Instead of Alabama locking down the victory, Auburn had a fresh start on the Tide 9. The clock read 3:19.

"Well," said Keith Jackson, "my goodness . . ."

On first down, Jackson sliced left into the defense, juke stepped, hopped forward, then—with whistles being blown—was slung to the ground by Russ Wood, the Tide's 6-foot-3, 218-pound lineman. It was a cheap shot, and as Auburn was being punished with a five-yard offsides call, Jackson glared toward the offender.

"Try that again," he said. "Just try."

The Tigers faced first and goal from the 14, and Campbell's pass to Woods in the corner of the end zone was too wide, too soft, too late. This was a serious problem—the arm wasn't big enough for the moment. On the next play, he faked a handoff to James, then flipped the ball to Jackson, who beat Wood around end and cruised for five yards back to the Alabama 9.

---

* Ed Hinton, a longtime sportswriter, lived near Teas in Atlanta. "Billy knew as soon as he threw that flag that he wanted it back," Hinton said. "It was Bear's last game, and that call ruined everything that was supposed to happen. The implications were enormous. Billy got phone calls about it. He was criticized about it. He was just sick. Billy had a drinking problem before he died, and every day he'd sit on his patio and drink and agonize over it. I'd tell him, 'Billy, you did the right thing.'"

Following a time out, Auburn returned for third down with the strangest of formations—O'Neal by himself behind Campbell, Jackson lined up as a tight end, two wide receivers wide right and one in the left slot. The ball was snapped and Campbell rolled out right. Covered one on one by the too small (5-foot-11, 195 pounds), too slow (4.65 40) Tommy Wilcox, Jackson ran straight to the 5-yard line, then cut hard right, where Campbell threw him a perfect strike. The running back headed toward the end zone and was met by Wilcox and Castille. The defensive backs converged on Jackson, hitting him so low that he sprung high into the air before landing on his head—just outside of pay dirt.

"He's a foot away!" yelled Keith Jackson. "Just a foot!"

It was now fourth down, with 18 inches standing between the Auburn offense and eternal glory. There was 2:30 on the clock.

On the sideline, Pat Dye knew *exactly* what to do.

On November 24, 1982, the day before Thanksgiving, Auburn's football team held its final full pads practice in preparation for the Iron Bowl.

By now, Dye and his staff had seen enough tape on the Tide to understand the Tigers were facing some uphill battles. In particular, Alabama's defensive line was enormous (the four starters averaged 251 pounds*), and no matter the experience and intellect of Auburn's coaches, no one had developed a fail-proof approach to moving mountains. Casey and Crowe, the two assistant coaches, watched hours of film on the Tide. "We have to figure out something," Casey said, "because we can't block these guys."

The plan: If you can't relocate a mountain, take a former prep high jump champion and soar over it.

Wrote Ryan McGee in an exceptional 2018 piece for ESPN.com:

> That afternoon, as the rest of the team practiced, the two coaches grabbed two of their players—Jackson and Campbell—and walked them to a side field, where a high jump pad was waiting. Campbell would take the "snap" and hand it off to Jackson, who worked to see how much momentum he could build from a standing start in the back right corner of the wishbone, only four yards behind the line of scrimmage. Meanwhile, Casey recalled, he was constantly reminding the 18-year-old to keep his hands on the football.

---

* Keep in mind, this was 1982.

The following afternoon, the entire offense practiced the play without pads. This time, Jackson would take the handoff and pretend to leap as the offensive line collapsed toward the ground. "If you saw us running that in practice," Jackson said, "you would have thought, 'What in the hell are they doing? They've lost their minds. They'll never run this goofy play.'"

Auburn's playbook was thick and fairly complex. Everything had a name that incorporated letters and numbers. On the quick, Crowe termed this one simply "Bo Over The Top."

"In forty-something years of coaching, that's the only play I've had where we put a player's name in the name of the play," Crowe told McGee. "But Bo is also the only guy we would've run that play with."

Dye turned toward the field, pumped his fist and screamed, "Go get 'em!" The clock read 2:30. The scoreboard read ALABAMA 22, AUBURN 17. It was fourth down. There was little at stake, save the happiness, sanity and sense of self-worth of a long-suffering college fanbase. From the stands, the chant of DE-FENSE! DE-FENSE! was loud and clear. This was a neutral sight game in name only. Alabama was the home team.

"Give the ball to Jackson over the top," Broyles suggested from the booth.

Keith Jackson ignored him.

The play had been run once earlier in the game, and Jackson leapt for a first down. "I thought it was a terrible idea to do it again," said Steve Wallace, Auburn's starting right tackle. "Alabama knew exactly what we were gonna do. Every fan in the stadium knew what we were gonna do."

"It was obvious in the press box," said Charles Hollis, covering the game for the *Birmingham News*. "Bo Jackson via air."

Shortly before the call, Dye had grabbed Wallace by the face mask. "We're going right behind your big ass!" he yelled. "Don't mess this up."

As Auburn huddled 10 yards behind the line of scrimmage, three of Alabama's four interior linemen dropped to hands and knees, a literal digging into the trenches. In football nonverbals, it was a declaration: *Bring it!* Ken Donahue, the Tide defensive coordinator, calculated a zero percent chance of Campbell dropping back to throw, so he stacked all eleven men at the line—a tightly packed pyramid of crimson and white. As Auburn's players finally approached, they broke into a familiar formation: Campbell standing under center, O'Neal directly behind him, James to the left, Jackson to the right. There were no wide receivers, just seven hogs up front.

Campbell sauntered forward. Looked left. Looked right. The Tide linemen were screaming, "Bo right! Bo right!" to one another. "You could see six or seven of their guys fill that hole," said Wallace. "This wasn't gonna be a surprise." Campbell took the snap, turned to his right and, with O'Neal and James slamming into the line, handed off to a charging Jackson. As soon as he took possession of the ball at the 2-yard line, number 34 planted his feet, bent his knees and soared over Wallace and right guard David Jordan. Alabama's linemen were pancaked toward the turf (Wallace: "It's a little dirty, but we had to knock their legs out."), and Jackson reached his zenith at the goal line, extended his arms aaaannnnnndddd . . .

. . . leaned forward for the score.

"As I was falling down I stretched out and lunged forward and got the ball over the goal line," Jackson said. "I looked over at the sideline at Bear Bryant and he had a look on his face like someone had walked along and stepped on his sandcastle. And the other coach [Ken Donahue] that told me Auburn would never beat 'Bama, he sat there and he looked like he had just swallowed a piece of shit. And I looked at him—I didn't say nothing, I just looked at him. I took my helmet off, I looked at him and I walked off the field."

Though the two-point conversion failed, Auburn now led 23–22 with 2:26 remaining. On Alabama's ensuing possession, strong safety Bob Harris intercepted a Walter Lewis pass, and the game was over. The generally stoic Dye leapt up and down. His players hugged and danced and screamed in holy delight. On the opposing sideline, Bryant's face turned expressionless. The Tigers were 1:45 away from perhaps the biggest victory in school history.

"All Auburn wants to do is run it around," said Keith Jackson. "Run around. Run the clock down."

On first down, Campbell handed off to James for a 5-yard gain. The Auburn sideline was giddy.

On second down, Campbell handed off to James for a 4-yard gain. The Auburn sideline was even more giddy.

It was now third down and one. Alabama called its second time out, and those watching the game on TV saw a graphic announcing Jackson and Lewis as the day's Chevrolet Most Valuable Players. The freshman had carried 16 times for 110 yards and a touchdown. It was a no-brainer.

There was 1:13 left.

During the break in action Campbell conferred with Casey along the sideline. Casey placed his right hand on his quarterback's shoulder and said, "Bo Over The Top."

So Campbell returned to the huddle, faced Jackson and said, "You're going over the top again."

It was the same exact play.

Snap.

Turn.

Handoff.

Jackson stepping.

Jackson planting.

Jackson soaring.

Jackson . . .

. . . fumbling.

While flying through the air, Jackson allowed the loosely cradled football (Keith Jackson: "He held it out there like a loaf of bread!") to meet the helmet of Alabama's Mike Rodriguez. It popped loose and was scooped up by Russ Wood. "Alabama's got it!" Keith Jackson said. "Can you believe it? Alabama is not dead yet!"

In the Auburn radio booth, Fyffe sounded as if he was about to vomit: "Our worst fears," he said, "may have been realized."

Bo Jackson dropped to the ground and lay prone. He held his helmet in his crossed arms for four seconds, until Campbell came to help him up. "Coming off the field," Jackson recalled, "I just said to myself, 'That could lose us the ball game.'" Hundreds of Auburn students had left their seats after the touchdown leap, anxious to storm the turf when the clock struck 0:00. "So we're down at the fence, and we can't see anything but we hear this loud groan," recalled Jeff Stumb, a *Plainsman* editor who attended as a fan. "Someone says, 'Bo fumbled! Bo fumbled!' Oh my god. No, please. Nooooo . . ."

Fortunately for Jackson, the Tiger defense held Alabama in check, forcing Lewis to scramble around under duress and uncork a series of misguided ducks.* When Campbell fell on the ball to seal the Tigers' 23–22 triumph, Auburn students and fans rushed the field, charged past the billy club–armed police officers ("They were pounding people," said Tim Dorsey, a *Plainsman* editor. "It was terrifying."), ripped down a goalpost, and tore out keepsake chunks of Legion Field's Astroturf. It was the biggest win in school history, and Chris Martin, Auburn's Huntsville-born senior linebacker, could barely contain his giddiness. "My girlfriend goes to Alabama,"

---

* Mark Stevenson, the *Auburn Plainsman*'s assistant sports editor, wrote of the moment: "The defense was so fired up that it could have stopped the Four Horsemen of the Apocalypse with Beelzebub himself calling the signals."

he said. "I've been catching it from her. I've been catching it from my family. I've been catching it from everywhere. But now I can go anywhere."

The next day's *Tuscaloosa News* ran the front page headline THE WALLS COME TUMBLING DOWN ON BAMA. *The Plainsman*, Auburn's student newspaper, countered with a staff editorial beneath the words OH HELL YES!!!!!!!!!!! It perfectly captured the spirit.

> Everyone was intoxicated with the moment and we all went berserk. Students ran full-bore into each other and fell to the ground. We jumped on each other. We hugged each other. And everything that Auburn means to all of us gushed out. It was the bond—that indescribable thing that joins all Auburn people together. There's no way to explain the rapture that causes so many otherwise respectable people to lose their minds. But it is very good.

Dye found himself raised off his feet and onto the shoulders of his players. Tears streamed down his cheeks. He and Bryant met at midfield, where old coach congratulated pupil on a plan well executed.

It is impossible to know what Bear Bryant was thinking. He looked at the scoreboard, in author Scott Brown's words, "like a man who'd lost a child." Maybe he was pondering his retirement from coaching, which would be announced two weeks later. Maybe he was questioning his decision to replace Lewis for portions of the game with the erratic Ken Coley. Maybe he was wondering how his team could roll up 507 yards of total offense and lose. Maybe he was hoping to get home in time for *The Love Boat* and *Fantasy Island*.

Or maybe, just maybe, he was wondering why, in God's name, he hadn't signed Vincent "Bo" Jackson.

CHAPTER 8

OFF BASE

Bo Jackson couldn't have known in the moment, but the goal line leap over the University of Alabama was far more than mere goal line leap.

With that flight into the end zone, a seismic shift took place.

Bear Bryant, the Alabama coach who had paced the Crimson Tide sideline for twenty-five years, retired two weeks after the Auburn loss, then died of a massive heart attack the following January. While Alabama's football program continued to fight for top recruits and high rankings, the next two decades brought three different head coaches and but one national title. They went from The Program to *a program*.

Granted, Auburn would never overtake Alabama for in-state love. But it found itself with a perception-altering moment, as well as the Heart of Dixie's new icon.

His name was Vincent Jackson.

Across the state everyone now knew him as Bo. Not long after the Bama win, Jackson and a pal were walking through a mall when they stumbled upon a kiosk peddling cheapish "Bo Over The Top" plaques featuring a glossy photo of the play. "My friend knew the guys selling them," Jackson recalled. "They said, 'Why don't you buy one and take it to Bo?' I was standing right there. I laughed and walked off."

"In the eyes of fans," said Mark Stevenson, the *Auburn Plainsman* assistant sports editor, "he was the biggest thing around."

On December 18, 1982, the Tigers capped off one of the best seasons in program history with a 33–26 win over quarterback Doug Flutie and Boston College in the Tangerine Bowl in Orlando, Florida. Jackson ran for 64 yards and two scores against the Eagles, and 829 yards and nine scores on the season.

The flight back from Orlando took an hour and a half, and Jackson slept the entire way. He returned to Bessemer for Christmas break, and slept. He went back to Auburn after New Year's and slept. For most college football players, the aftermath of a season serves as a blissful compilation of napping, eating, drinking, partying. It's the payoff for stadium steps and 110-degree practices and pulverizing hits to the head.

Jackson's break lasted eighteen days.

On January 5, 1983, the nation's most impactful freshman football player sauntered over to the Hutsell Track, Auburn's outdoor facility, to join Coach Mel Rosen's indoor team as a sprinter. This was one of the concessions Pat Dye was willing to make when recruiting the youngster—if Jackson was insistent on competing in track and baseball, he would be allowed.

At age fifty-four and in his twentieth season, Rosen had led his squad to four straight SEC track-and-field titles. When Jackson and the other members of the team arrived for practice, Rosen gathered them in a circle and gave a small introductory chat. Then—"OK, guys, so now everyone here is going to line up and do a timed mile. I don't care if you're a thrower, a hurdler, a distance runner . . ."

Jackson, quiet but confident, raised his hand.

"Coach," he said. "I can't do distance."

"Well, Bo," Rosen replied, "I'm sorry, but I don't make exceptions."

This was not entirely true. Years earlier Harvey Glance, sprinter and 1976 Olympic gold medalist, was ordered to shave his mustache.

"No," Glance said.

"Yes," Rosen replied.

"No," Glance said.

"If you don't, you're off the team," Rosen replied.

"I guess I'm off the team," Glance said.

"You can stay. Keep the mustache," Rosen replied.

Now Rosen faced a similar dilemma. Was he really going to lose an instant star attraction in the name of a meaningless 1,500? "I'll tell you what," Rosen said to Jackson. "Here's the clipboard. Write down all the times and hand them back to me at the end."

"That," Jackson said, "I can do."

A few days later, Rosen held a 60-yard time trial for his sprinters. Calvin Brooks, a teammate who would become one of the great 400-meter runners of the era, watched silently. So did the other Tigers. Most sprinters were sinewy and smooth. Jackson was a pile of bricks. "Shoot, I saw him come out of the block, with the size and speed he had," Brooks recalled. "It almost didn't make sense. That much power in one human."

Jackson made his collegiate track debut on January 22, 1983, at the LSU Invitational in Baton Rouge. He had practiced with Rosen's team a handful of times, skipping one day to take some swings in the batting cage. In Louisiana, beneath the roof of the LSU Fieldhouse, the competition was no joke. Jackson would be facing some of the region's fastest men, including Rice University's Vince Courville, who a week earlier ran the 60 in 6.10 seconds. "We didn't know exactly what to expect," Rosen said of the LSU meet, "or what kind of shape he'd be in."

As Jackson walked toward the starting line for the 60-yard dash, he knew nothing of the competition. Names. Times. Histories. It was all a blur. Courville, however, recognized Bo Jackson. "You know how sometimes you see someone and size him up?" Courville recalled. "Well, I see Bo at the line, and he's probably two hundred fifteen pounds. Just cut. A big ol' dude. I say to myself, 'This is the preliminary, so just run well, get rid of this guy, advance to the finals.'"

The gun was fired. Jackson darted from the blocks. "Just—gone, like dust," said Courville. "I thought this was gonna be super easy, and I look up and he's run a six-flat on me. I come in second. To a freshman football player."

Jackson officially clocked an electronically timed 6.18, which was (ho-hum) *the fifth fastest 60 in Auburn history and qualified him for the NCAA championships.* "Think about that," said Brooks. "Seriously, think about that. It was his first-ever meet." In the finals, Jackson led Courville by half a stride for much of the race before being caught at the very end. His time (6.20) was far from a disappointment. "He's probably one of the top ten sprinters in the country," Rosen said afterward, "and one of our first choices to be invited to the Olympic Trials in '84."

The headline appeared atop the sports section of the February 3, 1983, *Auburn Plainsman*—in big, bold type for everyone to see: BO AND HERSCHEL TO RACE IN DALLAS.

The accompanying article was fairly pedestrian, but the implication behind it was not. A mere six months earlier, anyone reading such words would have rightly asked, "Bo who?" Now not only was Jackson the phenom of phenoms, but he would be competing against Georgia junior Herschel Walker—the phenom of phenoms *before* Bo became the phenom of phenoms.

Jackson had followed up his LSU breakout with another stunning performance, clocking a 6.19 to win the 60-yard dash at the Auburn Invitational. Generally, on Auburn's campus, indoor track and field went unnoticed. Thanks to Jackson's presence, however, the sport started to matter.

Students attended events. Alumni attended events. The *Plainsman* covered meets. But—and this was a big but—members of the team took issue with Jackson's practice attendance record. "Bo didn't come," said Chris Fox, a distance runner. "Most of us loved being around track and field. Just everything about it. I never got that from Bo. It sort of seemed more like a chore."

"He'd show up when we had meets," said Brooks. "He'd come, run his six-something, take off. He was on the team, not really a part of the team. In his defense, he had so many things going on."

The Dallas Times Invitational was scheduled for February 5, 1983, and the day before Rosen drove Auburn's three participants (Fox, Jackson and Roger Jones, a distance runner) to Birmingham Airport for the flight to Dallas. En route, the car broke down on the side of the road, and Rosen glumly stared at the dashboard, which had gone dark.

"Coach," Fox said, "we can all get out and push the car to the side . . ."

Jackson interrupted. "I'll do it myself."

He opened the door, stepped outside and—with three full-grown men in their seats—shoved the vehicle a good thirty feet. "It felt like we were going twenty-five miles an hour," Fox said. "You could feel the energy and the power." Jackson had barely worked up a sweat.

The foursome made it to Dallas, and the next night Jackson v. Walker headlined the affair. In the twelve weeks since Georgia and Auburn met on the football field, much had transpired for the now-legendary Bulldog. First, he won the Heisman Trophy in a landslide. Second, he had begun (covertly) negotiating with a brand-new outfit, the United States Football League, and would soon leave college early to make $5 million playing for something called the New Jersey Generals.

Walker wasn't merely a big deal. He was a huge deal. He was also weird. Not just standoffish, but alien. Teammates barely knew him. His diet was often water mixed with a handful of peas, or an unseasoned slice of chicken. His body was his temple. He didn't flirt, or sip so much as a dollop of beer. In fact, Walker violated five hundred Deep South social norms by being engaged to a *white* coed—only overlooked by the Athens, Georgia, chapter of the Ku Klux Klan because, well, HE WAS HERSCHEL FUCKING WALKER!!! "Herschel was really distant," said Stanley Blalock, a Georgia wide receiver and sprinter. "He didn't talk to many people. I mean, Bo ran for Auburn but I knew him much better than I knew Herschel."

As Georgia's star was home most nights doing endless sit-ups before bed, Jackson was on the prowl. Even before he vanquished the Crimson Tide, he was having plenty of sex with plenty of women. Of late, his target was a fellow Auburn runner, Clara Hairston, who took one look at her teammate in shorts and singlet and considered herself hooked. "He was," she said, "just about the finest thing that walked this Earth."

"When Bo came to practices we'd work together," said Hairston. "Sometimes he'd walk me to class. I can't say we were exclusive, because I knew he was with *many* other women. But we were intimate on several occasions. Before he got a big head, he was great. And really fine."

As they lingered in a hallway waiting for a preliminary heat of the 60-yard dash, Walker and Jackson exchanged minimal pleasantries. The race was stacked—the two halfbacks were the draw, but other participants included Courville, former 1980 U.S. Olympic qualifier Stanley Floyd, and Alabama's Calvin Smith, a future Olympic gold medalist.

When the gun sounded, Jackson burst from the blocks. For twenty yards, he ran the perfect race. Head straight. Arms pumping. Legs churning. But then, lack of practice caught up, and pushing a rental car thirty yards caught up, and sexual conquests caught up, and inexperience caught up. He was passed by a flying Walker—who won in 6.10 seconds—then by Courville, Floyd and Smith. "He started his lean at the end of the race too soon," Rosen said. "Now Bo knows what he has to do to compete against these people."

Jackson's 6.25 failed to qualify him for the finals, but his coach hoped it was enough to convince his new star to devote himself fully to track and field and give up any of those fantastical baseball dreams.

Mel Rosen didn't stand a chance.

In 1990, Bantam Doubleday published Bo Jackson's autobiography.

The book, *Bo Knows Bo*, is filled with riveting details. In particular, Jackson is honest about his flaws and shortcomings. He rarely attempts to hide past mistakes, and lays his struggles bare.

On page 71, for example, Jackson delves into his early difficulties as a freshman member of the Auburn baseball team.

He writes:

> *I only had a couple of weeks of practice, then began playing baseball games, and I guess I didn't have my batting eye at first. I struck out my first twenty-one times up. I wondered if I was ever going to hit the ball again.*

Through the years, those first twenty-one at-bats have become the stuff of Auburn baseball lore. They provide hope. They offer proof that it never pays to give up. Why, as the decades pass, more and more of Jackson's former baseball teammates have comfortably settled into relaying the narrative.

Trent Hudson, Auburn catcher: "Every game, another three or four strikeouts until Bo was at twenty-one straight. If someone Ks four times in baseball you throw your hat out at him. A lot of hats were thrown at Bo."

Jamie Basso, Auburn outfielder: "When your starting center fielder strikes out twenty-one times in a row, you have to ask why he's in there."

Jerry Joe Chambers, Auburn infielder: "We were all sitting there going, 'If we struck out twenty-one times in a row like Bo has, Coach would pull us, scream at us and throw us in the batting cage. But not Bo. And, of course, his twenty-second at-bat he hit the ball four hundred feet."

There is one small problem: It's not true.

After failing to place in the 60-yard dash at the SEC indoor track-and-field championships, Jackson reported to Plainsman Park, where Coach Paul Nix's baseball team was slogging along through a 1–6 start. Nix, fifty years old and in his twenty-first season at Auburn, was a stern disciplinarian who berated his players via bullhorn throughout practices. His mantra—"I need a bunch of tough sons of bitches out here."—wasn't delivered warmly.

"We played Clemson one time, and during the game he made us sit at our positions and he came out of the dugout to scream at us, one by one, through his bullhorn," recalled Hudson. "It was so humiliating, Clemson's players walked off and left the field. If Coach Nix had something to say to you, it was only a bad thing."

Jackson's first collegiate baseball game would be played on the afternoon of March 8, against visiting Illinois State. Nix had barely seen the kid hit or throw or run, but he figured he couldn't hurt the Tigers' anemic lineup. So he plugged his new starting center fielder in the second slot of the batting order, and hoped for the best.

The Redbirds started Scott Becker, a hard-throwing freshman right-hander from Elgin, Illinois, and as he warmed up before the bottom of the first, the fifty or so spectators on hand observed in silence. Such was life at Plainsman Park, home to approximately 2,700 seats, few of which were ever occupied. Because no one had been warned of Jackson's baseball debut, no one in the sports information department did anything to promote it. Not that it would have mattered. Baseball wasn't much of a thing at Auburn.

With one out in the first, Jackson dug into the batter's box. The Tigers' home uniforms featured blue jerseys and white pinstriped pants, and Jackson—wearing number 29—fit his like an encased sausage. "We were all twigs," said Steve Childers, a pitcher. "Bo was a mountain."

There was no available scouting report, so Becker reared back and unleashed a fastball, which Jackson bounced on two hops to Paul Giersz, the Redbirds' 5-foot-9, 170-pound shortstop.

Whoosh!

Bo Jackson sped out of the batter's box and soared down the first base line. Giersz fielded the ball cleanly, pumped, stepped, released—and looked on as Jackson beat the throw by two full steps. "I did nothing wrong on that play," recalled Giersz, a future second-team Missouri Valley all-conference selectee. "Everything clean and right. Then I look up and it's, 'What the heck just happened?'"

"Bo should have been out by four feet," said Ward Yerby, an Auburn pitcher. "When we jogged back onto the field at the end of the inning, their guys were asking, 'What was *that* all about?'"

Later on in the Illinois State dugout, pitcher Doug Boehm tapped Giersz on the shoulder and said, "You know who that is, right?"

"Nope," Giersz replied. "But he's the fastest human I've ever seen."

"That's Bo Jackson," Boehm said.

"I don't know the name," Giersz said.

"Don't worry," noted Boehm. "You will."

Bo Jackson wound up going 2 for 5 in the loss to the Redbirds, with two RBI and an error.

His performance, alas, was a bit of a mirage.

Over the next sixteen games—largely against SEC foes Ole Miss, Mississippi State and Alabama—Jackson went a dreadful 1 for 19, including 12 strikeouts. Nix, to his (developmental) credit, refused to bench the kid. He knew talent when he saw it, and Jackson had plenty. In the second game of a doubleheader at Mississippi State, a Bulldog hit a high fly to the center-field wall. As soon as Jackson caught it, the runner on third casually tagged for home. Jackson leaned back and uncorked a 290-foot BB. The ball arrived at the same time as the runner, but catcher Dean Sunseri wasn't paying attention, and it clanged into the backstop. "It was a gimme with any other player," said Sunseri. "But Bo had a cannon attached to his body."

When the inning ended, Sunseri assumed he would catch an earful from his head coach.

"Sunseri!" Nix screamed. "Get over here!"

The catcher braced for impact.

"Don't worry, son," Nix said through a grin. "I had no idea he could do it either."

Jackson's arm was nuclear ("You could hear the ball sizzle as he threw it," said Chris Senn, a teammate). His speed was world class. Everything else was a mess. As word quickly spread of the football god on the diamond, so did the scouting report. "He couldn't hit a curveball to save his life," said Chambers. "He'd screw himself into the ground swinging at it."

"A slider away would eat his lunch for days," said Childers. "He couldn't touch it."

On March 29, Auburn bused the 105 miles north to Jacksonville State to play the Gamecocks. A capacity crowd at University Field chanted "Go Bo!" as Jackson approached the plate, then watched as he went 0 for 3 with three strikeouts. The Tigers reached a new low, falling 11-1 to Division II program.

Two days later, the Crimson Tide and Tigers met at Birmingham's Rickwood Field for the first-ever Alabama-Auburn Baseball Classic, and Nix's ball club was destroyed again, 12–3. After yet another 0 for 4 dud from Jackson, who was lowered to seventh in the lineup, Cecil Hurt of the *Tuscaloosa News* spared few words:

Alabama posted an eight-run third inning, giving the Tide a 12–0 lead. After that, the only suspense left in the evening was seeing how many times Bo Jackson, gifted running back turned slumping centerfielder for the spring, would strike out. Jackson fanned four times, lowering his season batting average to .100, and also committed an error in center, a performance that summed up the night—and much of the season to date—for Auburn.

"The bottom line is Bo was really, really raw," said Scott Tillery, an Auburn pitcher. "You knew he was a special athlete, but the coaching staff rushed him. He was a kid from a small high school who rarely saw good pitching, and suddenly he's hitting against future Big Leaguers. It was too quick. But I'll say this for Bo—through the hard times he still had fun with it."

By playing baseball Jackson was avoiding spring football practices— and there were few things that interested him less than football practices, particularly in hot weather. He also genuinely enjoyed the casualness of the sport. Football and track were intense. But baseball was lounging in the dugout, cracking jokes. It was spitting sunflower seeds into a bucket and crushing paper Gatorade cups with your spikes. Jackson reveled in the quiet solitude of center field—the green grass, the wide-open space, the crack of the bat, and tracking down a fly ball. On the football field, there were expectations of grandeur, and all eyes were on number 34. In baseball, if the team drew a hundred fans to its cruddy stadium, that was a large crowd.

Plus, his teammates were delightful.

Yerby was a bottom-of-the-barrel starter who went 3-8 with a 5.11 ERA for the Tigers. Coming out of Enterprise State Junior College a year earlier, his father, Ed—an Auburn alum who worked as a pilot for Southern Airways—offered his son two of the family planes should he turn down an Ole Miss scholarship to attend his alma mater. Ward signed with Auburn, and parked his Cessna 170 at Auburn University Regional Airport.

On off days, Yerby gathered teammates and flew over the dormitories where Auburn's coeds sunbathed topless. "Bo came up with me," Yerby recalled. "We'd circle around, check out the breasts, go back." Hudson, the junior catcher from Dunwoody, Georgia, made some extra cash by taking care of the pool at Fox Den Apartments near campus. "One day Bo came over to swim—just Bo and a bunch of girls," Hudson said. "Well, he's in the water, waist deep, and he says, 'Watch this!' He jumped flat-footed onto the deck of the pool. I'd have broken my knees. But he did it easily. I was floored."

On the road, Jackson roomed with Pat Visintainer, a pitcher from Vestavia Hills, Alabama. The slugger was a shy and quiet companion, but chuckled aloud watching Saturday-morning cartoons. On a mid-March road trip to Starkville, Mississippi, Nix made clear the bus would be leaving the Ramada at 10 a.m. sharp—"no exceptions." At 9:45, Visintainer bounded onto the vehicle, leaving Jackson behind to wrap an episode of Scooby-Doo. At 10, Jackson still wasn't on the bus. At 10:05, Jackson still wasn't on the bus. "Finally, at ten fifteen Bo walks down the stairs and gets on the bus," Visintainer said. "And we left."

Visintainer started against the Bulldogs, and was lit up in an 8–0 loss. The two teams were scheduled to meet again on Sunday, but since he knew he wasn't playing the pitcher stayed up late, then rushed out to the front of the hotel at 10:01 a.m. The bus was gone and Visintainer—dressed in full uniform—had to bum a ride to the field.

After arriving, he ran into Bill Davis, a fellow pitcher.

"Where you been?" Davis asked.

"I was at the hotel," Visintainer replied. "I thought the bus didn't leave until 10:15. It left at 10:15 for Bo."

Davis chucked.

"Hey, Pat," he said. "You're no Bo Jackson."

On October 23, 2013, a man named Emory Paul Jones was laid to rest at Peachtree Memorial Park in Norcross, Georgia.

He was fifty-two, and had spent twenty-seven years working in the banking industry before dying of a massive heart attack. He was a father of two, a husband, a Little League coach, and a devoted parishioner of Blackshear Place Baptist Church.

At the funeral, the Reverend Ty Blackburn, a longtime family friend, spoke of Jones's kindness and warmth. And then, before wrapping up, Blackburn shared the story of April 13, 1983.

The day Jones faced Bo Jackson.

God, Jones had *loved* telling that story. "When Dad was inducted into the Rotary he had to share something about his life," said Taylor Jones, his older son. "Of course, he talked about Bo Jackson."

Back in the early 1980s, Emory Paul Jones wasn't Emory Paul Jones. He was Paul "Dream" Jones, right-handed relief pitcher for the baseball team at Alabama Christian College, an NAIA-level Church of Christ school located in Montgomery.

Like the vast majority of his teammates, Jones was a solid high school ballplayer out of Duluth, Georgia, whose religious beliefs took him from the Greater Atlanta Christian School to the small campus of ACC. He was a goofy kid with a Mark Fidrych cut, thick glasses, and a Gumby physique. His nickname, "Dream," was an ode to his spot-on impersonation of the famed NWA wrestler Dusty "The American Dream" Rhodes.

The Alabama Christian players joined the program knowing their immediate baseball futures involved games against schools like Clearwater Christian and Jefferson State. Yet Tom Fletcher, the Eagles' coach, was friends with Nix, and the men agreed to a home-and-home series. "Paul's assessment was 'If we can't go over there and beat Alabama Christian, it'll send a message to our players,'" Fletcher said. "That was fine with me. The chance to play Auburn was a grand opportunity."

And so it was that, on a mid-April afternoon, "Dream" Jones walked to the mound at Harrison Field. A few handfuls of people sat in the largely empty bleachers. It was the top of the fifth inning, and the Eagles were trailing Auburn, 14–8.

Jones, a soft-throwing junkballer, tossed the requisite warm-up pitches to catcher Mark Courson before grabbing the baseball and looking in for the sign. Although the two schools rarely met, Jackson's raw strength didn't leave much mystery for Courson. Or in simpler speak: under no circumstances would he call for Jones to throw one of his high-70s fastballs.

Courson put down three fingers—forkball.

The pitch was delivered to perfection, and Jackson swung through the diving projectile for strike one. "Paul had a big hand," said Fletcher. "His ball really moved."

Jackson stepped out, then stepped back in. Once more, Courson put down three fingers. The forkball, again, befuddled Jackson, who watched strike two pass him by. "Paul could be very tough to hit," said Bruce Hill, Alabama Christian's center fielder. "He was all about trickiness."

The count stood at 0-2, and Jones was on the verge of a lifetime bragging moment: striking out Bo Jackson.

Courson called for another forkball.

The ball approached the plate like a floating melon, slow and plump and ready to be consumed. Jackson cocked his elbow, stepped forward, extended his arms and . . .

Gone.

But not just gone.

G-O-N-E.

Nobody said a word. "I took one step," said Hill, "then watched in awe like everyone else." The ball rose, and rose, and rose, and rose. Rose. And rose. And rose. Behind Harrison Field's left-field fence (which rested 330 feet from home) was Wares Ferry Road. The ball was still rising as it crossed the two-lane street. Still rising as it traveled above a line of eighty-foot-tall pine trees positioned thirty feet behind the fence. "There were these apartments about a hundred feet behind the road," said Fletcher. "It one-hopped those apartments." Thanks to gravity, there is a 96.7 percent chance the baseball landed somewhere on Earth and, in all likelihood, the state of Alabama. That, however, was never confirmed. Fletcher guessed it traveled 525 feet, and laughed decades later when asked whether it was the longest home run he had ever seen.

"Um," he said, "yeah."

Though the game continued, a gaggle of spectators bolted from the diamond to track down the baseball. Fletcher was supposed to be monitoring his team, but found himself momentarily terrified by the youngsters zipping across Wares Ferry Road, screaming, "Where'd it go? Where'd it go?"

"My heart went in my throat," he said. "That's a very busy road."

The final score, 19–14 Tigers, was highlighted by Jackson going 3 for 4 with two walks, two doubles, and the homer.

When the game ended, Jackson was asked about his afternoon and noted dryly, "It was like taking batting practice." He likely never again mentioned or thought of the Alabama Christian College game.

Yet until the day he died, Paul Jones spoke of the day Bo Jackson took him deep.

"Paul would say, 'Yeah, he crushed the ball. But it was *the* Bo Jackson,'" recalled LaDonna Jones, his widow. "It wasn't embarrassing. My husband wore it as a badge of honor."

Bo Jackson's freshman baseball run (during which he hit .279 with four home runs and 13 RBI in 68 at-bats) cannot be fully told without a final remarkable act—one few outside the program were ever made aware of.

It was seemingly just another day in a long season filled with days. With Nix and his coaches out recruiting, practice at Plainsman Park was a laid-back affair run by the players. "We weren't a very good team," said Chris Senn, the outfielder. "And most of us wanted to hurry up, finish working out, and go drink beers."

With no coaches available to throw batting practice, Senn stepped in. He was a big kid with a big arm—not good enough to pitch for the Tigers, but good enough to serve BP purposes. One after another, the Auburn hitters took their hacks. Then Jackson settled in for his turn.

The first pitch Senn threw was straight and over the plate, and Jackson hammered a line drive that exploded off his aluminum bat, slipped past the L screen protecting the pitcher, and cracked Senn in the skull, directly behind his right ear. He fell to the ground like a bag of rocks, and teammates—including Jackson—sprinted to his side. Senn was taken to East Alabama Medical Center, where he was diagnosed with a blood clot in the brain. Senn remained hospitalized for two weeks, missing the remainder of the season. He returned in 1984 for his senior year, but was never quite the same.

The years passed. In 2017, Senn's daughter, Anna Kathryn, worked as a student athletic recruiter at her father's alma mater. She wore a name tag at football games, and while standing on the sideline for Georgia-Auburn spotted a large man with a shaved head and earring. It was Bo Jackson.

"She wasn't supposed to go up and talk to famous alum," said Kathryn Senn, Anna Kathryn's mother, "but she felt led to introduce herself."

"Mr. Bo," she said, "my name is Anna Kathryn Senn."

Whoa.

"Your dad," Jackson replied. "Is it Chris Senn?"

"Yes," she said. "It sure is."

"You know I almost killed him in college," he said. "How is he doing these days?"

Anna Kathryn explained that while her father enjoyed more good days than bad days, the accident took something from him. Senn still suffered seizures and migraines. He had gone on to a successful career as a pharmaceutical rep, but it wasn't always easy. Anna Kathryn dialed her father's cell phone, hoping to connect him with Jackson. Chris refused to talk—he harbored no resentment, but didn't want to be a pest.

Nearly two years later, Senn received a random call from . . . Bo Jackson. He was going to be in Pensacola, Florida, on business, and hoped to drive to the Senn household in Dothan, Alabama, for a visit.

Some things needed to be said.

"Why don't we just pick somewhere closer to where you're gonna be," Senn suggested.

"No," Jackson replied. "I'm coming to you."

On September 13, 2019, Bo Jackson drove the two and a half hours to knock on the Senns' front door. As soon as he saw Chris, he hugged him and began to sob. Jackson couldn't hold back. Never one to publicly emote, it all came pouring out. Chris didn't quite know how to respond.

"All these years," Jackson said, "I've carried this guilt with me. All these years . . ."

Over the next two hours, Jackson and Senn sat in adjacent leather recliners, and the superstar tried to make right what had long felt wrong. He asked how much the family paid for seizure and anti-migraine medications, and offered to cover the costs (Senn assured him it was taken care of via insurance). He asked if they needed any help with . . . anything. Just name it. Anything at all.

"Bo," Senn said, "it happened. It wasn't your fault. I shouldn't have been on the mound. I was an outfielder pitching because I wanted to hurry up and get beer. You shouldn't be carrying this guilt."

Jackson told Senn that he had long felt he ruined his hopes for a professional baseball career.

Senn laughed.

"Bo, lemme tell you who ruined my career," he said. "Guys like you and [Mississippi State stars] Will Clark and Bobby Thigpen, who played in the SEC and showed me I wasn't at their level. You hitting me in the head had nothing to do with it. I promise."

Jackson sat and listened. He was quiet and cautious; comfortable, but heavy. The Senns own two dogs—a Weimaraner named Newt and a Lab-chow mix named Gus—and their enthusiasm for the guest broke some (but not all) of the tension.* Jackson was consumed by sadness and regret. Senn could see his words hadn't fully soothed his old teammate.

"Listen," he said, "please don't carry any more guilt. If I'm ever in trouble I'll call you, but I've had a great life. I have a great family. You need to let the guilt go."

When Jackson finally rose to leave, the men hugged for what felt like twenty minutes. There were no dry eyes, but also no hard feelings.

The guilt was gone.

---

* The Senn family's first dog was a cocker spaniel. Chris and Kathryn named him Bo Jack Senn.

CHAPTER 9

GREG PRATT

Greg Pratt was born bowlegged.

That wasn't something the doctors noticed on September 26, 1962, when Jessie Lee Pratt gave birth to her son inside a Philadelphia, Pennsylvania, hospital. But as the years passed, and the family relocated to Albany, Georgia, Greg's legs failed to grow normally. When he stood, his knees refused to meet. His feet pointed outward. "Physicians said he might not be able to walk by the time he reached thirty," said Jean Powell, Greg's younger sister. "When he was in elementary school, they broke Greg's legs to correct the problem."

It worked.

From 1976 to 1980, Pratt excelled as a three-sport star at Monroe County High. His specialty was football. Though only 5-foot-7 and 190-ish pounds, Pratt was powered by drive, heart, gumption and work ethic. "He never came off the field," said Gary Ellerson, a Monroe High teammate who went on to a three-year NFL career. "You hear me? Greg *never* came off the field. After kickoffs he'd just stand there and wait for whatever came next."

Pratt aspired to play big-time college football, but his height and physique (he was nicknamed "Junior Whopper" by teammates) proved obstacles.

So while Ellerson, an all-state running back, signed with the University of Wisconsin, Pratt settled for Tennessee State, an HBCU Division I-AA school. He spent one year on the Nashville campus, but minimal playing time resulted in misery. Come 1981, Pratt surrendered his scholarship to try and walk on at Auburn.

It didn't take Pat Dye and the coaching staff long to know they'd been gifted a gem. The kid played his ass off, blocked like a bulldozer and never appeared intimidated or nervous. After sitting out a transfer year, Pratt rushed for 106 yards in 1982, highlighted by a 15-yard touchdown scamper against Boston College in the Tangerine Bowl. It was the happiest time of his life. "He was a short, squatty thing," said Scott Selman, a punter. "But, boy, he could play."

Entering 1983, Pratt believed he had a legitimate chance to fulfill a dream and start alongside Jackson and Lionel James in the backfield of a national championship contender. Ron O'Neal, the incumbent fullback, had been ruled academically ineligible. So Pratt spent most of the summer on campus, trying to build muscle and shed some weight off his now-211-pound body. "He stayed at Auburn and ran and ran and ran," said Pat Arrington, an Auburn offensive lineman. "There were about twenty of us that hung around. We'd get up in the morning, work out, run, play golf, attend a class or two, and then we'd party hard every night. Greg was a part of that whole bunch."

On August 20, the Tigers' returning players were required to report at 7 a.m. for the official start of fall practices—physicals, then the training test. Now in his third season at Auburn, Dye was a firm believer in the powers of conditioning and endurance. In order to make the Auburn roster, all players had to pass the first-day trial—four timed 440-yard runs around the baseball field. "They gave you an ultimatum," said Chuck Clanton, a defensive back. "If you don't do this, you're not on the team. You can turn in your jersey, you won't be able to be in the team picture. That was a *really* big thing—the photo op with the team. Because no matter what happened to you the rest of the year, that poster would exist forever—you sitting right there with your legs crossed, helmet off, and that Auburn uniform clean and proud."

The coaching staff determined which positions would run together, based upon speed expectations. They had tight ends, defensive ends and fullbacks in a group—with the demand that each lap be completed in 80 seconds or less.

"Which," said Russ Carreker, a linebacker, "is not a walk in the park. Also, there was real pressure. The coaches made it clear that everyone in the group made it, or no one did."

For Pratt, more than the other backs, it was daunting. He wasn't built for either speed or endurance. One day earlier, he came to the field by himself to practice running. It wasn't a problem, but that was in a relaxed atmosphere, with decent weather and a cool breeze.

Like Pratt, Bo Jackson had remained at Auburn for much of the summer. The reigning SEC Freshman of the Year took classes toward his major in psychology, and also worked as a teller at the Colonial Bank. Unlike Pratt, though, he gave the 440s little to no thought. Jackson was naturally fast and, besides, was Dye really going to cut him should he fall short? The halfbacks, quarterbacks, wide receivers and defensive backs went first, and all cruised through the line with ease.

By the time Pratt's group readied to run, it was 11 a.m. The temperature was 95 degrees, the relative humidity was 49 to 50 percent, and there was no shade to be found. Pratt was far more nervous than he had been for any football game. The night before, he had called home in a state of panic. "Mama," he said, "I don't know if I can run that 440. I can't run like those other guys can."

The first lap went fine—Pratt hung with his teammates and crossed in less than 80 seconds.

A minute and a half break.

The second lap also went mostly fine—Pratt didn't look strong or confident, but again he managed to cross in less than 80 seconds.

A minute and a half break.

The third lap was awful—Pratt tripped and fell to the ground. Several teammates, led by Donnie Humphrey, a senior defensive end, rushed out to pick him up and push him to the finish line. "We all really wanted Greg to do this," said Joel Gregg, a fullback and one of Pratt's closer friends on the squad. "So Donnie made sure he got that one."

A minute and a half break.

The sun felt unyielding. Hydration wasn't emphasized. No coaches or trainers seemed overly concerned by a huffing, puffing, beaten-down Pratt. You had to finish a lap, then stand and bake, sweat pouring into your eyes, deep breaths choking on the cheesecake-thick slices of humidity. This was torture by design. You wanna hear 75,000 fans screaming your name on Saturdays? First survive hell.

"But some people," said Clanton, "just aren't built to run four 440s in under 80 seconds."

The fourth lap was a train wreck. Greg Pratt tried as hard as he could. That's the only way he knew to do things. But the heat plus the humidity plus the speed plus the pressure—he only completed the full distance by being hauled across the finish line by Jackson, James and a few others. Of the day's forty-four players, Pratt was the only one unable to do the four 440s. "We grabbed him, had his arms thrown over our shoulders," said Pat Mote, a long snapper. "Even if he wasn't gonna make the time, we wanted him to finish."

A few minutes later, Pratt wobbled toward James, who was now sitting on the grass. He face was pale, his eyes glassy. He could barely speak. "I think about this all the time, nearly every day of my life," James said. "Greg grabbed my waist and he was laying on my shoulder and he said, 'I can't breathe, Lionel. I can't breathe.'"

James told his friend to keep his hands above his head and inhale deeply. Herb Waldrop, the head trainer, saw Pratt was in pain, and hosed him down with a water spray, then took him to the training room via golf cart and draped him in cold towels. "He was talking," Waldrop said. "Although it wasn't very understandable."

When the training runs were wrapped, James, Jackson and the rest of the Auburn players returned to the locker room inside Memorial Coliseum. James sat on one of the wood benches, happy the ordeal was behind him. As he rested, he heard some mumbling coming from the showers, partly muffled by water shooting from a nozzle and reverberating off the tiles.

The voice was Greg Pratt, and he was slurring a line from the 23rd Psalm:

Yea, though I walk through the valley of the shadow of death, I will fear no evil; for though art with me; thy rod and thy staff they comfort me . . .

James entered the shower, where he saw Pratt, kneeling and ghostlike. The water was frigid—a questionable remedy, because it can elevate the risk of cold shock.

"Lionel," Pratt said, "tell my mama I'm gonna be OK . . ."

"Greg!" James said. "Come on, Greg!" James screamed for Bud Casey, the running backs coach, and the two men picked Pratt up and carried him out of the shower and onto the floor where he slumped, legs crossed. "He kept leaning right and falling to the ground," James said. "Eventually I put him between my legs and talked to him and looked at him. But his eyes were so far back in his head. They called a trainer down, and he looked at Greg and dialed 911."

James was upset, and Waldrop told him to go eat some lunch; that Pratt would be fine; that they would place some fluids into the fullback, get him to the hospital for a checkup and he'd be back to his old self in no time. One season earlier, also during a running drill, Pratt had been ferried to the hospital and kept overnight with symptoms of heatstroke. He survived in one piece, as he did a heat-related blackout during a 1980 workout with Tennessee State. So James and Jackson walked to a nearby cafeteria, where they grabbed food and spoke, in hushed tones, about their fallen teammate.

"Look," James told his friend, "they called 911. I'm guessing Greg is already getting better." In the distance, the players heard a siren. Joel Gregg watched as his unconscious teammate was strapped to a stretcher and loaded into the ambulance.

"What happened to him?" Gregg asked a trainer.

"Heatstroke," the trainer replied.

"Come on," Gregg said. "That looks like a lot more than just heatstroke."

When they finished eating, Jackson and James walked back toward the facility. They were greeted by dozens of Auburn football players on their knees, praying.

"What's going on?" James asked a teammate.

Silence.

"Yo, what's happening?" James asked again.

Pause.

"It's Greg. They took him in an ambulance. I don't think he's going to live."

James owned a car, and he and Jackson drove to East Alabama Medical Center, the nearest hospital, where Pratt had arrived at 1:31 p.m. More than fifty teammates followed in their own vehicles. "When we got there we saw a nurse walking down the hallway," said James. "We stopped her."

Jackson, not one to speak up, spoke up. "Excuse me," he said. "We're looking for Greg Pratt. He's our football teammate at Auburn."

The nurse flashed a somber look.

"I'm sorry," she said. "He didn't make it."

James went numb. Jackson held a pair of sunglasses in his hand, and threw them to the floor, where they shattered into dozens of small pieces.

Charles Hollis, the *Birmingham News*'s Auburn beat writer, followed the ambulance to the hospital and somehow worked his way inside. As he waited for news, he was confronted by Wayne Hall, the linebackers coach.

"You need to leave—now!" Hall said, then picked the reporter up and carried him toward the lobby exit.

"There were," Hollis said, "a lot of emotions."

Greg Pratt was pronounced dead at 2:35 p.m. by Jon Williams, the Lee County coroner. The cause was, in fact, heatstroke. He was twenty years old.

By the time Dye reached the hospital, Pratt's life was already over. "The doctor came out of the emergency room and told me that Greg had died of cardiac arrest," he explained. The Auburn coach asked to see his fullback, and was brought inside a small room where the body lay prone across a table.

Dye, all alone, stared down at Greg Pratt and sobbed.

The funeral was held on a Thursday afternoon at Third Kiokee Mission Baptist Church in Albany, Georgia.

Dye gave his players the day off, and two charter buses carried the Auburn football team 120 miles south to the hometown and last resting place of Greg Pratt. An Alabama State Police brigade escorted the Auburn buses to the state line. Upon reaching the Peach State, a Georgia State Police brigade took over. Many of the players had never attended a funeral before, and few—if any—of the white players had attended a Black funeral before.

The tiny wood building was overflowing with mourners. Ray Perkins, Alabama's new head coach, came to pay his respects. The Atlanta Falcons sent flowers. James, Jackson and Dye served as three of the pallbearers. "I was scared to death, to be honest," said Kyle Collins, a white Auburn H-back. "I came from an all-white public school and had never been around Blacks. It was really crowded and there was so much yelling and screaming. Just raw pain."

Pratt's casket was open, and people shuffled past, one by one. When it was his turn, Jackson—tears pouring from his eyes—removed a disposable camera from his pocket and snapped a picture. "I'd never seen that before," said Forrest Benson, a white teammate. "A few other Black guys took pictures, too."

After the service ended, Dye boarded the bus and asked whether the players wanted to go to the burial at Riverside Cemetery. The majority of hands were raised. "I'll be one hundred percent honest and admit I didn't want to go," said Collins. "But we went, and Greg's mother became very emotional. She lost her son. I will never forget that sadness."

Through it all, Pat Dye made certain to hug Jessie Lee Pratt on multiple occasions. He told her Greg would be missed. He expressed his faith in God and Jesus. He let her know that she would soon be presented with a $100,000 insurance payout via the university.

Auburn's football coach made the decision his players should run excruciatingly hard conditioning drills at 11 a.m. on a ninety-five-degree summer day in sweltering Alabama. It was a test of their manhood. Of their desire to be members of the Tigers football team.

He never felt compelled to apologize.

"[His] death affected me more than any one incident that has happened in my life," Dye wrote in his 1992 autobiography, *In the Arena*. "In some ways, it was more difficult than my daddy's death."

Dye devoted two pages of his book to Pratt's passing.

He misspelled his name every time.

When it comes to sports, there are requisite things we do in the aftermath of a tragedy.

First, for a day or two, we discuss what happened.

Then we explain how we'll never forget Willie Galimore or Lyman Bostock or Bryan Higgins or Thurman Munson or Greg Pratt.

Then we apply decals or patches featuring the number of our lost teammate to every uniform. In this case, all Auburn players would be wearing Pratt's number 36 on the back of their helmets.

Then we point toward the sky, a lot. With every home run. With every touchdown.

Then we move on—and, when competing for our attention spans against the lights and color and flash and pizzazz of organized college and professional athletics, the tragedy starts to feel as if it never actually occurred.

As if Greg Pratt never existed.

On the same day Auburn's players and coaches traveled to Albany, Georgia, for the funeral, the *Orlando Sentinel* ran an article headlined AUBURN LOOKS AT FULLWOOD AT FULLBACK. The piece, written by Frank Carroll, featured this quote from Bud Casey, the running backs coach: "If Brent [Fullwood] makes it, we'll have the fastest fullback in America. With halfbacks Bo Jackson and Lionel James, we'd have the fastest backfield in America."

The words were stated with tasteless exuberance, and deliberately so. Dye believed the 1983 Auburn Tigers were capable of contending for the national championship. But not if every spare minute was spent contemplating their dead fullback. So within twenty-four hours of Pratt's burial, the talk turned to an opening-night meeting with Southern Miss.

Entering his sophomore year, Jackson wasn't one to openly think of loss, or spend all of his time mourning a friend. Part of his greatness came in hyperfocusing on the task before him. If he needed to, say, push a couch, he could put 100 percent into furniture relocation. If he needed a good sleep, he'd place his head on a pillow, close his eyes and conk out for eight or nine hours.

Now, in the lead-up to the season, Jackson needed to focus on something new: moving his stuff into an off-campus trailer.

Thanks to a renovation of Sewell Hall, the Auburn athletic dormitory, athletes would spend the year residing in dozens of trailers. The vast majority of the housing was situated in the town of Auburn, as close to campus as possible. But when it came to Jackson and his two sophomore-year roommates—Lionel James and linebacker Jeff Jackson—the coaching staff faced what it considered a quandary.

While discussing the housing situation at a meeting inside his office, Dye was interrupted by one of his assistants, who asked, "Coach, what are we going to do about these n-----s dating white girls?"

The chatter around the table ceased. Dye's expression changed. His coaches were mostly Southern whites, and that came with an unspoken kinship of hunting and fishing and subtle (and sometimes not-so-subtle) racism. But Dye never fully embraced it. "Early on, when he was talking to the team, Dye said something I'll never forget," said Chuck Clanton. "He said, 'I don't care [what you are]. Here, you're just men. You're equals.'" Dye grew up in Blythe, Georgia, in a house built by his grandfather, and farmed peanuts, corn, wheat, oats, soybeans and cotton alongside his alcoholic father, Frank Dye. His family's employees were white and Black, and Pat's closest boyhood pal was Major Hardin, an African American kid whose dad sharecropped the land. "Lots of times I would go to Major's house instead of going home," Dye recalled. "Most of the time we didn't have a telephone; mama would just know where I'd be. [Major's mother] would throw me a pallet and a blanket on the floor; I'd fall in there and go to sleep. She was family, and I was family.

"I've got the advantage of having worked, Black and white, going down the cotton rows together. That's the way I grew up. The Blacks were as important as we were."

While serving as an assistant coach at the University of Alabama, Dye recruited the school's first Black scholarship player, running back Wilbur Jackson from Ozark, Alabama. "I told Coach Bryant that if I was going to recruit that area," he said, "I wanted to get the best player. And he happened to be Black. I'm more oriented toward people and production than I am what color they are."

So sitting in a meeting, hearing an employee drop the n-word and fret over Black players dating white women—it didn't fly with Dye. "Listen," he said, "I don't wanna hear about this bullshit. We bring these guys on this campus. They wouldn't be here if it weren't for football. We recruited them and got them to Auburn, and we put them in this fishbowl with almost all white people. So how can we punish them? How can we even be mad at them?"

And that was that.

Almost.

According to James, before housing was formally assigned he was pulled aside by Dye. "I know y'all are dating these white girls," he said. "We're gonna put you outside of town, just so I don't have to talk about it and y'all can do whatever you want to do."

The two (unrelated) Jacksons and James wound up situated in a trailer on Wire Road, several miles away from campus. "We were basically between Auburn and Tuskegee," James said. "Coach was pretty much saying, 'I don't want to deal with this, but y'all should live your lives as you see fit.'"

At the time, the solution didn't bother James or Bo Jackson or Jeff Jackson. They were all products of the South; all young men who knew white girls were off-limits. They didn't grow up seeing people lynched for dating out of race, but they grew up hearing one-generation-removed stories of people being lynched for dating out of race. Dye, in James's opinion, was doing nothing more than looking out for their well-being. "Coach loved his players, and I really believe Black and white didn't matter to him," he said. "But we didn't exist in a bubble, and there were realities he had to face."

Though it is impossible to state as fact, the case can be made that Auburn's 1983 schedule was the most daunting in college football history.

Of the eleven games, five came against teams that were slotted in the Associated Press's Top 25—with a sixth school, Florida, joining the rankings after the opening week. This was all by design. Unlike many of his peers, who enjoyed a buffet of cream puffs to lead off a meal, Dye thought his men needed to be tested. "To be the best," he'd say, "you need to beat the best."

Coming off a 9-3 season, the Tigers were ranked number 5 in the AP preseason poll, and Mitch Lawrence, the renowned *Rochester Democrat and Chronicle* scribe, had them at number 2. *Playboy* predicted Dye's club would wind up national champions. They returned all but two offensive starters, and lost only three starters on defense. Pratt's death was an emotional sledgehammer, but—from an X's and O's perspective—he was a relatively ordinary player. His replacement, sophomore Tommie Agee, stood out as an excellent blocker, a solid ball carrier and a team-first contributor.

On September 10, the most expectation-filled season in Auburn football history finally began at Jordan-Hare Stadium with a 24–3 cakewalk over Southern Miss. It was everything loyalists could ask for: a packed house of 73,500 fans, James rushing for 172 yards and Jackson for 73 more, the defense holding the Golden Eagles' new quarterback, Robert Ducksworth, to 63 yards passing. "I think they are quite a bit better than last year," said Jim Carmody, the Southern Miss coach. "We played a football game tonight against one of the better teams in the nation."

The triumph wasn't a mirage. Auburn was really good. But the victory seemed to set something off in the team that nobody within the facility saw coming: it made the players cocky. One newspaper writer after another came to campus to chronicle inevitable brilliance. AUBURN MAY BE NEW DYNASTY—*Great Falls Tribune*. WAR EAGLES ARE LOADED—*Hattiesburg American*. POLLSTERS HARBORING GREAT EXPECTATIONS FOR WAR EAGLES—*Jackson Clarion-Ledger*. "We were very overconfident," said Steve Wallace, the offensive lineman. "We thought we were just going to walk over the rest of our schedule. Which was crazy, because our schedule was loaded."

A week later, the Tigers hosted the University of Texas, America's number 3 ranked team. Throughout the lead-up, Auburn's players spoke breezily of the Longhorns, whose offense featured very few known playmakers.

More than 73,000 entered the building to clear skies and temperatures in the mid-eighties. The stadium was loud. The fight song was blared. When Texas's players—decked out in white duds with burnt-orange trim—ran onto the field, they were booed. When the Tigers arrived, they were greeted as conquering heroes. Save the number 36 stickers affixed to the back of their helmets, Greg Pratt barely existed. There was a big game to play.

Auburn kicked off to open the afternoon, and it didn't bode well. Kelvin Epps caught the ball in the end zone, started to run, momentarily froze, then bobbed and weaved his way to the Auburn 37, where he was prevented from going all the way solely by kicker Al Del Greco extending his left hand and grabbing Epps's ankle.

By the time the first quarter ended, the Tigers had accumulated only 51 total yards and trailed 10–0. At halftime, it was 20–0. "Texas," wrote Robbie Andreu of the *Fort Lauderdale News*, "made Pat Dye's team look like it belonged in the 1920s." The arrogance and hype surrounding the potential of a championship season was sucked from the building. Inside the Auburn locker room at halftime, Dye was stupefied. "I was embarrassed for our players," he said later. The coach could accept a good football team playing better than his men. But this was more than that—it felt as if Auburn weren't even trying. "You have a choice!" Dye screamed as he paced back and forth. "You can fight with everything you have to keep a dream alive, or you can wilt."

They wilted. Together, James and Jackson combined for 68 yards rushing. By the time the final whistle sounded, Texas walked away with a 20–7 triumph that felt far more one-sided. Akers, a conservative man opposed to boasting, could barely contain his giddiness. "It went, quite frankly, just like we planned it," he said—smiling widely.

In the immediate aftermath, Texas's players retreated to their locker room to whoop and holler and celebrate a program-affirming win. This wasn't just a big one. It was *the* big one. There was no reason to hold back. This! Was! A! Party!

And then Bo Jackson entered.

He was still in his uniform pants and the sweaty gray T worn beneath his jersey. Jackson went locker to locker and shook every hand. "Y'all took it to us," he told Jerry Gray, the star cornerback. "You deserve to enjoy this." When speaking with the media, Jackson took his praise further. "They came out and old-fashioned whipped our butt, and they didn't talk about us while they were doing it," he said. "I'd rather lose to a class team like Texas than play a team all up on its high horse, wanting to beat the crap out of you and brag on it."

When he left the room, the Longhorn players were shocked.

"Bo Jackson," said Gray, "is a class act."

Because the Texas matchup had been such a letdown, there was little demand for Bo Jackson to chat over the next few days.

Which was too bad. Because, suddenly, he was getting better at it.

Auburn's sports information director was a thirty-six-year-old alum named David Housel, who graduated with a journalism degree in 1969, left to become an editor at the *Huntsville News*, then returned to campus. Housel was a beloved figure—earnest, compassionate, never considered his players mere chips that came and went with the various seasons. He genuinely cared. And when it came to Jackson, and his stuttering problems, Housel viewed it as his responsibility to guard a young man with vulnerabilities of locution. So, early on, one-on-one interviews were rare, with the ahead-of-time warning to reporters that Jackson's speech required patience. "We protected Bo," said Housel. "I didn't want him to get spun around."

What happened next didn't merely improve Jackson's relationship with the media, but changed his life. Housel asked Patrick Waters, a longtime Auburn English professor who now served as the football team's academic adviser, to work with the star sophomore on his speech patterns. "A lot of the football players were from rural communities," said Waters. "And because of football's importance at Auburn, they were going to have microphones shoved in front of their faces and be asked to discuss all sorts of things. With a lot of these guys, God knows what you were going to get."

Jackson wasn't the only football player with such an impediment (Doug Smith, a defensive tackle, had an equally crippling stutter), but he was the most important to the school. So in the summer leading up to Jackson's sophomore year, Waters enlisted him in a class taught in the theater department, Interview Techniques for the Camera. It was headed by Professor Ralph Miller, who long ago had been inspired by a letter sent to the university president, then somehow passed his way. "It was a woman complaining that the grammar of the athletes didn't represent Auburn," Miller recalled. "And that something should be done about it."

That resulted in athletes first being sent to the speech department ("A failure," said Miller. "They were learning vowels and definitions, not keys to communication."), then to theater and Miller and Interview Techniques for the Camera. Jackson was nervous and uncomfortable. He didn't like people staring at him; hated people laughing at him. Deep down, he remained the young boy in Bessemer, punching classmates in the face whenever they ridiculed his words. Jackson had tried to suppress his discomfort with the stutter, but it was real and raw and humiliating. What Miller emphasized was . . . taking . . . things . . . nice . . . and . . . easy. Jackson tended to make the all-too-common mistake of rushing through words. Those who battle a stutter oftentimes attempt to push through a sentence, when the most effective approach is to gently ride the wave. So managing his obstacle meant doing a 180 and rolling along gradually. Instead of fighting to get past I-I-I-I, turn it into "I"—then a comfortable delay and an inhale. Wait for the next word. *Deep breath. Pause. Begin.* Before long, one could see a refreshed confidence within Jackson. He spoke slower and without the same terror. The stutter never fully vanished. But the upgrade was substantial.

"Bo really worked on it," said Miller. "I take no credit for the stutter improvement. What I did was teach him to put his best foot forward and think about what he was saying. In short, just to relax."

That advice did *not* apply to the Auburn football team as a whole. The Texas loss was devastating, and all one needed to do was look at the new AP poll (Auburn fell from fifth to eleventh) to see the damage. So while their next game would send the Tigers to Knoxville to face Tennessee, Dye was not playing games. Any of the early sensitivity he tried to show his players in the wake of Greg Pratt's death—gone. Any satisfaction over talk of championship contention—also gone. In case that wasn't clear, two days after the Texas loss the team suspended Chuck Clanton, the talented yet erratic defensive back, for three weeks after he missed a curfew and stayed out late Saturday night. The punishment was excessive: He would sit out games, move out of assigned housing, pay for his own food and complete two hundred stadium steps. Then, and only then, could he return.

Dye was trying to send a message. In the Longhorns game, Clanton played sloppily, getting beat on an 80-yard scoring pass. He was an easy target for a coach insisting those around him shape up.

"It was such bullshit," said Clanton, who quit the team and never graduated. "My teammates were like, 'Man, this motherfucker's been here three years and this is how you're gonna do him?' They all saw what Dye and those guys were doing to me. It pissed everyone off."

As intended.

The Tennessee Vols were a far inferior operation to Texas, but the Tigers practiced as if they were preparing to face the Washington Redskins. Drills were long and hot and grueling, and the pressure was intense. With one loss, Auburn could (conceivably) still compete for a national title, with two losses—not a chance.

So they traveled to Knoxville and, before 95,185 fans at Neyland Stadium, beat the crap out of the Vols, 37-14. It was neither artistic nor pretty—Tennessee had five fumbles, two interceptions, two missed field goals, a roughing the kicker penalty, a pass dropped in the end zone and a punt coverage screwup that resulted in an 81-yard Auburn touchdown return. But it was a quality triumph with a big performance from Jackson, who opened the scoring with a one-yard touchdown run. His 91 yards on 15 carries led all players. "I'm so happy for our guys," a visibly relieved Dye said afterward. "They came into the game off a tough loss last week and they were battered and bruised. We had to get back to basics."

Over the next two months, the Tigers rediscovered their groove. They beat Florida State, 27-24, when Randy Campbell hit James with a 15-yard touchdown pass with 1:59 remaining. They crushed overmatched Kentucky, 49-21, then did the same to Georgia Tech, 31-13, and Mississippi State, 28-13. A program deemed down was rolling through an extraordinarily difficult schedule. Jackson, for his part, was . . . good. Very good. He ran for 123 yards against the Seminoles, then another 123 against Georgia Tech. But considering the hype, which even included preseason Heisman chatter, his numbers were disappointing. Through the first seven games, Jackson accumulated 541 yards and 8 touchdowns. By comparison, Nebraska's Mike Rozier—the ultimate recipient of the award—was up to 1,064 yards and 9 touchdowns for a team that had yet to lose.

In Jackson's defense, he was playing through a bruised thigh. But he was also, yet again, somewhat exasperating. James, his backfield partner, was 6 inches shorter, 52 pounds lighter and possessor of $\frac{1}{100}$th of Jackson's athletic ability. Yet when he approached opposing 280-pound defensive linemen, he lowered his helmet and barreled ahead. James was a hardened practice player who squeezed every ounce of potential from his body. He sprained his right ankle early in the season. Nearly no one knew it. "Lionel was as tough as nails," said Greg Tutt, a defensive back. "You could hit him, and you could drop him, and he would always get back up and move forward."

Jackson was merely tired. Always. Too tired to run, too tired to lift, too tired to practice at full speed. In a revealing moment of truth, Jackson was asked by a reporter what he felt moments before kickoffs. "Sleepy," he said with a laugh. "Whenever Coach Dye says to go in, my eyelids get heavy."

It was funny, but not funny. Jackson was everything you'd want in a superstar, but the inconsistencies were maddening. He didn't seem to live for football. He liked it. Enjoyed it. "But you had to sometimes wonder with Bo whether it meant a lot to him," said Jack Crowe, the offensive coordinator. "You were sort of always looking for signs."

Here was a sign: On the night of October 28, less than twenty-four hours before the University of Florida would strut onto Jordan-Hare's field to play Auburn in an SEC battle, Bo Jackson vomited.

It began toward the end of a steak dinner inside the team dining room. Jackson excused himself, dashed to the nearest bathroom and—*blech*. He returned to his room, and continued to puke throughout the night. He slept, at most, two hours. He would feel better, try to lie down, then rush off to the toilet yet again. He thought it might be wise (inexplicably) to overload on vitamin C, so he gorged on oranges. Then he threw them up. Then he gorged on more oranges. Then he threw them up.

On the morning of the game, Jackson tried eating some peaches at the team meal.

Blech.

"When I got up this morning," he said, "I honestly didn't know if I'd be able to play or not."

Dye was aware of Jackson's stomach problems. He also knew his halfback was earning the reputation as a softie. So instead of checking in on his health, Dye ignored it. "I didn't ask him if he could play or not," he said.

With the five straight wins, the Tigers were back to number 4 in the national rankings and again starting to chirp national title chatter. The Gators, meanwhile, were the surprise of college football—initially unranked, now 6-0-1 and fifth in the country. The home team was installed as a 2½ point favorite, but only because of geography.

Although it is a given that Auburn's greatest blood rival is Alabama, there was a sliver of time in the early 1980s when, man to man, Tiger players reserved their most diabolical thoughts for all things Florida. It commenced during the 1982 game, a 19–17 loss, when the Gators took delight in late hits and chop blocks and all levels of trash talk. The hostility reached a new level when an insidiously industrious UF student screen printed, then sold, T-shirts featuring Pratt's number 36 with a line running through the digits, accompanied by the words AT LEAST WE DON'T KILL OUR PLAYERS.

In the days before the game, Jackson spoke little. He heard plenty. The banter. The T-shirts. Florida-Auburn was hyped as a matchup between the SEC's two leading rushers—Jackson (541 yards for a 77.3 ypg average) vs. Neal Anderson, the Gator sophomore with 625 yards and an average of 89.3 ypg. It was one thing to compare Jackson to Herschel Walker, Georgia's Heisman Trophy winner. But Anderson? *Really?*

"I'll tell you something about Bo," said James. "He had pride. If you challenged him, and it impacted his pride—watch out. Just . . . watch out."

Even if he puked his guts out?

"Even then," James said with a chuckle. "Maybe especially then."

Jordan-Hare, as always, was a zoo. The Tigers wore dark blue jerseys, the Gators white. There was no consensus from America's sports columnists as to what would transpire, only agreement that Florida's defense—led by linebacker Wilber Marshall—was nearly NFL-caliber. "We did a lot of hitting," said Tom Wiegmann, a Gators linebacker. "That's what we prided ourselves on—knocking you on your ass."

On the seventh play of Auburn's first possession, and no score, Casey—the offensive coordinator—called "57," a simple toss sweep toward the left. With the ball on the Auburn 45-yard line, Randy Campbell faked a handoff to Agee, pretended to give it to James, *then* pitched it wide and a tad late to Jackson. The halfback caught the ball on the run, stormed through a wide-open hole, swerved to the right of a smothering block from left guard

Jeff Lott and *flllleeeeewwww* down the field. Until Gators linebacker Alonzo Johnson briefly touched Jackson's hip at the Florida 32, not one opposing player laid a hand on him.

As soon as he extended past Johnson, Jackson hit a different gear. He swerved across the field, left to right, as an ocean of Gators followed. It offered the illusion of a surfer somehow emerging from the shadows of Shipstern Bluff—and Jackson, trailed by six Florida players, cruised diagonally into the right corner of the end zone to the sound of 75,700 fans losing their minds.

On its next possession, Auburn lined up in a tight wishbone set—no wide receivers, two tight ends, Agee behind quarterback, James to the left, and Jackson to the right. There was no trickery—Campbell quick pitched to Jackson, who followed as Agee took out the legs of Mark Korff, the encroaching inside linebacker. Jackson rocketed through the tiniest of holes, gained about 12 yards, and was brought down by Florida's free safety, Tony Lilly.

Well, kind of.

Tony Lilly had Jackson brought down. It was a done deal—arms wrapped around torso, ready to end the play. A 6-foot, 195-pound brick, Florida's free safety was a master of pulverizing opponents. "I thought I had Bo," Lilly recalled. "The angle was mine, not his, and I moved in for what was supposed to be a fairly routine tackle. But then I reached out, and he was just . . . I dunno. Impossible to stop. Damn near impossible."

Jackson shed Lilly, cut to the outside and, once again, was *gone*. The lone remaining defender with an angle was Ricky Easmon, a cornerback with elite speed. The chase was never really a chase. Jackson made speedsters look tortoise-like. He scored with ease.

By the time the game was over, Auburn could celebrate a 28–21 win and its new national ranking (third overall, behind Nebraska and Texas), and Jackson could celebrate his reemergence onto the national stage. He carried the football sixteen times for 196 yards (Anderson, by comparison, ran for a mere 36) and was named the Southeastern Back of the Week.

"There's one thing you learned from playing against Bo Jackson," said Alonzo Mitz, a Florida defensive lineman. "If you hit him early and wrapped him up, you might have a chance. But once he gets started, and his body starts moving, you're over. You're done. You give Bo an inch, he takes ten miles.

"Against us, he took twenty."

The Auburn Tigers were the 1983 national champions.

They had to be!

Right?

Had to be.

After the emotional Florida win, Pat Dye's team—powered by a revived and nonregurgitating Bo Jackson—went on one of the great tears in the program's history. The Tigers hosted number 7 Maryland, quarterbacked by the tremendous Boomer Esiason, and won handily, 35–23. (Recalled Esiason: "The first time I saw Bo run out onto the field I thought, 'What the fuck is that?' I played in the ACC. We had great athletes. But not like *that*.") They traveled to number 4 Georgia and—despite Jackson now battling strep throat—somehow beat a strong Bulldogs team 13–7, clinching the SEC title and a trip to the Sugar Bowl. To wrap the schedule, they met up with Alabama at Birmingham's Legion Field for what was dubbed a revenge encounter for the number 19 Crimson Tide, coached at this point by Ray Perkins. Yet instead of a return to state football norms, Jackson carved up the Alabama defense with 256 yards rushing, including scoring dashes of 69 and 71 yards. Auburn won, 23–20. "Tonight, Bo put his name in the record book at Auburn," Dye said afterward, "and established himself as a genuine Heisman Trophy candidate for the next two years." As Dye spoke, Jackson sat by his locker, chomping on an unlit cigar.

All told, Auburn's 10-1 record included wins against five ranked teams and a single loss to Texas, number 3 in the nation. Jackson, for his part, totaled 1,213 yards and 14 touchdowns, then was tabbed a first-team All-American, sharing a spot in the backfield alongside BYU quarterback Steve Young and Nebraska's Rozier.

Auburn and number 8 Michigan were slated to meet in the Sugar Bowl on January 2, 1984. The Tigers remained America's third-ranked team, behind undefeated Nebraska (who would play number 5 Miami in the Orange Bowl) and number 2 Texas (also undefeated, and scheduled to battle Georgia in the Cotton Bowl). Auburn had one narrow path to the national title: Should they win and both Nebraska and Texas lose, the crown *had* to be theirs.

On December 28, after a week's break for Christmas, then three days of practice, Auburn's football team arrived in New Orleans. As the players deplaned at the airport, they were handed Mardi Gras–style bead necklaces and greeted by the joyful sounds of a six-piece Dixieland band (as well as the strange sight of an adult man dressed as a giant crawgator). After a brief check-in at the Fairmont Hotel, the players and coaches were whisked away to a party on Bourbon Street hosted by the Sugar Bowl. Michigan would not arrive for another day, but Dye thought it important his team revel in the accomplishment. "We're going to try and enjoy the trip," he said. "But we still have to be ready to play Michigan."

Over the next few days, Dye's message to his players stressed a single theme: *You are playing to be national champions.*

Then again.

You are playing to be national champions.

And again.

You are playing . . .

The Tigers were installed as four-point favorites, and those affiliated with the program found it insulting. Though 9-2, the Wolverines were slow and plodding. Few gave them much of a chance.

In the lead-up to the game, Dye stressed team to the media. There was Randy Campbell. There was Lionel James. There was . . .

No one cared.

As the *Montgomery Advertiser* explained in a December 31, 1983, headline, NEW ORLEANS IS "BO TOWN." Though he spent most of his nonpractice time holed up in his hotel room, Jackson faced infinite questions over his week in the Crescent City, ranging from a far-fetched rumor that he would leave school early to sign with the Baltimore Colts ("I'm only interested in college sports right now.") to his sex life ("I don't have a girlfriend in Auburn or even date anyone in Auburn. I shouldn't say this, but the girls in Auburn think I'm gay. At least that's what I've been told.") to inevitable comparisons to Herschel Walker ("I'm not trying to fill Walker's shoes."). There was really no other story to be told—and besides, the majority of the college football media was assigned to Miami-Nebraska and Georgia-Texas. Which meant the majority of the college football media missed a moment that defied all boundaries of human physicality.

Two days before the game, Auburn's players and coaches held a light shorts-and-T-shirts practice inside the Superdome, home to the New Orleans Saints. Within the small world of sports mythology, there was a thing about the building's roof (which was 273 feet above ground) and the scoreboard affixed to a gondola (140 feet up). Since the Superdome's opening in 1975, only a single punter, Ray Guy of the Oakland Raiders, ever hit the scoreboard with a kick during a game.* Another, Vanderbilt punter Mike Wright, did it in a 1977 workout while goofing around. Both men, however, made contact when the scoreboard was 90 feet high—*not 140.*

Now, as the Auburn players stood goofing around, punter Lewis Colbert was doing his all to hit the scoreboard with a ball.

Punt! Miss.

Punt! Miss.

Punt! Miss.

Watching from nearby, Jackson picked up a football, stared upward, stepped and threw with all his might. The ball soared high into the air, hit nothing and returned to earth. So he tried again. This time, the flight path was perfect, and when ball collided with scoreboard a pronounced *THWONG!* reverberated through the building. "The ball sort of disappeared into the darkness," said Ben Tamburello, Auburn's center. "And everyone was like, 'Did you see that? Did you see what Bo just did?'"

For the next twenty minutes, one player after another attempted the feat—Randy Campbell and his backup quarterback, Pat Washington. Running backs. Wide receivers. Colbert took another shot with his foot. "Nobody could do it," Jackson recalled.

Two days later, Michigan and Auburn finally met, and the Sugar Bowl was . . .

Really (yawn) boring.

The Tigers came in with a plan, which was to run Jackson and James until the Michigan defense broke. The Wolverines came in with a plan, which was to play nine guys close to the line and dare Campbell to throw. "Those were the toughest, hardest-hitting white guys," said Jackson, who ran for 130 yards on 22 carries. "They were like bees. They'd hit you and fall off and somebody else would hit you. They'd get up and hit you again." All told, Auburn accumulated 21 passing yards and converted five of 15 third-down plays. Five times they drove inside Michigan's 25, and failed to score a touchdown. They lost three of four fumbles. It was like watching paint dry, then taking some extra time to inspect the dried paint. Attendance was listed as 77,893. Some stayed awake. The Wolverines led 7–6 with 23 seconds remaining, but Auburn's Al Del Greco kicked a 19-yard field goal for the 9–7 victory. The *Anniston Star* referred to Auburn's offense as "sputtering." That was charitable.

---

* This happened in the 1976 Pro Bowl—and was deliberate. "Any other game and I wouldn't have tried it," Guy later admitted to reporter Tim Botos.

Based upon his rushing totals, Jackson was named the game's most valuable player. He was handed a trophy and turned it down. "I don't deserve this," he said, glumly. "I just don't."

For a winning team, Auburn's players didn't feel like winners. This was a game they should have dominated by three touchdowns. "We didn't play like we needed to," said Pat Arrington, the offensive tackle. "We left a lot on the field."

But just when hope was dead, a couple of unpredictable happenstances unfolded.

First, after his team trailed Texas for much of the Cotton Bowl, Georgia quarterback John Lastinger scrambled for a 17-yard fourth-quarter touchdown, giving the Bulldogs a 10–9 win and wiping out the Longhorns' national title hopes.

Second, with 48 seconds left in the Orange Bowl and Miami up a touchdown, Nebraska's Jeff Smith took a pitch from quarterback Turner Gill and sprinted 24 yards into the end zone. As the nation's undefeated top-ranked team, all the Cornhuskers had to do was kick the extra point, walk off with a tie, and clinch a championship.

Instead, Coach Tom Osborne defied logic and went for the two-point conversion. Gill's pass to Smith was broken up by Miami's Kenny Calhoun. Final score: Hurricanes 31, Cornhuskers 30.

The Auburn Tigers were the 1983 national champions!

They had to be!

Right?

Had to be.

The number 1 team lost.

The number 2 team lost.

The number 3 team won.

"It wasn't complicated," said David King, the Auburn cornerback. "We did what we needed to do. The teams ahead of us did not. We're the winners."

One day later the Associated Press released its final poll, and Miami, ranked fourth a mere twenty-four hours earlier, was deemed the national champions. Nebraska was second. And Auburn, third at the start of the week, remained third. The UPI poll, released shortly thereafter, also had Miami sitting at number 1 with 30 of 40 first-place votes. This defied logic. Auburn's opponents had won *37 more games than they lost* during the season. Miami's opponents were 73-62-3. "Why would the fourth-ranked team jump over the third-ranked team after the third-ranked team won its bowl game?" said Gerald Williams, an Auburn defensive tackle. "There's no argument for it."

As word of their status trickled in, Auburn's players and staffers were overcome by disbelief and heartbreak. "It was," said David Housel, "one of the worst nights of my life." There were moments of regret ("We screwed the pooch a little," said Arrington. "We beat Michigan by a touchdown or more, we're voted number 1."), moments of self-reflection ("If only I'd played better against Michigan," said Campbell. "Maybe then . . ."), moments of powerlessness ("It showed that doing the right thing isn't always rewarded," said Larry Cooper, a defensive tackle). Truth be told, football fate had been out of the Tigers' hands from the get-go. NBC paid a king's ransom to televise the Orange Bowl, and the accompanying hype from both the network and the NCAA was that the game was "the" national championship.

When, a few days after the return from New Orleans, Dye held a final team meeting, the coach was in good spirits. He insisted the Auburn Tigers were the national champions, and everyone on the planet knew the truth.*

"Be proud of yourselves," he said. "Because I am proud of every one of you."

---

* Auburn did finish number 1 in the *New York Times* year-end rankings. Which meant little.

CHAPTER 10

PAYDAYS

When Chuck Clanton was a defensive back at Auburn University in the early 1980s, he would be asked—on occasion—why he chose to play for the Tigers. His answers varied, depending what words and thoughts entered his head. Maybe it was the beauty of the campus, or the passion of the fans. Perhaps he chose Auburn because he sensed a kinship among the players. Maybe he thought it would be great to help the underdog finally topple mighty Alabama.

"The whole thing," Clanton said decades later, "was bullshit."

Back in the late days of 1979, as a senior at Pine Forest High in Pensacola, Florida, Clanton stood out. He was a 5-foot-11, 175-pound wide receiver/cornerback with 4.4 speed in the 40. As a junior he led the state with 13 interceptions, and as a senior caught 31 passes for 425 yards. More than fifty major colleges were after him, and Clanton was torn. He verbally committed to Florida State. Then he switched to Auburn. Then back to Florida State. Then, finally, Auburn.

Why?

"Because," he said, "they paid my parents *a lot* of money."

Clanton's father, Cleveland, was a police officer. His mother, Joyce, worked in a chemical factory. They raised five children in a small house in a run-down neighborhood. "My dream was to play wide receiver in the NFL," Clanton said. "Why the fuck would I go to a wishbone team like Auburn if they weren't lining our pockets? But Auburn came along, and suddenly we're getting new cars, a new van. Suddenly my parents, who were arguing about bills a minute ago, are hitting up the casino. Mom and Dad told me if I picked Florida State, I'd need to find a new place to live. I had to go to Auburn."

Clanton's experience was hardly unique. One of his Tiger teammates, running back James Brooks of Warner Robins (Ga.) High, had been recruited by Georgia, Florida State, and Auburn. He told all three schools that his commitment would cost $100,000.

Auburn forked over the dough—ignoring the fact that Brooks was functionally illiterate. When asked how he managed to graduate college, Brooks admitted, "I didn't have to go to class."

Both Clanton and Brooks arrived during the Doug Barfield era, when rules were ignored and money changed hands and many Division I programs landed the best high school players by paying off the best high school players. It wasn't the worst-kept secret in sports, because it wasn't much of a secret, and in 1979 Auburn was placed on two years' probation by the NCAA for—among other crimes—having a booster exchange cash for a player's commitment and having boosters offer outlandish sums of money to buy players' allotted game tickets.

When Pat Dye took over in 1981, he pledged to run an operation of "class and integrity." In his autobiography, *In the Arena,* he wrote: "How do our coaches recruit? We sell our program. We sell Auburn. We sell the Auburn family. We work hard, but we want kids who want to come to Auburn. Each of our assistant coaches uses his own personality recruiting."

Only, it wasn't true. Not even close to true. "It was an unwritten rule in the South," said Tommy Sims, a University of Tennessee cornerback. "Wanna get rich quick—go to Auburn." Although the Tigers weren't quite the cesspool of slime that existed during previous coaching staffs, Auburn football was far from clean. And that became particularly clear in early August of 1984—when the money *really* started pouring in.

In many ways, it was the one time in his four years on campus that Bo Jackson was thought of strictly as a football player. Although he dabbled in both indoor and outdoor track as a sophomore (in January he ran in the Millrose Games, marking his first-ever visit to New York City), Jackson skipped playing baseball—a by-product of a tired body and a general disinterest in devoting his spring to the tyrannical, bullhorn-barking reign of Paul Nix, the head coach. So when he returned to Auburn on August 3, 1984, for the football team's first evening meal, it was with the campuswide belief that his single-minded focus would make him the next Heisman Trophy winner.

In the wake of the 11-1 season and shoulda-been national championship, Auburn's boosters were happy. *Really* happy. For many of the players, joining the program meant being rewarded for success. A high school recruit wasn't always paid to come to Auburn, but he often knew that membership had its privileges. That's why, according to cornerback David King, the team's parking lot "suddenly looked like a fancy car dealership." There were Mercedes and BMWs, shiny Cadillacs and souped-up Buicks.

Jackson drove black *and* red Pontiac Fieros and a red Nissan 240SX, as well as a brand-new 1983 Olds Cutlass, which he used to pick up Alexander Wolff when *Sports Illustrated* sent the young scribe to Alabama for a profile.

In particular, King remembered Jackson's new room at the renovated Sewell Hall. It featured a large-screen television a good decade before most Americans had large-screen televisions. He also owned what had to be the biggest boom box on campus—"when those things were really popular," King said. "Double cassettes, enormous speakers. The whole deal."

Was Bo Jackson paid to come to Auburn to play football? He has long denied it. Was Bo Jackson paid *while* playing at Auburn? Without question. In a May 4, 1990, session with Dick Schaap, the co-author of his biography, Jackson went on a lengthy riff about all the things Frelon Abbott, the booster loosely affiliated with the university, provided for him. Most of the material never appeared in the book . . .

JACKSON: "They get you locked in by giving you all this money and conning you and fooling you. I almost got in a situation like that, but I got out of it in a hurry because I saw it. I said, 'Look, here's this back what you gave me. Here are your boots back you bought me. Here. Take it. I don't want it.'"

SCHAAP: "That was while you were still in college?"

JACKSON: "Yeah. I thought this guy was my friend, but he was out for one thing—to make money for himself."

SCHAAP: "Is he still in Bessemer?"

JACKSON: "I don't know. After, I told him I don't want to have no more dealings with you, no more nothing, I told him this down at Auburn, no more dealings with you, no more nothing. He said, 'Well, if that's the case you're going to have to pay me back all the stuff I've given you.' I said, 'Hold it. Well, let's start right now. Take this shit, take this shit, take this shit and get the fuck out of my room.' . . . He did the same thing with some more players, which I tried to tell them but they wouldn't listen."

Dye insisted his players weren't paid. Which, in the tapdancing-around-the-rules world of the big-time college coach, was a see-no-evil-hear-no-evil approach to survival. But if he looked at their cars and he admired their snazzy outfits and he asked one for the time (and saw a player locate the answer on his new five-thousand-dollar Rolex), he had to have known what was transpiring. He simply didn't involve himself in it.

Which made sense. Because pretty much everyone in America was cheating. Alabama paid players. Georgia paid players. Tennessee paid players. Florida paid players. If a program wanted to compete at the highest level, and enjoy all the perks that came with filled stadiums and televised Saturdays and kids in Laguna Niguel, California, and Mahopac, New York, knowing the words to your fight song, it meant purchasing elite talent. And if someone like Bo Jackson—one of ten kids raised by a single mother in a tiny house—had the option of signing with the New York Yankees for $150,000, you damn well better offer incentives to turn it down.* "Everyone was throwing big bucks at us," said Tony Robinson, the University of Tennessee's star quarterback and a onetime prized recruit out of Tallahassee, Florida. "Especially in the SEC, winning didn't come cheap."

At Auburn, there were two primary methods for players to accumulate wealth.

First, the exchanges of dough—known, conveniently, as "The Handshakes." When members of the team jogged off the field after practices and games, they were greeted by adult men anxious to offer congratulations and well wishes via a firm handshake. "They were boosters, and in the hand was money," said King. "From the time you walked down to the stadium and back you got a couple of grand in hand. That's not including the money that got slid under the door, or what was mailed to you." Entering the 1984 season, King (a senior) was averaging $2,500 to $3,000 a week in payouts. It got to the point where he was sending his mother, Beatrice, weekly $300 bundles. "I lied to her," he said, "and told her I'd gotten a part-time job."

"You'd get a lot of money that way, but it still wasn't really enough," said Lionel James. "Think about it. Most of us arrived poor. So the money handed to us—we used it to buy food, we used it to do laundry, we used it to go out on dates. I had a car that I paid for. It needed gas. That money went to gas. It was against NCAA rules, but was it wrong? I don't think so."

According to King, Dye stayed out of it—mostly. "If you started to complain about a booster not getting you enough, it could be a problem," he said. "Next thing you know, you're in Coach Dye's office."

---

* In a June 9, 1984, *Orlando Sentinel* story, New York Yankees owner George Steinbrenner said he turned up information that proved Auburn had paid for Jackson's services. "I offered Bo Jackson $150,000 to sign with the Yankees and he turned it down," Steinbrenner said. When called for comment, Dye said, "Hogwash." Steinbrenner threatened to turn over his material to the NCAA. He never followed through.

Second, there were ticket sales. In the summer, before seasons began, all members of the team were presented with four tickets to every game. This was sanctioned by the NCAA as a way for family members to watch their loved ones compete. Yet at Auburn, players were encouraged to peddle their tickets to boosters with assistant coaches acting as the middlemen for ungodly sums of money. In 1983, for example, a good seat at Maryland-Auburn would go for $15 face value. A generous booster might fork over $250. "I was dumb my freshman year," said Clanton. "I sold my 44 tickets for $2,500. I was so happy. Then I told a teammate, and he said, 'Shit, $2,500? I sold mine for $7,000.' The next year one of our coaches told me he could get me $3,000. I said, 'Fuck, no. I want $7,000 like everybody else.'" Clanton settled for $6,000—then found more tickets to sell. All told, he said he made about $17,000 in ticket peddling over two years with the program. He was far from alone. Most of Auburn's players were in on the price-gauging ticket business. The bigger the star, the bigger the payouts. "Why wouldn't you do it?" one player said. "The coaches had no problem with it, the school also didn't have a problem. So what was so bad?"

"You might sell individual tickets for big games for more money," Clanton said. "Let's say a superstar is coming to play at Auburn. You keep your tickets for those games, sell at the last minute. Big dollars, baby.

"Big fucking dollars."

Entering his junior year, Bo Jackson seemed particularly happy.

Maybe it was all the money coming in.

Maybe it was that he switched majors, from psychology to family and child development—"[so] I could try to figure out why I was the type of kid I was: angry and aggressive and jealous," he said.

Maybe it was the increased national hype. He was the odds-on favorite to take home the 1984 Heisman Trophy. "Bo Jackson," said Gil Brandt, the Dallas Cowboys vice president, "is as good as any running back in the pros."

Maybe it was a fairly adventurous summer—instead of remaining on campus, Jackson traveled to the Talladega Institute for the Deaf and Blind to speak with disabled children, then to Phoenix to film a series of public service announcements for the NCAA. Lastly, he went to Dallas with his teammate, linebacker Gregg Carr, to take pictures and appear in a video for the *Playboy* Pre-Season All-American team.

Or maybe it was falling in love.

Over his first two years of college, Jackson had plenty of sex with plenty of women. Before games, after games. Before practice, after practice. They came in all shapes and sizes and races and ethnicities, and were largely disposable bodies who entered his sphere, enjoyed a quick spin, then (*poof*) left. This time was different.

Her name was Allison Elease Hines. She was an eighteen-year-old freshman nursing student at Livingston University, a midsize liberal arts college located in west central Alabama. In December 1983, one of Hines's classmates was Keith Mack, Jackson's former backfield partner and running buddy at McAdory High. "Keith was always talking about 'My friend Bo . . . my friend Bo,'" said Hines. "I didn't know who he was, as far as sports went. But one day he brought Bo over when I was there, and we hit it off. I liked that he was a little different. I mean, he was wearing plaid pants. What guy wore plaid pants? We exchanged numbers at that point, and a week or two later he asked me out."

Their first date was dinner at Quincy's Family Steakhouse in Birmingham. Midway through the meal a young boy approached, pen and sheet of paper in hand, and asked Jackson for an autograph.

Hines was bewildered. When the child walked off, she asked, "Why did he want that from you?"

"Well," Jackson said, "I'm known a little for playing football."

For the first time since high school, Jackson was smitten. He called Hines regularly. He tried to see her as much as possible. Unlike the coeds who conveyor-belted through his room at Auburn, she was different. Unimpressed by fame. Willing to talk back. Quick with a snarky retort. In some ways, she was not unlike Bo's mother, Florence, whose toughness and take-no-crap mojo scared some, impressed others.

Hines had two previous boyfriends, but none similar to Bo. He was shy, but confident. Handsome, but not overly cocky about it. "He'd acknowledge me in front of others and make me feel just as special," she told the *Opelika-Auburn News*. "I liked that."

When football practices started up at 6:30 on the morning of Monday, August 6, Jackson was in the best condition—mentally and physically—of his life. There was no wear and tear from baseball, and he had money in his pocket, a major he was excited about and a girlfriend he genuinely loved. Plus, with Lionel James off to the NFL's San Diego Chargers, there was no ambiguity over who would receive the majority of carries. "If we get beat," Dye said, "we're going to get beat with Bo carrying the ball."

It was Bo Jackson's time.

Based upon 1983 accomplishments, the Tigers were ranked number 1 in the Associated Press's preseason poll, directly ahead of Nebraska, Pittsburgh, Clemson and UCLA. Their new quarterback, Pat Washington, had a stronger arm than the graduated Randy Campbell, and their new halfback, sophomore Brent Fullwood, was a 6-foot, 196-pound sledgehammer of a runner who clocked a 4.4 40 during drills. As a senior at St. Cloud (Florida) High, Fullwood ran for 2,304 yards and scored 27 times. "I'd actually say, as an every-down back, Brent might have been better than Bo," said Jack Crowe, the offensive coordinator and speaker of sacrilege. "He never took plays off, and he attacked the defense."

In a bit of scheduling delectability, the Tigers would open on August 27 at Giants Stadium in the Kickoff Classic against the Miami Hurricanes—(undeserving) defending champions. Miami was brash and bold and the kings of trash talk. Their new coach, a former Oklahoma State head man named Jimmy Johnson, was cocky and shit-spewing. Their starting quarterback, Bernie Kosar, was one of Jackson's perceived Heisman rivals.

When Auburn's players jogged onto the field, resplendent in all white, they were greeted by light applause. When Miami, wearing orange tops, followed, boos rained down. Many of the Hurricanes held single index fingers in the air, an ode to their status as defending national champions. Translation: *We* have what *you* want.

Auburn didn't play terribly. Miami didn't play magnificently. But while the Hurricane offensive line opened enough holes for fullback Alonzo Highsmith to rumble for 140 yards on 22 carries, the Tigers slogged their way through the night. "We weren't in shape," said Smokey Hodge, an Auburn linebacker. "And Miami was." Jackson's stat line was good, if not quite Heisman-esque (20 carried, 96 yards). He played well, but suffered a mild left ankle sprain late in the action that slowed him down. The final score was 20–18, with Miami winning on a 25-yard field goal with 6:08 remaining. "We were the better team," said Russ Carreker, a Tigers linebacker. "But we were probably hungover from 1983."

Afterward, a stoic Dye stared down at a stat sheet and stated what seemed to be obvious. "I believe," he said, "those folks who ranked us number one made a mistake."

The softness of those words masked an inner outrage. The Miami defeat burned. In the near three-week gap between the Kickoff Classic and a September 15 matchup at the University of Texas, Dye demoted *every* offensive starter (save Jackson and tight end Jeff Parks) to second team. It was a furious coach sending a message, and it was not a fun time to be an Auburn football player.

Dye had fire in his eyes, and every newspaper article seemed to hype the Texas matchup as make or break for a season that began with enormous expectations. "It is as big a game as they have ever faced," wrote Phillip Marshall in the *Montgomery Advertiser*. "A loss to Texas will mean the nation's number one team in the preseason is out of the national championship race."

What went underreported was that Jackson's ankle remained swollen.

Six days before kickoff, Dye told the media that Jackson, "isn't doing too good." Four days before kickoff, Jackson appeared to be improved. On September 15, the morning of kickoff, Jackson seemed fine. When he walked to the hotel lobby for breakfast, there was no apparent limp. Spirits were high. The combined powers of medicine and medical tape would, once again, prevail.

Only thing is, the ankle hurt. Jackson didn't say so at the time, but before each step he winced, with each stair he took a deep breath. He later admitted his ankle was "swollen and messed up." But Texas' players didn't need to know such information. So he was fine and ready to go. Perfectly fine.

The game began at 6:47 p.m. on a hot Texas night at Memorial Stadium. Deep into the third quarter, Auburn regained possession on its own 23, trailing 21–19. On second down and 10, Jackson took the handoff from Washington, accidentally slammed into his own quarterback, stepped left, rushed through a wide-open gap and dashed down the field. "Look out!" bellowed Jim Thacker, the play-by-play announcer, "he can fly!"

Jackson was off to the races. But not in the manner in which a 100 percent healthy Jackson would be off to the races. Jerry Gray, the All-American cornerback, came slicing in from Jackson's left, forced the running back to the sidelines, leaped up onto his shoulders, wrapped his right arm around Jackson's helmet and dragged him down as a cowboy does a steer, 53 yards from the line of scrimmage. "It wasn't a play where I was trying to hurt someone," recalled Gray. "It was a play where if I didn't catch him, no one would." As the two fell, Jackson landed *hard* on his right shoulder and rolled onto his back. A wave of pain shot through his body. "I fell with my elbow down and it just pushed everything up," Jackson said. "Nobody catches me from behind, nobody runs me down from behind. And I mean nobody. If I get a step on you there ain't no way in hell that you're going to catch me from behind. But I was playing with a busted ankle, and he just ran up like I wasn't even running and just jumped on my back and rolled me to the ground. As soon as I hit the ground and jumped up I knew something was wrong." Jackson tried pushing his dislocated shoulder back into the socket, and it worked enough that he fooled Auburn's trainers into allowing him to play a few more downs. "The guy never even grimaced," said Yann Cowart, an offensive guard. "It had to hurt like hell."

Auburn lost, 35–27, and afterward Jackson (who once again made a quick stop to the Texas locker room to let Gray know there were no hard feelings) was diagnosed with a separated right shoulder. The next day he was taken to East Alabama Medical Center, where doctors said an operation was necessary. His season was over. There would be no Heisman Trophy. No national championship. Just months and months of rehab. On September 16, an orthopedic surgeon named Jack Hughston performed the surgery at the Hughston Clinic in Columbus, Georgia, then told David Davidson of the *Atlanta Journal* that Jackson needed to be confined to a sling for three to four months.

For perhaps the first time in his life, Jackson realized how much he truly loved the game of football.

"I cried," he recalled, "like a baby."

In the aftermath of his surgery, Jackson was as down as anyone had ever seen him. Although he never enjoyed practices, and his work ethic could run a bit cold, football was a big chunk of his life. Now his comfortable, neat world was spiraling. Auburn destroyed Southern Miss the following week, and captured six straight minus its star. Want to see a marquee athlete feel a little obsolete? Have his team win without him. Want to see that same marquee athlete lose his damn mind? Have that team go on a six-game tear.

Lonely, depressed and in need of support, Jackson encouraged Allison Hines to make a bold life change. "I was visiting him a good amount," she recalled. "But after he got hurt he said he thought I needed to transfer to Auburn to be closer to him. He felt very strongly about it."

Hines's parents, Orsie and Mary, were against such a rash move. Allison was young and immature, but she was also in love. She and Jackson had been dating for nearly a year, and she believed they were destined to marry. So Hines packed her belongings and enrolled at Auburn University as a nursing major. "I knew almost no one," she said. "I had an empty apartment. I was nervous. But I was young and dumb and I fell for Bo."

One Saturday afternoon around this same time, Jackson was cruising campus with Tommie Agee when he spotted a beautiful woman heading in the opposite direction. "So we decided to follow her," Jackson recalled. "[Then] we just happened to meet each other one day in the big building where they hold most of the classes, and we sat down and talked. Then I got her phone number, gave her mine and we went on a date."

Her name was Linda Garrett. Well, technically Linda Garrett *Robinson*. Three years earlier, on February 27, 1981, Linda had married a repairman named Eluard Robinson inside the Saint Ignatius Catholic Church in Mobile, Alabama. According to an announcement in the *Mobile Press-Register*, the reception was held at the Ramada Inn on Airport Boulevard. Cake was served.

Now, three and a half years removed, Robinson was an Auburn graduate student, armed with a biology and health sciences degree from Tuskegee. She was twenty-eight years old (six years Jackson's senior), separated (but not divorced) from Eluard. Linda was pretty in an unconventional manner—she looked *a lot* like Tina Turner from the mid-1970s Ike and Tina days. "Bo was such a nice guy," Linda said years later. "We were friends for a couple of months before the love thing started. We would go to lunch and he would tell me about his dates. Then things started to feel different between us."

Through the years, Linda and Bo have relayed multiple versions of their origin story. In 1989, she told Henri Rix of the *Tulsa World* that they met in the Auburn student lounge. In 1993, Linda told Carrie Muskat, a *Chicago Tribune* sportswriter, "I was talking to one of the professors and I said, 'Who is that guy?' I knew he had to be a big guy on campus because everybody sort of made way every time he came through." She added that they bumped into one another at a gas station and made a lunch date. In a 1990 conversation with Dick Schaap, Jackson's biographer, Linda said, "I never thought of him [romantically]. I certainly never thought it would get to [marriage]." Bo, too, has shared multiple versions of a similar saga—he saw Linda, liked her, fell hard and fast. There was only one match for him— Linda Robinson.

This was news to Hines. She said dating Jackson was difficult, because as soon as she arrived in Auburn women would shoot threatening glares her way. She wasn't Allison Hines, per se, but *Bo Jackson's girlfriend*. The phone calls followed—"I never knew who they were from," she said. "But it was a lot of, 'Bitch!'—then a hang-up." She assumed she and Jackson were exclusive. They saw one another daily; they would end calls with "I love you"; they spoke of ultimately marrying and having a family.

She had no clue about the other women—not merely Jackson's blossoming side romance with Linda Robinson, but also the staggering number of coeds he was bedding. "I was foolish," Hines said. "But, again, I was in love. I really loved him. So maybe that blinded me. I don't know."

Bo Jackson was released from Doctor's Hospital in Columbus, Georgia, on a Thursday in September. He returned to Sewell Hall, where—according to Agee, his roommate—"he's just been laying around the room watching television." An athletic department official lied to a *Huntsville Times* reporter and insisted Jackson was in good spirits. In a matter of weeks Jackson dropped from 228 pounds to 210. This was supposed to be The Year of Bo Jackson, and suddenly the Associated Press wire was carrying an image of a depressed Jackson, sitting in street clothes on Auburn's sideline, right arm in a sling. In one newspaper, the *Johnson City Press*, the picture was accompanied by two words: Bench Warmer.

Ouch.

On Tuesday, September 25, Jackson—the postinjury object of sports media frenzy—agreed to talk with the press after a stretch of silence. That afternoon, approximately thirty media members crammed into Sewell Hall, where the wounded running back . . . didn't show up.

It was awkward and a little infuriating. Housel tried explaining it to the attendees—Jackson, he said, called from his mother's house in Bessemer and expressed regret over not being able to return in time. But the reasoning did not go over well. "Because Bo Jackson is all of these things, he can close his hospital door and have somebody outside to guard it and not let in anybody he doesn't want to talk to," wrote Bob Mayes of the *Huntsville Times*. "And Bo Jackson doesn't want to talk to the media."

Eight days later, Jackson finally entered the lobby of Sewell Hall to offer up the state of Bo. By now reporters had grown to expect the tough-to-talk-to Jackson, and that's precisely what they encountered. Though not exactly rude, he was short and curt. When asked by Chris Welch of the *Huntsville Times*, "What will you do the next two years?" Jackson replied, "What would *you* do if *you* were in my shoes?"

Far from intimidated, Welch cracked, "Take the money and run."

The room burst into laughter. Jackson did not laugh. He sat and scowled toward the men—all his elders, all behaving as if this specimen running back were an animal in a zoo. He was in no mood for giggles and gags. No mood to dance a hopeful comeback jig. "I'm tired," he said. "Tired of having nothing to do but go to school. It's also not easy watching from the sidelines. I don't enjoy watching."

In the weeks that followed there were mounting questions as to whether

Jackson would ever play again for Auburn. The upstart United States Football League was throwing money everywhere—and it was tempting. "I can't say yes and I can't say no," Jackson said of departing. "I'll cross that bridge when I come to it." He would likely be selected once again in the June Major League draft. Just as Herschel Walker bolted Georgia and seemed to never look back, what was left for Bo Jackson to prove?

"Honestly," said Ed Hinton of the *Atlanta Journal,* "I think most of us figured he'd take off. That he was done as a college football player."

The suggestion began in early October. Maybe if everything goes well with rehab, Jackson can return for the December 1 Alabama game. Then a headline in the *Atlanta Constitution*—BO JACKSON MAY BE READY FOR GEORGIA (the Tigers and Bulldogs were scheduled for November 17). When *Birmingham News* readers woke up and retrieved their newspapers on October 30, they were greeted by the joyous headline, BO'S BACK! Wrote Charles Hollis: "It couldn't be. But, yes, it was number thirty-four all right. And he was taking snaps with the first offensive unit."

There were multiple motivations for Jackson. He missed the game. He missed his teammates. He missed stardom. But one overlooked at the time: he was being overshadowed by his replacement. In hindsight, it sounds crazy. Bo Jackson—overshadowed? And yet, in Brent Fullwood, Dye had a top-shelf ball carrier who ran with a ferociousness Jackson sometimes lacked. Fullwood was smaller than Jackson, but at 6-feet, 196 pounds, far from small. He was slower than Jackson, but his 4.4 40 was far from turtle-like. Unlike Jackson, shiftiness was a go-to—opposing tacklers didn't merely have to worry about being pulverized, but also juked. "I was a hard runner and I prepared myself to hurt people," said Tim Jessie, the halfback. "Well, Brent Fullwood was just that with more speed. The kid was a hard runner. And he could fly."

"In many ways," said Kyle Collins, the walk-on H-back, "Brent was as good a football player as Bo."

Against Southern Miss, Fullwood returned a kickoff for 96 yards, then scored on a 1-yard plunge. A week later, Fullwood ripped up Tennessee for 134 rushing yards, and *The Tennessean's* David Climer opened his game story with two words: "Bo Who?" On October 13, Auburn traveled to Tallahassee to play number 9 Florida State in a matchup that—even with Jackson—would have been considered a toss-up. Fullwood dominated in the most Bo ways possible. Not only did he score three touchdowns, but with 48 seconds remaining he plowed into the end zone from four yards out for the winning score in a 42–41 thriller.

Jackson had to watch all this unfold, then read about it the next day. Without their onetime Heisman Trophy candidate, Auburn was 6-2 and number 11 in the latest AP poll. Never known for his work ethic, Jackson raised the intensity. He lifted weights. He swam laps in the university pool. He *fought* to come back.

The return finally happened on November 3, when the Tigers headed to Gainesville to face number 13 Florida in an SEC clash of titans. In the week leading up to the contest, Jackson practiced sparingly and without contact. On Tuesday, a doctor gave him the OK to play, and Herb Waldrop, the Tigers trainer, slid up to Dye and said, "We've got to make a decision about Bo."

"What kind of decision?" Dye replied.

"Whether he's going to play or not," said Waldrop.

"What?" Dye said. "This week?"

Waldrop nodded.

"Lordy mercy," Dye said.

Jackson was activated.

Most of the Tigers had no clue Jackson was preparing for action until they arrived at Florida Field, entered the locker room and saw the training staff taping him up. This was the stuff sports movies are made of—a tight shot of our star sliding shoulder pads over his head; a knowing nod between teammates; an Ennio Morricone score blaring as the protagonist dives over the end zone for a game-winning score. A tearful mother in the stands. Doves flying off into the sunset. It was all too good to be true.

Outfitted with a body girdle hidden beneath a sparkling-clean uniform, Jackson was fool's gold. He was technically good to go, but not entirely comfortable doing so. His first run came with 7:25 remaining in the second quarter, and it gained two yards. His second run went for nine. All told, Jackson carried five times for 16 total yards. The Gators won, 24–3.

Afterward, no one was particularly happy. The loss stung. When asked by a reporter whether the now-snapped six-game winning streak meant the team was better off without him, Jackson's expression turned dark. "I don't think that's because of me," he said. "I think the opposition had a lot to do with it." Teammates wondered, quietly, whether this experiment actually made sense. Never mess with a winning streak. With Fullwood as the marquee attraction, the Tigers had been unstoppable. Jackson's return complicated things. The *Montgomery Advertiser* ran a piece headlined TIGERS SAY THEIR 0-3 RECORD WITH JACKSON IS COINCIDENCE. But was it? "I was glad to see him back out there," said Collins afterward. "But we've won six straight games and we felt like we could win without him."

One week later, the scheduling gods handed Auburn and Jackson the greatest of presents: the University of Cincinnati's football team. If the Bearcats weren't America's worst Division I program, it was only because the Indiana Hoosiers populated the earth. Cinci arrived in Alabama as 31-point underdogs; a 2-6 team with a defeat to a I-AA opponent (Youngstown State) and a recent 42-10 pummeling at the hands of the (no-so) mighty Temple Owls.

A few days before the game, Dye announced that Jackson would return to the lineup. When he trotted onto the field for the opening series, 74,750 fans at Jordan-Hare Stadium stood to offer an ovation. Though still tentative and far from 100 percent, Jackson ran through the Bearcats shredded-cheese defense for 58 yards and three touchdowns on eight carries. The final score, 60-0, was Auburn's most lopsided win in fifty-two years. "Jackson," said Dave Currey, the Bearcats coach, "was everything people had said he was."

The Tigers won again on November 17, this time beating Georgia at home, 21-12. Jackson looked vastly improved from the Cincinnati game, running for 83 yards on 18 carries. He was, once more, *the* Bo Jackson, and the upcoming December 1 Iron Bowl clash against unranked Alabama was expected to turn into the crowning moment of what had been an otherwise disappointing season. The Tigers wouldn't win the national title. Jackson wouldn't win the Heisman Trophy. But a leveling of Alabama might serve as a warm shower after plowing through the mud. "It meant," said Jessie, "absolutely everything."

Auburn entered as seven-point favorites and—thanks to Florida (the regular season SEC champion) serving out an NCAA probation—Sugar Bowl hopefuls. Jackson devoted much of the lead-up to reminding writers that, coming out of McAdory High, the Crimson Tide was skeptical of his potential. "The last two years," he told the *Anniston Star*, "the coach who recruited me [Ken Donahue] has eaten his words."

Donahue had now heard this story on at least a thousand occasions, and while he dismissed it as nonsense (he insisted he never said Jackson couldn't play immediately), he was well versed in the modern athlete creating a narrative. Plus, he and the 4-6 Tide had bigger issues. For the first time in twenty-seven years, they entered the Iron Bowl with a losing record.

The magic wasn't there under Ray Perkins, the second-year head coach who inherited a bare cupboard from the late Bear Bryant and whose steel-jawed, emotionless approach to running a 1980s college football team didn't work. The season was lost, and there was only one way to preserve some dignity.

"Coach Perkins," a reporter asked during a lead-up press conference, "what will a win over Auburn do for your football team?"

Perkins stared the inquisitor down, then shot back, "You're not from Alabama, are you?"

The writer shook his head.

"I didn't think so," Perkins said. "It would take me all day to answer that one."

In the days before the skirmish at Birmingham's Legion Field, Alabama's athletic staffers hung signs throughout the facility that read STOP BO. It was both mantra and game plan—should the Tide's defense keep Jackson in check, and force quarterback Pat Washington to throw, they'd have a legitimate shot at winning.

Alabama led 17-7 heading into the fourth quarter, and no one on the Tigers sideline could quite figure out what was going on. The Sugar Bowl was slipping away. Dye later admitted he overlooked the Tide. Auburn finally woke up with 9:25 left in the game, when—on a third and 7 from the Tigers' 40—Washington faked a handoff to a charging Agee, then rolled right before pitching the ball to Fullwood, who galloped 60 yards down the sideline for the touchdown. Jackson jogged in the two-point conversion, and with 9:11 to play Alabama's lead was sliced to 17-15.

"And," said Al Michaels, calling the game for ABC, "they set up for what they hope will be a game-winning field goal down the line . . ."

The momentum had shifted. On the ensuing possession, Alabama quarterback Mike Shula threw a high pass that bounced off the hands of fullback Ricky Moore and into the mitts of defensive end Kevin Greene, who returned the ball to the Tide 17. The Tigers offense jogged back onto the field—"Auburn," said Lee Grosscup, Michaels's color man, "has opportune field possession and could put this ball game away."

After two pathetic tries that went nowhere, the Tigers faced third and 11 from the Alabama 18. Washington handed off to Jackson, then watched as he trampled over Cornelius Bennett, the Tide's All-American linebacker, and high-kneed his way to the Bama 4. "How many teams on third and 11 are gonna run?" said Michaels. "But when you have Bo Jackson in the backfield, you might as well take the chance!"

It was now first and goal from the 4. The game was over. Auburn had

Jackson, Fullwood and Agee—three future NFL standouts. Its offensive line included two men who would also wind up playing professionally. Alabama was a mediocre team with little to no heart.

Following a holding penalty and two stuffed runs, Auburn faced a third and goal from the 9. Washington faked the handoff, then stepped, juked and bolted up the middle all the way to the 1-yard line. Tiger fans leaped to their feet.

"So now it's fourth and goal," said Michaels, "and Pat Dye has to make the decision. Do you go for what figures to be the sure field goal and go up by a point, or do you try for the touchdown? That's his decision right now."

Grosscup, long-ago first-team All-American quarterback at the University of Utah, took a second and added, "I think I'm going for the sure field goal."

"I do, too," Michaels said. "With all that's at stake for him right now."

The clock read 3:27. The ball was positioned two fingernails inside the 1. Dye and Jack Crowe, the offensive coordinator, conferred on the Auburn sideline. Earlier in the game, Alabama's Van Tiffin had kicked a 52-yard field goal with distance to spare. Dye couldn't get that out of his head. If Auburn went for three, there would still be plenty of time for the Tide to reach Tiffin's range.

"Field goal?" asked Crowe.

"No, no," replied Dye, shaking his head.

The noise inside Legion Field was earsplitting. Ron Middleton, the tight end, brought the play into the huddle and relayed it to Washington. It was "Lead Combo"—a sweep by Fullwood, with Agee and Jackson paving the way. The quarterback's job was to observe the defense and determine direction. A pitch to the right would be "56 Combo." A pitch to the left would be "57 Combo." A month and a half earlier, the call was used to score the winning touchdown against Florida State.

The Alabama defensive players held hands in the huddle, then placed all 11 men near the line of scrimmage. Auburn's offense set up—no wide receivers, just bulldozers up front, Washington at quarterback, Agee behind him and Fullwood to the left, Jackson to the right. Dye stood by himself, hands on knees. Based upon recent history, most everyone in the stadium (and certainly the Tide sideline) assumed the play would be Bo Over The Top II. Which made sense—there was little proof Jackson could be stopped.

From his spot, freshman free safety Rory Turner was freaking out. Less than a year removed from Gordon Central High in Decatur, Georgia, he chose Alabama because he wanted to chase a national championship, only to find himself on one of the worst Tide teams in decades. Perkins liked the way Turner attacked the ball, and nicknamed him "The Black Assassin." On the verge of yet another loss, Turner felt like anything but an assassin. He found himself thinking, *Please don't give the ball to Bo.*

"I was genuinely nervous because I knew Bo was about to get it," said Turner. "The coaches told me to be in the right place at the right time. But with Bo, was there really a right place?"

Washington called "56 Combo"—a Fullwood sweep right. He grabbed the snap from center and quickly spun to his left. Turner followed the football, not the backs. As Agee rammed straight ahead, Turner ignored him. Then—as Turner recalled it years later—"some weird stuff happened." Fullwood started drifting right. And Jackson . . .

Bo Jackson heard the incorrect play call. He was certain Washington had said, "57 Combo." Beyond certain. So (*glub*) he ran the wrong way.

"It was impossibly loud by the end zones, because the sound had no-where to go," recalled Freddy Weygand, a Tigers wide receiver. "Bo just didn't hear it right."

Jackson was supposed to bolt to his right and help clear a path for Full-wood coming around the corner. Instead, Jackson took a step and a half to his left, where he briefly bumped into Fullwood as Washington readied to flip the ball. Fullwood paused for a second, grabbed the pigskin and was met at the line by a trio of Alabama defenders. "When I saw [Middleton] block down," said Turner, "I saw the biggest hole in the whole wide world." Fullwood was first hit by linebacker Randy Rockwell, then cornerback Vernon Wilkinson. Finally, Turner slammed into Fullwood's midsection, forcing him out of bounds for no gain.

"Man, how could [Dye] do that?" Emanuel King, the Alabama line-backer, said afterward. "I don't guess he had much respect for our defense. But we were expecting Bo, either over the top or on a sweep. That's the man I've got to give the ball to if I'm Coach Dye."

Added Curt Jarvis, the Alabama noseguard: "When they decided to go for six, it was like a condemned killer getting a reprieve as he's being buckled in the electric chair." Just as the 1982 Iron Bowl would be forever remembered as "Bo Over The Top," the 1984 game was deemed "Wrong Way Bo." What goes forgotten is Auburn's defense actually stonewalled Al-abama on its next possession, and with nine seconds remaining and the score 17–15, kicker Robert McGinty shanked a 42-yard field goal that would have handed the Tigers the triumph.

Afterward, the Alabama locker room was a whirlwind of song and dance and hugs and screams. Some players sobbed for joy. Outside the door, fans stomped their feet and clapped their hands to the fading sounds of the song "Yea, Alabama." Moore, the fullback, yelled aloud, "Auburn's mouth is shut! Now they've got to listen to us! Now can't nobody say we're a bunch of losers!"

Across the way, the Auburn locker room was silent. Dye met with the media and pinned the loss on Jackson. "If I had known Bo was going the wrong way on the sweep," he said, "I would've gone for the field goal."

Jackson heard the words—heard *them all*. He pretended to not be hurt, but the cut was deep. No one on Auburn's offense had played well. Not Washington, not Fullwood, not the line. Hell, Jackson—still suffering severe shoulder pain—ran for 120 yards against Alabama. He gave everything he had, and refused to complain when his number was called.*

On December 27, Auburn wrapped its year with a trip to Memphis for a 21-15 win over Arkansas in the Liberty Bowl. Jackson was named MVP thanks to a game-winning 39-yard touchdown run, but it all felt anticlimactic. Of the 49,000 in attendance, a solid 98 percent seemed to be rooting for the Razorbacks.

"Loyalty," wrote Donny Claxton in the *Plainsman*, "should be made of sterner stuff."

---

* To his credit, Jackson was able to appreciate a good joke after the Alabama fiasco. His favorite: "How do you get to Memphis? Go to the Alabama one-yard line and turn left."

CHAPTER 11

A BAIRD MAN

In the late summer days of 1984, Paul Nix announced that after twenty-two seasons he would soon retire (aka: resign gracefully to avoid being fired) as Auburn's baseball coach. Nix was fifty-one, and the game passed him by. Once upon a time, Nix had guided the program to two College World Series berths. Now, wrinkled from too many days in the Alabama sun, his expiration date had arrived.

Though Jackson explained away his sophomore year sans baseball as a desire to focus on track, the number 1 reason he didn't return to the diamond was the unpleasantness of Nix.

Now, however, not only was Nix gone, but his replacement was a bundle of joy. On May 30, 1984, Auburn offered the job to Hal Baird, the thirty-four-year-old East Carolina head coach who took the Pirates to two Division I playoffs over the past three seasons. Pat Dye, who doubled as Auburn's athletic director, had known Baird from their East Carolina days, and after hearing one Nix complaint after another, believed him to be the perfect hire. In fact, one year earlier Baird asked Dye to serve as a reference for the open University of Florida job. The request was denied—Dye knew Nix wasn't long for Auburn, and there was only one man he wanted. "He's a proven winner," Dye said upon introducing Baird. "He's clearly one of the nation's outstanding baseball coaches."

Shortly after arriving, Baird asked Nix if he would be willing to chat over lunch, and the meeting was awkward. Baird had been told Nix voluntarily quit. "I didn't realize it wasn't a retirement by choice until I was sitting across from him," Baird said. "My comment to him was, 'Coach, these kids are your kids and this program is your program. You're welcome in this dugout any time you want.'"

Baird never saw Nix again.

The new coach happened to be friends with Bobby Wallace, Dye's football assistant, and after accepting the position he asked, "Any idea why Bo didn't play baseball last season?"

Wallace smirked knowingly.

"I'll tell you what," Wallace said. "He's gonna play this year."

A few days after Baird's lunch with Nix, Jackson stopped by the baseball office for a sit-down. Over twenty minutes, Baird explained what he was looking for, what he wanted, what he thought the program could become. "Bo," he said, "if you're game I'm very much looking forward to you being a part of this."

"I'll be there," Jackson replied.

"And those three words—*I'll be there*—are a mantra I could write a book about," said Baird. "Because Bo Jackson is the most literal person in the world. If he says something, you can go to the bank on it. If you ask him the same question twice he's insulted."

The Auburn football team played in the Liberty Bowl on December 27, 1984, and after a couple of weeks away from sports, Jackson reported to Plainsman Park for the first day of baseball practice. Baird and the Auburn players were uncertain what to expect. Jackson had not picked up a bat in nearly two years. "I thought, 'That's really not enough time to face Division I pitching,'" Baird said. "Boy, I was wrong."

The new coach was hardly a baseball novice. He pitched collegiately at East Carolina, then bounced around the minors from 1971 to 1976, spending the majority of his time in the Kansas City Royals system. Baird was one of *those* guys—good enough to win in the bushes, lacking enough to never get promoted past Triple A. Along the way, though, he played with some of the best in the game. George Brett. Frank White. Ruppert Jones. Al Cowens. Dennis Leonard. He watched and observed and took mental notes. And the one thing he was certain of: no one owned what Bo Jackson owned. "He's the only guy I ever saw who made marked improvement day by day," Baird said. "That's how superior physically he was.

"I saw four or five guys, total, who had the type of power Bo possesses; three or four who could run like he can; and three or four who could throw like he can. But those were twelve different people. It sounds like I'm talking about Superman. When I got [to Auburn], Pat Dye told me, 'Hal, you have the chance to coach the greatest athlete ever.' I thought he was exaggerating. He wasn't. Bo was the only person I ever saw who could alter the geometry of a baseball field. The ninety feet, the sixty feet, six inches—those are all baseball measurements wonderfully implemented to test a human's abilities. But Bo upset those balances. Ninety feet wasn't far enough for him. Expected home run distances weren't long enough for him. He would beat out two-hoppers to short; he would make three-hundred-foot throws. There was something to marvel at every single day."

The Tigers opened with a two-day, three-game series at Tennessee. Entering the February 23 doubleheader at Lower Hudson Field, Baird had still rarely seen Jackson play. His debut at bat came in the first inning, against Vols starter Steve Searcy. This was the type of pitcher Jackson hated—a left-handed control artist who painted the corners of the plate. Searcy threw Jackson a looping curveball that broke inside. Jackson tried checking his swing, but made contact on a soft roller back toward the left of the mound. "Easy out," recalled Baird. "Average grounder."

As Searcy casually pivoted to field the ball, Jackson galloped down the line. Greg Newsom, the Vols second baseman, screamed, "Hurry! Hurry!," but by the time the ball arrived, Jackson was three steps past the bag. "The pitcher did nothing wrong," said Baird. "He actually did everything right. But Bo defied physics." Auburn lost, 7–5, but won the nightcap, 6–5, when Jackson blasted a mammoth homer.

One day later, Jackson homered again—a three-run shot in the sixth, then a three-run triple in the ninth to lead Auburn to a 12–5 rout. Bobby Gaylor, the Vols' fantastic shortstop and a future pro, observed the spectacle with wide-eyed wonder. "I was at shortstop, probably a hundred feet away, and when he swung and missed you could literally hear the swoosh," said Gaylor. "I've played thousands of games at shortstop, and that's the only guy I've ever heard like that. I later learned that's the sound of torque. How amazing is that? You could stand a hundred feet away and hear the sound of Bo Jackson's torque."

Under Baird, the Tigers were rejuvenated. Were they a great baseball team prepared to fight for conference supremacy? No. But they were happy and peppy and engaged. Auburn opened at home on February 27 with a 22–7 dicing of Samford, during which Jackson went 3-for-3 and—with eyes closed, weight on the wrong foot—took a fastball from Joey Simms and sent it beyond a wall and bouncing through a parking lot. Over the season's first month and a half, Auburn fed on the corpses of lesser teams like Birmingham-Southern (Jackson hit two doubles and scored three runs in a 15-7 win) and Alabama-Birmingham (Jackson went 5-for-6 with a home run in a 14–11 thriller) while suffering sweeps at the hands of the SEC's two elite powerhouses, Mississippi State and LSU. Through fifteen games,

Jackson was hitting a conference-best .512 with 5 homers, 15 RBI and 20 runs scored for the 9-6 Tigers. "Bo isn't a polished baseball player," Baird said at the time. "But he's a *tremendous* athlete."

The day that stood out was March 17, when the Tigers boarded their dumpy team bus and traveled ninety miles south to the campus of Division II Troy State. For Auburn, playing at Pace Field against a lesser opponent meant nothing. For the hosts, the visit from Baird's club was Game 7 of the World Series.

The Trojans starting pitcher was Ron Warren, a twenty-one-year-old junior lefty later to be plucked by the Boston Red Sox in the 18th round of the 1986 Draft. Warren was a legit college ace who befuddled hitters with a snack bar of breaking balls. That's what happened in Jackson's first four at bats—all outs via curveballs. "You knew not to give him anything straight," said Warren. "So I tried confusing him." Troy State's cheering section, "the Troy Mafia," was made up of local bumpkins who came prepared to heckle opponents in the most vile possible ways. The Mafia was primarily retired factory workers, and they reveled in drunken orneriness. With each Jackson failure, the Mafia gained steam.

"You fucking suck . . ."

"Go back to picking cotton . . ."

In the sixth inning, Auburn had runners on second and third. Chase Riddle, Troy's head coach, walked to the mound, removed Warren and called in Scott Baldwin, a soft-throwing righty whose velocity topped out around 83 mph. A recent transfer from Lurleen B. Wallace Community College, Baldwin was new to the world of pitching to colossuses. Before returning to the dugout, Riddle offered some wisdom. "Don't throw strikes," he said in a thick drawl. "You throw this one three curves in the dirt, he'll chase 'em three times."

Baldwin gripped the baseball and peered in for the sign from Ray Stephens, his catcher. Four fingers—*changeup.*

The pitcher slid back, stepped forward and threw an absolutely picture perfect change. Jackson was as fooled as one can be—he read fastball, cocked his elbow, began his swing, then . . . *whoooooooa.* Leaning forward at a crumpled 65-degree angle, with only his left hand attached to the nub of the bat and his right heel high off the ground, Jackson somehow made herky-jerky contact and watched the baseball fly . . . and fly . . . and fly . . . and fly.

In Warren's retelling, the baseball soared halfway over an intramural field and 500 feet away from home plate. "Longest home run I've ever seen," he said. This is slight hyperbole. Jackson used his single arm and a grapefruit-size wrist to send the ball roughly 350 feet and over the right center fence. "How did he do that?" said Greg Frady, a Troy infielder. "I still don't know."

The members of the Troy Mafia said nothing.

The players of the Trojans bench said nothing.

Baird, watching and mock rubbing his eyes, said nothing.

Auburn won, 12–6, and those involved left certain they had bore witness to a once-in-a-lifetime feat of baseball strength.

Sixteen days later, that idea was put to shame.

The University of Georgia's Foley Field was far more high school complex than Division I baseball mecca.

Behind home plate stood an ugly two-story building, with a cinderblock concession stand on the first floor and a small wooden press box on the second. To reach their final writing place, media members had to *enter* the concession stand, dodge the stacked cardboard boxes filled with Twix and Coca-Cola and climb a rickety staircase. Fans sat in metal bleachers, separated from the playing field by a chain-link fence. There were no clubhouses for the teams—all players changed in the nearby football stadium, then walked over. "The facility was no better than an American Legion field," said Chip Caray, who announced Diamond Dogs (as Georgia's baseball team was known) games for the campus radio station. "It was primitive."

When Steve Webber, the University of Florida's pitching coach, took over the Georgia program in 1981, he knew Foley Field would be a recruiting thorn. No sane human could look over the facility and be impressed. "At the very least, we needed lights," said Webber. "So I brought it up through the years and finally we got them. It was a *big* deal."

The steel light poles and fixtures weren't particularly fancy, but they meant (at long last) the University of Georgia could host night baseball games.

On the evening of April 2, 1985, the school-record 3,217 spectators who stuffed into Foley Field were handed certificates that read, in cursive writing, I WAS THERE THE NIGHT THEY TURNED THE LIGHTS ON AT FOLEY FIELD.

The scheduling of Auburn was no coincidence. The Georgia athletic department—headed by athletic director/football coach Vince Dooley—was committed to making the night a big deal, and what could be bigger than having Georgia's enemy enter the facility? Not that Bo Jackson thought himself the Bulldogs' enemy. Or, for that matter, anyone's enemy. But as the comparisons to Herschel Walker intensified year by year, the number of scoffing Georgia loyalists also intensified. "It was always *the* debate," said Charles Odum, who covered the game for the *Athens Daily News*. "Bo or Herschel? Herschel or Bo? In Athens, there was no question—it was always Herschel Walker."

The Bulldogs broke out all the stops. In the lead-up, the Georgia Pep Band played a deafening "Glory, Glory!" Dooley walked to the mound alongside Julius Bishop, the long-ago Athens mayor and a Bulldog back in the mid-1930s. After Bishop tossed the first pitch to Bulldogs catcher Roger Miller, Georgia's players jogged to their positions accompanied by a standing ovation. Cameras clicked. Flashes flashed.

A few days earlier Webber informed Larry Lyons, a right-hander from Gainesville, Florida, that he would be starting the first night game. This was no small thing to a kid who, one year prior, was pitching for Middle Georgia Junior College in the tiny town of Cochran. Now he would be performing before a full house, against the nation's most acclaimed college athlete.

Lyons threw three pitches—a fastball that topped out at 89, a slider and a knuckle curve he learned from mimicking former Dodger All-Star Burt Hooton. His weakness was his heater. "He threw it straight a lot," said Doug Givler, a Bulldogs relief pitcher. "Larry was good, but if his fastball was off the other team was gonna hit it *really far.*"

Eight games earlier Baird had moved Jackson up in the lineup from sixth to cleanup, and in the top of the first he grounded out to Georgia shortstop Jimmy Harrell. As he jogged back to the Auburn dugout, Jackson absorbed a waterfall of verbal abuse from the Diamond Dogs loyalists who sat behind the right-field fence in an area referred to as Kudzu Hill. "It was a steep incline, and a lot of times people had to hold on to the Kudzu vines to keep from sliding down," said Ivan Aronin, a writer for the *Red & Black*, Georgia's student newspaper. "There was no alcohol allowed in the stadium, but because the hill was outside the fence people would drink as much beer as possible. And they would heckle the hell out of the opposing players."

When the half inning ended and Jackson trotted back to the outfield, the barbs turned ugly. Racist language. Homophobic language. Cursing. A couple of fans launched plastic footballs at Jackson. This continued frame after frame, until Jackson's next at bat in the top of the fourth, with no one on and the score tied at 2. As soon as he was announced, the Kudzu Hill gang started up.

Miller, the Georgia catcher, placed one finger down for an inside fastball. Lyons, who measured 6-foot-2 and 185 pounds, didn't quite know how to feel about this. "There were two things I thought about before pitching to Bo," said Lyons. "I didn't want to hit him, and I didn't want to get hit by him. He was an imposing man. His arms were like bazookas. He ran like a gazelle. Me? I was all about self-preservation." Lyons unfolded into his windup, then released the baseball. As it left his right hand and drifted gently toward the plate, two things became obvious:

1. It was a shit fastball.
2. It was straight as a dart.

Jackson timed it all perfectly. He drew his Easton back, stepped and—*Pop.*

No—*Pop!*

No—*POP!*

It sounded like a cement truck slamming into another cement truck—so loud that a number of writers inside the press box reflexively ducked.

"Then it all went *very* quiet," said Lyons.

"Never seen anything like it," said Givler.

"You had the normal chatter of a baseball game, and then when he hit the ball—it was like a vacuum," said Tommy Tomlinson, a Georgia student who attended the game and went on to become a renowned sportswriter. "All the noise stopped. I don't remember anything in my ears except silence."

The baseball blazed, comet-like, toward the left-center wall, some 405 feet away. It cleared the 85-foot-high center-field light pole and slammed into the actual light fixture—*as it was still rising.* Steve Carter, playing deep center field, never budged. Ronnie Wenrich, standing in left field, never budged. An All-SEC freshman from Middleburg, Pennsylvania, Wenrich realized the magnitude at hand. He had spotted Bigfoot. "It didn't look real," Wenrich said. "The only thing missing was the sparks flying off the ball. If I would have turned and started to run as soon as he made contact, that ball would have still beaten me to the fence. It looked like a Bugs Bunny cartoon."[*]

In thirty-nine days, a movie starring Robert Redford called *The Natural* would hit theaters and have audiences talking about fictional home runs disappearing into the lights. Bo Jackson's shot was real. "I remember

---

[*] On April 2, 2021, I emailed Lyons a copy of the game's box score. He replied, warmly, "Be sure to emphasize the groundout in the first!"

thinking that the ball must be flat on two ends," said Ed Thomas, a Georgia assistant sports information director. "The side where Bo hit it and the side where it hit the lights." As Jackson rounded the bases, no one was quite sure how to respond. Lyons could only chuckle. The meatheads on Kudzu Hill said nothing. Inside the Auburn dugout, mayhem ensued. Scott Tillery, a Tigers pitcher and engineering student, dug out a pad and pencil and tried calculating how far the unencumbered baseball traveled. His final number: *At least* 600 feet. When the ball bounced off the lights and fell toward the infield, Harrell, the shortstop, picked it up and rolled it outside a baseline.

"I have been to a lot of baseball games," said Tomlinson. "I have seen a lot of home runs. I've seen a good number of tape-measure shots. But I have never, ever, ever seen a ball hit that hard."

When the inning ended Jackson returned to the outfield, where—behind the right-field fence—the occupants of Kudzu Hill rose to offer a standing ovation, then bow in unison.

Jackson tipped his cap.

That easily could have completed a miraculous story. An unprecedented home run in a first-ever night game at a rival university. But no. Not with Bo Jackson.

In the sixth inning he returned to the plate, returned to face Lyons and belted his second home run of the game—this one merely a very long shot beyond the left-field wall. He was intentionally walked to load the bases his next time up but then—in the eighth—blasted his third homer. "It would almost be funny," said Lyons, "if he wasn't doing it to your team. And to me."

The Tigers led, 15–11, entering the top of the ninth, then put together an eight-run inning to seal a 23–11 drubbing. During that final frame, Jackson had one last moment in the spotlight. He smoked a line drive that traveled between first and second and into the right-center gap. As he cruised into second base with a stand-up double, the Kudzu Hill occupants sarcastically booed.

"They wanted the Bo show to continue," said Wenrich. "In a way, I think we all did."

The next afternoon, before Auburn and Georgia were to play one more game, Lyons was hanging by the batting cage when he saw Jackson sitting alone in the Tigers dugout. He sheepishly approached. "I just wanted to shake your hand," he said. "I've always dreamed of making a record book, and last night you allowed me to do that. Thanks, Bo."

Jackson held a mock stare before breaking into a cackle.

"Hey," he said, "it was my pleasure."

Bo Jackson was tearing up the diamond and scouts came calling.

This wasn't like his days at McAdory High, where bird dogs popped up behind a cage, in a parking lot, at the base of a field. No, this was significantly more professional.

You couldn't sneak up on Hal Baird. Whether it was Ed Creech from the Expos or Marty Maier with the Cardinals or Ellis Dungan with the Blue Jays, no one was going to slither around outside the system. So they arrived, they checked in with the head coach, they took their seats and they watched the Bo show.

Which was, recalled Dungan, "phenomenal." Jackson wasn't the SEC's best player—that honor belonged to Will Clark, Mississippi State's sweet-swinging first baseman. And he wasn't the most polished player—that honor belonged to Rafael Palmeiro, an outfielder also of Mississippi State. He didn't have the best instincts, his mechanics were rough, his baseball IQ was still TBD, he couldn't touch a curveball. But the things he did . . .

"I saw him hit a ball off the right-field wall at Auburn," Creech recalled. "The right fielder picked up the ball, turned around and by the time he hit the cutoff man Bo was on third base—standing up."

"I saw him play against Mississippi State," said Dick Egan, a scout with the Major League Scouting Bureau. "He was playing center, ran into the left-field gap, caught a ball at the wall and threw the guy out tagging from second to third. Didn't just throw him out—did it by five feet. He put on performances you never saw before, and would never see again."

In an April 18, 1985, article in the *Auburn Plainsman*, Pat Dye was praised for being open-minded and gracious about two of his stars— Jackson and wide receiver Trey Gainous—playing baseball. Which stood *mostly* true. But the anxiety was mounting. After the 1984 football season wrapped, Jackson told a handful of reporters that he needed to weigh his options in regard to returning for a senior season. "I'm not saying I'm leaving and I'm not saying I'm staying," he said. "I'm concerned about Bo Jackson, number one."

This was a terrifying thought. By now, Jackson was no mere football player. He was a collegiate supernova. He was the key to national championship hopes. He was the best opportunity for an Auburn player to capture the Heisman Trophy for the first time since quarterback Pat Sullivan in

1971. Entering 1985, never had more applications arrived at the university admission offices. Never had the bookstore sold more jerseys than the blue-and-white number 34s that flew off hangers. Never had baseball games been better attended. It was no coincidence that the Board of Trustees approved a $15 million expansion of Jordan-Hare Stadium that would increase seating capacity from 75,000 to 85,000.

The program and its boosters could continue funneling Jackson cash and goods. The legit fear, however, was they could no longer match the inevitably lucrative offer of a Major League franchise.

So Auburn did something else.

On Friday, March 29, the Bo Jackson–less Tigers football team commenced spring practices with many of the familiar faces and lofty expectations, but also in the midst of an enormous philosophical shift: the offense would operate exclusively out of the I-formation.

The timing was not coincidental. In the wishbone, Jackson shared ball-carrying duties with two other running backs. Now, at the top of the I, he would run a Herschel-esque thirty to forty times per game. When asked at the time, Jack Crowe, the offensive coordinator, smiled and said all the right things. *We have the ideal personnel. Bo is ready to blossom. This will be incredibly exciting.* It was nonsense. "I hated it," he recalled years later. "We were trying to make Bo Herschel Walker, but he wasn't Herschel. The wishbone was a good offense for us. To run out of the I, you have to be a bona fide all-out, go-to-war, I'm-gonna-live-and-die-with-what-I-do-today back. That was Herschel at Georgia. That wasn't Bo."

Crowe, however, was powerless. Bo Jackson couldn't leave. If that meant redesigning the offense into something the coordinator wasn't comfortable with—so be it. Offensive coordinators were a dime a dozen. Six-foot-one, 225-pound halfbacks with Olympic speed and Lou Ferrigno strength were not.

"I understood the deal," Crowe said. "My options were a bit limited."

Though Auburn's baseball team missed out on the SEC playoffs, the season had been a banner one. The Tigers posted a 30-22 record—the most wins for the school since 1978. Right fielder Paul Foster quietly set team records for hits (87), RBI (74) and batting average (.433), and Jackson's stat line (.401, 17 home runs, 43 RBI) was an ode to a ballplayer who had things figured out. "He's the most fundamentally crude awesome baseball player I've ever seen," said Rob Leary, Louisiana State's catcher. "His potential was limitless."

The baseball season ended on May 5 with a 4–3 loss to LSU, and over the next month all talk turned toward the June 3 Major League Baseball amateur draft. Kenny Gonzales, the Kansas City Royals scout who had been tracking Jackson for years, filed a report two months before teams would be making their selections. He referred to Jackson as, "A complete type player with outstanding tools; can simply do it all and didn't even play baseball last year. A gifted athlete; the best pure athlete in America today."

Wrote N. Brooks Clark in *Sports Illustrated*:

The scouts see Jackson playing centerfield and start rubbing their wings like a chorus of crickets on a summer night. Joe Campbell, a bird dog for the Dodgers, says he has never scouted anyone more talented. Dickey Martin of the Braves says Jackson has graded higher on ability than any prospect since Dave Winfield. And Dick Egan of the Major League Scouting Bureau says flatly, "He's got as much talent as Mickey Mantle or Willie Mays."

Were Jackson a lock to depart college for a professional baseball career, he would go number 1 overall. On May 27, however, Jackson told Charles Hollis of the *Birmingham News* that his plan was to return to Auburn for his senior season. "I will be back," he said. A beat—"Those are my plans now."

Ultimately, the risk of using a high pick, then having him reject your enticements, was too great. With the number 1 selection in the June draft, the Milwaukee Brewers grabbed B. J. Surhoff, a catcher from the University of North Carolina. Clark, the Mississippi State standout, went second to the San Francisco Giants, then Oklahoma pitcher Bobby Witt to the Texas Rangers. Finally, with the 511th slot in the 20th round, the California Angels took a shot and drafted Vincent "Bo" Jackson, outfielder, Auburn University.

Larry Himes, the team's scouting director, excitedly spoke of the limitless possibilities of Bo Jackson wearing a halo. He invited Jackson to visit during the team's July 4 through July 14 home stand, work out with the club, meet the stars and "get an idea of the atmosphere around a major league ballclub."

"Reggie Jackson spent 180 days in the minors," Himes told *USA Today's* Karen Allen. "Kirk Gibson spent 142. That's about what we figure Bo would need—500 to 700 at bats to get his rhythm and fine-tune his skills."

Gene Autry, the Angels owner, was a fabled showman who loved big-name veterans and sparkly headlines. His was the team of Reggie Jackson, of Rod Carew, of Bobby Grich and Fred Lynn and Doug DeCinces. As for scouting and player development, "He didn't really care," said Himes. "Drafts and draft picks didn't interest him." The Angels (really, Himes) had some thoughts on how to woo Jackson. The team compiled a packet of information showing the advantages of baseball over football, then had it delivered to Sewell Hall. It had Reggie Jackson, the franchise superstar, give Bo Jackson a call. At the time the Southeastern Conference enforced an (antiquated, unfair) rule where two-sport athletes couldn't play collegiately in one endeavor and professional in another. California was prepared to sue the SEC on Jackson's behalf, believing the conference had no leg to stand on. Alas, Bo Jackson wanted none of it. On June 25, he said, "I'm not going to California. It was nice of them to invite me, but there's really no reason for me to do that. I'm busy with school and getting ready for football now."

On February 14, 1985, the Auburn chapter of the Kappa Alpha Theta sorority hosted a "Love Auction." All students were invited to attend and bid on such hunka hunka hunks as university president James Everett Martin,* Aubie the mascot, linebacker Gregg Carr and—most notably—Bo Jackson.

Nothing *actually* happened—a few mock squeals when the fifty-one-year-old Martin waved to the crowd, laughs for Aubie, a couple of suggestive whistles toward Carr and Jackson. The winning bidders walked away with a hug, a Polaroid photo and a peck on the cheek. It was innocent fun.

Yet, to be a football player at Auburn in the mid-1980s was to oftentimes lather oneself in the pleasures of raw, youthful sexual suggestiveness. It all began during the recruiting process, when high school stars came to campus for an official visit and were greeted by members of the Tigerettes—aka (in university speak): "public relations representatives for Auburn's athletic department."

By sheer coincidence, the thirty or so members of the Tigerettes were all female students, all in shape, all attractive. They were mostly white, often blond, always bubbly and flirtatious. Generally speaking, the members of the Tigerettes didn't view their roles sexually. They loved Auburn and loved Auburn football. The perks of membership included free game tickets, occasional dining privileges at Sewell Hall and a photograph in the football program. When a high school recruit was invited to attend a first Tigers

* What could be more sexy than a middle-aged former Virginia Polytechnic Institute dean of agriculture and life sciences?

game, he would sit alongside a Tigerette, whose job was to make small talk and sell the university. When that recruit followed up with an official weekend visit, he would be assigned *two* Tigerettes to escort him to meals, take him bowling, show him the party scene. Afterward, Tigerettes were encouraged to write the recruit personal letters and call him long distance. "I saw it as a very Southern hostess thing," recalled Patti Henry, a mid-1980s Tigerette. "I mean, we wore uniforms to games and they were orange-and-blue polyester. We were not flirting around town in sexy outfits."

But the innocent ideals of the well-intentioned Tigerettes were not reality-based. In her 1991 *Atlanta Magazine* essay, "I was an SEC Recruiting Chick," former Tigerette Melissa Harris described her Auburn life as one of a gaggle of "comely college coeds . . . set out as bait for hormonal high school heroes."

Wrote Harris:

Most Tigerettes had something going for them in the face and/or bod department. In fact, anytime a seriously plain coed showed up in a Tigerette uniform, it was widely assumed she was descended from generous alumni or other well-placed persons. Sure that's sexist, shallow and unfair, but let's face it, high school boys aren't exactly known for their fascination with good personalities and academic achievement. My senior year, when Auburn was headed to the Sugar Bowl, the athletic department issued a poster of the Tigerettes assembled on the 50-yard line wearing blue jeans and players' jerseys. The poster said: "Auburn Tigerettes, Sweet as Sugar." Would anyone ever mistake that as an advertisement for the Future Nuclear Scientists of America?

"It was about selling sex," recalled Nedra Dodds, a former Tigerette. "That's what the Tigerettes were. You'd often have two girls and one guy. The guy is the pimp. We were teasing young high school students. That's exactly what we were for, and the message couldn't be more clear—*This is yours for the picking when you get here.*"

This was the world Bo Jackson entered when he signed with Auburn, and it was a world he very much enjoyed. "Bo never had to worry about women," said Smokey Hodge, an Auburn linebacker. "He would creep around, this woman, that woman."

Which is why what transpired exactly one month after the Major League Baseball draft was particularly shocking. On July 3, 1985, Allison Hines—the student who transferred from Livingston University to be closer to Jackson—celebrated her twentieth birthday with cake, well-wishes and a visit from her ex-boyfriend.

That's right—*ex*-boyfriend. After having dated for a year and a half, Jackson and Hines broke up. Theirs had been a tempestuous union, filled with the typical squabbles and arguments and splits-followed-by-reunions that accompany collegiate relationships. Hines was spoiled and high-maintenance. Jackson was the king of college sports. On this day, when he knocked on her door, stuck his head in, then fully entered, Hines was a little confused. Why, exactly, was he here?

"Bo came over to return an old ring of mine and to talk," she said. "He had bought an engagement ring before we broke up, but I didn't know about it. What's so funny is that rather than putting my old ring on he put the engagement ring on instead and I didn't even notice until about twenty minutes later. I wondered why he was looking at me so funny and when I noticed he said, 'We are officially engaged.'"

What?

"We're engaged," Jackson said. "We're gonna get married."

There was no proposal, and no explanation over the change of heart. "Young love," said Hines more than thirty years later. "It makes no sense." At the time, though, she was euphoric. Barely two decades on earth and betrothed to a superstar. She called her parents, who were less than enthusiastic. "Are you sure you wanna get married?" Mary Hines, her mother, asked.

"Yes, Mama," Allison replied. "I'm in love."

"I know," Mary said. "But that doesn't always mean marriage."

The daughter didn't want to hear it. This was why she transferred to Auburn; why she endured a long football season and an even longer baseball season; why she willingly ignored her hunch that Jackson was cheating on her and accepted the sparkly ring on her finger.

"I wanted happily ever after," Hines replied. "I don't think I realized that sort of thing is usually fantasy."

CHAPTER 12

SENIORITIS

When Bo Jackson was bored, he entertained friends and teammates by catching flies.

Not fly balls.

Flies—insects of the order Diptera.

It was the damnedest thing. Jackson and some pals would be sitting at a table, near a window, with a bunch of flies buzzing around. Two flies. Three flies. Maybe four or five flies. Then—*whoosh*. Captured. Or dead. Generally, both.

One time, at a baseball team cookout, eight or nine flies congregated against a nearby wall. Jackson turned to Trey Gainous, his teammate.

"I bet I could catch six of them at one time," he said.

Gainous laughed. *No chance.*

Jackson stood, sauntered over to the wall, reached back his right paw and swooshed it through the air. With his fist clenched, he returned to Gainous. "You think I got 'em?" he said.

"Hell, no," Gainous replied.

Jackson opened his pinkie and a fly flew out. He opened his ring finger and two more flies departed. He extended his middle finger and another fly took off. He extended the pointer, and a fifth fly made his way toward freedom. Jackson stared at Gainous, who shook his head. He unfurled his thumb, and the sixth fly sat contentedly still.

"The guy," said Hal Baird, Auburn's baseball coach, "could do absolutely anything."

Despite defenses keying on him, he was a 100-yard-per-game running back. Despite pitchers knowing his weakness, he batted .401 with 17 home runs and 43 RBI. Despite no longer participating in track, he was recently timed by NFL scouts clocking an unheard-of 4.13 40 inside the university's bubble—a jaw-dropping number for anyone in America, let alone a 6-foot-1, 225-pound mountain. Despite a hectic schedule, he was a solid 2.8 student in his family and child development major. Despite women chasing after him, he was engaged to be married. The football program had recently ordered all its players to submerge themselves in a water tank to have their body fat measured. A trainer explained running backs should be in the 8 to 10 percent range. "Bo was in front of me in line, and he was two percent," said Yann Cowart, an offensive guard. "Two!"

This is why, when Van McKenzie, sports editor of the *Atlanta Constitution*, was plotting the newspaper's 1985 football preview section, he envisioned Bo Jackson as Superman.

"But not just as Superman," recalled Ed Hinton, a staff writer. "His idea was he wanted Bo to be coming out of a phone booth with a lot of smoke and Bo is ripping open his Superman shirt, and where normally there's a Superman logo there's an AU logo."

One hiccup: Bo Jackson was a national figure and Heisman Trophy frontrunner with an image to protect and an increased awareness of his own Q rating. "Van told me to ask if he'd do it," Hinton said. "I figured there was no way."

The writer called David Housel, Auburn's sports information director, who said he would check. A day later, Housel reached out to Hinton.

"You're not going to believe this," Housel said, "but Bo loves the idea."

Photographer Rich Addicks traveled to Auburn, where Jackson was presented with his very own one-off Superman suit, complete with requisite red cape, red booties, yellow belt and orange-and-blue Auburn insignia. Addicks was setting up for the shoot at a phone booth across from Sewell Hall when he looked up and witnessed an unforgettable sight. "Bo was walking up the street toward me in his Superman outfit—just as if the real Superman were out for a casual stroll," Addicks recalled. "Well, a garbage truck is coming the other way. There are two trash collectors hanging off the back, and they start laughing at Bo. He looks at them and says, 'You guys better shut up, or I'm gonna fly over there and beat the crap out of you!'"

The final agreed-upon pose—Jackson standing before the phone booth, hands on hips, jersey and shoulder pads hanging from the door, smoke billowing around him—graced the cover of the August 25, 1985, Football '85 section. Even in the era of *Miami Vice* and *Flashdance* and Jordache, it was striking in its garishness. Bo Jackson looked like an erotic superhero stripper, pre-routine.

People *loved* it. The image went viral decades before images went viral, appearing in newspapers and magazines; popping up as conversation fodder on morning shows and late-night TV. To some, it was sexy. To others, it was bold. To a few, it was risible. Whatever the case, the picture kick-started the 1985 Bo Jackson Heisman Trophy campaign (aka: The Most Inevitable Heisman Triumph in History).

Entering the 1985 season, Auburn was again a favorite to win the national championship. With fifty-one lettermen returned to the roster, the Tigers trailed only Oklahoma in the Associated Press and United Press International polls. Yet title talk was dwarfed by Bo and the Heisman speculation. He had been considered a possibility to win in 1983. He had been considered the (pre-injury) frontrunner to win in 1984. Now, with full health and a strong supporting cast and the new Bo-centric I-formation offense, the BO JACKSON WINS HEISMAN TROPHY AWARD press release was all but written. In the lead-up to the Tigers' September 7 opener against the (piece-of-raw-meat-being-fed-to-a-lion) Southwest Louisiana Ragin' Cajuns, multiple articles broke down the Heisman race, placing Jackson far ahead of halfbacks Keith Byars of Ohio State and Napoleon McCallum of Navy and quarterbacks Robbie Bosco (BYU) and Chuck Long (Iowa). Whenever Jackson sat down for an interview, the Heisman was one of the first subjects broached—*Would he win it? Could he win it? What would it mean to his family? To the university? To the state of Alabama?* Jackson hated every moment of it. "I hope," he said, "the people who choose the Heisman don't put me on the top of the list now."

Auburn had Jackson conduct weekly press conferences in the lobby of Sewell Hall—soul-sucking endeavors that featured a disinterested, soft-spoken running back perched behind a desk. When Gary Binford of New York's *Newsday* arrived for a session, he was warned—"Bo doesn't really like this." Jackson entered fifteen minutes late. "I got hung up," he said, "at the dry cleaners."

Jackson had little to say and zero new to offer. Why, the most exciting moment of Auburn's preseason came days before kickoff, when Jackson, fullback Tommie Agee and halfback Tim Jessie went fishing on a nearby lake. Jackson stood on the shore while his teammates took off on a small rowboat. Jessie, an experienced outdoorsman, drew back his rod to cast. "I turn around and the hook is caught in Bo's lip," Jessie said. "His mouth is bleeding, his lip is bleeding and we can't get it out." The three knew they had to rush to East Alabama Medical Center, the nearest hospital, but also knew that someone would surely recognize Bo Jackson.

"If Coach Dye found out, we'd be dead," said Jessie. "D-E-A-D."

They entered via a rear door, and an emergency room doctor discreetly cut loose the hook. At ease, Jessie, Agee and Jackson walked through the lobby and out the front when . . .

"Holy cow! It's Bo Jackson! Mom! Mom! It's Bo Jackson!"

They were spotted by a little kid, who requested an autograph and asked the young men what the heck brought them to the medical center lobby. Jackson, honest to a fault, told the fish (hook) tale—which somehow went from boy to adults to the local media.

WOW, WHAT A CATCH! read the headline in the next day's *Anniston Star*.

"Coach Dye was not happy," Jessie recalled. "He talked to us—sternly—about that and placed some restrictions on what we could and could not do. Bo wasn't just a football star. He was *football*."

Because Dye was as much drill sergeant as coach, he prepared for the opener by selling his team on the idea that Southwest Louisiana was the second coming of the 1978 Pittsburgh Steelers. They were mean and tough and far more talented than their 6-5 record from a season earlier indicated. Sure, they lost their first game to Memphis State by a score of 37–6. But, good God, those Ragin' Cajuns could straight-up ball!

With 60,000 fans on hand at Jordan-Hare, Jackson put on a clinic. He scored his first touchdown with 11:39 remaining in the opening quarter, when he took a pitch from quarterback Bobby Walden on the Southwest Louisiana 7, ran through two holes and steamrolled over three opposing tacklers into the end zone. His second score occurred barely two minutes later. This time, at the Southwest Louisiana 47, he received another pitch, sliced left, cut outside and dashed down the sideline. One man, free safety Clarence Glenn, had the perfect angle and blistering 4.3 speed. He came within two feet of Jackson, then—*whoosh!* Gone. "Everyone said Bo owed me the Heisman," Glenn said years later. "Because if you look at all those early photos, it's him running and me behind him in molasses. I played against Thurman Thomas, against Emmitt Smith, against Barry Sanders. None of them compared to Bo. We couldn't touch the guy."

That wasn't the best of it. With 59 seconds remaining in the first quarter, Auburn had the ball on its own 24. Jackson snatched another pitch, observed the scrum before him and decided he would prefer to avoid it. So he cut outside, past one player and two players and three players and yet another lunging defensive back, and scampered 76 yards untouched. All told, Jackson's first quarter totals were six carries for 181 yards. He was once tackled for a loss when defensive lineman Chris Gannon grabbed him by the face mask and yanked him to the ground. As three yellow flags fell, Jackson glared toward Gannon. "Don't do that again," he said.

"Then," Gannon said, "he calmly walked away."

By the time the 49–7 razing wrapped, Jackson was staring at 23 carries for 290 yards and 4 touchdowns. He spent much of the fourth quarter in sweatpants and a T-shirt, signing autographs along the sideline as fans chanted, "Heisman! Heisman!"

After the convincing win over the Ragin' Cajuns, the Tigers vaulted Oklahoma in the Associated Press poll to once again become America's number one team. They faced a somewhat stiffer test a week later in a 29–18 home victory over Southern Miss, but Jackson's 30-carry, 205-yard, 2-touchdown afternoon not only bolstered his case for the Heisman, it resulted in a newly bequeathed nickname from the *Hattiesburg American*. "That's Bo," wrote Van Arnold. "As in RamBo."

With the increased scrutiny that accompanied Heisman front-runnership came the rare opportunity for the media to break through Jackson's shell. Yes, he could be ornery. But if one looked hard enough, the young man possessed a deep-down soft spot. Countless are the examples of Jackson loaning a teammate one of his cars, or giving a newcomer a few dollars, or offering a kind word to someone in need of one. Brian Bell, a freshman quarterback from Lutz, Florida, tore his right shoulder during a practice and was rushed off to the hospital. On the day he returned, Bell watched a large figure walk through his doorway. "I was in bed, and it was Bo carrying a plate of food for me," Bell said. "I was a no one. He didn't have to do that."

Jackson was the object of ceaseless charity requests, and despite a busy schedule he rarely turned any down. The day before Southern Miss, Jackson found himself ninety-four miles north of campus in Oxford, Alabama, visiting fourteen-year-old Jon Greenwood. On July 6, Jon's right leg had been severed from the knee down after a station wagon slammed into his bicycle. He spent two weeks in intensive care, then two more months in the hospital. "When I woke up, they said they had amputated my leg," he said. "I didn't know what that meant."

Jon lapsed into a depressive state, refusing to eat and dropping from 130 to 90 pounds. His dietician, Cindy Templeton, knew the boy was a football fan, so she wrote a letter to Jackson, requesting an autograph. Within forty-eight hours, the phone rang inside the Greenwood house.

Hello?

"Can I speak to Jon?"

Who's calling?

"This is Bo."

They spoke for twenty minutes. The next day, a package arrived filled with autographed photographs and media guides. Two days later—to Jon's shock—Jackson knocked on his front door and asked, "You have some time to talk?"

They sat alone on the porch. For half an hour, Jackson's main message was hope: keep plugging away, keep believing. "Bo's visit saved my life," Greenwood, a father of two and grandfather of two, said years later. "He told me about all his struggles as a child, and how he never had it easy but kept the faith. I can't say I was trying to kill myself, but I didn't want to live. He saved me."

Greenwood was one of many children Jackson took under his wing. Later in the season, a woman named Peggy England reached out to Auburn. She was with an organization, Gifts Incorporated, that helped the families of terminally ill children, and a ten-year-old boy named Rusty Scoggins was dying of leukemia. He was a Bo loyalist, and England arranged for the entire family to travel from Decatur, Alabama, to Auburn to meet his hero. Rusty's parents were poor—Harold worked as a pipe fitter, Sandra was a Kroger cashier. The Scogginses were escorted to Sewell Hall, where Jackson was scheduled to hold an 11 a.m. press conference. Rusty was sitting on a couch in the corner of the room when the session started, and Jackson stopped everything to introduce himself to Rusty.

"I'm Bo!" he said.

"I know!" Rusty replied.

"What happened next, I'll never forget," England recalled. "Bo told the media they all had to wait because he had a friend in the room." England explained to the reporters that Rusty was facing leukemia, and Jackson left to escort the boy to his dorm room, then ferried Rusty and his older brother Brandon to the nearby Auburn Mall. He treated each boy to a milkshake, bought both kids remote-control cars and gifted them Auburn hats and sweatshirts. "What he did that day for Rusty was unbelievable," said England. "I've worked with many people doing many lovely things. But Bo was an angel."

Jackson continued to send Rusty notes, to check in with England. A few months later Rusty was flown to Texas Children's Hospital in Houston for a transplant. It was not successful, and the family brought him home to Children's of Alabama hospital in Birmingham for end-of-life care.

England called Jackson. "Bo, I hate to bother you," she said. "But Rusty isn't going to make it."

Jackson sounded distraught.

"Ms. Peggy," he said, "I'd like to see him."

Days later, Jackson traveled to the hospital. The football star entered on his own, pulling up a chair by the bedside and sitting with Rusty for half an hour. When he exited, he opened his arms and engulfed England in a hug. Tears were pouring down his cheeks.

Rusty Scoggins died on March 7, 1986. He was buried at Johnson's Chapel Cemetery in Danville, Alabama.

The following day, a bouquet of flowers arrived at the home.

They were signed *Love, Bo.*

The Auburn Tigers had two weeks after beating Southern Miss to prepare for a trip to Knoxville to face the unranked Tennessee Vols in Neyland Stadium.

In those thirteen days, the Bo hype machine only grew. With 495 rushing yards, he was—by far—the nation's leading runner, and his stated goal was to exceed the 2,517 combined yards he gained over his first three seasons. On the Monday before kickoff, Ed Hinton of the *Atlanta Journal-Constitution* traveled to Knoxville to spend the week with the Vols. Johnny Majors, Tennessee's head coach, liked Hinton, and granted the scribe extra access. "I remember interviewing one of their nose tackles," Hinton said. "And when I asked about Bo he didn't hesitate. 'Oh, we're gonna handle him—no problem.'"

"How?" Hinton asked.

"We have loops and stunts they've never seen before," the lineman said. "They're not gonna know what hit 'em."

Hinton chatted with a handful more Vols, all of whom expressed confidence. Before leaving for the day, Hinton stuck his head in Majors' office. "Johnny, I wanna be up front," Hinton said. "Your players are saying they're gonna beat Auburn. They're really crowing. I'm gonna use it, and I wanted to tell you."

Majors grinned.

"Close the door," he said. "Sit down and give me a cigarette."

Hinton handed Majors a smoke.

"Eddie," he said. "We are gonna whup their asses. And we will stop Bo Jackson."

That night, Hinton called Van McKenzie, his sports editor. "Van," he said. "I get the feeling Tennessee is gonna beat Auburn."

"Aw, bullshit," McKenzie replied. "Auburn's got Bo Jackson."

"I'm telling you," Hinton said. "I'm *telling* you."

The game was nationally televised on ABC— the continuation of the Bo Jackson coronation world tour. "Some of the guys got to talking," said Tim McGee, the Vols star wide receiver. "Wondering, 'With the TV coming to see Bo, do you think they'll show us?'"

Before a raucous, orange-clad crowd of 95,000, a Heisman Trophy candidate put on a show—and it wasn't Jackson. A year earlier, after Auburn beat up Tennessee, 20–10, quarterback Tony Robinson entered the visiting locker room at Jordan-Hare and stood before his teammates. "Listen," he said. "When they come to our place next year, we're gonna put an ass whuppin' on 'em. I promise you."

Twelve months later, Robinson was determined to do right. He was hardly a prototype big-time 1980s quarterback. First, he was Black in the heyday of "Only whites are smart enough to play the position." Second, he was 6-foot-3 and about 187 pounds—lanky and sinewy (*Sports Illustrated* called him "fishing-line thin") and jaw-droppingly elastic. A poor kid from Tallahassee, Florida, Robinson had been paid under-the-table dough to attend Tennessee, then arrived and found himself one of *eight* incoming quarterbacks. Before long, most of the other seven were gone. "Tony could throw it eighty yards in the air," said Eric Swanson, a Vols receiver. "He would take these big drop-backs, seven or eight yards, feel the heat and make magic."

Auburn received the opening kickoff, but was held to three downs and a punt. Tennessee started out on its own 24, and after two middling plays faced a third and five from the 29. The Vols operated out of a traditional set—split wide receivers, a tight end, a halfback and a fullback. So skinny he wore orange wristbands around his ankles, Robinson dropped back five lengthy steps, looked right for a covered receiver, then took off like a Creamsicle flash. He ducked beneath the swinging right arm of defensive tackle Harold Hallman, sliced through a hole, sprinted past linebacker Ray Corhen and ran 30 yards untouched before a head-shoulder juke left safety Tom Powell lunging at air. By the time cornerback Kevin Porter brought Robinson down at the Auburn 32, Keith Jackson, broadcasting the game, yelled into the mic, "You don't think that is a natural quarterback, huh?"

Robinson jumped to his feet, pointed a right index finger toward the crowd and jogged back to the huddle. "Auburn's players had been calling me a sissy all week," he recalled years later. "I was yelling at them, 'Who's the sissy now? Who's the fucking sissy now?'"

Tennessee scored on a 3-yard Charles Wilson touchdown run to take a 7–0 lead, then scored again minutes later when Robinson hit wide receiver Tim McGee with a 37-yard bullet to the end zone. By halftime, the Vols were up 24–0, and all Keith Jackson and his sidekick, former Arkansas coach Frank Broyles, could talk about was the dazzling play of their quarterback. This, wrote *Sports Illustrated*'s Rick Reilly, transpired, "in front of most everybody with a Heisman vote and a television."

While Robinson's outing was brilliant enough to land him on the cover of the following week's *Sports Illustrated* (alongside the banner THE TENNESSEE WALTZ) and have Majors compare him to Joe Namath, it was upstaged by a moment midway through the third quarter. The Vols were still up by 24, and Auburn had the football at the Tennessee 35. On a third down and six, Jackson took the pitch, stepped awkwardly, continued straight ahead and was brought down after a four-yard gain. He stayed on for the next play, then turned toward Dye and, with 5:15 left in the quarter, trotted off the field.

Jackson spent the remainder of the game standing and watching from the sideline There was no ice on his knee, which was weird. None of the trainers ordered him to sit—also weird.

Afterward, it was explained to a bewildered media that Jackson—who was held to 80 yards on 17 carries in the 38–20 loss—had suffered strained ligaments in his left knee. Teammates went out of their way to defend the star, insisting he was a tough manly man who had to have felt plenty of hurt to leave the action. Plus, said Dye, "at that point in the game it didn't matter."

No one was 100 percent sure why Jackson removed himself, but it likely involved a combination of slight pain plus minimal-running-room frustrations plus self-preservation. "Our defense just got after him hard," said Doug Mathews, the Vols defensive coordinator. "He was used to running over people and dominating people, but our guys were very determined to make his life miserable. When he took himself out, it was a big win for the players."

"The mantra that week for our defense was 'Take Bo out of the game and make someone else step up,'" said McGee. "No one else stepped up. We took away their prized possession."

"Bo waved the white flag," said Robinson, "because we beat him the fuck up."

Afterward, inside the Auburn locker room, Jack Crowe, the offensive coordinator, was seething. No, he wouldn't do an interview! No, he didn't want to eat from the postgame spread! Nothing! Leave him alone and let him smoke his cigarettes in peace! "Bo took himself out of that game, and he deserved to be ripped," Crowe said. "I don't know how much was mental, how much was physical. But with a great athlete they're often the same thing. When I was asked about it by the media at the time, I lied my ass off. But he let us down.

"There are some things about Bo that are important. First, he was a baseball player who played football. Not the other way. I think he liked football well enough. But it wasn't a passion, and you saw that in his lazy practice habits. Bo was hard to manage. Nice kid. But a pain. He didn't love the game as much as we loved the game. If we were playing Alabama, you knew Bo was gonna give you 100 percent. If you weren't, you might get 100 percent, or 50 percent, or 10 percent. He sort of held us hostage, because he was so damn talented we had to keep him happy. But I'm not sure he was happy playing football. He definitely wasn't happy against Tennessee.

"So he took himself out. And we lost."

The aftermath of the Tennessee thumping was not kind to Jackson and Auburn.

The Tigers plummeted from first to fourteenth in the Associated Press poll.

Jackson was widely ridiculed as a quitter with a heart the size of a pebble. Paul Finebaum, the excellent *Birmingham Post-Herald* scribe, opined that Jackson's position for big games was "standing on the sidelines."

"He seems not quite the cinch to win the Heisman," wrote Bill McGrotha in the *Tallahassee Democrat*. Chuck Long, Iowa's splendid quarterback, was tearing up the Midwest. Tennessee's Robinson felt revolutionary. Robbie Bosco at BYU had a big arm and bigger stats. There were other Heisman options. Seemingly *better* Heisman options.

Until this unfolded . . .

OCTOBER 5, 1985

AUBURN 41

OLE MISS 0

Jackson: 38 carries, 240 yards, 2 touchdowns

OCTOBER 12, 1985
AUBURN 59
FLORIDA STATE 27
Jackson: 30 carries, 176 yards, 2 touchdowns

OCTOBER 19, 1985
AUBURN 17
GEORGIA TECH 14
Jackson: 32 carries, 242 yards, 1 touchdown

OCTOBER 26, 1985
AUBURN 21
MISSISSIPPI STATE 9
Jackson: 28 carries, 169 yards, 2 touchdowns

It was a remarkable stretch of dominance. Jackson stood at the top of the I-formation, and everyone knew he would receive the football. Yet nothing could be done. He ran over people, under people, through people. NFL scouts were mesmerized. Tony Razzano, the San Francisco 49ers director of college scouting, had been on the job for twenty-two years. He graded Jackson higher than any college player in history, and predicted his impact on the NFL could rival what Joe Namath brought to the American Football League. "I'm certain he'd be a star," Razzano said.

Buford Ray, a Green Bay Packers scout, filed that Jackson "can do more things than any back I've scouted. Have not seen anyone faster, quicker, stronger or more explosive."

During a particularly sparkling scamper against number 4 Florida State, Jackson was headed toward the end zone with one man to beat—a freshman cornerback named Deion Sanders. "I got down to about the ten, and you come out of nowhere like a hornet," Jackson told Sanders years later. "I didn't know you. I just knew you had on a Florida State uniform. So I just put the breaks on, swatted you down."

"You ain't put no breaks on!" Sanders countered. "You kept going. You didn't even break stride and just swatted me down."

After Jackson scored, Sanders walked to the Florida State sideline to be greeted by guffawing teammates.

"Hey," Sanders said. "At least it was Bo Jackson."

The biggest game of Bo Jackson's college football career was slated for November 2, 1985, when number 6 Auburn would host number 2 Florida.

The hatred for the Gators was raw. Two years earlier, after the death of Greg Pratt, Florida students sported T-shirts reading AT LEAST WE DON'T KILL OUR PLAYERS. That had yet to be forgotten. Plus, Florida was a dirty team filled with cheap-shot artists. "You know how you did in Bo?" said Alonzo Mitz, Florida's spectacular defensive lineman. "You tattooed his ass before he could get started."

Jordan-Hare was filled to capacity, and it was *loud*. This wasn't a game to Auburn's fans. It was a chance to cut the head off Darth Vader. "You waited all year to play the Gators," said Steve Wallace, an Auburn offensive lineman. "That, really, was our test."

The Tigers opened a 3–0 lead, but fell behind when Florida reached the end zone on a three-yard pass from Kerwin Bell to a wide-open Ray McDonald. The score was 7–3 at halftime, and while Jackson had been held to a mere 48 yards on 15 carries, he would certainly come out for the second half and dominate. That's what Bo did: he beat a defense up, wore it down, had his way.

Only . . . Jackson was badly hurt. We think. Maybe. Possibly. On his final carry of the first half, he was brought down after a 3-yard gain by linebackers Alonzo Johnson and Scott Armstrong. As Jackson fell to the ground, he caught an opponent's knee between his right thigh and a knee pad. It stung. He was ushered to the locker room for halftime, where team doctors determined Jackson had suffered a thigh bruise.

When Auburn returned to the field for the second half, Bo Jackson was nowhere to be found. He stayed in the locker room, replaced in the backfield by Brent Fullwood. With 13 minutes remaining in the third quarter, Jackson exited the tunnel. Fans screamed for the vision of hope. The score held at 7–3, and Bo Jackson—the man in the Superman outfit—was here to save the day.

Alas, Jackson spent all but three remaining plays on the sideline, fully dressed but a mere spectator. It was a sobering sight, and with no Bo to worry about, Florida held on for a 14–10 triumph that again expunged Auburn from national title discussions. What unfolded was one of the most stunning reputation thrashings in modern sports. Bo Jackson woke that morning as the Heisman Trophy no-brainer. He was now, again, a quitter. The metamorphosis began in the Florida postgame locker room, where Johnson shrugged when asked whether Jackson's disappearance surprised him. "I had the feeling he'd do that if we played good defense," he said. "I knew if he got hurt he would pull himself from the game."

Added Leon Pennington, a Gators linebacker: "Seems like Bo has a tendency to leave the ball game when the going gets tough. I'm not saying anything about Bo. It's just that, in football, you're going to get banged up. Sometimes you've got to play with pain."

It continued on the Auburn side. Jackson's status prevented other Tigers from speaking up, but plenty wanted to. Crowe, the offensive coordinator who had been upset by the running back's exodus vs. Tennessee, was yet again repulsed. "We needed this game," he said years later. "It was a must-win. I don't doubt he was hurt. But was it a serious injury, or was he just mentally done? Ask yourself that one."

In his press conference, Dye—as always—defended his superstar, insisting, "Bo didn't have anything to do with us not beating Florida." It was balderdash. Auburn redesigned its offense for Bo Jackson. Everything it did was based upon Jackson. The argument made Dye sound insincere.

The next morning, the same newspapers that regularly sang Jackson's praises went on the attack. In a piece headlined BADGE OF COURAGE WON'T GO TO BO, John Adams of the *Florida Times-Union* wrote that Jackson "should have chosen baseball yesterday. He could have been hitting instead of being hit. He could have been chasing fly balls instead of being chased. He could have been sitting on the bench without Auburn's offense feeling the weight of the world on its stooped back."

Jackson, Adams opined, "may win the Heisman but he won't win the Red Badge of Courage." Bill Fleischman of the *Philadelphia Daily News* suggested, "People are starting to wonder how much Jackson cares about helping the Tigers win football games." The Scripps Howard News Service sent out an article with the headline HAS ANYBODY SEEN THE "REAL" BO JACKSON?

The remainder of the season was a mixed bag. Jackson returned the next week for the East Carolina game, but ran for a paltry 73 yards on 14 carries. He came back strong by carrying 19 times for 121 yards in a win over number 12 Georgia, then 31 times for 142 yards in a last-second 25–23 loss to Alabama. In the shadow of the Florida fiasco, it felt reduced. Jackson was still, without question, the most physically imposing and impressive college football player in America. But was he the best? And could the best—*the absolute best*—have taken himself out of two games with minor maladies?

In short, was Bo Jackson worthy of the Heisman Trophy?

And, if not, who in God's name was?

Before the Internet, and before *SportsCenter,* and before 800,000 different ways to receive scores and stats and highlights, *Sports Illustrated* was the bible of American athletics.

This was true in the 1960s, true in the 1970s and certainly true in the 1980s, when an estimated 2.4 million subscribers read up on their favorite teams and jocks.

The magazine wasn't mere entertainment. It could make or break an athlete, and to appear on the cover of *Sports Illustrated* was no less an honor than a band landing the front of *Rolling Stone*.

In the first week of December 1985, the editors at *SI* had planned on entrusting the cover to none other than Auburn's Bo Jackson. But then the Florida game happened, and the East Carolina game happened, and the losing happened, and it became the en vogue thing to believe that, in reality, there was a better Heisman candidate *somewhere* out there.

Like, say, Joe Dudek.

Yes, Joe Dudek.

He was a Division III senior halfback at tiny Plymouth (New Hampshire) State; a 6-foot-1, 191-pound juke-and-go runner with good-not-great speed (4.55 in the 40) and video game statistics. On 210 carries, Dudek ran for 1,615 yards and 25 touchdowns. So what if he was competing against Westfield State and Framingham State? So what if no one outside of New England had heard of him? The kid was Brillo-tough and once, after having carried 34 times for 265 yards in a game and then collapsing from exhaustion, had to be removed from the field via ambulance.

No one within *Sports Illustrated*'s Manhattan offices knew of Dudek. But then a new college football writer—some kid out of Denver named Rick Reilly—mentioned that there was this small-college phenom who might be worthy of a page or two of ink. His name was Kudek. No, Hudek. No, Dudek. Mo Dudek. Eh, Joe Dudek. Of Plymouth College. No, Plymouth State. In Maine. Scratch that—New Hampshire.

Mark Mulvoy, the magazine's managing editor, was a Boston native with strong New Englander leanings. So Reilly was dispatched to Plymouth State, where he found a football player who symbolized—in his eyes—*everything* Bo Jackson did not. "I covered the Florida game where Bo took himself out, and everyone in the press box was like, 'What the fuck?'" recalled Reilly. "Bo was this larger-than-life figure who seemed soft. Dudek was this anything-but-larger-than-life figure who had to be taken away in an ambulance."

The initial plan was for Dudek to run as a short profile somewhere deep within the magazine's recesses. But Mulvoy and his cohorts got to talking, and they returned to a similar refrain: *Why not Joe Dudek for the Heisman Trophy? In fact, why not Joe Dudek on the cover?* "Look at Terry Bradshaw,"

Mulvoy said years later. "He should have won the Heisman Trophy but he played at Louisiana Tech. There are a lot of good football players who come from small schools."

When the December 2, 1985, issue of *Sports Illustrated* arrived in the mail, readers were greeted by one of the most shocking covers in the magazine's thirty-one-year history. Photographs of three college football players—Jackson, Iowa quarterback Chuck Long and Dudek—were laid out in a vertical row, accompanied by three small yellow boxes. Only the box alongside Dudek housed a red checkmark. The cover headline: THE THINK-ING FAN'S VOTE FOR THE 1985 HEISMAN TROPHY.

The accompanying piece, penned by Reilly and titled "What the Heck, Why Not Dudek?," lavished praise upon Dudek ("Maybe we've got it wrong. Maybe Dudek doesn't deserve the Heisman. Maybe the Heisman deserves Dudek.") while eviscerating Jackson.

Bo Jackson? *Puh-leeez*. In the two games of mortal consequence to Auburn fans this season, Tennessee and Florida, Bo had a thigh bruise. Auburn lost. Whatever happened to being carried off the field, you say? In big games, Bo grabs more bench time than Sandra Day O'Connor.

And a misconduct penalty for anybody who says Jackson could carry Herschel Walker's poetry journal. In the national championship of 1981, Walker carried 36 times with a famous subluxated shoulder. Georgia won. Against Clemson his junior year, Walker played with a broken thumb. Georgia won. Jackson, meanwhile, takes Auburn out of the Sugar Bowl with two Bo boo-boos.

Dudek did not know he would wind up on the cover until one afternoon when John Gardner, Plymouth State's sports information director, called the main office at Quincy High, where Dudek was giving a motivational pep talk. The running back was summoned to the phone, so he excused himself.

"Joe," Gardner said. "You got it!"

Got what?

"The cover!"

The cover of what?

"Of *Sports Illustrated*, Joe. Of *Sports* friggin' *Illustrated*."

In Iowa City, Long—a fantastic quarterback who would soon be selected by Detroit in the first round of the NFL Draft—picked up the magazine and thought two things:

1. "Well, at least I'm on the cover."
2. "Who the hell is Joe Dudek?"

"My father was genuinely furious, because he thought *Sports Illustrated* didn't like me," Long said. "But back then it was so huge to make the cover, I was just happy to be there."

In Alabama—well, in Alabama the reaction was not the best. Jackson was college football's top gun. And while, sure, the Tennessee and Florida sit-outs didn't look good, there was more to the story. The thigh bruise against Florida had resulted in some internal bleeding, which concerned team doctors. Later, in the win over Georgia, Jackson played spectacularly despite suffering two cracked ribs. Then, a few days before the Alabama game, Jackson went horseback riding with Tommie Agee and Tim Jessie. It had been approved by the coaching staff, because all three were somewhat experienced riders. "Everything is fine," said Jessie. "But then my horse kicks Bo in the [left] shin. And my gosh, it was this really loud crack. Just—CRACK! And Bo starts limping. And we're all like, 'Oh, crap.'" Jackson was diagnosed with a hairline fracture.

The Tide won on a last-second field goal, and few on the Legion Field turf knew Jackson was playing through agony. "[Reilly] made it sound like I was a coward who couldn't stand pain and didn't care about winning," Jackson recalled. "He was the worst asshole."

There was also some ugliness to the *SI* cover. The stereotypes were unspoken but clear—scrappy white kid who'll do anything to win vs. talented Black stallion unworthy of his physical gifts. To make ends meet, according to the magazine, Dudek worked a minimum-wage gig sweeping up Plymouth State's stadium after games. Jackson, by contrast, was a pampered crybaby. "It was a preposterous notion that Bo was soft," said Yann Cowart, an Auburn offensive lineman. "I tore up my knee vs. Alabama and let out a blood-curdling scream. I never, ever heard Bo scream or even complain. I saw Bo take hits that would have destroyed lesser men. He always just got up, kept going.

"Believe me, Bo was *tough*."

On the morning of Friday, December 6, 1985, Bo Jackson caught a Delta Airlines flight from Atlanta to New York's LaGuardia Airport to find out whether he would win the fifty-first annual Heisman Trophy.

Jackson was accompanied by David Housel, Auburn's sports information director. The running back was recognized by gate agents ("You're Bo

Jackson!"), and the two were seated in first class. Chicken was served ("Yes, please."). Champagne was offered ("No thank you, ma'am.").

One year earlier, Boston College quarterback Doug Flutie had been the prohibitive favorite to take home the trophy, and he nearly doubled the vote total of the runner-up, Ohio State's Keith Byars. This time, no one was quite sure. Bo was still the frontrunner, but the Dudek cover landed some blows, as did the presence of the other two invited finalists, Iowa's Long and Lorenzo White, a sophomore halfback from Michigan State who led the NCAA with 2,066 rushing yards—280 more than Jackson. "All anyone was talking about was Bo, Bo, Bo," said White. "And no disrespect—he was tremendous. But if you look at his 1985 numbers and look at mine, I win."

The award ceremony was scheduled for Saturday evening on the thirteenth floor of the Downtown Athletic Club in Manhattan. One night earlier, Mike Hubbard, Auburn's assistant sports information director, hit up Broadway for a performance of *Singin' in the Rain*, but Bo stayed in room 2110 of the Athletic Club, dialed for room service (two orders of escargot and the lobster tail) and slept. He woke up early the next morning, nervous but excited, and spent the day roaming the Big Apple. Around 4 p.m. Jackson returned to his room to change into his blue suit and red tie. Pat Dye had flown in that morning, and coach and star were seated side by side for the event.

The Heisman was voted on by 1,050 national media members, and the Long-over-Jackson movement seemed to have gained some steam. His numbers (26 touchdown passes, 2,978 yards) were terrific. The Hawkeyes were 10-1 and headed to the Rose Bowl. But was it enough? As Long rode the elevator to the top of the Downtown Athletic Club, Lisa Wells, his girlfriend, broke the silence and said, "Chuck, do you have a speech ready?"

"No," he replied.

"Well," she said, "you might actually win this thing."

He pulled out a napkin from his pocket and furiously jotted down some thoughts.

The Heisman ceremony was televised on NBC, which meant an hour needed to be filled for a presentation that took 120 seconds. For 55 minutes, Jackson, Long, White, their invited guests and other attendees sat in anguish, watching the network air a series of reheated highlight videos.

"It's the longest hour ever," said Long.

"A miserable stretch of time," added White.

At approximately 6:55 p.m., Eugene W. Meyer, president of the Downtown Athletic Club, faced the cameras. By now, Long, White and Jackson had been relocated to the front row, where they sat shoulder to shoulder to shoulder.

"On behalf of the members," Meyer said, "I'm pleased to announce the Heisman winner, in the closest vote in history . . ."

Time froze.

Long felt his palms pool with sweat.

White had a lump in his throat.

Jackson could hear his heart launching haymakers.

Tommie Agee, Jackson's roommate and fullback, sat on a sofa inside Sewell Hall, staring at the television, shaking.

Pat Washington, Auburn's quarterback, paced back and forth to Agee's side.

". . . Bo Jackson of Auburn."

Yes! Yes! Yes!

Jackson stood, gulped for air, shook hands with Long and White and approached the podium. Attendees politely applauded. Back in Alabama, however, the party was booming. Florence Bond's Bessemer house was overflowing with friends, relatives, reporters. When the result was announced, a sonic boom overwhelmed the greater Birmingham area. Bo called home moments later, and his mom—normally stern, disciplined, firm—was delighted. "She said the house was full," Jackson said. "She already had the champagne iced down." In Auburn, as soon as ". . . Bo Jackson of Auburn" escaped Meyer's lips, the world came to life. Students rushed to Toomer's Corner—the famous downtown spot where trees were toilet-papered after Tiger wins—and broke out the Charmin. "Toilet paper flew everywhere," wrote David Murphree in the *Opelika Auburn News*. "It hung like a curtain from traffic signals and looked surreal in the twilight." Soon members of the football team arrived. They instigated rolled-up toilet paper fights. They screamed and hugged and howled. Turner Evans, a Sewell Hall employee, drove his Chevrolet pickup to the scene, and Washington and Agee stood atop the truck's bed and led chants of "War! Eagle! War! Eagle!"

"It's great," Agee said. "You can't describe how it feels."

Jackson wound up with 1,509 total points, a mere 45 ahead of Long. Robbie Bosco of BYU finished third, White a distant fourth. Joe Dudek, with 56 points (including twelve first-place votes) wound up ninth. "When I see Chuck I blame him for me not winning, and he blames me," White said years later with a laugh. "We were two Big 10 guys, so we split the vote."

"Lorenzo might be right," added Long. "But Bo Jackson was the best football player in America. He deserved the Heisman."

CHAPTER 13

CLUTTER

One wins a Heisman Trophy, his life moves *fast*.

When the ceremony at the Downtown Athletic Club wrapped, Bo Jackson held a phone session with Alabama's media. Then he taped an interview for NBC's *NFL Today*. Then he taped an interview for CBS's NFL show. Then he taped an interview for CNN's *Sports Page*.

The next day, he was ferried via limo to Radio City Music Hall to appear on Bob Hope's All-Star Christmas Comedy Special, where the comedian introduced that year's collegiate All-Americans by calling them to the stage, one by one, and cracking nonjokes.

For example . . .

> *"This year's Heisman Trophy winner. How about that? Boy, he's some kind of open field runner. He is really tricky. In fact, he's so tricky that in the instant replays he's doing something else."*

Um, yeah.

Jackson returned to Auburn late Monday. While cruising down Samford Avenue he spotted roughly two thousand people, plus the Auburn band, milling outside Sewell Hall. "I thought I'd be coming back to quiet Auburn," he said. That night, Jackson and his pals hit the town. Generally a non-imbiber, Bo drank and drank and drank. "I was so drunk I passed out on the floor of a buddy's place," he said. "When I woke up in the morning I was sick as a dog. That was the last time in my life I was drunk."

On Tuesday, a severely hungover Jackson took two final exams he had missed because of all the Heisman hubbub and later held a press conference for local scribes. Then on Thursday he would have to fly *back* to New York City for the official Heisman Trophy award banquet and trophy presentation, held in the grand ballroom of the New York Hilton. He could bring multiple guests.

Three stood out.

One was Florence Bond, his mother.

One was A. D. Adams, his father.

One was Allison Hines, his girlfriend.

That Thursday morning, Bo and crew were taxied to William B. Harts-field International Airport in Atlanta, where they caught a Delta flight to LaGuardia.

Jackson checked his suitcase, and carried with him a backpack, a silver Walkman—and a secret.

Bo and Allison had now been engaged for half a year, and while no wedding date was set, there was a ring and a commitment. Hines had up-rooted her life to accompany her love at Auburn, and she spent the past year pursuing a nursing degree and serving as a member of the Tigerettes, the all-female-student-football recruitment team used to entice high schoolers. She believed it had been a good move. Auburn was great. Bo was great. And even if they occasionally squabbled, they always made up.

And now this!

"It was my first time in New York and my first time on an airplane," Hines recalled. "We had a limousine waiting for us at the airport, and when you walked in the door they gave you a little card—like a credit card—if you wanted to get your hair done or buy something. I was a girl from Alabama. I'd never experienced anything like it."

Back in Auburn, Linda Garrett-Robinson, the married graduate student who looked like Tina Turner, pulled hard for Bo's Heisman candidacy. After he had been announced the winner, she sent roses to his suite in New York.

She was also (ahem) two months pregnant with his baby

If it all sounds like a mid-1980s episode of *As the World Turns*, that's a fair take. According to a 1990 interview Linda did with journalist Dick Schaap, theirs was a love affair that began innocently. "Studying was very important to me," she said. "And Bo would just bring his books over. He'd just sit there and study along with me. We'd be in the same apartment but the contact was minimum.

"When I saw him for the first time I had no idea that it was really him. What awed me—his body just stands out. You can't help but notice him. Most people didn't understand Bo. I think they thought because he was so popular that he would run all over town, do all kinds of things." Linda told Carrie Muskat of *Chicago Sports Profiles* that she and Bo had not become serious until five months after meeting—roughly *a year* before the Heisman ceremony.

Allison was aware of Linda's presence, but presumed she was merely the nice married woman who helped tutor her fiancé. "That's exactly what Bo told me—she was his tutor. Just his tutor," Allison said. "I believed him. Why wouldn't I? But, looking back, there were some incidents I probably should have questioned. Just an example—she drove through my apartment complex a few times when I first moved to Auburn, which made no sense. Unless you lived in the building, there was no reason. And she was clearly around Bo a decent amount. I guess I was dumb. Or blind. Maybe just naive."

In a 1990 sit-down with Schaap, Jackson tried to explain what he was thinking—relationship-wise—around the time of the Heisman.

JACKSON: "[Linda and I] were friends for a long time, and we just fell in love."

SCHAAP: "That's the best way to do it."

JACKSON: "At the time I was trying to find an excuse to break up with this girl that I was engaged to, which she was a gold digger and her mother was manipulating the relationship between us. And I had to find an excuse. A way to get out of that."

When relayed the Schaap-Jackson exchange, Hines expressed bemusement. If Jackson had been so committed to ending the relationship, why didn't he tell her about Linda and, specifically, about Linda's pregnancy? If Jackson found her so repugnant, why that February did he agree to be interviewed for an *Opelika-Auburn News* piece headlined BO ENGAGED: HIS FUTURE BRIDE "WIND BENEATH HIS WINGS"? Why did he fly her to New York for the Heisman Trophy ceremony?

"We were engaged," Hines said, "and meanwhile he impregnated another woman—a *married* woman. But *I'm* the bad guy in this story?"

According to a 1989 profile in the *Tulsa World*, upon learning of Linda's pregnancy Jackson immediately proposed. "Bo said, 'Let's get married now,'" Linda recalled. "I said: 'No, no, no. I don't want you to marry me because I'm pregnant.' Bo said, 'I want to marry you because I love you, not because you're pregnant.'"

In New York, Hines knew none of this. She had no idea that her fiancé had been cheating on her for the past year. She certainly had no idea her fiancé had a second fiancée. She was just thrilled to be there, basking in the bright lights and standing alongside the talk of college football.

So, for that matter, was A. D. Adams.

In the four years since Bo left Bessemer to attend Auburn, his relationship with his father had improved *a bit*. The two still were not tight, and rarely spoke. But when he returned to town, Bo tried to stop by and visit A. D., his wife, Louise, and their children. Whether or not it was plausible, he desperately *wanted* to have a dad. In an extensive August 25, 1985, *Atlanta Journal-Constitution* profile, Jackson told writer Ed Hinton that he was "close" with both of his parents. A few years later, however, Jackson said it still, "pissed me off that on important days my father wasn't there."

Whatever the case, against Florence Bond's wishes A. D. Adams was brought to New York, where—for a day at least—he could bask in the glow of his famous son and answer questions about Bo's boyhood and pretend that, over the past twenty-three years, he had served as daddy dearest.

The ceremony, held on the night of December 11, merged length with boredom. It was largely an ocean of old white people, featuring a 5:30 p.m. cocktail reception, followed by a dinner dance at 7. zzzz. Music was performed by Lynn Oliver and his Orchestra. zzzz. Chef Luigi D'Angelo prepared veal Sorrentino, potato croquettes, and mousse au chocolate. zzzz.

At approximately 8 p.m., Bo Jackson was asked to come to the podium, accept the Heisman and say a few words. Thanks to the work he put in, Jackson was able to speak in public while minimizing his stutter. Still, this was not something he particularly enjoyed. That's why what followed shocked most everyone in attendance.

Clad in a black tuxedo, Jackson opened by asking his mother and father to stand. Absent for most of his son's life, A. D. Adams rose and waved to the crowd. He, too, was wearing a tux, and beamed from ear to ear. Florence sported a purple dress, and sat as quickly as she stood. Not Adams. He absorbed the undeserved applause a few beats too long. "These," Jackson said, "are the people that made it happen for me."

He asked other family members to rise, and a handful of siblings had their moments. Lastly, he mumbled, "and my girlfriend, Allison." *Girlfriend, not fiancée?* Hines waved clumsily.

Jackson proceeded to speak for twenty minutes. He spoke about his childhood in Bessemer, about his small house, about bullying other children. He spoke about dealing with criticism, about Auburn-Alabama, about being a good citizen. "I want people to see me not as an Auburn football player or a Heisman Trophy winner," he said. "But for what I can do for my community."

When he wrapped with "Thank you, and I love you," Jackson was met with a standing ovation. He stood for a spell, taking it all in.

This was Bo Jackson at his finest.

On New Year's Day 1986, Jackson's Auburn football run concluded in the most humdrum of ways. The Tigers traveled to Dallas, where they suffered their fourth loss of the season, a 36–16 beatdown at the hands of number 11 Texas A&M. When the Cotton Bowl PA announcer notified the crowd that Jackson (who ran for 129 yards in defeat) was voted game MVP, the news was greeted with indifferent silence.

This was hardly the way to cap a career.

Fortunately for Jackson, it wasn't quite done. Although he had nothing to prove to NFL scouts, and although the injury risk screamed *don't friggin' do this!*, on January 5 Jackson headed to Tokyo to play in something called the Ricoh Japan Bowl.

In the heyday of postseason college football all-star games, this was the weirdest of the bunch. The event debuted in 1976, when its sponsor, Sports Nippon Newspapers, aspired to commemorate the United States' bicentennial celebration with—according to the official press release—"something truly American."

Thus began the odd tradition of importing dozens of football stars to participate in a meaningless game in a half-empty stadium before fans who had no clue as to what they were witnessing.

U-S-A! U-S-A!

The Japan Bowl rosters (East vs. West) were comprised of all seniors, and it was a fascinating stew. Along with Jackson and Iowa's Chuck Long, the bold names included running backs Keith Byars of Ohio State and Allen Pinkett of Notre Dame, as well as Outland Trophy winner Mike Ruth (of Boston College) and UCLA kicker John Lee. Somehow, Joe Dudek made the cut, as did Columbia kicker Larry Walsh (who scored only 27 points for the 0–10 Lions) and someone named Ed Zeman, a "utility player" out of Fort Lewis College.

Jackson flew from Atlanta to Los Angeles, where he met up with the other participants to catch Japan Airlines flight 065 to Tokyo.

Because he was the marquee attraction, certain allowances were made. All players were assigned a roommate. Not Jackson. All players had events they *had to* attend. Not Jackson. All players had to pay for a companion.

Not Jackson.

"Being able to have a person come as your guest meant you were VIP," said Derek Taylor, a Baylor defensive lineman. "I was allowed no one."

Jackson actually brought two people along—Florence, his mother. And Linda Garrett-Robinson, his pregnant *other* girlfriend whom he introduced to teammates as "my fiancée."* Which could have been awkward, only—according to Allison Hines, his *other* fiancée—shortly after the Heisman presentation she and Jackson had a heated argument that resulted in (what she believed to be) a temporary breakup. Plus, Hines never knew Linda accompanied Jackson to Tokyo.

The flight lasted eleven hours. Coaches, sponsors and administrators sat in the front of the plane, the sixty-eight players—as well as six cheerleaders from the University of Illinois and six from the University of Washington—sat in the back. As soon as the Boeing 747 lifted off, flight attendants walked the aisles, handing out a near-bottomless supply of alcohol.

"The first eight hours of that flight, all we did was drink," said Todd Moules, a Penn State offensive lineman. "First it was American beer. Then it was American liquor. Then Japanese beer. And at the end we were drinking sake."

By the time the plane landed in Tokyo, the flight attendants were out of booze and the players were in various states of disrepair. Many were hungover. A few were still drunk. The cabin smelled of vomit and sweat. A bus took them to the Grand Prince Hotel Takanawa, where they were assigned rooms and presented keys to the twenty-four-hour hospitality suite—featuring an unlimited supply of soda, Gatorade, fruit and beer.

"It was crazy," said Ron Hadley, a Washington linebacker. "The coolers were loaded with Kirin beer. But the major sponsor was Sapporo. One of the days we're all in there, drinking our Kirins, and the head of Sapporo enters. He asked, 'Why are you all drinking Kirin?' We told him we liked it.

---

* Even by the standards of inconsistent college romances, it's truly all super weird. The flight to Japan departed on January 5, 1986—and for the duration of the trip Bo introduced Linda as "my fiancée." On February 9, 1986, the *Opelika-Auburn News* ran the piece headlined "Bo Engaged: His Future Bride 'Wind Beneath His Wings'"—concerning his engagement to Hines. Accompanying the article was a photograph of Bo, arm wrapped around Hines's shoulders. It was taken post-Japan. So, to review: Bo proposed to Allison. Bo impregnated Linda. Bo proposed to Linda. Bo brought Allison to the Heisman Trophy ceremony. Bo brought Linda to Japan and introduced her as "my fiancée." Bo was profiled in a newspaper story alongside his fiancée Allison.

He said, 'No! No! No!' When we came back a few hours later, all the Kirin was gone and the coolers were packed with Sapporo."

Did it matter?

"Beer," laughed Hadley, "was beer."

The participants had five full days in Japan before Sunday's game, and they used it in myriad weird and quizzical ways. Though approximately three Japanese citizens had heard of any of the players, there were department store autograph signings where one could wait on a mere forty-five-minute line to snag the signatures of such iconic figures as Bill Happel (Iowa wide receiver) and Andy Hearn (Georgia Tech lineman). There was an optional guided tour of Nikko, a parade through the streets of Motomachi featuring Illinois's cheerleaders and a night out at—according to the daily schedule—"The Disco."

Jackson and Minnesota linebacker Peter Najarian accepted an invitation to lunch with Shunichi Suzuki, Tokyo's governor. That was nice. But the lead-up to Sunday was primarily a blizzard of photo opps and gag poses with sumo wrestlers. Jackson was quiet and a wee bit shy on the trip, in part because he was traveling with his mother and pregnant girlfriend, in part because he was never overly comfortable around strangers. The majority of players recognized one another. Jackson seemed to know no one. He referred to peers by their schools—Hassan Jones was "Florida State," Chris Castelli was "Navy." He called Joe Dudek "Joe Dudek," because the two had recently appeared together on *Good Morning America*.

Wherever the players went, they were presented with gifts. A scarf. A camera. As everyone boarded the bus after one appearance, they were handed enormous red apples. "Most of the guys were like, 'An apple?'" recalled Roy Dunn, an SMU offensive lineman. "'What am I supposed to do with an apple?'"

Upon reaching the hotel, the party members exited the vehicle. Jackson had been sitting a few rows behind his mother, and when they met on the sidewalk she said, sternly, "Vincent Edward, where is your apple?"

"I don't know, Mama," he said. "I left it on the bus."

Florence Bond frowned.

"Vincent Edward," she said, "they didn't give you that fucking apple for you to leave it on the fucking bus. Go get it!"

She then turned to Linda Garrett—also apple-less. "You too, young lady."

The couple slogged back onto the bus to retrieve their fruit. Florence spun and faced Dunn—a human she had never before met.

"Young man," she said, "where is your apple?"

Dunn shrugged, then said to his teammates, "Hey, guys, let's all get those apples!" One by one, everyone followed.

"I can't speak for anyone else," Dunn said, "but I didn't want to face the wrath of Bo Jackson's mother."

As advertised, there was football to be played.

Mike White of Illinois coached the East team, Fred Akers of Texas coached the West. The men agreed the trip needed to be a reward, not a punishment. So each squad held three half-hour practices and operated offenses with six base plays.

Roughly fifteen minutes into the first East practice, Bo Jackson looked at White and said, softly, "Coach, I'm done. Bo don't wanna practice no more."

White was powerless. Plus, the hospitality suite had beer.

"OK!" he yelled. "You all heard Bo! Practice is over!"

The game was played inside Yokohama Stadium, with an 11:30 a.m. kickoff and an impossible-to-replicate quaintness. The uniforms—hideous green and yellow for the East, less-hideous red, white and blue for the West—were pieced together in Japan by people who had never watched the sport. Said Castelli, the Navy lineman: "We all had to cut the bottoms of the legs off because they were sewn too long." Cheerleaders were distributed two pairs of gloves—one East green, one West white—to better help fans know which team had done something well. When footballs were thrown through the air, everyone cheered no matter the result. If a player sliced through the defense for a nifty 25-yard run, there would be nary a peep. The stadium held 34,046 seats, and roughly half were filled. "Here's what I kept thinking to myself," said Scott Gieselman, a Boston College tight end. "'This was a long way to fly to play in front of a few thousand people.'"

The one thing everyone could agree on: Bo Jackson.

"Just *so* awesome," said Dudek. "Different level than every guy on that field."

"Allen Pinkett was my college teammate, and he was great," said Tony Furjanic, the Notre Dame linebacker. "But Bo was so fast, so powerful. He was a man. We were boys."

"They ran an isolation play that came my way," said Hadley. "Bo comes up, I hit him—and it's like hitting a brick wall. I made the play, but I suffered an incredible stinger in my shoulder. There was an acupuncturist on the sideline, and he was putting a needle in me. All because of Bo."

One participant who didn't appreciate Jackson's output was Illinois's Jack Trudeau. According to the East starting quarterback, Jackson was so anti-practice that even when he did attend, he didn't pay attention. On one early play in the Japan Bowl, Trudeau called for a simple play-action pass. "Well, Bo had no clue what we were doing and he ran into me," said Trudeau. "I stick my left arm out and Bo slams into it. I wind up breaking my left wrist." A few plays later, even with the damaged body part, Trudeau faked a handoff to Dudek and sprinted into the end zone. While sliding, his left knee caught on the turf and popped. "I blew it out," Trudeau said. "I had surgery and was on crutches for eight weeks. I couldn't go to the combine or the Senior Bowl or work out for anyone." Projected to be a first-round pick in the upcoming NFL Draft, Trudeau fell to Indianapolis with the 47th pick in the second round. "The Japan Bowl," he said, "cost me millions."

The same could not be said for Jackson. One of his closer teammates on the trip was David Williams, the Illinois wide receiver. Seven months earlier, the two had been in Miami for the *Playboy* Pre-Season All-American photo shoot. On a deep-sea fishing trip in the Atlantic, Williams spent twenty-five unsuccessful minutes trying to reel in an amberjack. Observing from a nearby perch, Jackson removed his shirt, grabbed the pole and yanked the overmatched, 185-pound sea creature onto the boat. "I still have no idea how Bo did that," Williams recalled.

Now, in the fourth quarter of the Japan Bowl, Williams was strutting his stuff. With the East far ahead, he sprinted down the field and caught a magnificent 58-yard bomb from LSU quarterback Jeff Wickersham for a touchdown. He was up to 176 receiving yards, and knew the MVP award would be traveling back to Champaign, Illinois. Williams sat next to Jackson on the bench and said, "Hey, Bo—the trophy is mine."

"Boy," Jackson said, "it ain't over yet."

The next time the East had the ball, Jackson took a pitch from Wickersham, followed a couple of blocks to the outside and zipped 57 yards down the field and into the end zone. "I had an angle on Bo," said Arizona defensive back Allen Durden. "He looked at me, grunted, sped up and—goodbye, Allen." It was his third score of the day, coupled with 171 rushing yards.

Back on the bench, Jackson plopped down alongside Williams. They smiled toward a nearby TV camera, and the Heisman Trophy winner's lips were not hard to read.

"That motherfucking trophy," he said, "is mine."

He was correct.

There was one last game as a college football player.

One final farewell.

A worn-down Jackson returned from Japan on Monday, January 13, and a day later arrived in Mobile, Alabama, to join the South team in preparing for the following Saturday's Senior Bowl.

If the other players viewed the experience as an opportunity to prove they were on equal footing with the Heisman Trophy winner/expected number 1 pick in the upcoming NFL Draft, that idea was squashed when—mid practice at a nearby high school field—they . . .

whumpa-whumpa-whumpa-whumpa

. . . heard . . .

whumpa-whumpa-whumpa-whumpa

. . . a sound . . .

whumpa-whumpa-whumpa-whumpa

. . . from above.

It was a helicopter, and as the craft descended toward earth and practice came to a pause, members of the South team laughed when the door opened and out stepped Bo Jackson.

"It didn't take us long," said Allyn Griffin, a wide receiver from Wyoming, "to see who the star of the show was."

Unlike the Japan Bowl, the coaching staffs of the two Senior Bowl squads came straight from the NFL. The North team was headed by Dan Reeves and his Denver Broncos assistants. The South team was headed by Leeman Bennett and the Tampa Bay Buccaneers crew.

This was no accident.

The Bucs had recently wrapped a god-awful 2-14 season, and with that sealed the number 1 selection in the draft. Jackson was the no-brainer, only there was talk (largely dismissed) that he *might* choose to instead pursue a Major League Baseball career. So Bennett and Co. craved exclusive access to their next franchise player.

"It was good to meet Bo today," Bennett told the media after Jackson fell from the skies. "What I've seen in watching him play in one day, I was pleased. Now that we've got our offense here, we're ready to work."

While the Japan Bowl was considered a vacation, the Senior Bowl practices were twice daily, with scouts lining the sidelines and whistles aplenty. It was hard and hot and pressure-packed, and while small-school participants like Vencie Glenn (Indiana State), John Offerdahl (Western Michigan) and Mark Collins (Cal State, Fullerton) viewed it as a golden ticket, Jackson could not have cared less.

So he simply didn't attend.

Once, en route to a workout, the team bus dropped him off at a lake to go fishing—"that was a little strange," said Kent Kafentzis, the Hawaii safety. Otherwise, he was a ghost. "We had really good running backs besides Bo," said Thornton Chandler, an Alabama tight end. "There was Dalton Hilliard [LSU], Kenneth Davis [Texas Christian]. And all week Bo isn't there. Well, Bo is announced as the starter and Ken is pissed. But let's be honest. Nobody was coming to see Kenneth Davis run the football."

Jackson, to his credit, did finally show up Friday for team picture day. As the players waited for the photographer, a discussion broke out: What type of car will you buy when you're in the NFL?

An airplane flew above. Jackson looked up and pointed. "That," he said, "is what I'm gonna have."

The game was held at Ladd Memorial Stadium, and the crowd of 40,646 viewed it as an opportunity to bid a hero adieu. That's why Senior Bowl organizers flew Jackson to the opening workout via helicopter, and also why they offered him a far larger payout than the $2,500 received by every member of the winning team and $2,000 for losing players. It made sense. "I might be wrong," said Warren Seitz, the Missouri wide receiver, "but I don't think I had too many fans in attendance."

Jackson would up carrying the ball a mere eleven times, but one of those was a 4th and goal from the 1 that had the North defense amped. On the day before the game, Broncos secondary coach Charlie West (serving as the North defensive coordinator) pulled Offerdahl to the side to go over short-yardage situations. "Here's what's gonna happen on any fourth down play," West said. "Bo Jackson is gonna get the ball and jump over the guard-center gap. We can't practice it without pads, but you need to jump into the gap immediately when the ball is snapped, and you need to go as high as you can without ever knowing where he is."

Now West's words circulated through Offerdahl's head. He was a nobody linebacker from a nobody school. He received a half scholarship to attend Western Michigan. He was only playing in the Senior Bowl because another linebacker had dropped out.

The ball was snapped. Jeff Wickersham, the LSU quarterback, turned and handed it to Jackson who—as promised—took the ball and leaped into the center-guard gap. Offerdahl closed his eyes, bent his knees and jumped.

"I took a running leap without ever seeing him," Offerdahl said. "Then I look up and I'm about to collide with a Mack truck."

THUD!

The two met in midair—l'il David vs. XXXXL Goliath. Offerdahl wrapped his arms around Jackson's waist and rode him to the ground.

Jackson's final line for the game (11 carries, 48 yards) impacted his future nary an iota. Neither did the South's 31–17 loss. But for Offerdahl—a projected sixth-round pick—the Senior Bowl changed everything. He would be selected in the second round by the Miami Dolphins, then go on to appear in five Pro Bowls. "That moment," he said, "put me on the map."

Years later, Offerdahl and Jackson found themselves reunited at a two-day celebrity golf tournament in South Florida. On the first day, Offerdahl reintroduced himself, and the two chatted. On the second day, Offerdahl brought along a Sharpie and a blown-up photograph of the Senior Bowl goal-line stand. He asked Jackson whether he might sign it.

The framed image hangs in the Offerdahl family living room.

There's an inscription.

NEVER AGAIN
—*BO JACKSON.*

CHAPTER 14

BUCKED UP

Sometimes people ask questions even though they know the answers.

For example . . .

Who would win in a fight—King Kong or the Hulk? (The Hulk, obviously.)

What's the best Hostess snack? (Duh, Ding Dongs.)

Who's the coolest member of Menudo? (Xavier.)

And in the early months of 1986: Will Bo Jackson play professional football or Major League Baseball?

So obvious was the answer that to engage in debate was illogical. Sure, Bo Jackson was an excellent ballplayer with all sorts of talents. But *clearly*, his future was the NFL. It had to be. He was the reigning Heisman Trophy winner and the best running back prospect to emerge from the collegiate ranks since Orenthal James Simpson departed Southern Cal in 1969.* Even though the stingy Tampa Bay Buccaneers held the first pick in the upcoming draft, there was no way the franchise would let a phenomenon like Jackson slip through its fingers.

Plus, there were the financial logistics: Should Bo Jackson choose baseball, he'd be languishing in the minor leagues for—at bare minimum—a year and a half. His signing bonus (based upon the average for first-round picks) would be in the $100,000 range. The NFL, by contrast, was a land of riches. The average first-rounder was gifted with (on average) $900,000 as soon as ink touched paper.

So as his time as a college football player faded and his life playing one final season on the Auburn diamond returned to focus, Jackson's dodging of the weekly "Football or baseball?" inquiries ("I'm not telling until the summer," he said at the time. "It's like getting dressed every day. You have

---

* Perhaps even better. The Blesto scouting combine, which graded college seniors for NFL teams, had Jackson rated slightly higher than it did Simpson when he entered the league.

to put on your clothes and it's the same way with the media.") felt almost amusing.

"He's going to the NFL," said Larry Himes, the California Angels scouting director. "I don't think he's going to be able to resist the hoopla and the dollars that go with the NFL Draft."

The Tigers baseball season opened on February 26, with a home game against Huntingdon College, an obscure NAIA school. There were approximately fifteen scouts sitting in the stands, notepads in hand, chronicling Jackson's every move. Bob Rossi of the Pittsburgh Pirates. Lamar North of the Baltimore Orioles. Joe Campbell of the Los Angeles Dodgers. Most knew Jackson's future was on the gridiron—but one could never be too careful. And while his lone contribution was an RBI double, with Jackson things were rarely as basic as they appeared in the box score. The double was hit into the left-center gap, and Jackson would have *easily* gone for a triple had Paul Foster, the runner in front of him, moved faster. It was a leopard chasing a water buffalo.

The 1-for-4 afternoon did nothing to hurt his stock. But the ensuing games weren't pretty. Because of all the postseason football award ceremonies, Jackson—who was skipping track and field to focus on his possible future endeavor—had only practiced with the baseball squad a handful of times. "He came really late," said Gregg Olson, a freshman pitcher. "Even for an athlete like Bo, jumping right into baseball takes adjustment time."

On March 24, the Tigers hosted Jacksonville State. The Gamecocks started a sophomore right-hander named Mark Eskins, who shut out Auburn for eight dominating innings in an 8–0 rout. Jackson only reached base a single time, when a curveball struck his thigh. Otherwise, the slugger whiffed once and dropped a routine fly ball for an error.

The next day, the *Los Angeles Times* ran this brief update on Jackson's progress:

> Bo Jackson's decision between football and baseball may be getting easier. Through 20 games of Auburn's season Jackson is hitting only .258 with seven home runs and 14 RBI. That, of course, is against college pitchers.

He *had to be* picking football.

On March 6, 1986, the *Tampa Tribune* published a profile of Bo Jackson that delved into the baseball v. football debate. The piece, written by Jim

Selman, was lengthy and well done, and included several revelatory nuggets.

One, in particular, should have leapt from the page.

Wrote Selman: "Jackson has retained Freland [*sic*] Abbott of Bessemer, Ala. as his 'business manager.'"

Frelon Abbott had first met Bo when the kid was a local on-the-rise high school phenomenon. He paid him to mow his lawn, and occasionally slipped him some dollars. A few years later, Abbott—an unofficial Auburn football booster—made it a priority to help the Tigers land McAdory High's star. Which, of course, they did. Once at Auburn, Jackson was presented with regular doses of money and material possessions via Abbott.

Now he was his "business manager."

The information failed to raise eyebrows. First, because it was buried in the middle of just another Bo Jackson newspaper piece. Second, because— intended or not—Jackson didn't use the term "agent" to describe his relationship with Abbott. He said, "business manager." An active SEC player could not have an agent. But . . . a business manager? It was murky.

In the midst of the college baseball season, Jackson had little to no time to devote toward the upcoming NFL Draft, which was scheduled for April 29. So he had Abbott handle any dealings with the Buccaneers. This was, again, very murky territory. Had Jackson been done with college sports, he could have used Abbott with no complication. He even could have signed a contract with the man. But as Auburn's center fielder, the only person allowed to chat with the Buccaneers on Bo Jackson's behalf was . . . *Bo Jackson*. Nobody else.

That's not what happened.

Who made the first call? All these years later, it's impossible to say. But somehow, Abbott and Phil Krueger, the Buccaneers assistant to the president, agreed that on the morning of Tuesday, March 25, the organization would send owner Hugh Culverhouse's private plane to Auburn Municipal Airport, pick up Jackson and fly him to Florida for a medical exam, then return him for that night's baseball game against the University of Alabama- Birmingham at Plainsman Park. "We didn't have access to the players that [morning]," said Hal Baird, Auburn's coach. "So we were a little in the dark as to what they were doing with their time."

As planned, Jackson boarded the jet, traveled the hour and a half to Tampa, landed and was ferried to the Buccaneers' facility for a physical. Culverhouse's plane brought Jackson back to Auburn later that afternoon, and touched down just as the Tigers were taking pre-game batting practice. "It was unusual for Bo to miss BP," said Baird. "I don't think he ever did."

Baird asked aloud: "Does anyone know where Bo is?"

"Oh," one of the Tigers said, "he's not back yet."

"Back from where?" asked Baird.

"He went to Tampa for a physical," the player said.

"What?" Baird replied.

"Yeah," the player said. "They sent a plane up and he's in Tampa taking a physical or something."

Shit.

"I knew," Baird said, "that was bad news. *Really* bad news."

The coach was well versed in the intricacies of college eligibility. The NCAA, as a whole, permitted athletes to be professional in one sport, amateur in another. The SEC, however, was steadfast in demanding 100 percent amateurism of its participants. A flight paid for by the owner of a for-profit team would make Jackson a pro. "We have had the rule for as long as I can remember," Boyd McWhorter, the SEC commissioner, said at the time. "People have to make that choice."

It was, of course, hypocritical nonsense. In Jackson's four years at Auburn, football season ticket applications increased by 1,700 annually. The school was making millions off of his presence, his likeness, his replica jersey, his name on stickers and pins and hats. A year earlier Jackson was prevented from appearing at the American Heart Association's "Walk for the Health of It" walkathon because it would violate "The Rules." Which rules? No one was sure. But there were rules. Plenty of rules. "The SEC clings to its pompous eligibility rules," wrote Bob Wojnowski in *Florida Today*, "like a bum clings to his dignity." Few secrets were worse kept than the one about enormous wads of bills being distributed to SEC football and basketball players. America's brightest high school stars weren't attending Georgia and Alabama and Auburn and Tennessee because they sought out educations at some of the nation's most academically so-so institutions. No—they were being paid, and McWhorter certainly realized as much. "The SEC had the screwiest rules," said Baird. "But they were rules that needed to be followed."

As soon as Jackson entered Plainsman Park to prepare for the night's game, Baird headed straight toward him.

"Bo," he said, "tell me what you've been doing."

Jackson informed his coach about the plane, then added, "It's fine. We had it checked out."

He stood 6-foot-1. He weighed 227 pounds. He ran a 4.13 40. There are few sights in sports history as simultaneously glorious and terrifying as Bo Jackson in the open field. (Courtesy of Auburn University)

Vincent Jackson

At McAdory High, Jackson was a subpar student who—despite academic shortcomings—was genuinely liked by teachers, coaches and classmates. (Courtesy of McAdory High School)

During his time at Auburn, many in the media (and some teammates and coaches) questioned Bo Jackson's willingness to play through pain. Here, after separating his shoulder a week earlier, he watches Auburn thrash Southern Miss in a 1984 clash. (AP Photo/ Charles Kelly)

After helping lead the Tigers to a Sugar Bowl victory over Michigan, Bo gleefully chomped on a cigar. (Courtesy of Auburn University)

Although he was a college megastar beginning as a freshman, Jackson fit in well with his Auburn teammates. (Courtesy of Auburn University)

After struggling as a freshman, then sitting out as a sophomore, Bo emerged as a baseball force and one of America's best collegiate sluggers. (Courtesy of Auburn University)

Jackson helps carry off Coach Pat Dye following the 1984 Sugar Bowl. Having been raised by a single mother, Bo embraced Dye as a father figure. (Courtesy of Auburn University)

Jackson hated dealing with adults, but loved engaging with children. Here, he challenges young Auburn fans to a sprint across the field. (Courtesy of Auburn University)

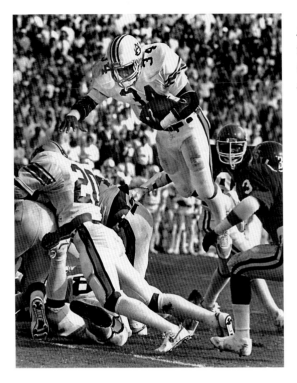

Jackson could not, technically, fly. But his athleticism often created that illusion. (Courtesy of Auburn University)

In April 1986, the California Angels flew Bo Jackson out to Anaheim to hang with team owner Gene Autry (*near left*) and slugger Reggie Jackson. It was a recruiting trip that went poorly. "Once I got to meet Reggie," Bo said later, "I was sorry that we have the same last name. He is an asshole." (Photograph by John Cordes)

Bo Jackson graciously accepts the 1985 Heisman Trophy in front of a fawning crowd at the New York Hilton. Among those in attendance were his parents, Florence and A. D. (Courtesy of Auburn University)

Bo Jackson's legendary physique was a by-product of genetics, not weight lifting. Throughout his time at Auburn, he let coaches know working out was not a priority.

(Icon Sportswire via AP Images)

There were strong ballplayers, there were stronger ballplayers—and then there was
Vincent Edward "Bo" Jackson, breaker of bats over knees. (Photograph by Brad Mangin)

Bo Jackson was genuinely pleased to meet NFL commissioner Pete Rozelle after being selected first overall in the 1986 Draft. But he knew he would never sign with the Tampa Bay Buccaneers. (AP Photo/ NFL Photos)

After the Kansas City Royals made him a generous offer to play baseball, Bo found himself manning the outfield of the Double A Memphis Chicks of the Southern League. (Edouard Bruchac/*Birmingham News*/Alabama Department of Archives and History)

Though he was never one of the guys, Bo did his best to fit in with his Kansas City teammates. Save for a strong dislike of third baseman Kevin Seitzer, relationships went smoothly. (Photograph by John Cordes)

Never a particularly graceful outfielder, Bo made up for inexperience with breath-taking speed and an explosiveness that allowed him to climb walls (like the one in Oakland) and rob home runs. (Photograph by AP Photo/Eric Risberg)

With Linda Garrett, his future wife, by his side, Bo Jackson exits the July 14, 1987, press conference held to announce his intention to play for the Los Angeles Raiders. (AP Photo/Dave Martin)

When Bo Jackson joined the Raiders, few knew what to expect. Before long, however, opponents learned what the Cardinals' Ken Harvey picked up here—the man was often unstoppable. (AP Photo/Al Messerschmidt)

Bo led off the 1989 All-Star Game with a home run against San Francisco's Rick Reuschel. He ended the night by claiming the Most Valuable Player trophy. (AP Photo/Lenny Ignelzi)

The aura of invincibility came to an end on January 13, 1991, when Bengals linebacker Kevin Walker tackled Jackson and, in the process, dislodged Bo's hip from its socket. In the immediate aftermath, he sat on the bench joking with his sons, Nicholas (*right*) and Garrett. Little did they know he would never be the same. (AP Photo)

Jackson's three years with Chicago failed to live up to expectations, but he was a positive clubhouse presence who played peacekeeper in an infamous August 4, 1993, brawl between the White Sox and Rangers. (AP Photo/Eric Gay)

Bo's final season with the California Angels served as a sad farewell to professional sports. Playing on an artificial hip, he was a shell of his old self. (Photograph by John Cordes)

Though Jackson's legacy begins with his baseball and football careers, his annual Bo Bikes Bama fundraiser has raised millions for charity. (AP Photo/ *Decatur Daily*, Gary Cosby, Jr.)

In the nearly three decades since his last appearance as a professional athlete, Jackson has devoted much of his (nonbusiness) time to walking America's greens and using his mythic power to hit drives into the stratosphere. (AP Photo/*Atlanta Journal-Constitution*, Curtis Compton)

Had Bo Jackson stayed healthy, he could have been one of the all-time great baseball players. "It was like Zeus came off the mountain," said David Cone, a Royals pitcher. (Icon Sportswire via AP Images)

Had Bo Jackson stayed healthy, he could have been one of the all-time great football players. Raved a Green Bay Packers scout: "I have not seen anyone faster, quicker, stronger or more explosive." (Icon Sportswire via AP Images)

"Who had it checked out?" Baird asked.

"My business manager," Jackson replied. "Frelon."

Shit.

"Bo," Baird said, "did you pay for the flight?"

Jackson shook his head.

"I don't see how this was OK," Baird said. "Maybe I'm wrong, but I don't believe there's any circumstance where you can take a free trip or do anything for a professional team."

Baird held Jackson out of that night's 11–5 win over Alabama-Birmingham. When the game ended, Baird called Pat Dye, the football coach/athletic director. "Coach, we've got a problem here," he said. "Bo made a trip to Tampa on the Buccaneers' plane. I'm pretty sure he just ended his eligibility."

Dye drove to Baird's office. It was eleven o'clock. Both men felt as if they'd been punched in the gut. Dye picked up the desk phone and dialed McWhorter's home number. First and foremost an academic, McWorter had earned a master's degree in English from the University of Georgia, then a doctorate at the University of Texas. He was a by-the-book man who believed rules needed to be followed.

Although Baird wasn't on the call, he sat across from Dye. Initially, the conversation pertained specifically to Jackson and the facts of the airplane trip. *This is what happened. This is when it happened. This is who was involved.* "But then I could tell in very quick order what was happening, because Coach Dye went nuts," said Baird. "He undressed that man like he was a yard dog. He was dog cussin' him, calling him every name in the book. He was citing all the things Bo Jackson had done for the conference."

Toward the end of the call, Dye said to McWhorter, "Well, let him pay the money back and restore his eligibility."

"That," the SEC commissioner replied, "won't be possible. He broke the rules. He's ineligible to play any more sports for Auburn."

Click.

The next morning, Baird summoned Jackson. He explained the violation, and that any further involvement on the baseball team was impossible. Jackson was fairly stoic throughout the conversation. He apologized and fought back tears. "Then," Jackson said, "I went behind the dugout and cried."

Later that day, Baird held a team meeting to break the news to his players. For the first time in forever, Auburn—led by one of America's greatest athletes—felt like a legitimate SEC contender. Now a baseball bat was being applied to the team's knees.

"I was devastated," said Steve Renfroe, the assistant coach. "Honestly, I cried and cried. Bo was the heartbeat of our team. And it'd be one thing were it his fault. But it wasn't."

Jackson gathered the belongings from his locker and vanished. Without their high-profile star the Tigers struggled, ultimately going on a pair of six-game losing streaks that flattened the tires on a magical season. "His loss was really demoralizing," said Scott Tillery, an Auburn pitcher. "First, because we liked Bo. But selfishly, with him on our team every game was electric because you'd have huge crowds, scouts, attention. As soon as he left, that changed."

Over the next few days a popular party game, Who Fucked Bo?, was a campus-wide rage. A good chunk of blame was applied toward the SEC— and with sound reason. "While all this was happening the NCAA basketball tournament was going on," said Baird. "The SEC office was empty, because reps were all over the country with basketball teams. So who knows who was managing the office and what was said to Bo's guy when he asked if it was OK to take a physical. There was so much confusion, and it cost a young man who didn't deliberately do anything wrong."

The primary suspect was the Tampa Bay Buccaneers and, specifically, Culverhouse. It was his plane that ferried Jackson to Tampa, back to Auburn and then out of college baseball. When reached by the Associated Press, the team assistant, Krueger, insisted that he spoke with an SEC official before the flight. "I asked for clarification as to what could take place during Bo's visit," he said. "I was told no negotiations, no talk of money or contracts, no signing of a contract, and no representation of Bo by an agent. We abided by those restrictions."

In the *New York Post*, columnist Dick Young slammed the Buccaneers, insisting the flight was a "put-up job" and that the team had to have been aware it would strip Jackson of his remaining eligibility. Wrote Young: "Now that there are to be no more at bats for the edification of big league scouts, it is felt that his baseball interest will wane. Pro football will have an open field."

This made little sense. The Buccaneers had the No. 1 selection. They wanted Bo Jackson, and thirty-four more college baseball games wouldn't have changed that. So why intentionally infuriate him? Why take lengths to cause Bo Jackson harm? "My dad said stupid stuff a lot, but he wasn't a vicious man," Gay Culverhouse, Hugh's daughter, said years later. "I don't know the precise truth, but I'm pretty sure my dad wasn't smart enough to purposefully destroy Bo's ability to play baseball. I think it happened inadvertently."

Jackson was incensed, heartbroken and more than a bit humiliated. But while he held a grudge against the Buccaneers, his ire was mainly directed toward Abbott, his sorta-kinda agent. In an April 5, 1985, *Atlanta Constitution* piece, writer Chris Mortensen tracked down Abbott and told him rumor was he now served as Jackson's agent.

"That's not true," Abbott said. "But call me next week."

There would be no next week. Or next month. Or next year. Four years after the flight to Tampa, Jackson expressed his feelings concerning Abbott to Dick Schaap, his biographer.

He did not hold back.

JACKSON: "I used to mow this asshole's grass while I was in high school. But up until this point, I can truly say there's only one person that I literally hate, and that's him. The way he tried to make a fool out of me. I don't even have to be in a pissed-off mood, if I'm driving down the road I visualize this guy standing in the road, and I just wipe him out."

SCHAAP: "He betrayed your trust?"

JACKSON: "Yeah. One person if I had a chance to get in a ring with, one person just to fight, I would kick his ass. We don't have to be in the ring. We could be out in the yard for five minutes. Just let me kick his ass."

SCHAAP: "Is he much older than you?"

JACKSON: "Yeah. I'll whup his ass. And he's a little weasel-type guy. A little weasel."

SCHAAP: "You said when the shit hit the fan. What happened?"

JACKSON: "Well, you weren't allowed to have agents in college, so I just said 'I'll let you advise me on some things. You're just an adviser. A family adviser.' So what he did—he got in cahoots with Hugh Culverhouse my senior year and I guess he had been putting out that he was my agent, which he really wasn't. Whenever people wanted to contact me or talk to me they would contact him. He would do this and do that and I would know nothing about it. He had set up a trip so I could go down and visit Tampa . . . on Hugh Culverhouse's jet. He checked and told me that everything was OK. He said they checked, they called the NCAA, they called the SEC office, and asked if it was OK for me to take the trip. And he said everything was OK. [After learning from Baird that he was ineligible] the only thing I could think about was that son of a bitch. He had screwed me in order to get himself some money. I think what he did with Culverhouse was Culverhouse said, 'Well, I'll give you this if you get him to come down, get him ineligible so we'll know that we have him.'

"And I kicked his ass out."

With his collegiate sporting career officially over, and with Frelon Abbott persona non grata, Bo Jackson had a couple of big events circled on his calendar.

First, on April 29, 1986—the NFL Draft.

Second, on June 2, 1986—the Major League Baseball Draft.

The problem: He needed guidance.

Back in the 1980s, large Division I football factories did a tremendous job when it came to producing NFL-caliber players, and a brutal job when it came to having them prepare for the next step. Not only had Jackson felt taken advantage of by a sketchy franchise (Tampa Bay) and a wannabe agent (Abbott), but he would leave Auburn 23 credits short of a degree in family and child development. And while that can certainly be pinned on the athlete, Dye and Co. took far too little interest in their players' intellectual pursuits. "Pat Dye was a good man," said Jeff Jackson, the Auburn linebacker. "But all those schools—Auburn included—were just concerned with keeping you eligible. You weren't taking classes that worked toward your degree. You were taking classes to play football."

"My mom was very academically inclined, and she'd always ask about my grades, my grades, my grades," said David King, an Auburn defensive back. "I didn't have the heart to tell her until years later that they were giving me grades without me doing the work. Just because I played football."

Bo Jackson was no dummy. But he was a small-town kid; sheltered and naive and prone to being used. So when the ugly aftertaste of the Frelon Abbott experience faded, he went about finding someone to trust. This ultimately led him to the office of Susann McKee, an Auburn-based Century 21 real estate agent whose daughter, Georganna, attended school with Bo. McKee was forty-one at the time, and had no experience in sports management. Bo, however, knocked on her door one day, introduced himself and said, "I don't trust anyone."

"Oh," replied McKee.

"But I know your daughter and I know about you," Jackson said. "I'm about to be the number one draft pick in the NFL, and I'd like you to manage me."

McKee was out of her depths. She *knew* she was out of her depths. But she also recognized the yearning in Jackson's face. The need for assistance. He told her about Abbott, and about the flight to Tampa, and about the potential to play football or baseball or (perhaps) both. He wasn't looking for a miracle worker. Just someone with his best interests.

A few days later, McKee reached back out to Jackson. "OK," she said. "I can help you as a manager. But you need a lawyer to handle contracts. Because there are things I don't understand."

McKee was friendly with a banker who did some work with Miller, Hamilton, Snider & Odom, a Mobile law firm that also had no experience in the world of athletics. A meeting was arranged, and what Jackson liked was the honesty. Jack Miller, the firm's founder, didn't try faking his way through the discussion with promises of a Toyota spot and fifty-room mansion. "We didn't know *anything* about sports law," Miller said. "But we weren't afraid of trying new things." Miller told Jackson he would be represented under the traditional lawyer-client relationship, as opposed to taking a percentage of his earnings. Again, the honesty soothed Jackson's psyche.

By now the NFL Draft was one month away, so Miller got to work. He assigned Tommy Zieman, one of the firm's partners and former head of the antitrust section of the state attorney general's office, to handle football, and Richard P. Woods, a firm employee and possessor of a tax degree, to take baseball.

Roughly three weeks before the NFL Draft, Zieman traveled to Tampa to meet with Krueger and Ward Holland, the Buccaneers treasurer. Around the same time, Woods was trying to grasp Jackson's baseball potential. The first pick in the upcoming Major League Draft belonged to the Pittsburgh Pirates, who told Woods they loved Jackson and thought him to be a remarkable prospect—but the risk of losing him to the NFL was far too great. The one franchise that seemed willing to use a high selection on Jackson was the California Angels, who had drafted him as a lark in the 20th round a year earlier. The team invited Woods and Jackson for a visit, and on April 21 they flew to Anaheim to attend a game.

Throughout his life, Jackson had responded to "Who's your sports hero?" with "Reggie Jackson." It wasn't particularly deep—the common denominator being a last name. But now Mr. October was the Angels' forty-year-old designated hitter, and on the field the two Jacksons met and shook hands for a photo op. A notorious egoist, Reggie told the assembled media that one day, with hard work, Bo Jackson could maybe become the next Reggie Jackson. Bo walked off, never forgetting the arrogance. "Once I got to meet Reggie," he said later, "I was sorry that we have the same last name. He is an asshole."

On Saturday, April 26, a mere three days before the NFL Draft, Zieman and Miller sat with Culverhouse in Tampa. The Buccaneers owner wasted no time with pleasantries. "He was basically saying that unless Bo Jackson asked to play with them, they weren't even going to make him an offer," recalled Zieman. "Which is a strange way to deal with a Heisman Trophy winner."

Zieman stressed to Culverhouse that baseball was a legitimate option, but was met with dismissive laughter. Jackson was a poor kid from East Bumfuck, Alabama. Was he really going to turn down millions of NFL dollars to stand in a minor league outfield and kick at the weeds?

"Culverhouse is a businessman, and one, I think, who only negotiates from a position of strength," said Zieman. "But he clearly didn't have that with Jackson, because Bo Jackson isn't driven by the dollar. He's driven by what Bo Jackson wants to do."

As the Draft neared, teams reached out to Tampa to see if the No. 1 pick was available. The Buccaneers' asking price, however, remained firm: Two marquee players and a first-round draft choice, or three marquee players yet to enter their primes. "That," said Leeman Bennet, the head coach, "is how we're looking at it." It was a joke. Just as Major League teams were reluctant to draft Jackson in the first round, NFL teams were reluctant to offer Tampa a king's ransom. What if, say, the 49ers gave up cornerback Ronnie Lott, halfback Roger Craig and nose tackle Michael Turner, and then Bo wound up a San Francisco Giant?

The other problem for the Bucs: there was no Choice 1A. The consensus second-best player in the draft was Tony Casillas, an Oklahoma nose tackle who projected to be a solid-yet-unspectacular pro. Purdue quarterback Jim Everett had a strong arm, Alabama defensive end John Hand was a 6-foot-6, 280-pound cinder block. But the Buccaneers could not make a serious case of bypassing Jackson for another Hercules. There was only one Hercules.

On the morning of April 29, Jackson and Zieman flew to New York City, and a white limousine (sent by the NFL) ushered them from LaGuardia Airport to the Marriott Marquis, where the draft was being held that night.

The event began at eight o'clock with Pete Rozelle, the league's commissioner, first welcoming spectators, then announcing, "First pick, first round, Tampa Bay."

Jackson, wearing a pinstriped gray suit and sitting backstage with Zieman, was nervous. He didn't want to play for the Buccaneers, but did aspire to be the No. 1 overall selection. So as the seconds ticked away, he could feel his anxiety building. *Had he played this right?* In Tampa, meanwhile, Bennett stared at the television before him at team headquarters. He repeatedly told Culverhouse that unless Jackson was a lock to commit, drafting him first overall would be a potentially epic—and historic—blunder. "I was guaranteed we'd sign him," Bennett said. "So I was OK with the idea."

From the galley, a soft chant turned loud: "Bo! Bo! Bo! Bo!"

Rozelle leaned into the microphone . . .

"With the No. 1 pick in the 1986 NFL draft, the Tampa Bay Buccaneers select . . . Vincent Edward 'Bo' Jackson, running back, Auburn University."

Jackson and Zieman hugged, and the top selection walked to the stage to shake Rozelle's hand. The commissioner gripped a football, and said to Jackson, "This is the ball you want, Bo."

"I'll admit," Jackson replied, "I can hit that better than a baseball."

There was no Buccaneer jersey for Jackson. Culverhouse was nowhere to be found—the team was represented by Bob Thompson, the Bergen (County, New Jersey) Community College athletic director and a pal of the owner. Jackson turned down an immediate offer to fly to Tampa and meet with media and fans, but was gracious. "I'm happy that the Buccaneers drafted me," he said. "It's nice to be the number one player picked."

Four weeks later, on May 28, Jackson (urged on by his representatives) agreed to give the Buccaneers something of a shot. He traveled to Tampa, held a quick press conference in Salon B at the Airport Hilton (said Jackson: "You sure have nice weather. It's nice to be in Tampa. I am looking forward to my stay here."), then grabbed dinner with a handful of Bucs players. The next morning he had breakfast with former defensive lineman Lee Roy Selmon, went on a sightseeing tour with receiver Theo Bell and learned he was going out for an intimate lunch with just the owner and the team's twenty-four-year-old quarterback, Steve Young.

It was Culverhouse's idea. He thought the articulate Young was an ideal recruiter. "You gotta sell him, Steve," Culverhouse said before the meal. "Sell him on the future of this organization."

"OK," Young replied. "I'll do my best."

The Buccaneers finished 2-14 in 1985, their third straight losing season.

The facilities were at a Division II college level. The roster was thin. The uniforms were effeminate. The offensive line was a rotting slab of rank meatsicles. "There was nowhere worse to play," said Ivory Sully, a veteran defensive back. "They put us up in a motel that was worse than a Motel 6. They fed us terrible food. They didn't care about winning."

Culverhouse was primarily known for being two things: cheap and bigoted. "He was a horrible human being," said Joe Henderson, the *Tampa Tribune* columnist. "He cared about the bottom line, and nothing else." Young, who had spent two years quarterbacking the Los Angeles Express of the upstart United States Football League, came to Tampa in 1985 and was thunderstruck by the incompetence. "I remember at one point I called my dad and said, 'I think I'm just gonna go to law school,'" Young recalled. "'I don't wanna do this.'"

But with Jackson in town, Young had a task. The two athletes and the owner went to one of Tampa's fancier steak houses, and after a few minutes Culverhouse looked at Young and said, "Let me leave you two guys to talk." He excused himself and walked from the table. Within seconds, Jackson leaned in. "Hey, man," he said, "I'm never coming here. Just so you know, there's no fucking way."

Young smiled. "Well," he replied, "I guess that ends my recruiting thing."

Culverhouse returned, and neither player let him in on the discussion.

"Bo was correct in his instincts," said Young. "You can be a losing team with a plan. You can be a losing team with direction. But the Buccaneers could not stop their own dysfunction. No sane person would choose to join that franchise."

Later in the day, a handful of Buccaneers players took Jackson bass fishing on Lake Tarpon. Again, this was Culverhouse's idea. The sun. The warm breeze. The camaraderie. Scott Brantley, a sixth-year linebacker out of Florida, was nothing if not blunt. "Bo," he said, "we'd love to have you. But you do *not* want to be a Tampa Bay Buccaneer. This place is a fucking joke."

The baseball thing still felt far-fetched.

When asked, Jackson told media members that he was "5%0" as it pertained to the two sports. But with the Buccaneers' all-around odiousness, the idea of shocking the system gained momentum. That was Bo Jackson in a nutshell: he gravitated toward the unexpected. Though never particularly rebellious, he believed in walking his own path, expectations be damned. So as the weeks passed and the inevitability of his NFL future seemed near-certainty, a turn toward baseball felt increasingly alluring.

On May 19, Jackson and Woods traveled to Toronto to meet with Pat Gillick, the Blue Jays general manager ("I'm here visiting and looking for a job," Jackson told Canadian reporters), and later that month Woods returned to Anaheim to break bread with Mike Port, the Angels' GM. Both franchises were genuinely interested in Jackson, but remained concerned about wasting a valued pick on the Tampa Bay Buccaneers' future halfback.

After returning from the West Coast, Woods was in his office when Baird, the Auburn baseball coach, called. A former Royals prospect, Baird retained close ties with the organization. In particular, he was in contact with Kenny Gonzales, the scout who tracked Jackson dating back to high school.

Baird knew how high Kansas City was on Jackson, and urged Woods to reach out to Art Stewart, the Royals' scouting director. Although he never saw Jackson play, Stewart gobbled up Gonzales's reports. The scout was of the belief that Bo Jackson—five-tool mega-prospect—was the (potential) second coming of Mickey Mantle. Hence, Woods and Stewart spoke, and the conversation concluded with Jackson being invited to Kansas City for a pre-draft meeting. On the afternoon of May 30, Jackson and Zieman arrived in Missouri and headed down to Royals Stadium for a matchup against the Texas Rangers. The men entered the building and came upon Linda Smith, the manager of scouting operations, sitting behind a large desk. She buzzed Stewart. "Art," she said, "standing in front of me is the biggest man I've ever seen. He looks like Adonis."

Jackson was introduced to Stewart and John Schuerholz, the skeptical general manager. He had visited Auburn to watch Jackson play as a college junior, and was overwhelmed by the power-speed combination. But this all felt ridiculous. "I think we're being used," Schuerholz said to Stewart shortly before Jackson's arrival. "I think we're being used for leverage they can use in football."

Throughout the long history of American sports, hundreds of agents worked teams against teams and leagues against leagues. Within the past few years the Royals had drafted three college football standouts (Stanford's John Elway, Pittsburgh's Dan Marino and Florida State's Deion Sanders). None wound up in Kansas City.

Shortly after Jackson stepped through the front doors, Schuerholz sat him down for a one-on-one.

"Bo," he said, "do you *really* want to play baseball?"

"Yes, I do," Jackson replied. "That's why I'm here."

"You're not using us for leverage?" Schuerholz asked.

Jackson looked him straight in the eye.

"Mr. Schuerholz," he said, "that is not something I would ever do."

A few minutes later, Jackson was escorted onto the field to observe batting practice. One year earlier the Royals had won the World Series via speed, defense and pitching. Only a single player, third baseman George Brett, cleared 100 RBI, and only two (Brett and first baseman Steve Balboni) had at least 30 home runs. Watching Kansas City's players swinging away, a sly grin crossed Jackson's face. "Hey, Art," he said to Stewart. "Not a lot of these guys hitting the ball out of the park, huh? This looks easy."

He zeroed in on the outfielders, who were throwing balls back into the infield. "Hey, Art," he said. "These guys don't throw so good. I could throw better than that."

It was cocky—but, Stewart thought, good cocky.

After BP Jackson strolled into the home clubhouse, where players were at their lockers preparing for the game. He shook hands with pitcher Bret Saberhagen and DH Hal McRae. George Brett, the team's biggest star and a die-hard football fan, introduced himself to Jackson. When it was time for agent and athlete to leave, he yelled out, "Good luck in football, Bo!"

Jackson stopped, spun and headed straight toward Brett. He pointed a finger in the superstar's face and roared, "Don't you bet on it!"

On the night before the Major League Baseball Draft, Richard Woods called John Schuerholz with some great news: The Kansas City Royals were Bo Jackson's preferred baseball destination. By now, it was clear Jackson was not going in the first two rounds. The risks were far too great, and many (including Schuerholz) remained skeptical.

Held via conference call, the draft began with the Pittsburgh Pirates selecting a University of Arkansas infielder named Jeff King. Inside the Royals draft room, the uncertainty was crippling. Gonzales, the scout whose life was largely devoted to all things Bo, swore Jackson would never sign with the Buccaneers. "You have to understand," he pleaded with Stewart, "he *hates* them. Passionately. He wants to play baseball, especially if it's for us."

"Do you think anybody else knows what you know?" Stewart asked.

"Definitely not," said Gonzales.

The Royals used their first pick (24th overall) on Tony Clements, a high school shortstop who would never pan out. The opening round passed without Jackson being selected, then the second and third rounds. Kansas City was playing a dangerous game of greatest-athlete-anyone-had-ever-seen chicken. As were the Angels and Blue Jays, clubs equally interested and terrified. As the fourth round began, Stewart looked at Schuerholz and said,

"If we blow the fourth-round draft pick with Bo Jackson, the franchise is not going to fold."

With the 103rd pick in fourth round, the California Angels tabbed . . . Paul Sorrento, a Florida State outfielder.

Deep breaths.

With the 104th pick in the fourth round, the St. Louis Cardinals tabbed . . . Mark Guthrie, a pitcher out of Louisiana State.

The Royals draft room broke out in cheers.

As soon as the noise dimmed, Stewart leaned into the phone and crowed, "The Royals select Vincent Edward Jackson, outfielder, Auburn University. Better known as Bo."

Most players hoping to be drafted would be sitting by the phone. Not Jackson. Most players hoping to be drafted would demand their agents reach out ASAP. Not Bo. Most players hoping to be drafted would be overcome by stress and drenched in sweat. Not Bo. He was in San Juan, Puerto Rico, scuba diving with friends. There was no phone or television nearby.

Jackson returned to Auburn the next day. A classmate spotted him in the Sewell Hall cafeteria and congratulated him on being tabbed by the Royals.

"I was?" Jackson said.

"Yup, you sure were."

Jackson called Woods, who confirmed the good news and arranged a series of remote interviews for Jackson with Kansas City's television stations. "The kid was on cloud nine," Woods said. "Up to that point, I would've bet that he would play football. I didn't know what he'd do—I don't think he made a decision—but because of how happy he was, I felt there was a great likelihood he'd play baseball. He was thrilled by getting drafted by the world champion Kansas City Royals."

More than a month had passed since the NFL celebrated Jackson as its No. 1 pick, and the Buccaneers had yet to make an offer. On the day his team took Jackson, Culverhouse promised reporters that "If it's a matter of money, I know we'll win. We'll make him the highest-paid player ever taken."

On June 13, Zieman and Miller flew to Tampa to sit across from Culverhouse. They had already told the Buccaneers they had no interest in swapping terms. They wanted the team to put its absolute best offer on the table. But these were the Buccaneers. Instead of presenting firm financial figures, they broached the topics of drug tests and skill guarantees. It was exasperating. When Zieman said any offer would have to be run by Jackson, Culverhouse snickered. "That's not the way agents do things," he said.

"No," Zieman snapped, "but it's the way lawyers do things."

One day later, Tampa Bay presented its offer: $4 million over five years, including a $1.5 million signing bonus ($1 million of which was an annuity that would kick in by 1998). An accompanying list of incentives could, at best case, bump the deal's value up to $7.6 million. On the bright side, it was an enormous jump from the four-year, $2.6 million deal the 1985 top selection, Virginia Tech defensive end Bruce Smith, landed with Buffalo. Zieman asked whether Tampa Bay could increase the numbers, to which Phil Krueger replied, "I could probably get it bumped up a few more dollars." Moments later, having conferred in private with the owner, Krueger said, glumly, "I went to talk to Mr. Culverhouse, and Mr. Culverhouse said, 'I won't raise it a penny.'"

To Jackson, none of this was surprising. From the day he lost his college baseball eligibility, he viewed Culverhouse warily. He didn't trust him, didn't like him, didn't want to play for him. "Culverhouse put an offer out and I said, 'No, I don't want it,'" Jackson recalled. "You're going to have to pay through the nose. I'm the first player taken in the draft, I'm the first-round pick, I'm the Heisman Trophy winner and I think I should name my price. You let everybody else name their own fucking price, so why can't I name my own price? Is it just the color of my skin?"

When Jackson ultimately rejected the offer, Culverhouse threatened to cut it in half. "And," the Bucs owner said, "you won't have a fucking choice."

In a peculiar way, Jackson loved this. *Loved.* The franchise he wanted nothing to do with was making his decision simple. "I told my lawyer to tell Culverhouse to go fuck himself," Jackson said. "And then when it was all said and done he pissed one of my lawyers off. My lawyer just got up and went to leave and then before he left he said [to Culverhouse], 'Now I see why you are such a tough person to work for. Because you're such an asshole.'"

The Royals, on the other hand, were honest and upfront. Wrote Michael Florence in the magazine *Business Alabama* . . .

Kansas City's offer was considerably less, amounting to $850,000, with $200,000 paid out in the first year ($100,000 salary, $100,000 bonus) and the remainder extended over the next two years. After the first year the continuation of the contract depended on mutual agreement. If Jackson wanted to leave baseball he had one day a year to terminate—October 1, 1986; July 16, 1987; and July 15, 1988. If he left baseball after the first year he was required to pay back the $200,000, minus taxes. After the second year, he had to return 50 percent of all money received.

The Buccaneers had offered four times more than the Royals. They were already sending out mailers featuring Jackson's photograph to potential season ticket buyers. Woods stressed this to Jackson—not in an effort to lure him toward football, but to make clear that a kid who grew up wearing only socks to elementary school was turning down *a lot* of money from an organization that would centerpiece him. Jackson was unmoved. "I'm not interested in anything Hugh Culverhouse has to say, offer or anything," he said. "And that's that." [Pause.] "The old cocksucker."

On June 20, Jackson and Woods flew to Memphis, home of Avron Fogelman, Royals co-owner and owner of the Memphis Chicks, Kansas City's Double A affiliate. By now the sports media was abuzz with rumors that Jackson just might skip over the NFL, so the Royals didn't send one of their chartered jets (with KC ROYALS painted across the tail) to bring Jackson to Tennessee. He and Woods traveled quietly via Fogelman's private plane. Once in Memphis, Woods, Fogelman, Schuerholz and Ewing Kauffman (the Royals' majority owner, who was wearing a royal blue suit Jackson later called "the most ridiculous thing I've ever seen") negotiated deep into the night as Jackson snoozed in a nearby chair. The hang-up was a small one: "If my client is going to turn down all the money the NFL is offering," Woods said, "he'd like to at least be able to say he's a millionaire."

"If we do that," Fogelman said, "will Bo sign?"

"We need to run it by him," Woods said, "but we believe he will."

The final offer boosted Jackson's earnings to $1,066,000. It also included two guarantees: 1. That Jackson would start his career no lower than Double A. 2. That he would be called up to the Majors before the end of the 1986 season.

Around 11:50 p.m., Woods looked at Jackson and said, "Are you ready to sign?"

Jackson smiled and said, softly, "I sure am."

Told the next day of the decision by Zieman, Culverhouse didn't scream or laugh or cry. He simply pulled out a cassette tape and played the recently released Dionne Warwick, Elton John, Gladys Knight and Stevie Wonder song "That's What Friends Are For." He said it gave him the proper perspective. Or something weird like that. "Keep smiling, keep shining, that's what friends are for," he told a (surely bewildered) reporter. "I don't think we're bums in this case."

The Tampa Bay Buccaneers—bums in this case—were left with nothing to show.

Bo Jackson chose baseball.

CHAPTER 15

MEMPHIS

The photographs were a bad idea.

Bo Jackson has never admitted such, because it's not his general makeup to publicly acknowledge this level of blunder.

But, again, the photographs were a bad idea.

On the afternoon of June 21, 1986, one day after agreeing to terms to pass over professional football for a career in baseball, Jackson found himself inside a banquet room at Royals Stadium, where the organization introduced its new high-profile addition to the local media.

Kansas City was hosting the California Angels that night, but nobody cared. This was about a generational athlete shocking America, about a generational athlete choosing love and honor over money. If nothing else, it had to be the most excitement in modern history generated by the addition of a fourth-round draft selection. So Jackson stood before a room overflowing with print, TV and radio reporters, wearing a gray suit and new Kansas City Royals cap, and offered the familiar ballplayer clichés about just being happy to be here and wanting to do his all to help the team win.

Then Bo Jackson joined the Royals to take batting practice.

He had absentmindedly left the bag with his baseball bats, glove and shoes on the private plane that carried him from Alabama, so Jackson was outfitted with a blue Royals No. 16 jersey, white pants, blue stirrups and a pair of blue Nike cleats. He sought out the biggest bat he could find, and settled upon first baseman Steve Balboni's 36-inch, 36-ounce Louisville Slugger. (In college, Jackson had used a 35-inch, 31-ounce aluminum Easton.)

As Kansas City's players took their cuts, Jackson lingered quietly to the side. He was the new kid at school. Finally, Mike Ferraro, the third base coach and batting practice pitcher, motioned for Jackson to approach the cage. A robust 40,646 fans would jam the stadium for the night's game, but now—an hour and a half beforehand—only a smattering bore witness. When Jackson walked in, things seemed to go quiet. The fans. The other players. The coaches. Reggie Jackson, California's designated hitter, entered the evening with 537 career home runs. He made certain to stand by the visitors' dugout and watch.

The uniform Bo wore appeared to be too tight. It wasn't. He was a 6-foot-1, 220-pound man. His neck was 19½-inches wide. His chest was 46 inches across. He had a 34-inch waist and 26-inch thighs. "Black & Decker biceps," wrote Gary Pomerantz in the *Washington Post*. Jackson tapped Balboni's bat on the plate, bent his knees, waited for Ferraro's pitch . . .

Miss.

Pitch.

Slow roller.

Pitch.

Pop up.

"I fouled off a few," Jackson recalled, "hit a few grounders."

Then . . .

WHAM!

Pitch.

WHAM!

Pitch.

WHAM!

There is a lazy cliché in sports—the ol' "No one had ever seen anything like it." Because, 999 out of 1,000 times, someone *has* seen something like it. Only, in this case literally no one had ever seen anything like it.

Wrote Dave Anderson in the *New York Times* . . .

Jackson did what Balboni (who hit 36 home runs last season) had never done, what a right-handed batter had never done—hit a ball that landed near the bottom of Royals Stadium's huge, crown-shaped scoreboard above and beyond the 410-foot mark in straightaway center field.

"It had to go 450 plus," [Royals manager] Dick Howser said. "The ball was carrying Saturday night, but I've never seen anyone hit one that far here straightaway."

Jackson's next shot soared through the air and—*plunk!*—dropped beneath the majestic waterfall 400 feet away behind the right-field fence. He followed with another in the waterfall. He slugged one into dead center, just over the 410-feet sign. His next one returned to the water. He didn't grunt when he swung, and there was no dirt flying from his heels. It was smooth and effortless. Whipped cream atop a bowl of berries. Sitting in the Kansas

City dugout, Buck O'Neil listened the way a conductor hears every note of his orchestra. A former player and manager with the Kansas City Monarchs of the Negro Leagues, O'Neil was now seventy-four and a team adviser. With each blast, his eyes widened. His smile grew. He jogged toward home plate to grab a thicker slice. "Listen, just listen, to the sound of Bo's bat," O'Neil said. "I've been around ballparks for some time and you don't hear that sound too often. I heard it years ago with Babe Ruth batting, and I heard it with Josh Gibson." He was hearing it once again.

When Jackson's session came to an end Fogelman asked an underling to fetch two of the balls from the water. "I'm keeping one, and Mr. K (Ewing Kauffman, the majority owner) gets the other," he said. "We've got a special young man here."

Reggie Jackson, rarely one to bestow praise, was nearly speechless. He had hit some bombs in his heyday. But nothing like this. "The man," he said, "is a killer."

But . . . the pictures.

They were a bad idea.

In his defense, Bo Jackson didn't know better. At Auburn, he dwelled within a cocoon. He was Bo. The Heisman Trophy winner. But the Royals players weren't screaming "War Eagle!" They were adult men, with wives and children and mortgages. So when Jackson arrived at the stadium the next morning, armed with a stack of 8½ × 11 glossy photographs of himself with the Heisman Trophy, it didn't fly.

Jackson maintained several men had requested pictures for their sons, and he was fulfilling a service. No one, however, remembered it that way.

The Angels-Royals game was scheduled for 1:35, which meant members of the team straggled in around 11. Most players found a signed Jackson picture on their chairs—left by the one and only Bo Jackson. "One of the things you don't do when you're an amateur," said Jim Sundberg, the seasoned catcher, "is come into a pro locker room with amateur stuff. I'm sure he meant it as a nice gesture, but . . ."

"It went over OK," said Bud Black, the starting pitcher. "And by OK, I mean not so well."

The first to speak up was Hal McRae, the forty-year-old designated hitter. He actually caught Jackson in the act, and followed the phenom around the room, picking a handful of the images up as soon as Jackson placed them down. When Jackson figured out what McRae was up to, he glared menacingly. The look may well have frozen water at Auburn, but it only emboldened McRae. "We don't care about your Heisman," the veteran said. "You ain't done nothin' up here yet."

Willie Wilson, the star center fielder whose résumé included two All-Star Game selections, a batting title and a Gold Glove, was equally appalled. "Who the hell put this fucking picture on my seat?" he yelled. "What the fuck am I supposed to do with this?"

Wilson took the photograph and flipped it onto the clubhouse rug. Multiple teammates followed, until it was raining Bo Jackson Heisman Trophy pictures. "I was one of the ball boys, and even we all thought it was pretty arrogant," said Brian Watley, fifteen years old at the time. "You're handing out a picture of yourself? To *these* guys?"

Sitting by his locker, legs folded, *Kansas City Star* opened to the sports section, Brett, a future Hall of Famer and already the greatest Royal of all time, found the whole scene delightfully outrageous. He laughed as the images whizzed past. When the storm subsided he bent over, grabbed some of the photographs and tucked them neatly onto a shelf within his cubby.

He found some masking tape and hung one on the wall.

"I thought it was great," Brett said years later. "There are a lot of things you need to excel at this level. Nothing is more important than self-confidence.

"That, Bo had from day one."

He stayed in Kansas City for ten days, and the whole experience (save the quickly forgiven photograph faux pas) was baseball nirvana. The clubhouse bins overflowed with snacks. The attendants fetched whatever you needed. The towels were all crisp and clean, the shower without a speck of mold.

But then reality set in. Until a contractually guaranteed September 1 callup, Bo Jackson was just playing Kansas City Royal. He was no more a member of the team than the ripped-up photographs that covered the clubhouse floor.

On Friday, June 27, Jackson arrived in Tennessee, where he would kick off his professional baseball career with the Double A Memphis Chicks of the Southern League. The team had no game that day, so Jackson strolled into dilapidated Tim McCarver Stadium (address: 800 Home Run Drive—directly across the street from a feed store and flea market) in the late morning for a press conference and a light practice. Because the Royals stressed speed over power, they urged their affiliates to have fields that emphasized those points. The Chicks, therefore, hired a local company, Kenny

Floor Covering, to remove the grass infield and replace it with a thin, rock-hard layer of artificial turf. That surface extended to the outer limits beyond the basepaths, and met up (somewhat clumsily) with a grass outfield. The rest of the stadium—"adequate and functional," wrote author Clarence Watkins—was an ugly mashup of additions and remodels. "It was an OK place to play," said Jeff DeWillis, a Chicks pitcher. "Our clubhouse was as big as a bedroom, and in the summer it got *really* hot in there."

Jackson seemed unusually loose in his media introduction, held inside a tent to accommodate the approximately 150 reporters. He cracked a few jokes. Deadpanned a bit. "For openers," he began, "it's hot here." He laughed, then told the third estate he was "happy as a lark" to be with the Chicks. Jackson admitted he knew no one's name, but added, "I can't wait to be with them."

Much like his first batting practice with the Royals, Jackson's Chicks debut was something to behold. "My first impression when he walked through the door of the clubhouse was, 'OK, 1980s baseball players do not look like this,'" said Terry Bell, a Chicks catcher. "We were all in shape, but thin. He blocked out the sun." The stadium was closed, so only players, coaches, a few officials and a smattering of media members bore witness to the day's BP session. Rich Dubee, the team's pitching coach/batting practice hurler, stood on the mound. Just twenty-eight, he spent six wayward years in the Royals minor league system before deciding his life would be better served instructing than playing. "Prospects come along all the time," he said. "Often it's mostly hype."

Because of his batting practice success in Kansas City, Jackson stuck with Balboni's Louisville Slugger (the Royals first baseball graciously gifted him with a couple). Dubee threw 28 pitches. Nine flew over the outfield wall. But not merely slightly over the wall, which stood 398 feet away. "He hit balls over the dawn," said Ed Allen, a Chicks outfielder. "At the time Memphis State had a practice field out there behind center field, and then there was a scaffolding. Bo's balls were hitting the dang scaffolding."

Jackson's debut was scheduled for three days later against the visiting Columbus Astros. In the meantime, he was able to adjust to new surroundings. Like the other Chicks players, Jackson would ultimately live in an apartment complex near the stadium. Until that was worked out, he called a suite inside the Hilton home. He paid no nightly fee (the Royals took care of it—as well as a room for his mother whenever she visited) and traveled lightly. Jackson drove a brand-new black Alfa Romeo with an Alabama vanity license plate that read TORQUE.

His teammates comprised a motley cast of baseball extras. A bit too short. A tad too slow. A fastball that lacked bite. A swing with too many holes. Most would go on to top out at Double or Triple A, and only two—third baseman Kevin Seitzer and catcher Mike Macfarlane—ever made serious contributions to the Major League club.

Jackson was interested in the other Chicks the way an about-to-retire elementary school teacher is interested in her students. He learned some of their names. He hung out on occasion. On the eve of Jackson's debut, Allen and his fiancée, Carolyn, were married at home plate before the opening pitch. The players stood in two rows—bats extended to form a tunnel—as bride and groom walked through. Jackson was a gracious participant. "Afterward a bunch of us went to Bo's Hilton suite to party," Allen recalled. "He let us hang out with him, talk, celebrate."

Finally, on June 30, the night of his first professional game arrived. In the lead-up, George Lapides, Chicks president and former sports editor of the *Memphis Press-Scimitar*, predicted this to be the most heavily attended sporting event in Memphis history. And while Lapides was largely a self-promoting blowhard, he wasn't exaggerating. The organization distributed two hundred press credentials, and ABC television was present to offer live cut-in shots of Jackson's at bats. The Royals flew in Dean Vogelaar, its vice president of public relations, to assist with the onslaught. Celebrities besieged Memphis to bare witness (OK, one celebrity—Peter Tork of the Monkees. He lived nearby). Jackson arrived thirty-seven minutes late to his pre-game press conference (excuse: a lost hotel key), but was already a big enough star to make it seem normal. He was a *huge* deal.

The stadium held 9,500 people, and a season-high 7,026 fans entered. As part of a promotion, months earlier Coca-Cola bought (on discount) thousands of seats for this particular evening and distributed the tickets for free to members of the area Boys and Girl Scouts. Lapides had forgotten about the arrangement until Jackson came to town, and when the Royals insisted his first game be June 30 . . .

Well, goddammit.

"It cost me over $20,000 to have Bo open (Monday)," Lapides whined. "I would have much preferred to have him open Sunday or (Tuesday)."

The Memphis skipper was a thirty-one-year-old mustached red ass named Tommy Jones. He played a few years in the San Francisco Giants organization, jumped into managing, and specialized in expletive-laced arguments with umpires. He was a tough guy who chewed tobacco by the bushel and believed he knew best when it came to all things involving his ball club.

Yet in regard to Jackson, Jones was a neutered chihuahua. The Royals said Jackson's first game should be June 30—it was June 30. The Royals said Jackson needed to DH before trying the outfield—he DHed. The Royals said bat Jackson seventh—Jones had no choice but to do so. It was a humiliating exercise. Like it or not, the Chicks' new No. 1 priority was Jackson.

The first official at bat came in the bottom of the first, with two outs, a runner on second and the Chicks already leading, 2–0. On the mound for Columbus stood Mitch Cook, a twenty-three-year-old right-hander from Wilmington, North Carolina. Cook was 6-foot-2 and 192 pounds, and the *Raleigh News and Observer* had once glowingly referred to him as a "flame-throwing right-hander." In 1981, the Chicago Cubs selected Cook in the third-round of the Major League Draft. At the time, he was a top-shelf prospect with electric stuff who, the Cubs believed, could wind up a rotation mainstay. Think Dave Lemanczyk with better movement.

As his minor league run progressed, however, Cook suffered repeated arm injuries. He was dumped on the Mets in 1983, then the Astros a year later. By 1986 he was in his second Double A season and fighting to walk the thin line between prospect and roster chum.

Jim Turpin, the Chicks public address announcer, introduced Jackson, and the crowd erupted into chants of "Bo! Bo! Bo!" The stadium thermometer read 90 degrees. "The air," wrote Joe Henderson of the *Tampa Tribune*, "was as thick as Texas-style chili." As he reached the plate, Jackson gazed toward the mound and saw a man headed in the opposite direction. Jackson was a phenomenon. Cook was the personification of faded potential.*

The pitcher looked at Jackson, then to catcher Jeff Datz for the sign. There was not much of a scouting report on the newest Chick, but word was out he could jack a fastball for miles and screw himself into the ground chasing junk. So Cook started him off with a couple of sliders and a curve, and the count sat at two balls, one strike. On his fourth pitch, Cook wound up and placed a slider just off the inside portion of the plate. Jackson swung hard, and the ball shot off his bat, took four long bounces, eluded Karl Allaire, the lunging shortstop, and rolled into center field for an RBI single. Arriving at first, Jackson pointed toward the Chicks dugout, then stood— hands on hips—and soaked in the standing ovation. ABC had interrupted its broadcast of San Diego Padres–Houston Astros to grace America with

---

* Tragically, Mitch Cook died at age fifty in 2013. He was survived by his wife, Megan, and two children, Morgan and Ross.

the moment, and its in-studio announcer summed things up with, "Bo Jackson's decision to play baseball—looking good through his first at bat."*

From the third base box Jones requested the baseball as a nice keepsake for Jackson. When the game concluded with a 9-5 Columbus win, the Chicks manager made sure to present Jackson with the ball.

"No thanks," the newbie said. "My trophy case is already full."

Jackson had gone 1-for-4 with two strikeouts and a grounder to the mound. It took about seven minutes to decide he hated the boredom of DHing. But he felt comfortable in the box, embraced the warmth of the crowd and was thrilled that Florence Bond, his mother, was flown in by the Royals for the occasion. In fact, the two were scheduled to have dinner after the game.

Just as soon as Jackson signed some autographs.

When Astros-Chicks ended, Jackson was escorted to the gate leading to the stadium's outfield bleachers. Once there, he was besieged by a *looooong* row of fans, all promised Bo Jackson signatures by the organization. So Jackson walked the line—"head down, eyes glazed, right hand moving with lightning quickness," wrote Billy Watkins of the Associated Press.

When a man asked whether he would sign "To Brian," Jackson said, firmly, "Can't personalize it." When a woman screamed "War Eagle!" he laughed. Mainly, he just wanted to head back to the clubhouse, take a shower and eat some steak and potatoes with Mom.

But he couldn't.

He needed to sign.

It was all part of Lapides's plan. From the moment he learned Jackson might join the Chicks, the team's forty-six-year-old president didn't see a ballplayer, but a walking ATM. Every day Jackson would enter the clubhouse and find a box filled with baseballs alongside a black Sharpie. He was required to devote at least thirty minutes after each home game to autograph sessions. "The front office was always trying to get me to get Bo to sit down and sign baseballs," said Steve Morrow, the team trainer. "Then they'd take them to the stands and sell 'em for five dollars a pop." One day Danny Zich, the fifteen-year-old Chicks batboy, was handed a case of balls to deliver to Jackson. "I don't have time for this," Jackson told the boy. "Lemme show you what my signature looks like."

---

* Watching from his home in Iowa was former Chicks infielder Dave Hoeksema, who had been released weeks earlier. "Bo was wearing my number [28]," Hoeksema said. "I remember telling my wife they gave Bo my uniform. That was pretty cool."

234 • THE LAST FOLK HERO

There are hundreds of mid-1980s Memphis Chicks fans who likely own a Danny Zich–signed baseball.

Lapides always had another corporate sponsor who "needed" a photograph with Jackson, another friend who wanted to shake his hand. Dave Lapides, George's seventeen-year-old son, was in high school, and one of his pals aspired to interview Jackson for the student newspaper. "No," Jackson told George Lapides. "I can't do that. I don't even have time for *USA Today.*"

The next day the high school scribe entered the clubhouse, pen and pad in hand, and said, "Mr. Lapides told me you'll talk."

Jackson exploded. "Look," he said, "I told him ten times I couldn't do this, but he insisted on bringing you here, embarrassing me and embarrassing you. I apologize, but I don't have time."

When the student left, Jackson sought out Lapides. "Do not," Jackson said, "do that shit to me again!"

While adjusting to Double A pitching would have been difficult regardless of circumstances, adjusting while doubling as a show pony was near impossible. After his debut single, Jackson fell into a deep slump. He went hitless in his next 14 at bats and with eight games down was batting .038 with one hit in 26 at bats. Curveballs on the outer part of the plate were Kryptonite. Fastballs on his hands were daggers. "He has great recognition," said Jones, "but he just swings at pitches he shouldn't because of his lack of experience." Jackson piled up four quick right-field errors. Newspaper columnists suggested it was all a joke ("[It shows] how little shame there is in having been a klutz on the diamond as a youth," wrote Donald Kaul in the *Philadelphia Daily News*). Headlines insisted he wasn't ready. Mitch Cook, of all people, summed up Jackson the baseball player by telling a reporter he belonged in Rookie ball.

On July 13, the Chicks were in Charlotte, North Carolina, for a four-game series. It was the finale of an eight-day road trip through the Carolinas, and Jackson found the whole exercise pure misery. The team bus was a glorified coffin, and as the hours rolled on and the temperature rose and some of his teammates' mediocre deodorant application skills started to manifest, all Bo wanted to do was jump out the window and find the nearest airport. "I rode with the team," said George Willis of the Memphis *Commercial Appeal.* "I vividly remember Bo standing up on the bus and saying, 'I will put it on my black card. Let's just rent a plane and fly.'" Jackson wasn't hitting, or even coming close to hitting. He had to do these press conferences in each new city (*"Bo, so now that you're struggling do you regret . . ."*). The autograph sessions were making his head explode. He couldn't eat at the local Wendy's without being besieged. The games could go on for hours and hours. Plus, on principle the daily $12 food per diem pissed him off.

It. All. Sucked.

Then, shortly before that night's game against the Orioles, Bo Jackson received something he desperately craved: great news. Back in Auburn, Linda Garrett, the graduate student he met (and impregnated), just gave birth to a boy, Garrett Lamar. Because Linda was still legally married to Eluard Robinson, the child's birth certificate read Garrett Lamar *Robinson*. And it wasn't as if Jackson were monogamous—Allison Hines, his on-again, off-again fiancée, made multiple visits to Memphis and knew not of Linda's pregnancy. But, complications be damned, it was Bo Jackson's son, and the ballplayer seemed genuinely giddy. Having been raised by a single mother, with a biological father who had little time for his boy, Jackson insisted he would be a present and loving parent. He didn't want to repeat the mistakes of A. D. Adams and leave a void in his offspring's life.

Later that evening, with 2,164 fans in attendance at Crockett Park, Jackson celebrated fatherhood. Dropped to eighth in the Chicks lineup, he came up in the top of the second inning with a runner on second and Joe Kucharski on the bump. In 1982, Kucharski had been selected by the Baltimore Orioles in the first round of the Major League Draft, but his career never took off, and now he was slumming in Charlotte (aka: baseball's hell hole). On March 16, 1985, a fire burned down much of the wooden Crockett Park, and the Orioles played in a charred shell with trailers for clubhouses. "My dream had been to make the Majors," said Kucharski, "and I was as far away as could be."

Carl Nichols, Charlotte's catcher, knew Jackson couldn't touch a slider. So that's what he called for—slider, low and inside. Pitching from the stretch, Kucharski reared back and threw a ball that crossed the heart of the plate. Jackson stepped, swung and watched the baseball fly over the WSOC-TV billboard in left field for his first home run. Before the game the Orioles had hosted a celebrity softball exhibition featuring stars of the local National Wrestling Alliance, and the building was unusually raucous. "It was the freakiest baseball crowd I'd seen in my life," said Jerry Holz, the Charlotte center fielder.

When the inning wrapped, Nichols walked into the Charlotte dugout shaking his head.

"What's wrong?" Holz asked.

"That Bo home run," Nichols said.

"Yeah?" said Holz.

"He broke his fucking bat on the swing," Nichols replied.

"No way," Holz said.

Nichols had grabbed the Louisville Slugger as Jackson rounded the bases and tossed it toward his bench. The wood was sliced like a cracked-open coconut. Later, the catcher presented it to Kucharski as a keepsake.

"I never won the Cy Young," he said years later with a laugh. "But I got the bat."

Jackson failed to get a second hit in the 12-4 Memphis win, but another moment stood out. For reasons no functioning human can explain, Crockett Park's right-field line was separated from the bullpen by a five-foot-high chain-link fence. It had been that way for years, and numerous ballplayers were nearly decapitated or castrated while charging a foul ball. Late in the game, Jackson was positioned in right when outfielder Ron Salcedo hit a towering pop down the line. "Bo starts running a hundred miles an hour," recalled Jim Benedict, a Chicks pitcher, "but the ball is coming down and coming down and coming down . . ."

"He was such a hard runner," said Terry Bell, the catcher, "there was no way in hell he could stop."

Roughly five feet from the fence, Jackson reached up with his glove and caught the baseball. In one shockingly seamless motion, he stopped on a dime, planted his shoes, bent his knees and leapt over the fence. "No hands," said Gene Morgan, a Memphis pitcher. Jackson landed on the other side in a dead stop, turned, planted his feet again and jumped back over the fence and onto the playing field.

No one could believe it.

"That," said Nichols, "was my real introduction to the baddest man around."

Thus began the Bo Jackson turnaround. A 1-for-3 with an RBI night against Greenville on July 15. A home run and a double, also against the Braves, a day later, then a towering grand slam (Read the Associated Press report: "[It] cleared the 360-foot fence in left center, 30 rows of permanent bleachers and 12-foot high signs") the afternoon after that against righty Robert Long. That shot measured—you will read this number correctly—554 feet. "I kept throwing him curves and he wouldn't chase," recalled Long. "Curve-curve-curve-curve. Finally my catcher signals fastball. There's a coaching tower in Memphis where coaches can watch practices. It went *over* that."

On July 21, Jackson was named the Southern League player of the week on the strength of an 11-for-26 seven-game stretch that included 7 runs, 3 triples, 3 home runs and 11 RBI. In baseball speak, the game was starting to come to him. "You made the mistake of thinking Bo's bat was slow," said Greg Cadaret, a Huntsville pitcher. "He didn't have a slow bat, he had a slow trigger. Once he picked up pitch recognition, we were in trouble."

Wherever Memphis played, fans arrived in droves. A massive 10,744 spectators for four games in Charlotte (as opposed to 4,703 for the previous four games). A tidal wave of 16,979 in Greenville (compared to 7,697 before). When Jackson expressed frustration with a bus trip to Chattanooga, the Royals forked over the dough to allow him to fly first class and feel pampered (Lapides lied, and told the local press he had stayed behind to shoot a commercial). It was money well spent. Against the Orlando Twins, he smoked a ground ball to *second baseman* Douglas Palmer—and beat the throw. "I'm still trying to figure that out," said Kevin Trudeau, the Orlando pitcher. Against Greenville, he struck out swinging through a curveball, and the pitcher—the fantastically named Thornton (Bean) Stringfellow—heard the bat whizzing through the air. "That's physically impossible, right?" Stringfellow said. "Not for nothing, that same series during warmups Bo was in foul territory in right field, picked up a ball and threw it to the bullpen in left field. Also physically impossible." Against Huntsville, he fielded a ball in the right-field corner and threw out a runner at home who started the play on third base. "The guy looked at the umpire like, 'No, no, no—that didn't happen,'" said Ron Higgins, a Memphis *Commercial Appeal* beat writer. "Yup, it did." Morgan recalled a throw Jackson unleashed from deep right field against Knoxville that defied all laws of physics. "Men were on first and second, and the guy on second was headed home," Morgan recalled. "Bo's body was pointed toward home, and mid-step a coach yelled, 'Third! Third!' Well, Bo changed his hip, his shoulder, his arm mid-motion and threw this sidearm bullet to third that got the runner who started on first. I could try that 1,000 times and never come close."

When the Chicks were home in Memphis, Jackson—always a bit wary of outsiders—fit in as best he could. Before every game at Tim McCarver Stadium he sent Adair Barton, a sixteen-year-old batboy, to the concession stand to grab him a Neapolitan ice cream. "Always with a one-dollar tip," said Barton. He'd grab Scott Crawford, the home clubhouse attendant, slam him to the ground and commence in WWF-esque wrestling matches. There were occasional house parties with the players and members of the Chicklets, the team's all-female squad of ushers/cheerleaders/eye candy. "He was very sweet," said Sherra Koerselman-Meyers, a Chick-let. Jackson's small apartment was sparsely decorated. On one wall, thumbtacked into the plywood, was his blue No. 34 Auburn football jersey. His Heisman Trophy sat on a small wood table alongside a photo of Jackson with Herschel Walker. That was about it.

Jackson was particularly warm toward Robyn Slone, the Chicks' first-ever batgirl. She was fifteen at the time, and Jackson treated her as he would a little sister. He referred to Robyn's mother, Norine, as "Mama," and visited the Slone household for barbecues. On the rare occasion it rained before a game, little Robyn and big Bo turned the tarp into a Slip 'N Slide and splashed through puddles. They played tag in the outfield. Shagged fly balls side by side. He once autographed a picture, and instead of just "Bo" or "Bo Jackson" wrote, IF I EVER LEAVE MEMPHIS, YOU WILL REMAIN IN MY HEART FOREVER. —BO JACKSON.

"People said he was hard to get close to, and I understand," said Slone. "But to me, he was a teddy bear. He made that summer so much fun."

On occasion, Jackson had visitors arrive in town, and it was up to Barton, proud owner of a silver 1979 Volkswagen Rabbit, to ferry them about. His main passenger was Florence Bond, who came regularly to see her son. "She was very friendly," recalled Barton. "It was a thrill for her." Linda Garrett, nursing a newborn baby back in Alabama, never made the trip (Jackson was unable to see Garrett until he was three months old), but Allison Hines did. In late July, she came anticipating a nice time with her man, but found photographs of an infant on a table inside his apartment.

"Whose baby is this?" she asked.

According to Hines, Jackson insisted it was not his child.

"But I didn't believe him," she said. "And that's when we were officially over. In Memphis, Tennessee, with me learning the man I still thought I was going to marry was a daddy."

By late-August, Jackson was batting .275 with 7 home runs and 25 RBI (.338 since his 4-for-45 start), and enough was enough with the Memphis Chicks.

He had done his time, adjusted to the professional game, proven his worth. In an interview with the Associated Press, Fogelman said Jackson had started to grate on nerves. "He speaks of himself in the third person a lot," he said, "as if he's bigger than being an individual."

Lapides added that Jackson, "is a nice guy. But I guess if I were back in the media, I would not like him."

Despite repeated condemnations from the Royals, the Chicks continued to milk Jackson for every dollop. It reached the point where if Fogelman or Lapides approached, Jackson spun and walked in the other direction. "It was a circus," Jackson later said. "I never had any problems with the guys on the team. But it was all the other stuff."

On the night of August 28, the Chicks were hosting the Chattanooga Lookouts with a scheduled 7:15 first pitch. Hampered by a slight right hamstring pull, Jackson wasn't scheduled to play. But he was expected to arrive early, get dressed, shag some fly balls, take a few cuts in the cage. There were four days remaining before his guaranteed advancement to the Royals.

At five o'clock, Jackson was nowhere to be found.

At six o'clock, Jackson was nowhere to be found.

At seven fifteen, Jackson was nowhere to be found.

A ball boy was sent to the parking lot—no black Alfa Romeo.

The team placed a call to his apartment—no answer.

Bo Jackson had exited the building. He packed up his belongings, yanked the football jersey down from the wall, shoved the Heisman Trophy in his trunk and drove off for Kansas City.

Inside Lapides's office, the heartache was real. The crowds would dwindle. The money would trickle in. Van Snyder autographed baseballs wouldn't pay the electric bills.

"None of us knew he had left," an agitated Lapides said. "We don't know who gave Bo permission to leave."

Answer: No one.

He was Bo Jackson.

And he was off to the Big Leagues.

CHAPTER 16

ROYAL

Steve Carlton was hanging on by a thread, and it was pathetic.

A mere four years earlier, in 1982, the longtime ace of the Philadelphia Phillies had won a baseball-best twenty-three games, and a fair argument could be made that the four-time Cy Young Award winner was the greatest left-handed starter in Major League history.

But then, as it does for all of us, everything began to fall apart. His velocity dipped. His ability to hit corners corroded. In his final outing of the 1985 season, the forty-year-old Carlton was lit up for five runs in five innings by the lowly Pittsburgh Pirates, and a scant 5,549 fans at Three Rivers Stadium watched in slumped indifference as his record fell to a pathetic 1–8. "He'll be back because he's tough mentally," Chuck Tanner, the Pittsburgh manager, said afterward. "I'd take him right now."

No, he would not.

The Phillies released Carlton midway through the 1986 season, and 10 days later he was snatched up by the San Francisco Giants. The Bay Area stay lasted but a month. After the Cincinnati Reds rocked him for seven runs and seven hits over 3⅔ innings, and the Candlestick Park crowd booed the legend as he trudged from the mound, Carlton was, once again, kicked to the curb. Because he rarely spoke with the media, the has-been issued a press release implying that his twenty-two-season run had come to a close.

CARLTON CALLS IT A CAREER, read the *Philadelphia Daily News* headline.

On August 12, the Chicago White Sox reached out.

Carlton immediately unretired, explaining, "I love the game. It's as simple as that." And as a first-time American Leaguer, he pitched surprisingly well. Not great. But good enough over his first four starts to be handed the baseball on the evening of Tuesday, September 2, 1986, when the Sox would visit Kansas City and participate in Bo Jackson's Major League debut.

Even without the presence of a 321-game winner, there was a weight to the event. Jackson had entered the Royals clubhouse a day earlier, one of four prospects called up to the Show. As soon as he stepped into the room, the rookie slugger—striking in a blue suit and tie—located his small locker area and was encircled by dozens of media members. He was fairly chatty and engaged until one writer asked three-straight times about the siren call of the NFL. "I don't see why the question of football comes up when I am playing baseball," he said. "Now I am a baseball player. And I expect baseball questions."

The tone was not congenial.

It was agitated.

He didn't start that first Monday, but when Jackson arrived at the stadium around four o'clock Tuesday afternoon, he walked over to the lineup card taped alongside coach John Wathan's locker and spotted JACKSON, RF in the No. 6 spot in the batting order.

"Oh, OK," he said aloud, to no one in particular. He then looked to see who was pitching for Chicago—Steve Carlton.

Jackson headed to his locker to change, where, while slipping a brand-new white number 16 jersey over his shoulders—he was approached by Charles Bricker of Knight-Ridder newspapers. "So, how are you feeling?" Bricker asked.

"I'm excited, sure," he said. "But I'm not jumping up and down. I'm not like that."

Because the defending World Series–champion Royals sat at 60-71 and 14 games out of first, and because Jackson's debut was (inexplicably) not announced beforehand, a piddling 17,418 entered the stadium. It had been, for Kansas City, a depressing year, the bottom falling out when manager Dick Howser was diagnosed with a brain tumor in July and forced to surrender his duties to third base coach Mike Ferraro. "That was devastating for all of us to go through," said Steve Balboni, the first baseman. "Try concentrating on baseball when the manager you love and respect has cancer."

The game began at 7:35—Carlton vs. Royals lefty Danny Jackson—and the first 1½ innings produced no runs for either team. When Royals second baseman Frank White stepped up to begin the bottom of the second, however, a buzz shot through the building. There, in the on-deck circle, was Bo Jackson.

It was impossible not to stare. His uniform was a latex glove. The contours of his forearms rippled beneath the lights. "His legs were so big," said Mike Kingery, a Royals outfielder, "it looked like he was wearing thigh pads under his uniform." With each practice cut, one could feel a jolt of power emanating from the tip of his Louisville Slugger. When White hit a soft fly ball to right, then jogged back to the dugout, the mood inside Royals Stadium shifted.

With White back on the bench, John Jessup, the Royals Stadium PA announcer, leaned into the microphone and, for the first time, uttered, *"Batting sixth . . . number 16 . . . Bo Jackson . . ."*

The fans rose to applaud.

Jackson wore blue Franklin batting gloves on each hand, and matching blue-and-white Saranac Pro wrist bands. The top button of his uniform was undone, and a white T-shirt peeked out from underneath. Jackson and Carlton were striking contrasts—the thin-but-pot-bellied Methuselah pitcher, with gray hairs peeking through his brown sideburns. The scene had a biblical tint—Isaiah 65:25: *The wolf and the lamb shall graze together . . .*

Catcher Ron Karkovice set up on the outside portion of the plate, and Carlton's first pitch was a loopy fastball that Jackson took for ball one. In the WFLD-Chicago broadcast booth, Frank Messer, handling the play-by-play, and Don Drysdale, the former Dodger ace, couldn't get past Jackson's size. "I'll tell you something," Drysdale said, "he was a *big* Chick . . ."

Jackson stepped out of the box, hit both of his Nike cleats with the head of his bat, slid his left hand down the barrel, planted his right foot in the rear of the box, wiggled his hips, swirled the bat around, gazed toward the sky, stepped in and awaited the next offering.

Karkovice had read his scouting report (fastballs away, off-speed inside) and placed down a single finger for the same exact pitch. Carlton again let loose a wobbly fastball, but Jackson reached and swung through it—*hard*—for strike one.

"Woo!" someone shrieked from the stands.

Jackson again stepped out, tugged on the brim of his helmet—and did something so casually that no one seemed to notice the physical preposterousness. He extended his arms in front of his torso, holding his bat horizontal to the ground. He wrapped his right hand around the knob, his left hand around the thick of the barrel, raised the bat above his head and pulled it—seamlessly, fluidly—back to his rear end without bending an elbow. He then—still, no hands removed, no elbows crooked—brought the bat back over his head and to his chest. This was twice repeated.* "The guy was a ballerina," said Mike Brewer, a Royals outfielder.

---

* Author's note: Try this at home. I did. As did my son, Emmett, and my wife, Catherine. None of us came close.

Karkovice signaled for a third-straight fastball, and once again placed his glove on the outside portion of the plate. Vintage Steve Carlton hits the mark 98 of 100 times. Geriatric Steve Carlton served a meatball that sailed over the heart of the dish. Jackson stepped and swung a hair late, and the ball exploded off his bat and traveled deep into foul territory along the right-field line.

The crowd, again, burst into cheers.

Rick Janssen, the Royals organist, started playing the requisite *dum-dum-dum. Dum-dum-dum.* [Higher] *Dum-dum-dum. Dum-dum-dum . . .*

Jackson wasn't nervous. This Carlton guy—there were better pitchers in Double A. He was throwing junk.

Dum-dum-dum. Dum-dum-dum . . .

Jackson stepped out. Stepped back in. Carlton looked in, misunderstood the sign, stepped off.

Dum-dum-dum. Dum-dum-dum . . .

Jackson returned to the box. Carlton's next pitch was a slider—once his bread and butter, now a rainbow trout swimming in polluted waters. The ball left his hand, cut across the plate and nearly took out Jackson's rear foot. A smattering of boos rained down.

The count was now 2 balls, 2 strikes.

Carlton was sizing the infant up. But Jackson had now seen the veteran's pitches, and they were slop. The fastballs—clocked at 83, 84 mph—were dogshit. The slider, a little less so. Odds are the next pitch would be another slider . . .

Carlton—a Big Bird–like 6-foot-4—wound up and threw. The slider again crossed the plate, but as it traveled left to right Jackson stepped, swiveled his hips and swung with a profound uppercut. The sound was audible—*CRACK!*—and as soon as he whipped the bat around, Jackson looked up toward the left-field stands to admire its flight.

"There's one!" said Messer. "A looooong drive. Waaaaay back. Thiiiiis ball iiiiissssss . . .

[Pause]

"Foul!"

The corner outfield stands were largely empty, and four or five fans scurried for the baseball. It landed *30 rows back*—an estimated 425 feet and close to a concession stand. John Hirschbeck, the third base umpire, made the call, but the ball sailed 50 feet above the orange foul pole and was tough to read. Onlookers booed. Jackson couldn't believe it. "It was so high it was like when someone kicks a field goal way above the goalpost, and you can't tell whether it's good," said Mark Gubicza, a Royals pitcher. "Either way, it was a crusher. Bo swears it was fair."

Jackson walked across the field and back to home plate, and as he did so everyone in attendance rose and presented the rookie with a boisterous standing ovation. "Will you listen to this," said Messer—clearly relishing the moment. "He's getting a standing ovation . . . *for a foul ball.*"

During Jackson's stroll, Janssen kicked off a spirited rendition of "If You're Happy and You Know It." Carlton wasn't happy—he nearly sired rawhide space travel. Jackson wasn't happy—he wanted the home run. The count was now 2 balls, 2 strikes. Jackson was back in the box, front foot extended to the side, squeezing the handle with both hands, then flipping up his right forearm followed by his left.

The sixth pitch was a low fastball that Jackson battered into foul territory along the right-field line. The count remained 2 and 2.

Carlton refused to engage the media, so this topic would never be broached. But the rookie was doing stuff that—under different circumstances—guaranteed a fastball to the temple. When the foul ball landed, Jackson took a few moments to walk in a wide loop around the standing Karkovice and Larry Barnett, the home plate umpire. It was a leisurely stroll in the park from a baseball embryo facing a guaranteed Hall of Famer. The audacity was both horrifying and—from the Royals standpoint—fantastic. This kid was fucking unafraid.

Janssen returned to the ol' *dum-dum-dum. Dum-dum-dum.*

Fans were standing.

Dum-dum-dum. Dum-dum-dum . . .

And clapping.

Dum-dum-dum. Dum-dum-dum . . .

This was epic.

Dum-dum-dum. Dum-dum-dum . . .

Carlton's next pitch was a two-seam fastball, again on the outside corner. It was perfectly positioned, and Jackson leaned forward a bit, extended his arms and hit a two hopper approximately 30 feet to the left of first base. As soon as ball left bat, Jackson dropped the wood and—*whoosh!*—took off. Head down, shoulders bobbing, legs driving. The Royals were a team built for speed—it's leadoff hitter, Lonnie Smith, had five seasons of at least 40 stolen bases. But this was a new stratosphere. John Wathan, the first base coach, never forgot the sound. "The pounding on the turf and the *huff, huff, huff,*" he said. "It was lightning."

Russ Morman, Chicago's rookie first baseman, had been thrust into action a month earlier when starter Greg Walker suffered a broken right hand. "Russ was way too far off the bag when Bo hit that ball," said Tim Hulett, the second baseman. "Greg never would have ventured that far. But Russ was a kid. He didn't know."

The Royals Stadium turf was, Morman recalled, "rubberized—you'd see little granules of refurbished tires in there," and balls that touched it wasted little time. So, already far off the bag, Morman tracked the baseball with his eyes, scooted to his right and made a fruitless backhanded stab with his mitt. The ball bounced past him and into the hole. Hulett sprinted behind Morman, snagged it with his glove in short right field and took a hop step while pivoting to his right hand. "I couldn't come in too hard, because on that turf balls took wicked in-between hops," Hulett said. "So I had to play it a little safe."

With Morman out of position, it was incumbent upon Carlton to leave the mound, receive Hulett's throw and beat Jackson to first. At the time, there were two living creatures who ran slower than Steve Carlton—Darren Robinson, 500-pound lead rapper from the Fat Boys, and Mosha, a three-legged elephant in Thailand. The pitcher did his best, but Jackson beat both the sidearm throw and the hurler by a solid two strides. "Not even close!" said Messer.

"Honestly, it wouldn't have mattered if Russ were in perfect position, if Steve got to the bag on time," said Hulett. "No way in hell were we catching Bo."

It took Jackson another dozen or so steps to slow himself, and when he turned back toward first he was greeted by yet another ovation. He removed his batting gloves, and Wathan flipped the ball into the dugout, where it was corralled by veteran outfielder Willie Wilson, then passed to Mickey Cobb, the trainer, for safekeeping.*

From their assigned seats behind home plate, a gaggle of scouts checked their stopwatches. No one uttered a word, because what they were reading made no sense. "We're all ashamed," recalled Art Stewart, the Royals' director of scouting. "We think we got him wrong."

Finally, one man spoke up. "I'll just say what I got," he said. "A 3.6."

Stewart nodded. He, too, had it at 3.6 seconds. As did all the other scouts. Wilson, who once stole 83 bases in a season, had a PR of 3.6—*from the left side of the plate.* The only right-handed hitter to ever clock a faster home-to-first time was Mickey Mantle, the New York Yankee Hall

---

* "I'll let him keep it," Jackson said afterward.

of Famer who did so in the early 1950s, when stopwatches were hardly precise.

"That whole at bat showed you everything you needed to understand about Bo's speed and Bo's power," said Bud Black, a Royals pitcher. "He hits that mammoth deep fly ball, and seconds later he's running down the line, and you can feel the vibrations in the dugout. You *felt* Bo Jackson running."

The White Sox wound up winning, 3–0, and Jackson grounded out in his other two at bats. But the imprint was set. Afterward, Ferraro kicked back in his office chair. He had seen many things in his lifetime of baseball, but this felt special. "One day," Ferraro said, "he will look back and say he got his first hit off a Hall of Famer. He can be proud of that."

Only years later did Jackson confess that, heading into the game, he didn't know the opposing pitcher was a 300-game winner, or a left-hander, or a guy who mixed sliders with fastballs. He didn't know he'd won four Cy Young Awards or two World Series championships or was named to ten All-Star teams.

Bo Jackson had never heard of Steve Carlton.

Two days after Jackson's Major League debut, Hugh Culverhouse transformed himself from (in Bo's mind) very pathetic to (in Bo's mind) historically pathetic.

He called Jackson's attorneys, Tommy Zieman and Richard Woods, and said this: "A new and exciting real estate deal of major proportions has emerged and if Bo Jackson chooses in time to return from baseball to football, I would be happy to include him in it."

The two representatives suppressed their giggles and promised they would get back to the Buccaneers owner ASAP.

They relayed the message to Jackson.

"Fuck that guy," he said.

Here it was, just two and a half months after the world said Jackson was deranged for bypassing the NFL, and life was but a dream. His body didn't hurt. He didn't have coaches screaming at him. Tampa Bay kicked off its season with a 31–7 shellacking at the hands of the 49ers, and its coulda-been halfback felt nary a pang of regret. "I don't miss it," he said. "There's nothing about football I miss." Jackson loved being in the Major Leagues; loved the Royals clubhouse.

Not everyone shared his enthusiasm.

When the Royals traveled to Arlington, Texas, to take on the Rangers on the weekend of September 5, Jackson's locker was situated alongside that of Wilson, the eleven-year veteran. A steady stream of reporters approached the rookie with interview requests. "Bo this, Bo that," Wilson said. "He won the Heisman Trophy, but he hasn't won the MVP yet."

A few days later, in another interview, Wilson complained that Jackson was being handed what wasn't deserved. "He's been pampered a lot," Wilson said. "They let him get away with a lot of things. [The front office] wants to draw people [to the stadium] the last month. That's what this is all about—dollars and cents."

Frank White, looking on, was asked for his take on the newcomer. "The less I say about Bo," he said, "the better it is for me."

The truth is, while Jackson's peacocking against Carlton was greeted warmly by many, it received a decidedly more negative review from Kansas City's veterans. To men like Wilson and White and catcher Jim Sundberg and outfielder Lonnie Smith (combined Major League experience: forty-seven years), rookies were made to be seen, not heard. "The veterans were nice to us," said Rondin Johnson, a second baseman promoted alongside Jackson. "But you had to show respect."

Though far from loud, Jackson walked with an air. After the infield hit against Carlton, he went 0 for his next six, including three strikeouts. George Brett, the standout third baseman, was astonished by how little the kid knew. "He got here and had no idea how to play baseball," Brett said. "He didn't have baseball instincts. A player with good baseball instincts doesn't have to think before he reacts. Bo had to think. He had to make decisions on the run. I don't think he knew which base to throw to, or where the cutoff man was. I don't think he knew when the good time to go from first to third was. On a base hit to left field with no outs, he would try to score from second. The coach would hold him up and Bo would keep going. He didn't understand that there are different ways to play when you're behind and when you're ahead.

"Bo wasn't ready for the Majors, and he wouldn't have been called up were he a college kid who didn't play football and wasn't the Heisman Trophy winner."

The worst part—*the absolute worst part*—was Jackson referring to himself in the third person. Dating back to mid-Auburn, it was never "I," always "Bo." And while some tried chalking this up to the stutter that still impacted his speech (though he was markedly improved from his early college days), Jackson did not, in fact, refer to himself as "Bo" because he tripped over "I." Nope. Bo referred to himself as "Bo" because—in the self-indulgent world of the 1980s—it felt and sounded sort of cool. So when a reporter wanted to know what Jackson admired about, oh, Rangers outfielder Odd-ibe McDowell, the reply would inevitably begin with, "Bo thinks . . ."

"[It] was something of a construct," wrote Michael Weinreb, a Jackson biographer, "manufactured for public consumption for marketing purposes, as a way for Bo to separate himself from his other celebrity."

This would have been OK were Bo a ten-year veteran. But Bo was a twenty-three-year-old rookie who had recently handed out unsolicited autographed photographs and couldn't hit a curveball for shit. "He was such a jag," said Melissa Isaacson, a reporter for the *Orlando Sentinel*. "Everything was Bo this, Bo that. I don't think there were many reporters at the time who didn't think he was an ass."

Jackson seemed to like the acclaim, not the attention. He treated journalists as if they were gum beneath his shoe. He rarely made eye contact and blew off requests. He would feel slighted when people ignored his greatness, but annoyed when folks dared ask about it. "If you needed him after a game for a one-paragraph utterance, all of which would take him fifteen seconds, he'd make you work," said Jack Etkin, the *Kansas City Star* beat writer. "First, he'd sit at a table and eat for a long time. He knew we were waiting, but it didn't concern him. That was not normal rookie behavior."

"He reminded me of what you'd read about Marilyn Monroe," said Jonathan Rand, the *Star* sports columnist. "The need for adulation, but also making you wait at his beck and call."

Of all the veterans, Brett was most sympathetic. The 1980 American League MVP knew what it was to be confined to a sports bubble, where the same stale questions arrived daily, where the expectations were Ruthian, where meals were regularly interrupted by a balding forty-year-old fan holding a scrap of paper and a Bic. He liked Jackson's feistiness. But early on in Jackson's stay, Brett noticed that he was rude to the clubhouse employees. "He treated us very badly," said Brian Watley, a Royals batboy. "The front office would tell us to go from player to player and get balls signed. Some of the players were great, some were not." Jackson, still scarred by the Memphis experience, was memorably awful. "I want two dollars per ball," he told Watley. "Otherwise I don't sign."

This continued for several days, until Brett—who referred to the rookie as "BoBo"—called Jackson to his locker for a talk. "BoBo," he said, "you can't do that shit. The batboys are here to take care of you. They're not *their* balls."

"Really?" Jackson said. "I had no idea."

Jackson apologized to Watley and Co. He had been done wrong by Frelon Abbott, the aspiring agent. He had been done wrong by Hugh Culverhouse, Buccaneers owner. He had been done wrong by George Lapides, Memphis Chicks president. His trust level was not particularly high. "He ultimately became the greatest guy ever to us," Watley said. "He was just new and feeling it all out."

Over the span of the next month, Jackson did things that caused jaws to drop. Dennis Cryder, the team's vice president of marketing, was first introduced to Bo outside a Royals Stadium elevator bank. He was wearing his 1985 World Series ring, and when Jackson shook his hand, "Bo's shake was so hard the ring punctured my skin," Cryder said. "I went to the bathroom and was washing blood off my fingers."

During a batting practice session at Royals Stadium, Jackson turned to Charlie Leibrandt, a veteran starting pitcher, and said, casually, "I'm gonna hit the scoreboard in center field."

"Bo," Leibrandt replied, "you're full of shit."

First pitch—*BOOM!* "OK, he didn't hit the board," Leibrandt said. "But he hit the brick facing up to the scoreboard, and that's 470 feet."

On September 14, Kansas City hosted the Seattle Mariners in the finale of a four-game series. The Royals were now fifteen games out in the American League West, the Mariners 19½. Befitting such a Monday-afternoon clash, the stadium was half empty.

Five years earlier, the Mariners had used the first pick in the Major League Draft to take Mike Moore, a hard-throwing righty from Oral Roberts University. Desperate for stars, the organization rushed him to Seattle after thirteen Double A starts and watched as he struggled with command and confidence. By the time he took the mound in Kansas City, he was a fairly run-of-the-mill Major League starter.

Through the first three innings, the Royals touched up Moore for a 3–0 lead. When the Mariners failed to score in the top of the fourth off Mark Gubicza, Jackson jogged in from right field, grabbed his blue-and-white helmet from the shelf and readied to lead off the inning. For reasons Jackson never explained, before the game he picked up one of Wilson's black Louisville Slugger R161 bats, liked the feel of the wood and the solid grip, and announced, "This is mine!" Now, exiting the dugout and armed with Wilson's northern white ash, he nodded toward Sundberg, the catcher. "Hey, Jim," he said. "Watch how far I hit this."

Sundberg was in his thirteenth season. He had played with some of the era's elite sluggers—Ted Simmons and Rusty Staub; Ben Oglivie and Bobby Bonds. Never before had a teammate uttered the words "Watch how far I hit this."

It was the smug arrogance of youth.

"OK, Bo," Sundberg said. "Let's see."

Moore was a gangly 6-foot-4, 205 pounds, all elbows and knees. His windup resembled a flamingo tucking its bill. He threw a nasty slider, a fastball and a slow curve that was a work in progress. In the second inning, he pitched Jackson inside, and coerced a feeble groundout to shortstop. Now Jackson reentered the box, cocked his bat and prepared to hit once again.

The first four pitches were a battle—two balls, two strikes, Jackson swinging for the fences, Moore busting him hard and inside. Catcher Scott Bradley placed three fingers down for a slider, then spotted his glove on the inner portion of the plate.

The pitch came in fast (which was good for Moore) and straight (which was awful for Moore), and Jackson swung. As soon as contact was made, every Mariner infielder and outfielder turned, craned their necks and observed. There were no false pretenses of making a play. The ball rose toward left-center, and Phil Bradley, Seattle's left fielder, gazed like a birdwatcher mesmerized by the path of an eagle. The baseball finally nestled on the top of a grassy bank in left field—475 feet from its place of origin. "It was like Zeus came off the mountain," said David Cone, a Royals pitcher. "No one had ever seen a baseball go that far."

"The ball landed by the flagpole," said Kingery. "*No one* hit balls by the flagpole."

The shot was both Jackson's first Major League home run *and* the longest home run in stadium history. When he returned to the dugout, Jackson winked at Sundberg and smiled as his teammates offered high fives. The fans stood and applauded, and refused to sit until Jackson—pushed up the steps by several Royals—raised his helmet for a curtain call.

"Bo," said Hal McRae, the Royals designated hitter, "is the strongest guy I've ever seen play."

The hype, of course, faded a bit—as did Bo Jackson's production. He hit only one more home run the rest of the way, and drove in a grand total of 9 runs in 82 at bats. His final average was a lowly .207. The strikeouts were plentiful (34 in total), as were the blunders (4 errors). Brett was right—the rookie wasn't Big League ready.

Of all the Royals veterans, the one who most resented Jackson was Wilson. He had always been The Athlete in Kansas City. He was the three-sport star at Summit (New Jersey) High who signed a letter of intent to play football at the University of Maryland. He was the cornerstone of the Royals' off-season basketball team. The fastest. The quickest. The strongest.

The highest jumper. "Until Bo came along," said Brett, "Willie was the best athlete I'd ever seen."

After Jackson was called up, Wilson devoted a portion of most pre-game stretching routines toward challenging him to a race. "Willie would beg and beg and beg, and Bo—who was fully committed to stretching—was always, 'No, no, no,'" said Steve Shields, a Royals pitcher.

Finally, during the last homestand, Wilson said, "Bo, you've pansied out all month. Can we *finally* race?"

"OK," Jackson replied. "I'll give you five yards."

Wilson was offended. "Fuck you," he said. "I don't need that shit."

The two players stretched along the first base line, and Brett jogged into the outfield, roughly 40 yards away, and yelled, "When I drop my hat, you guys race!"

Wilson and Jackson stood side by side, and Brett . . .

Ready.

Set.

. . . dropped the hat.

It was as if Wilson's feet were stapled to the turf and Jackson had a JT9D turbofan strapped to his back. The rookie left Wilson in his dust, and won by a solid seven yards. "It wasn't even close," said Shields. "Bo destroyed him."

A humiliated Wilson got back to his stretching. Jackson said nothing.

"So it's done," said Shields. "And Willie used to have this thing. There were open heating and air-conditioning ducts along the ceiling of the club-house. They were exposed. Willie kept a shopping cart by his locker, and he would take his shirt off, run up to the ducts, jump and slam his shirt over the ducts and into the basket."

The race was over. Stretching was over. Jackson returned to the club-house to change, and eyed the shopping cart. He grabbed it and pushed it to his turf. "Then Bo jumps—flat footed—and dunks his shirt over the duct and into the basket," Shields said.

Years later, he laughed in retelling the story. Not because it was funny. Because it was ridiculous.

"The veterans were right," Shields said. "Bo didn't know how to play baseball. But you can learn all the rules. What he had—that was 100 per-cent God gifted. And it was gonna take that young man awfully far."

CHAPTER 17

MIXED ROYALTIES

During his September callup with the Kansas City Royals, one of the team-mates Bo Jackson enjoyed chatting with was Greg Pryor, a thirty-six-year-old infielder in the final season of a decade-long Major League career.

The two shared little in common—Pryor was thirteen years Jackson's senior, as well as a married father of two daughters. But he was also comfortable in his status as a wizened guru. He knew his time was short, and wanted to enjoy it.

One day late in the month, Jackson plopped down alongside Pryor's locker and pointed to the photograph of an oil well hanging within the cubby.

"What are you doing playing baseball?" he asked. "Don't you wanna be in oil?"

Pryor laughed.

"Bo," he said, "you turned down $7 million in football money to take $500,000 for baseball. Who are you to talk?"

The numbers were off. But fair point.

"Greg," Jackson replied, "I'm just sitting here waiting for the right time."

He rose, patted the veteran on the shoulder and walked off. Pryor never forgot the words. "Bo *knew* what he was doing the whole time," he recalled. "There was no doubt to that man."

Within earshot, Jackson reassured everyone that he was a baseball player, and only a baseball player. He didn't miss football, didn't long for football, didn't even watch as the Tampa Bay Buccaneers endured a predictably miserable 2-14 season. Why, affixed to his lockers—first in Memphis, then Kansas City—were 8½ × 11 pieces of paper with a handwritten warning: DON'T BE STUPID AND ASK ME FOOTBALL QUESTIONS OKAY!

Yet behind the scenes, mechanisms were at play. Back May 1986, Jackson and his two attorneys—Richard Woods and Tommy Zieman—flew to Portland, Oregon, to meet with Karin Morlan, the head of Nike's "cleated promotions." Thanks to the recent blossoming of Michael Jordan and the

Air Jordan line of shoes, Nike was *the* place when it came to athletic apparel. Although Jackson was largely void of charisma, and still struggled with stuttering, he possessed something Nike craved: multifaceted sports talent. So while Morlan and Co. knew not whether Jackson would play football or baseball or (*pretty please with a cherry on top*) both, Nike longed for him to be the face of its upcoming shoe release—"a bulky contraption sealed with a strap [that] looked like a castoff from the production of *Ben-Hur*," wrote Michael Weinreb.

It was called The Trainer. Short for the cross-trainer.

Over the course of negotiations, Zieman and Woods insisted Jackson would not become a Nike pitchman unless the company forked over $100,000 per year for three years. This was astronomical dough. Jordan had received a five-year, $500,000-per-year deal that included royalties on Air Jordans and all Nike Air basketball shoes. But he was *Michael friggin' Jordan*. Most of Nike's other athletes were lucky to snag $5,000 annually.*

Something about Jackson, though, was deliciously appetizing to the company. Sure, it all may well go wrong. He could stick to one sport, stink, vanish. But he could also wind up the second coming of Jim Thorpe. "Bo was obviously a great athlete," said Phil Knight, Nike's founder and CEO. "He didn't talk a lot. But he was handsome, he had a beautiful smile and we had expectations."

Expectations didn't mean "great baseball player" or "great football player." It meant both. And while Nike knew there was no shot of Jackson ever signing with the Buccaneers, it was aware that once a calendar year passed, his name returned to the NFL Draft, available for any franchise willing to take a chance.

Which is where Chris Woods came in.

For two seasons, 1982 and 1983, Woods played alongside Jackson as a wide receiver with the Auburn football team. He was a good-not-exceptional Tiger, and after graduating, Woods jumped to the Canadian Football League, where over three years he excelled as a standout pass catcher and punt returner. When the NFL held a supplemental draft of CFL and USFL (United States Football League) players in the summer of 1984, the Los Angeles Raiders used the 28th overall pick on Woods.

"So by 1986 I'm ready to go to LA. and give it a shot," Chris Woods

---

* Around this same time, the shoe company Avia gave Dwayne "Pearl" Washington, a point guard drafted by the New Jersey Nets out of Syracuse, a five-year deal that paid $125,000 annually. Washington was an immediate flop, and served as a cautionary tale to betting on the trajectory of an athlete.

recalled. "Bo and I are both repped by Richard Woods, so he was kept in the loop when it came to what was going on with me." When Richard Woods told Jackson that Chris Woods was about to fly to California, meet Raiders owner Al Davis, take a physical and sign a contract, he reached out to his old teammate. This was while Jackson was in Memphis, sick of buses.

"Hey, Chris," Jackson said, "I have a favor to ask."

"OK," Woods replied. "Is everything OK?"

"Yeah, I'm fine," Jackson said. "Just do me a favor and tell Al Davis to draft me. Tell him that I definitely want to play football."

Chris Woods assured Jackson he would pass on the message—then did so. Davis, he recalled, was stunned.

"Really?" he asked Woods. "Are you sure he's being straight with you?"

Woods had no doubts.

"Bo," he said, "is straight with everyone."

In the aftermath of the 1986 season, the Kansas City Royals were aware of none of this. They knew Jackson was attached to a Nike shoe deal, but were never tipped off that the company was covertly applying two-sport pressure. From what they could tell, Jackson was all in on baseball.

Come October, the team fretted for nary a second in sending Jackson to Sarasota, Florida, for a miserable few weeks in the Instructional League—a place where young ballplayers gathered to enhance their skills and vets worked to rehab from injuries. One of the sport's worst-kept secrets is that an Instructional League assignment is the herpes of pro baseball—nobody wants it. The days are hot, dull, repetitive and relatively useless. Had the Royals known their future meal ticket was starting to itch for football, odds are they would have encouraged him to spend the offseason back home in Alabama, napping on a hammock, sipping from icy cold glasses of lemonade and spending some quality time in Auburn alongside Linda and their infant son Garrett.

Instead, he was stationed inside a clubhouse at tiny Twin Lakes Park and ordered to wake at six, arrive by seven and work on his outfield defense, throwing accuracy and baserunning. The man in charge was Joe Jones, the organization's field coordinator of minor league instruction and someone Jackson immediately abhorred.

Dating back to childhood, Jackson did not respond to yelling and ranting from anyone but his mother. Jones was a yeller and a ranter—and not Florence Bond. But there was more. He was a know-it-all who didn't know enough to advance past the low minor leagues in his seven years as a goodfield, no-hit second baseman. So why was Bo Jackson stuck here being drill sargented by a 5-foot-9, 150-pound aspiring baseball Napoleon? Why was a bush-league bum who batted .255 over his lifetime telling Bo how to hit? "Joe Jones is out there screaming at you like a high school coach, and all these minor league players that are fresh out of high school are terrified shitless of Joe Jones," recalled Jackson. "And he's telling us, 'Look, if you can't do what I say get the fuck out of here.' Who is this guy? Who died and made him God?"

Jackson's singular moment of joy came in an exhibition against a Japanese professional team, when the catcher stood in front of the plate, waved for his outfielders to back up and yelled, "Bo Jack-*sohn*! Bo Jack-*sohn*!" Before dipping into his crouch, the catcher bowed toward Jackson, who bowed back. "Bo then hits an absolute missile, like three-hopper up the middle, goes to second base and he does a pop-up slide into second base, safe," recalled pitcher Mike Butcher. "The Japanese players were in awe. So was I."

Jackson was slated to stay for a month, but after two and a half weeks of mosquitoes and humidity and loneliness and Joe Jones, he packed his bag and announced his imminent departure.

"You can't just leave and go home," Jones said.

"I came here on a fucking invitation," Jackson said. "I'd like to see someone stop me."

Jackson returned to Alabama, where he first visited his mother in Bessemer, then headed to Auburn to enroll in a winter class (he was still pursuing his degree in family and child development), work out with the Tigers baseball team, watch his favorite soap operas and finally meet his 3-month-old son, Garrett. Linda was living in a small off-campus apartment, and when Jackson arrived and the door was opened and son was presented to father, a switch flipped. Bo Jackson had been raised not merely without a dad, but with the knowledge that his dad resided across town and cared so little he rarely stopped by. He would never treat this infant before him with the callous indifference A. D. Adams had shown him.

"I knew then," Jackson said, "that the side of Bo Jackson which was a whore, really, running around and chasing women, was over. I had been around. I had been around a whole lot. And I was just tired of coming home to an empty apartment."

In February 1987, shortly before leaving for spring training, Jackson handed Linda Garrett a small box with a diamond ring inside. He looked her in the eyes and said, "I don't think it would be right for me to go to spring training without letting you have this."

It was his third (or fourth?) engagement to two women.

It's also the one that stuck.

The bitter taste of the Instructional League experience did not easily leave Bo Jackson's tongue. He refused to dwell on it. But as he prepared for his first-ever spring training at Terry Park in Ft. Myers, Florida, it was hard to feel wonderful about the Royals. First, Joe Jones was now the team's first base coach, which meant Jackson had to see his least-favorite dictator every . . . single . . . day. Second, in the offseason the organization pulled off a blockbuster trade, sending three players to the Mariners in exchange for a twenty-four-year-old power-hitting right fielder named Danny Tartabull.

The *Tampa Tribune* covered the deal with the headline SAY IT AIN'T BO!, and the corresponding story led with, "Bo Jackson, facing the stiffest challenge of his athletic life, has no blockers this time. He must clear his own path to the Kansas City Royals roster."

John Schuerholz, the general manager, made clear he expected Jackson to open the season with Triple A Omaha. Throughout his life, Jackson was always the person twenty steps ahead of the pack. He thrived on the understanding that he was special; that he was among The Chosen. Now the Royals were saying, *"Well, we hope you're special. But we're not so sure just yet."*

Even discounting Jackson, the team began spring training with plenty of drama. Dick Howser, the expected manager who stepped aside in 1986 because of brain cancer, resumed the position and, come early February, arrived in high spirits. On Saturday, February 21, he began the day with a press conference at Terry Park, and said that he expected to manage, "at least a couple more years." He sounded hopeful, but appeared shrunken. When he walked, he shuffled his feet. His eyes always seemed to be gazing downward. By the afternoon, Howser retreated to his office to rest. He could barely move. "All his energy had been sapped," said Schuerholz.

"I was in the elevator with Dick," said Jim Sundberg, the Royals catcher. "He was looking at me, but he didn't recognize me."

Two days later, Howser entered the clubhouse and—tears welling in his eyes—told the players he was resigning. Billy Gardner, the third base coach, was taking over. Howser had been the Royals skipper since 1981, and later that night he left Ft. Myers never to return. "He knew the truth," wrote Jack Ebling of the *Lansing State Journal*. "That wishing doesn't always make it so."

Howser died in June, at age fifty-one.

With the soft-spoken Gardner at the helm, the team held its first full workout on Sunday, March 1. For youngsters like Jackson and newbies like Tartabull, Howser's departure barely registered. It felt sad, but distant. He had never been *their* manager. "You compartmentalize things in baseball," said George Brett. "Even tragedies. You have to be selfish sometimes to be really good."

Jackson stepped into the batting cage for his debut cuts early that Sunday, and—with Gardner observing from mere feet away—it didn't go well. On the mound stood Steve Shirley, a thirty-year-old left-hander who had spent the past decade bouncing from the Dodgers' minor league system to the Lotte Orions of the Japanese Pacific League to the Pirates' minor league system to the Tigers' minor league system, back to the Dodgers' minor league system and now, the Royals, where he was a warm body who threw junk. Yet Shirley owned Jackson. He tossed ten pitches, none of which Bo hit fair. He missed three, fouled five others and let two pass by. "I'm not worried about it," Jackson said afterward. "Everybody has the first-day blues."

This felt different. Tartabull was a monster—mashing balls out of the park. Jackson, the man who willingly chose to depart Instructional League early, was a work in progress. And for all of the times he insisted he would not discuss football, there was *a lot* to discuss. The NFL Draft was less than two months away, and news outlets were floating rumors. First, CNN reported that Jackson had, indeed, agreed to terms with the Buccaneers.* Then the *New York Times* insisted the Denver Broncos were planning on acquiring Jackson's rights. Then Mike Lynn, general manager of the Minnesota Vikings, said his team was planning on drafting Jackson—"[not] in the first round, but we could take him any time after that."

A shrewd baseball man with the game's best poker face, in public Schuerholz expressed 100 percent confidence that Jackson was fully committed to baseball, and only baseball. Yet when the media vanished, and he could speak freely with colleagues, Schuerholz was concerned. He never fully bought Jackson as a ballplayer. At least not as a baseball-only ballplayer. Football was the more exciting game, the more marketable game. The money was enormous. Maybe, in some ways, Jackson was still using the Royals. That thought never escaped Schuerholz's mind, and caused him to think twice about giving the youngster an excuse to quit.

---

* The last time the Buccaneers spoke with Jackson was when the Memphis Chicks were playing in Orlando. Jim Gruden, Tampa Bay's director of player personnel, waited for Jackson to exit the team bus. "He was the last guy off," Gruden told Bob McGinn, the veteran sportswriter. "I forgot how big this guy was. He was wearing sunglasses. I remember saying to him, 'Bo, if things don't work out here I just want you to know we still love you in Tampa.'" Jackson smiled and walked off.

So, despite all reasons to send him to Omaha (a hot-and-cold spring training that resulted in a .290 batting average but a number of baserunning and outfield blunders), on April 4 Schuerholz asked Jackson for a moment alone.

"Bo, I wanted to congratulate you," the general manager said through gritted teeth. "You've made the twenty-four-man roster. Feel good about this, and help us win 110 games this year."

Without cracking a smile, Jackson said, "Let's make it 130."

Later, he was less diplomatic. "In my mind I was like, 'You assholes,'" he recalled. "I thought, 'You people will never learn. I'm not trying to be conceited, but I like making people eat their words."

The Royals returned to Kansas City the following day with Bo Jackson the starting left fielder.

"I guess I was the only one who didn't have any doubts about me," he told Bob Nightengale of the *Kanas City Star*. "People underrate me. Some do not like me. Some are jealous of me. But it doesn't matter to me, because I'm not trying to impress the media, the fans or anything like that. I just want to live up to my potential."

By late April, Jackson was hitting .338. He had 4 home runs and 15 RBI. Over the course of 17 games, he had reached above the Yankee Stadium wall to rob Dave Winfield of a home run, beat out a routine grounder to short against Boston to avoid a double play, smoked two homers and seven RBI against the Tigers and made a diving catch against the Yankees' Don Mattingly that defied physics. The all-around output was prompting members of the media to urge NFL teams to avoid drafting him. In a piece penned for the Associated Press, writer Doug Tucker opined that "The best available running back in this year's National Football League draft will be ignored—if the NFL is smart. Bo Jackson plays baseball. Oh, does he ever."

The Kansas City Royals were thrilled with Bo Jackson's first few weeks of the season.

The Los Angeles Raiders *loved* it.

L-o-v-e-d it.

Al Davis, the team's owner, managing general partner and overlord of all, had spent his twenty-eight years in professional football itching to buck the system and show the world the immense splendor that was his brain. He was the one who, back in the 1960s, emphasized the deep passing game when all others opted to run. He was the one who pushed for speed, speed and more speed when the longtime name of the game was power. Davis relocated the Raiders from Oakland to Los Angeles in 1982—defying a league that demanded they stay put. In a few months, Davis would testify on behalf of the USFL (United States Football League) in its antitrust lawsuit against the NFL.

Why?

Because he was Al Davis.

"Al didn't see taking chances as taking chances," said Jon Kingdon, the Raiders player personnel director. "He saw it as being Al."

So, with the April 28 NFL Draft approaching and Chris Woods's words ("Bo wants to be a Raider") floating through his cranium, Davis couldn't stop fantasizing over Bo Jackson. He was the perfect Raider. Fast as lightning. Sleek as a Thunderbird. Groundbreaking. Untraditional. A big middle finger to the rest of the league. Fuck, to the rest of the universe. Davis reveled in assembling rosters that (at first glance) made little sense. Los Angeles was the organization of Lyle Alzado and John Matuszak; of Ted Hendricks and Lester Hayes; of steroid freaks and chain smokers and ex-inmates looking for a fifth chance. Pull up your tits and punch the guy across from you in the mouth. *Those* were the Raiders.

Two years earlier, when Herschel Walker was playing for the New Jersey Generals of the United States Football League, Ron Wolf, the Raiders head of player personnel, had thought long and hard about taking a shot and drafting the former Bulldog with the 107th pick in the fourth round. He wimped out, however, and went with Jamie Kimmel, the Syracuse linebacker and inevitable disappointment. Seven picks later, Dallas grabbed Walker—a two-time Pro Bowler with the Cowboys. "We were pushing for Herschel pretty strongly," said Ken Herock, a Raiders' scouting executive. "Jamie Kimmel, what a stiff. Now we're going into the [1987] draft and Ron and I were both pushing for [Jackson]."

When it was time for the organization to make its first pick (fifteenth overall), the choice was John Clay, a 6-foot-5, 315-pound offensive tackle out of Missouri who would last one season with the team.

It's too early for Bo Jackson . . .

In the second round another offensive tackle, Bruce Wilkerson of Tennessee, came off the board. He played eight years in Los Angeles before winning a Super Bowl with the Packers.

It's still too early for Bo Jackson . . .

The Raiders grabbed a Penn State fullback, Steve Smith, in the third round (he was a member of the team for seven years), then quarterback Steve Beuerlein out of Notre Dame in the fourth (his rocky time in L.A. lasted three seasons).

Having traded their next two picks, Los Angeles wouldn't choose again until the 183rd slot in the seventh round. Jackson's baseball career made him too great a risk to select high. But Davis, Wolf and Herock were committed to using the team's final slot on the Heisman Trophy winner. One year earlier, Wolf evaluated Jackson at Auburn and gave him the highest score he had ever assigned a player. "I always felt . . . he'd become the first 3,000-yard rusher in the National Football League," Wolf said. "Once in a lifetime you get an athlete like that."

Now the Raiders just had to wait.

It wasn't altogether unlike the Royals nine months earlier, who hung tight until the fourth round of the Major League Draft. Like Schuerholz, Davis and Co. were concerned about someone swooping in at the last minute and ruining the master plan. But they also didn't know, with 100 percent certainty, that Jackson wanted to continue with football. They *thought* he did. They *heard* he did. But were they convinced beyond a doubt? Not exactly.

With the 182nd pick in the seventh round, the Miami Dolphins selected a running back. He was big—6-foot-1, 223 pounds. He was powerful. He was as good at track as he was at football.

He was Pittsburgh's Tom Brown.

Seconds later, the relieved Raiders announced they were taking Bo Jackson, running back, Auburn University. "Our feeling about him . . . he's a unique athlete," Tom Flores, the Raiders coach, said the next day. "We would honor his baseball commitment but we wonder if there is a possibility of dual profession. People have said no one could do it. We haven't talked to him, but maybe he would like the challenge."

On the afternoon of the draft, Jackson was back in Kansas City, preparing for an evening game against Baltimore. He was taking BP at Royals Stadium as the selection was announced, and when he completed his swings reporters gathered around for comment. Jackson sighed and turned toward Hal McRae, now the club's hitting coach. "I'm going to get a big sign," he said, "and write in big, black letters, 'I AM A BASEBALL PLAYER.'"

Pause.

"I'm a baseball player," he said. "Didn't you see me out here?"

Bo Jackson was a baseball player.

Only a baseball player.

No ifs, ands or buts. He played baseball. Got it? Only baseball.

And that was that. Davis and the Raiders kept their distance, knowing the mercurial Jackson would frown upon, say, a surprise Royals Stadium visit from Howie Long and Marcus Allen. They let the next few months of the baseball season play out, hoping something might stir their seventh-round pick in the direction of the NFL. When asked, Al Davis dropped mini-suggestions. Nothing major. Just thoughts. Microscopic ear worms. "We want him to look at it as a challenge to prove he is the greatest," Davis said. He explained the team was perfectly fine with Jackson as a two-sport guy. "We would have a two-week exemption to let him get ready to play," Davis said, "and then we would use him over the second half of the year and in the playoffs."

The greatest barrier facing the Raiders may well have been comfort. Jackson was *comfortable* in Kansas City. He lived in a spacious two-bedroom apartment (unit number 220, to be precise) on Wornall Road, and usually drove to the ballpark with Thad Bosley, a neighbor and veteran outfielder. "He was a nice guy, a good guy," said Bosley. "I took him to some stores and got him fitted for some suits. He was a little naive, so I wanted to help." Before the year wrapped, Bo and Linda (engaged to be married come September 5) and their toddler son, Garrett, spent a day with a real estate agent, looking for a home in Leawood, Kansas. "Bo wanted to be in the same neighborhood as George Brett," said Susann McKee, his representative. "So we were driving around with the realtor, and Bo saw a house he really liked. Only it wasn't for sale." Undeterred, Jackson knocked on the door and spoke with one of the homeowners—who told the heartwarming story of she and her husband building this amazing dream house, and how it meant the world to them, and how they were destined to retire there, and how the countertops were imported from Spain and the wood floors were . . .

Within a month, Bo, Linda and Garrett moved in. The 4,284-square-foot home featured a large backyard where Jackson could grill and nap and partake in his hobbies. The Royals viewed this as a great sign—Jackson seemed invested in the region. And, truly, he was. Jackson didn't seek out fancy restaurants or Broadway productions. He liked mowing a lawn, taking walks with Linda, going out every so often to eat a decent rib eye. Hunting, fishing. The idea of, say, New York's 8 million people held no interest. Jackson was a quiet man with quiet tastes. "I'd go over there sometimes to shoot a bow and arrows," said Ed Hearn, the Royals catcher. "Bo put a target right in the corner of his yard facing the middle of a four-way intersection. We're shooting these arrows, and a good number of them are missing the target and flying into the street toward traffic. Try to picture the scene—Kansas City in the mid-1980s, a big Black guy and a big white guy shooting arrows into cars, then politely retrieving them."

On multiple occasions, Jackson—a proud outdoorsman who lived for bagging white-tail deer—arrived at the clubhouse with a bow slung over his shoulder. After games he enjoyed setting up targets on one side of the room, then marching off paces, turning and firing arrows. "It was a deadly weapon," recalled Jonathan Rand, the *Kansas City Star* columnist. "He felt and behaved as if he could do whatever he wanted."

"With Bo," said Chris Browne, a batboy, "you learned to look both ways before walking."

With the small-market Royals, Jackson fit in as one of the guys. His stutter wasn't off limits as a mocking point. Neither were the Heisman Trophy photos of a year earlier. On two separate occasions he fell for the "Does this cake smell sour?" gag (Bo leans in to take a sniff, someone slams his face into the dessert). The room housed a Ping-Pong table, and Jackson was the Royals' dominant player. One day, as a gag, pitcher Bud Black invited a nationally ranked competitor and introduced him to Jackson as "my friend."

"Bo," Black said, "my guy is pretty good at Ping-Pong."

"I'll play the fool," Jackson replied, "if he wants to put some money down."

Black's pal threw the first game, and Jackson urged his teammates to wager on the follow-up.

"The guy starts playing," recalled Hearn, "and he spanked Bo's ass like he was a kindergartner."

Once in on the joke, Jackson laughed and laughed. This is what he wanted—to be normal and accepted. He had never been a mere piece, and it was refreshing. Were he playing for the Buccaneers, making all that money behind a dreadful offensive line, Jackson would have faced ceaseless questions from a ceaseless army of media intruders. *Why is this team so bad? Are you worth the money? Do you regret being here?* There was little of that with the Royals

Unfortunately for Jackson, there was also little consistency. Kansas City was never under the illusion that a man with such limited experience would maintain the hot start. But from May 2, when he was batting .307, until the July 12 launch of the All-Star Break, Jackson's average plummeted 54 points. He was second in the Majors with a staggering 115 strikeouts, and lacked any sort of plate consistency. The holes in his swing were the size of polar bears. At one point, Billy Gardner benched Jackson for a handful of games because—the skipper said—"he's swinging at a lot of bad balls that he wasn't when he was going good." Rick Bozich, the exceptional *Louisville Courier-Journal* scribe, penned a blistering column headlined ROYALS

SHOW PATIENCE WITH JACKSON, BUT HE BELONGS AT OMAHA AT THIS STAGE. "Name this kid Eddie Jackson, make him a former outfielder/tailback from Ball State, and you'd find him with Omaha, Memphis or Appleton, Wis.," Bozich correctly opined.

During a game earlier in the season, Jackson popped up on a ball that was deemed a balk. He dropped his bat and returned to the Royals dugout.

"Where ya going, Bo?" Gardner asked.

"I popped out," Jackson said.

"Yeah," Gardner replied, "but it was a balk."

"But they caught it," Jackson said.

"It was a balk, Bo," Gardner said. "That don't count. Get back in there."

He didn't know any better.

In hindsight, Bo Jackson's I'll-never-play-football stance was a lie.

When, in May, Davis made his "We want him to look at it as a challenge to prove he is the greatest" statement, it was no throwaway line. He was trying to entice Jackson. To dare him to try something bold and relatively unheard of. And, truth be told, it worked. Within days, Jackson and Richard Woods, his agent, began the discussions of whether a part-time leap to the NFL was realistic.

"Is it even possible?" Jackson asked.

"I don't know," Woods replied. "But I'll find out."

As the weeks passed, and his baseball output plummeted, and the boos began to fester, and talk of a Triple A demotion percolated, Jackson opened to the Raiders experiment. Though hardly a sports historian, he had once watched with great interest *"Jim Thorpe—All-American,"* the 1951 film about the multisport star who captured the imagination of a nation. "The more I thought about playing football and baseball," Jackson recalled, "the more it sounded like fun."

Finally, in early July, Jackson dialed up Richard Woods.

"Hey, I'd like to play both," he said.

"You sure?" Woods asked.

"I'm sure," Jackson replied.

"Well, I better call Al Davis and see if he's serious," Woods said.

Oh, Al Davis was serious. In 1986, the Raiders finished 8-8 and fourth in the AFC West. The team's slogan was "Commitment to Excellence," but nothing felt excellent about .500 football. Before long, Woods and Davis hashed out a five-year contract that paid $1.5 million annually while requiring Jackson to join the Raiders only after the baseball season was fully completed. Jackson's baseball deal spelled out that he could leave for football only if he did so by requisite dates and repaid a certain percentage of money earned. Nowhere, however, did it say he was banned from playing both.

On July 10, the Royals were in the middle of a three-game series at Toronto. Woods telephoned Avron Fogelman, one of Kansas City's owners, to request that his client be allowed to play football once the baseball season wrapped. Woods made it very clear Jackson wasn't quitting on the Royals, or even cutting out on the Royals.

Fogelman, Woods recalled, was relatively agreeable. Though far from thrilled by the idea, he didn't seem overly shocked or angry. When the conversation wrapped, it felt as if everything would work out with little drama. Again—Bo Jackson was not leaving baseball, per se. He simply wanted to be a two-sport star.

It all blew up.

Within minutes of hanging up the phone, Fogelman dashed off to Memphis International Airport, boarded his private jet and instructed his pilot to ferry him to Toronto. Once there, he checked into a room at the Westin and sent a pair of messages to Exhibition Stadium—one commanding Gardner to remove Jackson from the game (he was pulled for a pinch hitter in the seventh inning), one demanding Jackson immediately meet him at the hotel. Inside the Royals dugout, confusion reigned. There had been whispers about Bo and football. But why was Jackson suddenly being yanked for Thad Bosley? And where the hell was he going?

Upon reaching the Westin, an agitated, unshowered Jackson headed up to Fogelman's suite. He was furious—as was the owner. "We signed you to be a baseball player!" Fogelman said. "That was the deal! You said you were done with football!" Not one to back down, Jackson stood his ground. "I'm not leaving the team," he replied. "Who said anything about leaving the team?"

Fogelman paced back and forth, alcoholic beverage in hand. He genuinely liked Bo Jackson. Respected him, too. He was a nice kid who chose the Royals when he didn't have to. "I thought you love baseball . . ." Fogelman said. Jackson reiterated he did not want to leave the Royals. This wasn't about hating America's Pastime. This was about relishing a challenge.

Fogelman begrudgingly understood. In a past life he had owned the Memphis Rogues, a failed professional soccer team, as well as the Memphis Tams of the long-dead American Basketball Association. If nothing else, he could appreciate Jackson's sense of adventure and wonderment. He recognized the intrigue of playing two sports, as well as the inevitable Nike windfall. He hated it, but he got it. "OK," he told Jackson. "We'll work this out."

Later that evening, when reached by Bob Nightengale of the *Kansas City Times*, Fogelman seemed content. "Bo is a Kansas City Royal, and he's happy to be a Royal, and we have no problems," he said. "That's as far as we're concerned. Bo's happy, and if Bo's happy, we're happy."

If only it were that simple. Before departing the visiting clubhouse for his meetup with Fogelman, Jackson had asked an equipment staffer to clean *up* his locker. By sheer misunderstanding, the man cleaned *out* his locker—placing all the items into a series of cardboard boxes. This was witnessed by Kansas City's other players as well as members of the media, and wrongly interpreted as a single-fingered farewell to the Royals.

Jackson returned to Exhibition Stadium Saturday morning for the finale of the four-game series. By now, the news was out—NFL RAIDERS ARE CLOSE TO LANDING BO JACKSON, the *Washington Post* headline read. At his stall, Jackson was greeted by a sign—written on a sheet of paper in black ink—that said DON'T BE STUPID AND ASK ANY BASEBALL QUESTIONS. He tore it down and scanned the room for culprits. No one dared look his way. "We couldn't joke with him because he couldn't take it," Willie Wilson recalled. "He would want to fight you all the time." A few minutes later, the press was cleared from the clubhouse and Gardner stood before his players and said, sternly, "Bo has something he wants to say." Jackson rose, took in his teammates and insisted—without question, debate or argument—baseball was his top priority. The NFL, he insisted, would be a part-time endeavor. "I'm just thinking about adding a hobby," he said with a slight laugh. No one else appeared to chuckle.

Wilson, the most vocal Bo antagonist among the Royals, was particularly irritated. He had been the organization's first-round draft pick in 1974, a multitool phenom out of Summit, New Jersey, who quickly learned Black ballplayers still needed to bite their tongues and quietly absorb the game's inherent biases and indignities. Numerous were the times that Wilson felt disrespected or slighted. By a manager who spoke to him like a child. By teammates whose racism dripped from their gloves. But he became a two-time All-Star, and in the process developed the unlikely merging of rhino-thick skin and paper-thin sensitivity. That's perhaps why, from the time Jackson first stepped foot in Royals Stadium, Wilson was offended by the amount of attention, love and praise heaped upon a man who, in his view, was far more hype than accomplishment. A part of two Kansas City World Series teams, Wilson continued to feel unappreciated by the organization and its fanbase. Now, when the press was allowed back inside the room, he all but lofted a neon FUCK BO JACKSON sign above his head. "I guess he got the last laugh, didn't he?" Wilson told reporters. "He got us to believe him, and now we're the fools.

"It's bullshit," he added. "It's like Bo is bigger than the Royals. They treat him like a God. What it is, is the front office doesn't have any respect for the team. We've got guys playing here for years, then they let a three-month player come in here and tell them what to do. It shouldn't be up to Bo, man. It should be up to the front office to make a fucking decision. Aren't they scared about losing us? What about (Bret) Saberhagen? What about George (Brett)? What about Frank (White)? The front office hasn't got any respect for us, so why should we respect them. Tell them to take that to the bank. I don't give a damn. I'm so mad I can't stand it."

Brett, the king of Kansas City, considered Bo a friend. But he thought the timing was strange. Jackson was in a 3-for-21 slump that included 14 strikeouts. "He just hasn't looked like himself lately," Brett said. "And now he's opening himself up for some criticism if he goes bad. People will think he's thinking of football."

"It's obvious the game isn't about winning and losing anymore," added White. "It's about saving money, making money, putting people in the seats."

Later, during batting practice, Jamie Quirk, a veteran catcher with few shits to give, was asked for a take. He placed a bat between his legs and thrust his hips back and forth.

"Bo," Quirk said, "fucked us."

Jackson thought his teammates would understand (even appreciate) one expanding his athletic horizons. What he failed to grasp was the anger wasn't over sports, but favoritism. A good number of the Royals had contracts filled with conditions. Motorcycles—not allowed. Skydiving—also not allowed. Pickup basketball during the season—a big no-no. Now, out of the blue, a rookie (a damn rookie!?) was allowed to spend his off-seasons being pummeled by Andre Waters and Pepper Johnson? It made no sense.

Jackson started in left field against the Blue Jays, and when he struck out swinging in his first at bat, no one on the bench flinched. If Bo didn't wanna be there, why should anyone care? Such was Jackson's plight for much of the remainder of the baseball season. He was persona non grata to many teammates. One day, not long after the Raiders announcement (an official press conference was held on July 14, during which Jackson famously referred to football as "a hobby"), Bosley was lifting weights in the Royals Stadium home clubhouse. He sought some advice on bench-pressing, so Jackson leaned back and displayed proper form. "There wasn't more than fifty pounds on the bar," Jackson said. "And one of the ass-licking assistant coaches came by and saw me, thought I was working out [for football]."

The next day, the bench was gone.

"I went back and told those assholes, 'Look, the weights you got here I wouldn't waste my time trying to lift them,'" Jackson said. "'I got over thirteen thousand dollars' worth of weights in my fucking house, in my basement. If I want to lift, I can do it at my own house.'"

In his first home game since making the announcement, Jackson jogged into the Royals Stadium outfield and was pelted with boos and a bevy of plastic footballs—many with "IT'S A HOBBY" scribbled on the side. "Some of the fans there are with me," he said afterward. "As far as the fans that aren't, that's a personal problem on their part."

To his credit, Jackson didn't fret over whether he was liked or disliked. If Willie Wilson had objections—to hell with Willie Wilson. Same for Brett, Tartabull, Saberhagen and every other teammate. Same for the front office. Same for the fans. Jackson wasn't looking to make enemies, but he didn't fear them. If this meant sitting quietly by himself in the clubhouse, so be it. Baseball, to Jackson, was just baseball. Not life. "I don't back down to nobody," he said. "I'd rather not call names, but they're a bunch of babies on the Royals."

In the days following Bo Jackson's bombshell, members of the sports media found themselves discussing Royals and Raiders and Jim Thorpe and athletic greatness.

They also talked Vic Janowicz.

In 1950, thirty-six years before Jackson captured the award, Janowicz won the Heisman Trophy after a stellar junior season at Ohio State, during which he served as a running back, quarterback, placekicker, punter and safety. "He was absolutely great," said Wesley Fesler, the Buckeyes' coach. "He excelled in every phase of the game."

Yet instead of joining the NFL, Janowicz signed to play catcher with the Pittsburgh Pirates. He appeared in his first game against the Brooklyn Dodgers on May 31, 1953, with Dick Young of the New York *Daily News* marking the occasion by noting, "The former All-America from Ohio State made his big league debut as a pinch runner for [Johnny] Lindell—running without a football under his arm."

But after two seasons of forgettable baseball (a .214 average and 2 home runs in 83 total games), Janowicz jumped to the Washington Redskins. Much like Jackson's future leap to the Raiders, Janowicz arrived in the nation's capital *after* the 1954 baseball season wrapped. He had no pre-season drills, no football conditioning. Raved Joe Kuharich, Washington's coach: "He was in better shape when he showed up in Washington than some of the players who had been working out for two months."

The hype was short-lived. Janowicz played two seasons with the Redskins, suffered a serious brain injury in an automobile accident and never wore the uniform again. Years later, Washington acknowledged that Janowicz was "severely handicapped" by the lack of pre-season training.

In a *New York Times* column headlined BO JACKSON's "HOBBY," the fantastic Dave Anderson made the Janowicz comparison, and argued that the last man to jump from the Majors to the NFL served as a terrifying barometer for how this whole thing could go. Bo Jackson, according to Anderson, just *might* wind up as Vic Janowicz once did: forgotten.

On July 21, however, America was reminded why that fate was unlikely. Or, put differently: Bo Jackson was no Vic Janowicz. The Cleveland Indians were in town to play the Royals, and Jackson wasn't the happiest man around. His average was down to a paltry .251, and he had gone nine-straight games without a home run. A few days earlier, Schuerholz held a twenty-five-minute closed door session with the players to yet again discuss and move past the Bo situation (aka: *Can y'all please stop whining about this?*). Life inside the Kansas City clubhouse was uncomfortable.

On the morning of the game, Jackson was invited to go fishing on a nearby lake by Pete LaCock, a former Royal who lived in the area. The two would be joined by a pair of visiting Indians—pitcher Ernie Camacho and catcher Rick Dempsey. For about three hours, the foursome sat on a small boat, lines cast, joking and laughing and telling ballplayer stories. Major League seasons are long and unyielding. A few hours on the water is welcome medicine. "Once the bass stopped biting," Jackson said, "we started catching bullfrogs on rubber worms. We'd throw the worms up on the moss where the frogs were and the frogs would jump over and suck it up and we'd snatch them." At one point, Dempsey reeled in a particularly large bullfrog, and as he tried to remove the hook a two-foot-long water moccasin emerged from its throat. "I threw the damn thing back in as fast as possible," Dempsey recalled. "They're potent if they bite you."

What Dempsey remembered most was not the snake, but Jackson. He was refreshingly friendly and thoughtful. Down home as cornbread. "Really sincere," Dempsey said. "That's what struck me—the sincerity."

That evening, when Jackson approached the plate for his first at bat in the bottom of the second, he nodded toward a squatting Dempsey, brushed his bat against a kneepad and said, softly, "Hey there, Demps."

"Hey, Bo," the catcher replied. "Watch out for those moccasins."

Scott Bailes, the Indians starting pitcher, walked Jackson, who advanced to second on a wayward pickoff throw, then to third when Angel Salazar, the Royals shortstop, grounded out.

The next batter was Larry Owen, a .214-hitting catcher. There was one out, and as Jackson stood at rest, hands dangling by his waist, Jose Martinez, the third base coach, leaned in and said, "You're going home on anything hit."

Bailes's tossed a fastball over the plate, and as soon as Owens's bat connected with rawhide, Jackson took off. Tom Candiotti, an Indians pitcher, was sitting in the dugout along the third base line, wondering whether the vehicle before him was a Ferrari Testarossa or a Porsche 911 Turbo. "Holy shit, I'd never seen anything move like that," Candiotti said. "He was flying."

The Indians catcher was thirty-seven years old. He broke into the Majors with the Minnesota Twins in 1969, when Jackson was six. Through the years, his body had taken repeated beatings, but Dempsey—a relatively light 190 pounds on a 6-foot frame—refused to give in. Baseball was his life, and he would play as long as possible.

Owens's one-hopper went directly to Bailes. The pitcher fielded it cleanly, motioned toward third, then saw Jackson barreling down the line. He threw the ball to Dempsey, who straddled the plate. The baseball reached home three steps before Jackson's arrival, and Dempsey rotated his body toward third and braced for impact.

Jackson didn't run toward Dempsey's torso—he attacked it. Arms tucked, he uncoiled into a jaguar-like leap from five feet away, and slammed directly into the catcher's legs. *BAM!* The collision was loud and violent and the sort of thing children under thirteen cannot watch without a parent or legal guardian. Dempsey fell atop Jackson, then rolled to his back while holding up the baseball in his right hand.

Both men were out—Jackson at the plate, Dempsey for the remainder of the season with a shattered left thumb.[*]

"I could have hurt him real, real bad," said Jackson. "I could have hit him in the throat and took his head off."

Bo Jackson was ready for football.

---

[*] Two years later, Robin Ventura was a rookie third baseman for the Chicago White Sox when Carlton Fisk, the veteran catcher, motioned for him to meet at the mound. Jackson was standing on third with one out. "Listen," Fisk said, "if there's a fly ball to the outfield, I don't give a fuck if it's on line—you cut it off. No matter where it is, you cut it off and try to get the guy at second." Ventura was confused. "Have you seen the video of Bo running over Rick Dempsey?" Fisk said. "I'm forty-one-years old. He'll kill me."

CHAPTER 18
_____

THE DIFFERENT RUNNING BACK

Bo Jackson's final few months with the 1987 Kansas City Royals were, eh, not good.

First, the Royals fired their manager, the veteran Billy Gardner, and replaced him with John Wathan, a recently retired catcher who was only thirty-seven and garnered little respect within the clubhouse. Second, the sense of betrayal from many of his teammates had yet to subside. Jackson suspected many of the Royals were talking shit behind his back, and he was correct in that assumption. Third, Jackson played terribly. From the day he signed with Los Angeles, Jackson batted .188 with 4 home runs and 8 RBI while striking out 43 times in 112 at bats. He was benched in mid-August for the immortal Gary Thurman, and only returned to the lineup after the Royals (who finished in second place with an 83-79 mark) were feeling desperate. The team accused him of losing focus and dreaming of heavenly NFL days. They were likely correct.

The Royals wrapped their campaign on October 4, and eleven days later Jackson was scheduled to fly to Southern California and check in with his new team. Only, there wasn't a new team to check in with. Beginning on September 22, the NFLPA (National Football League Players Association) announced it would strike over the right to free agency, as well as better benefits and the end of Astroturf surfaces. That resulted in a canceled third week of the season, followed by three weeks of games featuring "fake" replacement players on the field and "real" self-exiled players marching in the stadium parking lots while gripping KILL THE SCABS signs. "I was one of those sign holders," said Trey Junkin, a Raider tight end, "looking like an asshole." Jackson made clear that he would not play until the legit Raiders were back in uniform, then watched as many of those legit Raiders—including star defensive linemen Howie Long and Bill Pickel—tucked their tails between their legs and crossed the picket line.

The strike finally ended after twenty-four days, and on October 17

Jackson—renting an apartment in nearby Redondo Beach—caught a ride to the facility with James Lofton, the veteran wide receiver. When Jackson stepped from Lofton's vehicle, he was spotted by Jerry Robinson, a veteran linebacker. "Hey, Bo," he said. "I knew you were here."

"How?" Jackson replied.

"Because," Robinson said, "the Brinks truck is parked out front."

Jackson walked through the front doors at 332 Center Street in El Segundo, passed a physical examination and earned his $500,000 reporting bonus. "To anyone who cares," he announced with a grin, "I just made my first half mil!" He found his locker, where a JACKSON 34 nameplate lorded from above and a JACKSON 34 white jersey dangled off a hanger.

To help its twenty-eight franchises adjust to the post-replacement world, the NFL announced rosters could (temporarily) contain as many as eighty-five players—forty beyond the norm. So in a seeing-your-grandma-naked level of awkwardness, the Raiders locker room was overflowing with four distinct categories of *Homo sapiens*:

1. Men like Chetti Carr (defensive back—Northwestern Oklahoma) and David Hardy (kicker—Texas A&M), who spent three weeks recapturing past gridiron glories but would soon return to their lives as plumbers, truck drivers and accountants.
2. Men like Long, Pickel and offensive lineman Bruce Wilkerson—who crossed the line to the dismay of their teammates and would have to face the consequences.
3. Men like cornerback Mike Haynes and quarterback Jim Plunkett—who dismissed those who returned early to work as one would a scurrying cockroach. "Howie was one of my best friends," said Mitch Willis, a Raiders defensive lineman. "But that didn't sit well with everyone. So when it was over, and we all had to sit in the locker room together—the air was thick."
4. Bo Jackson.

Los Angeles (which went 1-2 in replacement action) would continue its season with an October 25 home game against the Seahawks. Al Davis, the owner, requested a good number of the scabs to stick around to help scrimmage against the back-again Raiders and reacclimate the men to combat. That's why, on that first day, some initially failed to notice Bo Jackson in their midst. There were too many unfamiliar faces in too many unfamiliar jerseys.

Head Coach Tom Flores spoke to the players for about fifteen minutes ("I'm not asking you all to like one another. But I am asking you to be professionals."), then had them take the field, stretch and begin some drills. Two of the veteran Raiders, linebackers Matt Millen and Rod Martin, could not have been more excited. Both detested the strike and, in particular, the scabs. So when replacement running backs grabbed handoffs, Millen and Martin transformed into starving wolves staring down wounded squirrels.

"OK, Bubba," Martin said as the drills commenced. "Let's put some hits on these assholes."

"You got it," Millen said.

One halfback took a toss.

POW!

Another halfback ran a sweep.

BAM!

A fullback tried plowing up the middle.

THUD!

"We were just drilling these guys," said Millen. "For sport."

Joe Scannella, the offensive backfield coach, sent a different running back onto the field.

"Let's go!" Millen yelled. "Bring it!"

The different running back took a pitch from quarterback Vince Evans. Millen had the ideal angle on him—"everyone could see I was about to make the hit," he recalled. "And I'm just about ready to explode into him. Then the guy hits a gear . . ."

Millen reached out his arms, but the different running back motored past and into the secondary. When Millen returned to the huddle, he apologized. "That's on me," he said. "I don't know what happened."

"You're just rusty," Martin said.

The offensive and defensive units lined up for another play. This time, the different running back took a pitch and ran in the other direction. Once more, Millen closed in, extended—and missed. "Again, he hit another gear," Millen recalled. "Some scab running back is making me look like a fool."

Back in the huddle, Millen was mortified. "Guys, I'm so sorry," he said. "I can't touch that freakin' scab. I don't know what's wrong with me."

From beneath his silver helmet, Martin was guffawing.

"What's so funny?" Millen asked.

Martin laughed and laughed and laughed.

"You dumbass," he said. "That ain't no scab. That's Bo Jackson."

"Oh, thank God," Millen said. "Thank friggin' God."

Mickey Marvin, the eleventh-year guard, had paved the way for everyone from Mark van Eeghen and Arthur Whittington to Marcus Allen and Greg Pruitt. This was the first time—*ever*—he failed to begin his block before the ball carrier passed. "The coaches asked Bo to slow down a bit for Mickey," said Willis. "I mean, it was crazy."

Watching from a few feet away, Lofton looked at Allen, the team's star halfback. "Well," he said, "there goes your job."

Lofton was joking—sort of.

"When you play football long enough, you get used to norms," said Steve Strachan, a Raiders running back. "There are higher norms and lower norms, but everything is in a range. But when Bo came onto the field that first day, we were all seeing something we'd never witnessed before. We were seeing a different paradigm of an athlete. Someone that big moving in ways we'd never seen anyone else move."

Much like the Royals, many of the Raiders had taken offense to Jackson's "hobby" dismissal of their sport. Football was the world of broken arms and broken legs; concussions atop concussions. One either played through pain or found himself on the next flight out. The NFL was certainly no hobby. Robinson, who sat in the locker stall directly across from Jackson, was feeling anything but friendly after the first practice. He was sweaty, tired and itching for bed.

"Hey Bo!" Robinson yelled.

Jackson turned his way.

"You know what this is?" Robinson said, miming the pitching of a baseball. "You can't hit a curveball to save your ass. And this is harder than that. This is football. I'm not gonna treat you like some baseball brat. We won't have your food waiting for you, your shoes shined. None of that. So if you can't get your fucking ass in the end zone, get your ass back to Kansas City and stick to baseball."

Jackson looked surprised. "What did I do to you?" he asked. "I don't even know you."

"I'm Jerry, motherfucker," Robinson said. "And I'll tell you what you did. I saw you call football a hobby. Look around this fucking locker room. This is more than a hobby to us."

Jackson nodded. Point taken.

Besides the newness of it all, the other complication was the Raiders already had a star Heisman Trophy–winning halfback on the roster. Now entering his sixth season, Allen was on the short list of NFL's elite ball carriers, right there with the Rams' Eric Dickerson and San Francisco's Roger

Craig. He was an artistic runner whose sleek, slithery moves made him a darling of the NFL Films highlight reels. Yet even as Allen won the Super Bowl XVIII MVP award in 1984 and ran for a league-best 1,759 yards in 1985, Al Davis never took to him. There are 73,103 conspiracy theories, ranging from Allen once fumbling twice in a big game against Kansas City to Allen's pretty features and Hollywood tendencies to Allen (not Davis) appearing on the cover of the Lou Sahadi book *Domination: The Story of the 1983 World Champion Los Angeles Raiders*.

The bottom line: jealousy.

"If you asked, 'Who's the face of the Miami Dolphins?'—it would be Dan Marino," said a longtime Raider executive who requested anonymity. "'Who's the face of the Dallas Cowboys?' Tony Dorsett or Troy Aikman. Go through every NFL team, and there will be a player or two or three who symbolize everything. Lawrence Taylor with the Giants. Jim Kelly with the Bills, Joe Namath with the Jets. Now do the Raiders. There is no one—and that's by design. For Al, no one was ever going to be bigger than the emblem, the patch on the eye, the symbolism. Al would never allow a player to overshadow the team—or Al. And Marcus was coming far too close."

Davis could have traded the twenty-seven-year-old Allen to any team in the league, and received quality in return. For all his good attributes (an unquenching thirst to win, a love of the fans, a lifetime of charitable endeavors), however, the Raiders owner possessed a raw cruelty that bordered on barbarism. Davis had built up a foaming-from-the-mouth resentment of Marcus Allen—and he sure as hell wasn't going to present him with the gift of a fresh start. "Al wanted America to forget who Marcus Allen was," said Terry Robiskie, an assistant coach. "That was how you punished a star for being too big a star."

In Jackson, Davis acquired an unwitting anti-Marcus participant. He wanted to see Allen crumble; wanted to watch the pain as Allen sat on the bench, his world reduced to meaningless carries toward the end of blowouts. "Marcus was a great running back," said Flores. "But when Bo hit the practice field, the whole team went, 'Wow!'"

This was exactly what Al Davis hoped for.

Allen was thrilled by neither Bo Jackson's presence nor $864,000 salary for an abridged season (compared to Allen's $900,000 contract for a full year). But he was mature enough to recognize Jackson meant no harm. They were two members of the Heisman club being paid exorbitant mounds of dollars to play a child's game. And, not for nothing, Jackson was reasonably likable. He didn't come in demanding attention. He listened when Allen spoke, never interrupted, asked good questions. There was a surprising innocence to the man—why, roughly thirty minutes before the first practice was scheduled to end, Jackson was spotted eyeing the door to the locker room.

"Bo! Are you OK?" yelled George Anderson, the head trainer.

"Bo's tired," Jackson replied. "Bo's gonna take a shower."

Robiskie interrupted to explain that Flores wanted to go over some passing routes.

"Oh, oh—OK," Jackson said. "Bo will stick around."

"Nobody took offense," said Bruce Davis, an offensive lineman. "It was kind of endearing."

Jackson's goal was to suit up for the October 25 Seattle game. Toward the end of one practice, the coaches asked Jackson to be timed in the 40. The field was a bit wet from a recent rain shower, and some mud was peeking through the grass. Jackson—still wearing a helmet and pads—lined up on one end, and Flores and two assistants stood with stopwatches alongside a designated finish line.

Someone yelled GO!—and Jackson ran—"like an F-14 in cleats," said Long. He crossed the line, and the coaches compared their times.

"I've got 4.19," said Flores.

The other two nodded—same and same.

Richard Romanski was the Raiders equipment manager. Flores told Jackson to run again, but demanded Romanski stand by the line and make certain Bo wasn't cheating.

GO!

"I've got . . ." said Flores.

"What?" asked Romanski.

"No," said Flores. "This isn't right."

"What?" Romanski replied.

"I've got a . . . 4.17," Flores said.

The other coaches nodded—same and same.

Barely breathing hard, Jackson tapped Joe Madro, the team's personnel consultant, on the arm. "Bo is finished for the day," he said, and retreated to the locker room

Jackson stripped out of his uniform and walked toward the shower. Sitting nearby were three hulking linemen—Davis (6-foot-6, 287 pounds), Charley Hannah (6-foot-5, 260 pounds) and Sean Jones (6-foot-7, 280 pounds)—and they watched in awe as their new teammate, naked from head to toe, sat on the floor and churned out 250 sit-ups and 250 pushups.

Hannah looked at Jackson, then stared down at his own gut. "I feel like a fag," he said. "But I can't believe we're both men. Just look at him."

Flores told the team's beat writers that Jackson playing against Seattle was unrealistic. This didn't sit well with the newcomer. In his mind, unrealistic *was* unrealistic. Following his third practice, he informed Long that if he weren't activated for the Seahawks, he'd quit. "Those SOBs didn't get me here to sit on the bench," Jackson said. "If I'm not playing, I'm gone."

On the morning of October 25, the headline JACKSON TO MAKE DEBUT FOR RAIDERS appeared in the *Santa Maria Times*, and readers learned that Flores did, in fact, include the running back on the forty-five-man roster.

The kickoff was scheduled for 1 p.m. at the Los Angeles Coliseum, and Jackson arrived three hours early to begin his new journey. His locker was situated alongside the other running backs, and Jackson dressed as he had at Auburn. Shoulder pads just so, knee pads just so. Elbow pads, double wrist bands. He slipped on his pants, then his black jersey with the silver number 34. He grabbed his helmet, walked onto the field for warm-ups, stretched, did some drills . . .

And that was about it.

Seattle cakewalked to a 35–13 triumph, and Jackson never played. Flores later explained that once the Seahawks jumped out to the enormous advantage, there was no real use for the newcomer and his unfamiliarity with the playbook.

When asked afterward about his day, an irritated Jackson snarled "I've got nothing to say" before walking off.

Worst of all, the blowout served as a glorious NFL showcase not for Bo Jackson, but for Brian Bosworth, Seattle's brash rookie linebacker out of Oklahoma. Bosworth was twenty-two and rich (a ten-year, $11 million contract) and either (depending on viewpoint) a superhero or super villain. He wore his hair in a ridiculous bleach-blond, side-shaved quasi-hawk and had his ears pierced. He walked with an irritating strut unbecoming of one with such limited experience. In the advance for the game, Bo vs. Boz was a heavy talking point. It was the saga of two larger-than-large phenoms with big dough and big egos, and Bosworth showed little respect for his fellow newcomer. "Bo," he said, "has to prove himself."

Afterward, Bosworth admitted he was disappointed Jackson was kept out. "But," he insisted, "we'll meet again. I'm sure of it."

The big debut finally happened on Sunday, November 1.

It was weird, seeing the otherworldly running back take the field for the first time in unfamiliar threads, wondering whether he would fit in; wondering if the skills he showcased elsewhere would smoothly translate to his new surroundings.

But, of course, talent in one place is talent in another place, and the fans were overwhelmed by the brilliance at hand.

Such was Eric Dickerson's first game as a member of the Indianapolis Colts.

That was the big story come Monday's newspapers. Dickerson, the all-everything running back with the upright style and trademark goggles, had demanded a trade from the Los Angeles Rams, and his premier as a Colt was a success—10 carries for 38 yards, one catch for 28 yards, 0 knowledge of the playbook he picked up a day earlier, a 19–14 win over the Jets.

"Eric," Colts coach Ron Meyer said afterward, "has a chance to propel us into another echelon."

Oh. Right. Bo Jackson played his first game, too.

Not nearly as many people noticed. First, because he had suited up a week earlier; second, because the Dickerson trade was an earth-shaking blockbuster; third, because he wasn't listed as a starter for the Raiders trip to Foxborough, Massachusetts, to face the Patriots. But finally, with 13:07 remaining in the second quarter, Jackson jogged onto the field and lined up behind fullback Steve Smith, a few more inches to the rear of Rusty Hilger, the quarterback. His debut carry was a 14-yard off-tackle dash to the left— "showing both acceleration and the power to drag two or three opponents," wrote Bob Oates in the *Los Angeles Times*.

On the next play, Jackson was smothered for no gain by defensive line-man Kenneth Sims. Moments later Jackson took his first real lick when the 6-foot-5, 272-pound Sims laid into him with a punishing blow from the side. Jackson rose to his feet and jogged back to the huddle. En route, he noticed his right thumb was split wide open and gushing blood. Jackson had few fears in life—but needles were a big one. "I could see it was gonna take stitches," he said. "I was worried about that the whole game. I said, 'I don't wanna get shot with no fucking needle.'" (Come halftime, he was shot with a fucking needle.)

When the afternoon ended, the Raiders found themselves 26–23 los-ers to a team they should have thumped. Jackson's stat line—8 carries, 37 yards—was unmemorable, but what bothered him most was the fourth quarter, during which he mostly sat on the bench.

Following the game, a throng of media members congregated around Jackson's locker, waiting to hear from America's most famous backup halfback. They were quickly learning that the new star wouldn't be a joy to cover. "After I get dressed, please," he said curtly. "I need to go see the doctor. Can I get some room?"

In a trick he perfected on busy days with the Royals, Jackson used thirty-three full minutes to walk *slowly* toward the shower, take a *slow* shower, return *slowly* from the shower. By the time he had finished cleaning, the dressing room cleared out, save fifty (or so) reporters arranged in a semi-circle formation around his locker. "Jackson," wrote Dan Shaughnessy of the *Boston Globe*, "has a body bulging with potential, but he seems to get no joy from his work."

The questions began innocently enough . . .

Bo, how do you feel about your first game?

"It was nothing special, nothing spectacular."

Do you wish you'd played more?

"I played. I'm happy. It's fun to be playing any sport on a professional level."

Were the old college moves still there?

"It's still there. I wouldn't say I was as sharp as I was in college."

Do you wish you were on the field in crunch time?

"I expected to play, and I played. I don't have anything to say about the amount of time."

It was tense. The reporters had stories to write. Jackson had a life to live. No one really wanted to be doing this.

When Jackson motioned for the session to end, a final inevitable question popped up.

So Bo—which is No. 1 in your heart—baseball or football?

Jackson forced a grin.

"During football season, football is number one in my heart. Ask me that again next summer."

As an action figure, Bo Jackson was larger than life and dynamic and electrifying. He was handsome and powerful and a marketer's dream. Nike was working out a thousand different ways to turn his exploits into profits— and the company would achieve remarkable results.

But in person, before a sea of notepads and cameras, Jackson was a soggy grocery bag. Whether it be baseball or football, whenever possible he dressed in the training room to avoid the press. To ask a beat writer what he thought of Jackson was a flawed line of questioning. The beat writers never *knew* Jackson. "I can't say he was always unpleasant," said Mark Heisler, the *Los Angeles Times* writer. "He just basically didn't want to talk to us.

And when he did talk, he wasn't very interesting or engaged. We didn't offer anything he wanted. He was so huge upon arrival, he didn't care. He liked playing the games, but I don't think press attention mattered at all. We barely existed to Bo."

"Bo could be very nice one minute," said Roy Firestone, the famed ESPN interviewer. "And the next day, boy, it looks like he got out of bed on the wrong side and he's just distrustful and cynical and wary and suspicious and wanted to know your motives."

To his credit, Jackson didn't much concern himself with fame. He wasn't opposed to it. But the No. 1 directive was to return home each night to Linda and Garrett (the three were living together in the apartment) and watch TV and eat dinner and sleep well. He wasn't in Los Angeles to go Hollywood or hit the clubs ("I don't think I'll ever buy a place out here," he said. "My condo is twice as big as the one I had in Kansas City, but I'm paying five times as much as I did in K.C."). He was in Los Angeles to play football.

Over the next few weeks the Raiders succeeded in reminding America of their commitment to crappiness. They fell at Minnesota, 31–20, then at San Diego, 16–14. Jackson played well in both games, and began lining up in a split backfield with Allen. This would have had a greater impact were Jackson not still feeling out the playbook and the team not so woefully quarterbacked. The starter for much of the season was Hilger, a 1985 sixth-round pick out of Oklahoma State whose rise from nobody Okie to NFL signal caller was orchestrated by Davis. The kid reminded the owner of Kenny (Snake) Stabler, swashbuckling Raider quarterback of yore. So Davis demanded Flores play Hilger, then watched as he established himself as the second coming of Steve Pisarkiewicz. Early in the second half of the Vikings debacle, after Hilger's first pass wobbled off target and his second was intercepted, Davis dialed the red sideline phone (aka: The Owner Needs To Reach You ASAP Telecommunication Device) and screamed, "Get this fucker out of the game! He fucking sucks!"

Marc Wilson, Los Angeles backup/Davis's least-favorite-player-not-named-Marcus-Allen, entered. His second pass was picked off.

This was not what Jackson had anticipated. He was one of three Heisman Trophy winners on the roster (Jackson, Allen, quarterback Jim Plunkett). Sitting at 3-6, the Raiders were a talented team with a Super Bowl–winning coach. But they were stale bread, and while the Los Angeles Coliseum clientele could be notoriously rowdy, of late it was merely bored.

They needed a spark.

On November 22, the hated Denver Broncos came to town. They were 5-3-1 and headed for a second-straight Super Bowl appearance. The face of the franchise was quarterback John Elway, but the backbone and spiritual leader was a hard-hitting cornerback named Mike Harden.

In a pre-CTE era of professional football, men like Harden roamed NFL fields, looking for the next wide receiver to lay out. He was 6-foot-1 and 192 pounds, and he wrapped his forearms in thick medical tape so they could be used as billy clubs. "Mike was a badass," said Tony Lilly, a Broncos safety. "He was a corner who played like a safety."

Jackson and Allen would be starting side by side for the first time, and in the days before the game Raider offensive coaches emphasized avoiding Harden at all costs. Don't deliberately cross the field if he loomed nearby. Don't sprint in his direction. Harden was a player to run away from, not toward.

With 8:35 gone by in the second quarter and the Broncos up 13–0, Los Angeles faced a first and 10 from the Denver 35. A few weeks earlier, during a practice, Jackson took a pitch from Wilson and accidentally swept toward the right as his linemen and fullback all headed left. He realized his mistake (playbook memorization was not a Bo priority) after two steps, planted his foot and reversed direction. "That evening the coaches watched the film and they noticed that when Bo went right, the linebackers followed," said Strachan. "He was so fast and powerful that when he changed direction, no one could stay with him. The coaches decided to make it a play and use it. They called it 'The Bo Reverse.'"

Now, with Allen by Jackson's side at fullback, the Raiders called for their first Bo Reverse. Jackson snagged the pitch from Wilson, went a step and a half to the right, spun 360 degrees, turned left and watched as the two leading pursuers—linebackers Karl Mecklenburg and Jim Ryan—froze in their tracks. Brian Holloway, the veteran tackle, threw a devastating block to wipe out Ryan, and Jackson sprinted 10 yards into the secondary, where (shit!) Harden was licking his chops.

A 1980 University of Michigan grad, Harden had never played Jackson in college. With little professional tape available to study, he went into the Raiders game feeling somewhat blind. So as the running back approached, Harden presumed some sort of juke was coming. After all, no one in the league wanted to take a full-on lick from *the* Mike Harden. "I expected him to come out and shake me down," Harden said. "Get me off-balance."

Nope.

Bo lowered his right shoulder, jammed it below Harden's helmet and never stopped moving forward. Harden fell backward and onto his rear—a rabbit caught beneath a Corvette muffler. "Bo Jackson! Ohhhhh!" screamed Dick Enberg, calling the game on NBC. Jackson stomped atop Harden's crumbled body and charged down the sideline. Lilly, who witnessed the demolition, was being blocked by Lofton, the wide receiver. "James was actually holding me," said Lilly. "And I told him 'Don't let go of me! Don't let go! I want no part of this murder.'"

The last obstacle between Jackson and the end zone could have been cornerback Mark Haynes, who had dashed across the field to assist. But he, too, chose to pull up and avoid extreme contact. Immediately afterward, Haynes explained his decision to Lilly. "I saw him run over Mike," he said, "and I was like, 'Nah, man. I'm good.'"

With Jackson safe in the end zone, Bill Lewis, the Los Angeles guard, extended a hand toward Harden. "Man, Mike," Lewis said, "that *had* to have hurt."

Harden groaned and shuffled off.

Following the 23–17 Denver triumph, Harden stood by his locker and owned the humiliation. He was blunt and honest and appeared to have shrunk by at least a foot.

"It was," he said, "embarrassing."

All told, Jackson ran for 98 yards and 2 touchdowns on 13 carries. It was the best day of his brief Raiders career. "He's God's gift to halfback," said Lester Hayes, the Raider cornerback. "He's a godsend. He's unreal. He was destined to be a football player. He's a step beyond stupendous."

Next up was a trip to Seattle.

And a chance to meet Brian Bosworth.

CHAPTER 19

MONDAY NIGHT

In the history of modern organized professional sports, no athlete has benefited from mythology, hype and a misguided haircut quite like Brian Keith Bosworth.

Aka: The Boz.

Once, back in the early 1980s, he was little more than a promising high schooler out of Irving, Texas; his state's fifth-highest ranked prep linebacker who, on his official visit, sold the coaching staff at Oklahoma by noting, "I like your attitude. The other schools are concerned about winning their conference titles. You're concerned about winning the national championship."

Bosworth was redshirted as a freshman in 1983, then activated the following season. He was a solid contributor to a very good Sooners team. He worked hard and he hit hard. He knew the playbook.

That—zzzzzz—was about it.

On October 10, 1984, in the lead-up to that weekend's highly anticipated clash against the University of Texas, Bosworth was asked his opinion of the Longhorns. It was a throw-away question by a reporter doing his job.

"I didn't go to Texas because I don't like Texas," Bosworth said. "I don't like [Texas coach] Fred Akers. I don't like the city of Austin. And I don't like their color of orange. It reminds me of puke."

With those words, The Boz was born.

Brian was a fairly quiet kid with a 3.8 GPA as a marketing major. The Boz was a trash-talking, hard-hitting, cheap-shotting thug. Brian was a wonderful chef who enjoyed creating gourmet meals. The Boz was screaming toward opponents, "When I'm done with you, you're gonna have to fart to look out!" Brian was one helluva football player—a fast, powerful middle linebacker who twice won the Butkus Award as the nation's top linebacker. The Boz was a steroid-fueled freakoid whose muscles housed muscles. Brian was blessed with an angelic smile. The Boz wore a gold number 44 earring in his right ear and shaved his blond hair in—to cite Mike Tharp of the *San Francisco Examiner*—"a half-Mohawk, half-punk style. He resembles Sid Vicious on steroids."

Bosworth played three seasons for the Sooners, but by the end of 1986 his luck had run out. A little over a week before Oklahoma was scheduled to face Arkansas in the Orange Bowl, he tested positive for anabolic steroids and was banned from the game by the NCAA. He proceeded to infuriate fans and foes alike by walking the Sooners' sideline in a T-shirt that read NATIONAL COMMUNISTS AGAINST ATHLETES.

"He started becoming somebody that I didn't recognize," said John DiPasquale, a childhood friend. "The lines were becoming blurred."

Even Barry Switzer, the longtime Oklahoma coach with an appetite for renegades, was fed up. Though Bosworth had one remaining year of eligibility, Switzer said it would be best if he departed. So after declaring for the NFL Draft, then whining about the possibility of being picked by Indianapolis or Green Bay, he applied for a special June 12, 1987, supplemental draft. When the Seattle Seahawks grabbed Bosworth with the first overall selection, he moped and complained . . . before signing a ten-year, $11 million contract.

Were he a normal human, Bosworth would have arrived humbly in the Pacific Northwest. Instead, he presented himself as cocky, dismissive, rude and arrogant. The Seahawks were coming off of a 10-6 season, and the defense was packed with high-level veterans like safeties Kenny Easley and Eugene Robinson and linemen Jacob Green and Joe Nash.

The Boz paid them no mind. He was 30 percent athlete, 70 percent comic book villain. He and his agent, Gary Wichard, devised a marketing plan that was going to transform Bosworth into football's Michael Jordan. He appeared on *Good Morning America* and the *Tonight Show*, served as a guest weekend MTV VJ alongside Downtown Julie Brown. "It was supposed to be fun," Wichard said. "It was going to get us to Hollywood."

In the week before the Seahawks' season opener at Denver, Bosworth nicknamed Broncos quarterback John Elway "Horse Face" and promised to mangle the star quarterback. "I can't wait," he said, "to get my hands on Elway's boyish face." Come Sunday, ten thousand Broncos fans arrived at Mile High Stadium wearing T-shirts that read WHAT'S A BOZ WORTH? NOTHING on the front and BAN THE BOZ on the back.

The company that peddled the garments? Boz 44.

"We gave all the profits to the Children's Hospital," Bosworth recalled. "We just wanted to prove how oxygen-deprived Denver fans are."

Inside the Seahawks locker room, The Boz's act wore thin. And while he played fairly well at starting middle linebacker, hype exceeded reality. Bosworth was a boosted-by-artificial-enhancements creation with an enormous upper body, giraffe legs and tiny (size 9) feet. "He brought a lot of shit on himself," said Dave Krieg, the Seattle quarterback. "We were supposed to go to the Super Bowl that year, and he made it all about Brian Bosworth."

"Brian set himself up to get smacked down by someone," said Nash. "He was due."

Coming off of his stampeding of Mike Harden, Bo Jackson, like Bosworth, had much of the league abuzz. So as the Seahawks prepared to host Los Angeles on November 30, the anticipation exceeded the normal juice of AFC West rivals going head to head. The main event—Bo v. The Boz—would take place on *Monday Night Football*, before a predicted viewing audience of 20 million. It mattered little that the Raiders, at 3-7, were out of the playoff hunt. It also mattered little that the Seahawks were 7-3 and winners of five out of six. No. This was Balboa-Creed. Actually, this was bigger than Balboa-Creed. It was Hulk Hogan–Iron Sheik. Good v. Evil. There were Bo people, there were Boz people. You either liked the quiet running back whose exploits intrigued a nation, or you liked the cocky linebacker whose exploits infuriated a nation. You either wanted to see Bo stomp over Bosworth, or you wanted to see Bosworth pile drive Bo. "Boz came into the game as bigger than life and promoting himself every second of the day," said Nash. "And Bo just came in as Bo. Just his résumé. He wasn't talking about how great he was."

In the lead-up, Raiders team meetings were punctuated by players hyping up Bosworth to Jackson. Rod Martin, the veteran linebacker, found the exercise particularly blissful. "Every single day I was teasing Bo," said Martin. "'Man, Boz is a great linebacker. Boz is the best rookie in the league. That Boz is gonna run you over.'

"One day Bo says to me in his little stutter, 'N-n-n-no, he will not.'"

"Bo was not believing the Boz hype at all," said Steve Strachan. "Maybe some other guys were. Not Bo."

The game began at 6 p.m. on Jackson's twenty-fifth birthday, and the Kingdome was packed with 62,802 fans. It was a charmless building with the hardest playing surface in the NFL. "Such a beautiful city," said Al Michaels, who worked the *Monday Night Football* broadcast. "Such an ugly place to play."

The Seahawks went nowhere on their opening drive, and when the Raiders took the field a national viewing audience was treated to the rare sight of quarterback Marc Wilson standing before two Heisman Trophy winners in the same backfield—Allen as the fullback, Jackson as the half-back. On the first play, Wilson handed off to a charging Jackson, who took the ball toward the right, cut hard left, did a 360-degree spin and—*POP!*—was hammered by linebacker Greg Gaines, who wrestled him down. "I was trying to hurt Bo," Gaines said. "I know guys don't like to say that, but I would try and hurt the guys we feared." Bosworth arrived late and threw his weight atop Gaines to help complete the takedown.

A seventh-year veteran out of Tennessee, Gaines accepted the extended hand of Jackson, who helped him rise from the turf. "Good hit," Bo said before retreating to the huddle. Bosworth, on the other hand, could never allow a moment to pass. Though responsible for (at best) 4 percent of the tackle, he rolled away from the play, pumped both fists in the air and fired a loud *Whoooo!*

"As soon as I hit Bo I knew he was trouble," said Gaines. "It was punching a brick with your bare hand. There was nothing on that play for idiot Boz to celebrate."

Four plays later, Jackson rambled up the turf when a hit from Gaines dislodged the ball. Seattle recovered, and Bosworth once again celebrated as if he had cured cancer.

This, Jackson noticed.

The second quarter began with Los Angeles rolling down the field. It was second and 8 at the Seattle 42, and when Wilson handed off to Jackson a hole opened on the left side of the line. He soared through it, and 10 yards into the gallop was met head on by Easley, the NFL's best free safety. Jackson lowered his right shoulder. Easley lowered his left shoulder. The sound of the collision could be heard from the broadcast booth—*CRACK!* Easley tumbled like a piece of chopped pine. Initially, Michaels, Dan Dierdorf and Frank Gifford, the *Monday Night Football* broadcasters, overlooked the enormity of the collision.

When ABC showed the replay, the broadcasters caught on . . .

GIFFORD: "I looked at Dan, Dan looked at me and said, 'Hey, this guy is different.'"

DIERDORF: "I don't know. It might be better to get blocked than to have to tackle this guy."

On the next play, Jackson took a pitch right for four yards. But it wasn't an ordinary four yards. He was grabbed by defensive back Terry Taylor—

who refused to let go. Then grabbed by defensive end Jacob Green—who refused to let go. Safety Eugene Robinson arrived, and refused to let go. Nash came to help. As did linebacker Fredd Young. The last defender on the scene was Bosworth. Together, the *six* men with a combined weight of 1,396 pounds brought Jackson down as his legs churned and churned. This time, when he landed on his rear Bosworth didn't pump his fists or howl. He rose slowly, deliberately.

Three plays later, on second and 7 from the Seattle 14, the Raiders sent Jackson in motion and streaking into the end zone. Wilson floated the ball into his halfback's hands as he crossed through pay dirt all alone for his first NFL touchdown reception.

Were the game to end at that moment, Tuesday morning's watercooler chatter would be entirely about Bo Jackson and the plays he made against an excellent defense.

Alas, this was far from over.

One year before Bo Jackson teamed up with Marcus Allen to form an all-Heisman backfield, the Dallas Cowboys brought in Heisman Trophy–winner Herschel Walker to play alongside Heisman Trophy–winner Tony Dorsett.

On paper, it was a dream pairing. After leaving the University of Georgia, Walker spent three seasons tearing up the United States Football League. He was a 6-foot-1, 225-pound machine, and the idea of Walker and "Tony D" alternating carries sent shivers through the rest of the NFL.

It was a disaster.

Walker arrived in Dallas eager and happy to learn, but the veteran Dorsett wanted nothing to do with it. He hated that Walker made more money, that Walker generated more headlines, that Walker seemed more beloved. So when Walker asked questions like "Tony, what do I do on the sweep?" Dorsett's patented reply was "Figure it the fuck out."

Like Dorsett, Allen was far from giddy over another Heisman winner's arrival. Once upon a time, as a Southern Cal sophomore, he blocked ably for halfback Charles White, the 1979 Heisman Trophy winner. But those days were done. He had been an NFL superstar for half a decade, and relegation to the shadows didn't spark joy. But, as opposed to the oft-cantankerous Dorsett, Allen was one of the NFL's elite teammates. "He was the most professional athlete I've been around," said Chris Bahr, the Raiders kicker. "If Bo's presence was awkward for him, he never showed it. That took a very high level of self-confidence and class."

On the day Flores asked Allen whether he would mind playing fullback, there were two replies. The one in Allen's head ("Do I mind? Yeah, I mind.") and the one expressed in words ("Whatever will help the team, Coach."). For the remainder of the season, Allen devoted himself to leading the charge for Bo Jackson. Though often outweighed by 40, 50, 60 pounds, Allen's blocks were crushing. Any frustrations he felt were set free by slamming into an oncoming tackler. "Marcus was tougher than nails," said Flores. "He'd put his face in your chest and let you have it."

Against the Seahawks, Allen's blocking had set Jackson free on almost all of his marquee plays—he cleared out Robinson on the 12-yard scamper; he was the first to hit Taylor on the 4-yard tumble; he nailed a blitzing Young just before Wilson tossed the 14-yard touchdown pass.

Thanks to a booming 63-yard punt from Ruben Rodriguez, midway through the second quarter the Raiders found themselves in quite the hole, facing a third and 6 from their own 9. Though Los Angeles had dominated thus far, the score was only 14–7, and the Kingdome was *loud*. Fans stood, clapped, screamed, heckled. A stand here, and Seattle would get the ball back in terrific position.

The Raiders broke huddle. Allen and Jackson lined up behind Wilson—fullback to the left, halfback to the right. Tight end Todd Christensen packed in alongside right tackle Steve Wright, and tight end Trey Junkin packed in alongside left tackle Brian Holloway. Wide receiver James Lofton was split wide right. The play call was 17 Bob Trail—"The number one means we're going to the halfback," explained Terry Robiskie, the offensive coordinator. "The seven is for where the play is heading. The seven hole in the line between the left tackle and tight end. And 'Bob' means 'Back on backer,' so the fullback is blocking the linebacker."

Every walk from the huddle was a bit of an adventure for Jackson. He knew roughly half the playbook, and was prone to mixing his rights with his lefts. So this could work wonderfully. Or be a disaster.

Center Don Mosebar bent down and gripped the football in his right hand. The Seattle defense had four down linemen, plus two defensive backs across from the tight ends. As soon as the ball was snapped to Wilson, Allen charged left and sealed off Patrick Hunter, a cornerback lingering along the edge. "My job there is to force Bo to come underneath," Hunter recalled. "Which I kind of did. But then someone needs to catch him." Allen's block cleared a path for Jackson, who found himself running behind Dean Miraldi, the pulling right guard. Eugene Robinson eluded Miraldi, extended his arms and dove toward Jackson—who slapped him into the turf with a devastating straight arm to the helmet.

With that, Jackson found the left sideline and . . . *just . . . friggin' . . . took . . . off.*

"Find me a more electrifying play," said Jessie Hester, the Raiders wide receiver. "Ever."

The first opponent Jackson left in a vaper trail was Bosworth. The next man up was Easley, whose speed/power combination made him the prototype 1980s defensive back. Easley had the angle on Jackson, but as he closed in from the right that angle somehow vanished and Easley joined Bosworth in a cloud of nothingness. "Angles don't mean shit when it's Bo Jackson," said Robiskie. "He destroyed angles." The last player with a shot was cornerback Arnold Brown, a 1985 fifth-round draft choice out of North Carolina Central. Brown was fast, but nowhere close to Bo Jackson fast. "It's like little kids," said Dierdorf, "chasing a grown man."

At the Seattle 40-yard line, both Easley and Brown appeared on television screens. By the 30, only Brown's right arm could be seen. By the 25, Jackson was solo, and running so fast that as he passed George Dyer, the Seattle defensive line coach, the pieces of paper in his right hand went flying into the air. "His velocity sucked up my notes," Dyer said. "I spent a lifetime in football. That's the only time that ever happened." Krieg literally heard Jackson pass. Not the stomping of his feet or even deep breaths. "A whoosh," Krieg said. "All power." Jackson never slowed down or looked back—just ran into the end zone, out of the end zone and up the tunnel that led into the bowels of the Kingdome.

"There goes Bo!" raved Michaels. "And nobody catches Bo! Touchdown!"

The three-man booth giggled with delight.

Dierdorf: "He may not stop 'til Tacoma! He's gone!"

Michaels: "Portland!"

Gifford: "He just went by Spokane!"

The run covered 91 yards, and the aftermath should have been bottled. Three Raiders—Lofton, Rod Martin (arms aloft, helmet high) and Linden King—disappeared into the tunnel's darkness to seek out their teammate. Seconds later the four emerged, with Jackson cradling the football in his left hand. After saying something to King, he shifted the ball to his right hand, tossed it into the air, drew back an imaginary baseball bat and swung away.

"That wasn't Bo Jackson running 91 yards," said Taylor, the Seattle cornerback. "That was Superman. Seriously—that was the one and only Superman. There's no other explanation."

The Raiders were leading 27–7 midway through the third quarter, when again they marched down the field to the Seattle 2. By now, Jackson had accumulated 185 total yards—67 more than the entire Seahawks offense. It was third and one, and he lined up two steps behind Allen. This time the play call was a basic pitch to the left. There wasn't much suspense. Everyone in the building knew who would be running the football.

The Seahawks were in a goal-line defense, and the twenty-two men on the field were tightly packed together. Wilson accepted the snap and turned to pitch the ball. Jackson had started on the left hashmark at the 9-yard line, and by the time pigskin reached his hands he was at the eight and drifting outside. Paul Moyer, a veteran defensive back, tried making a tackle but was easily shoved aside by Allen. Jackson read the block, sliced behind it, pivoted his shoulders toward the end zone and, at the 2, encountered a last remaining obstacle.

The Boz.

From the start, Bosworth read the play perfectly. He knew exactly where Jackson was headed, and sprinted to the spot to implement—at long last—the great decimation of Bo Jackson. The collision was violent. Bosworth lowered his helmet, extended both arms and wrapped them around Jackson's waist. Lesser running backs would have fallen. Hell, lesser running backs *had* fallen. But the Raider was a bulldozer, and the Seahawk was an overhyped steroid bean bag. "Brian was an arm tackler," said Junkin. "But Bo wasn't going down from an arm tackle." The collision paused Jackson's forward momentum for a split second, but before one could blink his knees and legs and torso were combining to drag Bosworth into the end zone. Both men fell over, but Jackson quickly bounded up, glowered toward the prone Boz, then darted off to the sideline with football in hand.

"In Brian's defense," said Taylor, "nobody makes that tackle. Bo, at full speed, approaching a linebacker standing still? I don't care if we're talking Lawrence Taylor, Reggie White, God himself. No one's stopping Bo."

When he finally returned to his feet, a defeated Brian Bosworth—head down, hands on hips, white chinstrap dangling from face mask—tiptoed from the field, lesser than he had been before. The Seahawks wound up losing 37–14, with Jackson rushing for a team record 221 yards on 18 carries.

Within two years Bosworth—damned by injuries and underwhelming production—was out of the NFL.

"You could just see that single run shatter Bosworth's image of himself," said Steve Beuerlein, the Raider quarterback. "His ego was so big—nobody did that to the Boz. Nobody. Well, Bo did. When you're an NFL linebacker, and you start questioning yourself, you get taken advantage of. People target you and target your insecurities.

"That night, Bo killed The Boz. And then he buried the body."

CHAPTER 20

ICON

When Bo Jackson boarded the Raiders team bus and departed the King-dome, he assessed what had transpired as—simply—a football game.

A successful football game, sure. But a mere game, nonetheless.

Many athletes need to remind themselves to keep an even keel. They seek out sports therapists to assist with perspective and self-analysis. But Jackson was a natural. No victory was *that* big. No defeat was *that* devastating. Win or lose, his wife (now pregnant with a second child, Nicholas, who would be born on August 2, 1988) and son would be home waiting. "Bo's not a loner," said Susann McKee, his representative. "But he is a homebody."

What Jackson failed to understand, however, was that sports giants are constructed of moments, and with the 91-yard sprint down the sideline, then the *Monday Night Football* murder and cremation of Brian Bosworth, he morphed overnight into an unambiguous American sports giant. Or, as Jim Murray, the legendary *Los Angeles Times* columnist wrote, "Bo is the type of athlete you expect to find only in the pages of fiction."

Though the remainder of the Raiders' season proved uneventful (the team won one of its last four, and Jackson's heavily anticipated game at Kansas City ended with some mild boos, a sprained ankle and a mere three carries), Jackson had emerged. Nike was in the process of developing an ad campaign to revolve around his versatility, and his agents received a boatload of endorsement opportunities. He was a hot product.

If only he could stop behaving like such a baby.

Spring training was slated to begin on February 19, and—thanks in large part to his decision to pursue a hobby—Jackson was not being guaranteed a Major League job. That edict came from Royals skipper John Wathan, who told a reporter, "Bo knows he is going to have to make our club. For whatever reason, he wasn't the same Bo Jackson in the second half. We have to see if he's going to be the Bo Jackson of the first half of the year or the second half."

There was nothing unfair about the Royals' position. Jackson *had* batted .193 after announcing he would play football—"Bo doesn't want to admit it was the football decision," Wathan said. "But the media were getting on him, fans were throwing footballs on the field at him, players were making comments about it. When your peers talk about you, it hurts." Jackson *had* placed fifth in the Major Leagues with 158 strikeouts.* Jackson *had* been distracted. Jackson *was not* an engaged teammate. Jackson *did not* devote his offseason to baseball improvement (the Royals wanted him to play winter ball). Jackson *had* suffered a sprained ankle—the injury fear was always a concern for the Royals. Jackson *was* a mediocre outfielder. But instead of gracefully accepting the criticisms and the challenge, Jackson showed up to the team's brand-new $13 million spring training facility in Davenport, Florida, and acted the fool.

Approached by John Schuerholz, hand extended, Jackson rebuffed the gesture, turned and walked away. He had heard the Royals GM suggest he may well begin the season in Triple A Omaha, and it stung. "I don't speak to Schuerholz," he later explained. "Schuerholz's crackers don't sit well in my bowl of soup."

Both manager and general manager said Jackson would fight for the left-field job with Gary Thurman, the team's No. 1 selection in the 1983 June Draft. The two outfielders had played together at Memphis, and when Jackson was called up Thurman—hitting .312 with 53 stolen bases for the Double A ball club—felt wronged. "They took him instead of me," said Thurman. "And at the time I was a far more polished baseball player. It was disappointing."

Now Jackson was the disappointed one. Gary Thurman? Seriously? The Royals were going to force him to fight for a gig with . . . slap-hitting *Gary Thurman*? "These people," Jackson said, "got a screw loose some-fucking-where."

As was increasingly the case, Jackson took out his anger on the people who deserved it least: the sports media. Upon arrival, he made it clear that no reporters would be granted interviews, and no statements would be issued. Save for a single sit-down with Bob Nightengale of the *Kansas City Star*, he kept his word. When Michael Madden of the *Boston Globe* tried

---

* Carlton Fisk, the White Sox catcher, demanded his pitchers never throw Jackson a strike after the fifth inning, because he was so undisciplined he would chase everything.

breaking through by approaching Jackson on the field, he was told, "The embargo is still on. No talk. Talk can be cheapened."

At age twenty-five, one of Jackson's greatest shortcomings was a lack of introspection. He was confident and steadfast, but terribly poor at reading a room. If a sought-after athlete denies the media access, reporters wind up annoying those around him. So instead of Bo answering Bo questions, George Brett and Frank White and Gary Thurman and Kevin Seitzer were forced to answer Bo questions. It was hardly their first choice of an activity.

Jackson's moodiness extended to rude and uncooperative behavior when it came to signing autographs for teammates and opponents. In his mind, signatures were things to be profited off of. One only had so many years as marquee product, and he had to capitalize on such status. Part of professional sports ritual, however, involves the unspoken understanding that, when a peer asks for an autograph, you are required by etiquette and mutual understanding to deliver. Jackson, somehow, didn't receive the memo. The behavior began during his time with the Raiders, when he stood before the locker room of men and loudly declared, "I'm done signing autographs for y'all. Stop asking."

Stunned silence.

"It wasn't received well," said Trey Junkin, the tight end.

Depending on the day, with the Royals Jackson would either sign begrudgingly or not sign at all. He gave people grief for asking—"You're just gonna fucking sell it and make money off my name." Also, the item had to pertain to baseball—no Raiders jerseys or football allowed. Ballplayers used to confidently strolling through a clubhouse tiptoed up to Jackson and asked, meekly, "Um, Bo . . . would you mind autographing a jersey for my kid?"

Yes. Jackson *did* mind.

No. Jackson *wouldn't* sign. Not today.

In his 1990 autobiography, *Bo Knows Bo*, Jackson talked about hitting .333 during spring training, and how he "tore up" opposing pitching. This was a bit of an exaggeration. Jackson batted .298 with five home runs, which looked practically Ruthian compared to Thurman's flimsy .185 output. But he continued to swing wildly at off-speed pitches and butcher routes in the outfield. He made the team, coldly told Wathan and Schuerholz that, *duh, of course I made the team*—and got off to a hot start, batting .309 with nine home runs by the end of May.

But fun was hard to come by. On May 31, he ripped his left hamstring while falling across the first base bag and wound up on the twenty-one-day disabled list. By his July return, momentum was dead. His average dropped 60 points, and he looked (and felt) lost.

Through it all, Jackson harbored grudges, and he remained disdainful of the Royals. "Everybody was nice [to me] until that day in Toronto when I decided I was going to play football," Jackson said. "Or as they say, '*Try* to play football.' My name is mud. But I didn't worry about it, because the way I saw it, if the people were going to treat me like shit in baseball after the decision I made, I could just play football. People can't get to me mentally. I've said it time and time before. People in the front office, the fans, the press—the girders in that damn stadium will collapse and fall, you . . . can't hurt me. The stuff that they're saying about me and trying to do to me, you can't hurt a man that's been hurting all of his life. My tolerance level for pain is so high.

"The negative things that they were saying about me, the fans booing me, throwing footballs on the field when I got back to Kansas City—I'll never forget that. I'll never forget some of the things that people in the front office of the Royals said about me. I let my actions speak for me, and I shoved it right back up their asses, and they knew it. My uncle always told me, never get into a piss fight with a polecat—you'll never win."

There are two types of polecats. One is a metal bar used in hospitals to help patients gain balance. The other is a weasel-like animal related to the American skunk.

Within the confines of the Royals clubhouse, Jackson had his very own polecat (second definition). Not that Kevin Seitzer, All-Star third baseman and one of the game's better contact hitters, viewed himself as such. Two years earlier, he and Jackson had played side by side on the Memphis Chicks, and although there wasn't any noticeable animosity, the teammates shared little in common. Unlike Jackson, blessed by the Gods to be an athlete, Seitzer was your prototypical (aka: clichéd) scrapper—the white small-college kid (Eastern Illinois) who was drafted fairly late (eleventh round), but lived and died in the cage. Also unlike Jackson, Seitzer stapled every emotion, feeling and opinion to his forehead. During his rookie season, for example, Seitzer's hometown of Middletown, Illinois, planned on throwing a parade in his honor—until Seitzer made it clear he didn't like his hometown of Middletown, Illinois. "I doubt they'll ever have a Kevin Seitzer day," he said—more threat than reaction.

Seitzer was brash. Loud. Obnoxious. If you had a whitehead on your nose, he told you. If you farted, he was the first to announce it. "He was a gnat," said Danny Tartabull, the outfielder. "You know, the busy bee in everyone's conversation. Most guys, before they said something took the temperature. Not Kevin."

"Kevin was annoying," said Jeff Montgomery, a young reliever. "Not a bad person. But he pushed things when it was better to walk away."

Because he largely kept to himself, Jackson could be hard to read. Were you his pal? Were you not his pal? Sometimes he could be heard laughing. Other times he flashed the sternness of a judge. His size made him intimidating enough that rare was the Royal who challenged him. "The only time I actually saw someone stand up to Bo was [pitcher] Steve Farr," said Montgomery. "Bo had been told Steve was talking trash about him and he was mad. But that annoyed Steve. He went straight to Bo and said, 'Do you have a problem? If so, let's go—me and you.' Bo could have wrapped Steve up like a pretzel, but he didn't because he respected Steve holding his ground."

He did not, however, respect Seitzer. "He's one of the biggest ass-lickers we've got on the team," Jackson said. "He always puts his two cents in. And guys are like, 'Will you shut the fuck up?'"

One day, early in the 1988 season, the Royals held pre-game batting practice indoors, at the cages beneath the stadium. The team broke into groups of four, and Jackson's quartet included Seitzer, catcher Ed Hearn and infielder Bill Pecota. "[Kevin] is always the first in the cage," Jackson said. "He has to be the first to hit. So we're all back there, he takes his hacks, and I look down. I don't have nothing [on] but my sliding pants."

Jackson retreated to the clubhouse and threw on his shorts. When he returned, Hearn was wrapping his swings. Spotting Jackson, Seitzer theatrically jumped into the cage.

"Excuse me," Jackson said, "but didn't you just take your fucking turn?"

"Well," Seitzer said, "you should have been here . . ."

Three or four coaches, as well as a handful of teammates, were standing nearby. Jackson thought Seitzer was (as always) trying to peacock.

"Look, man," Jackson said, "will you just shut the fuck up and get out?"

He then entered the cage, where Seitzer—inches away—continued to lecture on protocol. "Kevin said to Bo, 'Fuck you—you weren't here,'" said Brian Watley, a Royals batboy. "Saying 'fuck you' to Bo seemed a little risky."

Jackson was not happy.

"Look, you better stop talking at me," he said.

Seitzer continued to bark.

"This is my last time telling you," Jackson said. "Don't say anything else to me, or I'm going to kick your ass."

Seitzer exited the cage, Jackson grabbed his Louisville Slugger, stepped in and missed the first pitch. Seitzer snickered.

Jackson threw down his bat, walked toward Seitzer ("With fire in his eyes," Hearn recalled), grabbed him around the throat with his left hand and shoved his head against the concrete wall. No one with the Royals had witnessed this fast of a Bo metamorphosis. Within seconds Seitzer's eyes rolled back.

"Look, you picked the wrong motherfucker to fuck with on the wrong day!" Jackson screamed. "As long as you're breathing air, don't you ever talk to me like that again! Motherfucker, I will break your neck!"

Dating back to his boyhood, Jackson's philosophy on dishing out an ass-kicking was fairly simple: If anyone steps in to end the ass-kicking, the ass-kicking intensifies. As several of the coaches and players tried separating the combatants, Jackson's grip grew vise-like.

"Bo!" screamed Bob Schaefer, the first base coach. "Bo! Bo! Let him go! Bo!"

Jackson wasn't listening. He was overcome by rage. Too much Kevin Seitzer. His arms, Schaefer recalled, seemed to be growing in thickness by the second. The veins bulged from his left bicep.

"The harder I squeezed, his eyes rolled back in his head," Jackson said. "And the harder they pulled on me, the stiffer my arm got."

By now Seitzer's feet were off the ground. His face was purplish-blue. "It was like a horror movie," said Tartabull. "Bo was Jason in *Friday the 13th*, and Kevin was the camp kid about to be murdered."

Finally, after what felt like an hour, Jackson released his hold, dropped Seitzer to the floor and stormed back to his locker. He picked up a bat and swung at the nearest wall. Wood and plaster exploded into little chunks.

Seitzer, meanwhile, was escorted to the training room, where he rested with an ice pack affixed to his neck. A still steaming Jackson rose from his stool and entered the room—followed by a half dozen curious/terrified/ wildly entertained teammates. Jackson stood over the battered Seitzer. "Don't you *ever* cross me again," he lectured. "If you do, I am not going to give those coaches time enough to grab me. I'm going to rip your asshole, and I mean that from the bottom of my heart. Don't you ever cross me again."

Seitzer nodded. About a half hour later, he tiptoed up to Jackson. The cocksureness was gone. "Bo," he said, "can we just forget what happened back there and be buddies?"

"No," Jackson said. "The shit don't work that way. You have said what you want to say, and you mean it, but now you want to come back and ass lick with me and say you're sorry? No."

Years later, Seitzer referred to Jackson as "a very good teammate, but not someone I knew that well. We weren't close."

Jackson was more blunt.

Kevin Seitzer could go fuck himself.

If one requires a sign that Bo Jackson's 1988 baseball season wasn't particularly joyful, all he needs to know is that the Kevin Seitzer suffocation was one of two highlights.

The other came on July 29, in Baltimore. At the time, Jackson's average was down to a season-low .259, and he was hitless in his last 14 at bats. As a team, the Royals sat at 49-52 and 12½ games behind Oakland in the American League West. It was *that* type of run.

Kansas City led 3–1 entering the top of the fourth, and Jeff Ballard—Baltimore's left-handed starter—was struggling. Frank White led off with a single, and two batters later Pat Tabler singled to left. Up stepped Jackson.

Ballard had never before faced Jackson. He looked at catcher Terry Kennedy for the sign—fastball. Pitching from the windup, Ballard glanced back toward White at second, started to lift his right leg into the air, turned his shoulder and . . .

Jackson raised his right hand toward Mike Reilly, the home plate umpire, to call time.

Reilly ignored him. Ballard was too far into delivery.

With the ball about to leave Ballard's fingers, Jackson realized there would be no assistance. He returned hand to wood and . . .

"He crushed it," said Ballard. "Just *crushed* it."

The ball sailed high over the green left-field wall and into the bleachers, an estimated 330 feet away. It wasn't the longest home run Bo Jackson would ever hit, but it was surely the longest home run in an at bat that was nearly aborted due to a time out. In the Baltimore dugout, manager Frank Robinson removed his hat and rubbed his forehead in disbelief. "My pitch was terrible," said Ballard. "But he deserves no less credit. What Bo did was awesome."

Statistically, the season was OK-ish. Jackson batted .246 with 25 home runs, 68 RBI and (egad) 146 strikeouts for a team that finished 83-79 and in third place. On the bright side, most of the Royals let any NFL antagonism go. It was an old story, and Jackson was a stubborn boot. Plus, he choked out Kevin Seitzer.

That scored clubhouse points.

On January 20, 1988, Tom Flores resigned as head coach of the Los Angeles Raiders.

He did so at a press conference inside the team's facility, standing before the franchise's signature emblem of a pirate wearing a football helmet.

Approaching his fifty-first birthday, Flores had guided the team to two Super Bowl titles over nine years. Wearing a dark suit and tie, the coach alternated between glum and relieved. "The timing is right for me to go about some other challenges," he said. "The timing is right for the Raiders to go about what they do best, and that's win football games."

Flores insisted it was his decision, only nobody with a functioning head bought it. The impatient Davis was fed up. He believed the Raiders roster was built to win, but 5-10 (the team's 1987 record) was far from winning. So he subtly suggested ("Tom—resign.") Flores step aside, then went about finding a replacement.

The owner loved promoting from within, but there was a realization that maybe the rest of the NFL had caught up with the Raiders. Davis purchased the franchise in 1966, and through the years the unflinching belief was the two keys to rings were a speed-demon wide receiver and a big-armed quarterback. That was the Oakland/Los Angeles Raider way: We will destroy you with the bomb.

Only, by the late 1980s, the Raider method had gone stale. The San Francisco 49ers' vaunted West Coast Offense—quick drops, slants and outs and running backs as pass catchers—was the way of the present/future. Faster, stronger players were entering the league, and most teams had a stable of fleet defensive backs to lock down equally fleet pass catchers.

So, against every impulse running through his body, Davis begrudgingly went outside the family. On February 29, 1988, the Raiders introduced Mike Shanahan as the team's eighth head coach. Just thirty-five, Shanahan arrived from Denver, where he had served as the Broncos' offensive coordinator and helped develop quarterback John Elway into a superstar. "I'm coming here with the thought of world championships," Shanahan said at the press conference. "I don't think there is a person in our organization who will be satisfied with anything less."

Shanahan said all the right things, but deep down he wondered whether he was voluntarily stepping atop a detonator. Whenever he asked peers about working for Al Davis, the replies were either grunts, curses, snorts or "Better you than me."

"My instincts told me not to take the job," he recalled, "even though it was paying more money than I had ever made. Yet I ignored my inner voice."

The Bo Jackson–less Raiders opened training camp on July 14, and it took the players approximately four seconds to realize the nightmare at hand.

Shanahan was stern and professional; a CPA taking over a thrash metal band. Davis had told him to "Do what needs to be done to turn this thing around," but in real time that translated to "Don't change a fucking thing." So when Shanahan made the rule players could no longer sit atop helmets during practices (a long-standing team tradition), Davis was furious And when Shanahan required suits for road travel, Davis was furious. And when normally ninety-minute practices were extended to two hours, Davis was furious. And when Shanahan tried firing some of the longtime assistant coaches, Davis was furious.

"Hiring Shanahan was the biggest mistake Al Davis ever made," said Trey Junkin, a tight end. "First, Mike tried putting in a system that did not align with the Raiders history. And second, Mike thought, as the head coach, he made all the decisions. He did not."

Los Angeles opened its season at home with a 24–13 beatdown of the rival Chargers, and Davis was dismayed. The offensive game plan was dinks and dunks and 28 (twenty-eight!?) handoffs to Davis's personification of human excrement, Marcus Allen. The new quarterback, Steve Beuerlein out of Notre Dame, was a game manager with a so-so arm and few impulses to launch 60-yard bombs. "At the end of that win the team was fired up," recalled Beuerlein. "It'd been 100 degrees and we wore black and played our asses off. I was really inspired."

Six hours after the final whistle, with Raiders Nation on cloud nine, the franchise traded Jim Lachey, arguably the best young offensive tackle in football, to the Washington Redskins for a lightning-armed quarterback named Jay Schroeder. It was a 100 percent Al Davis move, completed without consulting his coach, and he demanded Shanahan immediately start the new signal caller. "Al said to me as soon as the trade was done, 'You're gonna throw the ball down the field 10 times a game,'" said Schroeder. "'If you complete three of those, we score 21 points and win.'"

Before long, Davis was not only attending practices ("He wore this really strong cologne, so you'd smell him before you saw him," said Mitch

Willis, the defensive lineman), but undermining Shanahan. He pulled players aside to offer instruction. He whispered, "Don't listen to the shit Mike's
telling you. He's not a Raider." After one game during which Junkin cursed
out his coach, he was fined $5,000 for conduct detrimental to the team.
Junkin complained to Davis, who said, "You're not being fined. Just get
back out on the fucking field."

By the time Bo, Linda and their two sons arrived in Los Angeles on
October 11 (this time they rented the Santa Monica townhouse belonging
to Sean Jones, ex-Raider defensive lineman), the landscape was toxic. In
the offseason the team had used its first-round pick on Tim Brown, the
Heisman Trophy–winning wide receiver from Notre Dame, and also traded
for Willie Gault, the former Chicago Bears pass catcher with 4.2 speed.
Now, with Jackson, plus the presence of James Lofton and Mervyn Fernan-
dez, Los Angeles was built to sprint, with an owner who loved pedal-to-the-
metal football and a coach who wanted nothing of the sort. When he hired
Shanahan, Davis momentarily believed his team would be sitting atop the
AFC West. Instead, it was 2-4, with back-to-back losses to the Bengals and
Dolphins.

Jackson's first practice was October 12, and four days later he dressed
for the road matchup against Kansas City. With a new coach's new playbook,
there was much to learn, and during early drills Jackson and Marcus Allen
found themselves lined up behind Schroeder, now the starting quarterback.
Under Shanahan's watchful (and stubborn) eye, Schroeder was dropping
back three steps and dumping the ball off to the two running backs—"and it
was great," said Schroeder. "Bo for ten yards, Marcus for ten yards. I love to
throw deep, but when you have two nuclear weapons at running back, you
have to use them." Davis didn't see it that way. Pacing the field, reeking of
cologne and madness, he unleashed a string of expletives toward quarterback and head coach. "Throw the fucking ball down the field!" he ranted.
"Don't throw it to the backs anymore! What a fucking stupid philosophy!
We're playing like fucking pussies!"

In Kansas City, Jackson had hardly been a fan of John Wathan, the
team's manager. But compared to Shanahan, the Royals' skipper was
George C. Patton. Jackson watched perplexed as the Raiders' young coach
was undermined by Davis. He'd never seen anything like it. Pat Dye stood
up to everyone. Hal Baird stood up to everyone. Shanahan, by comparison,
was a wuss. Jackson referred to Shanahan as "someone that's never played
the game, that's only just studied it by being on the field or books." And
while this was incorrect (Shanahan played quarterback at Eastern Illinois),

the criticism was pointed. Was this Al Davis's team, or Mike Shanahan's team? "It was a lot of chaos," said Milt McColl, a linebacker who played seven years with the 49ers before signing with the Raiders. "With San Francisco we'd all be looking at the playbooks, studying. One time with the Raiders we were putting in a blitz and I asked the coach, 'If I blitz, who's covering the tight end over there?' The coach said, 'Um, let's hope no one notices.'"

"We had talent," said Mike Dyal, a rookie tight end. "But it was messy. Too many chefs in the kitchen."

On the morning of his first game, Jackson was back home in Leawood, Kansas, mowing his lawn and chatting with neighbors. He looked, according to Steve Springer of the *Los Angeles Times*, "like a typical Kansas City Royals baseball player enjoying his off-season." By the time he arrived at Arrowhead Stadium for the one o'clock kickoff, the cheerfulness vanished. As was the case a year earlier, fans threw baseballs from the stands. More than a hundred anti-Bo banners hung. Part of it was anger over a star local athlete deemed traitor; part of it was a 1-4-1 home team. When Jackson entered midway through the first quarter, he was lambasted by boos and taunts.

Despite limited practice, Jackson carried 21 times for 70 yards. With 5:49 left in the game, his one-yard touchdown plunge gave the Raiders a 27–10 lead. After scoring, Jackson looked toward the stands and launched the football toward the 77,078 spectators. "The fans were great," he said following his club's 27–17 triumph. "So I just gave the ball to them."

It made no sense. How could a guy carve up an NFL defense after three practices? If Bo Jackson was this great in his first game, what sort of amazement would he bring forth the following weekend, when the Raiders traveled to New Orleans to face the Saints?

The answer came quickly.

Los Angeles received the opening kickoff, and on first and 10 from their own 19, Allen and Jackson lined up in the I-formation behind Schroeder. The quarterback handed off to Jackson, who followed Allen right, sliced inside, then turned outside behind a block from Fernandez. He escaped the clutches of a diving Antonio Gibson and rambled 25 yards before being wrestled to the ground by free safety Brett Maxie.

On the next play, Jackson again lined up deep, with Allen a few feet to the right. Once more, Schroeder spun and gave it to his halfback, then watched as Jackson turned left, stutter stepped, cut outside of cornerback Van Jakes, turned the corner and steamed down the sideline to the Saints'

36. Upon being forced out of bounds, Jackson spiked the ball. Said Joe Namath, announcing the game for NBC: "The Saints' major concern—the speed of the wide receivers for the Raiders. But now they've gotta be concerned with Jackson the way he's running the football."

Roughly two seconds after his celebration, Jackson felt a tug in his right hamstring. He hobbled toward the sideline to seek medical help, en route passing Pat Swilling, New Orleans' standout outside linebacker. "S-Swilling," he said, a slight stutter. "I was about to put my f-f-f-foot in yo' ass."

The diagnosis was a pulled hamstring. Jackson never returned ("We were glad his ass was gone," said Swilling), and the Raiders were blown out, 20–6.

Back in Missouri, within the front offices of the Kansas City Royals, the sight of Jackson once again struggling with a football injury was greeted with both I-hope-he's-OK concern and I-told-you-so smugness. When Jackson first broached the idea of half a year in the NFL, Schuerholz wondered whether his body could withstand the rigors. Now the answer was fairly clear: it could not. Later in the season he suffered yet another injury (a pulled groin) while *taking off his uniform* following a win over the 49ers. (When asked, Jackson attributed the injury to "weird sex.") This wasn't Hercules. This was a man whose body required rest.

But Jackson refused to see it that way. His entire motivational circuiting was based upon the stubborn idea that he could conquer the unconquerable; that when others said, "No way," he said, "Hell, yes." The Buccaneers knew he wouldn't play baseball? Watch him. The Royals figured he wouldn't play football? Watch him. No one could possibly do back-to-back seasons? OK—check this out. Did it matter that he was, in fact, made of skin and bones, and that playing football was physically ruinous? Did it matter that he was a raw ballplayer who could only improve so much without off-seasons devoted to shortening his swing, sharpening his outfield routes, reading the moves of opposing pitchers?

For both the Raiders and Jackson, the remainder of the 1988 season was a dud. The team wound up 7-9 and third in the AFC West, Los Angeles Coliseum attendance plummeted (Wrote Scott Ostler in the *Los Angeles Times*: "On several occasions the roar of the crowd was drowned out by the din of aphids munching petals.") and Jackson never gained more than 100 yards in a game. He was . . . good. Some long runs. Some thrilling moves. But inconsistent and erratic and often hobbled. "Bo is a known quantity now and they're making him turn inside," explained Al LoCasale, a Raider executive. "He's still running over people, but when he runs over one now, there's another one right behind." In an unsightly 13–3 Week 10 win over San Diego, Jackson had successive runs of no yards, negative 4 yards, one yard, negative one yard, no yards, 13 yards (during which he fumbled away the ball), 9 yards and zero yards. Two weeks later, Jackson carried nine times for 25 yards against the Falcons, and Gary Pomerantz of the *Atlanta Constitution* opined, "Someone should have filed a missing persons report on Bo Jackson."

His body was tired. He wouldn't admit it—but his body was *definitely* tired.

Throughout the year, Davis worked hard to make life miserable for his team. It was all about ego and attention. Davis *needed* it. He second-guessed Shanahan, then denied second-guessing Shanahan. He told the press he was unhappy with his coach, but laughed off any rumors of a pending dismissal. His big offseason acquisition—surrendering a first-round pick for Gault—was blowing up in his face. The last thing Shanahan's offense required was yet another sprinter who blocked like a Squishmallow. Alas, Davis couldn't resist—and Gault wound up with 16 catches. Schroeder, his second big acquisition, was just as bad—all muscle, no touch, nervous feet. "When the Raiders broke the huddle and you had Marcus Allen on the left and Bo Jackson on right," said Martin Bayless, a Chargers safety, "you hoped Jay Schroeder would drop back to pass."

Over ten games, Jackson ran for 580 yards and 3 touchdowns. After the finale, he reassured Shanahan that he would return for 1989, but nobody was entirely certain. It had not been a fun campaign, just as baseball had not been a fun campaign. Jackson loved playing sports, hated the *business* of playing sports. And the hype. And the nonstop commitments. And fools like Kevin Seitzer and Mike Shanahan. The Royals, once again, were plotting to convince him to stick to the diamond—and that was irritating. For all anyone knew, Jackson might quit both professions to focus on fly-fishing.

"Just when you think you've got him figured out," George Brett said, "he'll move a little on you."

One thing was certain—1988 had not gone as planned.

Not even close.

CHAPTER 21

THE GREATEST YEAR I

Bo Jackson was happy.

That's one of the things people didn't understand about the man. Whether the Royals won or lost, he was generally happy. Whether the Raiders won or lost, he was generally happy. Yes, he preferred victories. But setbacks failed to impact him the way it did the majority of peers. He didn't live and die with the games he played. He didn't take stuff home and dwell on it.

Why? Family.

When Jackson impregnated Linda Garrett, then married her in 1987, he committed himself to being a family man. He didn't want to be like so many of the other athletes he knew—on-the-road dogs seeking out that next conquest. He had sewn his wild oats, and he was done with it. "People don't seem to realize there is a lot of loneliness in professional sports," he said in 1989. "People think we've got the world by the balls, can do whatever we want, but there are times when I'm so lonely, there are times I can't imagine what I would do without my family.

"Take George [Brett] for instance. George is one of the nicest guys you'll ever meet. But George is the loneliest man in the world. This guy's in his mid-thirties, he's not married, no kids. He doesn't have a relationship. There's nobody, and there's no way I could be like that."

No matter the sport, when Bo traveled he called Linda three times per day—in the morning from the hotel, in the afternoon before the game and in the evening when all was quiet. "I don't hang out at the bar," he said. "I don't go out with the guys. Guys try to get me to go out with them. [But] I'm not missing nothing."

In the wake of a fairly miserable 1988 baseball season, followed by a fairly miserable 1988 football season, Jackson entered the new year feeling content and whole. His oldest son, Garrett, was now two, and his youngest, Nicholas, five months. Jackson changed diapers and shopped for strollers and insisted he would never, ever, *ever* become an A. D. Adams sequel. He steeled himself to love and support his children.

So in the early days of 1989, as many teammates were making extra loot at autograph shows or playing winter ball in the Dominican Republic, Jackson was home with his wife and two boys, refreshing.

And then—once fully rejuvenated—the greatest year of any human being in the history of all human beings who have ever walked the planet commenced.

It began, strangely, in the woods of Dixie. Twenty-three days before reporting to spring training, Jackson traveled to Lowndes County, Alabama, to compete in the Buckmaster Celebrity Deer Hunt, during which he shot a 12-point buck alongside such sports notables as Davey Allison and Wade Boggs. It was as delighted as anyone had seen Jackson—decked out in camouflage, talking guns with fellow athletes, signing autographs for spectators more interested in the surrounding trees and grass than the tackling abilities of Harry Carson. The four-day event served as a reminder that, deep within the gruff exterior, Jackson was capable of real joy. Family, hunting, a good meal, a comfortable bed—it was there. Just difficult at times to find.

A couple of weeks later, the Royals signed Jackson to a one-year, $585,000 contract (plus a $50,000 bonus for winning the MVP, $25,000 for making the All-Star Game and $25,000 for earning a Gold Glove), thereby squashing any lingering rumors that he was still debating whether to go full-time gridiron. "Bo," Richard Woods, his agent, confirmed, "will continue to play two sports."

Jackson reported to Baseball City Stadium in Davenport, Florida, for spring training in outstanding shape. His body was healed. He still disliked Kevin Seitzer, but did his best to get along. He spoke to the media, and even smiled on occasion. When the Royals requested he remove his new hoop earring for the regular season, he never complained. "I liked him immediately," said Bob Boone, the recently acquired catcher. "Bo wasn't overly warm, but I think sometimes people confuse shyness with cruelty."

The general national consensus was that Kansas City *might* challenge the Oakland A's for American League West supremacy, but much depended on the starting rotation staying healthy and Jackson taking the leap from good-but-inconsistent to great.

Put succinctly: Could Bo reach his potential?

On March 5, he had an answer.

It was just a spring training game. Red Sox paying a visit to Baseball City. Sunny skies, temperatures in the mid-70s. Barbara Billingsley, the actress best known as "June Cleaver" from *Leave It to Beaver*, threw out the first pitch. Taking the bump for Boston was Dennis (Oil Can) Boyd, the herky-jerky, shit-talking right-hander about to begin his eighth Major League season. Boyd was a solid American League starter who relied on guile and smarts to get past opposing hitters. "I'd been hurt," Boyd recalled, "but I was beginning to feel healthy." Jackson came to the plate in the second inning, with Pat Tabler on second and two outs. Boyd hung a slider. Not a bad slider, by general definitions of the pitch, but one that seemed to rest comfortably atop the center of the dish.

Jackson swung, and the ball came off his bat as a loose cap explodes from a shaken bottle of Pepsi. It rose in a blink—clearing the outfield fence, then the 71-foot left-center scoreboard, then short hopping a 10-foot chain-link fence in the parking lot before landing on a patch of grass.

Andrew Hoppen, a Baseball City parking lot attendant, had heard the sound from the crowd (Hoppen: "It was an *ooh* noise. But not an ordinary *ooh* noise."), then saw the baseball settle. "I reached through the fence and worked it up with my hand," he recalled. "When it got to the top I flipped it to myself."

Within minutes, a handful of people sprinted into the parking lot.

"Did you see the ball Bo hit?" someone asked Hoppen.

"*That* was Bo?" he replied.

After the game, Hoppen was ushered into the clubhouse. He offered Jackson the ball, but the slugger declined. Instead, he signed it for Hoppen and handed him the bat used to hit it.

The next day Wathan, the Royals manager, had the distance officially measured. When the result was presented to him, he didn't believe it. When it was reiterated, he still didn't believe it.

Finally, he believed it—the baseball had flown *515 feet*.

"What did he hit?" someone asked Bob Schaefer, the first base coach.

"A Top Flite," he replied.

Did 1989 Bo Jackson seem like a vastly improved ballplayer from past seasons? Not entirely. He still struck out far too often (172 times), still didn't read developing situations with the smoothness of a George Brett or Frank White. But his base running was dramatically better, as were his outfield routes. He stopped trying to pull so many balls, and realized he could take advantage of his power by going both ways. "At the plate he's more patient," said Wes Gardner, a Boston pitcher. "He just looks more comfortable up there."

By the early days of May, his 9 home runs, 68 total bases, .624 slugging percentage, 16 extra base hits all paced the American League, and his 11 stolen bases led the *Kansas City Star*'s Bob Nightengale to speculate that Jackson may well become baseball's second-ever 40-40 player. "Bo Jackson doesn't talk about it," Nightengale wrote. "He refuses to even think about it. But his numbers are speaking loudly."

It was true—the numbers were speaking loudly. Yet it was a string of unprecedented, did-we-really-just-see-that? actions that kept opening eyes. The first was the spring training home run off Boyd. The second occurred on May 9 in Kansas City, when Jackson swung through a 3-2 fastball thrown by Cleveland pitcher Keith Atherton, stepped out of the batter's box, and snapped the bat—"Biff! Pow! Crack!" wrote Gib Twyman—over his right thigh, roughly 12 inches up the handle. *What in the world did he just do?* Read the *St. Louis Post-Dispatch:* "The legend of Bo Jackson continues."

"I would never, ever attempt to do that," said Willie Wilson, the Royals outfielder. "I would hurt myself."

The third—and least-witnessed—took place on May 15, inside the Metrodome in Minneapolis. The Royals and Twins were slated for the first of a three-game series, and beforehand Jackson jumped into the cage to take his BP cuts. He went through the motions—bam, bam, bam, bam—as Twins players watched awestruck from their dugout.

As the session wrapped, Mike Lum, the Royals hitting coach, yelled, "Bo, it's your turn! One last swing!"

Jackson dashed back into the cage, but this time on the left-handed side.

A public service announcement: Bo Jackson *did not hit* left-handed.

The batting practice pitcher threw a waist-high heater over the plate, and Jackson's swing was so naturally fluid one would think he had done it a thousand times before. The baseball ricocheted off the barrel and flew 450 feet, past the dome lights and off the Hardware Hank sign on the right-field upper deck—*the second-longest home run to right in the stadium's seven-year history.* Kirby Puckett, the Twins star center fielder, let out a howl. Jackson grinned his way and yelled, "I got work to do!" Then he walked off into the outfield, as if nothing out of the ordinary had occurred.

"He hit it lefty," said Tabler. "Lefty! Think about that. Just think about it. Lefty. And he was a righty. It's ridiculous."

One night later, Francisco Oliveras—twenty-six-year-old rookie right-hander—made his first Major League start for the Twins. Back home in Santurce, Puerto Rico, Oliveras's family gathered around a television situated near a satellite dish to watch their collective dream come true. Oliveras originally signed with Baltimore in 1980, and his long-awaited arrival was greeted as a holiday

Bo Jackson ruined everything.

In the sixth, he walked to the plate, dug in, sized up a junky Oliveras soft toss headed his way, reached out ("I hit it off the end of my bat," Jackson later said) and crushed it 404 feet into the upper deck just inside the right-field pole. Jackson was now the only right-handed hitter to ever reach the Metrodome's upper deck in right field. In Santurce, all the Oliverases went silent. There would be no victory celebration today.

"Hitting the ball the other way is one thing," said Roy Smith, a Twins pitcher. "But hitting it that far, that high—those balls never stay fair. To keep it fair and not have it slice. That's ungodly."

Bo Jackson was on a mega-roll. Then, on June 5, the Royals traveled to the Pacific Northwest to face the Seattle Mariners.

And Harold Reynolds.

In the mid-1980s, Major League Baseball was a land of speed and the speedsters who set the basepaths aflame.

The Oakland A's had Rickey Henderson. The St. Louis Cardinals had Vince Coleman. Devon White (Angels) and Gary Pettis (Tigers) terrified opposing catchers, as did Tim Raines in Montreal and Cecil Espy in Texas. There was a general order to a Big League lineup, and it almost always began with a man who could gallop like a stallion.

In Seattle, that meant Harold Reynolds.

Because he played for a bad team in a smallish market inside an enlarged sardine tin, the Mariners second baseman was no household name. Yet in 1987 he led the American League with 60 steals, then added another 35 the following year. Reynolds was wiry and explosive, and though he lacked Henderson's theatrics (fingers dangling, hands twitching), he manufactured runs.

"Harold wasn't just fast," said Mike Campbell, a Mariners pitcher. "He was dangerous."

The Monday-night Royals-Mariners clash inside the Kingdome was hardly one for danger. Or national interest. As always, the Jim Lefebvre-managed M's were a baseball afterthought. At 27-31, they already found themselves 10 games out in the American League West, and while Reynolds was terrific and a nineteen-year-old rookie phenom named Ken Griffey, Jr., was on a path toward greatness, the roster was largely a junkyard of scraps. The Royals, in third place with a 32-23 mark, were better, but no more sexy.

A lifeless crowd of 17,429 entered the stadium, and when the Royals jumped out to an early 3–0 lead it elicited little response. The Mariners, however, battled back, and tied the game at 3 with a bottom-of-the-ninth home run from Jay Buhner. When Kansas City failed to touch reliever Jerry Reed in the top of the 10th, Seattle found itself with a golden opportunity to eke out a win. On the mound for the Royals was Steve Farr, a thirty-two-year-old right-handed reliever who, Max Rieper once wrote, "never amazed anyone." Farr was the type of pitcher an opposing hitter wanted to see late in a game—low 90s, lots of off-speed garbage. "I got you out," Farr said years later. "I didn't scare you."

With one down and nobody on base, Reynolds beat out a roller to short-stop for an infield single. Next up was Scott Bradley, the left-handed hit-ting catcher and onetime New York Yankee prospect. A former University of North Carolina All-American, Bradley's bat contained minimal pop, but he was adept at making contact and moving base runners.

With the count full, Reynolds took a five-step lead, ignoring Rey Pala-cios, the first baseman who held him on. At the moment Farr lifted his glove, Reynolds took off, and when Bradley connected on the outside fastball Reynolds was halfway toward second and starting the turn toward third.

Bradley's liner went the other way, bounced off the warning track, and hopped up the blue left-field wall padding. Jackson sprinted to retrieve the ball, and by the time he grasped it Reynolds was steaming toward third with no plans on stopping. Bob Didier, the Mariners' third base coach, glanced toward left field, where Jackson was beginning to draw back his right arm. "When Harold passed me, he was running one hundred percent full speed," said Didier. "And you're not throwing out Harold Reynolds from three hundred twenty feet away when he's rounding third. No way in hell. Not possible. No chance. Zero. Zilch. Can't happen."

"I'm flying full tilt," Reynolds said. "Game over."

When Reynolds passed, Didier walked toward the dugout to celebrate the triumph. Bob Boone, the Kansas City catcher, was in his eighteenth Major League season. He knew the difference between hope and hopeless. "This was hopeless," he said. "When the ball was hit I thought, 'This ain't happening. Game over.'" Like Didier, Boone commenced the stroll toward his dugout, where other Royal players were reaching for their belongings. "I was halfway to the clubhouse," said Charlie Leibrandt, the veteran pitcher. "Why stay?" Farr's job was to run behind home plate in case of an errant throw. That's what pitchers were commanded to do. Not this time. "I wasn't even watching the play," he said. "I thought the game was over." So did the umpires—Larry Young, manning home plate, strolled absentmindedly down the third base line. Jim Joyce, the first base ump who was supposed to shift toward home, stood still and gazed off into the distance.

Because most eyes were focused upon Reynolds and his romp around the bases, it was easy to miss what was unfolding in the outfield corner. Much like Franco Harris's famed Immaculate Reception of seventeen years earlier, the cameraman filming the game for Seattle's KSTW 11 failed to capture the most important part of the action—which was Bo Jackson, one blue Nike cleat on the warning track, taking no hop, no step, no jump. Just rearing back and uncorking a flat-footed bazooka blast that soared high above shortstop Kurt Stillwell and in the general direction of home plate. "There was an old pitching machine, the Iron Mike," said Jeff Montgomery, a Royals pitcher. "It was a spring-loaded machine that just—*WHOMP!*— threw. That's what Bo did. Just—*WHOMP!*"

The first person to notice the spectacle was Bradley, who was rounding first when Jackson took hold of the ball. "I had this great view of Harold, this great view of Bo," he said. "At the initial glance there was no chance. Then it was, 'Hmmm . . .'"

Darnell Coles was the Mariners on-deck hitter. With Reynolds nearing the plate he flapped his arms while yelling, "You gotta slide, Harold! Yoooouuuuu gotttttttta sliiiiiiiiide!"

"In my head I'm going, 'Slide? What's he talking about?'" Reynolds said. "OK, I'll give it a courtesy slide."

Boone was a couple of strides off the plate when he became aware what might (but likely wouldn't) transpire. He froze in his tracks and stood nonchalantly, hoping to fool Reynolds into easing up. But then the ball neared. "I forget about the deke," Boone said, "so I can catch the ball and tag him out."

There had been ridiculous throws throughout baseball history. Launches by elite strongmen like Roberto Clemente and Dave Parker; Ellis Valentine and Rocky Colavito. But this was different—Jackson stood *320 feet away*, with one of the game's speediest men having the advantage of an enormous jump. There would be no cutoff or hop. Jackson's effort was a straight-shot, raw-brute-strength heave from wall-to-glove. "Nothing textbook about it," said Danny Tartabull, who was playing right field. "No polish."

With Reynolds closing in on home, Boone—helmet off, glove at head level, right leg extended, left leg bent at the knee—positioned himself two feet in front of the dish. Jackson's throw arrived at the catcher just as Reynolds was stepping with his right leg into an elongated feet-first slide. Boone grabbed the baseball and, in one motion, swiped downward toward Reynolds's shoes. He touched his left cleat three inches before it reached the plate.

Reynolds skidded across home and onto the adjacent dirt. He spun around on his rear and threw up both arms, a dramatic *Safe!* Only Young, the home plate umpire standing 45 feet up the third base line, pumped his right fist in the air—*Out!*

From afar, it was umpiring at its worst. None of the four officials were in position to make a definitive call. As soon as Young issued his ruling, Reynolds slammed his helmet to the ground and Didier blew up. "How can you call him out from here?" he screamed. "How can you call him out from here?" Lefebvre joined his coach in Young's face, pointing toward home, then toward third base, then toward home, then toward third base.

"I honestly didn't know if he was safe or out," Didier said. "That wasn't my argument. It was a matter of positioning."

Only after Lefebvre, Didier and Reynolds left the field did the reality of what transpired sink in for both ball clubs.

"What did we just see?" said Mariners pitcher Erik Hanson. "What in God's name did we just see?"

"It was unheard of," said Leibrandt. "No one else in the world makes that throw."

"We call it 'The Throw,'" said Didier. "There have been lots of great throws, right? But that's 'The Throw.'"

"It's the greatest throw I've ever seen in my life," said John Wathan. "The thing that got me was that it was a strike. And to think pitchers have trouble from 60 feet, 6 inches."

The Royals won, 5–3, in 13 innings, but afterward *all* anyone wanted to discuss was Bo Jackson and Harold Reynolds and the 320-foot launch. As soon as they entered their clubhouse, members of the Mariners crowded around a television monitor. Reynolds—who assumed a cutoff man made the final throw—forced his way to the screen, and watched the ten-second play, rewound it, watched, rewound. Sweet mother of Jesus—*he actually was out*. "It's crazy," Reynolds said after approximately fifteen viewings. "I was there. I was the one thrown out. I've seen it on replay, and I still don't believe it.

"I'm telling you right now, the guy is superhuman."

The replay was televised across the country, then televised again. It was quickly (and correctly) deemed the greatest outfield play human eyes had ever witnessed. Or sort of witnessed. "My feeling about Bo is really summed up in the video of that play," said Joe Posnanski, the longtime baseball writer. "We see him go to the wall, we see him begin to throw, then we see Reynolds. You know something incredible happened, but you don't know precisely what it was. There's no angle or footage of him throwing. That rarely happens, and it lends itself to mythology."

Combined with the steamrolling of Brian Bosworth, The Throw catapulted Jackson to a new level. He was not merely a star. He was Paul Bunyan.

Sixteen days later at Milwaukee, Jackson ended the top of the sixth by bouncing a one hopper back to Brewers pitcher Jay Aldrich. As soon as the baseball was tossed to first baseman Greg Brock, the camera panned to Jackson, who—walking back toward the dugout—grabbed both ends of his bat and placed it atop his helmet.

Step . . .

Step . . .

Step . . .

CRACK!

Jackson snapped the wood at the halfway point *on his head*, and the splintering sound filled much of Milwaukee County Stadium. As fans cheered the spectacle, Jackson folded the bat like a sheet of paper and handed it to Bob Schaefer, the first base coach. "That's my little claim to fame," said Aldrich, who pitched parts of three Major League seasons. "People ask about my career, and I'll say, 'Remember Bo Jackson snapping a bat over his head? That was me.'"

What never comes up is that Aldrich actually broke Jackson's bat on the pitch. The wood was cracked by the time Bo finished the task. "It's still cool," said Aldrich. "Still amazing. But maybe a little more mystique than raw strength."

With Jackson, mystique and reality overlapped, tangoed, snuggled. He never lifted a single weight (not true). He killed a bear with his bare hands (also not true). At Auburn he threw a football the length of a football field (true) then did it again seconds later (not true). He received roughly twenty pounds of fan mail per week (true) and ate half of it (not true). Jackson appeared on the cover of the June 12, 1989, *Sports Illustrated*, and inside Peter Gammons wrote, "At Royals Stadium, the rustle of anticipation begins as soon as Jackson takes his first step out of the on-deck circle toward home plate" (not true—it usually took two steps). Against Oakland on July 4,

Jackson smashed 2 home runs to give him 20 homers and 20 stolen bases at the halfway point. When asked whether he was focused upon becoming just the second 40-40 guy in Major League history, Jackson shook his head. "To hell with 40-40," he said. "You all are more concerned about it than I am" (true—he didn't care).

The numbers and achievements didn't particularly impress Jackson. Up in Beaverton, Oregon, however, it was far more important than mere statistics and SportsCenter fodder.

No.

It was the stuff of a merchandising revolution.

When Bo Jackson spoke, people tended to yawn.

That was the problem Nike faced in the two years since the athletic apparel company had signed the multisport athlete to an endorsement deal. Jackson was the world's greatest athletic specimen. He was faster than a speeding bullet, more powerful than a locomotive. He could leap tall buildings in a single bound (He *did* once jump over a car). For Christ's sakes, he played *two* professional sports at the highest level. "He was handsome," said Phil Knight, Nike's chairman. "He had a beautiful smile. Everyone knew his name."

But Bo Jackson was (yawn) boring.

Really friggin' boring.

He liked to hunt.

Yawn.

He was a good husband and dad.

Yawn.

He loved his mother and bought her a new car.

Yawn.

He played no instruments.

Yawn.

He didn't study the stock market.

Yawn.

He wasn't into astronomy or knitting or Irish set dancing or bargain shopping. He wasn't the world's biggest Dabney Coleman fan and didn't travel the world following Neneh Cherry. He spoke in a monotone, stuttered over certain words, avoided eye contact. He hated dealing with the media and oftentimes made autograph seekers feel like splotches of basement mold.

He was just . . . Bo.

"Our filter at Nike with Bo couldn't be charisma," said Liz Dolan, Nike's director of public relations. "It was performance."

That's why, in the spring and early summer of 1989, Nike's brain trust enlisted the Portland-based advertising firm Wieden + Kennedy to build a campaign around Jackson and a new multisport shoe the Air Trainer SC III. Better known as the "cross trainer."

A few months earlier, Nike had debuted its first cross trainer commercials, starring Raiders defensive lineman Howie Long and Joanne Ernst, winner of the 1985 Hawaii Ironman Triathlon. Long only played one sport, Ernst was recognizable to .0005 percent of the world's population and the spots came and went with nary a ripple. Three short ads featuring Jackson followed in August 1988—one with him riding a bicycle and asking, "Now, when's that Tour de France?," another with him dunking and pondering the splendor of "Air Bo" and a third featuring Jackson walking through a city neighborhood. They were unexceptional.

"Bo was a man of few words, so that was a challenge," said David Jenkins, Wieden + Kennedy's art director. "But he was the only person in the world playing professional football and professional baseball. It was pretty clear to us that he was the ideal person to tie a cross-training shoe to."

Jenkins was teamed up with Jim Riswold, Wieden + Kennedy's creative director. The two men lobbed ideas back and forth. They knew Jackson was quiet, handsome, powerful in appearance. They knew he had a charming crooked smile. One night, while out for drinks, Tom Clarke, Nike's vice president of marketing, asked Riswold and Jenkins, "So what are you gonna do with Bo? Bo Peep? Bo Derek? Bo Diddley? Bo . . ."

(Lightbulb)

Riswold and Jenkins had once worked on a commercial for Honda's line of motor scooters starring Bo Diddley, the famed singer, guitarist and songwriter. Both men relished the Diddley experience. He was punctual, appreciative, filled with stories. So now, leaving the bar, Jenkins's thinking was all about Bo Jackson and Bo Diddley. "You know," he told Riswold before they departed, "the only thing Bo Jackson can't do is play the guitar."

A few hours later, Jenkins's phone rang. "Dave," Riswold said, "I've got it!"

"What?" Jenkins asked.

"OK, so we see Bo doing all these things," Riswold said. "Baseball, football, basketball, running. All different sports. And then at the end we show him trying to play guitar with Bo Diddley, and it's the one thing he can't do. He can't do Diddley."

By week's end the men presented the idea to Nike's advertising department. Riswold acted out the different scenes—Bo skating, Bo shooting hoops, Bo hitting a home run. Jenkins pretended to be Diddley, jamming on a guitar.

They were greeted by a second of deafening silence, followed by rousing applause.

The agreed-upon catchphrase—"Bo Knows"—was easy to say and easier to grasp. Plus, Jackson would never actually have to utter a peep. The final project featured one-second snippets of Jackson participating in eight sports—baseball, football, basketball, tennis, running, hockey, cycling and weightlifting—as a cadre of superstars from the specific endeavors note, "Bo knows [fill in the sport]" and a Diddley guitar lick plays in the background. So there was Kirk Gibson, the Dodgers slugger, saying "Bo knows baseball" after a flash of Jackson taking cuts. Then Jim Everett, Rams quarterback, saying "Bo knows football" after a flash of Jackson running the ball ("It was the shortest take ever," Everett recalled. "I threw a ball, turned, said, 'Bo knows football.' Done."). Because of injury concerns, the hockey scene—Bo in a Los Angeles Kings uniform, slamming an opponent into the boards—was filmed from the waist up, with Jackson wearing socks atop a Kansas-based gymnasium floor. Wayne Gretzky, the NHL's all-time greatest player, was scripted to say "Bo knows hockey," but, according to Riswold, "Wayne was the worst-acting athlete I've ever worked with. I told the director (Jim Pytka) to just have him say 'No' because he couldn't do the line."

In the glorious, ten-second final scene, Jackson—in a Diddley-like hat—jams on a guitar alongside the musician, butchering every note (he wasn't actually playing). Diddley points and says, "Bo, you don't know Diddley."

When the minute-long advertisement was polished and presented, Phil Knight and Co. were flabbergasted. "It was perfect," said Knight. "One of the best commercials I've ever seen."

Nike just needed the ideal time for it to air.

On the afternoon of July 5, 1989, Major League Baseball announced the top vote getters for its upcoming All-Star Game.

Will Clark, the popular San Francisco Giant first baseman and Jackson's former foe at Mississippi State, headed all men with 1,833,329 votes.

Bo Jackson, with a paltry 1,748,696, led the American League.

As soon as Nike learned the star of its brilliant new advertisement would start the midsummer classic, it paid top dollar for the commercial to run during the game. This was something of a risk—should Jackson perform well, the timing would be hailed as genius. Should Jackson strike out twice and botch a few fly balls, Nike was doomed to—*"Just do nothing"*—ridicule.

"We had to go for it," said Knight. "It was too big of a spotlight to pass up."

When he learned about leading American League voting, Jackson did what he was programmed to do—act as if he didn't care. "It wasn't a surprise to me," he told writers. "I know what I'm capable of doing." Only Jackson (hitting .263 with 21 home runs and 59 RBI) *did* care. The honor was proof that the hard work was paying off; that he could play two sports and be spectacular at both; that all the naysayers were wrong.

The sixtieth All-Star Game was scheduled for Anaheim on July 11. One day earlier members of both teams congregated at Angels Stadium for official photographs, an hour-long workout and a skills competition. Wade Boggs, the Red Sox third baseman, was changing in the American League clubhouse when he bumped into Tony La Russa, the Oakland manager/A.L. skipper. "I think I'm gonna have Bo lead off tomorrow," La Russa said, "and you'll hit second."

Boggs walked over to Jackson. "Hey," he said, "we need a handshake or something. Just to look cool after you lead off with a homer."

"Boggs," Jackson said with a laugh, "you're crazy."

The All-Star Game began at 5:42 p.m., after the full rosters were introduced, after Doc Severinsen and the Canadian brass performed "O Canada" and "The Star Spangled Banner," after a formation of F-4 fighter jets soared above the stadium. It was televised via NBC, which meant Vin Scully (the Dodgers announcer) and Tom Seaver (the soon-to-be Hall of Fame pitcher) called the action. For the first inning, however, Seaver stepped aside as Scully was joined by the onetime lead sports announcer for Des Moines's WHO 1040-AM. Or, as Scully said: "Ladies and gentlemen, former president Ronald Reagan. And how good it is to have you here in the ballpark . . ."

Six months removed from the Oval Office, the seventy-eight-year-old Reagan appeared genuinely smitten by his surroundings. An hour earlier, he entered both clubhouses to meet the players. He went man to man down the line, and after shaking Jackson's hand turned to a Secret Service agent and said, "He has a very strong grip." Now nattily dressed in a blue suit, white shirt and blue tie, Reagan's voice remained silky smooth. His presence added something to the game. A sparkle. "You know it's a great honor for me," Reagan said, "after broadcasting several years in Iowa, and now I finally make it to the big time of a top sports network broadcasting job."

The top of the first was a rocky one for Oakland ace Dave Stewart, who surrendered two runs on three hits. When the inning wrapped, then the telecast returned from a commercial break, Scully engaged Reagan by noting that the president was once a two-sport athlete himself. The ensuing presidential monologue was long and winding and unnecessary, and also detracted from the remarkable scene at hand. On the mound for the National League was Rick Reuschel, the world's most improbable forty-year-old baseball star and that week's (equally improbable) *Sports Illustrated* cover subject. The San Francisco Giants ace was, at 6-foot-3 and 250 pounds, a Stay-Puft–size man, with a flabby, flappy chin, trench ditch necklines, a Goodyear midsection and a Groucho Marx mustache. His nickname was "Big Daddy."

So as Reagan blathered away, Reuschel completed his warm-up throws to Padres catcher Benito Santiago, then looked in as Bo Jackson—white uniform, blue Nikes, muscles exploding from his calves and hamstrings—stepped up. The crowd noise was an ambient hum, and Reuschel's first pitch was a low sinker that umpire Jim Evans called for ball one.

As Jackson dragged his rear foot along the dirt, then stepped out to gather himself and take a deep breath, Reagan snapped to attention. "That Bo down there," he said. "That's a pretty interesting hobby he has for his vacation. When baseball ends and he winds up playing football. I don't know if . . ."

Reuschel's second pitch was a sinker that started knee-high and then dipped toward Jackson's feet. Only, it didn't dip nearly enough. Just as Reagan was continuing his belabored thought (". . . there's ever been anyone doing that"), Jackson drew back his bat, stepped and took an absolutely perfect swing—arms extended, barrel sweeping through the zone, weight on the rear leg. As soon as the connection was made, Jackson knew it was gone. He looked up, paused in admiration, then mini-skipped into a trot. Reuschel was also aware—he pivoted his sandbag torso and gazed grumpily toward the sky.

"Hey!" Reagan said.

"He's remarkable!" said Scully. "And look at that one!"

This was no mere home run. The baseball traveled to dead center field, where it passed over Cincinnati's Eric Davis and the 404 feet outfield wall marker before landing atop the green mesh batter's eye some 448 feet away.

"It sounded like it was hit like a golf ball," said Tommy Lasorda, the N.L. manager. "Like it was shot out of a cannon."

"There's this beautiful moment in Southern California when you're watching a baseball game, and the air is perfect, the shadows are setting in, the light makes it look like a movie set," said Alex Williams, who covered the game for the *Orange Coast Daily Pilot*. "That's the precise moment when Bo hit his home run. It was bigger than a baseball moment. It was artistic."

As the ball touched down, six spectators from nearby seats scurried atop the mesh. The first to land a hand on rawhide was Edward Novitski of nearby Ontario. But before he could take hold, Novitski was tackled from behind, and Paul Cooper, a Brigham Young University law student in a white baseball cap, white T-shirt and a blue sweatshirt wrapped around his waist, stepped in. He grabbed the baseball, then held it aloft in the air for a national television audience of 16.5 million households.

Jackson rounded the bases to a standing ovation. At home plate he was greeted by Boggs, and the men—as choreographed a day earlier—shared synchronized shoulder pats (Moments later, Boggs would homer, too). When Jackson entered the dugout, he was showered by high fives, as well as a bear hug from Twins star Kirby Puckett. "Damn, Bo-Jack!" Puckett said. "What the fuck did you do to that ball?"

Inside the National League dugout, all twenty or so players were silent. It wasn't that they were upset by the home run. These things happen. No, they were in genuine veneration. "Nobody said a word," said Tim Burke, an Expos reliever. "I looked around the dugout and our mouths were hanging open. It was Major League All-Stars being rendered speechless by something they just saw. You do not find that. If you're used to playing at the highest level, you're used to seeing great players. But this was an absolute display of something that had us stunned. It was one of the coolest things I've ever witnessed."

"He was just a freak," said Howard Johnson, a National League All-Star and the Mets third baseman. "We were all excellent ballplayers. But he was a freak."

In New York City, Phil Knight and four other Nike executives were watching the game inside Mickey Mantle's Restaurant & Sports Bar at 42 Central Park South. As soon as the baseball left Jackson's bat, the table occupants went berserk—screaming and pointing and cheering and hollering. This was the precise scenario they'd dreamed of.

"It was magical," said Knight. "Everyone is looking at us like we're crazy."

"That was pure joy," said Dolan, Nike's director of public relations. "Because we knew something the other people in the room didn't—that this Bo Jackson campaign was about to explode."

According to Nike mystique, the new Bo Knows advertisement ran after the completion of the first inning, and millions upon millions upon millions of viewers responded in *"Holy cow! Did you see that?"* ecstasy. This, however, is slight fiction. The ad was actually scheduled to run midway through the fourth inning—and it did. Which was fine, because Jackson led off the bottom of the inning with a single against Burke, then two batters later made a spectacular belly flop dive into third.

The whole day was, simply, glorious—and if the commercial failed to serve as enough of a reminder, one could spot Nike-planted BO KNOWS signs throughout Angels Stadium, or open to pages 61 and 62 of the official All-Star Game program and see a Nike advertising spread featuring Jackson in five athletic endeavors and the bold words THE JACKSON 5. When Jackson (who went 2-for-4 with 2 RBI and a stolen base) was named MVP of the 5–3 AL win, all felt right in the universe.

Within days, Nike released one of the all-time great sports posters—a beefcake shot of Jackson, bare chested, in football shoulder pads with a bat wedged over his shoulders. Three words were printed along the bottom:

THE BALL PLAYER.

CHAPTER 22

THE GREATEST YEAR II

Because Bo Jackson was Bo Jackson, and the second half of his baseball seasons *never* matched the first half of his baseball seasons, the inevitable drop-off once again took place.

Not long after the All-Star Game he was relegated to the fifteen-day disabled list with a thigh injury, and upon returning he played well, but not like a franchise-carrying superstar. His batting average dipped, his power numbers fell, any talk of an MVP run went by the wayside. The Royals won a respectable 92 games, but (in the pre–wild card era) finished 7 games behind Oakland, the eventual World Series champions. Jackson's stat line (.256, 32 home runs, 105 RBI, 26 stolen bases) was the best of his career, but the 172 strikeouts pointed to a ballplayer who continued to require some fine tuning.

Still, Nike was thrilled—Jackson had joined Michael Jordan as the faces of the company. And the Royals were thrilled—Jackson was a franchise cornerstone who made the team a must-see attraction and had certainly improved.

And the Raiders.

Well, the Raiders weren't so certain.

Unbeknownst to Jackson or the local media, midway through the Major League season Al Davis had placed a call to the offices of the Green Bay Packers, who recently used the number 2 pick in the NFL Draft to select Tony Mandarich, the offensive tackle out of Michigan State. Mandarich was widely considered the greatest offensive line prospect in NFL history—he was 6-foot-6 and 315 pounds, ran a 4.65 40, did a standing long jump of 10 feet, 3 inches and bench-pressed 225 pounds thirty-nine times. Leading up to the draft *Sports Illustrated* placed him on its cover alongside the words THE INCREDIBLE BULK.

Mandarich was everything the image-obsessed Davis craved in a Raider—a snarling, tattooed tough guy who played dirty and talked trash and was in negotiations to fight Mike Tyson (his body also happened to be overflowing with performance-enhancing drugs, not that this concerned anyone).

Oh, and who insisted he would never go to Wisconsin.

That's the main reason Davis reached out to Tom Braatz, Green Bay's executive vice president of football operations, dangling the idea of a Bo-Jackson-and-some-draft-picks swap for the rights to Mandarich.

"You'd be gaining the greatest athlete the world has ever known," Davis pitched the Packers. "All for a guy who doesn't even wanna play with you."

Braatz asked for a night to consider, and the next day he informed the Raiders that Green Bay was going to roll the dice with Mandarich.*

Davis pretended it was no big deal, acted as if he expected the slight. But in the weird, oft-warped mind of the Raiders owner—where no player was bigger or more important than the silver and black—Jackson was beginning to wear out his welcome. On the surface it made no sense. Jackson was a quiet, soft-spoken sort who hated the media and longed to run hard while walking the world in silence. But with the Nike buzz and the All-Star Game and a blizzard of Bo Knows Mania, Davis's resentment grew. The Raiders owner was a devout reader of the *Los Angeles Times* and, in particular, Jim Murray, the paper's unparalleled sports columnist. One day, during the 1989 season, Davis had to digest this Murray offering:

> The team is just kind of an afterthought when Bo Jackson comes to town. Bo and the Ten Dwarfs. The hotel lobbies are jammed with people hoping not to see the Los Angeles Raiders but to get a glimpse of Bo Jackson. It's like a John Wayne movie, a Caruso opera. The rest of the cast is unimportant.

Each word hit Davis as a rusty drill hits a raw nerve. This was not his idea of a football team.

"Everyone knew Al wasn't a Marcus Allen guy," said Terry Robiskie, the Raiders offensive coordinator. "But he wasn't a Bo guy, either. His favorite line was always, 'He's not the show. He's not coming here to be the show. This isn't the Bo Jackson Show. He's gonna be *part* of the show. He's *a piece* of the show. So we're not going to make him the superstar. We're not trying to make him the focus.'"

---

* This would prove to be an enormous mistake. Mandarich remains one of the great busts in sports history.

Davis, a team executive explained years later, shunned the idea of a franchise cornerstone. "Al didn't want a Magic Johnson type for the Raiders," said the executive. "He certainly didn't want a Marcus Allen or Bo Jackson. To Al, the Raiders were about the emblem, the patch on the eye. Really, they were about *Al Davis*. He was the face of the Los Angeles Raiders. He had an enormous ego, and he needed people to think of him first and foremost."

Because Jackson lived in a cocoon—one where televised athletics were never watched (the last thing he *ever* wanted to do was sit through a ball game)—he failed to tell the Raiders his arrival date. He never called or wrote. It simply did not occur to him. No one with the team actually knew his telephone number. There were rumors Jackson might enter the facility on October 9, then October 10. He finally showed up in Los Angeles on October 11, explained that he had been catfishing on a lake and (because he paid attention to nothing) thought all was hunky-dory. Only it wasn't. With each Nike commercial that crossed his eyes, Davis recoiled. Allen, meanwhile, made it clear to the media that he was done serving as Jackson's fullback. "My problem is, I've been such a nice guy," Allen said. "I've been trying to make everybody happy, and I've been making myself miserable."

There was also the issue of the coaching staff. With Jackson still on the diamond, the team stumbled to a 1-3 start, and Davis fired the over-matched (and horribly disliked) Mike Shanahan. The new head man was Art Shell, the offensive line coach and legendary Raider offensive lineman. At age forty-two, Shell became the NFL's second African-American head coach. And while players were relieved to be rid of Shanahan, the new chief was a bit of an enigma. As a player, he was known for a steely demeanor. He was big (6-foot-5, 265 pounds), he was tough (he started 169 games over fifteen seasons), he was church-mouse-quiet with a gaze that could kill. As a coach, those attributes didn't necessarily translate. Shell did, however, have three important factors in his favor: (a) he wasn't Mike Shanahan; (b) he allowed players to sit on their helmets; and (c) Al Davis knew he could walk all over him.

Scratch that—four things . . .

(d) Bo Jackson

Davis's plans to knock Jackson down a few pegs were eradicated when Allen suffered a torn ligament in his right knee the week before Bo's arrival. As a result, Jackson was forced into immediate action, and on October 15 he carried the ball eleven times for 85 yards and a touchdown in a 20–14 victory over Kansas City. It was, once again, transcendental stuff—Jackson had practiced three times, twice without pads. "I probably thought it was a gimmick when he got there," said Bob Golic, a veteran nose tackle in his first season with Los Angeles. "Who practices three times and runs over an NFL defense? Well, Bo did. Because he's not fucking human."

Ever since he decided to play both sports professionally, most of Jackson's football achievements had been obscured by those on the diamond. Outside of the 1987 *Monday Night Football* game against the Seahawks and a stampeding of Denver safety Mike Harden, one would be hard pressed to pinpoint *"Oh my lord!"* gridiron moments that stuck in the American psyche. Some of this likely had to do with the visibility of the endeavors—a baseball player's face is exposed. He stands at the plate alone, in the outfield alone. Football, by comparison, is bloblike. A running back takes the pitch and vanishes into an ocean of similarly outfitted behemoths. "In football," said Greg Townsend, the Raider defensive lineman, "it's hard to get noticed."

On October 29, the Raiders hosted the Washington Redskins, and Jackson made his first start of the season. The opening half came and went with little note from the halfback—Jackson ran for 9 yards and his team held a 17–10 advantage.

Los Angeles received the second half kickoff, and began with first and 10 from its own 20. The unit lined up in the I-formation—Jackson deep, behind fullback Steve Smith and quarterback Steve Beuerlein. The first play was a handoff up the middle, and Jackson followed guard Steve Wisniewski for a gritty 7-yard pickup. On second and 3, Jackson and Smith stood side by side—fullback to the left, Jackson to the right.

"Blue 27!" Beuerlein barked.

Then again, "Blue 27!"

On those repeated words, Jackson jogged three steps to his left. Beuerlein yelled "Hut!," took the snap and immediately pitched to his on-the-move halfback. What ensued is a scene that combined football with the wildness of a 1970s grade B kung fu film. Smith (*hiyah!*) dove into the knees of Wilber Marshall, the incoming outside linebacker, and Jackson sprung loose. However, a pair of Redskins—middle linebacker Greg Manusky and free safety Todd Bowles—closed in for the stop. In a move that needs to be seen six or seven times to fully appreciate, Jackson headed directly toward the men and swiveled his hips and shoulders left without actually turning in that direction (*kiai!*). Bowles and Manusky launched their bodies toward the anticipated spot as Jackson stutter-stepped, pranced right then—BOOM!—exploded past both fallen corpses (*eeee-yah!*).

The next Redskin with a shot was Alvin Walton, the strong safety who sprinted forward from the center of the field. Walton extended his arms, leapt toward Jackson's hip, tried to grab hold—and was tossed aside (*kyup!*). "I hit him good—really good," Walton said. "But he wasn't going down." Cornerback Brian Davis arrived late, but could only tickle Jackson's ankles. "He was too much for one man to bring down," Walton said. "And too much for two."

"Bo Jackson rang guys' bells when he ran over them," said Robiskie. "He would lower his head and run over them and they'd wind up with a concussion. That run, which might be the best of all his runs—a lot of bells were rung."

Jackson bolted 73 yards down the field and for the touchdown. In the celebratory aftermath he jogged 10 yards out of the end zone and flipped the ball over his shoulder. The stadium's PA system blared Otis Redding's "I Can't Turn You Loose" while Tim Brandt, the CBS play-by-play commentator, bellowed, "And Bo knows he's gone!"

BO KNOWS FOOTBALL read the Jumbotron.

The Raiders won, 37–24, and Jackson totaled 144 rushing yards on 19 carries (a 45-yard fourth-quarter touchdown run was called back after a penalty). It was only his second hundred-yard day as an NFL player, and he later admitted the extra drive was supplied by Dexter Manley, the All-Pro defensive end who, early in the game, threatened to gouge out Jackson's eyes.

"Look," Jackson lectured Manley. "You shouldn't wish bad things on people because bad things can happen to you."

The run became Jackson's latest football moment. It was shown on endless replays, incorporated into a Nike commercial. "It was like, 'OK, we have a man who can't be stopped, and here's the proof,'" said Jeff Jaeger, the Raiders kicker. "Then you just counted all the Redskins who had Bo's cleat mark on their chests."

Davis was supposed to be happy. Under Shell's stewardship, his team won three of four, and Beuerlein and Jackson played brilliantly. But he turned pouty and irritable. Davis wanted to win—on *his* terms, with the TV cameras surrounding *him* afterward. Bo Jackson felt like the biggest story in sports. Not the Raiders. Not Al Davis. "Al couldn't deal with that," said Robiskie. "He was like a father to me. But his ego was very fragile."

Even worse, Davis was repulsed by Beuerlein, and not in the I-don't-like-mushrooms-on-my-pizza way of being repulsed. He had been Shanahan's preferred quarterback, and that was enough to damn him to the pits of hell. Beuerlein was a soft thrower who depended on touch over power. To

Davis, those attributes were unbearable. Even when Beuerlein played well, as he did against Washington, Davis refused to offer anything but venom. "Al hated me," Beuerlein said. "I never fully understood why, because I played hard and loved being a Raider. But he made it his mission to make my days miserable."

It was a weird time to be the Raiders owner. The team was surging without the discarded Shanahan (terrific). Beuerlein was the entrenched starter (bummer). Jackson was a mega-megastar who—on the back of a 73-yard touchdown run—was being hailed the team's new lord and savior (bigger bummer).

One week later, the Cincinnati Bengals traveled to Southern California and Jackson pieced together yet another monster performance, running for 159 yards and 2 touchdowns on 13 carries. "Bo," said Sam Wyche, the Bengals coach, "is as advertised." The gem of gems came in the first quarter, when he took a pitch, followed a Smith block to the sideline, blazed past Rickey Dixon, a speedy safety with a clear angle, and rambled 92 yards to the end zone. "I'm not trying to cut down the Bengals," Jackson later said, "but the holes [my offensive line] gave me, you could've driven a truck through 'em. My grandmother could have run through those holes." As he reached pay dirt, Jackson pulled out two imaginary six-shooters, fired them into the air then returned the (invisible) firearms to their (invisible) holsters. He was the first man in NFL history to have two 90-yard runs in a career, and was averaging 7.4 yards per carry.

Yes. *Seven point four.*

A couple of days later, Steve Bisheff of the *Orange County Register* wrote what most surely thought:

[Bo Jackson] is the best I've ever seen. The finest athlete of our time. No, make that of any time. Jim Thorpe, Jackie Robinson, Jim Brown and anyone else people care to mention in the same breath now have to be brushed aside. Next to Bo, they all seem to have been playing in slo-mo.

Bo Jackson belongs on his own pedestal. Don't put him in the Hall of Fame. Put him in the Louvre.

The problem with the 1989 Raiders is they were constructed by people (aka: Al Davis) who drank far too much coffee. Loaded with explosive individual performers (Bo! Marcus! Tim Brown! Howie Long! Willie Gault!), the inner-workings were soft. The Raiders didn't tackle well. Their corners were long in the tooth. They were sloppy and undisciplined. Davis knew what he wanted, and—dammit!—that's what he would get. Even if he were stuck in football past and savvier execs were running laps around Los Angeles.

"One day early on, I saw Al Davis and I said, 'Hey, Mr. Davis! How are you doing?'" recalled Golic. "Al looked at me and snarled, 'I ain't won a goddamn Super Bowl since 1984. How the hell do you think I'm doing?'"

Just as Los Angeles is a city of a thousand neighborhoods, the Raiders were a team of players going in a thousand different directions. There was little cohesion. Few off-the-field events. Jackson, for all his splendor, never uttered a word (literally not a single word) to most members of the roster. It was nothing personal—he was a to-himself guy who turned down nearly every interview request. "We had a tight locker room when we were together," said Mike Dyal, a tight end. "But I wouldn't say we all hung out together. It wasn't that type of team. And Bo just did his own things."

The back-to-back wins over Washington and Cincinnati were fool's gold. The *Los Angeles Times* ran a lengthy piece chalking up the newfound success to Shell's leadership ("Art is on the same par with Gen. George Patton and John Madden!" raved Lester Hayes, the veteran cornerback), ignoring the fact that his greatest strength was *not* being Mike Shanahan. He was an ordinary coach, with an ordinary team, and though Jackson stood out in back-to-back losses at San Diego (21 carries, 103 yards) and Houston (11 carries, 54 yards before leaving with a thigh injury), there was only so much he could do.

By the time Allen returned for a December 10 home meetup with the lowly Phoenix Cardinals, nobody was quite sure what to make of the Raiders. Because he insisted he would never again play fullback, Allen was listed as Jackson's backup. The general presumption was the men co-existed well and worked as a tandem. Which was sort of true, sort of naive. Allen rightly saw Jackson as an interloper on what had been his team. And Jackson later admitted he believed Allen talked garbage behind his back. "We get along fine when I'm there," Jackson said. "[But] I don't know what goes on when I'm not there. I've heard comments from his friends . . . I know he talks to his friend about this and that. But I don't worry about that."

One day, during a practice, safety Eddie Anderson mocked Allen, screaming in front of the team, "Hey, Marcus! Hey, Marcus! How does it feel to have a guy come in only half a year and make more money than you do?"

It was all in good fun, but Allen was humiliated and sulked off the field. "It stung him," said a Raider teammate. "Marcus had pride."

Interestingly, Allen's reappearance served as a reminder that he was the far more beloved player. As Glenn Dickey noted in his excellent book *Just Win, Baby*, Jackson "was sometimes a divisive factor, because he played only part of the season and because he had a tendency to come out of a game with what others regarded as minor injuries." The Raiders actually took two team photographs in 1989—the first shortly after breaking camp, the second a few days after Jackson arrived. "They explained to us the picture was worth more money with Bo in it," said Timmie Ware, a Raiders wide receiver. This did not play well.

Todd Christensen, the longtime tight end who was cut during training camp, viewed Allen as a brother, Jackson as an intruder. "Marcus is, to use a Hebrew term, a real mensch," Christensen said. "I saw him catch five passes in one game when he had a broken wrist—you could see the cast on his arm. Contrast that with Bo, who won't play because he has a sore tonsil."

Allen was one of the best blockers anyone had ever seen. Jackson wasn't a good blocker or a bad blocker—he was an absentee blocker. Refused to do it. Allen was willing to cross the middle of the field to catch any/all passes thrown his way. Jackson often had alligator arms, and surprisingly slippery fingers. Allen was an astute student of the game who could recite the playbook forward and backward. Jackson wore sunglasses to film sessions, and often fell asleep in the back row. "It's boring as shit," he complained. "We watch the same films 12 times per week." Were one to poll every member of the roster—*Marcus or Bo?*—it wouldn't have been close. "When I start ranking backs, first there's Marcus Allen, then there's Bo Jackson," said Trey Junkin, the tight end. "Bo was great, but Marcus was special. He could play any position on the field except the offensive and defensive lines. He did anything you asked. He was a leader, he was selfless, he was giving. Marcus made it impossible to hate Marcus."

"Bo wasn't human, he was a specimen," said Robiskie. "But I don't think Bo could play basketball. I don't think Bo could play golf. Marcus could do everything Bo did, only better. I always told people that if Marcus was in a phone booth and police were trying to arrest him, they better send in three officers. Because two wouldn't be fast enough to touch him."

The most conflicted was Davis, who fumed earlier in the year when Allen sat out training camp in an effort to earn the same money Jackson was receiving (Allen made $1.1 million for sixteen games, Jackson $1.356 million for eleven), as well as a contract extension. On the one hand, (Davis felt) Jackson's stardom was out of control and overshadowing the franchise. On the other hand, (Davis felt) Allen had no appreciation for all the organization had given him. Alas, Davis was stuck. He couldn't root for and against both of his featured backs.

The Raiders beat the Cardinals, 16–14, in an ugly game won when Allen sky-walked through the air for a one-yard plunge into the end zone. It was a far-from-satisfying afternoon for Allen, who only carried four times for 10 yards (Jackson, by comparison, ran for 114 yards on 22 carries), but it served as a reminder that the Raiders still had two star halfbacks on the roster.

Alas, the season once again ended with a thud. Los Angeles dropped its final two games (to Seattle and the Giants), and finished 8-8 and out of the playoffs for the fourth-straight year. Losing, however, failed to extinguish what had been a legitimately remarkable span for Jackson. Though he only played in 11 games, he ran for a team-best 950 yards and 4 touchdowns.

He was one of America's most famous athletes, and certainly its most marketable.

There was, after all, only one premiere two-sport phenomenon.

Until there were two.

CHAPTER 23

PRIME TIME

Bo Jackson started it.

That might sound juvenile, like two tykes fighting over Oreo cookies on the playground. But in this case, it's true.

Bo Jackson started it.

The reasons are probably a bit too deep to fully unfold here, but one should never overlook the latent power of insecurity upon an athlete's drive toward greatness. When it came to insisting he didn't care what teammates thought, what fans thought, what the media thought, Jackson was a Hall of Fame–level performer. He easily blew off criticisms, and treated reporters as flecks of dust atop his shoulder.

"I'll never forget the one time I tried to interview him," said Steve Mc-Gullam, a reporter for SportsChannel. "He was facing sideways with his legs propped up on a second chair, while holding a coffee and the *USA Today* sports pages, chewing a straw. I introduced myself and asked if he had some time to answer a few questions. He never looked over or acknowledged my presence in the slightest. It was as if I wasn't there."

McGullam's plight was one of a thousand.

But this was different. From the time he emerged as a two-sport megastar at Auburn, Jackson had worn the crown as America's one-of-a-kind athletic phenomenon. It was his title, and his title alone, and anyone who dared threaten it . . . well, no one would dare threaten it.

Until one day in February of 1989.

When Prime Time came to Fort Lauderdale, Florida, spring training home of the New York Yankees.

That's how he referred to himself. As "Prime Time." And "Prime." For four years, Deion Sanders had excelled as a defensive back and kick returner at Florida State, twice earning All-American honors and gaining national attention for his flamboyant mannerisms, his lavish jewelry, his sunglasses and high hats and fruit punch–hued outfits. Far less known was that Sanders also excelled on the diamond (Scouting report from Junior Ingram of the *Pensacola News Journal*: "Steady bat, outstanding defensive skills and the kind of speed only the very fast could comprehend."), and had been selected out of North Fort Myers High by the Royals in the sixth round of the 1985 Major League Draft (he was not interested). He played a year and a half of baseball at Florida State, and in 1988 was drafted by the Yankees in the 30th round. As was the case when Kansas City tabbed Jackson in 1986, it was a longshot that worked out. Sanders signed, and spent part of that summer in New York's minor league system. "The young man," said George Steinbrenner, the Yankees owner, "can be a star."

The following February, while waiting for the upcoming NFL Draft, Sanders was invited to Major League spring training. He arrived on February 24, sporting a long black leather coat, seven large Louis Vuitton bags and roughly fifteen pounds of gold necklaces cascading down his chest. "The first time I saw Deion he was with the Yankees, wearing a Mr. T starter set," said Tim Leary, a longtime Major League pitcher. "Gold chains, sunglasses, ice all over. I said, 'Who is this fucking clown?'"

Sanders represented everything late-1980s Major League Baseball was not. Sanders was *me-me-me*. Baseball was *us-us-us*. Sanders was "Let me tell you what *I* did." Baseball was "Listen to what *we* did." Sanders was celebratory after a win, casual after a loss. Baseball was magnanimous after a win, somber after a loss. Before his client reported, Eugene Parker—Sanders's agent—requested the Yankees bestow upon the newcomer a low uniform number (as opposed to the 67s and 74s given to minor league scrubs). He was presented with number 30—which for thirteen years belonged to Willie Randolph, the recently departed second baseman. "Get that number off his back!" Ron Guidry, New York's ace, screamed across the spring training clubhouse. "He hasn't earned that!"

From 208 miles away at the Royals' complex in Davenport, Jackson paid surprisingly close attention to Sanders's trial by fire. He hated what he was hearing, and waited for someone to ask his opinion.

On February 24, he was approached at his locker by Jerry Greene, the *Orlando Sentinel*'s lead sports columnist. Sanders, according to Jackson, was a hot dog and a flake. "He's got to decide if he's going to get by on his mouth or his talent," Jackson said. "The stuff he got away with in college just won't work in the pros.

"He doesn't know what real life is all about. Real life is being a professional in every sense of the word. If he tries some of that badmouth stuff in the NFL, they'll cut him in half."

Because spring training is interminable, the blossoming Bo v. Deion rivalry was media catnip. When asked about his new critic by *Florida Today*'s Peter Kerasotis, Sanders refused to mince words. "I think I can do anything I want," he said. "I think I can play for the Lakers if I had the chance. I'm tired of hearing Bo's name. The only thing he has on me is age."

The press was immediately all over this one. When the clubhouses opened midway through Reds-Royals at Baseball City on March 18, a fleet of reporters went straight toward Jackson. Sanders's latest sentiments were relayed.

"Fuck him," Jackson said. "I don't wanna talk about him. Deion Sanders is too big for me."

Glenn Miller, a reporter for the *Fort Myers News-Press*, mentioned he was from Sanders's hometown.

"I'm sorry," Jackson said.

A pause.

"Deion should take some advice from someone who knows what's out in the world," Jackson said. "Like somebody said, it's better to sit, look and listen and be thought a fool than to open your mouth and remove all doubt. I got nothing else to say."[*]

Later that summer, when Jackson was a BO KNOWS megastar and Sanders was slumming with Triple A Columbus, *Sports Illustrated*'s Dave Scheiber traveled to Ohio to profile the not-so-prime-time Prime Time. Five months had passed since Bo v. Deion, and the scribe was curious how Sanders felt about it all. The ballplayer was . . . confused. He admired Jackson. Wanted to be like Jackson. "He's always saying, 'The Kid,'" Sanders complained. "The Kid this. The Kid that. At this stage of my career I feel I'm so far ahead of where he was. He says, 'The Kid needs to be quiet,' Well, I think he's just jealous that somebody else is trying to do what he's doing."

Sanders stood correct: Bo Jackson was, indeed, jealous. He didn't admit such a thing, but beneath the rugged exterior and brooding manner was a man who valued his own mythology. When he snapped bats over his legs, Jackson never smiled or smirked or reacted in any way. Why? Because to do so would—to Jackson—reduce the value of the moments. Ballplayers who accomplished mighty feats were impressive, but ballplayers who accomplished mighty feats without so much as flinching—*that* was something. That's why he had no use for men like Reggie Jackson and Jose Canseco

---

[*] Jackson was sort of correct. The actual quote, attributed to Abraham Lincoln, is "Better to remain silent and be thought a fool than to speak and to remove all doubt."

and Sanders—publicity-obsessed showboats who needed to tell the world all about their splendidness. Jackson loved the looks fans flashed when he did things they couldn't. Mouths agape. Eyes wide. Holy crap. But talk himself up? Serve as his own hype man? Hell, no.

Only, for Sanders, it worked wonders. His agent, Steve Zucker, once referred to Sanders as "Bo Jackson with a personality"—and it was sort of true. But so what? Jackson didn't need to twist and shout to prove himself. He launched baseballs 500 feet and ran for 90-yard touchdowns. Deion Sanders? Please. Yes, he was a gifted football player who was selected by the Atlanta Falcons with the fifth pick in the 1989 NFL Draft. But as a ballplayer, Sanders was garbage. In fourteen games as a September call-up, he hit .234 for the Yankees. Plus, he was insufferable doing so.

When the 1990 Major League Baseball season began following a thirty-two-day lockout that wiped out most of spring training, Bo Jackson was no longer one of one.

He was still special, of course. Still a unique blend of power and speed.

But a bit of the uniqueness had vanished.

Sanders, who starred as a Falcons rookie the previous fall, cracked the Yankees' opening-day roster as a pinch runner and defensive replacement. He started his first game in left field vs. the Texas Rangers on April 14, and although he went 0-for-4 against Nolan Ryan and Gary Mielke, no Yankee Stadium seat emptied when Sanders stepped to the plate. "He was," said Matt Nokes, New York's catcher, "an electrifying presence."

Bo Jackson paid attention. Sanders was the fly in his tomato soup. As Prime Time was receiving love from the New York media (he was a character on an otherwise dreadful Yankee team), Jackson was actually taking some bullets in Kansas City. First, he used the time between football and baseball to return to Auburn's campus and complete correspondence courses in pursuit of his family and child development degree (he was 23 credits short). This led to the understandable question, "Does he have *any* interest in learning the game?"

Then there was the matter of money. Jackson was arbitration eligible, and submitted a request for a $1,900,001 contract for the 1990 season. The Royals countered with a $1 million offer, prompting Richard Woods, Jackson's agent, to say, "I use as a barometer Joe Carter. If Joe Carter is worth over $3 million, Bo Jackson is worth more than Joe Carter." It was one of the dumbest things a modern-era agent had ever suggested—Carter, the twenty-nine-year-old Padres slugger, had driven in more than 100 runs three of the past four seasons. He was steady and upbeat and (ahem) didn't swing wildly at every other off-speed pitch. "I don't know if Woods has watched so many Nike commercials that he doesn't know Diddley," wrote Gib Twyman in the *Kansas City Star.* "But Bo Jackson is not worth more than Joe Carter. Nell Carter, maybe. Maybe Jimmy Carter. But not Joe Carter."

Jackson lost the arbitration case. He also began the season on the cover of *GQ Magazine*—the subject of a widely read story by Alan Richman that made him sound whiny, unappreciative, incurious and moody. "I actually liked him," recalled Richman. "What I remember most is the baseball writers who covered him hated me being there, because he gave me time and he gave them none. I don't think I've ever been so unliked by a small group of people. But Bo clearly made their lives difficult. I can't blame them."

Linda, now his wife of three and a half years, would give birth to the couple's third child, a daughter named Morgan, on July 21, and that was wonderful. But otherwise, it all sort of stunk. On April 24, his mother, Florence, underwent exploratory surgery at a hospital in Birmingham, where several tumors were found and removed. The Royals were in Milwaukee, and the next morning Jackson caught a 6 o'clock flight to Atlanta, then a puddle jumper home. He arrived at the hospital, and couldn't believe the sight before him. "She was helpless," he said. "With tubes up her arms, tubes up her nose, and she was in pain." Jackson pulled up a chair alongside Florence's bed, held her hand and . . . waited. Through the years, Jackson had distanced himself from some of his kin. A good number of his siblings were casual acquaintances. It's the way these things often go with big families. Lives move in different directions. But now, as tears welled in his eyes, Jackson acknowledged it was the first time he had cried—*really cried*—since Greg Pratt's death at Auburn. "The more I looked at her, the more I realized how important your family is," Jackson said. "How your family's health and well-being is more important than anything else that's out there."

He wound up staying in Bessemer for four days, caring for Florence and cleaning the house. While home Bo learned that his oldest nephew, Ron, borrowed (without asking) his favorite pistol, a nickel-plated .38 with a rubber grip that he kept in his mother's bedroom. Perhaps it was the emotions of seeing Florence hospitalized. Perhaps it was the anger of having a cherished possession taken. Whatever the case, Jackson headed down to his nephew's high school and ordered the principal to have Ron delivered to the football coach's office.

Upon entering, Ron (who went by "Skip") was shocked to see his famed uncle.

> BO: "Hey, Skip."
>
> RON: "Hey, Uncle Bo. What are you doing here?"
>
> BO: "Skip, have you seen my pistol?"
>
> RON: "No. What pistol are you talking about?"
>
> BO: "My .38 that's been hanging on Mom's bedpost for the past four years."
>
> RON: "No, I ain't seen it."
>
> BO: "Don't lie to me, Skip. Please don't lie to me."

Ron insisted he knew not whereof his uncle spoke.

> BO: "I'm gonna ask you one more time. Where is my pistol?"
>
> RON: "I told you—I ain't seen your pistol."

Jackson rose, punched Ron in the face, slammed him into the nearby bathroom, grabbed him by the collar, pushed him up against the concrete wall.

"Bo! Bo!" the principal screamed. "That's enough! Bo!"

It wasn't.

"I busted his mouth, busted his lip," Jackson said. "Then I had to sit down and talk with him, because with everything that [went on] in the past week, Mom didn't need to be worried with no crap like that. Then I made him go back to class."

When Jackson returned to Kansas City five days later, the scene was also downtrodden. Predicted to contend for a World Series title, the Royals were a sloppy, undisciplined team with far too many key contributors three or four years past their prime (George Brett, now thirty-seven, started at first; Frank White, thirty-nine, started at second). "We had talent," said Brent Mayne, a rookie catcher. "But *a lot* of guys were on the way out." To take advantage of his speed (and make up for the soon-to-be thirty-five-year-old Willie Wilson's reduced range), Jackson was now starting in center.

Worst of all, for Bo, was John Wathan, the manager. Jackson simply did not respect his authority, and was particularly displeased on the night of April 21, when the Royals lost at Toronto, 5–1. Jackson had made the final out of the eighth inning, so when Kansas City prepared to bat in the ninth, he knew his odds of another at bat were slim. When pinch hitter Jeff

Schulz whiffed for the second out, Jackson walked down the tunnel toward the clubhouse. After the game he and Linda were going to drive to Buffalo to visit an infirm relative, so he wanted to make as swift an exit as possible.

The next day, however, Wathan called Jackson into his office. "We need you to be a team leader," the skipper said. "You can't be that selfish."

The steam rose from Jackson's ears.

"Listen," he said, "my wife is out there waiting on me, and I'm always going to be the first one off that fucking field and the first one undressed and in the shower and dressed and out of here. I don't care what you say, or what my fucking teammates say, because I'm a team player out on that field. But once we leave that field, fuck everybody I work with, because I am not going to take that shit home with me. I'm not going to sit up in the locker room and just emote over a fucking loss. If you're trying to use me as a scapegoat to let off your frustration, you're barking up the wrong fucking tree."

Wathan interrupted. "The thing is Bo, we really need more leadership . . ."

Bo didn't know leadership.

"I don't wanna be a fucking leader on this team," he said. "You've got too many pussies on this team. You got too many babies. You baby too many fucking guys around here. Wanna know why we aren't winning? You got too many small-assed brats on this team."

A day earlier, Kevin Seitzer—Jackson's baseball nemesis—complained to Wathan about Bo shooting arrows through the clubhouse. He wasn't the only player with the beef. From Brett to White to Wilson, nobody enjoyed having to dodge objects that could *kill you*. So the manager sent John Mayberry, the Royals hitting coach, to take care of it. "That," Jackson said of both Wathan and Seitzer, "is what I mean by 'pussy guys.'"

"In that case, Bo was right," said Steve Jeltz, a Royals infielder. "Nobody would ever say anything straight to Bo because they were too scared of him. He was a nice guy, but too many people found him intimidating and didn't approach directly."

A moody Bo was an irredeemable Bo. He always seemed grumpy and on edge. One teammate referred to him as "a bully—he was bigger than you and stronger than you, and he knew it." During a game against Cleveland, Buddy Biancalana, the former shortstop now doing color commentary for KMBZ Radio, suggested that Jackson appeared distracted. Afterward, Jackson tracked his onetime teammate down and threatened to beat him up. "He was gonna knock the crap out of me . . . *for a comment during a broadcast*," Biancalana said. "He definitely could have."

Throughout much of the season, Jackson broke up the boredom of day-to-day baseball life with scattered sit-down interview sessions with Dick Schaap, the veteran journalist hired by Doubleday to co-author an autobiography that would be titled *Bo Knows Bo*. The Q&As were all recorded by Schaap, then transcribed (by his son Jeremy) and converted into a 218-page book. Some of the talks were endearing—Jackson couldn't lavish enough love upon his wife and children. Some of the talks were educational—Jackson's approach to running the football, his thinking at the plate. But much of it was *angry*. Bo hated Wathan, hated John Schuerholz, hated Kevin Seitzer, disliked Willie Wilson and had little to no patience for most of his teammates or, for that matter, the planet's seven billion inhabitants. He found the Royals to be second rate, and still wasn't over the arbitration loss. For the first time in his three-plus-year Major League career, Jackson seemed to dislike baseball. At the All-Star break he was hitting .269 with 16 home runs and 49 RBI, solid numbers but not good enough to make the A.L. team.

During the two-day gap he stayed home in Leawood, Kansas, with Linda and the kids, hoping there was something salvageable in a season gone bad.

Back in 1986, Ed Allen was pretty sure he'd seen most everything baseball had to offer.

The Royals' third-round draft pick four years earlier, Allen spent his time in the minors bouncing from city to city and league to league. He was one of those guys who was good enough to hit professional pitching, but not good enough to *consistently* hit professional pitching. So he tried his best, failed more than he succeeded (a lifetime .240 average), and soaked in the splendors of life as a 20-something ballplayer.

"A lot of it blends together, because it's one game after another," said Allen, who went on to become an elementary school teacher. "But sometimes you see something so amazing, it sticks."

That something occurred in the summer of 1986, when Allen was the starting right fielder for the Memphis Chicks. The team was playing at Charlotte's Crockett Park, and an Orioles hitter slugged a ball to deep left. The outfield wall was approximately ten feet high, and Jackson turned and sprinted. Then—"and I'm not lying or exaggerating," Allen insisted—Jackson ran up the wall, caught the baseball, ran down the wall. "He scaled the thing," Allen said. "Like a real-life superhero."

Because the 1986 Charlotte O's averaged 17 fans,* few bore witness to

---

* OK, about 400.

the splendor. The moment came, the moment went, the moment vanished from time.

But four years later, on July 11, 1990, the Kansas City Royals traveled to Baltimore to face the Orioles. It was a game no sane fan would pay to see. At 38-45, lowly Baltimore was in fifth place in the American League East, nine out and going nowhere. The more-talented-on-paper Royals were even worse—a last-place 36-46 ball club that trailed Oakland by 15½.

The temperature was 71 degrees. A thirty-minute rain delay pushed the start back to 7:30 p.m. The pitching matchup was one only a masochist could love—Kansas City's Pete Filson (three days removed from a ⅓-inning, 4-earned-runs masterpiece) vs. Baltimore's Bob Milacki (the pride of Yavapai Community College). The listed attendance was 20,187. This was wildly inflated.

The on-field back and forth met expectations. The Orioles smacked Filson around for one run in the first, another in the second. The Royals answered back with five in the third. To his credit, Filson wasn't one to be easily ruffled. From 1983 to 1986, he had been a dependable lefty reliever for the Minnesota Twins. Then he tore the rotator cuff in his left shoulder and did the ol' bounce-around two step—spring training, minor leagues, winter ball, surgery. Traded to the White Sox. Traded to the Yankees. Released. Signed. Released again. When the Royals needed an arm to replace the injured Mark Gubicza, Filson was called up.

Leading off the bottom of the third for the Orioles was left fielder Joe Orsulak, a left-handed slap hitter. Filson reared back and threw a hanging slider. Orsulak swung, and hit the ball high and deep into the left-center gap.

It looked like it was about to fall.

It clearly was about to fall.

Suddenly, however, Jackson appeared out of nowhere like a greyhound chasing a tossed tennis ball. His legs were moving comically fast. His feet appeared to twirl like windmills. Running full speed, he raised glove toward sky and caught the ball approximately seven feet from the outfield wall.

"Bo is there!" screamed Gary Thorne, the ESPN play-by-play announcer.

However, according to $F = m\ (v/t)$ [where m is the mass of the object, v is the desired velocity and t = time], Jackson was screwed. He was running too fast, at too heavy a weight, to simply stop. He also was running too fast, at too heavy a weight to safely collide with the wall. "If I crashed," he said, "I probably would have re-injured my shoulder."

So Bo Jackson did something one simply doesn't do. Reaching the warning track, he took three stutter steps, planted his left foot in the dirt, raised his right knee and dug his corresponding cleat into the green padding—roughly five feet off the ground. Then, while still rising, he turned inward and planted his left cleat even higher—roughly seven feet off the ground. The wall shook, but Jackson kept rising. His next step—again, with his right foot—was near the wall's tippy-top. Literally, Vincent Edward Jackson walked *horizontally* across an outfield wall, his body somehow parallel to the ground. "He looked like he could have run along the wall for the entire stadium," said Filson. "I've never seen anything close to that." The Orioles bullpen was situated behind the wall, and several pitchers physically jerked back in their seats because they feared Jackson might run *into* them. With that, he leapt downward, landing on his left foot, then his right.

"Yo!" said Thorne.

The color commentator was Norm Hitzges, a veteran baseball observer. His contribution to the analysis was this: "Hahahaha."

That was all. Laughter.

Of all the crazy things Bo Jackson had done, this *had to be* the craziest. The wall wasn't even a wall—it was a chain-link fence cocooned in padding. "It gave and bent when you touched it," said Billy Ripken, the Orioles second baseman. "In our dugout after Bo's play we were looking at the wall, then wondering, 'Can a human being actually do that?' The general consensus was, 'No, a human cannot.'"

"There are some things in baseball you don't see every day," said Mark Davis, a Royals pitcher. "Maybe some things you see once a year. But that was once—ever."

Two people involved in the game (a 7–5 Orioles win) seemed unphased. The first was Wilson, who decades later swore he'd seen Jackson scale a wall during spring training. "I actually started betting guys on different teams that, during the season, Bo would run fully up a wall," said Wilson. "I made some real money off that moment."

The second was Orsulak, who tended to look at the first base coach—not the outfield—after making contact. In this case, he was running toward second when he looked up and spotted Jackson gripping the baseball. "I thought it was gonna be a triple, and then I saw I was out," Orsulak said. "But it wasn't until about ten years later that I learned I was the guy who hit the ball when Bo ran up a wall. Clearly I needed to pay more attention."

Over the next several days, dozens of Major Leaguers devoted their free ballpark time to trying to replicate Jackson's climb. The result was a comedy of pratfalls.

"That can't be done," said Johnny Oates, Baltimore's first base coach. "I went out and tried it a few days later. That was embarrassing."

"We had some really athletic guys go for it," said Erik Hanson, a Mariners pitcher. "They couldn't get three feet down."

"On our team, everyone went for it," said Steve Farr, the Royals reliever. "Most of us just bounced off the wall. Some of us didn't even get that far. It was a very clear reminder—there was Bo, and there was everyone else."

But was that true?

Was there Bo, and was there everyone else?

On July 16, five days after the wall climb, the Royals traveled to New York for a three-game series with the Yankees and Deion Sanders. Kansas City was now 39-47 and—were it not for the pitiful Bronx Bombers—clear front-runner in the American League's Ms. Cruddy Team Pageant.

New York's record was 30-54, and that was by luck. The club's best player, first baseman Don Mattingly, missed fifty games due to a crippling back injury. Its second-best player, outfielder Dave Winfield, was traded to California after it was learned George Steinbrenner, the Yankees' owner, had paid a known gambler $40,000 to dig up dirt on the slugger. Bucky Dent, the opening-day manager, didn't know how to manage, and was replaced in June by Stump Merrill, equally inadequate. "There was one game when Stump didn't realize our third baseman hit righty," said Tim Leary, a veteran pitcher. "That's a bad sign."

For the sake of this book, it would be romantic to suggest the one bright spot for New York was the exciting play of Deion Sanders. It would also be a lie. As good as Sanders had been as an Atlanta Falcon rookie in 1989 (and he was exceptional), he stunk as a Yankee. By the time the Royals came to town, Sanders was hitting .140 over 93 at bats. Despite this, he continued to defy logic and lob bombs Jackson's way. "It's hard at my position (defensive back) to play two sports," he told Phil Pepe of New York's *Daily News*. "If I was a running back like Bo Jackson, maybe . . ."

New York won the first game of the series 3–2, with neither Sanders nor Jackson making a dent. Afterward, several Yankees sent John Blundell, the team batboy, to the Royals clubhouse to have Jackson sign a few baseballs. "Bo was coming out of the shower, and he only had a towel on," Blundell recalled. "So he took the baseballs from me, leaned them one by one on his dick and signed. He did it to mess with me, but I was grossed out." When Blundell returned the autographed baseballs, he told the players, "You don't wanna know where these have been."

The Yankees and Royals were slated to meet again the following night, and once more Sanders (batting leadoff and playing center) and Jackson (batting cleanup and playing center) were in their respective lineups.

"I don't know who was pitching that night," Jackson recalled years later. "But it's gonna be the Bo and Prime Show."

The starting pitchers were Andy Hawkins for the Yankees, Storm Davis for the Royals. They are not remembered. The attendance was 26,777—also not remembered. The first batter of the game, Seitzer, flied out to right, then Kurt Stillwell flied out to center, then George Brett walked—none of that remembered.

With two outs and one on, Bo Jackson strode to the plate.

This is remembered.

"And here's Bo Jackson," said Phil Rizzuto, the Yankee announcer and Hall of Fame shortstop. "And he hit a couple in the center-field bleachers in batting practice. I mean, when he hits 'em it's a lot like the way Babe Ruth used to hit 'em. They go up high and then they start taking off . . ."

Hawkins's first pitch was a ball outside.

The second was a high fastball across the heart of the plate. Jackson swung through it—"Whoooo!" said Rizzuto.

The third pitch was fouled off.

The fourth pitch was a ball.

The fifth pitch Jackson fouled off.

"I tell you," Rizzuto said, "he has got arms and legs that are really muscular . . ."

Hawkins's sixth pitch was a belt-level fastball. Jackson stepped and swung, and as the ball rose en route to dead center, Rizzuto let out an audible moan. Sanders froze for a moment, then turned and sprinted toward the 408-foot marking on the blue wall. He leapt, grabbed the top of the wall and made a futile stab as baseball left building.

"I can't believe it!" said Rizzuto. "Man, he *is* strong."

Jackson nonchalanted his jog around the bases, but there was nothing nonchalant about it. He was inside Sanders's ballpark, tearing up the place. "Bo had a lot of pride," said Mark Gubicza. "He really did."

Jackson returned to the plate in the top of the third, with two outs and Brett again on first. The Royals were up 3–1, and Hawkins was struggling. Five years earlier he won eighteen games for the San Diego Padres, but the passing half decade had been unkind. "Andy had a very straight fastball," said Matt Nokes, New York's catcher. "He had some control and could change speeds, but his pitches were flat."

Jackson was booed as Bob Sheppard, the PA announcer, uttered his name.

"He can't keep throwing him that fastball," Rizzuto said as Jackson dug in. "He's gotta change speeds and put a little wrinkle on it."

As soon as the words left Rizzuto's lips, Hawkins threw yet another heater to the exact spot of the last one. Jackson swung, and the ball rose toward right field, and Rizzuto—as colorful a yakker as baseball ever knew—said the first thing that entered his mind: "Oh, no!"

Outfielder Jesse Barfield took about three steps, then froze. There was no point in fake pursuit. The baseball traveled three quarters of the way up the bleachers and 464 feet total. "I have never seen a right-handed hitter hit the ball that far the other way," said Barfield. "We used to call those the cheap seats. Bo gave them value."

Rizzuto had been teammates with Mickey Mantle and Hank Bauer; Elston Howard and Yogi Berra. But this . . .

"Holy cow," he said. "He just flicked his wrists."

There were boos as he rounded the bases. But not the thick, ugly boos Yankee fans reserved for Jim Rice and Dwight Evans. Listen closely, one could hear the faint sounds of amazement. Oohs and aahs. "Considering that Yankee team lost ninety-five games and everything went wrong, the stadium turned electric," said Blundell. "The power of Bo Jackson at work."

In the fifth inning, Jackson yet again prepared to hit. There was one out, and runners on second and third. Tom Seaver, future Hall of Fame pitcher and Rizzuto's partner in the booth, had just devoted several minutes to thrashing Hawkins and his "straight-as-an-arrow" pitches. As Jackson was introduced, Merrill—a squat man who stood 5-foot-8 and looked far older than his forty-six years—walked to the mound to confer with the struggling right-hander. This made no sense. The only reasonable decision was to yank Hawkins for a reliever. "He couldn't get Bo out," said Nokes. "But Stump left him in."

With first base open, the other option was to intentionally walk Jackson and pitch to Gerald Perry, the much less dangerous designated hitter. "You gotta figure the word from Stump is, 'Don't take any chances here,'" said George Grande, third man in the WPIX booth. "The base is open. Walk him."

The first pitch was a ball, far outside.

The second pitch was not a ball outside. It was yet another fastball over the plate. Jackson swung, and the orb again traveled over Barfield's head and into the right-field stands. This time none of the broadcasters said a word until Jackson was well past second base. "You don't throw Bo high," said Barfield. "Not sure how many times that needed to be reviewed."

He now had 3 home runs and 7 RBI, and New York's fans were on their feet. In the midst of a putrid season, they were finally seeing something worthwhile. And if that meant rooting for the enemy over Andy Hawkins and Stump Merrill, so be it.

Everything was going wrong for the Yankees and Sanders. The game was as an opportunity to go one-on-one against the only other ballplayer who walked his path. Sanders later admitted he knew he wasn't yet at Jackson's level. But he sought to prove they belonged on the same field.

In the bottom of the sixth, the Royals brought in right-handed reliever Mel Stottlemyre, Jr.—son of the former Yankee starter—to make his Big League debut. He was met with a warm round of applause, but quickly found trouble. Stottlemyre walked Kevin Maas with one out, then surrendered a double to Alvaro Espinoza, the shortstop. Roberto Kelly drove in Maas on a groundout, and the next man up was Sanders.

As he dug into the left side of the plate, Sanders was as threatening as a leaf. His stance was stooped and uneven—Omar Moreno in a funhouse mirror. His bat wiggled. His feet were oddly aligned. He had a nervous front-foot twitch. With the count full, Stottlemyre threw a fastball up, and Sanders—quick wrists, All-American reflexes—turned on it and smacked a line drive into the right-center-field gap. Because he was blessed with all sorts of superpowers, Jackson ran as hard as he could to his left, then leapt through the air. Only this time—unlike most times—he missed. The baseball shot past him and Jackson slammed to the grass, right shoulder first.

"It's by him!" screamed Grande, and Sanders flew from first to second. By the time right fielder Pat Tabler picked up the baseball by the wall, Sanders—helmet dislodged—was burning toward third. Tabler hit second baseman Bill Pecota with the relay, and Pecota turned and uncorked a rifle to catcher Mike Macfarlane. Were Sanders a precise baserunner, he would have beaten the throw by fifty feet. But his looping turns—while wildly entertaining—were the antithesis of efficiency. Macfarlane positioned himself a bit up the line, roughly five feet ahead of Sanders, and crouched down to make a low tag. The throw, however, bounced past him and into the glove of Stottlemyre, who was backing up. With instinct as his guide, Sanders jumped high into the air. His front leg cleared Macfarlane's glove, but his rear leg crashed into the catcher's head and caused him to flop—arms and legs sprawled like a scarecrow. Sanders somehow landed on the *opposite* side of the plate, rolled over, realized umpire Durwood Merrill had yet to make a call and crawled back to the dish at the same time Macfarlane was receiving the ball from Stottlemyre. When Macfarlane reached to tag a lunging Sanders, he inadvertently slammed the ball into the dirt and lost the grip. Sanders crawled over the catcher and pounded home with his right palm. The men were lying atop one another, and Merrill—never one to bypass the dramatic—extended both arms and bellowed, "Safe!"

Sanders stood, twice pumped his right fist, then high-fived Espinoza and Blundell while returning to the dugout.

"It was the most exciting play I've ever seen," said Blundell, who went on to a lengthy career as a Major League executive. "Because it wasn't Yankees vs. Royals. It was Bo Jackson vs. Deion Sanders."

Sanders, like Jackson one inning earlier, was graced with a standing ovation, and he returned to his dugout a hero. Suddenly the possibilities seemed endless. This kid had something. "That," said Grande, "is Deion Sanders at his best!"

As the Sanders Love Fest continued, an unfortunate sequence unfolded in center field. Jackson was slow to rise, and when Mickey Cobb, the trainer, walked out to the scene, he found a badly damaged man. Jackson's right side was throbbing. "You can't have a separated shoulder," Tabler told him. "You have a chance to hit four home runs." Jackson exited the field in excruciating pain, and dropkicked his glove midwalk. He was devastated—not only was he having the night of his life, but Sanders (friggin' Sanders) had gotten the best of him. "We were Yankees, but even we wanted to see Bo take another shot at it," said Blundell. "It was history."

Once he reached the dugout, Jackson stood on the floor and placed his hands on the top step in an effort to stretch. A nauseating popping sound filled the dugout—his shoulder escaping the socket. Jackson popped it back in. "That's enough," Cobb said. "We need to go inside."

The official diagnosis was a separated right shoulder, as well as minor tissue damage. Jackson would miss the next four weeks of the baseball season from hell.

Decades later, Sanders and Jackson developed a friendship that allowed them to laugh about the events of that night. In 2017 Jackson had his shoulder replaced and the rotator cuff reconstructed. In the days that followed, he dialed Prime Time's number. "Look here," Jackson said. "You need to call your attorneys because I'm suing you for messing up my shoulder. I'll settle with you for a lifetime certificate at Sizzler."

The two laughed.

Time heals all shoulders.

Because this is Bo Jackson, a little sprinkle of extra mythology needs to be added.

After a month on the disabled list, he returned to the Royals lineup for an August 26 matchup against the Mariners at Royals Stadium.

Pitching for Seattle was Randy Johnson, the unpredictable, flame-throwing left-hander. In his first at bat—on the *very first swing*—Jackson crushed the baseball 435 feet for a fourth homer in four straight at bats. The Royals won, 8–2.

Five days later, the Royals were in Seattle, and a few hours before the opener Johnson handed Steve Bunin, the Mariners' batboy, a soft leather football, a folded note and a Sharpie. "Do me a favor and take this over to the Royals clubhouse," Johnson said. "Ask Bo to sign it."

Bunin was terrified. "I'm wearing my white Mariners' batboy uniform," he recalled. "I'm sixteen, I've never shaved and I probably weigh a hundred and fifteen pounds. I see Bo in the middle of the clubhouse, dripping wet from a shower, wearing nothing but a tiny towel around his waist. By little, I mean waist bone to upper thigh. The towel is covering his manhood and not much else. To this day, this is the most muscular nearly naked human I have ever encountered."

Bunin gathered his nerve.

"Hi, Mr. Jackson," he said. "Randy Johnson sent me over to give you this."

Jackson opened the note, which read: *That was a hell of a shot off me last week. Big fan. Please sign. —R.J.*

Crumpling it with both hands, Jackson shoved the ball of paper into Bunin's rib cage. "Fuck that!" he screamed. "I ain't signing shit! Tell that motherfucker I'm gonna take his shit deep next time, too!"

Bunin scurried back to the home clubhouse. He knew not to bother the notoriously moody Johnson before a start, but tapped his shoulder and explained what transpired.

"Ah," Johnson said, "go back after the game."

"I don't know," Bunin whispered. "He was pretty mad."

"It'll be fine," Johnson said.

The Mariners won, 5–2, but Jackson went 1-for-3 with a run. As ordered, Bunin tiptoed up to Jackson, football extended.

This time, he was greeted by a large grin.

"No problem, kid," Jackson said. "I just get pumped up before games."

CHAPTER 24

HIP

On October 12, 1990, Timothy Finn of the *Kansas City Star* reviewed Bo
Jackson's recently released autobiography, *Bo Knows Bo.*

He did not like it.

> *Bo Knows Bo* is more than 200 pages of self-indulgent, narcissistic tripe.
> Jackson says early in the book that his nickname is short for bo'hog, the
> Southern term for a wild boar. Or should that be wild bore?
> Maybe Bo is really short for boast. The first 18 pages of this book are
> filled with testimonials from teammates, opponents, coaches and other
> athletes. They shamelessly compare Jackson to Ted Williams, Mickey
> Mantle, Secretariat, an F-16 and various other animals, aliens and im-
> mortals. Call it foreshadowing, with all the subtlety of a pitchfork to the
> forehead.

Finn's take is a bit harsh. The book, co-written by Dick Schaap, was actually a well-done as-told-to athlete autobiography that wound up perched
near the top of the *New York Times*'s bestseller list.

The larger point, however, was fair: Jackson could be a difficult man
to like.

When the Major League season ended (Jackson batted a career-high
.272 with 28 homers and 78 RBI in 111 games), he yet again refused to tell
the Raiders when he might report to camp. No one in the front office (Al
Davis, included) possessed his phone number, as did precisely zero Royals
executive. There was no good reason for this—employ*ers* (as a general rule)
know how to reach their employ*ees*. So when Art Shell, the Raiders coach,
was asked when he expected his halfback to arrive, he could only shrug
and say, "His rocket will land sometime between now and Monday."

Even when Jackson did finally show up, he carried with him the pec-
cadilloes that would have forced lesser men out of the league. For a player

four years into his NFL career, he *still* didn't really know the Raider playbook. For another, he continued to be an agnostic blocker and pass catcher. And, worst of all, he didn't work hard. Part of this was due to the ungodly merging of genetics and athleticism that allowed him to eat as he pleased and remain a rock. But through the years, Jackson had never been a grinder. He took pride in telling people he refused to lift weights, but instead of wide-eyed amazement, the better response would have been, *"Why?"* Jackson played two sports that beat a person up. There were no arguments to be made *against* maintenance. Yet he didn't run, didn't pump iron, didn't even eat healthily. He was a notorious layabout—and both organizations worried the result would be some crippling injury. "One of the things I thought about Bo," said Chris Bahr, the former Los Angeles kicker, "is that sometimes it seemed he just did enough to let people know how good he was."

Most members of the Raiders' were trying to hold on to a dream. They were in no position to criticize Jackson's methodology. But the beneath-the-breath grumblings were real. Marcus Allen was a far greater Raider than Jackson, and he busted his rear. Howie Long—also a far greater Raider, also a workhorse. Over the course of his first three NFL seasons, Jackson removed himself from three different games over injury concerns. Allen never requested off the field. *Ever.* Shell was happy to have Jackson's talent on the roster, but did he enjoy the hassle of having to reintegrate a foreign element into the foundation? No. Why, when Jackson entered the Raider locker room for the first time, several players walked past and muttered, "The baseball player is here." He held a press conference on his first day, and it was cringeworthy. Instead of warmly greeting the familiar faces, Jackson was defensive and obnoxious. When asked by a reporter "Who is Bo?" Jackson smugly replied, "You got twenty bucks?"—the price of *Bo Knows Bo*.

"Bo was not likable," said A. J. Jimerson, a rookie linebacker out of Norfolk State. "When he came in the room that first time, all the rookies were in awe. Like, 'That's Bo Jackson!' But we never bothered him because we knew Bo didn't want to be bothered. People literally told us that—'Bo does not want to be bothered.' So you wouldn't go up to Bo and say, 'Hey, man, how are you doing?' No way. And you couldn't ask him to sign an autograph, because Bo wouldn't sign anything. You know you're playing with the greatest ever. You just can't talk to him or treat him as a teammate."

When Jackson arrived the team was 5-1 and in first place in the AFC West. Although it went unsaid, many Los Angeles players felt his presence wasn't actually (cough) needed. Along with Allen, who ran for 296 yards over the first six weeks, Los Angeles' backfield featured former Buffalo Bill and Los Angeles Rams star Greg Bell (a two-time thousand-yard rusher), former Navy standout Napoleon McCallum (the NCAA's all-time leader in all-purpose yardage), fullback Steve Smith and Vance Mueller, a do-it-all hustler. "I'm the third-string tailback," Jackson said, "and I have accepted that."

It was, naturally, trash. Al Davis was not paying big bucks for a third stringer. So with Jackson's return, Bell was stashed on the injured reserve list with a phantom ankle injury. (Said Bell years later: "I was pissed. My ankle was just fine.")

Six days after showing up, Jackson played extensively in a 24–9 triumph over San Diego, coming off the bench to run for team highs with 12 carries, 53 yards and 2 touchdowns.

One moment stood out: During an otherwise nondescript scamper, Jackson was pulverized by Martin Bayless, the Chargers safety. The running back's helmet was dislodged from his head and went soaring through the air. San Diego's defenders whooped and hollered, as Jackson nonchalantly retrieved the object from the ground.

When the game ended, Jackson was asked about the play.

"That's part of my game plan," he said.

Um, what?

"I only snap three of the four buttons on my chinstrap."

Um, what?

"That way the helmet flies off. It makes you think you hit me hard. But you didn't."

Um, what?

"It's just a little psychology."

Does it work?

"Of course."

Los Angeles lost three of its next four games (much of the blame belonged to Jay Schroeder, Davis's strong-armed crush/among the league's worst starting quarterbacks), and then Jackson went on one of his tears— cruising for 117 yards on 13 carries in a 23–20 win over Denver, then 129 yards on 18 carries in a 38–31 thriller over Detroit, then 117 yards on eight carries in a 24–7 smackdown of Cincinnati. An oft-relayed criticism was that Jackson's statistics were padded by one long run per game; that the eye-popping yards-per-carry statistics were misleading. "He took your breath away," said Mark Heisler, the *Los Angeles Times* beat writer, "but when you get down to it, he wasn't very consistent."

The observation was both correct and misguided. Long touchdown runs were touchdown runs. Against the Broncos, Jackson broke free for a 62-yard scoring jaunt. Against the Lions it was 55 yards. And in the Bengals matchup, Jackson exploded for an 88-yard run—before being caught at the one-yard line by Rod Jones, a cornerback who ran the quarter mile at Southern Methodist University and boasted 4.27 speed. It was the only time anyone could remember a healthy Jackson being tripped up from behind. "Bo's fast," Jones said afterward, "but so am I."

In the final weeks of the 1990 NFL season, Bo Jackson (who ran for 698 yards and 5 touchdowns) was named to his first Pro Bowl team.

He also reached a decision: he would play one more NFL season, then walk away.

He wasn't loud about it. There was no press conference. Few—if any—of the Raiders were aware. But with age and experience, he was beginning to appreciate the finite nature of time, as well as all the experiences he was missing with his expanding family. Linda, now his wife of four years, was largely raising their three children solo, while simultaneously pursuing her PhD in clinical psychology at Auburn. Bo was sensitive to her needs and aware of the athlete wife's sacrifices. "When I leave the ballpark, I become a father and a husband," Jackson once explained. "And I don't resume that other role until the next morning."

Having been raised without a father, Jackson wore the pain of an ignored child. He didn't wish to inflict that on his own offspring. Plus, as much as he liked football, he never cherished the game. It was barbaric and brutal and left its participants in all sorts of disrepair. He'd seen retired Raiders invited back to a practice, limping on shredded knees and hallowed spines, sometimes flailing to grasp a memory that had escaped them. *What was my quarterback's name? Who was that game against? Where are my car keys?* The sport was unforgiving; the practices long and boring and graceless. Did he aspire for his sons to one day suit up and carry the pigskin? "No way," he said. "Never." Plus, while he felt a kinship with a handful of Royals (through the years a number of baseball teammates wound up on the sideline of Raider games), the same did not apply to his NFL brethren. With the sometimes exception of Long and Bill Pickel, a pair of Los Angeles defensive linemen, the Raiders were mere co-workers. Jackson much preferred the rhythms of a baseball season—beginning with the optimism of spring training and lazily winding its way through the months.

With a 12-4 record and the AFC West title, the Raiders entered the play-offs as a serious threat to reach the team's first Super Bowl in seven years. Jackson would enjoy it and hopefully raise the Vince Lombardi Trophy—then play one more season before devoting himself full time to baseball and fulfilling his destiny of becoming the next Joe DiMaggio/Mickey Mantle/Roberto Clemente (none of whom he would recognize).

As a divisional title holder and owner of the AFC's second-best record, on January 13, 1991, Los Angeles hosted 9-7 Cincinnati, the Central Division champion that destroyed the Houston Oilers one week earlier, 41–14.

On the night before kickoff, several Bengals came down with food poisoning. By two in the morning Boomer Esiason—one of the league's elite passers—was hallucinating. By three, he and a dozen teammates were attached to IVs and expunging tragic volumes of waste from multiple orifices. "I was up all night and uncertain whether I'd be able to play," Esiason said. "I don't think I've ever been that sick. I've always wondered whether Al Davis somehow food-poisoned us. It wouldn't be beyond him."

When he wasn't fretting over his legion of upchuckers, Sam Wyche, Cincinnati's head coach, was hyperfocused on stopping Bo Jackson. The *Los Angeles Times* referred to Jackson as a "Bengal Tamer." He'd faced Cincinnati two times, running for 276 yards (an average of 13.1 yards per carry). In the last two games against the Bengals, Jackson pulled off runs of 92 and 88 yards.

In the lead-up, Wyche was honest in his hopelessness. "He's so fast," he said, "that he is going to be gone before you can react."

Nike wanted to make certain its star client's first-ever playoff experience was viewed by the largest audience possible. Hence, a day before kickoff, the company purchased 9,000 tickets to the Los Angeles Coliseum, thereby ensuring a blackout would be lifted and the game could be televised in Southern California.*

The temperature was 60 degrees. It was windy, and the sky was cloudless. Oddsmakers had the home team as a seven-point favorite. Dick Enberg and Bill Walsh, the former 49ers coach, found themselves in the NBC broadcast booth. Since arriving in Los Angeles eight years earlier, the Raiders had sought out Lakers-like Hollywood buzz with little success. The team never had its own Magic Johnson, flashing a million-watt smile. It

---

* The NFL's blackout policy mandates that a game must be blacked out on local TV markets in the event that fewer than 85 percent of available seats have been sold seventy-two hours prior to kickoff.

never had the intimacy of the Forum, the sex appeal of the Laker Girls. On this afternoon, however, something clicked. The sidelines were overflowing with celebrities—boxer Evander Holyfield, rapper MC Hammer, actor James Garner. Jackson invited several Royals teammates, including pitcher Mark Gubicza and George Brett, the future Hall of Famer. The Coliseum was a centerpiece of sports and entertainment, and the main draw was Bo Jackson, backup.

Because Shell long ago abandoned the two-Heisman backfield, Los Angeles began with Allen at halfback, Steve Smith at fullback. The team's opening drive was fruitless, and after the Bengals were forced to punt on the next possession, the Raiders returned to the field with Jackson at halfback. His first carry came on second and 10 from the Los Angeles 39, and after slicing through the right side of the line and stomping over linebacker James Francis, he stumbled forward . . . and fumbled. The ball rolled from his arms and into the awaiting grasp of safety Barney Bussey. Cincinnati's defenders celebrated as if they'd won the lottery, and Walsh said, "This is what the Bengals had hoped for, and anyone who favors the Bengals knew they needed these types of things to happen."

Only, the officials blew it, deciding that Jackson had fumbled *after* hitting the ground. Despite righteous protestations from Cincinnati's staff, rules were rules. Jackson was credited with a 6-yard gain.

He didn't have another carry until early in the second quarter, when he burst through the middle of the field and was tackled after a 9-yard pickup. On the very next play, he again punched up the Bengals' gut for a second-straight 9 yarder. Then, for the third-straight time, Jackson grabbed the ball and chugged past the defensive line and into the secondary for 18 yards. After being brought down, Jackson pumped both fists in the air. "What can you say?" bellowed Walsh.

By halftime, Jackson had 43 yards on five carries, and while Los Angeles only led 7–3, there was an ominous feeling inside the Bengals locker room. "You knew what Bo was capable of doing, and you just sorta expected something amazing to happen whenever he touched the ball," said Tim Krumrie, the Cincinnati nose tackle. "You hoped for the best, you gave it your all, but you were aware that, with Bo, it was a matter of time.

"Honestly, your only hope was him getting hurt. But he seemed indestructible."

On that Sunday in early January, there was one uber-famous participant in the Bengals-Raiders game who:

- Was abandoned by his father.
- Was raised alongside multiple siblings by a belt/extension cord-wielding single mother who did not want her children playing football.
- Was highly recruited out of high school in both football and baseball.
- Played both ways on the high school gridiron, but starred at running back.
- Was brought up in an all-Black neighborhood but attended a majority-white high school.
- Scratched and clawed for everything he achieved.

There was also the Bengals' starting inside linebacker.

Kevin Walker's father, Robert, left home when his second of four children was only five, leaving Qrinne Walker to raise her kids on a bookkeeper's salary in a three-bedroom home on Yawl Avenue in West Milford, New Jersey. Though he longed to play in his town's youth football league, Kevin was forbidden by Qrinne. Instead of organized ball, he and his brother Robert would head down to the basement, slip tube socks over their sneakers and play one-on-one tackle football on the concrete floor. "I had one of those kiddie football uniforms that came in a plastic tube," Walker says. "It was a number 66 Packers jersey. Ray Nitschke. So I'd pretend to be Nitschke and we'd pound each other."

By her son's first year at West Milford High, Qrinne had a change of heart. Kevin was the freshman class president and an A student. A good kid. "I'm sure it terrified her," Walker said. "But she finally let me play."

In his first-ever prep game, Kevin returned a kickoff for a touchdown. Over four seasons he starred as the Highlanders' starting halfback and strong safety, as well as the baseball team's All-State power-hitting left fielder.

By his senior year, Walker was being recruited by many of America's college baseball powerhouses. His true passion, however, was reserved for the gridiron. "I loved everything about it," said Walker. "Wearing your jersey, putting on your helmet. Hitting. Being hit. The crowd noises. The smells. The feeling."

Walker signed at the University of Maryland as a running back. After a frustrating freshman year, his life was changed by Bobby Ross, the Terps' head coach. "Son," Ross said, "you run a 4.5. There are a lot of running backs who can run a 4.5. But I don't know of any linebackers who can run a 4.5 . . ."

As a Maryland junior, Walker noticed NFL scouts starting to take an interest. As a senior, he was one of America's best players and—with 172 tackles—leading ball hawks. When the Bengals grabbed him 57th overall in the 1988 Draft, Qrinne was overcome by emotion. "You have this dream," he said, "but you never know whether it'll really happen. Suddenly I'm playing against Dan Marino and Eric Dickerson and Joe Montana, thinking, 'Holy, cow! I've made it! I've really made it!'"

Walker did little his first two NFL seasons, but by 1990 he was starting at inside linebacker. Though never confused for Lawrence Taylor or Mike Singletary, he was a smart player who always seemed to wind up in the right spot at the right time. "Kevin was very solid," said Carl Zander, a Bengals linebacker. "He was definitely a head-in-the-game guy."

Through the first half of the Raiders matchup, much of Walker's life was devoted to keeping tabs on Jackson. Those first two 9-yard runs? The man who brought him down was Walker. That 17-yard gain? The man who missed—Walker. "We were sort of playing a variation of the Bears' 46 Defense that day, and I'd line up outside the tight end to give Bo and Marcus only one side to run," Walker said. "That doesn't mean they'd avoid my direction, but it would give them pause to head that way. If Bo got the ball and came toward me, I'd try and go right at him. If he went the other way, I was in pursuit."

The Raiders received the second-half kickoff, and started off on their own 23. On first down, with Allen behind him as the lone setback, Schroeder took a three-step drop and wildly misfired to a wide-open Mervyn Fernandez.

When the play ended, Jackson trotted back onto the field. The next call from Terry Robiskie, the offensive coordinator, was 28 Bo Reverse Left, which involved Allen lining up to Jackson's right, three steps forward. This was not the way to Marcus Allen's heart. If he said it once, he said it a hundred times: *I am not a blocking back.*

He was—for now—a blocking back.

The Raiders had wide receiver Tim Brown split far left, Fernandez far right. Tight end Ethan Horton was packed in alongside Rory Graves, the left tackle. Anticipating a run, the Bengals featured four down linemen, two safeties close to the line, linebacker Leon White directly in front of Horton and Walker—wearing number 59 with trademark blocky shoulder pads— prowling forward as Schroeder barked out the signals. By the time the ball was snapped, Walker was prepared to charge and—hopefully—cut off any advancements.

Within a second of taking hold of the football, Schroeder flipped it to Jackson, who followed Allen to the right. Walker was three steps into the backfield by the time the exchange took place, and as Jackson began his burst the linebacker tried cutting across the field in what would surely be a futile pursuit. Jackson, after all, ran a 4.17 40. Walker did not.

Allen's block on White opened a gaping hole, and Jackson squared his shoulders, raised his knees and was off to the races. "I was right there on the sideline," said Vince Evans, the Raiders' backup quarterback. "It looked like Bo was about to take it to the house." For 10 yards he sprinted untouched down the right sideline, and only slowed when Fulcher, the free safety, arrived from the far side of the field. With a quick stutter step, however, Jackson left Fulcher lunging in his vaper trail, and continued on his path toward the end zone.

Unfortunately for the Raiders, that one-tenth-of-a-second sliver in time—Fulcher stepping in, Jackson stopping-then-going—served as a delay. In that span Walker somehow returned from the depths and charged from Jackson's left. Jackson tried to keep him at bay with a left-handed stiff arm, but Walker ran through it and reached out both arms to wrap the torso. "I got on my horse from an angle and said, 'I'm gonna try and cut him off,'" Walker said. "Maybe I can get him on the ground."

It was, of course, not that easy. The running back kept heading forward, and the linebacker slid down Jackson's legs. He hung on to a right calf for dear life. "It was almost like Bo threw his torso forward," said Evans, "but the pull of the other guy pulled him back."

That's what finally brought Bo Jackson down—Herculean strength be damned, no man can run with a 238-pound anchor affixed to his calf. So as Jackson's body propelled forward, his right leg remained within Walker's grasp and his left leg (and, by extension, hip) was firmly planted in the turf. "The momentum of my body kept going," Jackson said, "and my left leg was extended to the point where I couldn't bend it and fall." By the time the play ended, Jackson had scampered 34 yards down the field. The Coliseum crowd went berserk—the Los Angeles Raiders were on the attack.

"This is just what the Bengals wanted to avoid!" said Walsh. "And just what the Raiders were expecting sooner or later to happen!"

There.

Was.

Just.

One.

Teeny.

Tiny.

Problem.

Bo Jackson wasn't getting up.

"I was one of the first over to him after the play," said Horton. "I was whooping and hollering—'Yeah, Bo! Great run!'"

Jackson, he noticed, didn't move.

"Come on, Bo!" Horton yelled. "Let's go!"

"I can't," Jackson replied stoically. "My hip—something's wrong."

As the fans cheered and the Bengals licked their wounds and the announcers offered praise, Jackson was rolling himself over, wondering what, precisely, had happened. He was quite certain his left hip popped out of the socket, so he wiggled his body and—he later insisted—popped it back in. He rose gingerly, but the pain was unfamiliar and intense. "It felt like somebody "had jabbed an ice pick up in there," Jackson said. He returned to his back, and the team's medical staffers, along with Shell, rushed to the field and surrounded him.

Once again, after several seconds, he lifted himself up, now sans helmet. Another round of cheers. It all appeared relatively normal. "He may have pulled a muscle as he was trying to pull away from a tackle," Walsh said. "Because he really wasn't hit on the knee."

Following a few clumsy steps, Jackson placed his right arm over the shoulder of H. Rod Martin, the team trainer, and his left arm over Napoleon McCallum, the running back. He was helped off the field. Once again Walsh, with a medical degree from the University of Random Guessing, diagnosed a pulled muscle.

But under closer inspection, there was reason for alarm. Bo Jackson's face was contorted. He appeared as if he were hurting. He also looked to be somewhat scared. None of this was normal. "There were tears in his eyes," said Jamie Holland, a Raider receiver. "That, I remember."

The general belief was that Bo Jackson's return was inevitable. He was constructed of cement and Tungsten, and after a few moments he would certainly grab his helmet and get back to the action. Only, that didn't happen. As Los Angeles began to pull away for a 20–10 win, Jackson entered the locker room, where the training staff cocooned his left leg from groin to thigh. "Bo knew something was really wrong," said Dan Land, a Raiders defensive back. "He wasn't naive about it." Jackson returned to the sideline, where he sat until the final gun. At one point he was approached by George Brett, gifted with a sideline pass. "Bo," Brett said, "you're OK, right?"

Jackson frowned. "Nah, George, I'm not," he replied. "I think my hip went out of the socket, then went back in."

Late in the fourth quarter, Jackson asked Mark Gubicza, also on the sideline, whether he could fetch his sons, Garrett and Nicholas, from the stands, where they were sitting with Linda. "Of course," said the Kansas City pitcher. By the time Gubicza brought them to their father, the game was nearly over, and Jackson appeared to be in shock. His face was expressionless. He said very few words. The whole Bo Knows ad campaign was fun exaggeration (he couldn't literally do everything), but Jackson considered himself to be indestructible. He could fight through any tackle, leap any obstacle. Pain was something others felt. Not Bo Jackson. Now, though, he was experiencing *excruciating* pain.

As soon as the final second ticked off the clock, Jackson—sons by his side—limped into the Coliseum's home locker room. Although Walker did nothing wrong, he sought Jackson out.

"Bo . . . Bo—I'm Kevin," he said. "I tackled you."

"I know," Jackson said.

"I'm so sorry," Walker said. "How are you feeling?"

"I'm sore," Jackson replied. "But it's no big deal. I'll be back next week."

Walker loved to hear that. "Well," he said, "I'll certainly be rooting for you."

The men shook hands, and Jackson shuffled off. "I've never spoken to him again," Walker said thirty-one years later. "That was the last time I saw him."

The Raiders were always known as a loose outfit, and the postgame locker room scene did nothing to dispute that. As soon as the injury occurred, Jackson should have been wheeled off and rushed to a hospital for testing. Instead, there he was, changing at his stall, showering, taking a handful of questions from the media before heading off on a cart. "It's a hip pointer," he told reporters. "I'm going to play next week."

It was not a hip pointer. No one (besides Jackson) said it was a hip pointer. There was no actual reason to believe it was a hip pointer. A hip pointer is a deep bruise to the ridge of bone on the upper outside of your hip. Hip pointers hurt. They don't hurt like *this*. "I had [hip pointers]," said O.J. Simpson, working the game for NBC. "They only come from a real jolt, such as a helmet hitting the spot. I saw him go down. It was something else."

Sitting in the Coliseum stands was Dr. Marcella Flores, a Portland, Oregon–based emergency room physician and the sister-in-law of Amy

Trask, an employee in the Raiders' legal affairs department. When the game concluded, Flores sought out Trask. "Amy," she said, "you better be concerned about Bo's injury."

"I don't think we're too worried," Trask said. "It's probably a bruise."

"I'm telling you, that didn't look like a bruise," Flores replied. "If I were you, I'd be very concerned about avascular necrosis."

Trask had never heard of such a thing. *Avascular necrosis?* Was that even a real injury? But she wrote it down and later approached Al Davis. "I think we might need to be aware of this," Trask said.

The Raiders owner listened. Or at least seemed to listen. Had he opened the nearest medical journal, he likely would have looked up "Avascular necrosis" and passed out. This wasn't, as Walsh twice suggested, a pulled muscle. It also wasn't, as Jackson thought, a hip pointer. Avascular necrosis, according to Cedars-Sinai, is a disease that "results from the short-term or lifelong loss of blood supply to the bone. When blood supply is cut off, the bone tissue dies and the bone collapses. If avascular necrosis happens near a joint, the joint surface may collapse."

Tony Decker, a longtime Division I athletic trainer, explained it simpler: "The blood supply to the head of the femur is disrupted. Blood is how our bones are nourished, so it leads to arthritic changes of the bone and everything becomes affected."

Back in 1990, not a whole lot was known about the condition. Some believed it could be treated with a cast. Others thought rest. A few hours after the game, Jackson went out to dinner with Linda and the children. When he rose from the table, a current shot through his hip. The next morning the Raiders had Jackson undergo an MRI (magnetic resonance imaging). He assumed the prognosis would involve rest and some sort of ice-heat healing thingamajig. Then a doctor pointed toward the image of Jackson's left hip.

"Do you see all that dark stuff?" the physician asked.

"Yes," replied Jackson.

"That's blood," the physician said, "in your hip socket."

For the first time in his twenty-eight years on earth, Jackson—who was standing as he received the news—felt light-headed and nauseous. He sat down. "Wow," he said. "I *really* injured myself."

No one—including Jackson—was 100 percent sure what it all meant. He was indestructible. Zeus and Paul Bunyan and Hercules and Superman. He didn't get injured, because Gods don't get injured. So this had to be a farce, right?

Right?

The Raiders issued a post-MRI statement: "Bo Jackson has an injury to his left hip for which he is now receiving treatment. There will be no status report until late in the week." Robert Rosenfeld, the team physician, maintained his belief it was not serious. "It's going to get well," he said before adding, "I really don't know what the injury is yet. That's the trouble." Calls to Richard Woods, Jackson's agent, went unreturned. The people at Nike were terrified. So were the Royals, who had long dreaded the inevitability of this moment.

Jackson suited up for one practice, but didn't touch the field. He was ruled out for the following Sunday's AFC title game at Buffalo, and the critics pounced. The *Santa Rose Press Democrat* ran a boxed listing of all the times Jackson had to sit with an injury (the implication: he's soft). Todd Christensen, the former Raiders tight end, was particularly nasty. "Bo Jackson's a baseball player," he said. "I can't think of a time when he played through an injury." Though Jackson certainly did not have to accompany the Raiders to Buffalo, he did so—even jogging gingerly across the field during pre-game. With the Bills up 41–3 at halftime, and the temperature a balmy 32 degrees, Jackson chose to spend the last two quarters of the 51–3 demolition inside the locker room. Again—understandable considering *his innards were bleeding*. The following day, Bob Keisser of the *Long Beach Press-Telegram* unloaded. "Bo Jackson showed his true colors Sunday in Buffalo," he wrote, "and they weren't silver and black."

Jackson read none of it. He flew back to California with the rest of the Raiders, bid a fond farewell at the airport and told a couple of his closer pals on the team he would see them "real soon."

His football career was over.

CHAPTER 25

REDUCED

On February 14, 1991, roughly five weeks after the injury, Bo Jackson found himself inside Kansas City's St. Luke's Hospital, having his left hip examined by Steven Joyce, the Royals' team doctor and a renowned orthopedic surgeon. Numerous tests were ordered—an MRI, a CAT scan, a bone scan.

The ballplayer knew what he wanted to hear: His hip was fine. He would return to being a phenomenon. His strength, willpower and devotion trumped a relatively mild malady.

That is not what Joyce had to report.

The diagnosis was a fractured dislocation of the left hip and cartilage damage in the hip socket. To be specific, it was development of early avascular necrosis—the worst-possible outcome. Bo Jackson's bone tissue was in the process of dying.

Before departing the hospital, a stunned, heartbroken and on-brand resilient Jackson urged Joyce not to disclose to the Royals the severity of the injury until the end of the business day on February 19, when his salary arbitration case was scheduled to be heard in New York. It was an awkward request—Joyce had been with the organization for more than a decade. Yet doctor-patient confidentiality laws trumped any doctor–ball club affections. "Bo did ask me not to speak to Royals' management," Joyce later explained. "It was a balancing act between being realistic with the Royals and being positive with the patient."

Thanks to the limited information, Herk Robinson, Kansas City's first-year general manager, was under the impression his star outfielder would return to full health. That's literally what Bo Jackson had been insisting to anyone who asked: I *will* be back, and I *will* be great. "Bo told me the injury wasn't anything serious," Robinson said. "I also spoke with Richard Woods and he also maintained there was nothing serious, nothing to worry about." Four days after Joyce's examination the Royals avoided arbitration and inked Jackson to a one-year, $2,375,000 contract—a $1.375 million raise from 1990. The injury, Robinson told the press, "is not considered serious," and Jackson would report to spring training, work on his recovery and be ready for Opening Day. Woods said his client was interested in signing a long-term deal with the club. "Would he listen?" Woods said. "You'd be stupid not to listen to anything."

Wrote Gib Twyman in the *Kansas City Star*: "If you are Diogenes, looking for an honest man, you needn't trudge in the direction of someone who hid his hip injury from the Royals."

On the morning of Wednesday, February 27, Jackson arrived at the team's spring training facility in Davenport, Florida. He was decked out in blue Nike sneakers, black Nike shorts, a Nike windbreaker—and silver crutches with foamy underarm padding. It was two days before his presence was required, and as he hobbled through the clubhouse entrance, teammates seemed genuinely taken aback. Was the indestructible Bo Jackson *on crutches*? Pitcher Mark Davis was one of the first to spot Jackson. He said, "Hey, Bo," then added with a laugh, "I lost another bet. I said you'd be ready by the first day."

Bret Saberhagen, Kansas City ace, waved from across the room and cracked, "Bo knows hip replacements!"

The joke bombed. "Sabes," Jackson said, "it's kind of serious."

Awkward silence.

Dick Kaegel, the *Kansas City Star* beat writer and one of the few media members Jackson didn't seem to hate, asked whether he would be ready for the April 8 opener against Cleveland.

"I don't know," Jackson replied. "We'll have to wait and see."

How were his spirits?

"I'm feeling fine," he said. "You know what's wrong."

Actually, nobody was entirely sure what *was* wrong. Jackson hadn't said a word. Joyce was gagged. Woods devoted his free time to reassuring folks his client would be ready. The team signed him to a fat new deal and expected results. Robinson appeared utterly clueless. It was all befuddling.

"I have a hip injury," Jackson said to the assembled scribes, the testiness mounting. "My main priority is getting well. I'm working now and I don't have time to talk to you guys."

With that, he changed into a black, purple and aqua wet suit and fuchsia slippers. "I'm going swimming, man," Jackson said, hobbling off toward a pool in the minor league facility. Later, he rode an exercise bike. "It looks good," said Nick Swartz, a team trainer, "from the standpoint of his range of motion."

It *did not* look good. Nothing about Bo Jackson looked good. The spectacle was pathetic. Jackson was your grandmother in a hospital bed, tubes attached to her body, face devoid of color, being told by those encircling her fading existence that she was doing *just great* and would be home in no time. John Wathan, the Royals manager, expressed hope to reporters that Jackson should start Opening Day. "It could be worse," Wathan added—only the sole way "it could be worse" was if a great white shark entered the Royals' pool and gnawed off Jackson's other leg, two arms and (for good measure) his head. This was as bad as it could get. Jackson was on crutches, pretending there was hope for a hip that was in the process of dying.

Over the next two weeks, the Royals camp morphed into Bo Jackson injury update central. Reporters from across the country descended upon the facility to behold what many seemed to believe would be another sports miracle. Though Jackson wasn't participating in team workouts, he was surely somewhere back behind the curtains—swimming, biking, lifting, turning rocks into crystals. "There were so many rumors," said Brian McRae, an outfielder. "Was he gonna lose his leg? Would he start Opening Day? The whole scene was a mess." On March 6, Jackson emerged to hold an actual twenty-five-minute mini-press conference. Wearing a black T-shirt, sunglasses and a scowl, Jackson leaned against a wall and looked out at an ocean of notepads and TV cameras.

REPORTER: "Will you be ready for Opening Day?"

JACKSON: "From the looks of things right now, if I had to choose, I'd have to say I would be ready. But I have to do what the doctors say simply because they know best."

REPORTER: "Is there any pain now?"

JACKSON: "There's no pain. I guess you can say it feels the best in the mornings when I wake up. They say that's really unusual because you should be stiff in the morning with the hip injury. But I don't get up with no problem. There's no pain."

REPORTER: "What is the exact nature of the injury?"

JACKSON: "It's a soft-tissue injury, and it's in the hip."

REPORTER: "Anything beyond that?"

JACKSON: "If it was, I wouldn't tell you."

REPORTER: "Has management or even players expressed disappointment that a football injury will impact your baseball job?"

JACKSON: "No, but are you looking for dirt?"

Beginning with the day Jackson signed with the Raiders in 1987, Royals executives had desperately wanted him to *not* play football. This was stated repeatedly—on occasion to Jackson, more often to his representatives. *What if he gets hurt?* Yet Bo Jackson refused to hear it. He was the guy who laughed at pain. Who thrived upon conquering the impossible. Much of his autobiography, *Bo Knows Bo,* was devoted to the very idea of refusing to allow naysayers to bring him down.

Many Royals—players and executives—found themselves intimidated by Jackson, and allowed him to walk over people and trample a franchise's norms. "Some would say Bo had a bully mentality," said Terry Shumpert, a Royals infielder. "And he did. But it wasn't necessarily a bad thing. He was aware of his status. You just knew not to punch Bo in the mouth." Jackson could shoot his arrows in the clubhouse because, well, who was there to say no? He could pin Kevin Seitzer against a wall and face no consequences because who was working up the nerve to reprimand him? He could play football and risk a career-ending injury because he was Bo Jackson. And you were not. "There was *always* the risk [with football]," Robinson said meekly. "Whether this is the one, I do not know."

Day by day, Jackson insisted he was on the road to recovery. And day by day, nothing supported this take. On March 15, Joyce ran more tests and, according to the *Kansas City Star,* found, "Jackson's condition worsening." That evening, George Brett, the team's longtime star, had a lengthy chat with his teammate. He was at his spring training rental, barbecuing, when Jackson stopped by. "He was as down as I've ever seen him," Brett said. "You could tell in his eyes, he was concerned for his own safety, his own health."

On the morning of Monday, March 18, Jackson flew from Orlando (where he cursed out a photographer hounding him in the airport) to Birmingham, then took a limousine to the Alabama Sports Medicine and Orthopedic Center, where his hip would be examined by Dr. James Andrews, one of the world's most respected orthopedic surgeons. Six years earlier, the Boston Red Sox misdiagnosed the shoulder injury of Roger Clemens, the team's hard-throwing ace. Clemens's agent sought a second opinion, and sent his client to visit Andrews—who correctly pinpointed a torn labrum. Word spread, and Andrews became the unofficial go-to physician when it came to professional athletic survival.

Jackson was hoping for a miracle. He had recently undergone more tests via Joyce, but the Royals doctor wanted to hold off with a prognosis until hearing Andrews's conclusions. The Royals, too, expressed eagerness to learn something—*anything*—new. "There's no point in conjecture until the entire examination process is complete," Robinson told the media. "We hope to tell everyone as much as we know about his condition on Tuesday."

Those words were uttered at approximately 8:30 Monday morning. By 3 p.m., Robinson held an official team press conference, where he stood behind a wood podium, cleared his throat, swallowed hard and read a twenty-seven-word statement: "It is with very deep regret that we announce that the Royals are asking waivers on Bo Jackson for the purpose of issuing him his unconditional release."

Wait.

What?

WHAT?!

The Royals were dumping Bo Jackson? Before word from Alabama?

What the heck just happened?

Answer: Joyce.

Shortly after Robinson's initial statement, the Royals' team doctor decided it was time to pull the GM aside and fill him in on the brutal reality: He had watched Jackson, and he had *twice* examined Jackson—and there would be no miracle comeback. His body was a Porsche 911, his left hip (and, by extension, leg) a concrete wheel. "Each succeeding test declined," Robinson said. "We were hoping for the best, praying for the best, but it didn't work out for the best."

What made the announcement all the more shocking was that Jackson—six hundred miles away in Alabama—was nowhere to be found. Robinson called Woods, his agent, to convey the news via phone *as Jackson was being seen by Andrews*. It was a classless and cowardly act. There was no reason the team could not have waited another day. Now, not only did Robinson tell Woods (as opposed to Jackson), but he held a press conference to let the world know.

"It was somewhere between awful and understandable," said Jim Eisenreich, the outfielder. "You don't treat someone that way. But he couldn't play."

"I'd been with the team for a while, and stuff like that no longer shocked me," said Mark Gubicza, the pitcher. "After we won the World Series [in 1985] they let go of six or seven bit players who were part of a great team. That was weird for me, but also a lesson about the Royals. They were a business."

A furious Jackson held his own makeshift press conference at the Alabama Sports Medicine and Orthopedic Center. With Andrews by his side, he said—in a defiant tone—"Don't count me out. I know deep down I'll be back playing baseball this year."

And this is what's remarkable about Bo Jackson. He *did* know. He always seemed to know. Even when it made no sense, and even when it defied logic. With a healthy left hip no longer a possibility and his powers fading like particles in the wind, Jackson maintained that he would regain it all.

Samson's hair grew back.

One way or another, Bo's superstardom would, too.

The next day, of course, was the saddest day.

When members of the Kansas City Royals reported to the clubhouse, they were greeted by the awful sight of Bo Jackson cleaning out his locker.

His nameplate had already been removed. Some cardboard boxes surrounded his stool. One by one, his former teammates filed in, looked toward the untoward scene, then looked away. This was a car crash—and in-their-prime athletes don't do car crashes. It's a reminder of the mortality one works to suppress. A blink ago, Jackson was throwing out Harold Reynolds, homering off Rick Reuschel, climbing the wall in Baltimore. Now, he was incapacitated. Shrunken. Useless. "We could pretend," said Bob Schaefer, the bench coach. "But he wasn't Bo Jackson anymore." Dark sunglasses covered much of Jackson's face, though one could spot tears streaming down his cheeks. He sat, and propped his left leg upon a chair and leaned his crutches toward the side. Several media members gathered around, and he accepted their collective presence less as hostile invaders, more as pallbearers. "I've had a better relationship with most of the guys here than I've had with my own brothers and sisters," he said in the slow, deliberate echoes of a man delivering a eulogy. Jackson paused, choked up a bit, paused again. This was harder than he had anticipated. "If there's any hurt that comes out of this," he said, "it's because I won't be able to play with my teammates."

Many Royals were sad. Many were not. The circus was leaving town. It was a relief. No more arrows. No more autograph rejections. "For the first time," wrote Joe Popper and Steve Cameron in the *Kansas City Star*, "there is a clear hint he won't be missed."

There was a game to be played—the Astros awaited at the nearby field. First pitch 1:05. Slowly, steadily, the Royals players and coaches—dressed in familiar blue and whites—said their farewells and streamed out the front door.

It felt, in a sense, as if Bo Jackson had never existed.

As if it were all but a dream.

The aftermath was not pretty.

The Royals placed Jackson on waivers, which meant for seventy-two hours any of the Major League's twenty-five other teams could claim his rights for a dollar, then pay the remainder of his $2,375,000 contract.

There was no interest in handing that magnitude of dough to a one-legged outfielder. If anything, the whole situation was treated as a joke, with Jackson as the punch line. A Seattle radio station sent the Royals a one-dollar bill to claim Bo for its office softball team. The Live Oak Gray Ghosts, a Little League baseball squad outside of Tallahassee, Florida, did the same. "Please advise Mr. Jackson that practice is on Mondays, Tuesdays and Thursdays and a missed practice means he will not start in Saturday's game," wrote Coach Daniel McKeever in a letter he faxed to Kansas City's offices. "He will have to supply his own jockstrap, cleats, glove and one baseball." In Wichita, the front office of the Double A Wichita Wranglers announced an upcoming "Bo Jackson Crutch Race" where participants would race from second to home via crutches.

The value of Jackson's Topps rookie card—a whopping nine dollars—plummeted. Companies seeking Bo Jackson's endorsement stopped calling. Read a headline in the *Tucson Citizen*: BO JACKSON GETS VERY LITTLE RESPECT.

Though the world seemed to love all things Bo, the sporting press never found him to their tastes. Now, at his lowest, its members went to work . . .

Ken Rosenthal, *Baltimore Sun*: "This was the chance he took: Play two sports, risk playing none. Bo Jackson ignored the past, disregarded the future. . . . Bo never pondered consequences. He simply followed his imagination."

Bob Ryan, *Boston Globe*: "He was doing it all on raw ability because he wouldn't devote himself to learning how to play the game properly. He long ago made a decision that it was more important to be Bo The Celebrity than Bo The Baseball Player."

Doug Krikorian, *Knight-Ridder News Service* (beneath the headline BO SIDELINED BY AN ILLUSION OF IMMORTALITY): "He blithely ignored the advice, and Nike turned him into a cult figure and multimillionaire with a series of clever commercials based on his two-sport gig. But Bo Jackson was immersed in self-deception."

One by one, baseball executives appeared from the mist to damn Jackson to Sheol. Joe McDonald, Detroit Tigers general manager, said, "I don't need

Bo Jackson to convince me players shouldn't be playing two sports." Added Bill Wood, Astros GM: "I think a lot of people are saying, 'I told you so.'"

On the afternoon of Friday, March 22, Jackson officially became a free agent when the waiver period concluded and the Royals submitted his unconditional release. "The final chapter in the Bo story is written," said Robinson with the grace of a rusted knife. "As of 2 p.m., the book is closed."

With that, any organization could sign Jackson without the anchor of the guaranteed money. According to Richard Woods, the agent, "twelve teams have reached out"—only, well . . . um . . . eh . . . he couldn't name them. Or wouldn't name them. In the same conversation, Woods guaranteed Jackson would return, noting that "I've talked to every expert in the world."*

It all felt *grim*. The Yankees sought the advice of six orthopedic surgeons, none of whom believed a pathway toward recovery existed. On the morning of Tuesday, March 26, Jackson made the New York television rounds, appearing on ABC's *Good Morning America*, then NBC's *Today*, then CBS *This Morning*. What was supposed to be the beginning of a media rehabilitation tour came off sad and desperate. Woods thought his client's efforts would reassure both potential endorsers and potential baseball employers. No—it was only a reminder that, at age twenty-eight, Bo Jackson was a thoroughbred heading for the glue factory.

Then, when all looked lost, Ron Schueler, the Chicago White Sox general manager, called.

It made some sense. Not a ton of sense. But some. The team was about to debut the $135 million "new" Comiskey Park, but remained second banana to the crosstown rival Cubs. So along came America's most famous ballplayer, available (albeit on one leg) for a discount price. Dr. James Boscardin, the team's senior physician, flew to Alabama and conferred with Andrews, then told the organization that while Jackson would never again run a 4.2 40, he *might* be able to resume playing baseball. Boscardin believed the hip injury was more like a series of fractures that could heal than one that would permanently destroy the bones. "Any time you can get an athlete of Bo's caliber," Schueler told Jerry Reinsdorf, the team owner, "you've got to take that gamble."

Translation: if this doesn't pan out (and it probably won't pan out), we'll survive.

---

* In 1991, there were approximately 20,000 orthopedic surgeons in the United States alone.

The three-year contract would pay Jackson a guaranteed $700,000 in 1991 (with incentives, $1.5 million). The following two seasons were option years that—if Jackson somehow went from one-hip non-wonder to a fully functioning ballplayer—would make him $2.9 million in 1992, $3.75 million in 1993. Because this was Bo Jackson (and Bo Jackson *was* athletic apparel), news of the White Sox deal was first spread by Liz Dolan, Nike spokesperson, who alerted the media the night before it became official.

In a Wednesday-morning press conference to introduce Jackson (who was decked out in a pinstriped shirt and black White Sox cap) to Chicago, Reinsdorf was honest in his expectations. "I'm approaching it with the idea that he won't play this year," he said. "If he's able to play, it's a bonus."

Schueler referred to the deal as a "shared risk"—which made no sense. What was the risk to Jackson? He either signed with the team or limped off to the Canasta and Bingo circuits.

The White Sox placed Jackson on the sixty-day disabled list, and Herm Schneider, Chicago's trainer, began piecing together a rehabilitation regimen heavy on two activities the ballplayer never much cared for: swimming laps and lifting weights. In a guest column for the *New York Times* (ghost written by Dick Schaap, the scribe behind his autobiography), Jackson expressed optimistic determination:

I'm going to get my hip back into shape.

I have to do it for all the people who say I can't.

I have to do it for me.

I've always had dreams of things I could do in baseball, things no one has ever done, dreams about home runs and stolen bases I've kept to myself.

And now that I've had a scare, now that I've been slowed down—temporarily—I want more than ever to make those dreams come true.

If I had to I could live without baseball, without football, without the cheers and without the boos.

I have no burning need for the spotlight.

But I've got something to show the Chicago White Sox for believing in me.

I've got something to show the Kansas City Royals for not.

I'm glad I'm still in the American League West, glad I'll get 13 chances a season to show the Royals what a dumb mistake they made.

It was hard to take Jackson seriously. The Royals begged him not to play football. He played football. The Royals warned him about the injury risk. He ignored them. The Royals could not justify paying more than $2 million for someone who was unable to take the field. He didn't want to hear it. The Royals liked upbeat clubhouse presences. Jackson was largely a sour puss. At one point, during the December 1990 winter meetings in Chicago, Herk Robinson checked around to gauge Jackson's (pre-injury) trade value. There was none. "If you knew what the Royals were offered for Bo Jackson, you'd laugh," said a rival general manager. "Fans have been making up deals with teams giving up two or three good players for Bo. But what the Royals could get are wimps. It's almost a joke."

It was simple: With or without two legs, Jackson's game was filled with holes. He didn't see them. Fans didn't see them. But he had one of the lowest clutch-hitting averages in the league. He struck out far too often. He was the fastest man in baseball, but stole few bases. His defense was—soup to nuts—below average. "Don't quote me," one Royals teammate said, "but go see if anybody around here remembers when Bo ever tried to move a runner from second to third."

During a press conference at the Sox spring training facility in Sarasota, Florida, Jackson vowed to return to Missouri and knock down the newly installed Jumbotron with a Ruthian homer. He insisted he was happy to join Chicago and finally play for a team that could win. "It was a personal vendetta of [Royals owner Ewing Kaufman] to get me out of Kansas City," Jackson told the Chicago media in a strikingly irrational rant. "I had some high-ranking people in that city tell me it was coming. I smelled the rat long before it died."

Later, in a chat with Tracy Ringolsby of *Inside Sports*, Jackson promised to, "haunt the Royals."

The White Sox were his new team, so Jackson spoke highly of the operation. But his arrival was as much about butts in the seats as it was home runs. Most Chicago executives presumed Jackson would either never play again or double as a poor man's Wayne Nordhagen. But, damn, the story line was amazing. And a White Sox cap in some of those Nike ads was the world's best free advertising. So why not peddle the fantasy? Why not string the fools along?

On April 8, 1991, the White Sox kicked off the season at Baltimore's Memorial Stadium and Jackson was back home fishing near Leawood, Kansas. "I'm not very good at spectator sports," he explained. "But I wish I could play baseball today." Ten days later, at the team's home opener (and Comiskey grand debut) against Detroit, Jackson donned a full White Sox uniform—white, with black pinstripes—for the first time. In the spirit of a fresh start, he wore number 8, and when the team was introduced to the capacity crowd of 42,191, Jackson set aside his crutches (which he still relied upon) and gingerly jogged from dugout to field. He was bestowed a king's ovation—the highlight of an afternoon that culminated in a 16–0 defeat.

Unlike old Comiskey, a circa-1910 rat-infested dump, new Comiskey came with perks. More concession stands. Larger space for the players to keep their possessions. And, best of all for a man trying to recover from a devastating injury, the $50,000 multidepth hydrotherapy pool inside the training area. "That was no accident," said Schueler. "Jerry contracted some people to come in, and they built that specifically with Bo in mind."

The pool was eighteen feet long, occupied 200 square feet and ran on a propulsion system that drove more than 25,000 gallons of water per minute through the side channels. The water supported the body and offered resistance. "You should have seen this thing," Schueler said. "It was like you were walking in the ocean against thirty-mile-an-hour waves." Members of the White Sox quickly came to refer to it as "Bo's Pool."

"Bo would be in there all the time," said Ken Patterson, a Chicago pitcher. "He was not messing around. He came to work."

At McAdory High, then Auburn, then Memphis, then Kansas City, Jackson was tagged as a maligner. And maybe that was a bit harsh. The sports world was forever home to uniquely gifted men and women who were able to coast as others grinded. Now, however, he was being told for the first time that it was either bust ass or go home. Slack off, and all of it—the baseball life, the Nike deal, the money—would vanish.

"Oh my God," recalled Matt Merullo, a backup catcher. "Watching Bo ride the bike, swim the pool—he just lived there, and Herm Schneider worked him *hard*. You knew the look when someone was hungry. Bo had it."

Schneider, thirty-nine years old and in his thirteenth year with the Sox, was unlike anyone Jackson had ever met. At Auburn, then with the Royals, the overarching rebound-from-injury philosophy began with healing and recovery time. In Chicago, it was blunt force trauma. "Herm doesn't like to rest injuries," said Tom Paciorek, a former Sox player. "He likes to go out and get them and beat them up."

Jackson stretched more than he ever stretched. He lifted weights (*serious* weights) more than he ever lifted weights. He swam nonstop—an endeavor that strengthened his hip while simultaneously making him miserable. It was not fun. None of it. He questioned whether the effort was worth the reward. But then he would see Schneider—lunchbox-shaped head, stern gaze—demanding more. More! MORE! The goal, the maniac trainer told him, wasn't to heal the hip. That was impossible. No, the goal was to strengthen every muscle that surrounded the hip. "[Herm] won't let you cheat yourself," Jackson said, "and he will talk to you like dirt if he has to, just to get you pissed off so you can do the work."

Come early June, Jackson was barely relying on his crutches. By late in the month, after another examination from Andrews, he and the organization were delighted. "X-rays definitely showed some improvement," said Schueler. "Everything so far has fallen into what he had hoped for." Jackson, Andrews determined, could start using both the Stairmaster *and* treadmill. Back in May, *The Physician and Sportsmedicine*, a medical journal, had declared Jackson done as an athlete—"despite Jackson's optimism," the piece read, "the consensus is he won't play again." Now, he was making tangible progress.

On July 16, several hours before the Sox faced Boston at Comiskey, Jackson—wearing baseball pants and a black pullover—walked from the dugout to the outfield alongside Schneider. For roughly twelve minutes, the men lightly tossed a baseball back and forth. Two Chicago infielders, Ozzie Guillen and Joey Cora, applauded from second base. A bunch of Red Sox players watched intently from the dugout lip. It was miraculous. Afterward, Jackson retreated to the stadium's enclosed batting cage, where he picked up a bat, stood next to the plate and hit seventy to eighty baseballs that were tossed underhand. Jackson hit the balls *hard*. "I'm not where I want to be," he said afterward, "but I will settle for where I am right now."

One day later, Jackson was back at the field, this time playing pepper (and looking spry) with pitcher Scott Radinsky and a clubhouse attendant. The day after that he took even more BP. Because the Jacksons had yet to purchase a home in the Windy City, Linda and the children were back in Alabama and Bo was living with Schneider and his family in Chicago's west suburbs. It was cozy, and came with all-you-can-eat refrigerator access and free transportation to Comiskey. More batting practice followed—beneath the stadium on July 18, again two days later. He was making solid contact, adjusting to the discomfort (but no longer pain) of a bum hip. Andrews offered an update to the media on July 20, raving about Jackson's "excellent" progress. Boscardin said the time had come for "a little running." No one had ever seen anything like this—Jackson still limped when he walked, but didn't limp jogging with a harness (a parachute-like device strapped to his back) in the outfield. "Explain that one," said Jeff Torborg, the Sox manager. "Because I couldn't."

For a man who never much cared for practice, Jackson embraced the challenge. He could see the incremental improvements; started to believe (truly believe) that he would be the same ol' Bo Jackson. It had always been so easy and, in a way, so joyless. "I have never had to work at anything," he said. "Everything has always come natural. You have to learn to walk before you can run." Now Jackson was looking around the White Sox clubhouse— at undersized infielders like Craig Grebeck and fighting-to-stick outfielders à la Warren Newson—and empathizing. He grasped the struggle.

On August 6, before that night's Yankees–White Sox game at Comiskey, Jackson changed into white pinstriped uniform pants, a black White Sox jersey and a baseball cap, strolled onto the field and, for the first time in nearly a year, took live outdoor batting practice alongside teammates. "I had butterflies in my stomach," he said. The stadium was largely empty, but those in attendance fell into a hush. Terry Bevington, the team's third base coach, tossed twenty balls to Jackson, and . . .

"He was awesome," said Torborg.

Not all of the baseballs were well hit. But most were. And six or seven flew over the left-field wall—not 500 feet over the wall, but over. The swing wasn't perfect. It was choppy. A tad labored. Jackson winced from time to time. A couple of cuts were late. Clearly, however, this was a professional hitter in a professional cage taking professional hacks. It wasn't a silly side show.

Jackson didn't shed tears, because Bo Jackson did not like to do (public) crying. But he felt the emotion. "It's a sense of relief," he said. "Like coming out of my shell all over again."

In the days that followed, Jackson continued to take BP. The swing improved, as did the power. On August 15, the team released Ron Kittle, the lumbering thirty-three-year-old slugger with a .191 average. Talk in the media was the roster spot *could* be granted to Jackson. With a 66-49 record, Chicago sat a game and a half behind Minnesota in the A.L. West. Adding a big bat to the lineup wasn't an unappealing idea.

First, however, Jackson required seasoning. On Friday, August 23, he was shipped out to Sarasota, Florida, home of the Class A Sarasota White Sox of the Florida State League. Though it read as a standard rehab assignment, this was anything but. Jackson needed to show what he could do against live pitching; to prove that this carnival wasn't mere carnival. "I'm not going to activate him just because he's Bo Jackson," Schueler said. "If he can't help the ball club, he's not going to be on the roster."

Locals rushed to the box office at rickety Ed Smith Stadium to purchase tickets for the Saturday matchup between the Port Charlotte Rangers and the Sarasota White Sox. An unprecedented 5,500 were sold in mere minutes (for a stadium that held 7,500), and fifty-nine media credentials were distributed. Sarasota's players learned of Jackson's forthcoming arrival while returning from a series three hours away in Vero Beach. Rick Patterson, the team's manager, stood before his men on the bus and said, "Hey, guys! I've got some news from the front office! Bo is gonna be in town to play some games with us!"

The average Sarasota player was twenty-two years old, and most would never sniff a Major League clubhouse. Jackson was the athletic icon of their boyhoods, and now he would be their teammate. "It was incredibly cool," said Mike Mongiello, the closer.

Jackson arrived in town on Friday afternoon. The doors to the clubhouse opened, and—as if responding to a director's cue—everyone stopped what they were doing to gaze upward. A teenage attendant entered, lugging a pair of massive black bags with WHITE SOX embroidered into the sides. Another youngster followed, this one carrying a small trunk. Schueler strolled through the entranceway, followed by Reinsdorf and, finally, Bo Jackson outfitted in a suit and walking with a marginal limp.

"It felt surreal," said Earnie Johnson, a twenty-three-year-old reliever. "Like, what was Bo Jackson doing here with us?"

The following night's game was scheduled to begin at seven o'clock, and the fans started to arrive six hours beforehand. The line extended down a sidewalk and around the block. "They came from all over," wrote Dan Le Batard in the *Miami Herald*, "traveling down appropriately named boulevards named Ringling and Circus." More than a thousand Bo Jackson/Sarasota White Sox T-shirts were rush ordered to sell at concession stands. Before spectators were allowed inside, Jackson took BP, and smacked 18 of the 40 balls thrown his way over Ed Smith's outfield walls. The kiddie ballplayers watched in astonishment. If this guy could hit like that with one healthy hip, what hope was there for the minions? "He was awesome," said Patterson. "The typical show you expect from Bo Jackson."

After batting practice ended, Johnson received a call on the clubhouse phone from back home in Kansas City. His father, Eddie, a fifty-seven-year-old maintenance supervisor with the Missouri Department of

Transportation, needed to have a double bypass surgery in the coming days. "But don't come home," dad told son. "You're having your best season. Stay with the team."

A disconsolate Johnson hung up, entered the manager's office and told Patterson what was transpiring. "My dad's having heart surgery," he said. "He doesn't want me to come home, but I feel like I need to." Jackson was in the adjacent training room having treatment done on his hip, and he overheard Patterson ask Schueler whether the organization could fork over dough for a flight to Kansas City.

A few minutes later, the skipper approached Johnson at his locker.

"Bo," he said, "wants to talk to you."

"Bullshit," Johnson said. This had to be a prank.

"No," Patterson said. "I'm serious."

Johnson reluctantly entered the stamp-size training room. Jackson was alone on a table.

"You Earnie?" he asked.

"Yup," Johnson said. "That's me."

Jackson motioned for the youngster to approach and extended his hand. "I'm Bo Jackson," he said.

Johnson—palms sweaty, tongue-tied—nodded and they shook hands.

"So I overheard the conversation about your dad," Jackson said. "You have to go home and be there for him. My mother was sick a few years ago, and I dropped everything I was doing. Drop what you're doing and be with your dad."

Then, the capper.

"Tell me if the White Sox don't pay for your flight," Jackson said. "I'll pay for it myself."

Chicago wound up arranging the trip, and Johnson traveled home to be by his father's side (the operation was a success). He went on to play two more minor league seasons, never advancing beyond Triple A Iowa. Thirty years later, as a husband, father of three and longtime physical therapist, Johnson could not get past the decency of the man.

"That's my all-time story," he said. "I've told it hundreds of times—the power of kindness. And it lasted all of five minutes."

The Saturday-night game was rained out. It probably could have been played, but following a thirty-minute downpour, the White Sox made the call to postpone. After all the work Bo Jackson had put in, the organization was not going to have him trip, fall and reinjure himself in the name of Class A baseball. A makeup day-night doubleheader was slated for Sunday.

At 7:24 p.m., shortly after the cancellation was announced, Schueler asked Jackson to say a few words to all the water-logged fans who had chanted, "We want Bo! We want Bo!" from the bleachers. The two men boarded a golf cart, and Schueler drove toward the spectators.

"I'd like to say we appreciate . . . I appreciate your support and loyalty," Jackson said in the emotionless tone of a man who wanted to be anywhere but here. "Sorry the game was called off. As they say, I'll see you tomorrow at noon. I'll be here. Will you?"

Schueler placed his foot atop the pedal and the cart drove off.

The forecast for Sunday afternoon was possible showers, and a thunderstorm pushed the noon Game One start back forty-eight minutes. Regardless, the stands were yet again packed with folks determined to witness the Christlike resurrection of Bo Jackson. Batting practice, as usual, was a show—Jackson launched eight balls out of the park, each one to *oohs* and *aahs*. Once done, he headed to the dugout to sign some cards. When a lovely day at the park devolved into men elbowing one another for positioning, Jackson placed his Sharpie to the side and banished all adults. "I don't like to sign autographs for hustlers because they abuse the privilege," he said, clearly (and correctly) irked. "I sign only for kids because they don't know what the word 'hustle' means."

As ordered by the White Sox, Patterson had Jackson DH and bat third in the lineup. The first-game starter for the Rangers was Juan Quero, a twenty-one-year-old Venezuelan. Jackson's premiere at bat came in the bottom of the first inning. He was greeted by a standing ovation, and Quero— throwing nothing but outside fastballs and changeups—coerced a harmless groundout to third. The next two Jackson at bats resulted in fly-out liners to right field (one resulting in a sacrifice fly), and he came up for a final shot in the bottom of the eighth. Now pitching for Charlotte was Johnny Maldonado, a 5-foot-11, 180-pound right-hander who two seasons earlier spent a month serving as the Class A Sumter Braves' ineffective closer.

With the count 0-1, Maldonado threw an outside heater. Jackson swung with all his might, but the ball merely trickled down the third base line, barely fair as it headed toward Jose Oliva, the Rangers' third baseman. By all measures of logic, reason and safety, Jackson was supposed to jog toward first, take the out and move on.

But, no. Jackson sprinted from the box and—ignoring his fragile left hip—chugged down the line. For a moment he was back at Auburn, back in

Kansas City. He was the Bo Jackson of old, wowing the world with freakish gifts of speed and strength. Sure, he ran with a jagged stride. But he somehow compensated. Olivia charged in, grabbed the baseball, took a couple of lazy pumps before tossing it across the diamond, where Randy Marshall, the first baseman, snagged the ball just before Jackson reached the bag. The umpire, a kid named Jeff Nelson, spread his arms to signal safe, and Maldonado, the entire rosters of both teams and all 4,459 paid attendees recognized a blown call when they saw one. But it mattered not. As soon as he ran through the base, Jackson—thrilled, relieved, pain free—playfully shook his hips and feigned exhaustion. He was clocked running 4.25 seconds down the first base line, a hair above average for a Big Leaguer. "He turned it on when he thought he was going to get a hit," said Duane Shaffer, Chicago's minor league scouting director. "That was encouraging."

Bob Molinaro, the Rangers manager, was furious with his third baseman's minimal effort. As the Bo-is-safe celebration took place at first, he yanked Olivia by the jersey into the dugout. "I look in their tunnel and I see bodies flying," said Kevin Castleberry, Sarasota's third baseman. "It's the first time I ever saw a manager and player beating each other up. I guess they weren't happy for Bo."

In the evening the Rangers and White Sox met again, and Jackson produced another infield single as part of a 1-for-3 showing. When the game ended, he and the other members of the Sarasota White Sox retreated to the clubhouse, where a catered five-course meal—paid for by a certain Nike spokesperson—awaited.

Thus far, the Bo Jackson Comeback Tour was going splendidly He played fairly well, he didn't get hurt, he took care of dinner. On August 26, Craig Dolch of the *Palm Beach Post* reported the White Sox were planning on calling Jackson up on September 2, where he would presumably make his highly anticipated Big League return against (of all teams) the Kansas City Royals.

There was one more test.

As soon as he polished off his postgame meal, Jackson headed for the airport and flew the three and a half hours back home to Alabama. He was joining the Double A Birmingham Barons for two more games. Despite Hoover Metropolitan Stadium, the Barons' three-year-old facility, being a mere ten miles from Bessemer, Jackson felt no pangs of nostalgia. He loved his mom, loved several of his siblings, kept in touch with a few coaches. All things being equal, though, he'd rather conduct business elsewhere, without the family obligations and ticket requests. This wasn't fun for him. It was work.

As was the case in Sarasota, Birmingham's players greeted their designated hitter with slack-jawed deference. His first game was scheduled for a Monday night against the Charlotte Knights, a Cubs affiliate. When Jackson entered the clubhouse, he introduced himself to the players, then popped his head into the office of Tony Franklin, the manager.

"You ready to go?" Franklin asked.

"You know it," Jackson replied.

As tradition dictated, players snuck peeks as Jackson changed into his uniform. These were men in their physical primes, but it was humbling. "You don't wanna stare," said Scott Tedder, a Barons outfielder. "But good lord. You're only teammates with a god once in your life."

If the reception in Sarasota had been a circus, this was a tsunami. The greatest athlete the state had ever produced was back, and Birmingham was invested. The Barons were a quality team with nine pitchers destined to occupy Major League rosters. They were exciting enough. But minor league baseball depends on exclamation mark moments. A big one had arrived. "It's like holding a golf tournament," said Marty Kuehnert, the Barons president, "and having Jack Nicklaus and Arnold Palmer show up."

With 11,859 bodies packed in and nary an empty seat to be found, before the game Kuehnert walked onto the field to hand Jackson an enlarged key to the city. As fans cheered, Jackson whispered, "What does this mean for me?"

Kuehnert grinned. "It means you get to pay the city's bills," he said. "You've got plenty of money, haven't you?"

Jackson batted third for the Barons. As he approached the plate for his first at bat with a runner on first, the PA system blared the audio from one of his Nike commercials. The fans (many wearing BO KNOWS shirts) rose to their feet, and after missing with his first pitch, Charlotte right-hander John Salles threw an outside fastball that Jackson bounced right back to the mound. Salles spun, rifled to shortstop Alex Arias, who slid his foot across second, then tossed to first to complete the double play. The out was meaningless. That Jackson felt no pain, showed no limp, reached for no body part was the joyful takeaway. He wound up going 2-for-4 with two singles, and few left disappointed. "I told everybody I knew how to get him out," Salles, a long-ago Fresno State ace, cracked. "He's on my Nintendo team, so I know how to pitch to him."

One night later, with another 10,000 fans watching and Charles Barkley in attendance and sharing a private skybox with Buffalo Bills stars Bruce Smith and Cornelius Bennett, Jackson . . .

. . . stole a base.

It came in the sixth inning. Nobody with the White Sox wanted Bo Jackson stealing. The Barons' staff was under strict orders not to have him steal a base, or even attempt to take an extra base. Bo would be the designated hitter—emphasis on *hitter*. But after Knights pitcher Chuck Mount walked Jackson to lead off the sixth, he strolled into a sizable lead and, on the third offering to first baseman Mark Chasey, jumped and ran.

Noooooooooooo!

Franklin was horrified—there went his managerial dreams. Mount was stunned—there had been no reason to hold the runner on. Catcher Dan Simonds figured it was some sort of an optical illusion. But, no, Jackson was dashing toward second with a slight trace of a limp but at what appeared to be a good clip. Simonds sprung from his slumber, cocked his right arm and threw down to second. Not only did Jackson beat the throw, but the baseball skipped past Arias and into center field. Jackson rose, turned and dashed toward third. The fans went bonkers. Inside the Barons dugout, teammates were startled. "Dr. Andrews was sitting with us, and he was really upset," said John Hudek, a Birmingham reliever. "He said, 'What is he doing? He just got that hip!'" Moments later, on a Chasey grounder to second, Jackson took off and charged toward home. "You could see Bo crouching, preparing to kill their catcher," Hudek said. "We didn't make enough money in Double A to be run over by a truck." Simonds got lucky—the throw didn't come home. "Seriously," Hudek said. "He would have been killed."

All told, Jackson went 6-for-19 in the minors, and even cracked a bat over his knee after making an out. Andrews was elated. "He may always have a detectable difference in his run and walk," Andrews said. "It may always look different than what he looked like prior to the injury." But—he added—"Bo Jackson has made amazing strides."

He left the Chicago White Sox with no alternative.

On Saturday, August 30, he was told to pack his gear and catch a flight to the Windy City. After overcoming the greatest challenge of his life, Jackson would be returning to the Big Leagues. He didn't cry when he learned the news. He merely smiled, and thought of all the people who deemed this an impossibility.

"It was," Hudek said, "a baseball miracle."

CHAPTER 26

THE RETURN

The only reason you are thinking about the 1991 Chicago White Sox is because you are reading this book.

Otherwise, they are forever condemned to baseball's dustbin of the forgotten. That's what happens when you go 87-75 and place second, eight games out of first. No one recalls you fondly. No one recalls you angrily. You come and you go and nary a soul speaks of you again.

Bo Jackson was activated from the disabled list on Monday, September 2, and in many regards the vanilla situation was ideal. Were manager Jeff Torborg's team in the midst of a pennant race, it would have been hard to justify Jackson's installation into the lineup. But with the (eventual World Series–champion) Twins running away with the American League West, Chicago was a baseball afterthought, ripe for some level of experimentation. "We were a little bit of a disappointment," said Torborg. "There were a lot of expectations coming into the season that probably went unmet. So you could say Bo arrived during a disappointing stretch."

His debut would come Monday night in the first of a four-game series at Comiskey against the (cue: Death Star music) *visiting Kansas City Royals.* Although he devoted a fair amount of time to tossing barbs at his former team, on the day before the game Jackson took a more genteel approach. John Wathan, the manager he didn't respect, was long gone—replaced by Hal McRae. Kevin Seitzer, his loathed teammate, was battling injuries and hitting a career-low .258. The outfielder brought in to replace him, a battered thirty-four-year-old Kirk Gibson, was a shell of his long-ago MVP self. The Royals sat behind the Twins, White Sox, A's and Rangers, a sad 10½ games out. It was hard to build up much animus. "Why should I seek vengeance against my former teammates?" said Jackson—momentarily forgetting that he, um, sought vengeance. "I had a lot of good moments over there."

When asked, members of the Royals expressed no apparent ill-will toward Jackson. Worse than that, they actually felt sorry for him. These were men who had once enjoyed a daily front-row seat to the Bo Jackson Experience, and the ballplayer they saw via Sarasota and Birmingham highlights was nothing of the sort. "Bo used to take a second to analyze what he had to do, then kick it into what he called that turbo shift," said Mike Macfarlane, the catcher. "It didn't look like he had that."

A crowd of 37,187 fans filed into the stadium—approximately 50 percent of whom purchased tickets to watch a man limp, 20 percent because it was half-price night and the remainder to experience the high of Koala Yummies Lunch Bag Night. The ambiance, Jerome Holtzman of the *Chicago Tribune* wrote, was circus-like. "It occurred to me," Holtzman opined, "what Bo really knows best is how to make money." Three hours before first pitch, the field was flooded with reporters and photographers. George Brett took one peek and cracked, "Is Mickey Mantle making a comeback or something?" Jackson's batting practice session had the feel of a member of the New Kids on the Block sprinting down Waverly to escape a throng of screaming girls. Reporters charged the cage, pens extended, pages flapping in the wind. "This isn't a White Sox game," added Tim Raines, a Chicago outfielder. "This is the Bo show." Jackson blasted two balls into the left-field stands, then two more to right. His swing appeared long and smooth. A bit less hip motion than before, but plenty good.

Torborg inserted Jackson (at designated hitter) into the sixth spot in the lineup, directly behind right fielder Dan Pasqua and in front of center fielder Lance Johnson. Starting for the Sox was Roberto Hernandez, a twenty-six-year-old right-hander making his Major League debut.

Were the world just, Hernandez's story would have been the talk of the evening. Four months earlier, while pitching for Triple A Vancouver, he learned that numbness in his pitching arm was caused by multiple blood clots. He immediately underwent surgery to have veins transplanted from his inner thigh to his forearm, and missed a chunk of the season. Now he. was back, making his first start for Chicago, and not a soul cared.

"It was actually good for me," Hernandez recalled. "I remember walking through the clubhouse and it looked like an All-Star Game or the World Series. There were so many reporters surrounding Bo Jackson's locker. I went unnoticed."

Jackson's return to the Majors formally commenced in the second inning, when—with one out and the bases empty—Gene Honda, the Comiskey public address announcer, bellowed, *"Now batting, number eight . . ."*

Everyone in attendance rose, marking Jackson's third standing ovation in a little over a week. He offered a slight nod of acknowledgment, then dug in against Luis Aquino, a fairly ordinary right-hander. McRae had watched Jackson's BP, and his advice (really, *command*) to Aquino was basic: No fastballs. Let Jackson and his crappy left hip try and adjust to off-speed stuff. Sliders, curveballs, a changeup here and there. Just no heat.

It worked. On the second pitch, Jackson got hold of an Aquino slider and grounded out back to the mound.

Jackson grounded out (on another slider) to third his next time up. After that, in the sixth, he flied out harmlessly to center. In the eighth, with Mark Davis now pitching, Jackson smoked a deep fly ball to center, allowing Robin Ventura to tag up from third. The White Sox wound up winning, 5–1, and the hero was Hernandez, who held the Royals hitless for six innings.

The story, though, was Bo. He looked good. He swung well. No body parts fell off. It was the most encouraging 0-fer of his lifetime. Maybe of any lifetime.

"This ranks at the top of my list," he said afterward, when asked to assess the night. "There were people that had written me off. But I am here and I am proud of this. I am going to go home and celebrate going zero for four with my wife."

The next day, Jackson found himself back in the lineup, once again going hitless. He flew out to center as a pinch hitter in the third game of the series, then finally connected for a pair of singles and three RBI in an 11–2 thrashing of the Royals on September 5. "Now that I've gotten those first couple of hits out of the way," he said afterward, "I guess it's time to try and live a normal baseball life."

This, sadly, would be impossible. Jackson exuded optimism, as did Torborg, Andrews, Herm Schneider—pretty much everyone involved with the grand Bo experiment. His muscles had been strengthened, his flexibility had been improved, he figured out ways to slide safely and run more protectively. Bill Melton, a former White Sox third baseman-turned-team community relations liaison, passed Jackson one afternoon, stopped and said, "You're the most beautiful naked man I've ever seen in a clubhouse." But, come day's end, Jackson's left hip remained damaged and decayed, and no amount of weight training or pool time could fix that. "Honestly, watching him was a bit sad," said Dave LaRoche, the White Sox bullpen coach. "He was in the training room all the time, but when he ran it was with a hitch. You recalled what he had been and hated what was taken from him."

Torborg committed himself to playing Jackson fairly regularly, but accompanied each appearance with bated breath and heightened anxieties. It was like watching a toddler work his way through a crowded room. He could do great. He could fall and smack his head against the television. Against the Rangers in Arlington on September 6, Jackson hammered a fastball from Nolan Ryan off the left-center-field wall for a double, then lined a run-scoring single to right center off Goose Gossage. It was beautiful. Three days later, at Oakland, he doubled and immediately felt discomfort shoot through his leg. He remained in the game for five more innings, but was ultimately pulled for a pinch runner. "He comes into the dugout, comes down the staircase, comes up next to me and says, 'Skip, I can't go—my hip is just killing me,'" Torborg recalled. "It stiffened up and caused him real pain." Four days after that, against California, Jackson ignored Torborg's *never, ever try to steal a base* directive and took off for second. He was thrown out by catcher Lance Parrish, popped up from a clumsy wrong-side-of-the-hip slide and scared the coaching staff to death. "That's the best I've seen him run," Torborg said afterward, shaking his head with each word.

Jackson's finest moment of a strange year took place at home against the Oakland A's on September 17. In the bottom of the seventh inning of a scoreless game, he came up against Ron Darling, a right-handed pitcher who had fanned nine while surrendering but one hit. "I struck Bo out the first two times, and it was easy," Darling recalled. "So maybe I got a little complacent."

Darling tried sneaking a fastball past Chicago's DH, and Jackson was not fooled. He extended his arms, swiveled his hips and destroyed the ball, sending it 417 feet into the center-field bleachers for the game's only run. It was his first homer since September 30, 1990, and Darling was dispirited. So, for that matter, was Tony La Russa, the A's manager. When the game ended, La Russa stormed into the clubhouse and destroyed the catered postgame spread. "That was really bad," said Darling. "The postgame spread in Chicago was famous for its tuna macaroni salad. It was phenomenal. I don't even like tuna macaroni salad, but you had to have it. And Tony was so mad he sent it flying everywhere.

"All because a man with one functioning hip homered off me."

And that was pretty much that. In 23 games and 71 at bats, Jackson batted .225 with 3 home runs, 14 RBI and 25 strikeouts. Although it was merely a so-so production, the White Sox saw hope. Ron Schueler, the general manager, predicted Jackson would return even stronger in 1992, and serve as the team's full-time designated hitter.

Jackson believed it, too.

Sports is fantasy.

It's not fantasy in the way Disney is fantasy, where an otherwise ordinary woman can work weekends at the Magic Kingdom, don a Little Mermaid costume and have little girls beg for autographs. But it *is* fantasy, in that we aspire to believe the people we're watching are more than mere people. They're gladiators of the Gods, capable of overcoming all obstacles and conquering unconquerable foes.

Or, put different: Despite Bo Jackson playing baseball on one good hip, the Raiders had hopes he might return for the 1991 season. Al Davis said he believed Bo could do it. Art Shell said he believed Bo could do it. Howie Long said he believed Bo could do it. Perhaps no athlete in the history of sports has inspired more people to begin a sentence with, *"If anyone can do it . . ."* than Bo Jackson.

Alas, it made no sense. Jackson ran *with a limp*. His hip was one good blow removed from exploding into a thousand pieces. Bo-Bosworth II would have ended quite differently.

That said, on October 10—as required under the language of his contract with the Raiders—Jackson took his NFL physical. And failed. Richard Woods, his agent, called Davis to deliver the news. The Los Angeles experiment was, sadly, over.

A few weeks later, during a promotional appearance at the Lakeview Sportmart store in Chicago, Jackson made it official. "As far as I'm concerned, I have to do what my doctors told me," he said. "And my doctors have said it's in my best interest to just play baseball. I can't argue with it."

With those words, Bo Jackson's NFL existence was supposed to come to an end. His lifetime numbers (38 games, 2,782 rushing yards, 16 touchdowns) failed to tell the story of a man who captured the imagination of football fans; who kept people expecting that next 90-yard scamper. He would go down in history as a bolt of lightning that vanished into the clouds.

Until something momentous occurred.

With little to no fanfare, on December 13, 1991, Nintendo Entertainment System released a new football video game for its home console. It was called Tecmo Super Bowl, because it was created by Tecmo, the Japanese gaming company, and featured all twenty-eight NFL teams and their full rosters. Two years earlier Nintendo's customers had been introduced to mere Tecmo Bowl (no Super), which was perfectly OK and certainly enjoyable, but included only twelve teams with limited players. The sequel, wrote Alan Siegel, "was designed to be a faster, supersized take on the original." Two Japanese men in their mid-twenties, programmer Akihiko Shimoji and director Shinichiro Tomie, pieced the game together. They had minimal knowledge of American football, so they pored over their nation's lone gridiron-related magazine (*Touchdown PRO*) and recorded the few NFL clashes that were televised on Japanese Broadcasting Corporation (NHK) satellite TV.

"Because I wanted to use unique formations and strategies," Tomie said, "I often watched the videos in slow motion while rewinding them and jotting down the players' movements on paper."

After consuming an ample amount of football, Tomie reached two conclusions:

1. He loved this wacky sport.
2. The large Black man wearing number 34 for the football club representing the greater Los Angeles municipality was 壮観 (spectacular).

"When I first saw him play on television, it was quite a big impact," said Tomie. "This raised the question, 'How do I represent that big impact through a game?' Specifically, how could I show his uniqueness in the game?"

The answer: Turn Tecmo Bo Jackson into an indestructible cyborg.

By 2022 standards, Tecmo Bo is an archaic bundle of silver-and-black pixeled cubes, stumps for legs and dated sound effects. But to control him as a character (which only required two buttons and a directional pad) is to practice the dark art of football wizardry. Hideshia Yamaguchi, who worked on the game as a project manager, later admitted player features were "exaggerated"—and a lie this was not. Against nearly any opponent, Tecmo Bo is unstoppable. To start with, he's faster than everyone—on the Tecmo rating scale, Tecmo Bo was an unmatched 75 for speed. Explained Ron Kantowski in the *Las Vegas Review-Journal*: "For context, Barry Sanders and Jerry Rice were next at 69. What it means in the game: If Tecmo Bo and Barry lined up for a 100-yard dash, when Tecmo Bo struck pay dirt, Barry would have lagged behind at the 12-yard line." He is also impossibly hard to tackle. He crashes through defensive lines and barrels over opponents. Myriad are the stories of a Tecmo Super Bowl game ending with Bo Jackson rushing for 800 yards and 12 touchdowns on 12 carries. "Bo Jackson," Tiger Woods once said, "is probably the best video game athlete of all time."

Were Tecmo Super Bowl merely another in the long line of forgettable sports releases, Tecmo Bo would have come and gone. Instead, it blew up. *Everyone* wanted Tecmo Super Bowl for Christmas. The game sold hundreds of thousands of units, and a decade and a half after the release, ESPN's Bill Simmons raved: "For fifteen years, the greatest force in video football was Bo Jackson . . . Video Bo was the best. Sports fans will argue about anything, but this particular subject has never been up for debate."

How big of a deal was Tecmo Bo? As of May 9, 2022, a YouTube video of him slicing through the Chiefs defense for a turning, twisting, back-and-forth, up-and-down, preposterous-beyond-preposterous 99-yard score had been viewed 2.7 million times (and counting).

Bo Jackson's epic stampeding of the Boz on *Monday Night Football*? A mere 471,000 times.

Here's something one might not expect about a man who valued his privacy, his family and his ability to hunt at most any moment: Bo Jackson loved Chicago.

He loved it more than Birmingham, and he loved it more than Kansas City. It wasn't New York, size-wise, which was terrific, but there was a lot to do and a lot to see, and it was surrounded by sprawling suburbs with all sorts of potential for happy family living.

So, in October 1991, the Jackson five left Leawood, Kansas, for good and moved into a 7,319-square-foot home in Burr Ridge, Illinois. The house had been built two years earlier, and was located in a gated community. It featured seven bathrooms, a spacious kitchen, an enormous backyard. The writer Carrie Muskat was one of the few media members ever invited inside, and she described the interior as "immaculate, expensive, and looks prepped for a *House Beautiful* photo shoot. Elaborate silk floral arrangements fill the entry and the adjoining dining room. There is a piano in the living room. Family photos peek from a nook." Jackson dug the tranquillity of the place (back in Missouri, people regularly rang his doorbell seeking autographs), but what he really cherished was what the home represented. It was *his*, based off of hard work. Jackson was less than three decades removed from arriving at elementary school without shoes, from having to leave his house to use a bathroom, from never being quite sure how plentiful the next meal would be. He was a bully who stuttered and seemed destined for reform school, if not a penitentiary.

Now he was able to gaze throughout his abode, and look at his wife and three children, and feel pride.

One more perk: the house was a mere eighteen miles west of Comiskey Park.

Entering the 1992 season, this would be no small thing. Though Jackson had been relatively pleased with his abridged return to baseball, he knew any longevity depended upon tenaciousness. So, through the winter, he spent between five and six days per week at the stadium, grinding it out alongside Herm Schneider in the pool, on the weight bench, on a training table. Even in the batting cage. In order to fully adjust to an uneven hip alignment, Schneider had Jackson alter his stance. "He's in a crouch more," he said. "And he's using his lower body more." The ultimate plan was unchanged—make the muscles around his left hip as firm and impenetrable as a bank vault. The pain was often unbearable, and Schneider was the only one Jackson could confide in.

Most sessions began with a familiar dialogue:

SCHNEIDER: "Are you sure you want to do this?"
JACKSON: "We have to."
SCHNEIDER: "Do you want me to push you?"
JACKSON: "If you don't push me, I'm not going to make it."

In early January, James Boscardin, the Sox team doctor, performed a full physical on Jackson, and offered the go-ahead for a trip to spring training in less than a month. The hip, he implied, had actually improved from the end of the 1991 campaign, and the White Sox were hoping Gene Lamont, the newly hired manager brought in after a lengthy coaching stint in Pittsburgh, could pencil in Jackson in for 400 at bats as a DH.

In truth, it was all a pipe dream. The diagnosis was aspirational, not reality-based. When the injury occurred in the early days of 1991, Jackson's left side was an eighth of an inch shorter than his right. In the year since, the bone compacted, and his left side was a full inch shorter than his right side. The limp was more pronounced than ever, and there was nothing Boscardin or Schneider could do about it.

Jackson headed to Sarasota on February 14, and within a few days it was clear this would not work. He walked with a limp and ran with a limp.

The man behind a Nike marketing bonanza purchased a pair of loafers because he was unable to bend down and tie his shoes. The hip clearly hadn't improved. If anything, Jackson looked significantly worse. "The first time I saw Bo run, I knew he wasn't gonna play that year," said Lamont. "It was so painful for him."

On February 16, the Los Angeles Lakers held a ceremony inside the Forum to retire Magic Johnson's number 32 jersey. The guard had left the game three months earlier after a positive HIV diagnosis, and at thirty-two was just three years Jackson's senior. Bo observed the festivities from his Sarasota condo, and tears welled. It all seemed to come and go so quickly. For Johnson, sure. But also for Jackson. He had been warned, oh, a thousand times. Don't blink—*you'll miss your career.* But this metamorphosis was unexpected. He had been healthy. Now he was damaged goods. Watching Johnson stand center court, looking both thankful and remorseful, Bo understood. "Some of the things he said really made me sit back and think," Jackson said. "It makes you put your priorities in order and give thanks every day you're even allowed to wake up."

Spring training proved disastrous. He went 2-for-2 in the exhibition opener against Pittsburgh, but the statistical line told little of the story. On a first-inning double (which should have been a triple) off John Smiley, he hobbled into second base. Jackson later scored on a wild throw, but the 90-foot scamper home was no scamper. He was barefooted, running atop shards of glass. Each step looked worse than the one before it. Two innings later, he was on first when Sammy Sosa* grounded toward second. Jackson began to run, then stopped after four steps. Anyone who had seen Willie Mays stumble in the outfield as a New York Met, or watched Bjorn Borg's recent attempted comeback (with wood racket), knew what they were observing: the bottom.

When, in the fourth inning, he was pulled for a pinch runner, Jackson exited the field to a standing ovation. But this wasn't a you're-the-best standing ovation. No. It was a you're-a-shell-of-your-former-self-but-we-still-love-you standing ovation.

And it was horrible.

Against the Detroit Tigers a few days later, Jackson hit a double-play ball to shortstop Alan Trammell, but stopped running after a handful of clumsy steps. Trammell flipped it to Lou Whitaker at second, who looked up and saw Cecil Fielder, the first baseman, signaling with both hands for

---

* Yes, Sammy Sosa was on the 1992 Chicago White Sox.

him to hold the ball and spare Jackson the humiliation. The act itself—born of respect—*was* humiliating.

A few days later, Bernie Lincicome of the *Chicago Tribune* called Jackson "a cartoon." He wrote that "Bo knows denial" and Chicago was "no more than a rest area on the vanishing Bo highway."

"He cheated himself at both [sports]," Lincicome opined, "but he invented a legend. Bo Jackson is not the first to trade dignity for cash. It may be the only common thing he did."

On March 9, in an exhibition game against the Orioles in St. Petersburg, Jackson hit a ball off Rick Sutcliffe that soared between second and third. Cal Ripken, Jr., Baltimore's All-Star shortstop, lunged to his right, but failed to make a play. The baseball rolled into the outfield, where it was picked up by left fielder Brady Anderson.

Then, and only then, did Jackson begin his—in the words of the *Tribune*'s Alan Solomon—"unbalanced, high-step waddle toward first base." He had spent the entirety of the play watching from home.

Seconds later, a man who once ran a 4.13 40 was removed for Joe Hall, pinch runner/long-ago fourth fastest member of the cross country team St. Mary's High in Paducah, Kentucky. "It's like pinch hitting for Ted Williams," Mike Littwin wrote in the *Baltimore Sun*. "It's like pinch jumping for Carl Lewis. Heck, pinch running for Bo is like dubbing Brando." Jackson dragged his left hip all the way from first to the third base dugout, a bellhop lugging a stuffed duffle. It was unbearably sad. The author A. A. Milne once noted, "How lucky I am to have something that makes saying goodbye so hard"—and the sentiment applied here. The fans stood and applauded. This felt like a goodbye.

"I wanted to go up in the stands and shake every man's hand," Jackson said afterward. "And hug every woman and child for that."

The following morning, a somber, reflective Jackson told the media that his season—and maybe athletic career—was over. The White Sox placed him on waivers, and after Jackson went unclaimed the team signed him for the major league minimum of $109,000. This way, he could continue to be a part of the organization and use the facilities to rehabilitate.

His plan was to undergo hip replacement surgery in the coming months, and hope for the best.

"This injury has opened my eyes a whole lot," he said. "I took a lot of things for granted. I haven't always been the most delightful person to work with when it comes to trying to get a story. Not only that, but just simple, everyday things. Now I've got to think about everything I've got to do—getting in and out of the truck, going up and down the stairs, just getting up and going to the bathroom in the morning.

"Like they say, the Lord works in mysterious ways. There's a lot of professional athletes out there that take life for granted. God's got his own way of reaching out and telling you, 'Hey, plant both feet on the ground.'"

With that, he hobbled off.

Alone.

On the morning of April 4, 1992, Dr. Linda Jackson—recent recipient of a PhD in education from Auburn University—drove her husband the eleven miles from their home to Palos Hills, Illinois, where he was scheduled to undergo a major left hip reconstruction (aka: replacement) surgery at Palos Community Hospital.

The surgery was performed by a team of doctors, including Boscardian and Andrews, and lasted two hours. Though it was reported in the media as a fairly normal procedure, little here was, in fact, normal. The vast majority of those who underwent artificial hip replacements were seniors suffering through arthritis. The remaining 15 (or so) percent needed a new hip thanks to an accident, or a birth deformity, or a couple of other random predicaments. Bo Jackson's circumstance was one of a kind.

"The operation went smoothly," the medics said in a post-operating statement, "with no complications."

Five days later, Jackson returned to his sanctuary in Burr Ridge. His hip was supposed to hurt. He was ordered to stay immobilized and rest. Instead, he headed out to the Chicago Bulls game.

Yes, that is correct. The surgery was Saturday. Exactly one week later, Bo and Linda invited friends to the house to celebrate. Steaks were grilled. More than $600 was spent on three bottles of champagne. The crew then drove downtown to catch Pacers-Bulls at Chicago Stadium. Jackson was introduced to the sold-out arena, and waved proudly, purple (yes, purple) crutches to the side.

"I was looking forward to this," he said. "I never looked forward to anything in my life. I couldn't wait to get rid of that person with the limp."

The White Sox opened at home against the Seattle Mariners on April 13, and there was Bo Jackson yet again, hopping around on those purple crutches, smiling in the clubhouse, cracking jokes ("I'm running like a John Deere!" he yelled to Frank Thomas, the first baseman), yukking it up (as much as Bo could yuk anything up) with reporters. He had been chauffeured to Comiskey by Carlton Fisk, the veteran White Sox catcher who also lived in the suburbs and was out with a foot injury.

When it came time for the ceremonial first pitch, Jackson—standing along the box seats near the Sox dugout—was handed a baseball by Eleanor Daley, mother of Chicago mayor Richard Daley. The 42,290 on hand gave a rousing ovation. Jackson waved, smiled and tossed a perfect strike to Ron Karkovice, the White Sox catcher lingering feet away. Asked afterward whether this was the beginning of a comeback, Jackson grinned. "It ain't over 'til the fat lady sings," he said. "And she ain't even got up to the mic yet."

It was one of the exceptional moments of his life.

Two weeks later, in Bessemer, his mother died.

Florence Bond had been sick with colon cancer, but few outside of the family's inner circle knew just how sick. Bo was with his mother on her final days, and Linda and the children flew to Birmingham to meet up with the rest of the family and lay Florence to rest. "It was *so* bad," said Susann McKee, Bo's representative. "I've never seen Bo that sad, that devastated. He didn't have a dad. At least a dad who served as a parent. His mother was everything to him. She was a strong woman who raised all those kids on her own. Bo idolized her."

At a time when Jackson needed a parent to turn to, no one was available. Florence had been his rock. He ran ideas by her, discussed plans with her, sought out her blessing and approval. He had not communicated with A. D. Adams in more than three years, and wasn't about to start now. "I still have a lot of open wounds not having a father around when I was growing up," he said. "Up to this day, my father and I don't speak.

"I tried to have a relationship with him, gave him my number, said, 'Dad, call me. I'll fly you in.' Can you imagine? I'm Bo Jackson, one of the so-called premier athletes in the country, and I'm sitting in the locker room and envying every one of my teammates whose dad would come in and talk with them after the game. I never experienced that."

Following a small funeral for only family and close friends, Florence was buried at Highland Memorial Gardens in Bessemer. Her late husband Joseph had passed nineteen years earlier, and Bo had his remains moved from Pine Hill Cemetery, a ratty, unkempt field of weeds and dirt, and placed by her side. There is one headstone with both names, and in small writing the words REST IN PEACE MOM & DAD. A statue of Jesus Christ watches from ten or so feet away. The section where Florence and Joseph lie is named The Garden of Resurrection. It is quiet and beautiful.

In the years that followed, when Jackson returned to Alabama he would sleep in his old house, in his late mother's bed, beneath his late mother's comforter, head atop her pillow. He half figured to see her there, cooking up something in the kitchen, complaining about a neighbor, asking about her grandkids. "I expect to walk up and hug her," he said. "And I can't do that anymore." From this point on, Jackson wrote his mother's nickname—"Bebe"—on his batting glove and inside his shoes.

Throughout history, plenty of celebrities have milked tragedy for attention. That was not Bo Jackson's way. McKee issued a statement asking for privacy, and her client refused all interview requests. When he was able to regroup and return from Bessemer to Chicago, he did so inspired by the resolve Florence Bond had taught him.

He would work his tail off to return to Major League Baseball.

As the White Sox stumbled through a season that concluded with a third-place finish, Jackson was nowhere to be found. Schueler told no one of the man's whereabouts. "We don't want eight camera crews rushing over there every day," he said. Jackson had, in fact, relocated to Phoenix, Arizona, where he rented a home and trained under the guidance of an unusual man recommended by the White Sox front office. His name was Mack Newton.

A former conditioning coach for the Oakland A's, Newton was the director and chief instructor at Newton Tae Kwon Do. Which, in and of itself, didn't count for much. But the forty-seven-year-old was also a pioneer in physical therapy. Back in the early 1970s, Newton, an Army enlistee, suffered severe injuries while serving in Vietnam. His right ankle was torn open by bullets. His left knee and hips were mangled jumping out of a helicopter. He was returned to the United States and shipped off to a VA hospital for rehab, but found the therapy techniques to be mechanical. So, via trial and error, he developed his own recovery program; one that was steeped in the motivational outlooks of philosophers ranging from Brian Tracy to Ralph Waldo Emerson. "It's a very advanced and specialized form of rehabilitation," he said, "that combines flexibility and muscle reorientation." The Newton Plan was to stretch and exercise the damaged area of the body until it felt and behaved normally. Newton called it "remodeling"—the merging of aggressive isometrics and tons of muscle work. Most physical therapists believed, post–hip replacement, the proper methodology was to avoid weights and place little to no stress on the joint. Newton disagreed. "That approach," he said, "makes the person limp forever."

By the late 1980s, word was spreading about this black belt in the desert with unusual methodologies. When Phoenix Cardinals quarterback Neil Lomax suffered a debilitating left hip injury, he turned to Newton. "We're talking sit-ups, push-ups, weight work, shoulders, legs, everything," Lomax recalled. "Every area of your body, you just do a complete overhaul." In 1987 Newton had his own hip replaced with a rotating plastic joint, and utilized the methods he swore by to regain full usage of his legs and return to competitive tae kwon do.

Newton was the first national voice to express belief in Jackson's comeback. He was asked for his opinion by Casey Tefertiller of the *San Francisco Examiner* a few weeks before the hip replacement surgery, and replied, "I have to say a qualified yes [to Jackson returning]. If rehabilitation is done properly, if he had the attitude that he wants it real, real bad, then he has a chance. If he has a strong will and has a strong desire, it can happen."

Jackson moved to Arizona three and a half weeks after the surgery, and he and Newton got to work. By May 9—roughly a month after the operation—Jackson was walking without crutches and only the slight aid of a cane. Ten days later, any sign of a limp was gone. "As an athlete, he just recovers faster," Newton said. "We've only been working three days and, frankly, it's astonishing, the amount of progress. Bo is a phenomenon, there's no question about that. It's obvious in three days he's not your run-of-the-mill individual."

From the start, Newton promised Jackson his program was three times harder than the roughest football training camp. This was a lie—it was a hundred times harder. But it also worked. Newton put Jackson through physical hell. "My rehabbing was the hardest thing I've ever had to do," Jackson said. "You've got to pay the price, and I've paid my dues.

"It was twenty-four hours a day. There was a certain way to walk, a certain way to sleep, shower, get in the car. How hard was it? If you combined all the years I played sports—twenty-three years into one year—that's how hard."

By late summer, Jackson was physically stronger than he'd ever been. His hip no longer hurt. His body was a rock. Not only was he not limping, but he was nearly running. When he first met Jackson in person, Newton looked at his battered condition and wondered, deep down, how far this might go. In September, he guaranteed the *Boston Globe* that Jackson could be penciled in for spring training '93. "You can't even tell which hip it is," he raved.

Not long after wrapping up with Newton in Arizona, Jackson found himself back in Kansas City for a charity engagement. At the time, the city's only indoor batting was called Grand Slam USA. One night, shortly before the ten o'clock closing time, Mike O'Malley, a seventeen-year-old part-time employee and senior at Blue Valley North High, was sweeping the floor when the phone rang.

O'MALLEY: "Hello?"

JACKSON (from a car phone): "This is Bo Jackson. I'll be there in 15 minutes."

O'MALLEY (sarcastically): "OK—*Bo Jackson*. I'll see you."

It was, obviously, a crank call.

Jackson pulled up in a Mercedes-Benz 500SL convertible. He jumped out, bat in hand, head to toe covered in Nike workout gear, and said he wanted to hit. After getting past the shock, O'Malley set up the machine that threw fastballs and curveballs. He cranked it to the highest level and stood behind a screen and roughly fifty feet in front of Jackson.

"Kid," Jackson said, "you might wanna put on a helmet."

The first pitch was a curve that sailed inside and missed Jackson's hip by about three inches. "That was scary," said O'Malley. "I adjusted the machine, and for the next half hour every ball came right back toward my head. I've never seen anything like it."

When the cage work wrapped, Jackson grabbed a glove, motioned toward some nearby fields and instructed O'Malley to stand 90 feet away. Then 100 feet. Then 120 and 130 and, ultimately, 225 feet. "He was flicking his wrist," O'Malley said, "and throwing these darts right to me." That went on for an hour.

"It's time to run," Jackson said.

"Run?" thought O'Malley. *"You have one hip."*

The two removed their shirts—Jackson starring as Lee Haney, O'Malley as Richie Cunningham. They lined up and began a series of fifty 40-yard sprints. "I was 152 pounds, maybe 6 feet tall, and I could not keep up with him. With a replaced hip."

It was 2:30 in the morning by the time Jackson was ready to wrap. He shook O'Malley's hands, thanked him profusely and sped away in the Mercedes.

"It was clear," O'Malley said, "he wasn't slinking away into the sunset."

Inside Nike's offices, Jackson's initial injury had been deemed a death blow to his marketing career. He was still under contract for another year, but nobody wanted to buy athletic shoes from a wounded warrior. Now, however, there was a glimmer of hope. Three years earlier, during the 1989 All-Star Game, Nike debuted the Bo Knows ad campaign in electrifying fashion. This time, midway through the July 14, 1992, midsummer classic, the company brought forth a new thirty-second commercial. It featured Denis Leary, a young, fast-talking comedian, staring into the camera while pacing (often in front of Jackson doing some sort of exercise), holding a toothpick and snarling: "Hey, no more questions about Bo's hip, OK? No more questions about football, baseball, advertising. Shut up. You thought it was over? Wrong. It ain't over 'til the hip socket sings. OK? So Bo's got a bum hip? So what? Look what he's doing with that hip. He's hitting the bike, he's hitting the weights, he's wearing the shoes. As a matter of fact he's in the pool, wearing the shoes, riding the bike with a hundred and twenty pounds of weights strapped to his neck, OK? And what are you and your good hip doing right now? Watching commercials! I think you hear me knocking. And I think I'm coming in. And I'm bring Bo and his big, bad hip with me."

The spot was funny, resilient, bad-ass.

And a promise that Bo Jackson wasn't done just yet.

CHAPTER 27

A HOG'S HEART ON A FENCE POST

The most enriching year ever wasn't supposed to be the most enriching year ever.

Bo Jackson had won the Heisman Trophy at Auburn, was the number one overall pick in the NFL Draft, made his Big League debut with a hit off of Steve Carlton, led off an All-Star Game with a home run, threw out Harold Reynolds, climbed a wall in Baltimore and starred in one of the biggest advertising campaigns of all time.

So how, in God's name, could 1993 be the most enriching year of Bo Jackson's athletic life? When now, at age thirty, he had a 3- to 5-pound titanium-plastic contraption embedded within the left side of his body where a diseased hip once resided? When the biggest scar anyone had ever seen zipped—crescent-like—from his left buttocks halfway down his thigh?

The most enriching year? Made no sense.

As promised, Jackson not only arrived in Sarasota for spring training, but showed up a day early. Herm Schneider, the team trainer/Bo's former landlord, immediately had him out on the grass inside Ed Smith Stadium, running the bases, taking batting practice, fielding grounders at first base, where Lamont suggested he might see some time. The forty-minute session was observed by only a handful of people, but it was inspired. There was neither noticeable limp nor pain. Jackson felt great and looked great. The one-legged glue mule of a season earlier was not merely planning to DH, but also play first *and* the outfield. "Anything," Jackson said, "to help the team out." First, however, he had to make the roster—one that at the moment overflowed with nine outfielders. Chicago had until March 25 to either exercise Jackson's 1993 option for $910,000 or buy him out for $150,000. Nothing was guaranteed.

The White Sox started full-squad workouts on February 24, and during his first batting practice session Jackson took a fastball from closer Bobby Thigpen and sent it 390 feet over the chain-link fence in right center. His teammates hooted and hollered—but it was hard for Schneider and James Boscardin, the team doctor, to relax. The prosthesis was strong and secure, and would do Great Grandma Norma and her weekly shuffleboard efforts quite well at the Sunrise Lakes Senior Center. This, however, was unchartered turf. Jackson was not only the first Major Leaguer to ever try playing with an artificial hip—he was the first *professional athlete* to ever try playing with an artificial hip.

The prosthesis was top of the line. But it was embedded into the femur, which made anyone competing in a high-impact world (like, say, baseball) vulnerable. "The top part of the thigh is so much stronger," Boscardin said. "It's reinforced there. Just below the prosthesis is where it's subject to stress. If he catches a spike or collides with another player, he could snap it in two." There was also a material issue. Although the 1993 hip was significantly upgraded from the original Teflon models of the 1960s, the reliance on a plastic cup with metal joints spelled trouble for particularly active people. With usage, the two materials would inevitably rub together, causing microscopic bits of plastic to flake off and the hip to loosen. "My advice to patients is, once you have your artificial hip, you can walk, climb stairs, swim or ride a bike," said Dr. Robert Fitzgerald, Jr., a nationally known hip replacement specialist. "But I advise against activity involving running and jumping."

Mark DePaolis, a Brooklyn Center, Minnesota–based physician, put it bluntly: "The constant abuse of competitive sports," he wrote, "might turn his new hip into a rattling peanut in a shell."

Jackson didn't want to hear the negativity. He was here, basking beneath the Florida sun, fighting for his career. Plastic cups? Metal joints? No, thank you. "Screw the doctors," Jackson said when confronted with the potential for catastrophe. "I am living for myself, not some Dr. Seuss who can't cure the common cold."

He started at DH in the spring training opener against Pittsburgh, going a no-limp-to-be-found 1-for-4 with a single to left off Mariano de los Santos. Jackson reached first and smiled contentedly. The Pirates players and coaches stood to cheer. So did his teammates. Jackson grinned toward the dugout. Ozzie Guillen grinned back. The shortstop had missed all but 12 games in 1992 with two torn ligaments in his right knee, and now the men—who spent hours upon hours of rehab time together—referred to themselves as "Club Handicap." Jackson was over the moon. "Hitting is just like sex," he said afterward. "Once you learn how to do it, you don't forget."

Two days later, against Texas, Jackson made his debut as a first base-

man. Imagine Keith Hernandez, arguably the greatest defensive first baseman in baseball history. Now subtract smoothness, know-how, comfort and
precision. Jackson missed a tag (error one), kicked a ball (error two) and
threw away a ball (error three)—all in the third inning. But he went 2-for-3
at the plate, and nothing hurt. So, no, he would never be a wizard around
the bag. He could still rope.

Such was spring for Jackson and the Sox. There was minimal pain. His
swing looked solid. His speed (4.3 seconds to first) was satisfactory. His
defense resembled a John Ritter skit. Lamont insisted Jackson would only
stick if he could contribute beyond DHing, so before long he was in the
outfield. In a game against the Yankees, Paul O'Neill hit a sinking, curving
liner toward left. Jackson charged in, stuttered a bit, watched as the ball
bounced, but slid to block it with his chest. "I liked the way he went after
it," Lamont said. In another matchup, this one against the Pirates, Jackson
sprinted home and clumsily toppled atop the plate on his left hip. "There
was an audible gasp," wrote Joey Reaves of the *Chicago Tribune*, "and then
all of McKechnie Field erupted in applause."

No one was dumb enough to believe the old Bo Jackson might return.
This wasn't about that. Boston ace Roger Clemens offered a blunt assessment, telling reporters, "Everything that was there when he was with Kansas
City before he got hurt, I don't see now. He's average. I guess." But . . . so
what? Evolution is a cornerstone of sports survival. Rookie phenoms don't
remain rookie phenoms. Guys who threw 95 at age twenty-two inevitably
need to develop other pitches. You go from powerful and swift and mighty
to crafty and creative. You work the angles. It's how Julius Erving played
sixteen seasons of high-level basketball. It's how George Blanda stayed in
the NFL until age forty-eight. You don't stand pat. You don't live in a plastic
container. You evolve. You morph.

Bo Jackson was the best story line in baseball. A diamond-shaped soap
opera. Everyone on the White Sox was rooting for the miracle. Everyone
in the Chicago media seemed to be shitting on the miracle (BO JACKSON
IS A MARVEL, BUT HE'LL SOON BE PUT OUT TO PASTURE, read a headline in
the March 13 *Chicago Tribune*). Jackson, resident grump in Kansas City,
arrived each day with a smile on his face and a pep in his step. He opened
up more to the media. He joked with teammates. He no longer had his
gifts to take for granted, and it was liberating. Bo Jackson was one of the
guys. Spirited Ping-Pong games in the clubhouse. Buying meals for rookies. Talking trash and cracking jokes. Spring training happened to coin-
cide with prime hog hunting time in Florida, and after workouts Jackson

headed off for Myakka State Forest with his bow and arrows. "One day he shows up in the morning with this big hog," said Rick Wrona, a White Sox catcher. "One of the staff guys had a smoker, and the whole team ate wild hog for lunch. It was awesome."

The Chicago clubhouse was a riveting mix of personalities. There were well-respected veterans (catcher Carlton Fisk, outfielders Ellis Burks, Tim Raines and Lance Johnson), journeymen galore (Ivan Calderon, Mike Huff), surly brooders (George Bell), nonstop yappers (Guillen) and penis-flicking pranksters (Steve Sax—literally a penis-flicking prankster). The pitching staff had the cocky young Jack McDowell and the cockier, younger Alex Fernandez. The biggest enigma—and biggest star—was Frank Thomas, a twenty-five-year-old first baseman coming off back-to-back 100 RBI seasons. Thomas was one of the best players in the game, but a selfish prick of a teammate. At 6-foot-5 and 240 pounds, he was an intimidating presence who moped with the best of them. "Frank was a douchebag," said one Chicago standout. "I judge people by how they treat those they don't need to be nice to. Frank treated the clubhouse guys like garbage."

"Just a baby," said Lance Johnson. "That year the coaches decided they would hit Frank fifth to protect some guys in the lineup. He refused. Just said, straight up, he wouldn't hit fourth or fifth. I heard that and thought, 'There goes our shot at the World Series.' Because everyone would just pitch around him. Which they did."

Over the course of his first three seasons, Thomas learned (as Bo once had) that if you're really good, and really big, and stomp all over people, no one will stand in your way. Jackson, however, endured none of it. Both men had played football and baseball at Auburn (not together), and Jackson knew Thomas well enough to regularly say, with authority, "Frank, seriously, shut the fuck up."

"Bo was the best thing for Frank," said Doug Mansolino, the first base coach. "No one else on that team had the authority to tell Frank he was being an asshole. But Bo did."

This is not the only reason Jackson (who batted .372 with 9 RBI and a team-leading 16 hits in 13 spring training games) wound up making the 25-man roster. It's not even the number one (Jerry Reinsdorf, the White Sox owner, knew Jackson equaled huge merchandising opportunities) or number two (power bat off the bench) reasons. But unlike in Kansas City, Jackson's clubhouse aura now mattered. If he could help The Big Hurt (as Thomas was known) mature, the built-to-win-Sox might just contend.

When Ron Schueler, the GM, called him on March 24 to break the big news, Jackson was speechless. Not all that long ago, as a Royal, he scoffed at the audacity of anyone thinking he was unworthy of a Major League spot. But times had changed, and perspectives had changed. Jackson immediately thought of his late mother, and the lessons of resiliency Florence Bond had passed his way. He then thought of all the scores of doubters who deemed this quest a joke. Lastly, he thought about playing with an artificial hip—something no one believed could happen. "I've reached my goal—to be on the '93 White Sox," he told the media upon solidifying his place. "The next thing I want to do is help bring a World Series trophy to the South Side of Chicago."

If one looked closely, he might notice tears in the man's eyes.

If, deep down, Bo Jackson thought making the roster meant contributing in major ways, the opening series at Minnesota was a cold splash of water to the face.

He sat on the bench the entire time.

The first home game was slated for the afternoon of Friday, April 9, against the visiting New York Yankees, and when Jackson arrived at the park he looked over the lineup card and saw, yet again, he was not listed. This wasn't shocking. Gene Lamont told Jackson where he stood, and that was as a bat off the bench and occasional DH. Still, it was a bit dispiriting.

There were a stadium-record 42,775 fans at Comiskey, and through five innings not much had gone as planned for the hosts. The Yankees lit up starter Wilson Alvarez for four runs over the first three innings, then knocked around reliever Donn Pall. By the bottom of the sixth, New York led, 7–4, and the Yankees brought in veteran left-hander Neal Heaton to face catcher Ron Karkovice (who grounded out), Guillen (flied out) and Dan Pasqua, the burly left fielder who generally either hit baseballs very far or missed baseballs very badly.

Because Heaton and Pasqua were both lefties, Lamont summoned for the right-handed Jackson to yank his 35-34 Easton from the rack and pinch hit. Inside the Comiskey press box, Doug Abel—the team's public relations director—announced via microphone, "Bo Jackson will be hitting next for Chicago."

One reporter cracked loudly, "Since when do they announce on deck-batters?"

Since Bo Jackson.

Out in the right-field bleachers, Greg Ourednik, a sixteen-year-old high school student from nearby Schererville, Indiana, had begun his exit strategy. His beloved Sox were losing, the weather was miserable (a blustery 45-degree day). So Greg; his father, Allen; brother, John; and a family friend, Ron Serpe, were gathering their stuff, making sure nothing was left on the ground, when a buzz filled Comiskey. Jackson was entering the on-deck circle.

"Wait," Greg told his companions. "Let's just see Bo hit."

Now in his twelfth and final Big League season, Heaton was a thirty-three-year-old journeyman whose once-quality stuff was somewhat ordinary. Like everyone else in the world, he was well aware of Jackson's journey. Respected it even. But he also knew the old Bo Jackson was dead and gone, and that before him stood a carbon copy on a bionic hip. So as soon as the ovation died down and Jackson stepped to the plate, Heaton peered in for the sign from catcher Mike Stanley—fastball.

The pitch was a good one, right over the outside corner of the plate. Jackson took it for strike one. "Be ready," Allen Ourednik told his son. "This one's coming to you."

Heaton and Stanley had only worked together a handful of times, but they were on the same page. Jackson would be looking a fastball, so catch him off guard and fire off a changeup (Heaton's best pitch).

Heaton lifted his right knee to the sky, brought back the ball and released. The pitch was not a good one—straight over the outside portion of the plate, perfect for a slugger who liked to extend his arms. Jackson stepped a hair late, and when he made contact the baseball headed toward right field, a weird location for a dead-pull hitter. At first it appeared to be a warning-track fly ball. But then the wind took hold. And right fielder Danny Tartabull (Jackson's former Royals teammate) drifted toward the wall. Closer to the wall. Ken Harrelson, calling the game for Chicago's SportsChannel, raised his voice. "Tartabull goes back! Looks up! You can put it on the board! Yes! Bo Jackson! In his first at bat in the '93 season, homers to right field! What a moment this is for that man!"

Harrelson, one of the game's great announcers, underplayed the significance. Few believed Jackson would make the team. And here he was, staring upward as his home run left the park, converting the masses and offering a free lesson on perseverance.

Comiskey exploded into cheers, and Greg Ourednik was wowed by his good fortune. The ball soared off Bo Jackson's bat, traveled 400 feet and—as his father promised— nestled perfectly into the boy's raised hands as a gaggle of nearby fans also tried stabbing it from midair. "Dad! Dad!" Greg screamed. "Look!"

Jackson slowly rounded the bases, a man happy to soak it all in. There was no limp to be seen. He was running on adrenaline and confidence. Jackson thought about Florence, his late mother, from second base all the way until touching home. Heaton, watching from the mound, was neither happy nor angry. "I could appreciate all Bo went through," he said. "If you're gonna give one up, that's not a bad one."

Jackson entered the White Sox dugout, but was pushed back onto the field for a curtain call. With the Royals and Raiders, he had never been a man of the people. Now, lathering in the joy, he thrust his helmet into the air with his right hand, soaked in the love, then returned to the safety of a bench. Comparing it to *The Natural*, Bernie Lincicome of the *Chicago Tribune* wrote: "It had to come against the Yankees, naturally, before the fullest house yet at a new Comiskey opener. Fiction has never been Bo Jackson's enemy."

When the inning ended and the Sox returned to the field, Ellis Burks, the right fielder, walked toward the outfield wall. "Hey!" he yelled into the bleachers. "Who's the guy who caught the ball? Bo wants to talk to him."

Ourednik was escorted to the home clubhouse, where Jackson was waiting in his white pinstriped uniform. The teenager knew all about the comeback, the late mother, the meaningfulness of the afternoon. A year earlier, he submitted a report on Jackson for his Lake Central High English class. "We had to write about a person we looked up to," he recalled. "I really admired Bo." Now, sans hesitation, Ourednik removed the ball from his jacket pocket and handed it over.

"Here's the ball, Mr. Jackson," Ourednik said.

"Thank you so much," Jackson replied. "I'm going to have this bronzed and placed atop my mother's tombstone."*

He shook the teen's hand, presented a signed bat and ball and posed for a quick photograph.

All these years later Ourednik, now forty-five and a Chicago resident, has the items framed inside his house. "It's one of the best memories of my life," he said. "Mainly because it meant so much to someone else."

On Thursday, April 15, the White Sox arrived in Boston for a four-game series at Fenway Park scheduled to kick off the next afternoon.

After settling in at the Marriott Copley Place, Bo Jackson took Ellis Burks for lunch.

---

* For whatever reason, he never did.

For six years, Burks had been one of the Red Sox foundational players—a four-tool outfielder who the team planned to build around. After a back injury wiped out much of his 1992 season, however, Burks was kicked to the curb. Boston chose not to go to salary arbitration, and refused to offer a contract. The White Sox swooped in and signed him to a one-year deal for $500,000.

Now, returning to Beantown for the first time, Burks was overcome by emotions. He was mad at the franchise, hurt by the rejection, saddened by the lack of any loyalty. Mostly, he was jumpy. This was terribly uncomfortable.

"Let's go eat," Jackson told Burks. "I'll pay."

They met in the hotel lobby, and Jackson hailed a taxi and had it ferry them to what he promised would be a terrific meal.

"I was thinking surf and turf," Burks said. "Or maybe Italian."

Ellis Burks had never tried sushi. He barely knew sushi was a thing. Raw fish, right? Eel, maybe? He gazed over the menu, and stared blankly across the table toward his teammate. "Don't worry," Jackson said, "I'll order for you."

The food, Burks recalled, was fantastic. Even better was the conversation. Jackson explained that, in the grand scheme, none of this was a big deal. Baseball was a business, and Boston made a stupid business decision. The best thing Burks could do was relax and force his old employer to see the errors of its ways.

In his first at bat the next afternoon, Burks blasted a homer off of Danny Darwin. It remains one of the most memorable moments of an eighteen-year career.

"I took Bo's football mentality into that game," Burks said. "I felt relaxed, but also energized. That's entirely because of Bo.

"Plus, now I love sushi."

Burks's lifelong affection for spicy tuna rolls sums up Jackson's contributions to the 1993 White Sox. His statistics (.232, 16 home runs, 45 RBI, 106 strikeouts in 284 at bats) tell the story of a below-average Major Leaguer who earned his position largely based upon the powers of name and narrative. In his midseason report card, Joey Reeves of the *Chicago Tribune* gave Jackson a C+. It was fair—Jackson wasn't very good.

But he was simultaneously great. Great with a quick word. Great with advice. Great with a sharp sense of humor and great with the presence to distract from struggles and hardships. After a loss at Toronto, Thomas blamed his misplaying of a fly ball on the SkyDome's air-conditioning unit causing an unnatural drift. On the bus back to the Hilton International, Jackson walked toward the driver and picked up the intercom speaker. "Paging Frank Thomas!" he said. "Paging Frank Thomas! Frank! Frank! The fucking retractable roof was open, Frank! The fucking roof! Wasn't no A/C unit!"

Lots of Major League teams hazed their rookies in ways that bordered on cruel. One day, while the Sox were in Milwaukee, Jackson spotted rookie pitcher Jason Bere sitting alone and eating lunch at the hotel restaurant. Jackson pulled up a chair, ordered a tuna melt, asked Bere about his childhood, his family, how the season was going. "It was so cool," Bere recalled. "Bo genuinely talking to a nobody like me. Then he got up and left me the bill." Bere chuckled. "That," he said, "was the extent of his hazing." The same year, pitcher Roberto Hernandez was in Seattle hours before a night game, shopping for a new jacket inside a posh leather boutique. He felt a tap on the shoulder, spun and saw a smiling Jackson. "Ma'am," the veteran said to the shop manager, "whatever jacket this young man wants, it's on me."

"He was such a tremendous teammate," Hernandez said. "The best."

When the White Sox traveled to Oakland, Jackson instructed the whole team to meet inside the lobby bar of the Airport Hilton, where the players commandeered the pool table. Like the old days in Kansas City, the White Sox set up a Ping-Pong table in the middle of the clubhouse, and like the old days in Kansas City, Jackson dominated. His hand was enormous enough to hold the paddle as one would a tortoiseshell, fingers wrapped around the perimeter. He rarely lost. "Man, he was really good," said Wrona. "I'd try challenging him all the time."

One afternoon, as Jackson was emerging from the shower, Wrona—paddle in hand—barked, "You don't want none of this!" Jackson approached the table, dropped the towel wrapped around his waist and said, "Hit one to my backhand, soft."

"What?" Wrona said.

"You heard me," Jackson said. "Not too hard."

Wrona served, and Jackson returned the ball with his erect penis—*twice*. Howling ensued. "He hit a Ping-Pong ball with his dick!" Wrona said. "With his dick!"

Steve Sax, the veteran second baseman who came to Chicago after three years with the Yankees, was among the impressed. Sax was—depending on which teammate fills out the poll—"crazy," "wild," "super weird" and/or "warped."

Sax loved Jackson. He especially loved discussing Jackson's penis. During the first homestand of the season, Sax had been approached by a handful of New York beat writers. He greeted the familiar scribes not with "Hello" or "Bug off," but—"Guys, I am here to officially report that Bo Jackson's dick is like the arm of a young Black boy holding a plum." Later in the season, he adjusted his descriptive flair. "Bo's penis," he'd say, "is a hog's heart on a fence post."

Though he certainly longed to play and produce, Jackson was more at ease than he had been with the Royals. He tasted superstardom, and no longer craved it. He relished being one of twenty-five, as opposed to number one of twenty-five. During a Sox trip to Cleveland, Thomas was signing pre-game autographs when Jackson and Wrona exited the dugout to cross the field. The fans' attention shifted from Frank to Bo—thousands of people screaming, "Bo! Bo! Please sign! Bo! Bo!"

"Ricky Ro," Jackson said to Wrona, using his nickname, "I will trade my popularity for yours in a heartbeat, and I'll throw in a toaster."

Jackson was at his finest in late June, when the White Sox—sitting atop the American League West for much of the season—headed to Cleveland for a three-game series against the Indians. On June 22, Carlton "Pudge" Fisk, the team's forty-five-year-old catcher, had set the all-time games caught record with his 2,226th appearance behind the plate. It was an enormous deal; the capper on a sure-to-be Hall of Fame run. The White Sox anointed it "Carlton Fisk Day," and presented the legend with his very own Harley-Davidson (driven onto the field by Jackson—who came up with the idea for the gift). Afterward, the normally cold and stoic Fisk told the media it was the most gratifying day of his twenty-four-year career. "This is it, number one," he said. "Even more emotional than the day I was married. I would like to say it was a culmination of a career, but that would sound like it's the end."

It was the end.

On the morning of Monday, June 28, roughly six hours before he was scheduled to report to Cleveland Municipal Stadium for Game 1 of White Sox–Indians, Fisk was summoned to Schueler's thirteenth-floor suite inside the Radisson. The catcher presumed it would be a chat over the team's direction. Nope—Schueler came to the Sixth City to tell Fisk (batting .189 at the time) he was being released. "I don't think he expected it," Schueler said afterward. "He still thought he was going to be here all season."

Chicago's players reported to the stadium and learned the news. It was not received well. If this sort of thing could happen to Fisk, it could certainly happen to them, too. Plus, why did the White Sox even have Fisk travel to Cleveland? Why not do it at home? "Everyone was pissed," said Scott Radinsky, a Chicago reliever. "It was such fucking bullshit. There was a lot of uneasiness during BP. What the fuck is going on here?" Joey Cora, the second baseman, placed two pieces of masking tape on the back of his helmet and wrote THANKS—72 (Fisk's uniform number) in black marker. Thomas grabbed his helmet and taped Fisk's number above his own. Bere chalked 72 onto his cap. Walt Hriniak, the hitting coach, was close to tears.

As the recent victim of an organization discarding once-precious goods, this one cut Jackson. He urged his teammates to calm down, and in the clubhouse before the game explained that everyone in the room—from star to scrub—needed to prepare for such a moment. "We're products," he said. "Just know that—you're a product and then one day they dump you on the side of the road."

Fisk spent the hours after his dismissal enjoying the miniature refrigerator inside his room at the Radisson Plaza, then made his way to the stadium. "It was something," said Wrona. "He comes to the park, bum-rushes past security and gets into the clubhouse during the game." Fisk's apparent goal was to reach the White Sox dugout and either: (A) Rip Gene Lamont a new one; or (B) Distribute daisies to his teammates while thanking them for so many cherished experiences.

"I'm pretty sure it's A," said Wrona. "Definitely A."

There was a tunnel, roughly 30 yards in length, between the clubhouse and the dugout. The intoxicated Fisk stumbled down the walkway, feet stomping ever so loudly, when he was intercepted by Jackson.

"Pudge," Jackson said. "You don't wanna do this."

Fisk *did* want to do this.

"Pudge," Jackson said again, his arm over the ex-catcher's shoulder. "It's not worth it. Please, man. Go back to the hotel. We'll have a party for you later . . ."

Fisk retraced his steps back up the tunnel, through the clubhouse, into the bowels of the stadium and walked toward the left-field bleachers, where he wound up leaning over the wall and chatting with Chicago's relievers. He was drunk and angry. "He didn't know what to do with himself," said Pall, "after all those years of going to the park every night."

When the game ended with a 2–0 Indians win, Jackson announced a farewell soiree on the second floor of a gentleman's club in the Cleveland Flats. "It was only White Sox players there," said Wrona. "By the end of the evening Carlton was on the stage and there were eight to ten strippers up there with him, riding him. That's what I remember. It was a really fun night, and a cool thing for Bo to organize." The final tab was four thousand dollars, and Jackson paid for most of it. He didn't drink a sip of alcohol—"I felt I had to chaperone," he recalled. "I put it on myself to stay sober because that's the last thing we needed was for somebody on the team to get in trouble and to do something stupid."

Jackson had a few on-field moments of note. An amazing throw from right to nail Yankees shortstop Mike Gallego tagging from second to third. A towering home run against Baltimore's Rick Sutcliffe. A ninth-inning two-RBI single off the Brewers' Doug Henry to break a 1-1 tie. Two that stand out have little to do with actual baseball skills. On July 16, at the start of the eighth inning of a game at Milwaukee, White Sox first base coach Doug Mansolino engaged in a heated argument with John Jaha, the Brewers first baseman. From the Milwaukee dugout, manager Phil Garner spared no "Fuck you" in his verbal onslaught toward Mansolino.

"Are you talking to me?" Mansolino said.

"Fuck you, asshole!" Garner said.

The 5-foot-9, 180-pound Mansolino charged toward Garner, en route taking a wild swing at Rocky Roe, the first base umpire. "I'm in the Brewers dugout getting the absolute shit kicked out of me," Mansolino said. "I'm on the bottom of the pile being beaten like a redheaded stepchild, and when I finally escape and leave, Al Clark, the crew chief, throws me out of the game."

"What about fucking Garner?" Mansolino yelled.

"You can't run into a dugout," Clark replied. "You're out of here."

Mansolino headed straight toward Clark, fist cocked, when from behind he felt two steel beams reach around his waist. It was Jackson. "I'm going crazy, totally out of my mind, screaming, 'Al, you want a piece of me? Al, you want a fucking piece?'" Mansolino said. "Bo carried me down the tunnel, up the ramp, up the two flights of stairs into the clubhouse and set me down on a chair. Then he said, 'You're not leaving.'

"I owe Bo my career. He saved me from committing manslaughter."

Nineteen days later, the White Sox were in Texas playing the Rangers. These were two franchises that bore the scars of repeated beanball wars against one another. During batting practice, Jackson was chatting with Robin Ventura, the team's young third baseman, about that night's opposing starter, Nolan Ryan. "If he hits you, don't rip your helmet off," Jackson said. "Use your helmet like a football helmet. And then when you charge the mound you don't run to the pitcher, you run to second base. You take the pitcher and take him off the back of the mound and he'll fall on his ass. Do not go to the mound and stop."

With one out in the third and the White Sox up 2–0, Ryan nailed Ventura with a fastball on the right side of his back. Chicago's cleanup hitter threw down his helmet (wrong!), ran straight for Ryan (wrong!)—*"Noooooooooo!"* yelled Jackson—and was placed in a headlock by the forty-six-year-old ace. Four right hands to the skull followed, then a fist directly to Ventura's face. "All I could think about when it happened was 'What's Robin thinking?'" said Jeff Huson, a Rangers infielder. "You don't charge the highest authority." The video wound up on nightly sportscasts across the continent. Overlooked by the blind eye was Jackson—now about 235 pounds of solid muscle—walking through the scrum of Rangers and White Sox players and coaches and, one by one, lifting them away like paper plates off a picnic table. After several moments Ryan, pinned at the bottom of the pile, felt himself starting to suffocate. "I thought I was going to black out and die," he said, "when all of a sudden I see two big arms tossing bodies off of me. It was Bo Jackson. He had come to my rescue, and I'm awful glad he did."

That night, a couple of hours after the Rangers 5–2 victory, Jackson was resting inside his room at the Radisson Suites when the phone rang.

"Bo," a man with a slight twang said, "it's Nolan—Nolan Ryan."

This was unexpected.

"Listen, pal, I just wanted to call and thank you for saving my life . . ."

On the afternoon of September 27, 1993, Dave Fleming arrived at Comiskey Park to put a final touch on a fairly miserable baseball season.

One year earlier, as an out-of-nowhere rookie starter from the University of Georgia, Fleming pieced together a 17-10 record and 3.39 ERA for the lowly Seattle Mariners, at one point prompting the *New York Times* to run the headline WHO IS DAVE FLEMING? AND WHEN WILL HE LOSE?

Fast forward 365 (or so) days, and Fleming was learning the hard truths of the Big Leagues: hitters figure you out. So while the soft-throwing left-hander came to Chicago sporting an 11-4 record, the statistics were misleading. His ERA was an alarming 4.44. He'd been hammered in three of his last four starts. His ball was staying up in the zone. "I wasn't the same guy," Fleming said. "Winning in the Majors is hard enough. But sustaining—it's even harder."

With a 78-78 mark, Seattle was 12 games behind the White Sox in the American League West and merely playing out the circuit. But for

Chicago, the night's game was particularly meaningful. With a win over Fleming and the M's, the White Sox would clinch their first division title in a decade.

"It felt like a playoff game," Fleming recalled. "The atmosphere was energized. I loved pitching in those circumstances."

Before a jam-packed Comiskey, Fleming and Chicago's Wilson Alvarez found themselves in an old-school pitcher's duel. For 5½ innings, neither team scored a run, and only five total hits were racked up by the two clubs.

In the bottom of the sixth, Fleming tired. Ellis Burks led off with a single to left. Craig Grebeck followed with a bunt single. Thomas flied out, then George Bell struck out.

With two outs, Bo Jackson stepped up. By now it was clear his time in the game was short. Jackson's batting average was down to .224, and his play in the outfield had been atrocious. A DH with dwindling power, no speed, no position and an artificial hip had a limited shelf life.

Fleming wasn't an ideal matchup for Jackson. Yes, he was a lefty. But he was a lefty who worked spots, exploited weak points, dissected hitters in order to overcome so-so velocity. In other words, undisciplined free swingers (like Bo) *hated* him. With the runners on first and second, Fleming pitched Jackson carefully. A fastball inside for ball one. Another fastball for ball two. A fastball back outside for ball three.

Now, when Fleming peered in for the sign, catcher Dave Valle dropped four fingers—another changeup. The pitcher nodded, glanced back at Burks on second, flashed a look toward Grebeck on first, faced home, raised his crooked right leg high into the air and let fly one of the absolute worst pitches of his life. "For whatever reason I didn't think he'd be swinging," Fleming said. "He's a guy with a flair for the dramatic. How stupid of me." The baseball fluttered toward home and Jackson unloaded. His swing was exquisite—left leg up, right elbow cocked, hips parallel to the ground, bat head level, but with a slight skywards tilt. Fleming immediately twisted his neck and looked toward the outfield, as did Jackson. Brian Turang, the left fielder, froze for a moment, giving the impression this was a mere long out. But then he turned to run, reached the warning track and stared upward.

Jackson's shot cleared the outfield wall by about six feet, landing directly in the palms of a teenager sitting in the front row. "You can put it on the board!" screamed Ken Harrelson, the announcer. "Yes! A three-run homer! By Bo Jackson! And the Sox lead it! Three! To! Nothing!"

Everyone in the stadium stood. Not *most* everyone. Everyone. All 42,116. Approaching second, buoyed by the noise and the moment, Jackson punched his right fist in the air and, a second later, his left fist. Fireworks exploded over the scoreboard beyond center field, and at home he was greeted by a series of high fives. Approaching the dugout, Jackson was swallowed in a bear hug from Guillen, cofounding member of Club Handicap, then an endless string of hugs and butt slaps. The fans refused to sit. The organist continued to play. The fans still refused to sit. The organist still continued to play. Ventura, the next hitter, was in the batter's box, but his moment would have to wait.

After Jackson walked halfway down the dugout, Guillen and Burks urged him to take the curtain call the fans were longing for. Jackson hated these things. He was a ballplayer, not a Broadway performer. Not a showboat. Not a ham. Not a . . .

He hopped up the two steps, removed his helmet with his right hand, passed it to his left and thrust it into the air. He then drew back his right fist, punched upward and screamed a gladiator-like, "Yeah!"

"The big moment," said Harrelson. "He's a big moment man."

The White Sox wound up winning, 4–2.

The American League West was theirs.

Dave Fleming pitched parts of but two more Major League seasons. Decades later, as a fourth-grade math teacher at Chatfield-LoPresti Elementary in Seymour, Connecticut, he occasionally talks to students about failing, and shows them the YouTube video of the home run.

"It's life," Fleming said. "The highs, the lows. It's all part of the journey. Plus, it's not like I gave up a home run to a nobody. That's Bo Jackson, the greatest athlete of all time.

"I can live with it."

There should be a happy ending to all of this.

If you've ever seen *Major League*, or *Major League II*, or even *Major League: Back to the Minors*,* you know how this goes: The band of wacky misfits, playing for a team that generally loses, finds a way to shock the world, capture the championship and get back together with Rene Russo.

Unfortunately for the 94-68 White Sox, runaway champions of the A.L. West, the champagne celebration that followed the win over Seattle was as good as it got. They would go on to play Toronto in the American League Championship Series, and while the six-game matchup was somewhat competitive, the Blue Jays were a deeper club. "Just better than us," said Tim

---

* Don't see *Major League: Back to the Minors*.

Belcher, a White Sox pitcher. "Sometimes it's OK to admit you lost to the superior team."

Jackson wasn't one of those kids who grew up dreaming of World Series glory, but now that the Sox were *this* close he hungered for the experience. Perhaps that's why as Chicago—playing before its home fans—lost the first two games, Jackson sat on the bench and brooded.* Thanks to a triceps injury, Thomas was forced to DH, and Lamont played reserve outfielder Dan Pasqua—not Jackson—at first. The move was reasonable: Jackson manned the position with the dexterity of a potted fern. But for the first time all season, he lashed out to the press. "We have been one bat short for two days and we've been missing one bat for two games," he said. "Now we have to go to Toronto and play catch up."

It was a direct shot at the 0-for-6 Pasqua ("I understood," Pasqua said years later. "Bo was frustrated."), and Lamont was incredulous. Of all the moments to complain, why now? Regardless, Jackson was inserted into the lineup for Game 3, and went 0-for-4 with three strikeouts in Chicago's 6–1 victory. "Bo didn't have much to say in the clubhouse after [the win]," wrote Jerome Holtzman in the *Tribune*. "And so far as is known, none of his teammates expressed anger that he struck out three times." Two days later, in a 5–3 Game 5 defeat, Jackson twice came up as the potential tying run. Twice, he struck out. "I really don't have an excuse," Jackson said. "I saw the ball good, but I just didn't get it."

Midway through the series, Jackson ran into Nathalie Dixon, mother of Blue Jays pitcher Dave Stewart, in a restaurant. He approached her table, offered his hellos, then added, "The next time we face your son, we're going to kick the shit out of him." Nathalie immediately called her child and relayed the conversation. Stewart's blood boiled.

"Guys who talk a lot," Stewart told the media, "let everybody know they're fools when they don't deliver."

Stewart started Game 6 at Comiskey. He held the White Sox to two runs over 7⅓ innings in his team's series-clinching 6–3 win. Jackson spent the night on the bench. All told, the man who openly whined about his club lacking a bat (*his* bat) wrapped the ALCS a pathetic 0-for-10 with a walk and six strikeouts.

---

* It didn't help the White Sox that on October 6—the same day the series began—Michael Jordan of the Chicago Bulls announced his retirement from the NBA. A Comiskey Field press box that was supposed to be stuffed with reporters suddenly turned ghost town. "It upstaged everything," said Jay Mariotti, a *Chicago Sun-Times* columnist. "It was like, 'White Sox? Who are the White Sox?'"

"Oh, those Chicago White Sox Jacksons," wrote Dan Shaughnessy in the *Boston Globe*. "There was Shoeless Joe; now there is Clueless Bo."

The Blue Jays went on to beat the Philadelphia Phillies in the World Series, the White Sox went home to ponder a tremendous season that ended poorly.

Less than a month after his final swing, Jackson was told Chicago would not pick up his $2.41 million option for 1994, and he was presented a $150,000 termination fee and waived. "Although Bo is eligible to become a free agent, that does not eliminate the possibility that he could still be a member of the White Sox next year," Schueler said in a statement.

Those words were stated on Friday, November 5. Two evenings later, Jackson was handed a couple hundred bucks to sit at a table and sign autographs at the grand opening of a Marshalls inside the Charlestowne Center Mall in St. Charles, Illinois.

The store's slogan: "Never, never, never pay full price."

CHAPTER 28

THE CIRCUS ACT

All the right things were said.

The White Sox appreciated everything Bo Jackson had done for them. He was inspiring and heroic. He taught youngsters the right way to approach the game. He was professional and smart and one of baseball's great icons. He was named the American League's Comeback Player of the Year by *The Sporting News,* and it was well-deserved.

"Bo," said Jerry Reinsdorf, the team owner, "is one of the great stories of our time."

All the right things were said.

Inside the team's executive offices, however, there wasn't much debate over whether the thirty-one-year-old DH with the .232 average and severe physical limitations should return for another season on the South Side. Actually, scratch that. There was no debate. When the White Sox offered Jackson salary arbitration, it was only a formality of public kindness. They knew—correctly—he would reject it.

And with that, on January 8, 1994, Bo Jackson became a free agent.

Save for a brief exchange with the Oakland A's, no teams cared. This was hardly a surprise. Jackson had recently fired Richard Woods, his longtime agent, and replaced him with Arn Tellem. But no matter who was handling the negotiations, it wasn't going to be easy. The benefits of adding Jackson to a team (solid clubhouse guy who can return a Ping-Pong ball with his penis) no longer outweighed the negatives (couldn't play, body attached to an artificial hip that might fall apart at any moment). So if Jackson were to continue as a ballplayer, it would take some genre of special circumstance that made his reduced impact worthwhile.

Luckily, he found one.

On the afternoon of Friday, January 7, 1994, Whitey Herzog, vice president and general manager of the California Angels, caught a ride to Los Angeles International Airport with Bill Bavasi, his assistant. His plan was to fly home to St. Louis for a weekend of relaxation with the family and return Monday.

On Sunday, the phone rang in Bavasi's Mission Viejo home.

"Bill, it's Whitey," Herzog said. "I'm not gonna be on that flight."

"All right," Bavasi said. "Just let me know when I should pick you up."

"No," Herzog replied. "That's not it. I'm resigning, and you'll be taking over as GM."

Um, oh.

Bill Bavasi, thirty-six years old, was now calling the shots.

Best known as the son of Buzzie Bavasi, long-ago GM of the Brooklyn/ Los Angeles Dodgers, Bill spent most of the past decade working as the Angels' director of minor league operations—a far cry from running the show. He was well regarded and genuinely liked, but inside the organization it felt as if the Tiffany's janitor had been promoted to store manager.

The worst part: the Angels cupboard was bare. Coming off of a dreadful 71-91 season, California boasted a farm system with a bushel of prospects two or three years away and a Big League roster populated by stiffs, geriatrics and geriatric stiffs. "I got the position, looked around and realized we weren't good," Bavasi said. "And then, about a week later, Arn Tellem called."

The conversation was brief. Jackson was a free agent. He had some potential business dealings in Southern California. He wanted to play one last season, and would happily DH, man a corner outfield, come off the bench, pinch hit, knit booties. "He can really help with some of your younger guys," Tellem said. "He'll be a positive influence, I assure you."

The Dallas Cowboys and Buffalo Bills met in Super Bowl XXVIII on January 30, 1994. It was a game Bo Jackson once aspired to play in. Instead, that morning he agreed to a one-year, $1 million contract with the Angels. The news appeared on page C13 of the *Los Angeles Times* sports section, just below a blurb about Cammy Myler becoming the first American woman to win a World Cup luge race. In the article, Bavasi raved about Jackson adding to the club's outfield depth. Years later, he admitted that was a whole lot of phony hype. "I'm gonna be honest," he said. "We looked at ourselves in the mirror and thought, 'Hey, we can definitely use a circus act to have people come to the ballpark.' Because we had a terrible team."

This is what it had come to for Bo Jackson. He was a circus act. A gate attraction. The one-legged wonder. Fifty-nine years earlier, the Boston Braves signed a forty-year-old free agent named Babe Ruth to waddle the outfield, tip his cap to fans, sign some autographs and partake in the postgame buffet. Such a pathetic vision prompted Edward J. Neil of the *Burlington Free Press* to note that Ruth, "has dropped faster from public sight and the public mind than any great athletic hero of his time. No one asks anymore, 'Where's Ruth? What's he doing?' He's lived like a goldfish so long, complaining all the time that he had no privacy, yet loving the crowds, the hero-worship, the excitement just the same."

Now here was Jackson, Ruthian of the modern day—not nearly as accomplished, yet just as iconic and seemingly just as sad. He had become a sympathy hire. "I'm just being truthful," Bavasi said. "He wasn't really brought in to help us win." The introductory press conference was well attended, and Jackson appeared to be in good spirits. He viewed himself as a fourth outfielder. He had again worked throughout the winter with Mack Newton, and was down ten pounds (and 2 inches off his waist) from the end of the previous season. Asked how his life had changed with a new hip, he cracked, "I spend a lot of time at the metal detector at the airport."

Jackson arrived early at the team's Tempe, Arizona–based spring training facility on Saturday, February 19. He was introduced to Ken Higdon, the Angels' equipment manager and man who matched players with uniform numbers. For three seasons Jackson had donned number 8 with the White Sox, and felt kinship with the digit. Higdon explained that—technically— the number *probably* remained available, but that there was a bit of a hiccup. One year earlier, on April 22, 1993, MaryAnn Flora, wife of California infield prospect Kevin Flora, was driving outside of Van Horn, Texas, when she lost control of her car and flipped into the air. Both MaryAnn and her four-year-old nephew, Alec, were killed.

Playing for Triple A Vancouver at the time, Kevin Flora was desolate. He missed nearly all of the remainder of the season, then lasted a week in the Arizona Fall League before breaking down. The Angels asked him to play winter ball in a Latin American country, but he refused—it would bring back too many memories of his time with MaryAnn in Venezuela.

Flora had only three big league games to his résumé (all from 1991), but was being invited to camp as a longshot competitor for the second base job. His presumed uniform number lined up perfectly with MaryAnn's birthday: February 8.

Higdon told Jackson the story. Without hesitation, he said, "Give me another number. I'll take 22."

"I knew Bo was joining the team and that he wore number 8," recalled Flora. "So when I got to my locker and saw number 8 hanging there, I was surprised. Kenny explained what happened. That meant so much to me.

He's Bo Jackson. Goodness. He could have taken the number and nobody would have said a word."

Through the early days of camp, Jackson impressed teammates with his long BP blasts and a generally upbeat demeanor. He couldn't move a lick side to side, but otherwise there was optimism. When asked about his new slugger, Buck Rodgers, the veteran manager, told reporters, "Bo can be a bargain or Bo can be a bust. But like Adam said to Eve the first time they met, 'Stand back, because I don't know how big this thing will get.'"

His official spring training debut came against the Rockies on March 4. In the eighth inning of a tie game, Jackson headed to the plate to face Marc Pisciotta, a twenty-three-year-old righty who had been recently plucked from Pittsburgh in the Rule V Draft. The bases were loaded, and when the count went to 3-0 Pisciotta took a second to appreciate the magnitude of the deity before him. Pisciotta's entire 1993 had been spent at Class A, and now he was about to try and throw heat past Bo Jackson. "Shit," he thought to himself, "just don't groove one."

The outside fastball traveled in at 92 mph, and Jackson reached and powered it over the outfield wall at Diablo Stadium. The Angels won 7-6, and afterward Gene Autry, team owner, entered the clubhouse to offer a personal congratulations. "Hopefully you'll be doing the same thing in six months," he said.

"Does this mean I've got a job?" Jackson replied.

Autry flashed a grin and a thumbs-up.

Pisciotta, for his part, was sent back to Pittsburgh.

Jackson made the opening day roster, of course, because seats don't fill themselves. And, from the start, his was a Jekyll and Hyde presence. He had loved everything about the White Sox, and this new world was a major comedown. The Angels' clubhouse was fine, but without an ounce of fire. Jackson cut off the media for much of the year, but whenever ESPN wanted time he made certain to break his silence. He was (as usual) unpredictably moody, once approaching the club's *Orange County Register* beat writer and saying, menacingly, "Are you Lawrence Rocca?"

"Yes."

"I'm going to kick your ass," Jackson barked. "Don't ever talk to me again."

While sitting in the press box trying to digest what had transpired, Rocca heard *THUMP! Pause. THUMP! Pause. THUMP!* against the window. It was Jackson from below, throwing baseballs at him.

After the game, one of the Angels pitchers pulled Rocca aside. "I saw what happened," he said. "Don't let Bo get to you. He's an asshole."*

John Weyler of the *Los Angeles Times* was cobbling together a lengthy profile of Chili Davis, the team's best hitter. He asked Jackson for his thoughts. "Chili fucking Davis!" Jackson screamed in mock anger before the entire clubhouse. "I don't have the time to talk about Chili fucking Davis!"

Weyler slunk off, a bit unnerved.

Such was (oftentimes) Jackson the Angel. Rude. Indifferent. Exceptionally crude. When a team employee broke his arm, Jackson signed the cast—in permanent black marker—BO JACKSON, 12" COCK. He gave shortstop Gary DiSarcina the nickname "Horsecock," which was funny the first, second, third, fourth, fifth and fiftieth times it was uttered. Then it got old. "I was Horsecock," DiSarcina said years later with a laugh. "There are worse nicknames."† Unlike his time in Chicago, Jackson no longer fully devoted himself to the comeback. He rarely lifted weights, didn't seek out a nearby pool. Mack Newton sent Jackson to California with a series of essential hip exercises, the majority of which were ignored. This was his last dance, and he wanted to cruise. So extra BP—meh. Bonus time stretching—nah. When he wasn't in that day's lineup, Jackson could usually be found back in the clubhouse, talking on the phone inside the manager's office, legs propped up on a chair, game on mute from a nearby television. "Sometimes we'd go get him so he'd talk with us," said Rex Hudler, an Angels infielder. "You wanted to pick his brain." Unlike Chicago, where the fan intensity was always dialed up to an eleven, in sunny, suburban Anaheim loyalists were far more concerned with beating traffic. It failed to feed Jackson's competitiveness, and his indifference reflected such.

But just when one thought Jackson was going full Hyde, Jekyll emerged. On an off day Jackson invited the team's batboys and equipment managers to his home, where he cooked up thirteen chickens, two slabs of ribs, corn on the cob and corn bread. "I just wanted to show them how much they are appreciated," he said.

One of the Angels' youngest players was a twenty-two-year-old rookie left-hander named Brian Anderson. Jackson liked the kid, and decided to adopt him as a protégé. Anderson made his first start of the season in Milwaukee on April 10, holding the Brewers to one run in 8⅓ innings for a 4–1

---

* In Jackson's defense, Rocca was abhorred by most of the Angels. Years later, he admitted it was justified. "I was an awful beat writer," he said.

† There really aren't.

California triumph. "It was my first Major League win," said Anderson. "I think Bo was happier than I was."

On the bus from County Stadium to Milwaukee's General Mitchell International Airport, Jackson pulled out a shoe-size cellular talking device and demanded Anderson surrender his mother Janice's phone number back in Geneva, Ohio.

"Hello?"

"Yes, is this Janice? Janice Anderson?"

"Yes it is."

"Mrs. Anderson, this is Bo Jackson."

"No, it's not."

"Yes, it is."

"No, it's not."

"Yes, it really is. And I wanted to tell you that your son picked up his first Major League win tonight, and I bet you're so proud of him. Because we sure are. Here, I'll hand him the phone . . ."

Throughout the season, Anderson and Jackson watched the soap opera *The Young and the Restless* together. Jackson rented a home near Dana Point, roughly forty minutes south of Anaheim, and one night he asked Anderson, "Rook, what are you doing after the game?"

Nothing.

"You're coming with me."

First, the two men headed to a nearby hotel bar to have drinks with some of Jackson's pals. Then they stopped at Jack in the Box for burgers, fries and sodas. Then they headed for Jackson's home, where Anderson was told to stay for the night. They woke up late the next morning (an off day) and had lunch. "Bo had a phone in the bathroom," said Anderson. "I snuck in there." Back in Ohio, his closest friend was a guy named Tim Leonard. Anderson dialed his number, and Leonard picked up.

"Tim," he whispered, "I'm at Bo Jackson's house! On his toilet! Using his telephone!"

When the Angels traveled to Boston for a July series against the Red Sox, Jackson phoned Mark Dalesandro, a rookie catcher, in his room at the Marriott Copley Square. Since his callup in June, Dalesandro had been deemed Jackson's coffee rookie—meaning in the third inning of home games he was required to retreat to the clubhouse and fetch Jackson a cup of joe with two creamers and a good dose of sugar. Sometimes, to mess with the kid, Jackson snarled, "This ain't right—make it again." And Dalesandro would complete the task again.

"But now we're in Boston," Dalesandro recalled, "and Bo ordered me down to the lobby."

"Why, Bo?" Dalesandro asked.

"Just come down," Jackson replied.

"Bo took me shopping," Dalesandro said. "He spent about $1,000 on suits, shoes, belts for me."

That same season, Dalesandro was called upon to pinch hit against Seattle's Randy Johnson. It was his fourth Big League at bat, and he was petrified ("My leg was actually shaking," Dalesandro said.). As Dalesandro walked back to the dugout after striking out on three pitches, Johnson flashed a brush-off hand gesture from the mound. Jackson stormed to the dugout's top step. "Hey, Johnson, you fucking pussy!" he screamed. "Why don't you try that fucking shit with me! I beg you—try that shit with me, you bitch! It will not end well!"

"He had my back," Dalesandro said. "And I was a nobody."

When he aspired to be, Jackson was uproariously funny. On one team flight, with the air-conditioning on the fritz, he stripped to his underwear, flexed, posed and spread across three seats. "Wake me," he announced, "when we get there." Another time, a rookie pitcher named Andrew Lorraine was holding court with a couple of reporters when Jackson walked past, making fire engine noises.

"What's that about?" Lorraine asked.

He looked downward. Bo had set his right cleat aflame.

Jackson drove a Harley-Davidson. Few things brought such joy as cruising up the Pacific Coast Highway on his bike, the sun shining, the temperature just right, a scent of Pacific Ocean wafting through the air. "The coolest thing I've ever seen was Bo Jackson driving to the ballpark on his Harley," said Hudler. "I can still picture it—sunglasses, a skull cap, a leather vest without a shirt, those big ol' arms flexing in the sun."

When Jackson played, he was a semi-reasonable offensive option. Most of his numbers (.279, 13 home runs, 43 RBI) compared favorably to his final season in Chicago. He remained a power threat. "He hit a ball in left center into the upper deck of our stadium," said Chili Davis. "Not the upper deck—the second upper deck. I'd never seen anyone do that." It was estimated to have traveled roughly 500 feet. At Minnesota in April, he doubled off the auxiliary light standard on the roof of the Metrodome—"Most of us would have to take a fungo bat to hit that SOB," Rodgers raved.

Against Detroit in late May, he hit a two-run homer, a two-run single and a sacrifice fly to drive in five and help the Angels win, 7–5.

Beneath the hood, though, the engine was overheating. He started 44 games in the outfield, far too many for an artificial hip. His running was noticeably labored. He could not change directions or come to a full stop. "It looked like his hip was hurting all the time," said DiSarcina, the shortstop. "When I was out there I knew I had to cover a little bit more ground."

"If he'd run for a ball down the left-field line, he couldn't react as a healthy outfielder would," said Mark Leiter, a relief pitcher. "You couldn't get mad because he did what he could. But balls would get past him and he couldn't stop, turn and get it. A lot of times you had doubles turned into triples." In the rear of the Angels dugout, the team stashed a special stretcher, just for Jackson. It had a clamp attached to the side, and would secure his leg and hip should either come out of place. "It was explained to me," said Hudler, "that there was a small risk Bo could break his hip a certain way and bleed to death."

At some point every season, all baseball teams find reason to believe they will compete. For the 1994 Angels, any sense of optimism lasted all the way until April 10, when their record stood at 4-2. They lost the following day, then the day after that, then the day after day, commencing a startling run of futility that saw California drop 16 of its next 21 ball games.

Everything that could go wrong went wrong. J. T. Snow, the twenty-six-year-old first baseman, demanded a trade but hit .220 and spent much of the season in the minors. Harold Reynolds, thirty-three and brought in to play second, batted a cool .232 and covered zero ground (Jackson and Reynolds regularly engaged in trash talk about the Kingdome throw from five years earlier). Mark Langston, staff ace, missed much of the season with bone chips in his throwing elbow, and starting catcher Greg Myers was lost because of torn cartilage in his left knee. None of the five members of the opening-day rotation posted an ERA below 4.22. On May 14, the Angels blew a 7–0 lead to the Mariners. In the aftermath of a 9–5 loss to Seattle a day later, Rodgers vented to the press about his lack of quality arms. "You have to realize John Dopson has been released (by another team)," he said in a subdued rant. "Mark Leiter has been released. Joe Magrane has been released. And we're trying to find spots for them on our club. You've got to look at what we've got to start with."

Rodgers was fired later that week, and replaced with Marcel Lachemann, the Florida Marlins pitching coach. It changed nothing.

As the wretchedness manifested itself, paying customers stopped coming. The Angels averaged 24,010 fans per home game, good for 20th in the Majors. In fact, Jackson's most Barnum and Bailey–esque achievement occurred in a mostly vacant Angels Stadium, while the team was holding a 4 p.m. pre-batting practice stretch along the left-field line. Throughout most of the season, a construction crew had been working to repair damages in the left-field upper deck. On this particular day, one of the welders spray painted BO KNOWS IRON on a beam near the tippy top of the facility.

"Bo, look at that sign," Reynolds cracked. "That dude says you've got no iron." (Iron is a ballplayer word for "money.")

Some of the Angels waved toward the construction guys, and a welder removed his mask, gazed downward and held out his hands in a throw-me-a-ball manner. Jackson grabbed two baseballs off the grass, walked toward the outfield and stood beneath the welder, who measured approximately 200 feet off the ground. Jackson dropped one ball, cocked back his arm and threw the other to the worker. The baseball hit him square in the hands, bounced off his palms and fell to the earth.

"Holy shit!" screamed Reynolds.

"Jesus!" said Hudler.

"Did he just . . ." said Lachemann. "Did that just . . ."

"There was no way that just happened," said DiSarcina. "No way."

Jackson bent, picked up the other ball, threw again. For the second time, it traveled directly to the construction worker. For the second time, he dropped it. Jackson gave a mock wave of indignation and returned to stretching.*

"Chuck Finley was one of the best pitchers in baseball," said Hudler. "He watched it all, said, 'That's nothing.' Then he made the same throw and couldn't even come close."

By late June, the Angels were bobbing around ten games under .500 and any playoff thoughts had drifted away with the Santa Ana winds. "It's a good thing we don't play for Colombia," Jackson cracked, "or we'd all be dead." Rod Carew, the team's hitting coach, bashed the Angel players as "selfish." Veteran Dwight Smith, Jackson's closest pal on the team, was traded to Baltimore. Jim Edmonds, a cocky rookie outfielder whose lack of humility irked the clubhouse, started eating up Bo's playing time. Lachemann

---

* Around this time, Bavasi toyed with the idea of asking Jackson whether he would consider becoming an Angels relief pitcher. "Less stress on the hip," the GM said. "And Bo clearly had the velocity to pull it off. But it was unrealistic and I didn't want to disrespect him. So I never brought it up."

viewed Jackson as a pinch hitter, and little more than a pinch hitter. In a rare start in left field at Yankee Stadium on July 7, Jackson struck out four times, booted a ball, juggled another ball and spewed enough venom toward home plate umpire Durwood Merrill that he was fined. "I have no excuse," Jackson said afterward. "No excuse at all." The lowest point came in a 12–3 home loss to the Yankees. Jackson went 1-for-4 with a homer, but bungled two balls in left field. Afterward, he sat by his locker and did the one thing players on an awful team should never do: he bashed the fans. "I've never seen anything like this in my life," he said. "It's no wonder why we play like shit here. Guys can't wait to get on the road with the kind of fans we've got here. We might as well be playing on the road 162 games a year with the way we're treated."*

This was not how 1994 was supposed to go. Jackson wanted out of California, out of a baseball uniform, out of the spotlight. It was embarrassing, being Superman without his powers. On a slow news day (and there were many with this dreadful outfit), Bob Nightengale of the *Los Angeles Times* asked Jackson whether he would play another season. It was one of those questions reporters have to try, even if the answer is inevitably delivered in the form of a filibuster. Only, this time, Jackson teed off. "Politics have screwed this game up," he said. "And I get sick of all the political bullshit."

He was referring to the increasingly dark cloud hovering above the Major League season—a potential players strike. Much of the dispute had to do with a proposed salary cap that owners insisted upon and Donald Fehr, the union head, dismissed as a craven attempt to limit payrolls. When the season started, most believed the dispute would work itself out. Yet as the weeks passed, and the sides remained miles apart, hope frayed. "It got really sour, really quickly," recalled Anderson. "I started preparing for the worst." On July 13, after consulting with player representatives, Fehr told Major League Baseball that if good-faith negotiations did not begin shortly, a strike would prove inevitable and potentially wipe out the Fall Classic for the first time since 1904. The Players Association set a line-in-the-sand date of August 12.

A few hours before the Angels' 5–3 setback to Kansas City on August 9, Jackson called his travel agent and had her book a refundable (just in case) 8:30 a.m. flight to Atlanta for the day of the strike. His plan was to rent a car, drive to Bessemer, Alabama, dump his stuff inside his late mother's home, then start fishing. "They better hope the strike lasts at least a week,"

---

* Upon further review, the lowest point probably came a week later, when Texas' Kenny Rogers tossed a perfect game against the Angels.

he said with a grin, "because it will take that long for them to find me. I'm gonna have myself a good ol' time, and who knows, maybe I won't be coming back."

For most, the idea of a strike was catastrophic. The financial repercussions, the loss of a year of prime physicality, the little perks (luxury flights, five-star hotels) that made life extra special. Ballplayers are creatures of regimentation, and the interruption of patterns can be terrifying.

Jackson, though, was not terrified. He was exhausted. Beginning when he arrived at Auburn as a freshman twelve years earlier, his existence had been sports, sports and sports. It made him wealthy beyond his wildest dreams. But it also beat much of the life out of him. Not all that long ago he was a kid in Bessemer, hitting baseballs for miles, tucking a pigskin beneath an elbow. He played for the innocent fun, and quickly learned that—should all go right—he wouldn't have to work in a mine or a factory. He could go to college, he could turn pro, he could supply financial security to generations of Jacksons.

And it was worth it. All of it. But now he was a gimmick, too proud to quit mid-season but aware enough to recognize a look of pity when he spotted it plastered upon the faces of peers. The name Bo Jackson was supposed to mean something—power and pride and two-sport dominance. But if this charade continued, that would forever change. Jackson knew it. He didn't say so aloud, but he knew it. The realization followed him, day to day, like an unpleasant stench.

The final game was played in Anaheim—Royals v. Angels in a Wednesday night battle royale of teams no one cared about. More than three years removed from his Kansas City exile, Jackson harbored no lingering animus. The vast majority of preferred teammates (George Brett, Frank White, Bret Saberhagen) were long gone. These Royals meant nothing.

With the looming sense of finality, and the season now a lukewarm stew of hopelessness, Lachemann gave Jackson the sympathetic start in left field.

He came to the plate for the first time in the second inning, and stared out at Tom (Flash) Gordon, the Kansas City starter and a man Jackson once took under his wing. It is possible Jackson realized this would be his final Big League game, and that he used a moment to absorb the sights and sounds. It is more likely, however, that a man who had little need for sentimentality merely aspired to hit a round object with a wood stick.

Jackson singled to right, and what followed is one of the most remarkable professional sports moments *no one bothered to remember*. With Greg

Myers at the plate and Mike Macfarlane—his old teammate—catching, Jackson took a five-step lead off first. Then, when Gordon began his delivery, Jackson bolted. It certainly wasn't as it used to be. The sound of a thoroughbred. The power of a diesel train. The speed of Houston McTear. But Bo Jackson running hard remained a sight to behold. On the Angels bench, Hudler held his head in his palms. "Noooo!" he yelled. "Bo! What are you doing?" Lachemann was equally appalled. No one had given the green light. Yet, somehow, Jackson slid into second, beneath the tag of shortstop Greg Gagne, and popped up in a cloud of dust, safe.

Some of the 19,605 in attendance politely applauded. Most, however, knew not that they had just witnessed Jackson's sole steal attempt of the season.

The game lasted 2 hours and 32 minutes. It concluded with a 70 percent vacated stadium, a 2–1 California win and a glum understanding that the 1994 Major League season was likely over.

About twenty minutes after the final pitch, Bavasi was sitting in his box high above the playing surface, alone with his thoughts and a moribund sense of doom. He gazed downward, through the darkness, and movement caught his eye. A man wearing long underwear, no shirt, and no shoes was jogging out from the Angels dugout and across the infield. Upon reaching second base, he looked to make certain no one was watching, then bent at the waist, dropped his arms and yanked the bag from the ground.

Base tucked beneath his right elbow, the man walked back to the dugout, down the flight of steps and vanished.

Bavasi would never forget the moment.

Bo Jackson wanted one last keepsake.

CHAPTER 29

AFTERMATH

On the afternoon of April 28, 2021, I was walking across the campus of Auburn University—notepad in hand, pen tucked behind my right ear—when I ran into Mia Burcham, eighteen-year-old freshman from Huntsville, Alabama.

Over the course of the previous forty-five minutes, I had roamed the school's 1,875 acres (well, not *all* of it), curious as to how many of the first hundred students I encountered might recognize the name of a man who last played a college football game some thirty-five years ago.

I figured, with the passage of time and the softening of legend, Bo Jackson would be, at best, familiar. Go to Syracuse and ask students about Jim Brown. Go to Notre Dame and inquire about Rocket Ismail. Even Ricky Williams at Texas, Carson Palmer at USC, Keita Malloy at Delaware. When we're in college, everything takes on an air of permanence. In reality, though, time serves as a conveyor belt, and legends tend to be legendary only to those who witness the transcendence. As soon as the observers depart, newly created icons replace old.

To my shock, however, *everyone* knew Bo Jackson. The club volleyball player who wore uniform number 34 for Bo. The math major whose dad insisted he visit Bo's campus statue. The kid from Tallahassee who didn't even root for Auburn. On and on. I'd asked seventy-five students, all between the ages of eighteen and twenty-three, whether they'd heard of Bo Jackson—and all seventy-five answered with an enthusiastic yes.

So I reached Mia, who was sitting at an outside table, studying. I explained I was a journalist, then—"Quick poll question: Do you know who Bo Jackson is?"

She looked at me, somewhat embarrassed.

"I think I've heard the name," she said. "Who is that?"

I told Mia about the kid from Bessemer who won the Heisman Trophy, then went on to play two professional sports. I alluded to Bo Knows and Bosworth and Harold Reynolds and . . .

She grinned sheepishly.

"To be honest," Mia said, "I like soccer. Not football."

I spoke with twenty-four more Auburn students, and all twenty-four knew the legend of Bo Jackson.

That's ninety-nine of a hundred.

That's preposterous.

When Bo Jackson removed second base from its moorings, then faded into the shadows, he never looked back, and certainly never looked back with regret. As planned, he caught a flight to Atlanta, drove to Bessemer, went fishing and threw whatever sporting equipment he had into a box or closet or trunk or whatever. There was no hardware room, and zero inclination to show visitors the Heisman or All-Star Game MVP trophies (if he could even find them). He indicated little to no interest in keeping up with teammates, and almost no one in baseball or football possessed his phone number. In fact, when the Angels' beat writers asked players for their contact information, Jackson jotted down phony digits. "I tried calling once," said Lawrence Rocca of the *Orange County Register*. "Didn't work." The baseball season, of course, ended prematurely, and the World Series was never played. Bo was done, and quite happy about it.

The Jacksons committed themselves to remaining in suburban Chicago, where all three children (Garrett, 8, Nicholas, 6, Morgan, 4) were settled. In April 1995, Kendal Weaver of the Associated Press reached America's most famous thirty-two-year-old retiree, who raved of his new life. "After eight months, I've really gotten to know my family," he said. "That is the big thing behind it."

What surprised Weaver was that Jackson already plotted out his next career. He had recently signed with the William Morris Agency in an effort to pursue acting. It was an eyebrow-raising move for a man insistent that he wanted nothing more to do with the spotlight (but clearly wasn't entirely ready to leave it). Jackson began working with Stephen Eich, an independent producer who trained thespians. He studied at Steppenwolf, the famed Chicago theater company founded by John Malkovich and Gary Sinise. Before long he'd lined up a bunch of bit spots on TV shows like *Moesha* and *Married . . . with Children*. There were multiple opportunities to play "Bo Jackson," and nearly all were turned down. He dreaded the idea of becoming a caricature of himself.

Before long, Jackson was going on a long string of motion picture auditions—and being rejected every . . . single . . . time. He read for more than fifty parts in movies ranging from *Waiting to Exhale* and *Alien 4* to *Dumbo Drop* and *Heat*. "I knew this wasn't going to be easy," he said. "I wasn't going to give up." The big break arrived in early 1996, when he found himself in front of Mali Finn, casting director for an upcoming movie based upon the John Grisham novel *The Chamber*. The project already enlisted Gene Hackman for the lead role, then added Chris O'Donnell, Faye Dunaway and Lela Rochon. Jackson read for a small part—that of Sergeant Clyde Packer, a death row prison guard who befriends a bitter racist (played by Hackman). Finn was hooked as soon as Jackson entered. ("He owns the space," she raved.) James Foley, the director, offered him the gig.

Filming started on March 6, 1996, at the Parchman Farms Prison in Indianola, Mississippi, and Jackson came to find the movie business to be painfully dull. Mississippi was unbearably hot and humid. The cast was housed in a fleabag motel in nearby Cleveland—"there was nothing but a Country Platter for food and a Walmart for entertainment," said Rochon. "Me and the hair stylist were so bored, we'd walk around the Walmart like it was a mall."

When Jackson was involved in a scene, it would be shot twenty to thirty different times, from all sorts of angles. When he wasn't involved in a scene, the hours dragged like a damp rag. The whole ordeal was hurry up and wait. Jackson, ever the athlete, craved movement and physicality.

Because he was a deep member of the cast, he did not receive his own trailer. He'd sit on a chair inside a tiny Winnebago and count the minutes until it was time to shoot. Though not a sports fan, Foley knew Jackson's résumé. "I had a huge trailer, and I gave it to Bo to use," he recalled. "He moved in there, and was genuinely appreciative. He did well in the movie. He really did. But it's the grace and appreciation that stuck with me. He was a rookie in our world, and he behaved as someone trying to make it."

As was the case in sports, Jackson largely kept to himself. He didn't roam Walmart with Rochon, never traded war stories with the notoriously gruff Hackman, wasn't cracking jokes with O'Donnell.* He was on time, pulled off his lines, returned to his dwelling. Day after day. "I remember meeting him for the first time," said Rochon. "He opened his trailer door, and he was wearing hot pants and had the most muscular legs I'd ever seen. I thought, 'Wow, that's Bo Jackson. He looks like he can do some things.' That's pretty much the only conversation we had."

The one person Jackson formed a kinship with was Bobby McFadden, a

---

* Recalled Foley: "Chris O'Donnell was one of my big mistakes. I didn't want him in the movie, but he was a person of the moment and I relented."

former Parchman guardsman who had been hired as the project's technical adviser. At the time McFadden was working as a Mississippi state trooper, and Jackson begged to come along on a night patrol run. "Bo was really into it," McFadden said. "He actually backed me up at a vehicle stop. I said to him, 'If something happens, grab that shotgun.' He grabbed it.

"That movie had a bunch of California people coming down to Mississippi. You could tell they didn't think much of our way of life. But Bo was country. He was one of us. I loved the guy."

The Chamber hit theaters on October 11, 1996, and nobody liked it. Roger Ebert called the film, "not a serious movie about anything." Grisham dismissed it as "a disaster." Dunaway was nominated for a major award—a Razzie for worst supporting actress.* Jackson earned positive reviews for his limited screen time, and appeared at the Hollywood premiere wearing—a bit desperately—sunglasses at night. *The Chamber* wound up grossing $14.5 million in the United States, wonderful had it not cost $50 million to make.

The entire experience turned Jackson off to acting. He landed bit parts in two more films—the 1997 Tone Loc–Ernie Hudson classic *Fakin' da Funk* (he played a preacher) and, a year later, Jim Wynorski's direct-to-video nonthriller *The Pandora Project*. In that one, Jackson teamed up with the third or fourth Baldwin brother, someone named Erika Eleniak and Epstein from *Welcome Back, Kotter* to deliver a fifteen-second performance that literally no *Homo sapien* is able to recall.

"He was in the movie?" Wynorski asked years later. "I honestly have no memory of that."

Acting didn't wind up grabbing Bo Jackson the way he thought it might, and that was fine. He had other interests.

In no particular order, over the ensuing two and a half decades Jackson kept a promise to his mother by returning to Auburn and graduating with a bachelor of arts degree in family and child development; threw his name behind the Bo Jackson Signature Portable Gas Grill (made of superior quality 316 marine-grade stainless steel!); used his mother's sweet potato pie recipe to start Bo Jackson's Homemade Sweet Potato Pie (pumpkin, peach and pecan pies also offered and sold frozen in stores); worked with the White Sox as a team ambassador (aka, wave and sign autographs) and the Royals as a spring training instructor; introduced Bo Jackson's Better Bar—an energy bar (don't try the blueberry cheesecake flavor—you've been warned);

---

* Dunaway was eked out by Melanie Griffin for her showing in *Mulholland Falls*. An argument can be made for both women.

starred alongside Neil Diamond in a music video for the Dallas County Line song "Honk If You Love to Honky Tonk"; served as the president of the HealthSouth Sports Medicine Council; was inducted into the College Football Hall of Fame; cofounded a food-processing firm called N'genuity; had his uniform number retired by Auburn; hung with Desmond Tutu after the two men were presented International Quality of Life Awards by Auburn; fell deeply in love with an array of soap operas (*Guiding Light* was a favorite); held a celebrity golf tournament (and played a ton of golf); had his other hip replaced; joined the board of the Burr Ridge Bank & Trust and the Bo Jackson Elite Sports Complex; threw out the first pitch before Game 2 of the 2005 World Series at Comiskey and the 2010 Home Run Derby at Angel Stadium; hunted for all genre of animals; put three children through college and—on the highly lucrative sports memorabilia front—earned the reputation as a notorious pain in the ass.

It's true—and fair. Jackson is a well-regarded man who gives charitably of his time (and money) and refuses to be one of those retired athletes who bemoans the way things once were. But he is far from warm and bubbly, and oftentimes quite suspicious of the motives of anyone not named Bo Jackson. Along those lines, there are endless stories of Bo turning down an autograph request. Bo playing in a celebrity golf tournament but treating fans like rotted meat. Bo making demands that exceed normal expectations.

Several years ago, Jackson and Greg Townsend, his former Raiders teammate, were appearing at an autograph show inside the Anaheim Convention Center. Townsend had heard that Bo would be participating, so he brought a helmet, a jersey and a football to be signed. He saw Jackson from afar, and approached warmly.

"Bo!" Townsend said. "How you doing, champ?"

"Oh, man!" said Jackson with a smile. "They'll let anyone in here. Great to see you, Greg." The men hugged like long-lost football brothers.

Townsend opened a bag and pulled out the items. "Bo, would you mind doing a fellow Raider a solid and signing these for me?"

Jackson's mood darkened.

"Greg," he said, "I've gotta charge you."

Townsend laughed.

"No, really, Greg," Jackson lectured. "This is business."

Through the years Townsend had asked dozens of former teammates to sign objects. In turn, he had dozens of former teammates ask him to sign objects. Money was never exchanged. Not once.

This time, the bill came to $410—which Townsend paid in cash.

"Bo, this is bullshit," Townsend said as he walked away. "I'm gonna tell every guy I run into that you made me pay. You're a fucking asshole. Always have been."

Jackson moved on to the next customer.

A similarly strange incident took place on February 1, 2013, when Jackson and former Detroit Red Wings star Steve Yzerman traveled to Saskatoon, Canada, to appear at the annual Kinsmen Sports Celebrity Dinner. That morning, shortly before both retired stars were to host a press conference, a local TV reporter named Kevin Waugh was preparing to leave the CTV network offices for the event. A coworker, Cory Tomyn, slipped him a Bo Jackson football card. "If you're gonna see Bo," Tomyn said, "can you ask him to sign this?"

Waugh grabbed the rectangular slip of cardboard and placed it in a pocket. He headed to the press conference, asked some questions and, before leaving, plunked the card on the table, whipped out a Sharpie and said, "Bo, will you please sign this?"

The silence could slice granite.

"Bo," Yzerman said, "just sign the damn card."

Jackson grabbed the pen, scribbled his name and pushed it back toward Waugh.

"Thanks," the reporter said.

That night, Waugh did his daily 6:30 sportscast before heading to the TCU Place in downtown Saskatoon for the event. As he entered, he was confronted by an event official. "Bo's looking for you," he said.

"For me?" replied Waugh.

"Yeah," he said. "He wants the card back."

"What card?" asked Waugh.

"The one he signed today," the man replied. "Bo wants it back."

"I don't even have it," Waugh said. "I gave it to someone."

"Well, you better get out of here," the man warned. "Because Bo is absolutely furious."

A few other officials urged Waugh to take off. This was the strangest moment of his media career. Unsure what to do next, Waugh visited the bathroom to urinate. Jackson spotted him from afar, and followed. He entered the room, saw Waugh by the urinal and said—mid-pee—"Give me the card back!"

"Bo," Waugh replied, "I gave it to my coworker. He lives thirty miles south."

"Well," Jackson said, "I want the card back before the night is over."

"Um, OK," Waugh said.

He left the event, never to return.

"Bo Jackson is six foot two and huge," Waugh said. "I'm a thirty-eight-year-old sportscaster. That's not a fight I win."

It was later explained that Jackson had recently signed an exclusive deal with a trading card company, and the item he signed for Waugh was of a different corporation.

"Which, of course, doesn't make the way he behaved right or any less strange," Waugh said. "I mean, the man followed me into a bathroom."

Bo Jackson's life is everything he wanted it to be. Which is to say, fairly pedestrian and uneventful. Though I devoted a great deal of time toward uncovering the post-sports world of Bo Jackson, there isn't a ton to uncover. Approaching sixty, he lives comfortably in a large house, with a loving wife of 35 years. He has three children and (as of 2022) one grandchild. He hunts and fishes as he pleases, drives a simple Dodge truck, shovels his own driveway, grills his own steaks. He watches almost no sports (save for golf), and could not care less whether the Raiders or Royals or White Sox or Angels win, lose or tie. He will never be inducted into the Baseball or Pro Football halls of fame, and it bothers him nary an iota. When people ask if he regrets having played football, he shrugs. Regret? Bo Jackson doesn't do regret.

Every so often, someone will wonder whether, were medicine and technology more advanced, Jackson's injury would have turned out differently. Or, to be specific: Had Bo Jackson's hip been yanked from the socket in 2022, would he be able to continue on the path toward sports immortality?

The answer: Yes.

And no.

Over three decades, major advances have been made in hip replacements. One of the biggest is the usage of ceramic, as opposed to metals and plastics, when creating the hip and surrounding parts. "Ceramic on ceramic results in much less wear and tear and erosion," Dr. Lee Rubin, a renowned orthopedic surgeon, explained. "With the materials we use now, which are so much more resistant, you can have all the muscles attach around the hip, then allow the athlete to recover and train at a significantly higher level than back in the day."

Rubin noted the comeback of Andy Murray, the British tennis star who spent years trying to play through deterioration in his right hip. In early 2019, he finally underwent hip resurfacing surgery—a replacement alternative that didn't exist for Jackson. Instead of completely removing the femoral head, doctors inserted a metal rod into Murray's femur, and the joint was coated in a metal shell (much like capping a tooth). Five months later, Murray returned to the court, teaming up with Feliciano Lopez to beat the top doubles seed at Queen's Club in London.

Rubin believes many athletic careers could have been saved had modern hip technology been available through the decades. So, for that matter, does Edwin Su, a New York–based orthopedic surgeon who has performed more than one thousand hip and knee replacements and was involved in the hip resurfacing surgery that allowed veteran NBA guard Isaiah Thomas to continue his career after a devastating injury.

Su was raised a Bo Jackson fan, and remembers well the injury that brought him down, as well as the mixed-bag comebacks. He believes (no, *knows*) that, had the injury occurred in 2022, Jackson's future would have been significantly brighter. "The one professional sport I don't advise people returning to is football," Su said. "It's just too physical. But with modern procedures, he could have continued playing baseball for a long time at a high level. Would he have lost a little speed? Probably, just because it's major surgery. But there would have been no limp, no stiffness. The explosiveness still would have been there."

Late in my reporting, I was asked by an editor whether—post-injury—Jackson ever considered a career as a coach or broadcaster. Both thoughts made me snort aloud. The idea of Bo Jackson breaking down a pitcher's mechanics, or explaining proper positioning to a young outfielder, is laughable. He was a natural, and naturals don't do nuance and rarely grind. His studying of an opposing defense usually went thusly:

"Who are we playing this week?"

Denver.

"OK."

Also, the whole process would have put Jackson to sleep. As peculiar as it sounds, sports were boring to Bo. These days, when he reports to spring training as a guest instructor, it's 90 percent cracking jokes with old friends, 8 percent enjoying the free food, 1 percent signing autographs, .5 percent napping and .5 percent instructing. Maybe less.

What he does do, however, is empathize. It's not always apparent, with mistrust of strangers. But, deep down, Jackson's friends, teammates and family members agree he is genuinely compassionate.

Which is why April 27, 2011, hit him so hard.

It was the day when an unprecedented sixty-two tornadoes touched down in Alabama, devastating the state. Fifty-eight deaths were confirmed in the immediate aftermath by the Alabama Emergency Management Agency, and that number ultimately swelled to 238. A state of emergency was declared. The Tennessee Valley Authority closed three of its Alabama-based nuclear power plants. Power lines were down everywhere—much of Tuscaloosa was destroyed, and the entirety of the city was without energy. Hospitals were overwhelmed. More than 1,400 National Guard soldiers were deployed to assist. "The whole house caved in on top of that car," recalled Randy Guyton, a Concord, Alabama, resident who, along with his family, took cover in a Honda Ridgeline parked in the garage. "Other than my boy screaming to the Lord to save us, being in that car is what saved us."

From his home in Burr Ridge, Bo Jackson watched the TV in horror. These were his people suffering. Sure, he hadn't lived in Alabama in decades. But it remained the state that nurtured him, developed him, taught him sports and hunting and compassion and love. It was the birthplace of his wife. The birthplace of his mother.

He *had* to help.

Enter: Bo Bikes Bama.

On the morning of April 24, 2012, Jackson met privately with Bryce Ferguson, an eleven-year-old boy whose parents and little sister all died in the tornadoes. "He lost everything" an emotional Jackson said, "but he is standing tall." With that Jackson—joined by approximately one hundred enlistees—hopped up on a custom Trek bicycle and embarked on a five-day, three-hundred-mile ride from Henagar, Alabama, to Tuscaloosa. The plan was to use the event to raise money for the Alabama Governor's Emergency Relief Fund. Jackson enlisted a bevy of celebrities—ranging from Scottie Pippen and Ken Griffey, Jr., to Picabo Street and Lance Armstrong—to ride with him. "I conjured up the idea about a month after the tornado hit last year," he said. "I asked my wife about it. She thought I was crazy."

The event turned into an annual sensation, and by 2020 more than $2.1 million had been raised for charity. "It's everything you need to know about Bo Jackson," said John Montgomery, who worked PR for Bo Bikes Bama. "He's one of Alabama's favorite sons and he knows it. But he never wants it to be about him. He's not super commercial. He's not looking for the spotlight. He's not very accessible and he doesn't like being bothered.

"But when the state of Alabama needed a superhero, it realized it had an exceptional one the whole time."

"His name," Montgomery said, "is Bo Jackson."

ACKNOWLEDGMENTS

On May 1, 2020, I was sitting on a bench in the back of my house, speaking via phone with my mother, when a blocked number popped up.

"Mom," I said, "hold on one second. Lemme get this."

Click.

"Hello?"

Mr. Jeff Pearlman?

"Yes?"

He didn't have to introduce himself. I knew the voice.

But he did.

This is Bo Jackson.

Four days earlier I had sent Bo some of my work, along with a note telling him that my tenth book would concern, well, him. "I am asking for your blessing on the project," I wrote, "as well as the chance to speak with you about your one-of-a-kind life. Which absolutely fascinates me."

Though widely known to be surly and standoffish, Jackson could not have been warmer. He was driving his car somewhere in suburban Chicago, en route to pick up dinner for his wife, Linda. "I'm in traffic," he said with an agitated chuckle. "It's gonna take me forty minutes to get a damn chopped salad."

He went on to tell me that he was happy and content and comfortable in his out-of-the-spotlight existence and that (dammit!) no, he wouldn't grant me an interview for what, from day one, I have referred to as "the definitive Bo Jackson biography."

"It's nothing personal," he said, "I like the quiet, subtle life. I like my privacy. I don't have any problem with you writing a book. You're a writer. I get it. But I've had so many people through the years wanting to write a book."

We chatted for about a half hour. He reflected on his 1990 autobiography, *Bo Knows Bo*, as well as his charitable work. He told me his current high comes from "helping people—it's my rush." Which I loved to hear. As our chat wound down, I told Bo I would keep him abreast of my progress, and that—hopefully—we'd talk again. He wished me luck and, before hanging up, uttered something that has stuck with me. "Everyone wants to do a Bo book," he said, "but nobody realizes how hard that would be."

Bo Jackson was right. Well, sorta right. Not *everyone* wants to do a Bo book. But damn if it wasn't hard.

The first person I'd like to thank is, in fact, Bo Jackson—for the greatness, for the inspiration, for the mystique. And also for taking the time to call. Although he kept his word and we failed to speak again (I sent him several letters. I'm guessing they made wonderful kindling), I never felt any hostility or anger. Truth be told, by reaching out, Bo allowed me to say "Yes" when folks inevitably asked if he knew about the project.

"Is he doing it *with* you?"

"No," I'd reply, "but we spoke and he doesn't seem to mind."

In this business, one takes what he can get.

Like sports, books are a team effort, and for nearly two decades I've thrived in large part because I'm surrounded by an incomparable squad of loved ones and peers. My agent, David Black, is the king of goodness and serves as equal parts guardian, spokesperson and friend. Lucy Stille, my other agent (you know you're money when you have an "other agent") is the perfect blend of angel and Rottweiler.

Michael J. Lewis has now suffered the pain of proofing all ten of my books, and deserves the Rich Kotite Medal of Honor for such valor. Casey Angle, friend and fact-checker, is simply as decent and kind a person as walks the globe, and the wonderful Amy Balmuth has graduated from "Bo who?" to a PhD in the Life and Times of an American Icon. David Rosenthal is the best editor I've ever worked with, and a one-thousand-times-better guy. Ashley Brouwer is proof that plenty of roses grow in Alabama. Paul Gutierrez is the Vince Ferragamo we all need to know.

So many contributed to this project. I will never, ever, ever, ever, ever forget the kindness and hospitality offered by Angela Woods and family— who gave me the royal Bessemer treatment and a guided tour for the ages. Michele Souli's vast gifts as a genealogist helped me grasp the winding Jackson family history. (Seriously, if you're a writer in need of roots, Michele's gold.) Brad Mangin is one of America's great sports photographers and a dear friend/helper. Daniel Lubofsky charged way too little for his transcription skills. Luca Evans is a future journalism star who—on his rise to ink dominance—did his old professor some research solids. Bruce Weber is a people-find godsend. Megan Wilson is the Steve Grogan of publicists, Tommy Brown of the Auburn University Library went above and beyond, as did James Huxtable, my *Playboy* stash provider, and Glenn Clark, Joe Orsulak Society CEO. George Nunnelley, Auburn's assistant director of communications, walks Christ-like across media relations water. Oh, and John Carvalho went above and beyond.

Though decades removed from her turn as a University of Illinois cheerleader, Wendy Rosman's Japan Bowl artifacts were worthy of a hundred pom-poms. Mack Liederman serves as the Tecmo Bowl guru the world wants and needs. I have been several decades chronicling sports and I was lucky three former Major Leaguers standouts consider me decent enough to serve as sports verifiers. Shawn (Mazel) Green, Brian (Dog Fancy) Johnson and Dave (The Pride of Mahopac) Fleming—my gratitude is boundless.

So many athletes contributed to this book, and to try and name them all would take far too long. But I want to acknowledge the pure loveliness of Lionel (Little Train) James, Bo's friend and college backfield mate who died several months after speaking with me. His joy and sense of nostalgia radiated through the phone.

I hate lists, but here's a list of peeps who made *The Last Folk Hero* a thing: Ivy Givens (HarperCollins's five-tool phenom), David Eber (president of the Faye Dunaway Fan Club), Peter Hubbard (Tupac Shakur fan), David Robinson (finder of folks), Tamara Cottrell (the queen of Tuskegee yearbooks), Shawn Yaple (restroom archer), Michael and Max Vosburg (father-son purveyors of Bo love), Mary Beth Newbill (department head of Southern history and government documents at the Birmingham Public Library). Daniel Atkins, Lucas Montoya and Davin Decaro (Da Boys of Discord), Gary Miller (my Atlantic Ocean bass-fishing correspondent), Greg Campbell (assistant director of communications at Mississippi State), Andy Greenberg, Jeff Pinkston, Adam Lorber, Jim Hecht, Ramon Maclin, David Pearlman, Ian Browne, Mac Engel, Mirin Fader, Meghann Cuniff, Shane Summers, Andrew Murphy, Katherine Nails, Larry Rubama, Jonathan Eig, Howard Bryant, Michael Dolan, Erik Sherman, Poppy Pearlman, Norma Shapiro, Leah Guggenheimer, Chris and Jessica Berman, Jordan Williams, Isaiah Williams, Laura Cole, Richard Guggenheimer, Jon Wertheim, Dan Wetzel, Cory Giles, Shawn Anderson, Patrick Shuck, Marisa Elliott, Jack Silverstein, Elizabeth Newman, Timothy Bella, Mike Brodsky, Tim Mocco, Chris Herring, Russ Bengtson, Kevin DiBattisto and Ron Clements. Rest in peace to Dan Furman, a great man.

There are few journalism peers I admire as much as my friend and colleague, ESPN's Jeremy Schaap. There are few legendary scribes I revere as much Dick Schaap, Jeremy's late father and the co-author of Bo Jackson's 1990 autobiography, *Bo Knows Bo*. While completing this project, I aspired to create a continuation of Dick Schaap's work. Whether I succeeded or failed is up to the reader. But I tried to feel his presence throughout.

In case you failed to notice, this book is dedicated to my mother, Joan Pearlman. If there is a single person who taught me to appreciate the beauty of a Bo Jackson touchdown run . . . eh, it wasn't my mom. Or my dad, Stan Pearlman. Truth be told, neither of my folks know a damn thing about sports. But they know everything about supporting their kids. Which is even better.

While filling out college applications, my daughter Casey was asked by Chapman University to list her role model. She wrote, "Bo Jackson." And, yeah, it was a bit of a reach (her role model is obviously Brent Fullwood). But Casey's Bo love is real—and if you need proof, check out the poster hanging above her bed and the elation when Bo kindly Tweeted her warm birthday wishes. My son, Emmett, meanwhile, has gifted me with many late-night chats about Bo, and his ear for dialogue and narrative is way beyond his years. As Tyler, the Creator once said, "If the world was ending, I think I would grab some Cinnamon Toast Crunch."

When Catherine agreed to marry me twenty years ago, I don't think she foresaw two decades of ceaseless conversations about Doc Gooden and Brett Favre, Barry Bonds and Bo Jackson. But if love means never having to say you're sorry, I will refuse to apologize for the ten million *hence*s and *hell*s my wife has had to cut from my copy.

It is an honor to be on this side-by-side journey with such a rare jewel. I know.

A NOTE ABOUT SOURCING

Although Bo Jackson politely turned down repeated interview requests for this book, more than two decades ago Dick Schaap—co-author of Bo's autobiography, *Bo Knows Bo*—generously donated to Auburn University's library hundreds upon hundreds of pages of notes and interviews (as well as the actual cassette tapes) from his sessions with Bo dating back to 1989 and 1990. It was an invaluable resource that I am eternally grateful for. All unattributed Jackson quotations in *The Last Folk Hero* are from those chats.

NOTES

PROLOGUE

1 *On the night of September 15, 1991*: *Kenosha News*, "Sox Makes Emergency Landing," Sept. 17, 1991.

CHAPTER 1: "THE LITTLE ROCK CHUCKER"

10 *The headline atop the next day's*: "Negroes lack bond, stay behind bars," *Birmingham News*, Dec. 1, 1962.

10 *Despite the city's 39.6 percent Black population*: "Birmingham's Population: 1880-2000," Birmingham Public Library, *http://www.bplonline.org/resources/government/BirminghamPopulation.aspx*

14 *"loved and adored by many who called him Daddy"*: "A. D. Adams," *chambersfuneralhome.com*, July 30, 2010.

14 *"I was best known in the community for throwing rocks,"*: Richman, Alan, "Only Bo Knows Bo," *GQ*, March 1990.

16 *In 1979, a study conducted*: "Teen girl study: More sex activity, pregnancies, fewer hasty weddings," *Orlando Sentinel Star*, Oct. 17, 1980.

18 *"My older brother and cousin said I was tough*: "Bo Stories," Sporting News, p. 10.

CHAPTER 2: A BLACK BRUCE JENNER

24 *"My mother was the motivator,"*: "Bo Knows Bo," Nike VHS. 1991

26 *In the spring of 1979, the McAdory track team*: Hick, Tommy, "Lee dominates 4A state meet," *Selma Times-Journal*, May 6, 1979.

29 *The next afternoon's* Birmingham News *wrote of "Timothy Reese"*: Pennington, Steve, "Washington has two TDs in Minor win," *Birmingham News*, September 8, 1979.

33 *"Vincent Jackson began his track career"*: Pilkinton, Gail, "McAdory High's Vincent Jackson is all-around athlete, but in track no one believes he's just a soph," *Birmingham News*, April 16, 1980.

34 *Not only did Jackson win the long jump*: Reimer, John, "21 marks fall in first day of prep meet," *Montgomery Advertiser*, Feb. 9, 1980.

34 *On May 3, Jackson led McAdory to the state 3A boys*: Weathers, Ronald, "McAdory 3A champ, Gardendale girls second in 3A track," *Birmingham News*, May 4, 1980.

34 *Two weeks later, at the same venue*: Pilkinton, Gail, "Metro sports looks at 'gold medalists' in West area for '80," *Birmingham News*, July 7, 1980.

CHAPTER 3: EMERGENCE

35 *Vincent's mother worked all the time*: Van Hoose, Alf, "'Bo' Jackson, your decision is a rough one," *Birmingham News*, June 2, 1982.

36 *"People think a man is important. They're OK in their place"*: Richman, Alan, "Only Bo Knows Bo," *GQ*, March 1990.

36 *"I saw my daddy once a month, twice a month,"*: Appearance on *The Phil Donahue Show*, Nov. 9, 1990.

36 *He and his wife, Jody, had been sweethearts*: "Joanne Holcombe 'Jody' Atchison," *Birmingham News*, April 11, 2018.

38 *Starting alongside Mack and Mason*: "McAdory 28, J. Valley 6," *Birmingham Post-Herald*, August 30, 1980.

39 *"McAdory crushed Dora 36–6"*: Lloyd, Charles, "Jackson runs up 31 points as McAdory wallops Dora," *Birmingham News*, Oct. 4, 1980.

40 *"Vincent Jackson provided a dramatic ending"*: Seale, Race, "Jackson's kick gives Jackets two-point win," *Birmingham News*, Oct. 11, 1980.

40 *On October 24, against visiting Brookwood*: "McAdory gains on Midfield as Pats lose in area to 'Dogs,'" *Birmingham News*, Oct. 25, 1980.

41 *"Vincent probably would have had better stats"*: Grant, Robin, "Life's a game for Jackson and he knows how to win," *Birmingham News*, May 15, 1981.

44 *"Art," Gonzales said, "I saw this player down here"*: "The Art of Scouting," p. 23.

44 *"He found out when she took her coffee break"*: "The Art of Scouting," p. 25.

44 *On April 14, 1981, after striking out five batters*: Pilkinton, Gail, "Jackson wins West sports award," *Birmingham News*, April 14, 1981.

44 *Jackson's windup resembled that of Luis Tiant*: Chass, Murray, "Yanks Sign Tiant, 37, to Pitch Two Years for $500,000," *New York Times*, Nov. 14, 1978.

45 *At the Class 2A-3A Jefferson County Track Meet*: Bynum, Cary, "Jackson cops MVP honor, Parsons too," *Birmingham News*, April 16, 1981.

45 *A few weeks later, in the state outdoor*: Grant, Robin, "Life's a game for Jackson and he knows how to win," *Birmingham News*, May 15, 1981.

45 *Just for kicks, Jackson ran a leg*: Weathers, Ronald, "Mountain Brook Junior High captures its third state title," *Birmingham News*, May 3, 1981.

45 *"I never did figure out the proper way to throw the discus*: "Bo Knows Bo," p. 53.

46 *On July 20, 1981, the cover of the new* Sports Illustrated *featured*: Faces in the Crowd, *Sports Illustrated*, July 20, 1981

47 *"It's a real nice feeling,"*: Grant, Rubin, "He's a Face in the Crowd," *Birmingham Post-Herald*, July 24, 1981.

CHAPTER 4: DON'T MESS WITH BO JACKSON

50 *Back two decades earlier, Abbot had been a basketball standout*: "Meet the cagers—McAdory," *Birmingham News*, Jan. 13, 1961.

51 *"This kid Jackson is out front, leading a play"*: "In The Arena," p. 155.

51 *"Like dominoes. I never saw anything like it."*: Underwood, John, "Bo's Two Way Stretch," *Life Magazine*, Oct. 1987.

53 *Lucious Selmon, the University of Oklahoma defensive line coach*: "The Courting of Marcus Dupree," p. 336.

54 *Tennessee and Nebraska invited him to make visits*: Heisler, Mark, "It's The Bo Show, Part II: Kansas City, Here He Comes," *Los Angeles Times*, March 30, 1988.

54 *Houston came hard*: Kilgore, Mike, "Versatile Vincent Jackson leads All-Metro Squad," *Birmingham News*, Dec. 12, 1981.

54 *"Every coach in the South tried to recruit the kid,"*: Denman, Elliott, "Rutgers facing 'Superman' test," *Asbury Park Press*, Nov. 4, 1982.

55 *"Vincent Jackson kicked the extra point"*: Ward, J. W., "McAdory 20, Jones Valley 14," *Birmingham News*, August 29, 1981.

56 *Jackson performed admirably, catching a 37-yard*: "Midfield wins with field goal," *Birmingham News*, Sept 5, 1981.

56 *Recruiting-wise, Evans was closer to Dupree status*: Marshall, Phillip, "Impressive: Recruiting pressure grows, but Allan Evans unchanged," *Montgomery Advertiser*, Jan. 29, 1982.

58 *"Auburn was my second choice,"*: Marshall, Phillip, "UA Coach's Words Sent Bo to Tigers," *Montgomery Advertiser*, November 28, 1984.

59 *On the third weekend of September 1981*: "In The Arena," p. 157.

60 *"I think I asked Bo one other time if he was coming to Auburn*: "In The Arena," p. 157.

60 *After splitting their first two games*: Mize, Mitch, "McAdory 15, Oxford 7," *Birmingham News*, Sept. 12, 1981.

61 *A week later, after a 48–20 takedown of Dora High*: Callaghan, Charles, "McAdory explosion nets 528 yards, 48 points against Dora," *Birmingham News*, Oct. 3, 1981.

61 *The members of BAQ were no joke*: Brown, D. Winston, "Ghost Children," Creative Nonfiction No. 28, Essays from the Edge, 2006.

62 *One of its leaders, eighteen-year-old Kenneth Blaylock*: Monte, Jeanette, "Court rejects penalty claim," *Pensacola News Journal*, March 24, 1982.

CHAPTER 5: THE EPITOME OF SUPERMAN

63 *The team finished 8-2, and Bo Jackson*: Kilgore, Mike, "Versatile Vincent Jackson leads All-Metro squad," *Birmingham News*, Dec. 12, 1981.

63 *When, that December, the* Alabama Journal *ranked*: Lumpkin, Karen, "Lee, Stewart Among Best," *Alabama Journal*, Dec. 2, 1981.

63 *But in McCalla, at McAdory*: Marshall, Phillip, "Indoor meet begins Friday," *Montgomery Advertiser*, Feb. 4, 1982.

64 *Beforehand, he told peers his goal was to smash four state records*: Crenshaw, Jr., Solomon, "McAdory's Vincent Jackson sets three state marks at track meet," *Birmingham News*, Feb. 15, 1982.

64 *"When you are 6-foot-1, weigh 215 pounds*: Marshall, Phillip, "'Bo' should wear an 'S' on his chest," *Montgomery Advertiser*, Feb. 7, 1982.

65 *Julian Mock, a Cincinnati Reds scout*: Booher, Kary, "How the Royals drafted Bo Jackson," *Springfield News-Leader*, June 6, 2011.

66 *Against Thompson High, he blasted a shot that*: "Bo Knows Bo," Nike VHS, 1991.

67 *"There's somebody from Auburn at just about all our games,"*: Ray, Darryal, "Big League Offers Worrying Tiger Coaches?," *Alabama Journal*, May 12, 1982.

70 *Over the course of the season he set state records*: "Bo Stories," p. 16.

71 *In the following day's* Birmingham News, *writer Rick Lowry*: Lowry, Rick, "Ailments can't stop Jackson from taking 2nd decathlon," *Birmingham News*, May 23, 1982.

75 *Gus Poulous, a Yankee scout who had watched*: "Yankees draft Vincent Jackson, call him top prospect," *Birmingham Post-Herald*, June 8, 1982.

75 *"They can't understand why he won't talk,"*: Kausler, Jr., Don, "Jackson won't change his mind, says coach," *Birmingham News*, June 9, 1982.

76 *"This confuses me a little"*: Kausler, Jr., Don, "Jackson won't talk with Yanks," *Birmingham News*, June 10, 1982.

CHAPTER 6: VILLAGE ON THE PLAIN

84 *Dye—referred to as a "benevolent tyrant of the old school"*: Nuwer, Hank, "Dye's Way Is The Only Way," *Inside Sports*, Jan. 1984.

84 *He was raised on a farm*: Haywood, Matthew, "Pat Dye Delivered," *West Alabama Gazette*, Aug. 25, 1983.

84 *He rarely wore shoes*: Nuwer, Hank, "Dye's Way Is The Only Way," *Inside Sports*, Jan. 1984.

86 *The Tigers, sports editor Stuart Blackwell noted*: Blackwell, Stuart, "The winning Dye era," *Auburn Plainsman*, Jan. 26, 1984.

86 *"Auburn's returning football players were on the practice fields"*: Hinton, Ed, "Auburn shows optimism by the dawn's early light," *Atlanta Constitution*, Aug. 24, 1982.

87 *Evans—his presumed rival—was left in the dust*: Young, Larry, "Evans puts frustrating year behind," *Auburn Plainsman*, May 26, 1983.

88 *"Vincent 'Bo' Jackson was everything Bear Bryant wanted in a running back"*: "Auburn's Jackson may be new phenom," Associated Press, Aug. 28, 1982.

88 *"We're glad we have a player the fans feel excited about"*: Bragg, Rick, "Bo Jackson may be spark for Tiger offense," *Anniston Star*, Sept. 9, 1982.

89 *"Maybe," Dye recalled thinking, "that's a sign he is nervous."*: "In the Arena," p. 162.

90 *Jackson scored from the Wake Forest one-yard*: Rutledge, Jerry, "Jackson begins college career with fast start," *Anniston Star*, Sept. 12, 1982.

90 *"[Jack Crowe and I] were walking off the field after the game"*: McGee, Ryan, "The legend of Bo Jackson and 'Bo Over The Top,'" *ESPN.com*, Nov. 23, 2018.

91 *He was an instant phenomenon*: Ray, Darryal, "'Go Bo' Bumper Stickers; Alabama On TV," *Alabama Journal*, Oct. 4, 1982.

92 *The event was held every April*: "The Village on the Plain," p. 222.

92 *"The brothers were nice guys"*: Bowlin, Sean, "You let the bands in your house," *Auburn Plainsman*, Oct. 14, 1982.

93 *"The evidence tends to support the widespread perception"*: Driscoll, James G., "Unless you're Bo Jackson, outrunning poverty easier said than done," *Fort Lauderdale News*, Dec. 22, 1985.

93 *"When I first came here, I could walk on campus"*: Bowles, Billy, "Black students at Auburn battle feelings of isolation," *Detroit Free Press*, Dec. 15, 1985.

94 *Jackson—who received an endless number of "lust letters"*: Sonja Baucom and Abby Petiss, "Best of Friends," 1983 Auburn Golmerata.

95 *"Failure to get Jackson the ball,"*: Bobcock, Mike, "Jackson's lack of playing time questioned," *Lincoln Star*, Oct. 4, 1982.

95 *"Both are big, strong and outrageously fast"*: Stevenson, Mark, "Bo and Herschel share more than number 34," *Auburn Plainsman*, Sept. 30, 1982.

95 *"This is not football,"*: Ray, Darryal, "Gators and Tigers Bask in Southeastern Spotlight," *Alabama Journal*, Oct. 29, 1982.

96 *It had been a mere thirteen years since*: Cole, Nick, "Auburn's first African-American football player has died," *www.saturdaydownsouth.com*, Jan. 13, 2016.

97 *Jackson even fumbled an exchange with Randy Campbell*: Craig, Brent, "Breaks go against Auburn in tough loss to Gators," *Auburn Plainsman*, Nov. 4, 1982.

97 *But despite the Tigers being outgained*: Marshall, Mike, "Gator victory leaves Auburn destiny questionable," *Auburn Plainsman*, Nov. 4, 1982.

CHAPTER 7: BUS STATION

98 *"SEC football players,"*: Harris, Melissa, "I was an SEC Recruiting Chick," *Atlanta Magazine*, Dec. 1991.

99 *"Bo could be another Herschel Walker,"*: Ray, Darryal, "James Is The One Who Captures Dooley's Eye," *Alabama Journal*, Nov. 11, 1982.

99 *Georgia took a surprisingly close 19-14*: Legge, Ed, "Little James gave AU chance," *Anniston Star*, Nov. 14, 1982.

99 *Long considered one of the two or three most revered*: Stevenson, Mark, "AU-UA: game of streaks," *Auburn Plainsman*, Nov. 18, 1982.

100 *"In general, Alabama people think of Auburn followers"*: "The Uncivil War," p. 15.

100 *Entering the 1982 meeting, Alabama had won twenty-eight of the forty-six*: Stevenson, Mark, "AU-UA: game of streaks," *Auburn Plainsman*, Nov. 18, 1982.

100 *Alabama was once ranked in the Top 5 in every poll*: Blackwell, Stuart, "Forget 17-16, AU to break Alabama jinx," *Auburn Plainsman*, Nov. 18, 1982.

100 *After a loss to LSU in Birmingham, Don Kauser, Jr., of the* Birmingham News: "The Last Coach," p. 483.

102 *Citing a lack of a "winning attitude"*: Marshall, Phillip, "Ken Simon dismissed from team," *Montgomery Advertiser*, Nov. 19, 1982.

103 *The Auburn-Alabama kickoff was scheduled for 11:35 a.m.*: "The Uncivil War," p. 43.

103 *"Dye intended to walk into Legion Field"*: "The Uncivil War," p. 43.

103 *"Everything else in the state stops that day,"*: "Where Football Is King," p. 29.

103 *Keith Jackson, however, wasn't so certain*: "Touchdown Auburn!," p. 195.

105 *One season earlier he tore his quadricep*: Linn, Jennifer, "Campbell begins as number one," *Auburn Plainsman*, April 8, 1983.

105 *"He is not fancy or flashy or even a very good passer"*: Ray, Darryal, "No mistake, AU was winner," *Montgomery Advertiser*, Nov. 28, 1982.

107 *The defensive backs converged*: "SEC Football's Greatest Games," p. 36.

107 *On November 24, 1982, the day before Thanksgiving*: McGee, Ryan, "The legend of Bo Jackson and 'Bo Over The Top,'" *ESPN.com*, Nov. 23, 2018.

110 *In the Auburn radio booth*: "Touchdown Auburn!," p. 198.

110 *"Coming off the field"*: Mayes, Bob, "Tigers' Bo Jackson is a reluctant hero," *Montgomery Advertiser*, Nov. 28, 1982.

110 *When Campbell fell on the ball to seal the Tigers' 23–22*: McBride, Lee, "Wild Auburn fans tear up field, roll Toomer's after Bama victory," *Auburn Plainsman*, Dec. 2, 1982.

111 *"My girlfriend goes to Alabama"*: Stevenson, Mark, "Hysteria hits as Auburn ends jinx," *Auburn Plainsman*, Dec. 2, 1982.

111 *"Everyone was intoxicated with the moment"*: "oh hell yes!!!!!!!!!!" *Auburn Plainsman*, Dec. 2, 1982.

111 *He looked at the scoreboard*: "The Uncivil War," p. 51.

CHAPTER 8: OFF BASE

112 *Not long after the Bama win*: Melick, Ray, "Bo Jackson," *Birmingham Post-Herald*, Dec. 1, 1983.

112 *On December 18, 1982, the Tigers capped off*: Buchalter, Bill, "Campbell's secret proves Tigers' biggest weapon," *Orlando Sentinel*, Dec. 19, 1982.

114 *"We didn't know exactly what to expect,"*: Ballard, Perry, "Bo Can Go," *Auburn Bulletin*, 1983.

114 *"He's probably one of the top ten sprinters in the country,"*: Ballard, Perry, "Bo Can Go," *Auburn Bulletin*, 1983.

114 *The headline appeared atop the sports section*: Johnson, Jon, "Bo and Herschel to race in Dallas," *Auburn Plainsman*, Feb. 3, 1983.

115 *First, he won the Heisman Trophy*: Rogers, Thomas, "Walker Wins Heisman," *New York Times*, Dec. 5, 1982.

116 *When the gun sounded, Jackson burst from the blocks*: Marshall, Mike, "Trackers travel to MTDU after Indiana Relays win," *Auburn Plainsman*, Feb. 10, 1983.

117 *The Redbirds started Scott Becker*: Bloodwood, Bryan, "ISU believes pitching bolstered by new faces," *The Pantagraph*, Sept. 9, 1982.

119 *On March 29, Auburn bused the 105 miles*: Lewis, Terry, "Time was right, but Tigers weren't," *Anniston Star*, March 30, 1983.

119 *"Alabama posted an eight-run third inning"*: Hurt, Cecil, "Tide romps past Auburn," *Tuscaloosa News*, April 1, 1983.

121 *And so it was that, on a mid-April afternoon*: Webb, Donnie, "Auburn belts Ala. Christian," *Montgomery Advertiser*, April 14, 1983.

CHAPTER 9: GREG PRATT

126 *He spent one year on the Nashville campus*: "Tragedy at Auburn," *The Tennessean*, August 21, 1983.

127 *They had tight ends, defensive ends and fullbacks*: Davidson, Davis, "Pratt death a result of heat stroke," *Atlanta Constitution*, Aug. 23, 1983.

128 *"Mama," he said, "I don't know if I can run that 440*: Woody, Larry, "Pratt Gave His Life to Game He Loved," *The Tennessean*, Aug. 26, 1983.

129 *Herb Waldrop, the head trainer, saw Pratt*: Davidson, David, "Auburn's Dye downplays running," *Atlanta Constitution*, Aug. 23, 1983.

129 *The water was frigid*: Rawlings, Sally, "How a cold morning shower in winter can boost your energy levels," *Sydney Morning Herald*, June 13, 2020.

129 *One season earlier, also during a running drill*: "Auburn Player Collapses at Practice, Dies," *Washington Post*, Aug. 21, 1983.

129 *He survived in one piece, as he did a heat-related blackout*: Woody, Larry, "Pratt Gave His Life to Game He Loved," *The Tennessean*, Aug. 26, 1983.

130 *Greg Pratt was pronounced dead at 2:35 p.m.*: Marshall, Mike, "Pratt dies after run," *Auburn Plainsman*, Sept. 29, 1983.

131 *"The doctor came out of the emergency room"*: "From the desk of David Housel," p. 186.

131 *He let her know that she would soon be presented*: Marshall, Mike, "Pratt dies after run," *Auburn Plainsman*, Sept. 29, 1983.

132 *"[His] death affected me more than any one incident*: "In The Arena," p. 181.

132 *"If Brent [Fullwood] makes it, we'll have*: Carroll, Frank, "Auburn looks at Fullwood at fullback," *Orlando Sentinel*, Aug. 25, 1983.

133 *"I told Coach Bryant that if I was going to recruit*: Shearer, Ed, "Dye Sees Changes In South's Athletes," *Daily Advertiser (Lafayette, La.)*, Dec. 31, 1983.

134 *Coming off a 9-3 season*: Lawrence, Mitch, Top Twenty College Ratings," *Rochester Democrat and Chronicle*, Sept. 2, 1983.

135 *On September 10, the most expectation-filled season in Auburn football*: Rutledge, Jerry, "defense clears path for Auburn's title hopes," *Anniston Star*, Sept. 11, 1983.

135 *"Texas," wrote Robbie Andreu of the*: Andreu, Robbie, "Florida's SEC title hopes at stake," *Fort Lauderdale News*, Oct. 29, 1983.

135 *"I was embarrassed for our players"*: Borden, Paul, "Big showdown never arrived," *Jackson Clarion-Ledger*, Sept. 18, 1983.

136 *"It went, quite frankly, just like we"*: Mizell, Hubert, "'Horns coach: It went, quite frankly, just like we planned it," *Tampa Bay Times*, Sept. 18, 1983.

136 *"They came out and old-fashioned whipped our butt*: Chapin, David, "Auburn's Jackson a class act," *San Antonio Light*, Sept. 14, 1984.

138 *So they traveled to Knoxville and, before 95,185*: Cox, Bill, "Shattered dreams: Auburn licks error-prone Vols," *Jackson Sun*, Sept. 25, 1983.

138 *"I'm so happy for our guys,"*: "Auburns turns it on, tags Tennessee 37-14," *Tampa Bay Times*, Sept. 25, 1983.

139 *In Jackson's defense, he was playing through*: Bliss, Ron, "Dye says injured Tigers can't rest," *Montgomery Advertiser*, Oct. 5, 1983.

139 *"Sleepy," he said with a laugh. "Whenever Coach Dye says*: Yang, Catherine, "Quote of the Day," *Times-Advocate (Escondido, Cal.)*, Oct. 10, 1983.

139 *He thought it might be wise (inexplicably) to overload on vitamin C*: Cook, Ben, "Bo is bad medicine to the Gators," *SEC Sports Journal*, Nov. 4, 1983.

139 *"When I got up this morning"*: Davidson, David, "An ailing Jackson is the star," *Atlanta Constitution*, Oct. 30, 1983.

140 *Florida-Auburn was hyped as a matchup*: "Head to Head Battle," *The Town Talk (Alexandria, La.)*, Oct. 27, 1983.

141 *He carried the football sixteen times for 196 yards*: "Jackson selected as Back of Week," *Anniston Star*, Nov. 1, 1983.

142 *They traveled to number 4 Georgia*: Finder, Chuck, "Auburn's Jackson is ill, but hold all those get-well cards for later," *Atlanta Constitution*, Nov. 9, 1983.

142 *"Tonight, Bo put his name in the record book at Auburn"*: "Auburn trips Bama, 23-20, wins SEC title," Associated Press, Dec. 4, 1983.

143 *As the players deplaned at the airport*: "Auburn arrives," *Selma Times-Journal*, Dec. 29, 1983.

143 *"I'm not trying to fill Walker's shoes."*: Welch, Chris, "Bo Will Make Own Footsteps at Auburn," *Huntsville Times*, Dec. 31, 1983.

144 *Since the Superdome's debut in 1975*: Davy, Jimmy, "Superdome Awes VU Players," *The Tennessean*, Oct. 2, 1977.

144 *All told, Auburn accumulated 21 passing yards*: Stott, Charlie, "Sputtering Tigers give Michigan boot," *Anniston Star*, Jan. 3, 1984.

144 *They lost three of four fumbles*: Moffit, David, "Bo Jackson: 'We should be No. 1,'" *Daily Spectrum (Saint George, Utah)*, Jan. 3, 1984.

145 *Based upon his rushing totals*: Wilson, Austin, "Game's MVP shuns award," Associated Press, Jan. 3, 1984.

145 *The UPI poll, released shortly thereafter*: "Auburn caught in the bowl trap," *New York Daily News*, Jan. 8, 1984.

146 *"It was," said David Housel, "one of the"*: Barnhart, Tony, "Auburn Wins 1984 Sugar Bowl, but National Championship Still Eludes Title," *www.allstatesugarbowl.com*, 2008.

CHAPTER 10: PAYDAYS

147 *Back in the late days of 1979, as a senior at Pine Forest High*: "Auburn Signs Chuck Clanton," *Pensacola News*, Jan. 2, 1980.

147 *He told all three schools that his commitment would cost $100,000*: "The James Brooks Illiteracy Scandal," *www.diverseeducation.com*, Jan. 6, 2000.

148 *When Pat Dye took over in 1981*: "From the desk of David Housel," p. 190.

148 *"How do our coaches recruit? We sell our program"*: "In the Arena," p. 178.

151 *Maybe it was that he switched majors, from psychology*: "Bo Knows Bo," p. 78.

151 *He was the odds-on favorite to take home the 1984 Heisman*: Oates, Bob, "Bo Jackson Wins Most of Preseason Accolades," *Los Angeles Times*, July 25, 1984.

151 *Maybe it was a fairly adventurous summer*: Housel, David, Auburn Sports Release, May, 1984.

152 *In December 1983, one of Hines's friends and classmates*: Dye, Missy, "Future Bride 'Wind Beneath His Wings'" *Opelika-Auburn News*, Feb. 9, 1986.

152 *"If we get beat," Dye said, "we're going to get beat*: Weaver, Kendal, "Auburn Tigers gave solid shot at grid title with Bo Jackson," *Desert Sun (Palm Springs, Cal.)*, Aug. 17, 1983.

153 *As a senior at St. Cloud (Florida) High*: Reese, Earnest, "Auburn getting ready for Brent and Bo show," *Atlanta Constitution*, Aug. 14, 1984.

154 *"It is as big a game as they have ever faced,"*: "Bo's Eyes On Texas," *Montgomery Advertiser*, Sept. 11, 1984.

155 *Upon returning to Alabama*: Melick, Ray, "Jackson's Out!" *Birmingham Post-Herald*, Sept. 17, 1984.

155 *On September 16, an orthopedic surgeon named Jack Hughston*: Davidson, David, "Jackson operated on, will miss rest of season," *Atlanta Journal*, Sept. 17, 1989.

155 *"I cried," he recalled, "like a baby."*: "Bo Knows Bo," pp. 80–81.

156 *Three years earlier, on February 27, 1981, Linda had*: "Robinson-Garrett," "February ceremonies unite couples," *Mobile Press-Register*, Feb. 28, 1981.

156 *Linda was pretty in an unconventional manner*: Rix, Henri, "Bo's wife supports her favorite superstar," *Tulsa World*, Aug. 10, 1989.

156 *"I was talking to one of the professors"*: Muskat, Carrie, "Lofty goals," *Chicago Tribune*, Aug. 1, 1993.

157 *Bo Jackson was released from Doctor's Hospital*: "Auburn's Bo Jackson released from hospital," *Pensacola News Journal*, Sept. 21, 1984.

157 *He returned to Sewell Hall*: Mayes, Bob, "Bo Still Says No," *Huntsville Times*, Sept. 22, 1984.

157 *In a matter of weeks Jackson dropped from 228*: Maselli, George, "Collins living a fantasy as Bo Jackson's fill-in," *Tallahassee Democrat*, Nov. 2, 1984.

157 *Bo Jackson is a running back who is going to become*: Mayes, Bob, "Sneaking a Peek Behind Bo's Door," *Huntsville Times*, Sept. 19, 1984.

158 *"I can't say yes and I can't say no"*: Maselli, George, "Collins living a fantasy as Bo Jackson's fill-in," *Tallahassee Democrat*, Nov. 2, 1984.

158 *"It couldn't be. But, yes, it was number thirty-four all right"*: Hollis, Charles, "Bo's back! Auburn's star runner gets in," *Birmingham News*, Oct. 30, 1984.

158 *A week later, Fullwood ripped up Tennessee*: Climer, David, "War Eagles Destroy Vols," *The Tennessean*, Sept. 30, 1984.

159 *Never known for his work ethic*: Walsh, Mick, "Even Injury Couldn't Keep Jackson Down," *Columbus Enquirer*, Nov. 15, 1984.

159 *"We've got to make a decision about Bo."*: McCollister, Tom, "Jackson likely to start for Auburn," *Atlanta Constitution*, Nov. 7, 1984.

159 *Outfitted with a body girdle*: Murphy, Mark, "To Teammates' Surprise, Jackson Comes Back," *Columbus Ledger-Enquirer*, Nov. 4, 1984.

159 *His second run went for nine*: Marshall, Phillip, "Jackson's return not enough for AU," *Huntsville Advertiser*, Nov. 4, 1984.

159 *"I don't think that's because of me!"*: Mayes, Bob, "Jackson's Return Shaky," *Huntsville Times*, Nov. 6, 1984.

160 *"Jackson," said Dave Currey, the Bearcats coach*: "Auburn, Bo Jackson make believers of Cincinnati," *Jackson Sun*, Nov. 12, 1984.

161 *"Coach Perkins," a reporter asked during a lead-up*: Rutledge, Jerry, "This is it for Bama," *Anniston Star*, Nov. 30, 1984.

161 *Dye later admitted he overlooked the Tide*: Herndon, Mike, "Wrong Way Bo: Remembering the 1984 Iron Bowl 30 years later," *Al.com*, Nov. 28, 2014.

162 *"Field goal?" asked Crowe*: "The Uncivil War," p. 79.

162 *Ron Middleton, the tight end, brought the play into the*: huddle "Braggin' Rights," pp. 308–309.

162 *The Alabama defensive players held hands in the huddle*: McCollister, Tom, "Tide turned Dye call into big mistake," *Atlanta Constitution*, Dec. 2, 1984.

163 *"Man, how could [Dye] do that?"*: McCollister, Tom, "Tide turned Dye call into big mistake," *Atlanta Constitution*, Dec. 2, 1984.

164 *Outside the door, fans stomped their feet*: McCollister, Tom, "Tide turned Dye call into big mistake," *Atlanta Constitution*, Dec. 2, 1984.

164 *"If I had known Bo was going the wrong"*: Reese, Earnest, "Bo blasts critics, might forgo his senior year," *Atlanta Constitution*, Dec. 5, 1984.

164 *"Loyalty," wrote Donny Claxton in the* Plainsman: Claxton, Donny, Small turnout in Memphis showed little loyalty to AU," *Auburn Plainsman*, Jan. 10, 1985.

CHAPTER 11: A BAIRD MAN

165 *Once upon a time, Nix had guided the program*: "Former Auburn Baseball Coach Paul Nix Passes Away," *www.auburntigers.com*, April 13, 2009.

165 *"He's a proven winner"*: "Auburn hires Baird as baseball coach," *Selma Times-Journal*, June 1, 1984.

167 *"I saw four or five guys, total"*: Clark, N. Brooks, "Which way you gonna go, Bo?" *Sports Illustrated*, May 13, 1985.

167 *Auburn opened at home on February 27*: "Plumb's 2 HRs lead Auburn," *Alabama Journal*, Feb. 28, 1985.

167 *Jackson hit two doubles*: Peters, Dan, "Shelton's HR Spurs Blazers Past Hawks," *Montgomery Advertiser*, March 7, 1985.

168 *"Bo isn't a polished baseball player,"*: Bobcock, Mike, "Bo plays baseball," *Lincoln Journal Star*, March 15, 1985.

169 *Auburn won, 12–6, and those involved*: "Auburn routs Troy," *Anniston Star*, March 18, 1985.

170 *In the lead-up, the Georgia Pep Band*: Aronin, Ivan, "Bo blasts Bulldogs in first night game at Foley Field," *The Red & Black*, April 4, 1985.

171 *Miller, the Georgia catcher, placed one*: Martinez, Michael, "Bo Jackson Has a Choice: Football or Baseball," *New York Times*, May 19, 1985.

174 *On Friday, March 29, the Bo Jackson-less*: Icolano, Jr., Paul, "Dye's Tigers begin spring drills with new look," *Auburn Plainsman*, April 1, 1985.

174 *When asked at the time, Jack Crowe*: Icolano, Jr., Paul, "Thunder, lightning brand I-formation," *Auburn Plainsman*, April 11, 1985.

175 *"The scouts see Jackson playing"*: Clark, N. Brooks, "Which way you gonna go, Bo?," *Sports Illustrated*, May 13, 1985.

175 *"I will be back," he said*: Hollis, Charles, "Scouts call Bo best they've seen, another Winfield," *Birmingham News*, May 30, 1985.

175 *He invited Jackson to visit during the team's*: Allen, Karen, "Another Jackson in Angels' plans," *USA Today*, June 19, 1985.

176 *The Angels (really, Himes) had some thoughts*: Ballard, Perry, "Jackson Not Interested In Angels' Offers," *Opelika-Auburn News*, June 25, 1985.

176 *On February 14, 1985, the Auburn chapter*: "Personals," *Auburn Plainsman*, Feb. 14, 1985.

176 *It all began during the recruiting process*: Blackwell, Mary, "From Barfield to Chizik, Auburn's Tigerettes and Tiger Hosts have adapted to evolving recruiting culture," *thewareaglereader.com*, Sept. 11, 2012.

177 *In her 1991 Atlanta Magazine essay*: Harris, Melissa, "I was an SEC Recruiting Chick," *Atlanta Magazine*, Dec. 1991.

178 *"Bo came over to return an old ring of mine*: Dye, Missy, "Bo Engaged," *Opelika-Auburn News*, Feb. 9, 1986.

CHAPTER 12: SENIORITIS

181 *In the lead-up to the Tigers' September 7 opener*: Rosenberg, I. J., "The Heisman," *Birmingham News*, Aug. 25, 1985.

181 *"I hope," he said, "the people who choose"*: Finebaum, Paul, "Is this Bo's big year?" *Birmingham Post-Herald*, Aug. 26, 1985.

181 *"Bo doesn't really like this."*: Binford, Gary, "Making a Run for the Heisman," *Newsday*, Aug. 27, 1985.

183 *All told, Jackson's first quarter totals were six carries*: Murphy, Mark, "The Bo Show," *Inside The Auburn Tigers Newsletter*, Sept. 1985.

183 *After the convincing win over the Ragin' Cajuns*: Nissenson, Herschel, "Auburn vaults to top of poll," *Longview News-Journal*, Sept. 10, 1985.

183 *They faced a somewhat stiffer test*: Arnold, Van, "Duckworth's exit break for Auburn," *Hattiesburg American*, Sept. 15, 1985.

183 *On July 6, Jon's right leg had been severed*: Webb, Donnie, "Auburn star makes winning visit," *Anniston Star*, Sept. 14, 1985.

184 *Later in the season, a woman named Peggy England*: "Bo Stories," pp. 60–61.

185 *In those thirteen days*: Shearer, Ed, "Bo Jackson sets lofty rushing goals," *Birmingham Post-Herald*, Sept. 10, 1985.

186 *"Some of the guys got to talking"*: Reilly, Rick, "The Vols Had a Ball," *Sports Illustrated*, Oct. 7, 1985.

186 Sports Illustrated *called him "fishing-line thin"*: Reilly, Rick, "The Vols Had a Ball," *Sports Illustrated*, Oct. 7, 1985.

187 *Jackson spent the remainder of the game standing and watching*: Scarbinsky, Kevin, "Bruised knee sends Bo to sideline," *Birmingham News*, Sept. 29, 1985.

187 *Plus, said Dye, "at that point"*: "Auburn's Jackson defends action," *Clarion-Ledger*, Oct. 3, 1985.

188 *Paul Finebaum, the excellent*: "Jackson's disappearing act sabotages Tigers' high hopes," *Birmingham Post-Herald*, Nov. 3, 1985.

189 *Tony Razzano, the San Francisco 49ers director*: McGinn, Bob, "The McGinn Files: Bo Jackson's 'legendary' talent is a curiosity 30 years later," *The Athletic*, Sept. 18, 2020.

189 *"I got down to about the ten"*: "21st and Prime Podcast" conversation between Bo Jackson and Deion Sanders, Oct. 26, 2020.

190 *On his final carry of the first half*: Scarbinsky, Kevin, "Bruised Bo wanted to play—'I just couldn't,'" *Birmingham News*, Nov. 3, 1985.

190 *"I had the feeling he'd do that if we played good defense,"*: Adams, John, "Badge of courage won't go to Bo," *Florida Times-Union*, Nov. 3, 1985.

191 *"Seems like Bo has a tendency to leave the ball*: Reilly, Rick, "Their Hall-mark is winning," *Sports Illustrated*, Nov. 11, 1985.

191 *Jackson "should have chosen baseball yesterday"*: Adams, John, "Badge of courage won't go to Bo," *Florida Times-Union*, Nov. 3, 1985.

191 *"People are starting to wonder how much Jackson cares"*: Fleischman, Bill, "Jackson Putting Heisman Ahead of Team, Critics Say," *Philadelphia Daily News*, Nov. 5, 1985.

192 *This was true in the 1960s*: "Sports at a Glance," *Independent Record (Helena, Mt.)*, Jan. 9, 1982.

193 *"Maybe we've got it wrong"*: Reilly, Rick, "What The Heck, Why Not Dudek?" *Sports Illustrated*, Dec. 2, 1985.

193 *Dudek did not know he would wind up on the cover*: Guay, Victoria, "Where are they now? Plymouth State football legend Joe Dudek," *fosters.com*, Dec. 6, 2009.

195 *One night earlier, Mike Hubbard*: Broadway Lumpkin, Bill, "Bo's busy day stirs memories," *Birmingham Post-Herald*, Dec. 9, 1985.

196 *Tommie Agee, Jackson's roommate and fullback*: Lumpkin, Bill, "Jackson now part of history," *Birmingham Post-Herald*, Dec. 9, 1985.

CHAPTER 13: CLUTTER

197 *When the ceremony at the Downtown Athletic Club*: Lumpkin, Bill, "Bo's busy day stirs memories," *Birmingham Post-Herald*, Dec. 9, 1985.

197 *"I thought I'd be coming back to quiet Auburn"*: Ballard, Perry, "A Hero Returns Home," *Opelika Auburn News*, Dec. 10, 1985.

197 *That night, Jackson and his pals hit the town*: hard "Bo Knows Bo," p. 91.

199 *Linda told Carrie Muskat of* Chicago Sports Profiles *that she*: Muskat, Carrie, "Introducing The Bo Jackson Family," *Chicago Sports Profiles*, Aug. 1993.

199 *"Bo said, 'Let's get married now,'"*: Rix, Henri, "Bo's wife supports her favorite superstar," *Tulsa World*, Aug. 10, 1989.

200 *In an extensive August 25, 1985*: Hinton, Ed, "Super Bo," *Atlanta Journal-Constitution*, Aug. 25, 1985.

201 *"I want people to see me not as an Auburn"*: Nissenson, Herschel, "Bo shows a different side at the Heisman Trophy presentation," *Birmingham News*, Dec. 13, 1985.

201 *On New Year's Day 1986, Jackson's Auburn*: Canning, Whit, "Texas A&M's Bryant just as valuable as Jackson," *Fort Worth Star-Telegram*, Jan. 2, 1986.

201 *Somehow, Joe Dudek—the Division III*: Long, Shep, "Lion kicker Walsh to play in Japan Bowl," *Columbia Daily Spectator*, Jan. 3, 1986.

205 *The next time the East had the ball*: "Jackson Scores 3 Touchdowns To Lead East over West in Japan," *Montgomery Advertiser*, Jan. 13, 1986.

206 *"It was good to meet Bo today,"*: "South offense (Jackson) arrives for Senior Bowl," *Alabama Journal*, Jan. 15, 1986.

CHAPTER 14: BUCKED UP

210 *"I'm not telling until the summer,"*: "Jackson Wins Award, Fields More Questions," *Montgomery Advertiser*, Feb. 11, 1986.

210 *"He's going to the NFL,"*: Selman, Jim, "Which Way Will Bo Go?" *Tampa Tribune*, March 6, 1986.

210 *The Tigers baseball season opened on February 26*: "Auburn '9' Wins Opener, 5-4," *Selma Times-Journal*, Feb. 27, 1986.

210 *The Gamecocks started a sophomore right-hander*: Williams, Chuck, "Eskins 'cuffs Tigers," *Anniston Star*, March 25, 1986.

210 *"Bo Jackson's decision between"*: "Oh My! Dodgers Work at Training," *Kenosha News*, March 16, 1986.

211 *"Jackson has retained Freland* [sic] *Abbott"*: Selman, Jim, "Which Way Will Bo Go?" *Tampa Tribune*, March 6, 1986.

212 *"We have had the rule for as long as I can"*: Finebaum, Paul, "Bo's Confusion Not His First Mistake to Hurt Auburn," *Birmingham Post-Herald*, March 31, 1986.

212 *In Jackson's four years at Auburn*: "The National Collegiate Athletic Association: A Study in Cartel Behavior," p. 46.

212 *A year earlier Jackson was prevented*: "Rules to Keep Jackson from Walkathon," *Montgomery Advertiser*, May 17, 1985.

212 *"The SEC clings to its pompous eligibility rules,"*: Wojnowski, Bob, "Dumb Rule Cost Jackson," *Florida Today*, March 30, 1986.

214 *"I asked for clarification as to what could"*: "Plane Ride Innocent Bo-bo," *The Tennessean*, March 30, 1986.

214 *"Now that there are to be no more at bats"*: Young, Dick, "Bo's Boo-Boo," *Wausau Daily Herald*, April 3, 1986.

215 *In an April 5, 1985* Atlanta Constitution *piece*: Mortensen, Chris, "What's with Bo? It Depends on Who and When You Ask," *Atlanta Constitution*, April 6, 1986.

218 *"Culverhouse is a businessman"*: Florence, Michael, "The Kansas City Deal," *Business Alabama*, Oct. 1986.

218 *The Buccaneers' asking price, however*: "Bucs Want to Sign Bo before Draft," *Opelika-Auburn News*, April 13, 1986.

218 *The consensus second-best player*: Forbes, Gordon, "NFL Draft Preview," *USA Today*, April 19, 1986.

219 *From the galley, a soft chant turned loud: "Bo! Bo! Bo! Bo!"*: Florence, Michael, "The Kansas City Deal," *Business Alabama*, Oct. 1986.

219 *"This is the ball you want, Bo."*: Johnson, Joey, "The Commissioner Speaks," *Tampa Tribune*, April 30, 1986.

219 *"I'm happy that the Buccaneers drafted me,"*: Henderson, Joe, "Jackson's Plans Will Follow His Heart," *Tampa Tribune*, April 30, 1986.

219 *"You sure have nice weather*: Selman, Jim, "Bo Visits Tampa, but Nothing's New," *Tampa Tribune*, May 22, 1986.

219 *The next morning he had*: McEwen, Tom, "Recruiting Time for Bucs and Bo," *Tampa Tribune*, May 22, 1986.

221 *On May 19, Jackson and Woods traveled to Toronto*: "Bo Jackson Takes Swing By Baseball," *Albuquerque Journal*, May 20, 1986.

221 *The men entered the building*: "The Art of Scouting," p. 30.

221 *That's why, shortly after Jackson*: "Bo Jackson visits Royals Stadium," *Longview News-Journal*, May 30, 1986.

221 *"Bo," he said, "do you* really *want to play baseball?"*: "The Art of Scouting," p. 30.

222 *Jackson stopped, spun*: "The Art of Scouting," p. 31.

222 *"Do you think anybody else*: "The Art of Scouting," p. 32.

223 *"The kid was on cloud nine,"*: Florence, Michael, "The Kansas City Deal," *Business Alabama*, Oct. 1986.

223 *"If it's a matter of money, I know we'll win*: Wojnowski, Bob, "Culverhouse: We won't lose Bo to bucks," *Florida Today*, April 30, 1986.

224 *"Kansas City's offer was considerably less"*: Florence, Michael, "The Kansas City Deal," *Business Alabama*, Oct. 1986.

225 *They were already sending out mailers*: Dodd, Dennis, "Bucs built their ticket-selling campaign around Jackson," *Kansas City Star*, June 22, 1986.

225 *He and Woods traveled via Fogelman's private plane*: Jackson, Bo, "Bo, on Bo," *Kansas City Star*, April 27, 1987.

225 *On June 20, Jackson and Woods*: "Jackson to Hold News Conference," *Tyler Morning Telegraph*, June 21, 1986.

225 *"If we do that," Fogelman said, "will Bo sign?"*: Florence, Michael, "The Kansas City Deal," *Business Alabama*, Oct. 1986.

225 *Around 11:50 p.m., Woods looked at Jackson*: Marshall, Phillip, "It's Baseball for Bo," *Montgomery Advertiser*, June 22, 1986.

225 *He simply pulled out a cassette tape*: "Bucs' owner says gamble on Jackson was worth it," *Montgomery Advertiser*, June 22, 1986.

CHAPTER 15: MEMPHIS

226 *In college Jackson had used*: "Bo Knows Bo," p. 106.

227 *His chest was 46 inches across*: Robinson, Cindy, "Bo: Is Heisman winner worth Royals treatment?," *San Bernardino Sun*, Sept. 18, 1986.

227 *"Black & Decker biceps,"*: Pomerantz, Gary, "For Jackson, the Proof Will Be in the Pounding," *Washington Post*, July 6, 1986.

227 *"Jackson did what Balboni"*: Anderson, Dave, "Bo's Blast: 450 Feet Plus," *New York Times*, June 23, 1986.

228 *"Listen, just listen, to the sound of Bo's bat,"*: "Jackson commands attention," *Pittsburgh Press*, March 25, 1990.

229 *The first to speak up was Hal McRae*: "Inside the Park," p. 188.

230 *The rest of the stadium*: "Baseball In Memphis," p. 77.

230 *For openers," he began, "it's hot here."*: Fleming, Mike, "Bo wows 'em in Memphis," *Lompoc Record*, June 29, 1986.

230 *Jackson admitted he knew*: "'Happy as a lark' Bo Jackson ready to have fun in minors," *Wilkes-Barre Citizens' Voice*, June 28, 1986.

230 *Jackson drove a brand-new black Alfa Romeo*: Gretz, Bob, "Bo returns to Auburn," *Kansas City Star*, Feb. 7, 1987.

231 *Jackson arrived thirty-seven minutes late*: Henderson, Joe, "Jackson: 'I'm ready to play,'" *Tampa Tribune*, July 1, 1986.

231 *"It cost me over $20,000 to have*: Henderson, Joe, "Jackson: 'I'm ready to play,'" *Tampa Tribune*, July 1, 1986.

232 *On the mound for Columbus*: "East well represented," *Raleigh News and Observer*, June 30, 1981.

232 *Jim Turpin, the Chicks public address announcer*: Zapadka, Pete, "Plum's George is teammate of Bo Jackson in Memphis," *Pittsburgh Post-Gazette*, July 3, 1986.

232 *"The air," wrote Joe Henderson of*: Henderson, Joe, "Jackson: 'I'm ready to play,'" *Tampa Tribune*, July 1, 1986.

233 *"My trophy case is already full."*: "Bigger Than The Game," p. 211.

233 *When the Astros-Chicks ended*: Watkins, Billy, "Bo's debut a hint of superstardom, *Pensacola News Journal*, July 2, 1986.

234 *George's seventeen-year-old son was in high school*: "Bo Knows Bo," p. 109.

234 *After his debut single, Jackson fell*: "Jackson's Hitting .065; Team Stresses Patience," *Associated Press*, July 7, 1986.

234 *"He has great recognition,"*: Katz, Michael, "A Royal welcome for Bo," *New York Daily News*, Sept. 2, 1985.

234 *"[It shows] how little shame there is in having*: Kaul Donald, "Bo Jackson gives hope to baseball fans," *Philadelphia Daily News*, July 16, 1986.

236 *"[It] cleared the 360-foot fence in left center*: "Bo slams Greenville," *Greenville (S.C.) News*, July 18, 1986.

236 *The shot measured . . . 554 feet*: "Bo Jackson on a streak after slow start," *Courier-Journal*, July 22, 1986.

237 *Wherever Memphis played, fans*: "Southern League says thank you to Royals for singing Bo Jackson," *Courier-Journal*, Aug. 5, 1986.

237 *When Jackson expressed frustration with a bus*: "Bigger Than The Game," p. 211.

239 *"It was a circus," Jackson later said*: Eisenbath, Mike, "Minors Low Point For Bo," *St. Louis Post-Dispatch*, April 21, 1990.

239 *"None of us knew he had left,"*: "Bo's departure catches team by surprise," *Lincoln Journal Star*, Aug. 30, 1986.

CHAPTER 16: ROYAL

240 *"He'll be back because he's tough mentally,"*: Emert, Rich, "Pirates add to Carlton's troubles, defeat Phillies, 6-3," *Pittsburgh Press*, Sept. 15, 1985.

240 *After the Cincinnati Reds rocked him*: Fernandez, Bernard, "Carlton Calls It A Career," *Philadelphia Daily News*, Aug. 7, 1986.

241 *He didn't start that first Monday*: Bricker, Charles, "Jackson's debut: A hit, a near HR and a pro's poise," *Detroit Free Press*, Sept. 4, 1986.

243 *John Hirschbeck, the third base umpire*: Dolson, Frank, "Bo Jackson proves he's where he belongs," *Arizona Daily Star*, Sept. 14, 1986.

245 *"We're all ashamed,"*: "The Art of Scouting," p. 36.

246 *"One day," Ferraro said, "he will look back*: Tucker, Doug, "Jackson Debut Nearly 'Spectacular,' *Sheboygan Press*, Sept. 3, 1986.

246 *"A new and exciting real estate deal*: McEwen, Tom, "Culverhouse still pitching for Jackson," *Tampa Tribune*, Sept. 5, 1986.

246 *"I don't miss it,"*: Garber, Greg, "On NFL's Opening Day. Bo Shows No Remorse," *Hartford Courant*, Sept. 7, 1986.

247 *"Bo this, Bo that,"*: "Bo Jackson just wants to be one of the fellas," *Vancouver Sun*, Sept. 9, 1986.

247 *"He's been pampered a lot,"*: Robinson, Cindy, "Bo: Is Heisman winner worth Royals treatment?," *San Bernardino County Sun*, Sept. 18, 1986.

248 *"[It] was something of a construct,"*: "Bigger Than the Game," p. 277.

250 *For reasons Jackson never explained*: Posnanski, Joe, "The Legend of Bo," joeposnanski.substack.com, April 16, 2021.

250 *When he returned to the dugout*: Dodd, Dennis, "Jackson ignites Royals with 475-foot shot," *Kansas City Times*, Sept. 15, 1986.

250 *The fans stood and applauded*: Rappaport, Ken, "What a blast!" *Associated Press*, Sept. 16, 1986.

250 *"Bo," said Hal McRae, the Royals*: McKenzie, Mike, "Everyone agrees, Jackson's first homer was something to see," *Kansas City Times*, Sept. 15, 1986.

CHAPTER 17: MIXED ROYALTIES

253 *So while Morlan and Co. knew not*: "Bigger than the Game," p. 178.

254 *Instead, he was stationed inside*: Smith, Paul C., "Royal Treatment," *Tampa Tribune*, Nov. 19, 1986.

256 *"Bo Jackson, facing the stiffest challenge*: Johnston, Joey, "Say It Ain't Bo!," *Tampa Tribune*, Jan. 29, 1987.

256 *"He knew the truth,"*: Ebling, Jack, "Dick Howser Gave It a Royal Shot, but Cancer Is Tough Foe," *Lansing State Journal*, Feb. 25, 1987.

257 *First, CNN reported*: Selman, Jim, "Bucs Says Jackson Deal Is Only Rumor," *Tampa Tribune*, Feb. 16, 1987.

257 *Then the* New York Times *insisted*: "Broncos Seek Jackson," *New York Times*, Feb. 21, 1987.

257 *Then Mike Lynn, general manager of the Minnesota*: Hartman, Sid, "Dick Biddle to handle 'U' defense," *Star Tribune*, Feb. 24, 1987.

258 *"I guess I was the only one who*: Nightengale, Bob, "Jackson assured spot on KC's roster," *Salina Journal*, April 5, 1987.

258 *Over the course of 17 games*: Pomerantz, Gary, "Bo Jackson a Fair Catch for Royals," *Washington Post*, April 24, 1987.

258 *"The best available running back*: Tucker, Doug, "NFL officials should ignore Jackson in upcoming draft," *Longview News-Journal*, April 16, 1987.

259 *Two years earlier, when Herschel Walker*: McGinn, Bob, "The McGinn Files: Bo Jackson's 'legendary' talent is a curiosity 30 years later," *The Athletic*, Sept. 18, 2020.

260 *"I always felt . . . he'd become the first 3,000-yard*: McGinn, Bob, "The McGinn Files: Bo Jackson's 'legendary' talent is a curiosity 30 years later," *The Athletic*, Sept. 18, 2020.

260 *With the 182nd pick in the seventh round*: "Brown can provide the blocks for Pitt to build on," Weiss, Jon, *Pittsburgh Press*, July 28, 1985.

260 *"Our feeling about him. . .he's a unique athlete,"*: Heisler, Mark, "Raiders Had Nothing to Lose, a Lot to Gain," *Los Angeles Times*, April 30, 1987.

261 *"We want him to look at it as a challenge*: "Two sports for Bo?" *Philadelphia Daily News*, May 4, 1987.

262 *On multiple occasions, Jackson:* "Gourmet taste," *Asbury Park Press*, May 11, 1987.

262 *At one point, Billy Gardner*: "Bo Jackson will sit out a few games," *Tampa Bay Times*, May 14, 1987.

263 *"Name this kid Eddie Jackson*: Bozich, Rick, "Royals show patience with Jackson, but he belongs at Omaha at this stage," *Louisville Courier-Journal*, May 19, 1987.

263 *"Is it even possible?"*: "Bo Knows Bo," p. 123.

265 *"Bo is a Kansas City Royal*: Nightengale, Bob, and Jonathan Rand, "Bo Jackson wants to be a two-sport athletes," *Kansas City Times*, July 11, 1987.

265 *"We couldn't joke with him because*: "Inside the Park," p. 188.

266 *"I guess he got the last laugh, didn't he?"*: Nightengale, Bob, "Players react angrily to Bo's permission slip," *Kansas City Star*, July 12, 1987.

266 *"It's obvious the game isn't about winning and losing*: Heisler, Mark, "Bo Jackson to Cultivate New Hobby: Playing for Raiders," *Los Angeles Times*, July 12, 1987.

267 *"Some of the fans there are with me,"*: Dodd, Dennis, "Taunting Bo becomes new hobby for fans," *Kansas City Times*, July 17, 1987.

267 *"He was absolutely great,"*: "Ex-Heisman winner Vic Janowicz dies," *The (Lebanon, Pa.) Daily News*, Feb. 29, 1966.

268 *"He was in better shape when he showed up*: "Vic Janowicz Makes Shift to Pro Grid," *The Marion (Ohio) Star*, Nov. 19, 1954.

268 *Years later, Washington acknowledged*: Anderson, Dave, "Bo Jackson's 'Hobby,'" *New York Times*, July 16, 1987.

269 *Tom Candiotti, an Indians pitcher*: "Car and Driver Tested: The 13 Quickest Cars of the 1980s," *www.caranddriver.com*, May 12, 2020.

CHAPTER 18: THE DIFFERENT RUNNING BACK

270 *Beginning on Sept. 22, the NFLPA*: Cosentino, Dom, "The 1987 NFL Players Strike Created The Modern NFL," *Deadspin*, Jan. 25, 2018.

271 *The strike finally ended, and on Oct. 17*: Heisler, Mark, "A Hobby Horse," *Los Angeles Times*, Oct. 18, 1987.

276 *"Those SOBs didn't get me here to sit on the bench,"*: Notes from Dick Schaap's interview with Howie Long, June 18, 1990.

276 *On the morning of Oct. 25*: "Jackson to make debut for Raiders," *Santa Maria Times*, Oct. 25, 1987.

277 *"Eric," Colts Coach Ron Meyer said afterward*: Rowe, John, "Dickerson is upstaged in Colts debut," *Bergen Record*, Nov. 2, 1987.

277 *His first carry was on off-tackle dash*: Oates, Bob, "Pride and Poise May Still Be There, but Ability Seems Lacking," *Los Angeles Times*, Nov. 2, 1987.

278 *When the afternoon ended*: Shaughnessy, Dan, "Jackson's newest job leaves him speechless," *Boston Globe*, Nov. 2, 1987.

279 *"I don't think I'll ever buy a place*: "Shaky or Not, Maybe Bo Needs a Roommate," *Los Angeles Times*, Dec. 7, 1987.

279 *Early in the second half of the Vikings debacle* Heisler, Mark, "Flores Gets the Call, Hilger Gets the Hook—Raiders Get Beat," *Los Angeles Times*, Nov. 9, 1987.

280 *"I expected him to come out and shake*: "Raiders' Bo Jackson blasts his way into NFL," *Napa Valley Register*, Nov. 24, 1987.

CHAPTER 19: MONDAY NIGHT

282 *Once, back in the early 1980s*: Kensler, Tom, "Sooner Crop Has a Strong Texas Accent," *Daily Oklahoman*, Feb. 11, 1983.

282 *"When I'm done with you*: "The Boz," p. 105.

283 *The Boz wore a gold number 44 earring*: Tharp, Mike, "Oklahoma has turned itself into the Land of Boz," *San Francisco Examiner*, Sept. 17, 1986.

283 *He proceeded to infuriate fans*: Henry, Jim, "Orange Bowl drew little interest— and wasn't very interesting," *Tampa Tribune*, Jan. 3, 1987.

283 *"He started becoming somebody that I didn't recognize,"*: "Brian and the Boz," ESPN 30 for 30, 2014.

283 *He appeared on Good Morning America*: Fame for 15 (TV series), "Dangerous Games: Brian Bosworth/Valerie Solanas," March 15, 2002.

283 *"It was supposed to be fun,"*: Plaschke, Bill, "Bosworth's Second Take: Reality," *Los Angeles Times*, Aug. 27, 1996.

283 *In the week before the Seahawks' season opener at Denver*: "Elway Shuts Up Seattle's Bosworth," *Los Angeles Times*, Sept. 14, 1987.

283 *"I can't wait to get my hands*: Ruiz, Steven, "How Brian Bosworth duped thousands of Broncos fans into raising a lot of money for charity," *USA Today*, July 6, 2017.

Chapter 20: Icon

291 *"Bo is the type of athlete you expect*: Murray, Jim, "Bo has easier time hitting a cornerback" *Los Angeles Times*, Nov. 26, 1987.

292 *"Bo knows he is going to have to make our club*: "Bo not assured of KC job," *Santa Cruz Sentinel*, Jan. 28, 1988.

292 *But instead of gracefully*: Isaacson, Melissa, "Cozy facilities luring baseball teams," *Orlando Sentinel*, Feb. 21, 1986.

293 *When Michael Madden of the Boston Globe*: Madden, Michael, "Bo speaks, sort of," *Boston Globe*, March 16, 1988.

293 *In his 1989 autobiography, "Bo Knows Bo,"*: "Bo Know Bo," p. 150.

293 *Jackson batted .298 with five home runs*: Kaegel, Dick, "Bo bucks odds again, wins Royals starting left-field job," *Kansas City Times*, March 29, 1988.

294 *One is a metal bar used in hospitals*: Ashby, Ted, "'Polecat Kept in Closet With Other Useful Items," *Boston Globe*, Jan. 24, 1964.

294 *During his rookie season, for example*: "The Seitzers vs. Middletown," *Manhattan Mercury*, April 24, 1987.

297 *Kansas City led 3-1 entering the top*: Kurkjian, Tim, "Brett, Jackson homer to Rock Ballard, Orioles, 6-2," *Baltimore Sun*, July 30, 1988.

298 *"The timing is right for me to go*: Heisler, Mark, "Flores Steps Down as Raider Coach but Did He Get a Push," *Los Angeles Times*, Jan. 21, 1988.

298 *Only, by the late 1980s*: "Slick," p. 328.

298 *"I'm coming here with the thought*: Hasen, Jeff, "Raiders hire 35-year-old coach," *Kenosha News*, March 1, 1988.

300 *they rented the Santa Monica townhouse*: Watson, Vikki, "Bo is trustworthy," *Kansas City Star*, Oct. 10, 1988.

301 *On the morning of his first game*: Springer, Steve, "Bo's Typical Sunday," *Los Angeles Times*, Oct. 17, 1988.

302 *The diagnosis was a pulled hamstring*: "Saints surge by Raiders," *Santa Rosa Press Democrat*, Oct. 24, 1988.

302 *When asked, Jackson attributed*: "Bo's Boo-Boo," *San Francisco Examiner*, Nov. 20, 1988.

302 *"On several occasions the roar of the crowd*: Ostler, Scott, "Los Angeles Turns Tables on Raiders, Abandons Them," *Los Angeles Times*, Nov. 21, 1988.

303 *"Bo is a known quantity now*: "Quote Department," *Los Angeles Times*, Nov. 16, 1988.

303 *In an ugly 13-3 Week 10*: Heisler, Mark, "It's a First for Raiders, They Share West Lead," *Los Angeles Times*, Nov. 7, 1988.

303 *"Just when you think you've got him figured out"*: Heisler, Mark, "Bo Tells Shanahan He Will Return," *Los Angeles Times*, Dec. 20, 1988.

Chapter 21: The Greatest Year I

305 *It began, somewhat strangely, in the woods*: Polk, Alan, "Bo nips Davey in Buckmasters obstacle course race," *Montgomery Advertiser*, Jan. 29, 1989.

305 *"Bo," Richard Woods, his agent*: Nightengale, Bob, "Bo signs rich contract with Royals," *Kansas City Times*, Feb. 16, 1989.

305 *When the Royals requested*: Nightengale, Bob, "Look who's suddenly a contented Royal—Willie Wilson," *Kansas City Star*, March 31, 1989.

306 *Not a bad slider*: Buckley, Steve, "Bo, Royals take Oil Can for a ride," *Hartford Courant*, March 7, 1989.

306 *"What did he hit?"*: Buckley, Steve, "Bo, Royals take Oil Can for a ride," *Hartford Courant*, March 7, 1989.

306 *"At the plate he's more patient,"*: Kaegel, Dick, "Bo's performance raises some eyebrows," *Kansas City Times*, April 24, 1989.

307 *"Biff! Pow! Crack!"*: Twyman, Gib, "This game's just a snap for Jackson," *Kansas City Star*, May 10, 1989.

307 *"The legend of Bo Jackson continues."*: Smith, Mike, "Eye Openers," *St. Louis Post-Dispatch*, May 11, 1989.

307 *The baseball ricocheted off the barrel*: Kurkjian, Tim, "First place doesn't mean first-rate in AL East," *Baltimore Sun*, May 21, 1989.

307 *Kirby Puckett, the Twins star center fielder*: Gammons, Peter, "The Big Stick," *Sports Illustrated*, June 12, 1989.

308 *Back home in Santurce, Puerto Rico*: Konkle, Matthew "Rookie gives Twins a lift," *St. Cloud Times*, May 22, 1989.

308 *"I hit it off the end of my bat,"*: "Bo Stories," p. 105.

309 *On the mound for the* Royals: Rieper, Max, "The 100 Greatest Royals of All-Time - #47 Steve Farr," *www.royalsreview.com*, July 1, 2008.

309 *"I'm flying full tilt,"*: Covering The Bases interview with Daron Vaught. March 3, 2021.

309 *"I wasn't even watching the play,"*: Nightengale, Bob, "Long throw faster than a speeding Mariner," *Kansas City Star*, June 6, 1989.

310 *"In my head I'm going*: Covering The Bases interview with Daron Vaught. March 3, 2021.

310 *"So I forget about the deke,"*: Nightengale, Bob, "Long throw faster than a speeding Mariner," *Kansas City Star*, June 6, 1989.

311 *"It's crazy,"*: Nightengale, Bob, "Long throw faster than a speeding Mariner," *Kansas City Star*, June 6, 1989.

312 *Jackson appeared on the cover*: Gammons, Peter, "The Big Stick," *Sports Illustrated*, June 12, 1989.

313 *"To hell with 40-40,"*: "Jackson's two homers lift Royals past A's 10-1," *Springfield News-Leader*, July 5, 1989.

315 *Because of injury concerns, the hockey scene*: Rossen, Jake, "Bo Knows Everything: Remembering Nike's Legendary Bo Jackson Ad Campaign," *mentalfloss.com*, May 21, 2020.

315 *On the afternoon of July 5, 1989*: Walker, Ben, "Retired Schmidt, injured Canseco win All-Star voting," *Springfield News-Leader*, July 6, 1989.

316 *"It wasn't a surprise to me,"*: "Baseball's main attraction—The Bo Jackson Show," *St. Joseph (Mo.) News-Press/Gazette*, July 10, 1989.

316 *For the first inning, however*: Chardy, Alfonso, "WHO's on first against proposed Radio Marti," *Fort Worth Star-Telegram*, July 8, 1982.

316 *An hour earlier, he had entered both clubhouses*: "21st and Prime Podcast" conversation between Bo Jackson and Deion Sanders, Oct. 26, 2020.

318 *"It sounded like it was hit like a golf ball,"*: Morgan, Chris, "Bo Jackson's 448-Foot ASG Blast Turned Ronald Reagan Into a Fan," *fanbuzz.com*, July 13, 2021.

318 *As soon as the ball touched down*: Churm, Steven R., and Jean Davidson, "For American League, a Field of Dreams," *Los Angeles Times*, July 12, 1989.

CHAPTER 22: THE GREATEST YEAR II

320 *Mandarich was widely considered*: Telander, Rick, "The Big Enchilada," *Sports Illustrated*, April 24, 1989.

321 *The team is just kind of an afterthought*: Murray, Jim, "Houston a Poor Host to Galloping Ghost," *Los Angeles Times*, Nov. 20, 1989.

322 *Because Jackson lived in a cocoon*: "Raiders lose Allen, but Bo should arrive today," *Sacramento Bee*, Oct. 11, 1989

322 *"My problem is I've been*: "Allen says no to move for Bo," *Sacramento Bee*, Oct. 7, 1989.

322 *"No departing talk, no handshakes*: "You're Okay, It's Just a Bruise," p. 228.

325 *[Bo Jackson] is the best I've ever seen*: Bisheff, Steve, "Bo is the best ever," *North County Times*, Nov. 6, 1989.

326 *"Art is on the same par"*: Heisler, Mark, "Chalk It Up to Old-Line Approach," *Los Angeles Times*, Nov. 9, 1989.

327 *As Glenn Dickey noted*: "Just Win, Baby," p. 220.

327 *Allen made $1.1 million for 16 games* Noland, Eric, "Allen's ligament is fine, but his career may not be," *Los Angeles Times*, Dec. 10, 1989.

CHAPTER 23: PRIME TIME

330 *"Steady bat, outstanding defensive skills"*: Ingram, Junior, "FSU's Sanders: Football is it for now," *Pensacola News Journal*, Sept. 3, 1986.

330 *"The young man," said George Steinbrenner*: Dodd, Rustin, "When Bo met Deion: Two transcendent stars, a feud and a night at Yankee Stadium," *The Athletic*, July 15, 2020.

330 *He arrived on Feb. 24*: Kay, Michael, "Flashes," *New York Daily News*, Feb. 25, 1989.

330 *"Get that number off his back!"*: Kay, Michael, "Yankees dim on Neon Deion," *New York Daily News*, Feb. 26, 1989.

331 *"I think I can do anything I want,"*: Kerasotis, Peter, "Horner's brilliance cut short by injury," *Florida Today*, March 13, 1989.

331 *"He's always saying, 'The Kid,'"*: Scheiber, Dave, "Decisions, Decisions," *Sports Illustrated*, July 3, 1989.

332 *First, he used the time between*: Nunley, Deana, "Bo Jackson returns to college," *Birmingham Post-Herald*, Jan. 19, 1990.

333 *"I don't know if Woods has"*: Twyman, Gib, "Bo-nanza premature for Jackson," *Kansas City Star*, Jan. 18, 1990.

337 *"If I crashed into the wall,"*: Marcello, Brandon, "Why did Bo Jackson run up the outfield wall in 1990?," *www.al.com*, Jan. 13, 2019.

338 *The color commentator was Norm Hitzges*: "Orioles Card 'O' The Day," *www.oriolescards.blogspot.com*, May 6, 2000.

339 *"That can't be done,"*: Boswell, Thomas, "What Bo Knows: Playing's The Thing," *Washington Post*, April 21, 1993.

340 *"I don't know who was pitching that night,"*: "21st and Prime Podcast" conversation between Bo Jackson and Deion Sanders, Oct. 26, 2020.

343 *"You can't have a separated shoulder,"*: Dodd, Rustin, "When Bo met Deion: Two transcendent stars, a feud and a night at Yankee Stadium," *The Athletic*, July 15, 2020.

343 *Once he reached the dugout*: "21st and Prime Podcast" conversation between Bo Jackson and Deion Sanders, Oct. 26, 2020.

CHAPTER 24: HIP

345 *"Bo Knows Bo is more than 200 pages*: Finn, Timothy, "Bo By Bo," *Kansas City Star*, Oct. 12, 1990.

345 *His rocket will land*: Baker, Chris, "Shell Waiting for Bo's Rocket to Land," *Los Angeles Times*, Oct. 12, 1990.

346 *When Jackson entered*: Dufresne, Chris, "Bo Holds Annual Coming-Out Party," *Los Angeles Times*, Oct. 18, 1990.

347 *"I'm the third-string tailback,"*: "Bo knows he'll be ready to play Sunday," *The Californian*, Oct. 18, 1990.

347 *"That's part of my game-plan,"*: Cox, Bob, "Jackson makes mark in his seasonal debut," *News-Pilot*, Oct. 22, 1990.

348 *And in the Bengals matchup*: Downey, Mike, "Bo Comes Up Short, but Not the Raiders," *Los Angeles Times*, Dec. 17, 1990.

348 *He also reached a decision*: Conklin, Mike, "Bo to concentrate on only baseball," *Chicago Tribune*, Nov. 20, 1991.

348 *"When I leave the ballpark"*: Brown, Ben, "Bo's private side always stays home," *USA Today*, Nov. 22, 1988.

349 *Because this was its star client's*: Stewart, Larry, "TV Blackout Is Lifted," *Los Angeles Times*, Jan. 12, 1991.

352 *When the Bengals grabbed him 57th overall*: Free, Bill, "Walker first Terp, goes to Bengals; Dolphins pick Edmunds in 3rd round," *Baltimore Sun*, April 26, 1988.

353 *"The momentum of my body kept going,"*: ESPN Sports Century, "Bo Jackson."

354 *"It felt like somebody,"*: ESPN Sports Century, "Bo Jackson."

355 *"It's a hip pointer,"*: "Jackson could miss AFC final," *North County Times*, Jan. 15, 1991.

355 *"I had [hip pointers],"*: Craig, Jack, "Simpson made the call," *Boston Globe*, March 19, 1991.

356 *A few hours after the game*: Popper, Joe, and Steve Cameron, "The fall of the rising star," *Kansas City Star*, April 14, 1991.

356 *"Do you see all that dark stuff?"*: ESPN Sports Century, "Bo Jackson."

357 *"Bo Jackson's a baseball player,"*: "Chatter Box," *North County Times* (Oceanside, Cal.), Jan. 20, 1991.

357 *"Bo Jackson showed his true colors*: Keisser, Bob, "Of Todd's woes, Bo's no-shows and Super Bowls . . ." *Long Beach Press-Telegram*, Jan. 23, 1991.

CHAPTER 25: REDUCED

358 *On. Feb. 14, 1991, roughly six weeks after*: Dufresne, Chris, "Royals Cite Hip Injury, Cut Jackson," *Los Angeles Times*, March 19, 1991.

358 *"Bo told me the injury wasn't anything serious,"*: Cameron, Steve, "Royals watching Jackson's injury," *Kansas City Star*, Jan. 30, 1991.

359 *"Would he listen?"*: Kaegel, Dick, "Royals' season opener is sold out," *Kansas City Star*, Feb. 21, 1991.

359 *"If you are Diogenes, looking for an honest man,"*: Twyman, Gib, "Bo's act becoming sideshow," *Kansas City Star*, June 8, 1991.

359 *Pitcher Mark Davis was one*: Kaegel, Dick, "Opener is goal for Jackson now," *Kansas City Star*, Feb. 28, 1991.

359 *Bret Saberhagen, Kansas City ace*: Twyman, Gib, "Royals could see Jackson feared worst from injury," *Kansas City Star*, March 17, 1991.

361 *"There was always the risk,"*: Cameron, Steve, "Doubt is cast on Jackson's health," *Kansas City Star*, March 16, 1991.

361 *On March 15, Joyce ran more tests*: Popper, Joe and Steve Cameron, "The fall of the rising star," *Kansas City Star*, April 14, 1991.

361 *"He was as down as I've ever seen him,"*: Twyman, Gib, "Royals could see Jackson feared worst from injury," *Kansas City Star*, March 17, 1991.

361 *Six years earlier, the Boston Red Sox*: "Explaining Dr. Andrews, the brand," *SB Nation*, Sept. 15, 2013.

362 *"It is with very deep regret*: Cameron, Steve, "Royals choose to release Jackson," *Kansas City Star*, March 19, 1991.

363 *"I've had a better relationship*: Kaegel, Dick, "Jackson felt end could be at hand," *Kansas City Star*, March 20, 1991.

364 *A Seattle radio station sent*: "Bo Jackson in Little League?" *San Francisco Examiner*, March 22, 1991.

364 *The Live Oak Gray Ghosts*: "Live Oak Gray Ghosts want Bo," *Miami Herald*, March 22, 1991.

364 *In Wichita, the front office*: "Promotion makes fun of injury," *Kansas City Star*, April 25, 1991.

364 *The value of Jackson's Topps rookie card*: Pugh, Tony, "Jackson Action," *Miami Herald*, March 25, 1991.

364 *Companies seeking Bo Jackson's endorsement*: Foltz, Kim, "Despite injury, Bo Jackson still in endorsement game," *Tampa Bay Times*, March 25, 1991.

364 *"This was the chance he took*: Rosenthal, Ken, "Bo knew it all: It might cost him everything," *Modesto Bee*, March 20, 1991.

364 *"He was doing it all on raw ability*: Ryan, Bob, "No two ways about it," *Boston Globe*, March 19, 1991.

364 *"He blithely ignored the advice*: Krikorian, Doug, "Bo sidelined by an illusion of immortality," *Raleigh News and Observer*, March 21, 1991.

365 *One by one, baseball executives*: "Two Sports Too Many, Even for Bo Jackson," *Asheville Citizen-Times*, March 21, 1991.

365 *"The final chapter in the Bo story is written,"*: Cameron, Steve, "Jackson release official," *Kansas City Star*, March 23, 1991.

365 *According to Richard Woods, the agent*: "12 teams express interest in Bo," *Wichita Eagle*, March 29, 2021.

365 *The Yankees sought the advice*: Ringolsby, Tracy, "Will Bo Ever Play Again?" *Inside Sports*, June 1991.

365 *Dr. James Boscardin, the team's senior physician*: Verdi, Bob, "Signing Jackson an All-Star move," *Chicago Tribune*, April 4, 1991.

365 *he believed the hip injury was more*: Solomon, Alan, "A closer look at Bo encourages doctors," *Chicago Tribune*, April 5, 1991.

365 *"Any time you can get an athlete*: Robinson, Alan, "Chicago puts up the dough for ailing Bo," *Salina Journal*, April 4, 1991.

366 *The three-year contract would pay*: Solomon, Alan, "Sox make a small bet on Bo," *Chicago Tribune*, April 4, 1991.

366 *I'm going to get my hip back into shape*: Jackson, Bo, "A Fielder's Dreams," *New York Times*, April 8, 1991.

367 *"If you knew what the Royals*: Popper, Joe and Steve Cameron, "The fall of the rising star," *Kansas City Star*, April 14, 1991.

367 *"Don't quote me,"*: Popper, Joe, and Steve Cameron, "The fall of the rising star," *Kansas City Star*, April 14, 1991.

367 *Later, in a chat with*: Ringolsby, Tracy, "Will Bo Ever Play Again?," *Inside Sports*, June 1991.

368 *"I'm not very good at spectator sports,"*: Jackson, Bo, "Play ball without me (for just a bit," *Sacramento Bee*, April 14, 1991.

368 *In the spirit of a fresh start*: Marran, David, "Thud! New Comiskey opens to a 16-0 White Sox embarrassment," *Kenosha News*, April 19, 1991.

368 *The pool was 18 feet long*: Johnson, K. C., "Comiskey rehab pool the wave of the future," *Chicago Tribune*, Sept. 13, 1991.

368 *"Herm doesn't like to rest injuries,"*: Baumbich, Charlene, "When they're down but not out," *Chicago Tribune*, Oct. 4, 1992.

369 *"X-rays definitely showed some improvement,"*: "Sox say Bo's hip improved, but still no word on return," *Chicago Tribune*, June 19, 1991.

369 *In May, Physician and Sportsmedicine, a medical journal*: Warren, James, "Who knows," *Chicago Tribune*, May 23, 1991.

369 *On July 16, several hours before the Sox*: "Bo takes first swings since last October," *The (Moline, Ill.) Dispatch*, July 17, 1991.

370 *Andrews offered an update*: "Docs say Bo making excellent progress," *The Dispatch (Moline, Ill.)*, July 21, 1991.

370 *"I have never had to work at anything,"*: Patterson, Ken, "Bo learns patience in his comeback," *Anniston Star*, Aug. 27, 1991.

370 *"I had butterflies in my stomach,"*: Viorva, Jeff, "Jackson just wants to work," *Northwest Herald*, Aug. 8, 1991.

370 *"He was awesome,"*: "Bo takes batting practice with White Sox," *Herald and Review (Decatur, Ill.)*, Aug. 7, 1991.

370 *"It's a sense of relief,"*: "Bo gets some swings in live batting practice," *Journal Gazette (Mattoon, Ill.)*, Aug. 7, 1991.

370 *On Aug. 15, the team released Ron Kittle*: "Number's up—Sox release Kittle," *The Dispatch (Moline, Ill.)*, Aug. 16, 1991.

371 *"They came from all over,"*: Le Batard, Dan, "Bo Jackson fever strikes Sarasota ballpark," *Miami Herald*, Aug. 26, 1991.

371 *"He was awesome,"*: Korzenowski, Scott, "Bo show a no-go," *Fort Myers News-Press*, Aug. 25, 1991.

373 *"I'd like to say we appreciate*: Korzenowski, Scott, "Fans only get a glimpse of superstar," *Fort Myers News-Press*, Aug. 25, 1991.

373 *When a lovely day at the park*: Strauss, Joe, "Bo plays two cautiously as comeback begins in Class A," *Atlanta Constitution*, Aug. 26, 1991.

373 *Now pitching for Charlotte*: Brunson, Dennis, "Maldonado fills Richey's shoes in Braves' pen," *The Item (Sumter, S.C.)*, Aug. 6, 1989.

374 *As soon as he ran through the base*: Le Batard, Dan, "No: 'It was fun,'" *Anniston Star*, Aug. 26, 1991.

374 *"He turned it on when he thought he was going to get a hit,"*: "Bo makes return to baseball," *Associated Press*, Aug. 26, 1991.

375 *"It's like holding a golf tournament,"*: Aiello, John, "Bo takes comeback to Barons," *Montgomery Advertiser*, Aug. 27, 1991.

375 *As fans cheered, Jackson whispered*: "Bo goes 2-for-4 in debut with Barons," *Selma Times-Journal*, Aug. 27, 1991.

376 *"He may always have a detectable*: Flanagan, Jeffrey, "Jackson hitless but happy, healthy," *Kansas City Star*, Sept. 3, 1991.

CHAPTER 26: THE RETURN

377 *"Why should I seek vengeance*: "Bo Jackson to return Monday," *Kansas City Star*, Sept. 1, 1991.

378 *"Bo used to take a second*: Kaegel, Dick, "Royals plan Jackson strategy," *Kansas City Star*, Sept. 2, 1991

378 *A crowd of 37,187 fans filed*: Solomon, Alan, "The show is hardly all Bo's," *Chicago Tribune*, Sept. 3, 1991.

378 *It was, Jerome Holtzman of the*: Holtzman, Jerome, "A little bit of history and a lot of show business," *Chicago Tribune*, Sept. 3, 1991.

378 *Four months earlier, while pitching*: MacIntyre, Iain, "Canadians' ace Hernandez facing serious arm surgery," *Vancouver Sun*, May 18, 1991.

379 *"Now that I've gotten those first*: Diedrich, Robert W., "Jackson's patience prevails, collects 2 hits," *Northwest Herald*, Sept. 6, 1991.

380 *Against the Rangers in Arlington*: DeMarco, Tony, "Bo shows Rangers he still knows," *Fort Worth Star-Telegram*, Sept. 7, 1991.

380 *"That's the best I've seen him run"*: Solomon, Alan, "White Sox notes," *Chicago Tribune*, Sept. 15, 1991.

381 *"As far as I'm concerned*: Conklin, Mike, "Bo to concentrate on only baseball," *Chicago Tribune*, Nov. 20, 1991.

382 *On December 13, 1991*: Siegel, Alan, "The Legend of 'Tecmo Super Bowl,'" *The Ringer*, Nov. 17, 2016.

382 *"Because I wanted to use unique formations*: Raguse, Lou, "The Fathers of Tecmo Super Bowl," *louraguse.com*, Feb. 26, 2016.

382 *Hideshia Yamaguchi, who worked on the game*: Robinson, John, "Sports Video Game Rankings (1-5)," *ESPN.com*, May 10, 2013.

383 *"For context, Barry Sanders and Jerry Rice were next at 69*: Kantowski, Ron, "5 things about Bo Jackson, unstoppable video game star," *Las Vegas Review-Journal*, July 18, 2020.

383 *"For 15 years, the greatest*: Simmons, Bill, "Who's better than Bo?" *ESPN The Magazine*, Sept. 1, 2003.

383 *"immaculate, expensive,*: Muskat, Carrie, "Introducing The Bo Jackson Family," *Chicago Sports Profiles*, Aug. 1993.

384 *"He's in a crouch more,"*: Solomon, Alan, "Bo knows that his future is murky," *Chicago Tribune*, Feb. 18, 1992.

385 *The man behind a Nike marketing bonanza*: Vorva, Jeff, "Jackson's hip a hot topic again," *Northwest Herald*, Feb. 7, 1993.

385 *The guard had left the game*: Solomon, Alan, "Bo knows that his future is murky," *Chicago Tribune*, Feb. 18, 1992.

385 *He went 2-for-2 in the*: Walker, Ben, "Bo's designated problem: running," *Northwest Herald*, March 6, 1992.

386 *Against the Detroit Tigers*: Wulf, Steve, "It Hurts Just To Watch Him," *Sports Illustrated*, March 16, 1992.

386 *He called Jackson "a cartoon."*: Lincicome, Bernie, "He still doesn't know it's over," *Chicago Tribune*, March 11, 1992.

386 *On March 9, in an exhibition game*: Solomon, Alan, "Bo hobbles off field—for now," *Chicago Tribune*, March 11, 1992.

386 *"It's like pinch hitting for Ted Williams,"*: Littwin, Mike, "Now it's what Bo can't do, but the fans are still his," *Baltimore Sun*, March 10, 1992.

387 *On the morning of April 4, 1994*: "Bo satisfied after surgery," *Anniston Star*, April 5, 1992.

387 *The vast majority of those who underwent*: Anstett, Patricia, "Doctors fear Bo Jackson's hip will fail," *Detroit Free Press*, March 2, 1993.

387 *Five days later, Jackson returned to*: Vorva, Jeff, "Bo knows how to stay optimistic," *Northwest Herald*, April 14, 1992.

387 *"I'm running like a John Deere!"*: "Bo knows the mound," *The Dispatch (Moline, Ill.)*, April 14, 1992.

388 *The White Sox opened at home against*: Solomon, Alan, "Jackson, Fisk limp in together," *Chicago Tribune*, April 14, 1992.

388 QUERY: Endnote was empty but reference still in text. Pls confirm deletion is intentional.

388 *"I still have a lot of open wounds*: Nightengale, Bob, "Do You Know Him?" *Los Angeles Times*, April 4, 1994.

388 *"I tried to have a relationship*: "Raising a Modern-Day Knight," p. 73

389 *From this point on, Jackson wrote*: Terry, Mike, "Bo knows life after baseball," *San Bernardino County Sun*, July 10, 1994.

389 *"We don't want eight*: Furman, Wade, "ChiSox planning on Jackson comeback," *Rock Island Argus*, July 2, 1992.

389 *His stomach had been torn open by bullets*: Nolan, Kate, "Fitness guru speaks out," *Arizona Republic*, Oct. 26, 2005.

389 *"It's a very advanced and specialized form of rehabilitation,"*: "Jackson in Phoenix for rehab," *Tucson Star*, May 9, 1992.

390 *He was asked for his opinion*: Tefertiller, Casey, "Expert: Bo might play again," *San Francisco Examiner*, March 28, 1992.

390 *"As an athlete, he just recovers faster,"*: Goodykoontz, Bill, "Bo gets hip to Valey with rehab, tae kwon do," *Arizona Republic*, May 10, 1992.

390 *"My rehabbing was the hardest*: Donnellon, Sam, "Bo turns the other cheek to skeptics," *Philadelphia Daily News*, March 3, 1993.

390 *"It was 24 hours a day*: Boswell, Thomas, "What Bo Knows: Playing's the Thing," *Washington Post*, April 21, 1993.

390 *"You can't even tell which hip it is,"*: Cafardo, Nick, "Sox Hope to Catch up with Pena's Agent," *Boston Globe*, Sept. 7, 1992.

CHAPTER 27: A HOG'S HEART ON A FENCE POST

393 *When the biggest scar anyone*: Vincent, Charlie, "Jackson Has Long Odds in Battle to Become Baseball's Bionic Bo," *Detroit Free Press*, Feb. 28, 1993.

393 *"Anything," Jackson said, "to help the team out."*: Conklin, Mike, "Recovering Stars Hold Key for Sox," *Chicago Tribune*, Feb. 22, 1993.

394 *"The top part of the thigh*: Reaves, Joey, "Bo Setback? Sox Doctor Tells Fears," *Chicago Tribune*, Feb. 25, 1992.

394 *Although the 1993 hip*: Anstett, Patricia, "Doctors Fear Bo Jackson's Hip Will Fail," *Detroit Free Press*, March 2, 1993.

394 *"The constant abuse of competitive sports,"*: DePaolis, Mark, "The Bionic Bo Jackson Knows Better," *Minneapolis Star Tribune*, March 30, 1993.

394 *"Hitting is just like sex,"*: Twyman, Gib, "Bo Has Done All He Can, but It Won't Be Enough," *Kansas City Star*, March 7, 1993.

395 *A day later, against Texas*: Reaves, Joey, "Jackson's Debut at 1st a Success—He's Still Alive," *Chicago Tribune*, March 8, 1993

395 *In a game against the Yankees*: "Bo's Stock Rises Even as He Slides," *Chicago Tribune*, March 19, 1993

395 *"There was an audible gap,"*: Reaves, Joey "Bo's Safe—and Sound–after Slide," *Chicago Tribune*, March 16, 1993.

395 *"Everything that was there*: Holtzman, Jerome, "Verdict Is Still Out on Jackson's Value to Sox," *Chicago Tribune*, March 25, 1993.

397 *"I've reached my goal*: Reaves, Joey, "Sox Roster Includes Bo," *Chicago Tribune*, March 25, 1993.

397 *Inside the Comiskey press box*: Guyette, Rob, "Bo Jackson Adds on to His Legend," *Green Bay Press-Gazette*, April 10, 1993.

399 *"It had to come against the Yankees*: Lincicome, Bernie, "'Bo, The Movie'? It's a 'Natural,'" *Chicago Tribune*, April 10, 1993.

400 *In his midseason report card*: Reeves, Joey, "Joey Reeves' Sox Report Card," *Chicago Tribune*, July 15, 1993.

402 *"This is it, number one,"*: Vorva, Jeff, "Fisk Catches Record," *Northwest Herald*, June 23, 1993.

402 *"I don't think he expected it,"*: Reaves, Joey, "Schueler's 'Rough' Decision Hits Sox Players Emotionally," *Chicago Tribune*, June 29, 1993.

403 *"He didn't know what to do with himself,"*: Reaves, Joey, "Schueler's 'Rough' Decision Hits Sox Players Emotionally," *Chicago Tribune*, June 29, 1993.

404 *The final tab was four thousand dollars*: Nightengale, Bob, "Do You Know Him?" *Los Angeles Times*, April 4, 1994.

405 *"If he hits you, don't rip your helmet off,"*: Bo Jackson interview on the Rick & Bubba Show, WZZK-FM, May 17, 2017.

405 *"All I could think about when it happened*: "Nolan Ryan: The Making of a Pitcher," pp. 317–320.

408 *"We have been one bat short*: "Bo Jackson Back in Lineup as Sox Go after AL Game 3," *Daily Chronicle (DeKalb, Ill.)*, Oct. 8, 1993.

408 *"Bo didn't have much to say*: Holtzman, Jerome, "Mouthy Bo, Bell Pick a Bad Time," *Chicago Tribune*, Oct. 9, 1993.

408 *"I really don't have an excuse,"*: "Bo Whiffs with Game on the Line," *Herald and Review (Decatur, Ill.)*, Oct. 11, 1993.

408 *"Guys who talk a lot,"*: Ford, Bob, "Stewart Remains Quietly Confident despite Needling," *Philadelphia Inquirer*, Oct. 12, 1993.

409 *"Oh, those Chicago White Sox Jacksons,"*: Shaughnessy, Dan, "No-Action Jackson," *St. Louis Post-Dispatch*, Oct. 12, 1993.

409 *"Although Bo is eligible to become*: "Bo Can Become Free Agent after Sox Waive Option Year," *The Pantagraph*, Nov. 6, 1993.

CHAPTER 28: THE CIRCUS ACT

410 *"Bo," said Jerry Reinsdorf*: Sullivan, Paul, "Bo Knows He's Joining the Angels," *Chicago Tribune*, Jan. 31, 1994.

412 *Such a pathetic sight prompted*: Neil, Edward J., "Babe Ruth's Dive into Obscurity a Speed Record," *Burlington Free Press*, Aug. 2, 1935.

412 *He viewed himself as a fourth outfielder*: Gazzolo, Jim, "Are Angels Smart or Just Desperate?," *The Californian*, Feb. 1, 1994.

412 *One year earlier, on April 22, 1993*: Nightengale, Bob, "Worst Is Over," *Los Angeles Times*, Feb. 26, 1994.

413 *The Angels won 7-6, and afterward*: "Jackson Hits Slam in Win over Rockies," *Santa Maria Times*, March 5, 1994.

416 *At Minnesota in April*: Nightengale, Bob, "Angel with an Attitude Steals Show," *Los Angeles Times*, April 7, 1994.

417 *Against Detroit in late May*: "Jackson's power still there as he collects 5 RBI in Angel win," *The Signal (Santa Clarita, Cal.)*, May 27, 1994.

417 *"You have to realize John Dopson*: Nightengale, Bob, "Angels Fire Buck Rodgers as Manager," *Los Angeles Times*, May 18, 1994.

418 *"It's a good thing*: "Quotable," *Santa Rosa Press Democrat*, July 22, 1994.

418 *Rod Carew, the team's hitting coach*: Weyler, John, "Carew Blasts Angels After Latest Shutout," *Los Angeles Times*, June 30, 1994.

419 *In a rare start in left field*: Nightengale Bob, "Timing Isn't Right for Bo and Angels," *Los Angeles Times*, July 8, 1994.

419 *"I've never seen anything like this in my life,"*: Nightengale, Bob, "Bo Says Fans Hurting Team" *Los Angeles Times*, July 24, 1994.

419 *"Politics have screwed this game up,"*: Nightengale Bob, "Jackson Won't Decide Until Winter," *Los Angeles Times*, June 20, 1994.

419 *He was referring to the increasingly dark* Chass, Murray, "Owners Terminate Season, Without the World Series," *New York Times*, Sept. 15, 1994.

420 *A few hours before the Angels' 5-3*: Nightengale, Bob, "Royals Have Angels Folding Tens in 11th, 5-3," *Los Angeles Times*, Aug. 10, 1994.

CHAPTER 29: AFTERMATH

423 *"After eight months*: Weaver, Kendal, "No Knows Retirement," *Daily News Leader (Staunton, Va.)*, April 5, 1995.

423 *Jackson began working with Stephen Eich* Hevrdejs: Judy and Mike Conklin, "Bo Getting to Know about Being a Rookie in the Film World," *Chicago Tribune*, Oct. 11, 1996.

423 *He studied at Steppenwolf*: "Bo Faces Big Test as Guard in Movie," *Orlando Sentinel*, April 6, 1996.

424 *He read for more than 50 parts*: Haysom, Ian, "Bo's New Act," *Star-Phoenix (Saskatoon, Canada)*, Sept. 30, 1996.

424 *Finn was hooked*: "Bo Knows Acting; He's 'Visually Charismatic,' Director Says," *Pensacola News Journal*, Oct. 9, 1996.

424 *Filming commenced on March 9, 1996*: "Saturday Will Be First Day of Shooting Movie in Indianola," *Enterprise-Tocsin (Indianola, Miss.)*, March 7, 1996.

430 *Fifty eight deaths were confirmed*: "Storms Persist, Death Toll Rises," Reeves, Jay, and Holbrook Mohr, "'Devastation,'" *Montgomery Advertiser* April 28, 2011.

430 *"The whole house caved in on top of that car,"*: Bluestein, Greg and Holbrook Mohr, "Devastation," *Anniston Star*, April 29, 2011.

430 *On the morning of April 24, 2012*: Reeves, Jay, "Bo Leads Bike Tour for Tornado Relief," *Montgomery Advertiser*, April 25, 2021.

430 *The plan was to use*: Murschel, Matt, "Jackson gives back with 'Bo Bikes Bama' ride," *Sun Sentinel*, April 16, 2012.

430 *"I conjured up the idea*: Abramson, Mitch, Christan Red, Michael O'Keefe and Eric Barrow, "Bo to the Rescue," *New York Daily News*, March 25, 2012.

BIBLIOGRAPHY

Allen, Marcus, with Carlton Stowers. *Marcus: The Autobiography of Marcus Allen*. New York: Thomas Dunne, 1997.

Allen, Marcus, with Matt Fulks. *Road to Canton*. Champaign, Illinois: Sports Publishing, 2003.

Bagley, Joseph. *The Politics of White Rights: Race, Justice, and Integrating Alabama's Schools*. Athens: University of Georgia Press, 2018.

Barnhart, Tony. *Southern Fried Football: The History, Passion, and Glory of the Great Southern Game*. Chicago: Triumph Books, 2000.

Bolton, Clyde. *War Eagle: A Story of Auburn Football*. Huntsville, Alabama: The Strode Publishers, 1973.

Brown, Scott and Will Collier. *The Uncivil War*. Nashville: Rutledge Hill Press, 1995.

Browning, Al. *Kick 'em Big Blue*. Montgomery, Alabama: Five Points South Productions, 2001.

Bryant, Paul W. and John Underwood. *Bear: The Hard Life and Good Times of Alabama's Coach Bryant*. Boston: Little, Brown and Co., 1974.

Burnett, Jason. *Early Bessemer*. Charleston, S.C.: Arcadia Publishing, 2011.

A Circular of Information about Bessemer City, Alabama. New York: The South Publishing Company, 1889.

Colbert, Lewis, with George Littleton. *Lewis Colbert: The Unlikeliest Auburn Tiger*. Montgomery, Alabama: The Donnell Group, 2011.

Cromartie, Bill. *Braggin' Rights*. Atlanta: Gridiron Publishers, 1994.

Devaney, John. *Bo Jackson: A Star for All Seasons*. New York: Walker Publishing, 1988.

Dickey, Glenn. *Just Win, Baby: Al Davis & His Raiders*. New York: Harcourt Brace Jovanovich, 1991.

Dye, Pat. *I Believe in Auburn and Love It*. Auburn: Auburn Network, 2003.

——. *In the Arena*. Montgomery, Alabama: The Black Belt Press, 1992.

——. *After the Arena*. Montgomery, Alabama: The Donnell Group, 2014.

Edson, James Stewart. *War Eagle! The Tigers of Auburn.* Auburn: Alabama Polytechnic Institute, 1951.

The First 50 Years: Bessemer Hall of History Museum. Birmingham, Alabama: Banner Digital Printing & Publishing, 2020.

Fleischer, Arthur A. III, Brian L. Goff, and Robert D. Tollison. *The National Collegiate Athletic Association: A Study in Cartel Behavior.* Chicago: University of Chicago Press, 1992.

Flynt, Wayne. *Alabama in the Twentieth Century.* Tuscaloosa: The University of Alabama Press, 2004.

———. *Keeping the Faith: Ordinary People, Extraordinary Lives.* Tuscaloosa: The University of Alabama Press, 2011.

Forney, John. *Above the Noise of the Crowd: Thirty Years behind the Alabama microphone.* Huntsville, Alabama: Albright & Company, 1986.

Fyffe, Jim. *Touchdown Auburn!* Montgomery, Alabama: The Donnell Group, 1996.

Glier Ray. *How the SEC Became Goliath.* New York: Howard Books, 2012.

Gold, Eli. *Crimson Nation.* Nashville: Rutledge Hill Press, 2005.

Greunke, Lowell R. *Football Rankings: College Teams in the Associated Press Poll,* 1936–1984. Jefferson, N.C.: McFarland & Company, 1984.

Griffith, Lucille. *History of Alabama: 1540–1900.* Northport, Alabama: Colonial Press, 1962.

Groom, Winston. *The Crimson Tide: The Official Illustrated History of Alabama Football.* Tuscaloosa: The University of Alabama Press, 2010.

The Heisman: Sixty Years of Tradition and Excellence. Bronxville, N.Y.: Adventure Quest, 1995.

Hill, Mike. *Open Mike.* Atlanta: 13th & Joan: Chicago, 2020.

Hollis, Dan W. *Auburn Football: The Complete History, 1892–1987.* Auburn, Alabama: Auburn Sports Publications, 1988.

Housel, David. *Auburn Saturdays to Remember.* Auburn, Alabama: The Village Press, 1973.

———. *Football Vault: The Story of the Auburn Tigers, 1892–2007.* Atlanta: Whitman Publishing, 2007.

Jackson, Bo and Dick Schaap. *Bo Knows Bo: The Autobiography of a Ballplayer.* New York: Doubleday, 1989.

Knight, Phil. *Shoe Dog.* New York: Scribner, 2016.

Lewis, Robert. *Raising a Modern-Day Knight: A Father's Role in Guiding His Son to Authentic Manhood.* Colorado Springs: Focus on the Family, 2007.

Marshall, Phillip. *Auburn Tigers*. Guilford, Connecticut: The Globe Pequot Press, 2015.

Mayfield, Mark. *Miracle Moments in Alabama Crimson Tide Football History*. New York: Sports Publishing, 2018.

Morris, Willie. *The Courting of Marcus Dupree*. New York: Doubleday, 1983.

Murphy, Mark. *Game of My Life: Auburn*. Champaign, Illinois: Sports Publishing, 2007.

Nomel, T. C. *Reading the Psalms as an Auburn Fan*. Scotts Valley, California: CreateSpace Publishing, 2011.

Plexico, Van Allen, and John Ringer. *Decades of Dominance: Auburn Football in the Modern Era*. Auburn, Alabama: White Rocket Books, 2013.

Rhoden, William. *Forty Million Dollar Slaves*. New York: Three Rivers Press, 2006.

Ribowsky, Mark. *Slick: The Silver & Black Life of Al Davis*. New York: Macmillan, 1991

Rogers, William Warren, Robert David Ward, Leah Rawls Atkins, and Wayne Flynt. *Alabama: The History of a Deep South State*. Tuscaloosa: The University of Alabama Press, 1994.

Scherer, George. *Auburn-Georgia Football: A Hundred Years of Rivalry*. Jefferson, N.C.: McFarland & Company, 1992.

Scott, Richard. *SEC Football: 75 Years of Pride and Passion*. Minneapolis: Voyageur Press, 2008.

Schuerholz, John. *Built to Win*. New York: Warner Books, 2006.

Shanahan, Mike, with Adam Schefter. *Think Like a Champion*. New York: HarperCollins, 1999.

Simmons, Ira. *Black Knight: Al Davis and His Raiders*. Rocklin, California: Prima Publishing, 1990.

Skotnicki, Michael. *Auburn's Unclaimed National Championships*. Self-published, 2012.

Smith, Alex Martin. *SEC Football's Greatest Games*. Guilford, Connecticut: Rowman & Littlefield, 2018.

Stewart, Art, with Sam Mellinger. *The Art of Scouting*. Olathe, Kansas: Ascend Books, 2014.

Stutsman, Douglas. *Auburn vs. Georgia: The Deep South's Oldest Rivalry*. Charleston, S.C.: The History Press, 2017.

Thomas, Landon. *The SEC Team of the '80s*. Auburn, Alabama: Tigers Publishing, 2004.

Townsend, Greg. *All Time*. Newport Beach, California: Celebrity Publishing, 2012.

Trask, Amy with Mike Freeman. *You Negotiate Like a Girl*. Chicago: Triumph Books, 2016.

Walsh, Christopher J. *Where Football Is King: A History of the SEC*. Lanham, Maryland: Taylor Trade, 2006.

Watkins, Clarence. *Baseball in Memphis*. Charleston, S.C.: Arcadia Publishing, 2012.

White, George R. *Bo Didley: Living Legend*. Rochester, Kent: Castle Communications, 1995.

Williams, Chette. *The Broken Road*. Winston-Salem, N.C.: Looking Glass, 2013.

Williams, Horace Randall. *100 Things You Need to Know about Alabama*. Atlanta: Whitman Publishing, 2016.

Wilson, Willie, with Kent Pulliam. *Inside the Park: Running the Base Path of Life*. Olathe, Kansas: Ascend Books, 2013.

INDEX